FISHING *in* OREGON

FISHING *in* OREGON

NINTH EDITION

Madelynne Diness Sheehan

Flying Pencil Publications

Scappoose, Oregon

Fishing in Oregon © 2000 by Madelynne Diness Sheehan and Dan Casali.
Maps © 2000 by Flying Pencil Publications.
Photographs © 2000 by photographers or entities credited in captions.

Published by Flying Pencil Publications. Address all inquiries to:
Flying Pencil Publications
33126 SW Callahan Road
Scappoose, Oregon 97056
Phone 503-543-7171, Fax 503-543-7172

Cover photograph by Richard T. Grost: *Deadline Falls on the North Umpqua River.*

Book design by John Laursen, Press-22, Portland, Oregon.

Printed in the United States of America.

10 9 8 7 6 5 4 3 2 1

Library of Congress Control Number: 00-130982

ISBN: 0-916473-14-7

Publisher's Notice: Water-related sports, and travel associated with them, are by their very nature hazardous. Risks include, but are not limited to, those related to terrain, weather, equipment, wild animals, errors in judgment, and physical limitations (not the least of which is the inability of humans to breathe while underwater). This book does not describe every hazard associated with fishing in Oregon. Furthermore, despite diligent efforts, it may contain errors of typography, cartography, or content. This book's maps are for planning reference only, not for navigation. Flying Pencil Publications and the author shall have no liability or responsibility with respect to physical harm, property damage, or any other loss or damage asserted to be caused directly or indirectly by the information in this book. We sigh and regret that our society has reached such a litigious state that it is necessary to include a paragraph like this in a book about goin' fishin'.

Contents

LIST OF MAPS

HOW TO USE THIS BOOK

Fishing in Oregon is presented in eight chapters corresponding to the eight angling zones of the *Oregon Sport Fishing Regulations*. To look up a specific water, use the Index on page 352.

Waters are listed alphabetically within each chapter. Chapter introductions describe the varieties of fishing available in the zone and the zone's outstanding characteristics, climate, road and trail conditions, and availability of visitor facilities. We have also shared our choice of *best fishing* for each of the eight zones. Each *best water* is identified by a fish icon beside its name. These are absolutely not the only high quality fishing opportunities in Oregon, but they do provide a starter set of fisheries to explore.

Fishing in Oregon is more than twice the size of the first edition offered by this publisher in 1984, but there is still much we didn't include. We regret having to abandon an earlier intent to provide a running history of the management of important fisheries. There was just too much to say about what, when, and how to get the most out of fishing Oregon today. Nor could we go into as much detail as we'd have liked explaining the "why" behind current regulations. For further information about specific fisheries and regulations, call the Oregon Department of Fish and Wildlife district office nearest that water. All ODFW district office contact numbers are listed on page 345 in the Appendix.

While *Fishing in Oregon* refers to angling and boating restrictions in effect at the time of publication, anglers and boaters should refer to the current regulations for the final word. In particular, readers might be on the lookout for changes in regard to streams in eastern Oregon that support Great Basin redband rainbows (Silver Lake, Goose Lake, Ft.

Rock, Catlow, and Malheur Lake watersheds). There is also talk of reopening some Umpqua basin cutthroat fisheries.

Road and trail directions to each water are generally given in the opening paragraphs. Angler services and facilities are listed near the end of each write-up. Occasionally, dealing with some of our larger and more complex fisheries (e.g. Deschutes, Columbia, Snake), we have used sub-headings to help you navigate through the text. For additional information about National Forest roads and campgrounds, call the relevant ranger district office, listed in on page 345 in the Appendix.

A Fishing Resources Directory on page 344 in the Appendix, lists contacts (with phone numbers and web addresses) for further information. These include several businesses around the state that have generously offered to serve as local information sources for our readers.

The Appendices also include three specialty lists: Appendix 5 is a list of fisheries especially suitable for youngsters; Appendix 6 lists fisheries accessible to the disabled; and Appendix 7 lists warmwater fisheries. Use these in conjunction with the Index.

Most folks use *Fishing in Oregon* to look up specific waters, or browse it like a catalog or the Sunday newspaper. But a few dedicated fanatics do read it cover to cover and thus discover there's a lot of useful general information about Oregon fishing tucked into miscellaneous write-ups. I have yet to think of a way to direct readers to those bytes of tactical advice, definitions of Oregon fishing terms, and historical lore, so I leave you to discover them on your own some day when the water's out of shape or your rig breaks down.

Map Symbols

Symbol	Description	Symbol	Description
⌐	boat ramp	5	Interstate
Λ	campground	26	U.S. highway
♀	spring	22	state road
▫	community or other site	4210	Forest Service road
⊼	day use (no camping)	← *streamflow*	direction of current flow

ACKNOWLEDGMENTS

Sincere thanks to the men and women of the Oregon Department of Fish and Wildlife (ODFW), who are holding steady at the helm through some rough sailing. Their efforts and sincere concern for Oregon fish are appreciated. They have given generously of their time and knowledge.

In particular, I would like to acknowledge the assistance of the following ODFW biologists: Tim Bailey, Reese Bender (good fishing in your retirement), Don Bennett, Wayne Bowers, Keith Braun, Bob Buchman, Kin Daily, Nick Duncan, Curtis Edwards, Mike Gray, Bob Hooten, Wayne Hunt, Chris Kern, Mark Knoch, Bill Knox, Dave Loomis, Steve Mamoyac, Steve Marx, Rhine Messmer, Ray Perkins, Steve Pribyl , Tom Rumreich, Joe Sheahan, Terry Schrader, Brad Smith, Mark Wade, Tim Walters, Jimmy Watts, John Weber, George Westfall, and Jeff Ziller. Special thanks to Laurie Hansen and Rod Lemeni of ODFW's Portland Information office who keep me informed of queries they *can't* answer by referring to their copies of *Fishing in Oregon*.

Individual anglers around the state have shared information about their home waters.Thanks to Ron Byrd for your help on the new Nestucca map, Dennis Dobson for doing the same for the Trask, Bill Davis for being *Fishing in Oregon*'s unofficial roving man-on-the-stream throughout the past five years (taking me to task for errors and providing unsolicited but much appreciated updates for the new edition), Bob Judkins of the Oregon Bass and Panfish Club for mobilizing members to provide many of the warmwater fishing photos in this edition, Larry Kenney, Jim Molitor, Jack Ryder of the Oasis Cafe in Juntura for checking the accuracy of the expanded Malheur River coverage, and Will Trout. Thanks to April Curtright of NSIA, Clyde Zeller and Ian Caldwell of the Oregon Department of Forestry, and Matt Walker of Tillamook BLM. Recognition to Dan Casali for his contributions to earlier editions of this book. Special thanks to my fishing buddy and friend Terry Hines of the Lady Anglers who proofed the final draft instead of going fishing during the home stretch, to Judith Irwin who kept my grammar and sentence construction up to acceptable standards, and to Myra Clark and Lynn Kertell who assisted with map construction, layout, and invaluable graphics production advice. Thanks also to the photographers represented here: Mark Bachman, Dennis Frates, Richard Grost, Bud and Marcia Hartman, Terry Hines, Mac Huff, Nancy Huff, Jeffrey Kee, Jerry Korson, Jim Liddle, John Ramsour, Dan Reynolds, Scott Richmond, Randy Sampson, Mitch Sanchotena, Phil Simonski, Mark VanDuser, Lynn Hokanson Welsh, Bill Wagner, and Ken Witty.

Thanks to John Laursen of Portland's Press-22 for the handsome book and cover design, and to Richard Grost for the beautiful cover photograph.

REFERENCES

Atlas of Oregon Lakes; Daniel M. Johnson; Portland State University; Portland, Oregon.
Fishing in Oregon's Best Fly Waters; Scott Richmond; Flying Pencil Publications.
Fishing in Oregon's Cascade Lakes; Scott Richmond; Flying Pencil Publications.
Fishing in Oregon's Deschutes River; Scott Richmond; Flying Pencil Publications.
Oregon Atlas & Gazeteer; DeLorme Mapping.
Trout and Beyond; John Shewey; Frank Amato Publications.

INTRODUCTION

If you're reading this Introduction, chances are the rivers are out of shape or your rig broke down. Well, welcome to the ninth edition of *Fishing in Oregon*. This essay is the last thing I (the publisher) am insisting that I (the author) compose after writing nonstop for 18 months. I have already emptied my brain of almost everything useful to you, and we would both most assuredly benefit more from a day spent staring at a river. But publishing tradition calls for an Introduction, and I am conservative in that regard if in no other.

It's been raining enthusiastically since 1995, so this edition reflects the healing power of timely autumn rains, lively spring freshets, and brimming reservoirs. This is a cheerful book for the most part, focusing on appreciation of our state's fishing opportunities. Which are many. It recognizes as facts changes that have occurred in Oregon angling since the last edition was published in 1995. It doesn't blame or lament. Instead, it attempts to provide the information you need to choose where to fish, depending on your fishing preferences and goals.

In case you hadn't noticed, this is no longer the Wild West, and you can't keep everything you catch just because it bites and looks good to eat. If harvest is your aim, use *Fishing in Oregon* in conjunction with the current angling regulations to hone in on the appropriate fisheries—rivers with strong runs of finclipped hatchery steelhead, finclipped coho, or fall chinook; streams with hatchery trout, an over-abundance of brookies, or wild trout but no juvenile steelhead; smallmouth bass and other warmwater species in backwaters and sloughs; rock, bottom, or surf fish; sturgeon or walleye; almost everything that thrives in lakes and reservoirs. We're far from bereft of catch-and-keep opportunities in this state.

On the other hand, if you're yearning to fish wild steelhead, wild coho, chum salmon, bull trout, coastal cutthroat, searun—resign yourself to catch-and-release, and rejoice that they're still here despite the years of drought, El Niño, lost habitat, and too many dams. Remember that the chase and the hook-up are the most fun anyway. And when people ask you why you bother to fish if you can't bring it home as fillets, remind them that nobody eats golf balls either.

If you've been fishing Oregon long enough to feel reverent about our native fisheries and indignant about their

Maddy Sheehan. Photograph by Marry Stupp-Greer

decline, consider what you can do to help reverse the trend. Donate money or time to an organization working to restore fish habitat or change policy at the state, regional, and federal level such as the Northwest Sportfishing Industry Association, Northwest Steelheaders, Oregon Trout, and Water Watch of Oregon. Help form a watershed council in your community, or join one of the 50 or so councils already working to implement *The Oregon Plan for Salmon and Steelhead Restoration*.

At the very least, abide by and support regulations and legislation aimed at protecting and restoring our fishery resources. Consider introducing youngsters and Oregon newcomers to fishing in order to insure the perpetuation of sportfishing's friendship base. And teach them angling ethics (obey the rules, take only what you need, do no damage, leave the environment better than you found it).

The ninth edition of *Fishing in Oregon* has been painstakingly assembled as a guide to Oregon's fisheries as they are today. I offer it to you to use as an escape from life's dramas. Those of you who are just getting to know us—explore, enjoy, and become a friend. Old friends—keep alive the vision of what has been and can be.

Good fishing forever.

— *Maddy Sheehan*

This book is dedicated to my husband, Mike Sheehan, whose own dedication to doing both good work and good works is a continuing source of inspiration, and to my daughters, April and Melissa Mejias, who are well on their way to becoming women of valor.

FISHING *in* OREGON

FISHING IN OREGON'S
NORTHWEST ZONE

The Northwest Zone is defined by the Pacific Ocean, which alternately laps and roars against its west flank at beach, bay, and rocky cape. The ocean fills valley cauldrons with morning fog, and launches flotillas of clouds that condense over the Coast Range and replenish the region's dozens of rivers and streams. The ocean cools the summer breeze, moderates the winter chill, and is a constant presence in the tang of air, the dripping green of moss-draped trees, and the ubiquitous company of seagulls.

A dozen great rivers pour out of the Coast Range and into the Pacific off the northwest Oregon coast. Spring and fall chinook, chum, and coho salmon rear and return here, as do anadromous rainbow trout, called *steelhead* for the metallic gray of their heads and backs after two years in the ocean. Cutthroat trout reside in most tributary streams, available at this time for catch-and-release fishing only. Some go to sea and return pounds heavier and silvery blue as *searun*.

The tidewaters of these rivers offer unique fishing opportunities. Alsea, Nehalem, Nestucca, Siletz, Siuslaw, Tillamook, and Yaquina are among Oregon's most productive bays. Fall chinook, in particular, use the bays as a staging area before making their run for upstream spawning grounds. Some bays, like Tillamook, have strong spring chinook fisheries, too, as well as late summer fisheries for *jack* salmon, the immature salmon who arrive prior to the adult fall runs. Crabbing is generally good in summer and fall, and catches can be made in winter if you can bear the cold. Clams are abundant in the tidal flats. Sturgeon move into many of the bays in late winter and are popularly fished through early spring. Redtail perch and many varieties of rockfish are caught from bayside docks and rocks, including the jetties that help pacify the entrance to the ocean, known as *the bar*.

The offshore fisheries in this zone include chinook, halibut, cabezon, lingcod, kelp greenling, seabass, sea trout, red snapper, striped perch, and rockfish. In some years, albacore tuna are also available within a day's run. Some bays provide easier offshore access than others. Depoe Bay, created by two small streams rather than a one or more major rivers, offers the zone's safest portal to the Pacific as well as outstanding near-shore reefs.

Redtail perch can be fished in the surf along the Northwest coast's miles of public beach. Look for the presence of mole crabs at low tide, a favorite redtail forage. Sandy beach-

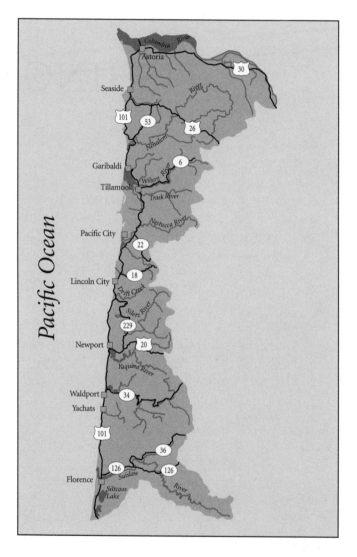

es with stream inlets, troughs parallel to the shore, or an adjacent south jetty can be particularly productive.

With the discontinuation of trout stocking in Northwest Zone streams, more trout are being released into its lakes. In addition to a sprinkling of forest lakes in the Coast Range (Town, Hebo, Barney, Lost, Olalla), there are many small lakes tucked among the sand dunes from Ft. Stevens State Park in the north to the Oregon Dunes National Recreation Area at the southern edge of this zone. Many of these lakes receive larger trout especially grown to add spice to the sport in addition to 8-inch legals.

Warmwater species are also available in many of the dune lakes, as well as in the zone's few big lakes (Devils, Lytle, Silt-

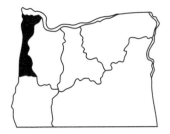

The Northwest Zone includes all waters draining directly to the Pacific Ocean north of, but not including the Umpqua River drainage; and tributaries of the Columbia River entering downstream of the City of St. Helens. Portions of the tributaries below the railroad bridge (near the mouth) are included in the Columbia River Zone.

THE BEST FISHING IN OREGON'S NORTHWEST ZONE

ALSEA RIVER
Good fishing for wild fall chinook and hatchery winter steelhead.

KILCHIS RIVER
Best chance to catch (and release) chum salmon in Oregon.

NEHALEM RIVER, NORTH FORK
Catch and keep fall chinook, finclipped coho and winter steelhead, or hike and fish for (catch-and-release) wild winter steelhead in a handsome coastal forest setting.

NESTUCCA RIVER
A real gem for spring and fall chinook, and for both hatchery and wild winter steelhead.

SILETZ RIVER
Steelhead (mostly fin-clipped and available for harvest) are in the river and can be fished year-round.

SILTCOOS LAKE
Big largemouth bass, plentiful panfish, and the biggest and most abundant cutthroat trout on the mid-coast.

SIUSLAW BAY
Rivals Tillamook Bay for fall chinook abundance.

TILLAMOOK BAY
A popular access to offshore fisheries, some of the coast's best bay fishing for spring and big fall chinook, and excellent opportunities to hook keeper sturgeon.

TRASK RIVER
An excellent river to fly fish for wild winter steelhead, pick up finclipped hatchery strays in summer, or catch spring and fall chinook.

WILSON RIVER
Always one of the top 10 producers of salmon and steelhead on the Oregon coast.

YAQUINA BAY
One of the most popular and productive bottom fish bays on the coast, with a good bar and easy access to productive offshore halibut and bottom fish grounds.

coos, Tahkenitch). Siltcoos is the queen of Oregon's coastal lakes, a nationally known largemouth bass fishery that floats in the mist like a big Scottish loch at the edge of Siuslaw National Forest. It lures anglers with the opportunity to land trophy-size bass and offers the coast's best chance to catch and keep big cutthroat trout.

Largemouth and smallmouth bass, yellow perch, crappie, bluegill, and catfish are plentiful in the many sloughs along the lower Columbia River, which forms this zone's northern boundary.

The Northwest Zone is accessed north to south by scenic Hwy. 101, which hugs the coast except for a brief inland detour around the Three Capes (Meares, Lookout, and Kiwanda). Roads inland follow the major rivers as they breach the forested slopes of the Coast Range. The primary east-west roads are paved, though mostly two-lane and poorly lighted for night driving. Passing lanes are provided in areas of steepest grade, and slow-vehicle turn-outs help ease congestion. A network of logging roads connects watersheds and main roads, accessing tributaries and upper reaches. Though open to public use, most are unpaved, with portions less than two-lane. When traveling them during weekdays, keep an eye out, and an ear tuned, for logging trucks.

The highest point in the Coast Range (Saddle Mt.) is only 3,282 ft., but snow and ice can make driving hazardous from November to May, and severe rainstorms and fog are possible year-round. The northwest zone averages over 180 days with measurable rainfall each year. A pleasant side effect of this deluge is moderate temperatures. Averages vary from about 40 degrees in winter to 60 degrees in summer. Summer warming (such as it is) is delayed at the coast, with seasonal highs occurring in late August.

Settlements in the mountains are limited to the lower elevations at either end. Campgrounds are sparse along the rivers, but state parks with camping areas dot the coast, and private RV parks and a wide variety of accomodations are available along Hwy. 101.

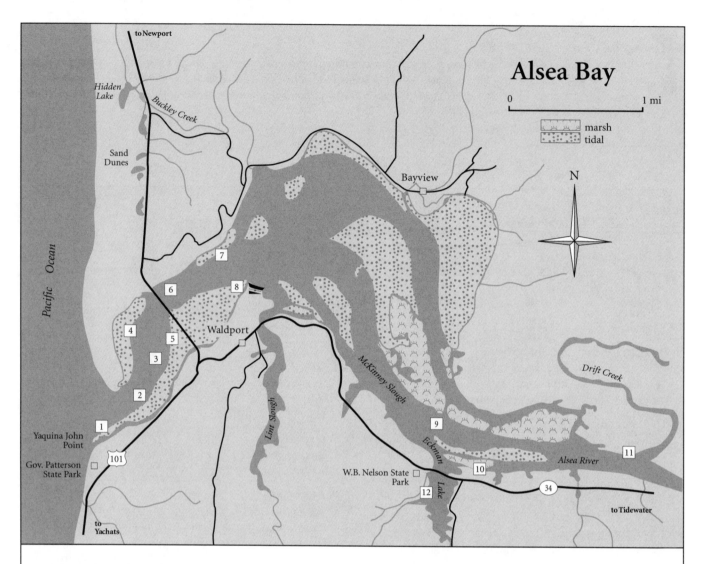

Alsea Bay

0   1 mi

marsh
tidal

N

1. Secondary Channel. Bank fish for salmon in fall.

2. Sand Bar.

3. Lower Main Channel. Fish for fall salmon, crab.

4. Lower Bay Flats North. Dig for clams, cockles.

5. Lower Bay Flats South. Firm sand, not mud; walk out at low tide and fish for coho and chinook in late Aug., perch all summer; dig cockles.

6. Mid-Channel. Hwy. 101 bridge to Waldport docks best area for perch; salmon and crab available.

7. Old Bridge Flats. Park below old bridge and walkout for cockles at low tide, perch at high and low.

8. Public Docks.

9. Mouth of the Alsea. Troll for salmon July-Sept., jacks September to October., sea-runs June to October; no perch above Eckman Slough.

10. Softshell Clams. Park off road across Eckman causeway.

11. Tidewater. Fish for chinook.

12. Eckman Lake. Bank fish for stocked trout and largemouth bass.

ALDER LAKE. One of Oregon's dune lakes, a 3-acre trout lake in Siuslaw National Forest, 7.6 miles north of Florence. Alder is west of Hwy. 101, about ½ mile north of Sutton Lake. Look for the sign to Alder Dune Campground on the highway.

Alder is stocked with legal rainbows. Buck Lake is ¼ mile south and Dune Lake is ¼ mile farther. Both are similar to Alder in size and fishing. There is a campground at the north end of Alder Lake. Recommended for youngsters.

ALSEA BAY. Intensely fished for fall chinook, offering calm and productive waters close to its boat ramps. Alsea Bay is a good place to introduce family and friends to salmon fishing. Six miles long, with tidewater extending about 12 miles upriver, it can be reached in about an hour from Corvallis by way of Hwy. 34. Hwy. 101 approaches it from north and south.

A good number of moorages along the bay from Waldport up to Tidewater offer launching facilities and rental boats. Many fish are caught right in front of the moorages, convenient to hot coffee.

The salmon season currently opens mid-August, with best fishing in September and October. Jacks and adults arrive simultaneously. Best fishing is in the lower main channel and at the mouth of the Alsea. Bank anglers work the lower south side bay flats below Hwy. 101.

Spring chinook are present from May through July, and coho return September through November, but the bay is currently closed to fishing for both.

Trolled herring, feathered spinners, Kwikfish-type lures, and Hot Shots are effective for adult salmon. Cluster eggs drifted under a bobber seem to attract the young jacks.

Perch fishing is good in the bay from spring through fall. Perch are caught from the Hwy. 101 bridge to the public docks at Waldport, and from the Old Bridge Flats at high and low tide. There are no perch above Eckman Slough. Shrimp, clam necks, kelp worms, and sand crabs are all available locally for bait.

Searun cutthroat can be found in the bay from June through September. Fishing for them is catch and release. Most anglers prefer to pursue them in the river where they can be tempted with flies and spinners that allow a safer release.

ALSEA BAY offers calm, productive waters for fall chinook close to its boat ramps. Photograph by Scott Richmond.

Crabbing continues to be good here. The most popular area is the main channel below Lint Slough. The best hard shell catches are made in September and October. Cockles are dug in the south shore's Lower Bay Flats, which have comfortably firm sand rather than mud, and in the Old Bridge Flats above the 101 bridge. Both cockles and gapers are dug in the smaller north shore Lower Bay Flats. Softshell clams are available in the flats above Eckman Lake.

Flounder are no longer plentiful in Alsea Bay or in any other bay on the Oregon coast, though they are occasionally caught.

Services and supplies are abundant along the bay, with motels and restaurants in Waldport. There is a Siuslaw National Forest campground 5 miles south at Tillicum Beach.

ALSEA RIVER

A highly regarded winter steelhead and fall chinook stream, about 55 miles long, heading in the coast range west of Corvallis and entering the Pacific Ocean at Waldport. The main river hosts both hatchery and wild steelhead. The Alsea is closely followed by Hwy. 34 from its mouth to above the confluence of the North Fork. Good secondary roads follow its major tributaries. The mouth is reached by Hwy. 101.

The Alsea continues to maintain a strong run of hatchery-reared winter steelhead. At this time, about 2,000 fish are caught annually.

Steelhead appear in late November, with peak catches in December and January. Fish are often available through the end of March. There's a lot of good water, with a fair share of snags and tackle-grabbing boulders. Popular steelhead spots are at the head of tide (about two miles above the community of Tidewater), the Hatchery Hole, Barclay Drift, The Maples (at Lake Creek), and the Strawberry Patch. Wild (non-finclipped) steelhead must be released unharmed.

A healthy run of wild fall chinook moves into the bay in late August. During low water, best fishing is in tidewater. Once the

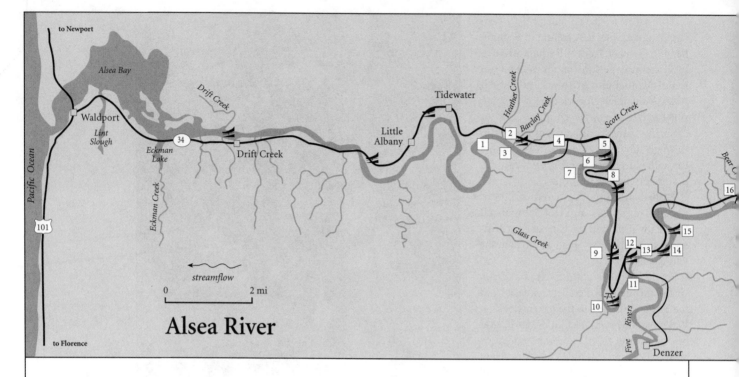

Alsea River

1. Sand Hole. Head of tide; private property; boat-fishing only.

2. Barclay Hole. First good hole above tidewater; good low water hole for salmon or steelhead.

3. Barclay Hole, South Bank. Ask permission to access good private bank fishing; cross river on Boundary Rd. then turn rt. on SouthBank Road.

4. Scott Creek Hole. Ledges and channels; fish just below creek; bring lots of tackle.

5. Hellion Rapids. Deep hole just below rapids.

6. Hootenany Trail. Forest Service access trail up to Rock Crusher Hole; trail runs under edge of highway.

7. Rock Crusher Hole. Rocks, ledge, channels.

8. Mike Bauer Wayside. Public boat ramp; popular for plunking; wheelchair accessible.

9. Blackberry Campground. Public boat ramp; deep holes; overnight camping with RV spaces; nice forest trail.

10. Maples Hole. Deep plunking water; boat ramp, parking, picnic area.

11. Five Rivers Bridge. Productive fishing from bridge to Maples Hole; channels, ledges, rocks, holes. good bank access with productive slots close to shore.

12. Five Rivers Boat Ramp.

13. Old Put-in Hole. Plunking hole upstream of road bend.

14. Low Water Bridge Put-in. Good bank angling.

15. Stony Point Boat Ramp. Good gravel put-in with parking at Transformer Hole; good bank fishing upstream.

16. Forest Service Campground

17. Bear Creek Lodge. Bank fishing just above lodge.

18. Digger Mt. Mill Bridge. Good fishing above & below; private property; ask permission to fish.

19. Private Park. Access fee.

20. Fall Creek Boat Launch. Popular boat slide into Fall Cr. ¼ mile above Alsea; drift into Alsea.

21. Missouri Bend Park. Log skid; picnic facilities; lots of parking.

22. Salmonberry Bridge. Boat launch; good drifting and plunking.

23. Campbell Park Put-in. Fish just below.

24. Mill Creek Boat Ramps. Upper limit for boats; fish the stretch from boat ramps up to Mill Cr.; accessible good drifts throughout.

25. Alsea Ranger Station. Bank access with permission; ask at farm houses.

26. Fish Hatchery. Winter steelhead, especially during high water, between hatchery and Hwy. 34.

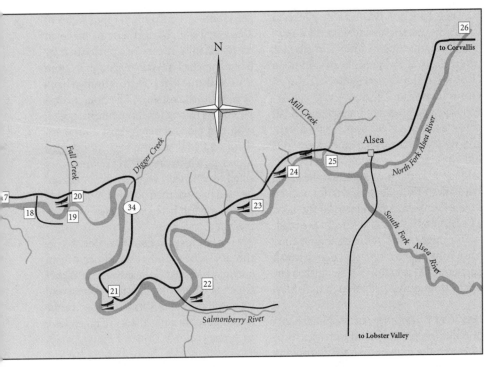

river level rises, salmon are caught from the head of tide up to Fall Creek (the upstream deadline for salmon fishing). Most salmon are taken by trolling in the bay, but casting can produce fish up to the forks. Anglers use medium to large flies and lures as well as sand shrimp and eggs.

Searun cutthroat move up into the river in mid-August. Though their numbers are depressed here as in other coastal streams, you can still fish for them in the Alsea with reasonable expectation of success. Fishing is strictly catch and release, so don't use bait. A small Rooster Tail (yellow or white) or flies with a little flash in sizes 6 to 10 can be effective.

There are a number of spots where boats can be launched, some of which have small user fees. Rental boats, supplies and accommodations are available at Waldport, in the Alsea Bay area, and at several points upriver. Boats and other personal flotation devices are allowed downstream from Mill Creek. There is a Forest Service camp 17 miles upstream from Waldport.

Flood level on the Alsea is 18 ft., with best fishing at river levels 4-6 ft. A gauge reading is available. See Appendix.

ALSEA RIVER, NORTH FORK. A beautiful stream (well suited to fly angling) with a large run of hatchery winter steelhead. It enters the mainstem Alsea at the town of Alsea. It is easily accessed from county and logging roads running north and west from Hwy. 34.

Winter steelhead are present in large numbers from December through February. Steelheading is productive throughout the stream, but the highest concentration of fish and anglers is in the one-mile stretch from the Hwy. 34 bridge to the hatchery. Get permission to access the river across private land. The folks at the hatchery sometimes know of landowners willing to allow public access. Best catching is during periods of extended high water.

Catch and release fishing for wild cutthroat trout is generally good when the season opens in late May and holds up for several months. The river is closed to all salmon fishing. Angling from a floating device is prohibited in the North Fork.

ALSEA RIVER, SOUTH FORK. An excellent wild cutthroat stream, with opportunities to catch surplus hatchery steelhead for the table. This fair size fork of the Alsea (average width 40 feet) flows into the main river from the southwest at the town of Alsea. County roads access it and many of its tributaries, with BLM land bordering much of its run. To reach the stream from Hwy. 34, follow the South Fork Rd. south at the town of Alsea.

The South Fork offers good catch and release fishing for wild cutthroat both above and below its falls at r.m. 9. It has good trout cover, though limited food sources. If the water is clear, light leader fly fishing is your best bet.

ODFW often transports hundreds of surplus hatchery steelhead to the South Fork near Tobe Creek (r.m. 3). The fish hold there for some time before heading out to sea. Call the North Fork Hatchery for release dates. See Appendix.

The nearest campground is on the

The ALSEA RIVER *maintains a strong run of hatchery-reared winter steelhead. Photograph by Jeffrey Kee.*

South Fork about 7 miles southeast of Alsea. Continue south onto Glenbrook Rd. when the South Fork Rd. cuts east.

ARCH CAPE CREEK. A fair stream for catch and release searun cutthroat in spring and late fall. Only 4 miles long, it flows into the ocean 6 miles south of Cannon Beach, off Hwy. 101. Arch Cape Creek has some good pools and brush, but it is surrounded by mostly residential property, so be sure to ask permission. There is a campground at Oswald West State Park.

BARK SHANTY CREEK. Deadline on the North Fork Trask River for winter steelhead fishing. The creek itself is closed to all angling.

BARNEY RESERVOIR. Headwaters of the Trask River and the drinking water source for the city of Hillsboro. Difficult to find within a maze of primitive logging roads, this 450 acre reservoir on the coast range divide opened for recreational use in 1999.

If you can find it, Barney offers catch and release fishing for a good population of wild cutthroat trout and as many brown bullhead catfish as you'd care to keep. Before heading out, get a current copy of the fire protection district map (NW Oregon, Forest Grove District) from the Oregon Department of Forestry. This map was recently updated, so it may be reliable for a few more years.

The reservoir is most easily approached from the west by following the North Fork Trask Road. (Stay on the main dirt road.) From Hwy. 47 in Yamhill, the reservoir is about 20 miles by way of a network of unmarked logging roads. Begin by turning off the highway onto Pike Rd., which becomes Turner Creek Rd. At the sign for Trask Mountain Tree Farm, keep right on the main road (which begins the Mainline Rd.). From there, follow the map, and look for "Barney" painted on a tree to the left near an intersection. After a downhill grade, you will pass the first arm of the reservoir. There are a number of turn-outs where you can park and walk down to the lake.

This fishery is open to the public on a trial basis. Be especially fastidious about cleaning up after yourself to preserve access. Use artificial lures and flies only.

BATTLE LAKE. A two-acre easy hike-in lake in the Siuslaw National Forest west of Hemlock, offering fishing for stocked trout. From Tillamook, head south on Hwy. 101, 11½ miles to Hemlock. Turn left on East Beaver Rd. (next to Bear Creek Artichokes) and proceed 3 miles to the end of pavement. Turn right on Forest Rd. 8172 and go about two miles to a gated spur road on the right. Parking is limited, but seldom a problem. Hike down the gated road about 1¼ mile and look for a short road on the left, which leads to the lake. The lake itself if not visible from the road.

You might want to bring a float tube since bank angling is limited due to brush and terrain. Legal rainbows are stocked annually from early April through mid-May.

BAY CITY RESERVOIR. A ½-acre impoundment lightly stocked with legal trout (formerly the source of Bay City's drinking water). From Bay City, travel north on Fifth Street; take a right on Ocean, then a left at the stop sign. Continue ½ mile, turning right at the "Y" onto Patterson Creek Rd., then right onto Jacoby Creek Rd. Head uphill at the next "Y." During the rainy season, the road is gated due to poor road conditions. The hike from the gate is about ½ mile.

The reservoir is stocked with rainbows trout once in mid-April. Take only what you can use immediately, and leave plenty for others to enjoy.

BEAR CREEK (Lower Columbia). A tributary of the Columbia, managed for wild cutthroat and steelhead. The stream flows through industrial timberland into the Columbia near Swensen, east of Astoria. A locked gate during most of the year prohibits motorized vehicles, but anglers on foot or mountain bike are welcome. The gate is unlocked during deer and elk season (October and November). Be a good visitor. Pack out whatever you pack in to preserve access.

BEAVER CREEK (Lower Columbia watershed). Fished primarily for warmwater fish near its mouth. The creek flows about 25 miles west from near Rainier to the town of Clatskanie. It is crossed several times by Hwy. 30 and approached by secondary roads.

The most significant fishery is for bass and panfish near the mouth, where the creek enters the Columbia in a series of connected sloughs northeast of the town of Clatskanie. It can be approached by boats launched in Wallace Slough or from the Clatskanie River. There is limited bank access at road crossings. The slough complex offers fishing for about fifteen species, with crappie and perch most abundant. April and May are the best months for these fish, which can run to 5 pounds. Very small wobblers or weighted streamers can be used to catch them, or an abundance of non-game fish here can be used for crappie bait.

A sparse population of resident cutthroat can be found in the upper stream and may be fished catch and release. Beaver Creek is currently open for salmon and steelhead fishing to within 200 feet of the lower falls, but only a few are taken here each year.

BEAVER CREEK (Lincoln Co.). A short coastal stream, offering catch and release opportunities for resident and searun cutthroat trout. It flows into the Pacific about 6 miles south of Newport. A county road follows the creek east from Hwy. 101.

Sea-run cutthroat are in the stream from July through September. A small wild winter steelhead run returns to the creek and can be fished catch and release in the lower 3 miles up to the county bridge at Ona. Coho enter in October and November, but the creek is closed to salmon fishing.

A scenic coastal marsh at the lower end of the creek offers nice boating and bird watching opportunities. Ona Beach State Park near the mouth east of Hwy. 101 provides picnic facilities and a well-maintained boat ramp.

BEAVER CREEK (Nestucca watershed). A good cutthroat stream with lots of cover and many deep pools, traditionally fished for searun. This stream enters the mainstem Nestucca River at the town of Beaver, about 15 miles south of Tillamook on Hwy. 101. It has small runs of chinook winter steelhead that can be fished up to the fishing deadline at the West Beaver Creek confluence. It is closed to coho fishing.

BENEKE CREEK. A good early season trout stream with some searun showing in early fall if the water rises. This creek enters the Nehalem River at Jewell and is about 14 miles long if you include its tributary, Walker Creek. A good road follows the stream. Fishing for resident and searun cutthroat is catch and release. The creek is closed to fishing for both salmon and steelhead.

BIG CREEK (Clatsop Co.). A popular winter steelhead stream with limited public access. Most fishing on Big Creek is for hatchery-reared (finclipped) winter steelhead and coho.

The creek enters the lower Columbia sloughs near the town of Knappa. County roads cross and follow it south from Hwy. 30 near Knappa Junction.

Good numbers of winter steelhead and coho salmon ascend Big Creek, heading for the hatchery at r.m. 5. In most years, the steelhead catch exceeds 2000, with peak fishing in December and January, and a bite that continues through March. Coho show in October. The stream is open for chinook fishing in late spring and fall, but most chinook are caught from August through November.

Best access to the fishery on Big Creek is from the hatchery deadline to about ½ mile downstream. There is also ½ mile of public access on the east bank between the old highway bridge and the new one. If you find the space a little cramped here, head over to the nearby Klaskanine, where there are usually equal numbers of fish and fewer anglers.

At this time, Big Creek is closed to all fishing above the hatchery, where efforts are being made to restore searun cutthroat and wild steelhead populations. Check current regulations for deadlines. Hook and bait restrictions may be in effect to minimize harm to wild fish.

Columbia River management regulations apply to Big Creek downstream of the railroad tracks that cross the creek near its mouth. Emergency closures on this stretch have been common.

BIG CREEK RESERVOIRS. Two 20-acre reservoirs on the north edge of Newport offering year-round fishing for bass, catfish, and stocked trout, including some of trophy size.

The reservoirs are just north of Yaquina Bay, accessible from Hwy. 101 by way of Big Creek Rd. just north of Hotel Newport and south of Agate Beach. Because the reservoirs are used as the water source for the city, motors are prohibited. Most anglers fish from the bank beside the road which crosses between the two reservoirs.

ODFW stocks these lakes heavily with rainbow trout in March, April, May, and again in the fall. Big trophy-size trout are stocked in spring. Look for largemouth bass and brown bullhead in the upper reservoir around the lily pads and reeds. Bait or spinner and bait combinations seem to work best here.

There are no boat ramps. Light-weight boats can be launched in the lower reservoir, but shallows around the upper reservoir make launching there difficult. Float tubes would be perfect. Recommended for youngsters. Wheelchair accessible.

BIG ELK CREEK. A major tributary of the Yaquina river with good bank fishing for wild fall chinook and hatchery reared winter steelhead. Big Elk enters the Yaquina at Elk City. To reach it from the coast, drive east on Hwy. 20 from Newport to Toledo, then head south on the Elk City Rd. The road continues up Big Elk about 22 miles to Harlan.

The steelhead run is at its peak here in December and January. Fall chinook are generally most abundant in October. Resident cutthroat provide good fishing in May and June. Currently, all cutthroat fishing in the creek is catch and release as elsewhere on the coast, but check the regulations for a possible relaxation of restrictions here.

BLIND SLOUGH. A long narrow finger of the Columbia River upstream from Knappa, offering a classic mix of Columbia River cold and warmwater fishing opportunities. Covering 194 acres, it is approached by county roads heading north from Hwy. 30 in the vicinity of Knappa Junction.

The slough has long been a favorite for warmwater fishing. Largemouth bass to 5 pounds, large yellow perch on their spawning migration in March and April, crappie, and catfish are all available.

Fall chinook move into the slough in September, followed by coho and coho jacks in October and November. These fisheries are regulated by Columbia River Management. Check The Daily Astorian, The Oregonian, and the ODFW Web site for season openings.

A spring chinook netpen program similar to that in Young's Bay was begun here in 1997 to support both recreational and commercial fishing. The first significant re-

turns are expected in 2000. If all goes well, commercial fishing will take place during the weekdays, with weekends the best time for recreational anglers. Springers should enter the slough beginning in mid-April and linger through June.

Blind Slough can be fished from the public easement off the north bank road. Most other property along the slough is privately owned, but it can't hurt to ask for permission to access the water. Be a respectful visitor, and you'll be welcome to come another day. Leave no trace.

Most anglers fish Blind Slough from boats. The closest launch is at Aldrich Point. Head downstream to the slough.

Blind Slough connects to several other smaller sloughs which can be productive for bass and panfish.

BLUE LAKE (Tillamook Co.). Once a 3-acre cutthroat lake on the south side of the coast range divide, Blue lost its fishery when the dam blew out. It's hardly even a pond now, with roads very deteriorated. No reconstruction is planned at this time.

BRADBURY SLOUGH. All the Columbia river bass and panfish species can be found in this good size slough just west of Quincy, about 3 miles northeast of Clatskanie on Hwy. 30. Two other sloughs, Johns and Deadend, are connected to it. Small boats can be launched, and there is some access from bridges and the county road. It is only lightly fished.

BROWNSMEAD SLOUGH. Offers good bass and panfish, just east of the community of Brownsmead. The Brownsmead junction on Hwy. 30 is 20 miles east of Astoria, and the town is located 5 miles north. The slough is over 10 miles long and holds good water levels with tide gates. Banks are steep, and bank access is limited except from county roads and bridges. One unimproved boat ramp near the middle of the slough is suitable for launching light-weight craft or float tubes.

White and black crappie are abundant, and there are lots of yellow perch, and yellow, black, and brown bullhead. Bluegill and largemouth bass are occasionally taken. Bottom fishing with worms is best for catfish and perch. Use a bobber to fish for crappie and bass.

BUCK LAKE. One Oregon's dune lakes,

about 4½ miles north of Florence, ¼ mile south of Alder and Dune lakes. About 5 acres, Buck is stocked with rainbow trout and may have some bass. Park on the highway shoulder just south of Buck Lake Trailer Park. A trail on the west side of the highway leads a few hundred feet to the lake. Fish from the sand dune on the south end. Best fishing is in April, May, and June before the water warms. There is a Forest Service campground at Alder Lake.

BURKES LAKE. See **SHAG LAKE.**

BUSTER CREEK. A small early-season cutthroat stream flowing west into the Nehalem River near Tidesport, about halfway between Elsie and Jewell. The middle reach of the stream can be reached by the Grand Rapids Road and by Wage Road, which cross both forks of the creek southeast of Jewell.

In early season this is a good cutthroat stream, but it is hard to fish because of the brush. Angling for the cutthroat is catch and release. A dark fly sliding off riparian vegetation might raise some interest.

CAPE MEARES LAKE. Tillamook County's largest lake, tucked between Tillamook Bay and the ocean, supporting trout, largemouth bass, brown bullhead catfish, and bluegill. The lake was created by diking on the Cape Meares side of Tillamook Bay. To get there from Tillamook, head west on Third street, then right onto Bayocean Rd.

Though the lake has about 90 surface acres, it is never deeper than ten feet. Aquatic vegetation is quite thick in places along the edges, and gets worse throughout the summer.

It is stocked from mid-March through early May with legal rainbow trout, and there are usually some nice holdovers from the previous season. If you think you've hooked an aquatic cheetah, chances are you're into one of the adult hatchery-reared steelhead that ODFW plants here when they have a few returns in excess of their hatchery stocking needs. Count these twenty-inchers as trout in your daily take (no steelhead tag needed).

Largemouth bass are established here, but because reproduction is low, you might consider releasing bass unharmed in order to help maintain the fishery. Look for bass around clumps of rushes or along the riprap of the dam road. A cove at the west end has a lot of woody structure that should attract bass. Bluegill and brown bullhead are present in small numbers.

You can fish along the road or at a sturdy public dock just off the main road. You can also drive out the dike access road on the east shore, park at the end (don't park along the narrow road), and walk the short distance back to the lake. There is a boat ramp just past the angling dock. Speed limit on the lake is 5 mph. Tillamook Bay and nearby beaches offer alternative saltwater fishing opportunities. There is a campground 10 miles south at Cape Lookout State Park.

CARCUS CREEK. Tributary to the Clatskanie River, flowing from the south and meeting the Clatskanie about 8 miles southeast of the town of Clatskanie near the Firewood School. This is a nice little wild cutthroat stream, but it takes a good deal of brush beating to fish it. Beaver ponds have been known to make the trip worthwhile.

Access is through private timberland (Longview Fiber and Olympic Resources at this time) which allow non-motorized public access. Use a current fire protection district map (NW Oregon, Forest Grove District) to make your way through the maze of logging roads. Carry a shovel and a gallon of water or fire extinguisher during fire season.

There is a spectacular 100-ft. waterfall high up the creek where it flows through Carcus Creek Park, an undeveloped county park surrounded by private timberland. Access is challenging, but worth a visit by the hearty and adventurous.

CARNAHAN LAKE. A private 9-acre lake west of Hwy. 101 about 5 miles north of Gearhart, and just north of Cullaby Lake. Maximum depth is 15 ft., and the lake is very weedy. It is closed to public access.

CARTER LAKE. A typical dune lake with good trout fishing, one mile long and 400 feet wide. It is reached by Hwy. 101 about 9 miles south of Florence. The lake is on the west side of the highway. A very brushy shoreline makes it difficult to fish from shore in high water years. Carter is stocked with legal rainbows and occasional brood fish to 12 pounds.

There is a public campground at the east end of the lake with a concrete boat ramp, parking, and picnic facilities.

CEMETERY LAKE. A 10-acre Clatsop County fishery for black crappie, warmouth, bluegill, largemouth bass, and yellow perch. It is connected by pipe to Smith Lake. The lake is open to public use, with access through the Astoria cemetery.

CHAMBERLAIN LAKE. Quite prominent on most maps, this 11-acre lake is located at the Scout camp just south of Cape Lookout State Park. It is not open to public angling.

CAPE MEARES LAKE offers trout fishing with an expansive bay view and fresh salt air. Photograph by Scott Richmond.

CLATSKANIE RIVER. Flows through the town of Clatskanie and enters the Columbia River about mid-way between St. Helens and Astoria. Do not confuse this with the Klaskanine River, which is near Astoria. The Clatskanie River is a good all around stream, about 26 miles long, featuring cutthroat trout as well as a good steelhead run and a few coho.

Roads parallel and cross the river in many spots and it has several good tributaries. The headwaters can be reached from the St. Helens-Vernonia Rd. by taking the gravel road north to Apiary. The lower stream is best reached from Clatskanie. Gravel and boulders make it an ideal fly stream, but there are brushy areas where a spinner will work best. Fishing for all cutthroat and wild steelhead is catch and release only, so the use of bait is discouraged.

Resident cutthroat are present throughout the system. Sea-run cutthroat linger in the lower river from July until September before moving upstream.

The Clatskanie has a nice wild winter steelhead run, and finclipped hatchery stock from a discontinued stocking program should continue to show up for a couple more years.

There's lots of private land along the lower river, but landowners continue to be generous about allowing access. Be a courteous, no-trace visitor. Supplies are available in Clatskanie.

CLATSKANIE SLOUGH. Very good bass and panfish water, connected to the lower Clatskanie River and accessed by county roads north of Clatskanie on Hwy. 30. The slough is controlled by tide gates. There are no boat ramps, but light-weight boats can be launched at the road crossing. Bank access is limited to a few vehicle and foot bridges. Good size yellow and black crappie and brown bullhead are plentiful. Perch, bluegill, and bass are present but not numerous. Bobber and worm are probably your best bet. This fishery is recommended for youngsters.

CLEAR LAKE (Clatsop Co.). An 8-acre largemouth bass fishery on private property, one mile north of Warrenton.

CLEAR LAKE (Lane Co.). A mixed fishery for the adventurous angler. Located about 3 miles north of Florence on Hwy. 101, just north of Munsel Lake, Clear Lake is quite

Photograph by Scott Richmond.

prominent on maps. It is about 160 acres, with naturally reproducing largemouth bass, yellow perch, and trout. There is no public road to the lake, but there is some public access on the west shore after a grueling one-mile hike through sand dunes and swamp.

CLEAR LAKE (Tillamook Co.). Not to be confused with Spring Lake, about a mile down the road. A small, poor cutthroat lake, about 3 acres and very shallow, it is located just south of Rockaway on the east side of Hwy. 101. It supports cutthroat trout, but isn't very productive. It is surrounded by private land, and public access is doubtful.

CLEAWOX LAKE. Popular because of its location within Honeyman State Park a few miles south of Florence. Stocked with legal rainbows as well as larger trout grown to trophy size, the lake also has good populations of largemouth bass and crappie, with yellow perch, brown bullhead, and bluegill available. It's a good bet in early season before the campers get too numerous. The lake has about 82 surface acres. Motor boats are prohibited.

COFFENBURY LAKE. A 50-acre trout lake within Fort Stevens State Park, about 2 miles west of Warrenton. The lake is long and narrow, in a deep depression between sand dunes. Its maximum depth is 9 feet near the north end, and it is easily reached by a good road.

Coffenbury is stocked annually with legal trout and a few adult steelhead. Best fishing is earlier in the season. Although

Coffenbury supports some yellow perch and brown bullhead, it is not a very productive warmwater fishery.

There is a trail all the way around the lake and several fishing docks. Boats are allowed on the lake, but there is a 10 mph speed limit.

Ft. Stevens is one of Oregon's most extensive state parks, including a full service campground, bike and hiking trails through coastal forest, as well as access to some of the state's finest surf fishing and razor clam beds. Razors are especially tender and can grow to 6 inches. They are best dug on a minus tide close to the surf. Check with ODFW for open seasons and quality assurance (Razor clams are subject to a natural toxicity that can be fatal. Their quality is monitored regularly by the Dept. of Agriculture.)

Coffenbury is recommended for youngsters. Docks are wheelchair accessible but lack safety edges..

COLLARD LAKE. A private 32-acre lake about 3 miles north of Florence and one mile east of Hwy. 101. The lake supports yellow perch, bluegill, brown bullhead, and largemouth bass, but there is no public access at this time.

COOK CREEK. A fair wild cutthroat and-steelhead stream flowing southeast into the lower Nehalem, about 7 miles from the town of Nehalem. The creek is about 18 miles long, including tributaries, and enters the Nehalem at a point shown as Batterson on most maps. A gravel road parallels the creek.

A good fly stream with lots of boulders

Charter boat operators provide gear and know-how for halibut trips out of DEPOE Bay. Photograph by John Ramsour.

and gravel and not too brushy, it has quite a few cutthroat. It offers 5 miles of good catch and release angling for winter steelhead up to the south fork.

Coho and fall chinook spawn in Cook, but the creek is closed to all salmon fishing.

CRABAPPLE LAKE. A swampy 22-acre lake in Ft. Stevens State Park. Fish it early in the season for largemouth bass and yellow perch before weeds choke out access. You'll need a boat or float tube to get beyond the weeds. There are lots of sunken logs to attract the fish. There is a day use fee to enter the park.

CREEP AND CRAWL LAKE. A swampy 5-acre pond in Ft. Stevens State Park, offering bluegill fishing in early season. By midsummer the lake is usually weed-bound. You'll need a boat or float tube to get beyond the weeds. There is a day use fee.

CRESCENT LAKE (Tillamook Co.). An 11-acre lake 5 miles north of Tillamook Bay on Hwy. 101 near Manhattan Beach. Just north of Lytle Lake (and connected to it), Crescent covers 11 acres, but has grown increasingly shallow due to siltation.

Activity by resident beavers has restricted boat access, but this is a great place to observe a good looking beaver dam and maybe even catch a few of the engineers at

the construction site..

Largemouth bass are present, and stocked trout drift down from Lytle. Crescent itself is no longer stocked.

CRIMM'S ISLAND SLOUGH. A Columbia River slough 6 miles northeast of Clatskanie, with known populations of white and black crappie.

CRONIN CREEK. A wild cutthroat stream entering the Nehalem from the east, about 10 miles south of Elsie on the lower Nehalem Rd. Sea-run cutthroat are present in late fall. Only the stretch below Nehalem River Rd. is open to public access.

CULLABY LAKE. A good place to take the family for panfish and stocked catchable trout. It is east of Hwy. 101, 12 miles south of Astoria. The lake is a long and narrow 220 acres, about 1½ miles from north to south and usually less than ¼ mile wide. Its depth ranges 6 to 12 feet.

Cullaby is stocked with legal trout and usually provides excellent angling from spring through late fall for good-size crappie, bluegill, perch, brown bullheads and largemouth bass. There's a lot of good habitat for warmwater fish, including overhanging brush and submerged vegetation.

Bullhead fishing is excellent at the south end of the lake, especially in March. For

bass, try working the snags on the east bank of the lake where the weeds aren't so thick. A boat is essential to reach the fish later in summer when the lake chokes up with aquatic weeds. Winter perch fishing can be very good in the deeper water.

A county park with boat ramp and picnic areas extends halfway around the west side of the lake. There are docks at the north end and mid-way around the lake. Motorboats and water-skiers can be a problem for angling on summer weekends, but a 10 mph speed limit keeps the north end of the lake relatively calm.

DEADWOOD CREEK. Tributary to Lake Creek in the Siuslaw watershed with catch and release angling for wild winter steelhead. It joins Lake Creek from the north about 30 miles upstream from Florence, accessed from Hwy. 36 (Florence to Junction City) by a paved road that parallels its length. Best fishing is in early season for primarily wild winter steelhead. The creek is closed to all angling April 1 to December 31 to protect spawning chinook. The closest campground is at Indian Creek, one mile north of Hwy. 36 at Indianola.

DEER ISLAND SLOUGH. A large bass and panfish slough on the lower Columbia west of St. Helens, 35 miles west of Portland. Access is from the town of Deer Island on Hwy. 30. It connects to Goat Island Slough. Boats can be launched from the county road. About 15 species of fish are present, with crappie, perch, and brown bullhead most numerous. Some good size bass are taken on plugs and spinners. It is bordered by private property, but landowners have been generous with access. Ask permission. The slough can also be reached from Shell Beach.

DEPOE BAY. Oregon's safest portal to the open sea, south of Siletz Bay and crossed by Hwy. 101 about a hundred miles from Portland by way of highways 18 and 101. The bay itself is only lightly fished, fed by two small streams.

Its channel to the Pacific is extremely narrow, and boats coming in and out usually have quite an audience on the highway bridge and at the state park rest area on the bluff. Commercial fishing boats makes daily trips from June through October in pursuit of bottom fish, and for halibut and salmon in season. Charter boats are available. The bay itself is best fished from its shoals at low tide for rockfish, perch, and other bottom species.

There is a large public boat ramp and parking area on the south side of the bay. Although its access to the open sea is considered one of the least hazardous on the coast, precaution when entering the ocean is always advised. Check with the Coast Guard crew based on the bay. All boats venturing "outside" should be safety equipped, with a spare motor.

Salmon start showing well outside the bay in late June. Both coho and chinook are fished on trolled wobblers, spinners, or herring. At times the fish are right on top, but anglers often have to go deep for them. Most fishing takes place within a few miles of the buoys marking the channel entrance. There are forty to fifty thousand angler trips out of Depoe Bay each year, and the average catch per trip is often the highest on the coast. Private boaters fish the reefs as far south as Yaquina Head Lighthouse (a few miles). Reefs north of Depoe extend to the mouth of the Siletz. Fish 8 to 30 fathoms for lingcod, rockfish, greenling, and cabezon. Halibut are caught as well, especially to the north. Following the commercial boats is an acceptable tactic for locating good fishing grounds.

Charter boats make trips of two hours, four hours, and all-day. They can't guarantee your limit, but they have the equipment and know-how to locate fish, and you'll be in safe hands. Charter operators supply rods, tackle and bait. Bring warm clothes and rain gear.

Salmon and Pacific halibut fishing seasons and quotas are determined annually by the Pacific Fishery Management Council. General regulations are published in the spring of the year, but in-season changes are common. Always check before planning a trip to fish either of these species. See Appendix for information sources.

In addition to salmon and halibut, private boat operators also pursue lingcod, black seabass, cabezon, kelp greenling, sea trout, red snapper, rockfish, and striped perch using herring, sand shrimp, and many different kinds of jigs. One of the best bottom fishing spots out of Depoe Bay is Government Reef to the north.

Depoe Bay is also the center of a productive shoreline reef fishery. There's good fishing from the rocks north and south of the channel, as well as at Pirate Cove and Boiler Bay a little farther north, and at Whale Cove and Cape Foulweather to the south. Best fishing from the rocks is in spring and on calm winter days. Peak catches are made in February and March during the spawning period. Fishing from the rocks is considerably slower in summer, but can still be productive.

Anglers use both bait and jigs. Cut herring is a favorite bait for lingcod. Kelp greenling and striped perch seem to prefer sand shrimp. Check with local tackle shops for bait, jig, and hook recommendations. In recent years, the ling population has suffered a decline, and regulations reflect the effort to protect adult spawners. At this time, harvest is limited to one fish per day with a keeper slot length of 24-inch minimum and 34-inch maximum. Check current regulations.

DEVILS LAKE (Lincoln Co.). A large coastal lake with about 700 surface acres, featuring bass, panfish, and a fair trout fishery. It is located off Hwy. 101 a few miles south of Lincoln City. Hwy. 18 through McMinnville offers the best route from the Willamette Valley. A serious aquatic weed problem in years past is being successfully addressed by introduced grass carp. It is illegal to fish for the carp.

Legal rainbows are stocked from spring into early summer, providing the bulk of the trout fishing here, with the average fish measuring 12 inches. Carry-over rainbows reach 16 to 20 inches.

Warmwater fish (brown bullhead, channel catfish, black crappie, yellow perch, and largemouth) are less numerous now that the weeds are under control.

Devils Lake State Park at the southeast corner of the lake has a campground, boat ramp, and picnic area. There is a launch fee at the park. Several other boat ramps around the lake are free.

DIBBLEES SLOUGH. A Columbia River slough west of Rainier. It is southwest of the popular salmon beach known as Dibblees Beach, accessed by county roads and by boat from the Columbia at Rainier. It can also be reached by the river road under the Longview Bridge. Crappie and brown bullhead are the main catch here, with bottom bait and bobber the best technique.

The slough is used for log storage, and log rafts offer good shelter for panfish.

Casting under the log rafts often produces crappie. Do not stand on log rafts to fish here or elsewhere on the river.

DRIFT CREEK (Alsea watershed). A good size stream with native runs of salmon, steelhead, and cutthroat trout, opening into Alsea Bay about 3 miles east of Waldport. About 30 miles long and 30 to 60 feet wide, it carves a narrow canyon through thick woods, including stands of old growth timber. Its lower waters can be approached from the north side of Alsea Bay by a road running east, and by boat from the bay itself. Logging roads bisect the upper stream, and several marked trails make the steep descent into the canyon. It's a 1200 foot drop over 2 miles on the Horse Creek Trail, 1000 feet on the Harris Ranch Trail. This is a pristine roadless area of old growth timber.

The creek offers good catch and release fishing for resident cutthroat trout from late May throughout the season.

It also hosts important runs of coho, winter steelhead, and searun cutthroat and is considered a key watershed in the effort to restore the coast's anadromous fish populations. The creek is monitored closely by the US Forest Service. Most steelhead in Drift Creek are wild and must be released unharmed. A good, healthy run of wild fall chinook present in late October and November may be fished for harvest.

Boat moorages and public ramps are available on Alsea Bay for explorations of the lower creek, which is heavily posted against bank fishing.

DRIFT CREEK (Siletz watershed). A good coastal cutthroat stream with important runs of wild winter steelhead and fall chinook. Drift Creek enters Siletz Bay at Cutler City, one mile north of the Siletz River Rd. 229. It flows about 18 miles with average width 35 feet. About one mile north of Kernville, a road heads west from Hwy. 101 and follows Drift Creek more than 10 miles. Access within the first 8 miles requires a hike south to the stream. The upper water is reached by the Drift Creek Trail and by logging roads.

Drift Creek offers high quality catch and release angling for wild winter steelhead from January through March and for cutthroat trout in summer. The fall chinook run is strong, with fish available in October and November.

Like Drift Creek in the Alsea drainage, this Drift Creek is considered to be a key watershed in the effort to restore anadromous fish runs. Stocking of hatchery steelhead has been discontinued, and all non-finclipped steelhead must be released.

Road access is limited, and best angling is available by hiking through roadless areas above and below Drift Creek Camp. The camp is at about stream mile 12. Another camp is located about 5 miles up on Schooner Creek. Devils Lake State Park, north of Taft on Hwy. 101, also provides camping facilities. Supplies and accommodations are available in the Siletz Bay area.

DUNE LAKE. An Oregon Dunes lake featuring stocked trout. It is north of Sutton Lake. See ALDER LAKE for directions.

ECKMAN LAKE. A 45-acre lake with trout and warmwater species adjacent to the lower Alsea River off Hwy. 34, about 2 miles east of Waldport.

Eckman supports brown bullhead catfish and some large largemouth bass. Look for them in the deep channel along Hwy. 34. Legal rainbows are stocked in early season. Cutthroat trout are also present and must be released unharmed. There is a boat ramp here but no campground.

ECOLA CREEK (a.k.a. Elk Cr.). Flows directly into the ocean after a 10 mile run. Historically, a good resident cutthroat and winter steelhead stream, with small runs of coho and searun. Good numbers of wild winter steelhead appear in the creek in December. Best fishing is in January and February. Hatchery steelhead occasionally stray into Ecola and may be kept if caught. Salmon, cutthroat, and non-finclipped steelhead must be released unharmed.

The creek is currently closed to all angling from April 1 till November 1. It opens for winter steelheading up to the forks, about a mile above Hwy. 101.

ELBOW LAKE. A 13-acre lake south of Tahkenitch Lake, on the west side of Hwy. 101. The lake is visible from the highway. Pull off the highway and park by the south shore, where light-weight boats and float tubes can be launched. Fish for rainbows trout and yellow perch along the brushy shoreline and among the downed trees. Best bank access is along the highway. Recommended for youngsters.

ERHART LAKE. A good, small, very scenic rainbow lake on the west side of Hwy. 101, about 8 miles south of Florence near Siltcoos Lake. This is a beautiful little lake, reminiscent of those in the high Cascades. Generously stocked with rainbow trout, it holds up well into summer. You'll lose less gear if you toss flies rather than hardware .

Erhart is heavily fished through spring, mostly from shore. A trail leads down to the lake from the highway. There is a little gravel road that goes around to the far shore where you can bank fish or launch a light-weight boat or float tube. There are good campgrounds nearby.

ESMOND CREEK. A tributary of the Siuslaw, offering excellent catch and release angling for wild cutthroat. It flows about 10 miles, entering the Siuslaw just beyond mile post 10 on the Siuslaw River Rd., which cuts south off Hwy. 126 between Richardson and Austa. A landslide at its upper end forms Esmond Lake. A beautiful road follows the creek to within ½ mile of the lake. Begin fishing at its confluence with the Siuslaw.

ESMOND LAKE. A very deep three-acre lake created by a large landslide near the upper end of Esmond Creek. It contains a good wild cutthroat population. A ½-mile trail leads in from the end of Esmond Creek Rd. This lake is truly in the middle of nowhere. A float tube would be very useful.

EUCHRE CREEK (Pronounced Yoo-ker, . A fair cutthroat stream entering the Siletz River about 24 river miles above the bay, 4 miles downstream from the town of Siletz. Hwy. 229 crosses it just above its mouth.

Not heavily fished, it affords good cover for trout, rich food sources, and fair cutthroat fishing in early season. It's easy on tackle, too. Only about 10 miles long and about 25 feet wide, it has a good population of wild cutthroat trout. Fishing for them is catch and release at this time.

FIVE RIVERS. A major tributary of the Alsea River, flowing about 18 miles from the south. It enters the Alsea 20 miles upstream from Waldport, 23 miles west of the town of Alsea off Hwy. 34. A good road follows the stream to its headwaters.

Five Rivers has many nice pools and bedrock ledges, and offers good catch and release fishing for cutthroat well into the season. Wild winter steelhead are available for catch and release angling January through March.

There's a popular crayfish fishery here June through August. Place traps along the bedrock ledges.

Five Rivers has an important run of wild coho salmon, generally present in late October and November, but the river is closed to coho fishing at this time. It is open for fall chinook, however, and catches can be good below the mouth of Lobster Creek.

Camping along the river is limited to undeveloped sites among the blackberries. There is a developed campground on the Alsea toward Waldport.

FLOETERS POND. One of a group of small hike-in cutthroat lakes on private industrial timber land in rural Columbia County northwest of Portland (see also Gunners Lakes). Covering only about 3 acres and difficult to reach, it offers wild cutthroat angling in spring and early summer. The lake is dominated by snags and fallen logs, and at times beavers have dammed the outlet. Not exactly pristine, it can be heavily used at times as the site of clandestine parties by local young folk.

The pond is about 5 miles southeast of Vernonia and 3 miles north of the Columbia County line. To get there, follow a trail south from the Scappoose-Vernonia Hwy. 1½ miles east of the BLM picnic area on the East Fork Nehalem. It's a 1½ mile hike south to the lake.

It can also be accessed by bushwhacking down from logging roads in the vicinity of Gunners Lakes. Carry a current fire protection map (NW Oregon, Forest Grove District), as well as a shovel and gallon of water or fire extinguisher during fire season. Be a courteous, no-trace user to protect continued public access. Be especially careful with fire.

FOGARTY CREEK. A small stream flowing into the ocean through Fogarty State Park, about 4 miles south of Siletz Bay. A few cutthroat are taken in the upper section, but its too small for much angling.

Some perch and kelp fish are fished from the rocks at the outlet. There is a nice picnic area on the creek, but overnight camping is prohibited.

GEORGIA LAKES. Two deep trout lakes opposite the Siltcoos Lake outlet and campground off Hwy. 101. Access is from the east side of the highway. Follow Hobbit-like trails around the lakes, through big ferns and moss-covered old growth spruce. Both lakes are stocked with legal rainbows. Other lakes in the vicinity include Perkins, Erhart, Carter, and Lost.

GNAT CREEK. A fair stream for wild cutthroat, with a good run of winter steelhead, primarily of hatchery origin. It enters the lower Columbia by way of Blind Slough, crossing Hwy. 30 a few miles east of Knappa. About 9 miles long, it heads near Nicolai Mt. and has a lot of beaver ponds in its headwaters.

Steelhead are stocked in Gnat and return to the stream from November or December to March. Coho may also be present, including finclipped strays. Only finclipped steelhead and coho may be kept. Fall chinook enter Gnat already ripe for spawning and should be left undisturbed.

GOAT ISLAND SLOUGH. A 55-acre slough on the Columbia River northeast of Columbia City at Reichold Chemical Plant. Look for white crappie, brown bullhead, largemouth bass, bluegill, and yellow perch. There is public access at the south end only.

GUNNERS LAKES. Two very small wild cutthroat lakes tucked into private industrial timberland in Columbia County's Nehalem Mountains. The lakes are open for public fishing and are approached by a network of unsigned and active logging roads that emerge and vanish from year to year, making access an adventure.

At the time of this writing, the approach from Hwy. 30 is as follows: turn south on Scappoose-Vernonia Highway, then left on Chapman Rd. (not Chapman Grange Rd.). Set your odometer at zero. Bear left at the first major fork and continue uphill on rough gravel. At 3.6 miles, fork to the right at a broad U-shaped intersection. At 4.7 miles, take the left fork and head uphill. Bear right at 5.3 miles. and again at 5.6 miles. The smaller lake is .2 miles from this turn (difficult to spot on your way in). The second, larger lake is on the left at 6.6 miles from the Chapman Rd. turn-off. Signs placed by the Scappoose High School Environmental Club announce you've made it. Four-wheel drive is not necessary in dry weather, but drive slowly to protect your tailpipe and undercarriage.

The State Forest Service patrols these roads during the dry season, and fire restrictions are in effect at that time. Visitors must carry a shovel and a gallon of water or fire extinguisher.

Upper Gunners Lake is the more approachable and productive of the two. An inlet flowing through partially submerged timber, visible across the lake from the road, attracts fish in late summer, though catches are also made from the little clearing beside the roadside culvert. A succession of game trails through the marsh grass can get you around the lake with considerable effort. A float tube would be useful. Camping is not allowed at either lake.

There is a third lake in the area, Floeters Pond. To reach it, follow the directions above, but head straight across the broad U-shaped intersection at 3.6 miles and continue to the dead end. Floeters is downhill about 300 feet.

HEBO LAKE. A 2-acre cutthroat lake 3½ miles east of the Hebo Ranger Station on the Hebo Mt. Rd. From Hebo, take Hwy. 22 ¼ mile east, then turn left onto Forest Rd. 14. At 4 miles, watch for a sign directing you to the lake. The access road is gated in winter, but it's a short walk in.

Hebo is shallow throughout and contains good trout forage. It is stocked with legal cutthroat from early April through mid-May. Additional fish are provided for Free Fishing Day activities.

Small boats can be launched, and electric motors are allowed. Fish are caught using all methods.

There is a trail around the lake, and a developed campground open in summer. Recommended for youngsters. Barrier-free piers provide an opportunity for disabled anglers.

HULT RESERVOIR. A wild cutthroat fishery with bass and panfish opportunities, about 4 miles north of Horton, 10 miles from Triangle Lake.

Hult provides fair angling for largemouth bass in spring. There is a good bluegill and brown bullhead population (average size 9 inches). The reservoir has a small boat ramp. Only electric motors are allowed.

HUMBUG CREEK. A fine catch and release cutthroat stream, about 9 miles long, entering the Nehalem south of Elsie. Hwy. 26 parallels the creek and crosses both the east and west forks. Humbug has some boulders and gravel, but it is primarily a bedrock stream.

Working a spinner or streamer along the ledges can be effective. Use hooks size 10 or larger to avoid hooking and possibly injuring juvenile steelhead and coho. Cutthroat must be released unharmed.

INDIAN CREEK. One of the best wild steelhead streams in the Siuslaw drainage. Indian is a major tributary of Lake Creek, joining Lake Creek about 2 miles north of Swisshome. The creek is about 10 miles long and averages 30 to 40 feet wide. A county road follows the stream north from Hwy. 36, about 40 miles west of Junction City. There is a lot of private land along the stream, but there is some access through public forest land.

Indian Creek is closed to angling April 1 to December 31 to protect spawning chinook. There is a US Forest Service campground at mile post 1½ on Indian Cr. Rd.

KAUPPI LAKE. A 5-acre lake on private timber land 5½ miles south of Birkenfeld (probably not worth the 12 to 14 mile trek currently required to reach it). The lake is no longer stocked due to weed problems, though it does have a few wild cutthroat and stunted crappie. Kauppi was never easy to find. Now it also requires a long hike since the private Crooked Creek mainline road is closed to public motorized traffic. Weeds seal the lake in late summer, and there are lots of logs and snags. Deepest water (10 feet) is on the eastern edge. Best access is probably now from Pittsburg, south of Big Eddy on the Nehalem. Check a current fire protection map (NW Oregon, Forest Grove District).

KILCHIS RIVER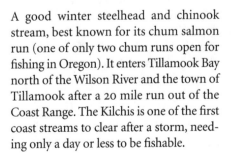

A good winter steelhead and chinook stream, best known for its chum salmon run (one of only two chum runs open for fishing in Oregon). It enters Tillamook Bay north of the Wilson River and the town of Tillamook after a 20 mile run out of the Coast Range. The Kilchis is one of the first coast streams to clear after a storm, needing only a day or less to be fishable.

The KILCHIS RIVER offers Oregon anglers a good chance to catch (and release) chum salmon. Photograph by Richard T. Grost.

The chum salmon population is currently very low, and fishing for them is restricted to catch and release during a short season mid-September to mid-November. Chum are smaller than chinook (averaging 8 to 20 pounds) and are identifiable by their color (silvery green and bronze when fresh, red and olive with broad vertical bars when closer to spawning). Use pliers for releasing them to avoid their sharp fangs. Check current regulations.

Winter steelhead are the river's strongest run. The average catch weighs 6 to 9 pounds. Steelhead are available November through March with peak catches in mid-December and January. The wild run is generally later, in February and March. Fish to 20 pounds have been taken late in the season. Summer steelhead were once stocked here and some still enter the river in May, lingering till fall.

Fall chinook are holding their own in the Kilchis, arriving late, with best catches often in November. A handful of spring chinook (both wild and hatchery strays) are generally ignored by anglers.

The upper Kilchis is gravelly with scant cover, but the lower river has very good trout habitat. Catch and release cutthroat angling can be good here, though the river's searun population, which shows in August, has been severely depressed in recent years.

There's reasonably good access to the Kilchis, which flows through the Tillamook State Forest, though boating is limited to the lower 6 miles. Boaters can put in at Mapes Creek Landing (also known as the Logger Bridge) about three miles up Kilchis River Rd., or at the county boat ramp 2½ miles farther up. The take-out is an improved public ramp called Parks Landing, about 200 yds. above Hwy. 101 on Alderbrook Rd.

Bank anglers have only a couple of options on the lower river, which flows through private land. One downstream owner currently allows access for a modest fee. Note the coin box at Curl Rd. Bridge. The only other bank opportunity is at Mapes Creek, with room for about 20 anglers. But from Kilchis County Park upstream, the river flows through public land, with the river road following closely. There are many pull-outs with trails down to the river, and better fishing than ever since the floods of '96 rearranged things a bit.

Flood level on the Kilchis is 11 feet with optimum fishing 7 to 6 feet and acceptable levels between 7 and 5.3 feet. Use the Wilson River gauge reading to estimate the condition of the Kilchis. See Appendix. At 4 feet the Kilchis runs low and clear, and bottoming out in a boat can be a problem.

Supplies, accommodations, tackle, and advice are available in Tillamook.

KLASKANINE RIVER. A tributary of the lower Columbia (not to be confused with the Clatskanie), offering excellent opportunities to catch and keep coho, spring and fall chinook (virtually all of hatchery origin), and finclipped winter steelhead. Heading in the coast range west of Jewell, the Klaskanine flows about 20 miles into Young's Bay near Astoria. The fish pack in here just as thick as at popular Big Creek to the east, and there's usually more elbow room on the banks.

From Astoria, Hwy. 202 skirts the shore of the bay then follows the North Fork Klaskanine about five miles before cutting over to the South Fork. The South Fork can also be approached near its mouth by a road south out of Olney. The South Fork flows through mostly private timberland, but the current owner (Willamette Industries) allows walk-in public access. Be a courteous no-trace visitor. Pack out what you pack in to preserve the privilege.

There are hatcheries on both forks of the river, but the North Fork produces fish for the Klaskanine itself, while South Fork catches are more likely to be wild.

Spring chinook enter the bay in early April and are usually plentiful in the North Fork by the time the river's chinook season opens in late May. Fall chinook make their run for the hatchery in July and early August and are fished through November and December. There are no known wild chinook in the river. Some chinook stray into the upper river, but most are caught from the North Fork Klaskanine Hatchery downstream.

Jacks (immature salmon) offer a lively fishery in themselves. Arriving in September and remaining through the winter, they can be fished using small spoons and spinners, and eggs with bobbers. This is an especially good fishery for youngsters.

Winter steelhead are in both forks from Thanksgiving through the end of the season. The North Fork is heavily stocked with finclipped steelhead, and good numbers are caught. A few hatchery steelhead may stray into the South Fork, but that stream isn't stocked, so be prepared to re-

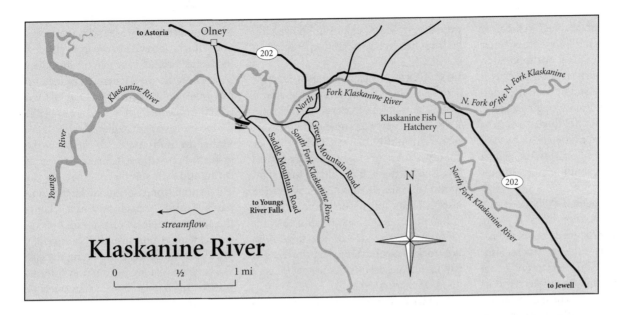

Klaskanine River

streamflow

0   ½   1 mi

lease most of your catches there.

The Klaskanine provides good trout habitat, with quite a few boulders and gravel bars and some good but brushy holes. All cutthroat are wild and must be released unharmed. Sea-run cutthroat return to the river in late August or early September, depending on the rainfall.

From the bay to the head of tidewater, the Klaskanine is best accessed from boats. Anglers motor up about ½ mile from the primitive public boat ramp at the head of tide just off the Youngs River Loop Rd. To reach it, follow Hwy. 202 to Olney, then turn south onto Youngs River Loop. The ramp is on the south bank just across the bridge.

Above tidewater, the river is almost exclusively fished from the bank. The major concentration of fish and anglers is right below the hatchery on the North Fork. Park at the hatchery and walk through the grounds to fish about a hundred yards from the deadline ropes downstream. Anglers also fish from the bridge adjacent to the county boat ramp on Young's Loop Road, and there is a public fishing easement at an undeveloped Klaskanine County Park (mile post 11 on Hwy. 202). To reach it, turn right just upstream of the private RV park. The road continues through a big field and down to the river. The easement extends downstream about ¾ mile. Smiley's Hole, at the confluence of North and South forks, is currently closed to public access by the landowner, but it can't hurt to ask permission to cross over to the river.

Special bait and hook restrictions may be in effect at some times of the year. Check the regulations.

KLICKITAT LAKE. A tiny trout lake in the headwaters of the North Fork Alsea River near the divide between the Yaquina and Alsea basins. It has small wild cutthroat in abundance.

From Philomath on Hwy. 20, follow Hwy. 202 southwest. A little less than 2 miles west of Marys Wayside, turn right to follow BLM Rt. 10, which heads up the North Fork. Klickitat is on the left, about 12 miles up this windy gravel road. It is fed by Klickitat Creek, which enters the lake at the northwest corner. Use a Siuslaw National Forest map to navigate.

LAKE CREEK (Siuslaw watershed). A major tributary of the Siuslaw River, offering the best opportunity for winter steelhead in the Siuslaw system. It joins the river at Swisshome.

From Eugene, follow Hwy. 99 north to Hwy. 36, which leads to Triangle Lake. Hwy. 36 follows Lake Creek downstream to its confluence with the Siuslaw. The mouth of Lake Creek is about 42 miles west of Junction City.

Lake Creek is extremely clear since Triangle Lake (created by a landslide on the creek) serves as a sediment trap. It really has to rain to muddy it up. A ladder at the falls just below Triangle Lake allows salmon and steelhead access to an additional 100 miles of spawning ground.

A favorite of Eugene-Springfield anglers, the creek has runs of both hatchery and wild steelhead that show up in December,

with peak catches in February and March. The creek also has chinook and coho, but is closed to coho fishing. Check the regulations for chinook opportunities. Lake Creek is closed to trout fishing above Greenleaf Creek.

There are drift boat put-ins at the mouths of Indian and Green creeks and near the mouth of Deadwood Creek. There is a Class 4 rapids (The Horn) about one mile below the mouth of Indian Creek. It is extremely dangerous and should not be run by drift boats. Take out ¼ mile above the rapids at the highway gravel pile site. Konnie Fishing Access below the Horn can be used for a good drift down to the take-out at Tide on the mainstem Siuslaw (about 4 miles).

Lake Creek flows through a lot of private land. Don't trespass.

LEWIS AND CLARK RIVER. A wild steelhead and cutthroat stream, tributary of Young's Bay on the lower Columbia. To reach the river from Astoria, follow the Hwy. 101 Business Route south to Miles Crossing, then continue south on the Lewis and Clark Rd., which follows the stream for some distance before heading over to Seaside. Much of the river flows through private land, but there is some public access.

Steelhead can be found in the river from December through March. Most, if not all, are wild and must be released unharmed. Few are found above the city of Warrenton water intake. Only a few salmon spawn in the Lewis and Clark. If you happen upon them, give 'em a break.

There is good public access to the river in the vicinity of the Warrenton Water Treatment Plant. Heading north on Hwy. 101 from Seaside, turn right onto Lewis & Clark Rd. At its intersection with the Lewis & Clark Mainline Rd. (a logging road at the top of a steep grade) there is room to park near the locked gate. Hike (or bicycle) down the first spur on the left, which reaches the river in about ¾ mile. Fish upstream or down.

Logging roads behind the locked gate are perfect for mountain bikes. If you're walking or biking the roads on weekdays, keep an ear tuned for logging trucks. Fishing is prohibited within 200 feet of a dam (there are four dams on the river and its tributaries in this area). There is a wonderful variety of good steelhead water along the 400 Line Rd. below the water treatment plant.

LILY LAKE (Lane Co.). An opportunity for the hardy to fish for native cutthroat in a pretty meadow setting near the ocean. This small lake is west of Hwy. 101, about 10 miles north of Florence. Take Baker Beach Rd. to the trailhead (unsigned). A ¼-mile trail leads to the lake, along the edge of a swamp and through a genuine bog. Don't underestimate this trail.

Lily is lightly fished for good reasons, but it does have pretty, wild 14-inch cutthroat. A float tube might make the trip worthwhile, since the lake has a thick border of reeds. Fishing is restricted to catch and release angling with barbless hooks and artificial flies or lures.

LITTLE ELK RIVER. A fair wild cutthroat stream, tributary of the Yaquina River, joining the Yaquina near Eddyville on Hwy. 20, the Newport-Corvallis Hwy. Only 11 miles long and fairly small, it is followed by Hwy. 20 upstream from Eddyville.

LOBSTER CREEK. A major tributary of Five Rivers of the Alsea River system. It joins Five Rivers about three miles upstream from the mainstem Alsea. Lobster has a healthy population of wild cutthroat and small numbers of salmon and steelhead. It is currently closed to all fishing.

LOST LAKE (Clatskanie watershed). Formerly a small beaver pond with native cutthroat in the headwaters of the Clatskanie River, it was truly lost when its beaver dams were destroyed by persons unknown. Too bad, but here's to perservering beavers.

LOST LAKE (Nehalem watershed). A 15-acre rainbow lake on private timberland east of Spruce Run Park on the Nehalem River. From Hwy. 26 near mile Post 27, turn right onto Quartz Creek Road. At abouty 3 miles turn right onto the August Fire Road. After about 2 miles, turn right onto Lost Lake Road, which reaches the lake in about 2 miles. Don't count on signs.

Maximum depth is 20 ft., near the center of the north end. Rainbow fingerlings are stocked periodically, and quite a few run 14 to 18 inches by late summer. There's good carry over, too.

It's a fairly popular lake, but angling success tapers off after the first months of spring. It's difficult to get a boat in the water, but quite a few anglers troll, with spinner and worms favored. A few people fish it late in summer with good results on both flies and bait. Small live crayfish fished near the bottom have produced some big ones. It's pretty snaggy, so bring plenty of tackle.

Be a courteous no-trace visitor to private timberland. Respect the landowner's request that you not camp or light fires to help preserve public access.

LOST LAKE (Lane Co.). An early season trout lake, covering 6 acres, east of Hwy. 101 mid-way between Tahkenitch and Siltcoos lakes. The dirt access road off Hwy. 101 just south of Carter Lake is closed to cars, but anglers can park on the highway shoulder and walk in.

A good early season lake, it is stocked with rainbows in spring and has some resident cutthroat. A float tube isn't necessary to fish this narrow water. There are campgrounds north and south on Hwy. 101.

LOST LAKE (Westport Area). A small private lake with some bass, about 2 miles southwest of Westport. A gravel road leads from Westport to the lake. It offers spring fishing for local anglers with permission from the owners.

LYTLE LAKE. A 65-acre coastal lake with large trout and largemouth bass. Lytle is just north of Rockaway on the east side of Hwy. 101. It is connected to Crescent Lake.

Lytle contains both rainbow and cutthroat trout and is stocked from mid-March through early May with legal rainbows. If you'd like to be sure to catch a few innocents for the frying pan (or introduce a newcomer to the excitement of fishing) call the Tillamook office of ODFW for a stocking schedule. Larger fish are available for the more patient angler.

Shallow and prone to heavy weed growth, Lytle is best fished for trout in spring and early summer.

The small population of largemouth bass here could be easily over-fished, hence the catch and release restriction. Average size is 5 to 6 pounds, with some to 9 pounds. Woody structure along the east side and reeds along the highway offer attractive bass habitat. Best catches are made in summer and fall.

There is a public boat ramp with parking off 12th St. on the northeast shore , and a fishing dock near Hwy. 101 with ample parking on the highway shoulder. Other pull-outs along the road provide additional bank access. Resign yourself to near-constant wind and be prepared to deal with weeds. Supplies, facilities, and services are available in Rockaway.

MAGRUDER SLOUGH. A good warm-water fishery on the lower Columbia River, lightly fished. Magruder is on Hwy. 30 about 3 miles east of Westport and is about 5 miles long. Most surrounding land is private, but permission to bank fish is usually given. County roads and bridges also provide access. Light-weight boats can be launched in a few spots.

This is primarily a still-fishing show due to heavy vegetation. Crappie and bullhead are numerous. Bluegill, perch, and a few bass are also present.

MAPLE CREEK. A fair wild cutthroat stream about 10 miles long, flowing into Siltcoos Lake from the northeast. County roads follows the stream. You'll need a map. The creek flows through private property, so ask permission before you approach the stream. Largemouth bass can be found near the creek mouth. Maple Creek is an important refuge for wild salmon and steelhead and is closed to fishing for them.

MARIE LAKE (Tillamook Co.). A little 6-acre pothole at Twin Rocks east of Hwy. 101. It supports largemouth bass.

MAYGER SLOUGH. A lightly fished Columbia River slough 3 miles NW of Downing, east of Crimm's Island. It supports white crappie and bluegill.

MERCER LAKE. A good trout lake with lots of big, wily bass and some of the best perch fishing on the coast. Mercer has over 340 surface acres east of Hwy. 101, about 5 miles north of Florence. A county road leads from the highway around the south shore. The north shore road deadends at the head of the valley, offering no access to the lake.

Mercer can be fished year-round for bass, though spring is most productive after the water begins to warm. Good catches are made along the shoreline where fallen logs and lily pads offer cover. Mercer's largemouth are plentiful, though reputed to be difficult to catch. Local bass clubs like to fish the lake at night, perhaps to avoid other recreational water sports which can be a nuisance to anglers at the height of summer. The areas around the Mercer Creek outlet and the inlet creeks in the upper arms are worth a try.

Of the several species of panfish in the lake, yellow perch are most plentiful and worth the effort. The average catch is 7 to 10 inches, with some to 14 inches. Try fishing around the docks.

The lake is stocked with rainbow trout each spring, and good catches are made well into the summer. Larger carry-over trout are also available.

Mercer has a brushy shore that makes bank angling difficult. There is a resort on the lake where supplies and rental boats are available. The resort boat ramp is closed to general public use, but there is a public ramp about 2½ miles around the south shore over a narrow bumpy road. There are no campgrounds on the lake.

MIAMI RIVER. A good coastal river with a variety of fish, including a run of chum salmon. About 14 miles long, it enters Tillamook Bay just east of Garibaldi. In addition to chum, the Miami has a good native cutthroat population, winter steelhead, fall chinook, and coho. The Miami River Rd. follows the stream between Hwy. 101 south of Garibaldi and Hwy. 53 north of Mohler. The most popular stretch flows through agricultural land. Public access is limited.

Most fish in the Miami are wild, though

Using forceps to release the MIAMI's chum salmon will save your fingers from the fangs that give these fish the name "dog salmon." Photograph by Scott Richmond.

there are occasional hatchery strays. A fair winter steelhead run peaks early in January, and a run of larger steelhead (12 to 18 pounds) enters the river in late February and early March. The forest stretch above the old mill, about 5 miles upstream from Hwy. 101, is particularly good for early season steelheading.

There is a fair fall chinook run, and coho are present in late October, though the fishery for them is closed. The Miami and nearby Kilchis River share the distinction of having the only chum salmon runs of any size on the Oregon coast. However, these populations are now greatly diminished. Fishing for chum is currently limited to a brief catch and release season from mid-September to mid-November. Chum can be caught on corkies and small spinners. They will also take a fly more readily than other salmon species. Green is the favorite color for both flies and lures.

The Miami is strictly a bank fishery, and not much of that. Most of the lower river is posted against trespassing, and there are no public fishing easements. A few landowners allow access when anglers ask permission. Some post a sign granting permission for a small fee. You can also fish on Tillamook State Forest land about 5 miles upstream from Hwy. 101.

Flood level on the Miami is similar to that of the Wilson River, 11 feet. Optimum fishing is at 6 feet, with acceptable levels between 5.3 and 7 feet. Use the Wilson River gauge reading to determine the status of the Miami. See Appendix.

MIDDLE LAKE (Clatsop Co.). Prominent on maps, this lake is located in the headwaters of Bear Creek in the Astoria watershed and is closed to public access.

MILES LAKE. A small trout and catfish lake west of the road between Woods (on the lower Nestucca) and Sand Lake, several miles north of Woods. The lake is under private ownership at present.

MUNSEL LAKE. A good trout and bass lake with about 93 surface acres, very deep and lightly fished. It is the southernmost of a chain of three lakes that includes Clear Lake and Collard. Clear is difficult to access, and Collard is privately owned with no public access.

Munsel is about 2½ miles north of Florence east of Hwy. 101 on Munsel Lake Rd.

Don't be fooled by the clarity of the water. There are plenty of fish here. Trout fishing is good in the spring and holds up well into summer. Munsel is stocked with legal rainbow trout each season and with a good number of trophy-size trout that the hatchery fattens to 5 pounds before releasing for public sport. Most anglers fish from boats, as a brushy shoreline limits bank fishing. Trolling is very popular.

Munsel has a fairly small largemouth bass population, but it makes up for low numbers with quality and size. Bass to 7 pounds have been taken on plugs and lures. In spring, fish the shallow coves. Later in the year, fish the creek inlet to the north and around the docks. Catch and release would be a good idea here to preserve the fishery. For the pan, consider fishing the lake's healthy population of plump yellow perch.

There is a county boat ramp at the lake, and a boating speed limit is strictly enforced. The lake has steep sides with logs around the edge, so a boat is useful to reach good fishing. There is no campground on Munsel. The nearest camp is a pretty one at Sutton Lake about four miles north.

NEACOXIE LAKE (a.k.a. Sunset Lake). See **SUNSET LAKE.**

NECANICUM RIVER. A pretty little stream, about 22 miles long, that adds considerable charm and interest to the drive from Portland to the coast along Hwy. 26. It is most popularly fished for winter steelhead, both wild and hatchery. It heads in the Coast Range near Saddle Mountain and joins the Pacific at Seaside.

Winter steelhead enter the river in November. The hatchery run peaks in December or January. Wild steelhead enter later, with good fishing in February and March. Only finclipped steelhead may be kept. Most steelheading takes place below Necanicum Junction where the landscape begins to flatten out a bit.

There's no river gauge on the Necanicum, but a gauge reading for the North Fork Nehalem is a good guide. See Appendix. A river height of 40 to 50 inches is best. The Necanicum usually takes about two days to clear after heavy rain. Steelheading is best when the river is dropping after a period of high water.

The Necanicum has a fair native cutthroat population, with searuns returning plump and feisty in late August. There is some nice fly water in the lower stream above tidewater, and fly fishing for searun cutthroat in late summer can be very good.

Fall chinook of hatchery origin are fished in tidewater. After the first fall rains, local anglers fish for chinook right in town from Seaside's many little bridges. The river is closed for coho.

The Necanicum is a shallow stream and gets very low in summer, but it can be drifted in winter and early spring. A rubber raft may be a better choice than a drift boat. Most boaters launch at Klootchie Creek County Park (home of the big Sitka Spruce off Hwy. 26). The most convenient

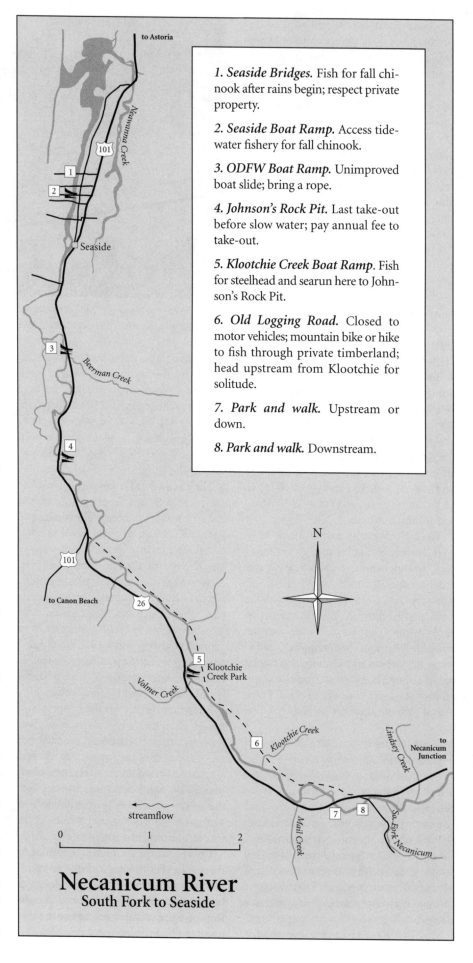

1. Seaside Bridges. Fish for fall chinook after rains begin; respect private property.

2. Seaside Boat Ramp. Access tidewater fishery for fall chinook.

3. ODFW Boat Ramp. Unimproved boat slide; bring a rope.

4. Johnson's Rock Pit. Last take-out before slow water; pay annual fee to take-out.

5. Klootchie Creek Boat Ramp. Fish for steelhead and searun here to Johnson's Rock Pit.

6. Old Logging Road. Closed to motor vehicles; mountain bike or hike to fish through private timberland; head upstream from Klootchie for solitude.

7. Park and walk. Upstream or down.

8. Park and walk. Downstream.

Necanicum River
South Fork to Seaside

take out is Johnson's Rock Pit near the Hwy. 101 Bridge, since the river gets slow and unproductive for steelhead below that point. Johnson's charges an annual fee to use their facility. See Appendix. Free public alternatives include an ODFW access above the golf course just south of Seaside off Hwy. 101 (unimproved slide; bring a rope), a public ramp in Seaside next to the School District Administration Office, and a ramp north of Broadway.

Bank anglers might want to avoid the heavily fished water between Klootchie Creek Park and Johnson's by heading upstream from the park. An old logging road along the river between Klootchie and the South Fork is a perfect track for mountain bikes. Just below the South Fork confluence, you can park a car and walk in to fish about 1¾ miles through private timberland. Access to the river in its run through public forest is limited only by thick timber and underbrush.

In Seaside, there's public bank access between the Seaside Convention Center on First St. and the 12th St. Bridge. Anglers also fish from the many little bridges during salmon season. Few steelhead are caught in this slack water section of the river. Ask permission to access the river through private property elsewhere on the lower river.

NEHALEM BAY. The first bay south of Cape Falcon, fourth largest on the Oregon coast, with fair fishing both in the bay and offshore. To reach Nehalem Bay from Portland, drive west on Hwy. 26, then turn south on Hwy. 101. Or take Hwy. 6 to Tillamook, then Hwy. 101 north about 23 miles. It takes about an hour and a half to reach the bay from Portland. Tidewater extends to Eck Creek on the main Nehalem.

Angling activity in the bay in spring and early summer focuses on bottom and surf fish. Good size perch, rockfish, and greenling, and an infrequent flounder are taken on shrimp, clam necks, and kelp worms. Good catches are made from the south jetty and from the rocks off Hwy. 101. Best fishing is on the incoming tide. Anglers also anchor and fish for these species in the lower channel, but beware of frequently rough conditions in the lower bay. Fishing the surf for perch from beaches north and south of the bar can be excellent.

In early summer, chinook appear at the Nehalem bar. The Nehalem bar can be very dangerous, especially in high winds. Get an update on conditions from local moorage operators or the Coast Guard.

Salmon stay outside the bay until late summer. Jack salmon are the first to enter after the early fall rains. They are taken on cluster eggs, small lures, and spinners. Adult chinook enter sometimes as early as August, followed by a small run of coho. Only finclipped coho may be kept.

Chinook are caught in the bay until November. Early season catches are near the mouth, then the run moves upstream. Bay anglers generally troll herring higher up the bay, spinners closer to the mouth. Trolling with the tide (either incoming or outgoing) is generally most effective. Bobbers produce in the deeper holes.

Crabbing is generally good in summer and fall. Most crabs seem to leave with the freshets in winter and spring, but some good catches are made even in late winter if you don't mind the cold. Best crabbing is in the lower channel. Rings and bait are available at most moorages. Softshell clams are easily dug in the flats about 3 miles up from the mouth. Follow Bayside Gardens Rd. to the dead end. There are about 400 acres of digging flats here. There are other small flats along both sides of the river, but the best spot is the large cove across from Wheeler.

There is a small local fishery in the bay for sturgeon. Bring sturgeon gear along when you're salmon fishing. Between tide changes when the salmon bite is off, put away your salmon rod, bait up for sturgeon, and see who comes along.

Several moorages offer boat rentals, tackle, bait, and other supplies from Brighton upstream to Wheeler. Nehalem Bay State Park, south of Manzanita, has pleasant sites for trailers and tents, picnic areas, boat ramp, bike trails, horse camp facilities, and ocean access.

NEHALEM RIVER. A big, temperamental river, offering opportunities to catch and release large wild steelhead and cutthroat. Chinook can also be fished. It is the third longest river on the Oregon coast and is slower to clear than smaller streams in the area, flowing 118 miles before entering Nehalem Bay at the town of Nehalem.

Hwy. 53 crosses the lower river near Mohler. The Lower Nehalem River Rd. follows the river upstream to Hwy. 26 at Elsie. County Rd. 202 follows the upper river through Jewell, Birkenfeld, Mist, Pittsburg, and Vernonia.

The Nehalem is very accessible to the Portland metropolitan area and is popular with steelheaders and salmon anglers. It's also an excellent cutthroat stream, though

Most NEHALEM salmon are caught in the bay, but some big summer chinook can be found in the river in June and July. Photograph by John Ramsour.

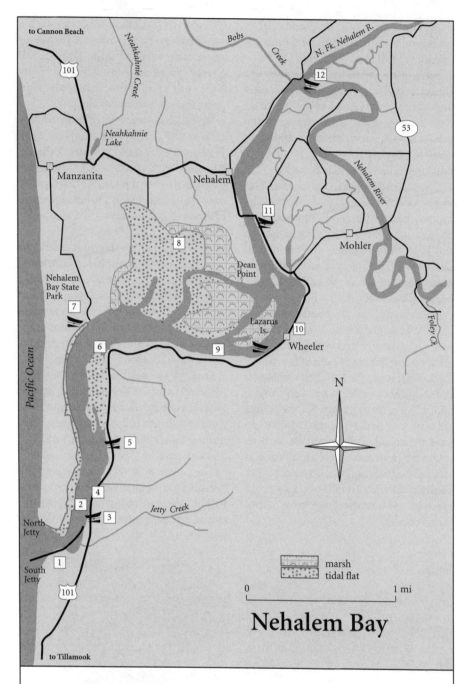

Nehalem Bay

marsh
tidal flat

0   1 mi

1. South Jetty. Fish for perch, rockfish, greenling, salmon in fall; access from beach or at Jetty Fishery.

2. Lower Channel. Anchor and fish for perch, rockfish, greenling; troll for salmon; crab year-round

3. Jetty Fishery. Public boat ramp; jetty access.

4. Hwy. 101 Rocks. Frequent turnouts access rocks for pile perch.

5. Brighton Moorage. Public ramp.

6. Fishery Point. Downstream boundary for coho; fish up to forks.

7. Nehalem Bay State Park. Boat ramp, picnic area, camping.

8. Mud Flats. Softshell bed; approach from end of Bayside Gardens Road.

9. Upper Bay. Troll for salmon, searun cutthroat.

10. Wheeler Marina. Public boat ramp.

11. County Boat Ramp.

12. Aldervale. Unimproved but decent boat ramp used as take-out from North Fork.; small boat access to chinook and coho in early season.

its searun population has been hard hit by poor ocean conditions.

The mainstem is not stocked with hatchery fish of any species, but there is a hatchery on the North Fork Nehalem (which joins the big Nehalem in tidewater), and hatchery strays are not uncommon in the mainstem. Anglers are urged to keep hatchery (finclipped) fish caught in season in the big Nehalem, and are required to release wild (unclipped) steelhead, coho, and cutthroat.

Although most Nehalem salmon are caught in the bay, there is a small summer chinook run that is lightly fished in the river in June and July. Chinook jacks run upriver in August and are fished up to the falls at r.m. 17. The Nehalem is closed to coho fishing, but finclipped coho strays may (and should) be kept.

Steelheading on the Nehalem gets underway in December, with best fishing often in March. The best steelhead water is in the lower 13 to 14 miles, most of which is accessible only by boat. The highest put-in is the Beaver Slide below Lost Creek on Nehalem River Rd. about 100 yards downstream from the State Forest Guard Station. This is a steep slide that requires manually guiding a boat about 10 yards downhill to the river. Take-out opportunities are at Roy Creek Park or Aldervale. The drift from Roy Creek to the Aldervale ramp receives less fishing pressure and can be productive. There are additional boat ramps in tidewater near the communities of Wheeler and Nehalem.

Bank fishing opportunities on the Nehalem are limited. Anglers can fish at Roy Cr. Park and at Falls County Park on the lower river. Above Nehalem Falls, the river flows through a mix of private and public land owned by the state or counties (Tillamook, Clatsop, and Columbia). A very popular stretch flows through Spruce Run County Park off the Nehalem River Rd. south of Elsie. A little farther downstream, anglers can fish close to the mouth of the Salmonberry River (though a private landowner prohibits access to the most productive water at the confluence). Country parks in the vicinity of Vernonia offer limited bank fishing opportunities.

Much access to the river through private land in the Nehalem watershed as elsewhere in Oregon has been lost in recent years due to the behavior of a few bad actors. At this point, anglers are urged to ac-

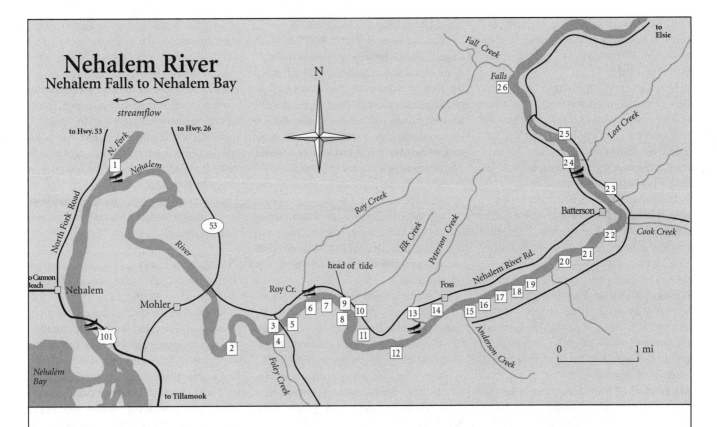

Nehalem River
Nehalem Falls to Nehalem Bay

1. Aldervale. Take-out for N. Fork.; early fall salmon fishing.

2. Liverpool. Plunking in tidewater.

3. Foley Creek Drift. Drift boats fish NW side; plunkers access from south bank.

4. Stump Hole. Another good cutthroat spot early and late in day.

5. Fence Hole. Good August and September fly-fishing for cutthroat.

6. Walker Hole. Right across from Roy Creek.

7. Easom Drift. Just below big rock.

8. Middle Easom Drift. Slow water from here on down.

9. Twilight Hole. Watch for jacks right after first fall rains, September through October.

10. Rock Crusher Drift.

11. Winslow Drift. Doesn't look as good as it is, though holding fewer fish than in days gone by.

12. Upper Winslow Drift. Long straight gravel bar drift; better slow down going through here.

13. Mohler Sand & Gravel. Gravel bar put-in or take-out; park along county road.

14. Freezeout Hole. Sun never shines here, plunkers; pretty water, drifters.

15. Foss Drift. Fish below at piling close to brush.

16. Anderson Creek Hole. Fish lie along south bank; boat drift only.

17. Lindsay Riffle. Best for plunkers; still eddy on north side holds fish; drift upper end at low water.

18. Clover Patch Hole. Excellent for plunking during high water; good drifting in low water; good drift water between here and Lindsay.

19. Stone Hill Hole. Good drifting; brushy banks.

20. Cattle Guard Hole. Plunker's paradise, both banks; drifters down the middle.

21. Rock Hole. Strictly for plunking.

22. Batterson Riffles. Overhead pipeline about ⅔ way down.

23. Sacrifice Hole. A real tackle snatcher but produces good salmon.

24. Beaver Slide. Put-in only; slide drift boats down bank; park adjacent to county road.

25. Lost Creek Hole. Nothing between here and the next one except for pros; big boulders, some fish in pockets.

26. Nehalem Falls. Good bank access at County Park; good holes & drifts upstream are often far apart; limited boating above this point; don't boat the falls.

cept and obey no trespassing signs, ask permission to cross private property, and be respectful no-trace visitors when permission is granted.

Flood level on the Nehalem is 14 feet. Best fishing is at 4½ feet, with acceptable levels between 4 and 5.2 feet. Plunkers do well with the river as high as 9 ft. The Nehalem is slower to clear than smaller coastal rivers. A gauge reading for the Nehalem is available. See Appendix.

Accommodations and supplies are available in Wheeler and along Hwy. 101 north and south of Nehalem Bay. Watch for well-marked closure regulations at Nehalem Falls about 2 miles above Cook Creek.

NEHALEM RIVER, EAST FORK. A small stream with wild cutthroat and winter steelhead. It flows into the Nehalem at Pittsburg, 2 miles north of Vernonia. A good road parallels the stream through forest land open to public access. It can also be reached from Scappoose by way of the Scappoose-Vernonia Rd. north from Hwy. 30. All fishing in the East Fork at this time is catch and release.

NEHALEM RIVER, NORTH FORK

An opportunity for catch and keep salmon and steelhead angling at a pace reminiscent of the old days on Oregon's coastal rivers. The North Fork is within easy driving distance, though a world away, from the Portland metropolitan area. From Hwy. 26, follow Hwy. 53 south to the North Fork Hatchery at milepost 8. From Hwy. 101 at the town of Nehalem, follow the North Fork Rd. upstream to its junction with Hwy. 53.

Like many coastal streams, this one offers several different fishing environments, all of them productive. There's the fast-moving high gradient stretch above the North Fork Hatchery, where anglers can walk along a private gated road, accessible only to foot traffic and mountain bikes, and cast to wild fish in a pristine rainforest environment. There's the popular bank fishery at the North Fork Hatchery, a generally good-natured fishing carnival when the runs of steelhead and coho are in. And there's the boat fishery, with challenging technical whitewater and productive pocket water from the hatchery to the first take-out at Ericson's, and a slower more contemplative reach through rural agricultur-

al land from Ericson's to Aldervale.

The season on the North Fork begins in August when a healthy run of wild fall chinook enters the stream. Jack salmon enter the river in September and October. The chinook fishery continues through November. Finclipped hatchery coho usually appear in early November. The hatchery run of winter steelhead enters around Thanksgiving, followed by a strong wild run from January through February and into early March some years.

Cutthroat offer good catch and release fishing in early spring, late summer, and fall. Sea-run cutthroat can be hooked in the river's tidewater from July until the rains come.

For boaters, there are two drift options on the North Fork. The first is from the North Fork Hatchery to Ericson's, a private pay-to-use concrete ramp at milepost 11½. This float includes some wonderful pocket water but requires negotiating a serious set of three rapids (the Jack, Queen, and King) which demand expert boating skills. A rubber raft with a rowing frame and floor is much safer in this stretch than a driftboat. A second drift, suitable for novice boaters, is from Ericson's to the Aldervale ramp near the river's mouth. This float is considerably more sedate and may hold fewer steelhead at times, but you'll undoubtedly make it home safe and dry. There's some pocket water in this stretch as well as good holes and drifts. In the big holes, look for steelhead close to the brushy shore. In the deep stretch below Boykin Creek, add extra lead to reach steelhead that may be using the depth for cover. Shuttle service is currently available through Ericson's. See Appendix.

The vast majority of bank-caught salmon and steelhead on the North Fork are taken at the hatchery. In addition to being the final destination for the river's hatchery runs, a barrier to migrating wild fish keeps them in the hatchery hole until the river rises sufficiently. The hatchery grounds offer about 300 yards of riverbank below the intake and another 100 yards above it. That's room for about 50 anglers. Drift fishing is the only acceptable technique here when there's a crowd. Come early to reserve your rock. A barrier-free dock is available for handicapped anglers.

Below the hatchery, resident landowners have been known to give permission to fish. Be a good guest. Above the hatchery,

a generous local landowner allows hiking and mountain bike access to several miles of good pocket water. This is an opportunity to fish strictly catch and release for wild salmon and steelhead. Be a courteous no-trace visitor to keep access open. Occasional hatchery fish stray into this reach. If you catch a finclipped salmon or coho above the hatchery, ODFW urges you to keep it in order to protect the integrity of the wild population.

Best fishing is when the river level is 36 to 44 inches. A gauge reading is available. See Appendix

NESKOWIN CREEK (a.k.a. Slab Creek). Enters the ocean at Neskowin, about 4 miles south of Nestucca Bay. Hwy. 101 follows much of the stream above the town of Neskowin. The creek is currently closed to fishing in spring and summer but opens for catch-and-release winter steelhead fishing in November. Check the regulations.

There is a Forest Service campground about 5 miles south of Neskowin. Supplies and accommodations are available in town.

NESTUCCA BAY. Created by the Big Nestucca coming in from the northwest and the Little Nestucca from the southwest, forming a wishbone shaped tidal area that offers a variety of bay fisheries. Just 20 miles south of Tillamook by way of Hwy. 101, it's a quick trip here from the Willamette Valley. Because it's a very shallow bay, boaters must be alert to depth and tide, or find themselves high and dry on the flats at ebb. The water deepens above Pacific City.

Fall chinook provide the primary salmon fishery in the bay, entering the estuary in August and September. Spring chinook move quickly through the bay in May and early June and are better fished in the rivers. The bay and its tributaries are closed for coho. There is an annual closure for all salmon fishing from the north point of Cannery Hill seaward for ½ mile from June 16 to August 15.

Salmon anglers drift and float eggs and use herring or trolled spinners. Bobber fishing with eggs is also productive. The Airport Hole, across from the airport below the Pacific City boat ramp, is a popular spot in the upper bay. There's also good trolling mid-bay. Lower bay trollers need to be wary of tide conditions and

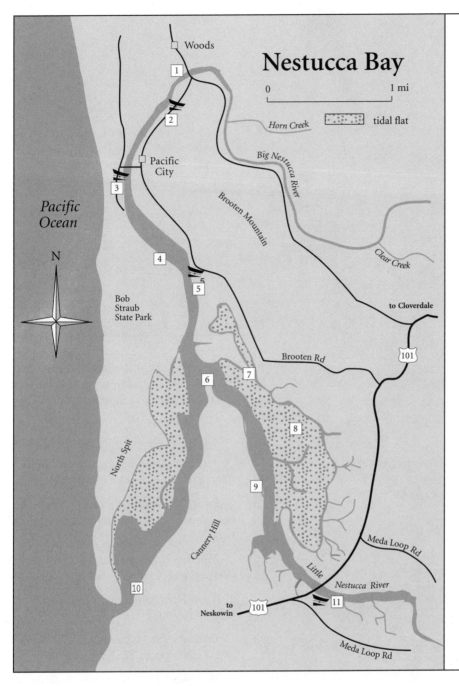

Nestucca Bay

0   1 mi

tidal flat

Pacific Ocean

N

Woods

Horn Creek

Big Nestucca River

Brooten Mountain

Clear Creek

to Cloverdale

Pacific City

Bob Straub State Park

North Spit

Brooten Rd

101

Cannery Hill

Little Nestucca River

Meda Loop Rd

to Neskowin

101

Meda Loop Rd

1. *Upper Tidewater.* Troll for fall chinook August to October; bank fishing at county park.

2. *Nestucca Ramp.* Gravel ramp with limited parking.

3. *Pacific City Ramp.* Improved public ramp south of town; accesses lower bay; good fishery for fall chinook in airport hole.

4. *Mid-Bay.* Troll for fall chinook; use caution (subject to shifting shoals).

5. *Fisher Landing.* Bank angling from parking area for fall chinook (Guardrail Hole) August to October; limited parking; unimproved ramp.

6. *Cannery Hill.* Salmon deadline extends seaward during closed season; fish for perch, greenling in channel off rocky point; accessible by boat only.

7. *Little Nestucca Flats.* Softshell flats; marker on road indicates access trail; limited parking.

8. *Softshell Flats.* Best digging on the bay for softshell clams; boat access.

9. *Little Nestucca Channel.* Troll for fall chinook, occasional perch in lower reach.

10. *Mouth of Bay.* Can be productive but dangerous boat fishery for fall chinook, perch, greenling, crab; bank fishery accessed by hiking through park.

11. *Little Nestucca/101 Ramp.* Improved ramp; bank access above the bridge; fish for fall chinook Aug.-Oct.

rough water. Bank anglers can fish for chinook at the Guard-rail Hole at Fisher Landing, an unimproved public ramp south of Pacific City off Brooten Rd. It is also possible to bank fish the mouth of the bay by hiking the north spit through Bob Straub State Park.

Perch are available in the shallows of the lower bay and in the Little Nestucca Channel, and surf fishing for perch is good anytime off the beach at Bob Straub State Park. For perch, time your fishing to the tide. Off the beaches, fish the incoming tide. Inside the bay, fish the last two hours of high tide. Greenling are also available

near the mouth and at the mouth of the Little Nestucca.

Sea-run cutthroat make an appearance in late summer, and there is a small fishery for them in the upper tidewater. Fishing for them is catch and release only, so use spinners, Kwikfish-type lures, and other artificials rather than bait. Crab can be taken in the lower deep areas of the bay. Steelhead pass through the bay but are primarily caught in the rivers.

The best softshell clamming in the bay is on the Little Nestucca Flats just off Brooten Rd., about 2 miles south of Pacific City. Almost any minus tide exposes the beds, and

since you can't get out to fish the bay then anyway, you might as well dig in.

There is a novel summer fishery off Cape Kiwanda north of Pacific City. A fleet of dories launches from the beach and fishes 6 to 7 miles off shore. The skill of the dory operators is legendary, and their catch rate is very high for chinook, lingcod, snapper, and halibut. Even if you don't go out yourself, it's interesting to watch the dories break through the surf. A good road leads to the dory launching area. It should be noted that launching through the surf should not be attempted by novices. Charter dory rides may be available.

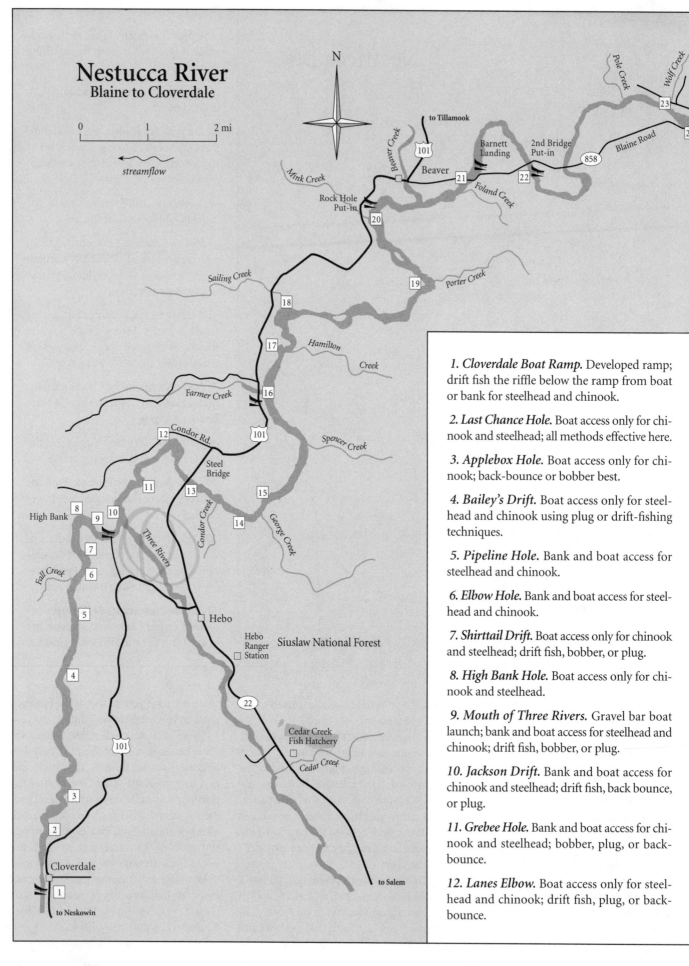

Nestucca River
Blaine to Cloverdale

0 1 2 mi

streamflow

N

to Tillamook

Pole Creek

Wolf Creek

4t Pu

23

24

Beaver Creek

101

Barnett Landing

2nd Bridge Put-in

Blaine Road

858

Mink Creek

Beaver

21

22

Foland Creek

Rock Hole Put-in

20

Porter Creek

19

Sailing Creek

18

Hamilton Creek

17

16

Farmer Creek

101

Spencer Creek

Condor Rd.

12

Steel Bridge

13

15

11

Three Rivers

Condor Creek

14

George Creek

High Bank

8

9

10

7

6

Fall Creek

5

Hebo

Hebo Ranger Station

Siuslaw National Forest

4

22

Cedar Creek Fish Hatchery

101

Cedar Creek

3

2

to Salem

Cloverdale

1

to Neskowin

1. Cloverdale Boat Ramp. Developed ramp; drift fish the riffle below the ramp from boat or bank for steelhead and chinook.

2. Last Chance Hole. Boat access only for chinook and steelhead; all methods effective here.

3. Applebox Hole. Boat access only for chinook; back-bounce or bobber best.

4. Bailey's Drift. Boat access only for steelhead and chinook using plug or drift-fishing techniques.

5. Pipeline Hole. Bank and boat access for steelhead and chinook.

6. Elbow Hole. Bank and boat access for steelhead and chinook.

7. Shirttail Drift. Boat access only for chinook and steelhead; drift fish, bobber, or plug.

8. High Bank Hole. Boat access only for chinook and steelhead.

9. Mouth of Three Rivers. Gravel bar boat launch; bank and boat access for steelhead and chinook; drift fish, bobber, or plug.

10. Jackson Drift. Bank and boat access for chinook and steelhead; drift fish, back bounce, or plug.

11. Grebee Hole. Bank and boat access for chinook and steelhead; bobber, plug, or back-bounce.

12. Lanes Elbow. Boat access only for steelhead and chinook; drift fish, plug, or back-bounce.

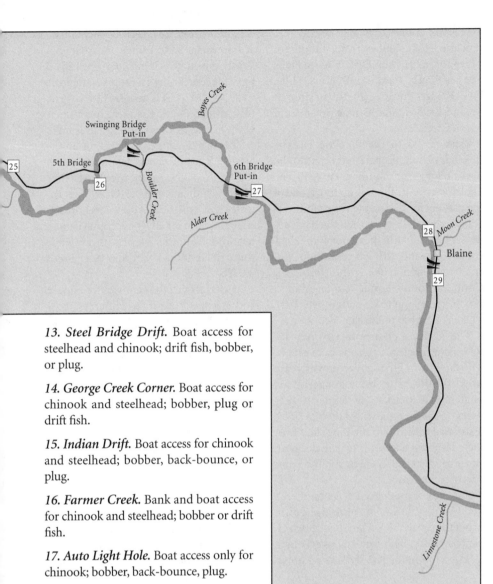

Supplies, facilities, and good advice are available in Pacific City. There's a gravel boat ramp beside the sporting goods store in town, and another public ramp a couple of miles south of town. You can also launch at Fisher Landing off Brooten Rd. and at the Little Nestucca Ramp off Meda Loop Rd.

If you have access to a small plane, the airport is less than 100 yards from the estuary, with marinas within walking distance. It's only an 1800 ft. strip, so be sharp. Best approach is from the south.

NESTUCCA RIVER

Also known as the Big Nestucca, a real gem of an all-around stream. This big river flows 55 miles, running 50 to 100 ft. wide in the lower stretch. Easily accessed, it is crossed and followed by Hwy. 101 from Pacific City to Beaver. County Rd. 858 follows the river upstream from Beaver into the Siuslaw National Forest. From inland, the Nestucca can be reached by county roads west from Carlton.

A nice run of spring chinook enters in April, peaking in June and July. Bigger runs of fall chinook and coho begin in late August, though the river is closed to coho angling. Fall salmon remain in tidewater until the rains begin and reach the upper river in October. Even then, the majority of anglers fish the river below Hebo, since the salmon population thins out above Three Rivers and Beaver Creek.

The Nestucca's searun cutthroat population is benefiting from the years-long closure on cutthroat harvest and on fishing the tributaries and upper river. Look for searun in August as high up as r.m. 25 near Blaine. Fishing for them is catch and release.

Steelhead are in the river year-round. Scrappy 4- to 7-pound summer steelhead (all hatchery) appear in tidewater in April. In good years, August can find them almost nose to tail throughout a 20-mile section of the river. Winter steelhead enter the river in late November or early December. There are more hatchery fish in the mix through February, and more wild fish in March and April. Nestucca winter steelhead average 10 to 14 pounds, but 20-pounders are also available. Only fin-clipped steelhead may be kept. If the challenge of the chase and the thrill of the hook-up are your primary steelheading

13. Steel Bridge Drift. Boat access for steelhead and chinook; drift fish, bobber, or plug.

14. George Creek Corner. Boat access for chinook and steelhead; bobber, plug or drift fish.

15. Indian Drift. Boat access for chinook and steelhead; bobber, back-bounce, or plug.

16. Farmer Creek. Bank and boat access for chinook and steelhead; bobber or drift fish.

17. Auto Light Hole. Boat access only for chinook; bobber, back-bounce, plug.

18. 101 Camp Hole. Bank and boat access for chinook and steelhead.

19. Porter Hole. Boat access for chinook; back-bounce or bobber.

20. Rock Hole Put-in. Bank slide; bank and boat access for chinook and steelhead.

21. First Bridge Put-in. Developed boat ramp; bank and boat access for chinook and steelhead; drift fish or plug.

22. Salt Rock Hole (2nd Bridge). Bank slide for boats; bank and boat access for steelhead and chinook; drift fish.

23. Wolf Creek. Bank and boat access for steelhead; drift fish or plug best.

24. Old Fourth Bridge Hole. Developed boat ramp at 4th Bridge; boat access only for chinook and steelhead; drift fish, back-bounce, or bobber.

25. Tony Creek Hole. Boat access for chinook and steelhead; drift fish, back-bounce, or bobber.

26. Pig Pen Hole. Boat access only for steelhead and chinook; drift fish or plug best.

27. Sixth Bridge Put-in. Bank slide; bank and boat access for steelhead and chinook; drift fish or plug best.

28. Moon Creek. Bank slide put-in; bank access for chinook and steelhead; drift fish or bobber best; salmon fishing deadline.

29. Upper Nestucca. Lots of good access; look for turn-outs and walk down to river; drift fishing and spinners best up here.

goals, you'll enjoy fishing in March and April when angling pressure drops off. Wild Nestucca winter steelhead are a real thrill on the line. Fish the deep holes and stay out of sight if fishing from the bank. Morning and evening are the best times.

Bank access to the lower river is at a premium these days, with many private access points (formerly open to the public for a small fee) now leased to a private fishing club. There are only a few generous landowners who still share their good fortune with the general public for a modest fee. To retain that access, be a considerate visitor. Pack out everything you pack in, and bring an extra garbage bag to pick up after less thoughtful anglers.

Currently, there is bank access to the lower river at the Cloverdale Boat Ramp, Pipeline Hole, Elbow Hole, mouth of Three Rivers, Jackson Drift, Grebee Hole, Farmer Creek, Camp Hole, Rock Hole, First Bridge Put-in, Salt Rock Hole at Second Bridge, Sixth Bridge put-in, and Moon Creek.

Bank access to the Pipeline Hole is through private property adjacent to the parking lot at the mouth of Three Rivers. Look for a pay-to-fish box at the left end of the parking lot (facing the river) and contribute your dollar. To reach the bank access at Jackson Drift, head north on Hwy. 101 at Hebo and turn left on Condor Rd. (first road after crossing the Nestucca). Continue about ½ mile to a farmhouse (on the right)opposite a barn (on the left). There is a paybox at the gate.

The Nestucca offers a variety of water for boating anglers, from novice to expert. The float from First Bridge downstream offers the best water for less experienced boaters. It includes some rapids but presents no major hazards other than those associated with all riverboating. This float includes access to some premiere steelhead water between Beaver Creek and the Three Rivers confluence.

For more experienced boaters, there's good floating from Fourth Bridge down. Scout the water above Third Bridge, which can be tricky. The water above Fourth Bridge requires expert skills and knowledge of the river. Be especially wary of hazards between Sixth Bridge and Swinging Bridge put-in, which includes The Falls, a tight squeeze through a dropping rapid. A water level of 6 feet is necessary to navigate this stretch. Boating is ideal in summer when the Nestucca is running a little high.

The only developed boat ramps on the Nestucca are at Cloverdale and Fourth Bridge. Boat access at the mouth of Three Rivers is from a gravel bar. Other boat accesses are bank slides. Four-wheel drive is recommended for all Nestucca put-ins and take-outs. Shuttle service is available through Nestucca Valley Sporting Goods in Hebo.

Anglers fishing the Nestucca for salmon and steelhead use many different techniques. Drift-fishing, plugs, and back-bouncing are all effective in faster water. Bobbers are best for fishing slow water and big holes. Spinners can be productive throughout the river when the water is clearer. The Nestucca muddies quite rapidly after a good hard rain and doesn't clear quickly. Best fishing is generally when the river is less than crystal clear.

Flood level on the Nestucca is 18 ft. Best fishing is at 4½ ft, with acceptable levels between 3.6 and 5.4 ft. A river gauge reading is available. See Appendix.

Tillamook County, the Dept. of Fish and Wildlife, the Highway Dept., and local anglers have all pitched in to make launching

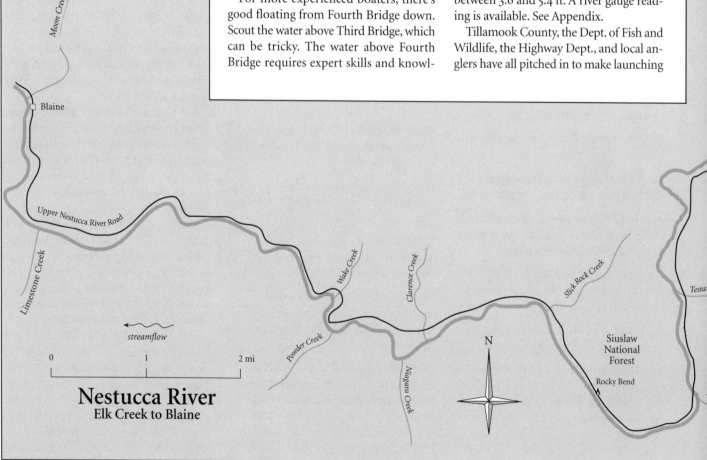

Nestucca River
Elk Creek to Blaine

places available. There are public boat ramps at Pacific City, Cloverdale, Three Rivers, and Farmer Creek as well as put-ins (more and less developed) upriver.

The character of the river changes dramatically above Moon Creek, the deadline for salmon fishing. The terrain grows steep, and the river quickens its pace. More than half the land bordering the river in this stretch is publicly owned (Siuslaw National Forest and BLM), with private land generally associated with private homes on the river.

The Upper Nestucca River Road follows the river through its canyon, offering excellent access from frequent and obvious turn-outs. Designated a scenic by-way, the road is mostly paved and can be accessed either from Beaver on the west or from

Most boat launches on the NESTUCCA are bank slides. Photograph by Richard T. Grost.

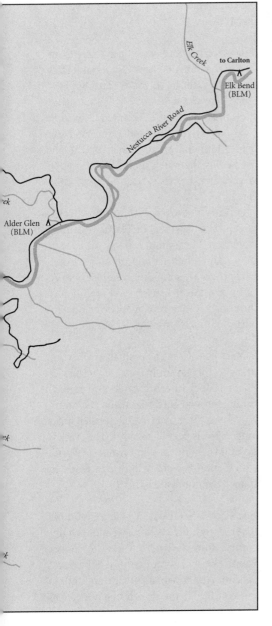

Carlton on the east.

From Moon to Elk Creek, the river is fished primarily for winter steelhead. The hatchery run generally peaks in this stretch in December and January. The wild run appears beginning in February, with fish still present as late as June many years. Most anglers fish from the bank, though the river is wadeable in many places-throughout this stretch and can even be crossed with care. Drift-fishing and spinners are best for the upper river.

The Nestucca is closed to all angling above Elk Creek. Of its many tributaries, only Beaver Creek and Three Rivers are open for fishing at this time. Read the regulations carefully for hook and bait restrictions at some times of the year.

There's a camping at Castle Rock on Three Rivers and at five campgrounds on the upper river. Three of the campgrounds (Elk Bend, Fan Creek and Dover) are within the angling closure area above Elk Creek. All BLM campgrounds on the Nestucca have drinking water and charge a fee. The camps are open for drive-in use from May through November. In winter, park at the gate and walk in.

Several boat rentals and moorages are available in tidewater. Supplies and accomodations are available in Hebo on Hwy. 22

and along Hwy. 101 from Beaver to the mouth.

NESTUCCA RIVER, LITTLE. A fair stream for wild winter steelhead, wild cutthroat trout, and fall chinook. It heads in Yamhill County and flows past the community of Dolph on Hwy. 22, from which point a road follows the stream closely down to its mouth. It enters Nestucca Bay about 3 miles south of Pacific City.

Fall chinook return to the Little Nestucca in October with the rains. Some coho also show in October, but angling for them is prohibited. Most steelhead in the Little Nestucca are wild, with peak returns in December and January. Fishing for cut-

throat and searun is catch and release only. All non-finclipped steelhead must be released unharmed.

The river is open from the Hwy. 101 bridge upstream to the Forest Service bridge at Dolph. Below the Hwy. 101 bridge, see regulations for Nestucca Bay. The Hwy. 101 crossing is a popular place for bank casting.

Supplies and accommodations are available in Pacific City. There is a public access area with parking facilities at the Hwy. 101 crossing, and bank access continues in the Siuslaw National Forest.

NETARTS BAY. Of little importance to anglers, but popular for clamming and crabbing. Netarts Bay is the sixth largest in the state in total area, about 7 miles long and quite shallow for the most part, with few channel areas more than 10 feet deep at high tide. No major rivers feed the bay, and of the dozen small streams that flow into it from the east, none harbor many salmon or steelhead.

It's a quick hour and a half run from the Willamette Valley to Netarts, about 4 miles southwest of Tillamook. The road follows the bay's eastern shore.

Clamming is the main attraction at Netarts, with many good flats. The big flat off the spit at Cape Lookout State Park and the little flat on the north bay shore near the mouth yield tremendous numbers of cockle, butter, gaper, and littleneck clams and a few razors. Whiskey Creek Flats and Wilson Beach are less productive but worthwhile. Moorage operators make trips to these flats when the tides are favorable and will help you get started. Check current regulations for catch limits.

Netarts is one of five major crabbing bays on the Oregon coast, with good populations of both dungeness and redrock crab. As in all bays, the winter rush of fresh water draws crab out into the open sea. They usually return in September, October, and November. In low-water years, good numbers of crab are in the bay year-round. Crab rings and bait are available for rent locally, but you'll need a boat, as there are no piers here.

Perch can be plentiful in Netarts, with best catches made in April and May. Try the north end and the area known as the Boiler Hole, just south of the county boat launch.

Kelp greenling, tomcod, and other bot-tomfish are occasionally caught in the bay in summer and fall. Sand shrimp, clam necks, or kelp worms are good bait and can be purchased locally. Wind a few turns of pink thread or strands of fluorescent yarn around your baited hook to secure it.

In October and November a few coho and chum salmon enter the bay, but Netarts is closed to all salmon angling.

Oyster beds in Netarts (as in all Oregon bays) are privately owned and off-limits for public harvest.

Netarts is a safe bay for family fun, as the water is so shallow that boat accidents are rare. Stay away from the Netarts bar, though, which is shallow and rough, a good spot to flip a boat if you are inexperienced. Veteran boaters cross the bar in calm weather to fish the reef beyond Arch Rocks for rockfish, halibut, and other bottomfish.

Several outlets on the bay rent boats and sell tackle and bait. There are motel accommodations and agood county boat ramp in Netarts. Lookout State Park, just south, offers camping facilities.

NORTH AND SOUTH LAKES. Two ponds on the ridge line above Hebo Lake. North lake is about ½ acre, South is 5 acres. See Hebo Lake for directions. Beyond Hebo, follow Forest Rd. 14 another 5¾ miles. North Lake is close to the road. South lake is about 1¼ miles farther. North is stocked with legal rainbows once in early April. South Lake is stocked in April and May. The roads leading to these lakes are unimproved and can be rough. Trailers are not a good idea here. Light-weight boats or float tubes can be useful.

NORTH GEORGIA LAKE. See **GEORGIA LAKE.**

OLALLA RESERVOIR. A 120-acre reservoir on Olalla Creek, tributary to the Yaquina. Owned by Georgia Pacific, it is open to public fishing for bass, panfish, and trout. From Toledo, follow Hwy. 20 east about a mile, then turn left (north) on Olalla Rd., which reaches the reservoir in less than 3 miles.

Legal rainbow trout are heavily stocked each year, as well as trout of larger size, specially grown for this fishery. Surplus hatchery steelhead (as many as 500 some years) may also be available to catch and keep. Count them towards your daily trout limit.

Though Olalla isn't a great warmwater fishery, it does support brown bullheads, yellow perch, bluegills, and some mid-size largemouth bass. Submerged timber added to the reservoir by local organizations provide additional bass habitat.

Olalla has steep sides except for a couple of shallow bays on the east side. The best warmwater fishing is in these bays. There is no good bank fishing.

Vehicle access is limited to the dam area, where there is a boat ramp. Only electric motors are allowed. If you're thinking of launching a float tube to fish for bass, it's a long kick from the launch area to good bass habitat.

PEBBLE CREEK. A small tributary of the upper Nehalem (13 miles long), entering the river from the south at Vernonia, offering catch and release fishing for wild cutthroat trout.

PERKINS LAKE. A very clear 5-acre trout lake in the Oregon Dunes National Recreation Area about 10 miles south of Florence. The lake is just west of Hwy. 101 and a few miles north of Tahkenitch Lake. Park on the old Hwy. 101 shoulder. You can bank fish or launch a small boat from the old road along the north shore. The shoreline is very brushy, so a boat or float tube is helpful.

Perkins is stocked with rainbow trout. Green baits, spoons, or Flatfish seem to work best. Fly angling can pay off later in the season when fishing pressure drops. Large trout are sometimes taken. There's a campground at Carter Lake about one mile north. Other nearby lakes include Erhart, Georgia, North Georgia, and Lost.

PLYMPTON CREEK. A small creek, tributary to the Columbia in the vicinity of Puget Island, offering catch and release fishing for wild cutthroat trout. Its mouth is near Westport on Hwy. 30. About 8 miles long, it heads near Nicolai Mt. The creek is closed to angling for salmon and steelhead, which enter the creek dark and ready to spawn. Do not disturb them.

PRESCOTT SLOUGH. A 9-acre Columbia River slough off Hwy. 30 west of the decommissioned Trojan Nuclear Power Plant, featuring a smorgasbord of bass and panfish. West of Trojan and the entrance to Prescott Beach, the slough first appears as a narrow ditch paralleling the highway, then heads toward a grove of trees. You can slip a canoe, float tube, or light-weight boat into the water, or fish from the tall grass on the banks. Each tide brings new recruits of largemouth bass, with best fishing near the Columbia River confluence and along the base of the adjoining bluff. White crappie and brown bullhead are also available, as well as yellow perch, bluegill, and warmouth bass.

QUARTZ LAKE. A small but fairly deep cutthroat lake on state timber land near Jewell. The lake is south of Hwy. 26, about 2 miles east of the Jewell junction. Follow Quartz Creek Rd. south of Hwy. 26, 2½ miles west of the big Sunset Rest Area. It is also possible to get to the lake from Elsie.

The land surrounding the lake has been logged, and the lake is brushy and hard to fish. There are lots of snags. About 4 acres, Quartz has produced some nice cutthroat.

RECREATION LAKE. See TROJAN POND.

RILEA SLOUGH. At National Guard Camp Rilea, about 3½ miles southeast of Warrenton. The public is welcome to fish for yellow perch, white crappie, largemouth bass, and bluegill, except during Guard maneuvers. Rilea joins Sunset Lake by way of a narrow channel through which you can take a boat. The camp is a well-tended, pleasant place for a day's outing. See also Slusher Lake. Call the armory for information. See Appendix.

RINEARSON SLOUGH. A Columbia River slough that has suffered from heavy water withdrawals and now offers only poor fishing for a small population of bass and panfish. The slough is northwest of Rainier, some 45 miles from Portland. It can be accessed from the Columbia downstream from Longview Bridge. A number of side roads to the south aproach the slough. Crappie, perch, bluegill, and bass may be present. Access is privately owned, but permission to fish is usually granted.

ROCK CREEK (Nehalem watershed). A very clear wild trout and steelhead stream, open for fishing up to the former Keasey Dam site at r.m. 15. It flows into the upper Nehalem at Vernonia. A county road follows the creek from the northwest side of Vernonia to Keasey. Private logging roads

farther upstream are gated but open for walk-in or bike-in angling. You can also reach the stream from the Sunset Rest Area at about mile post 30. Keep your ears tuned for log trucks at the upper end.

Rock Creek has a good native cutthroat population that may be fished catch-and-release, and a wild winter steelhead run open for catch-and-release fishing after November 1. All non-finclipped steelhead must be released unharmed. The run peaks in December and January. This is a good fly stream, resistant to muddying. It does flow through a lot of private land, so ask permission for access.

SALMON RIVER (Lincoln Co.). A fairly short coastal stream with strong hatchery runs of fall chinook and coho. It also offers good catch-and-release fishing for wild winter steelhead. One of two Salmon rivers in Oregon, this one heads in the coast range in northern Lincoln County and flows 24 miles to the ocean north of Lincoln City. It is followed by Hwy. 18 from McMinnville for most of its length and is crossed by Hwy. 101 a few miles above its mouth.

A salmon hatchery above Otis, at about r.m. 4, releases thousands of fall chinook and coho into the river annually, and attracts almost equal numbers of anglers during the return migration. The Salmon River is primarily a bank fishery, as most of the riffles are shallow gravel bars. Unfortunately, bank access is limited, with most salmon angling taking place just below the hatchery and at the Hwy. 101 bridge downstream. The hatchery is on the North Bank Rd. Anglers fish ¼ mile stretch downstream from the hatchery on both north and south banks. Park at the hatchery in pull-outs off Hwy. 18.

At the Hwy. 101 bridge, anglers park and fish from the bank both upstream and down. Downstream from the bridge, the banks are public land, part of the Cascade Head National Scenic Research Area. Boat anglers launch at the ramp on Three Rocks Rd. below the bridge and motor up to popular holes. Few anglers boat higher than ¾ mile. When the river is high enough to allow boating up to the hatchery, fishing is usually off.

Sea-run cutthroat are the first migrants to appear in the river, entering in late July. Fishing for them is catch and release. Chinook enter the river in August, followed by

coho. Peak catches of both are made in September and October.

Steelhead are in the stream from December through March. All non-finclipped steelhead must be released unharmed. Hatchery steelhead are no longer stocked. In the Rose Lodge area off North Bank Rd., anglers fish for steelhead from the Rose Lodge bridge and from roadside turn-outs.

Above Rose Lodge, the river passes through a corridor of state land (the Van Duzer Corridor) and offers high quality opportunities for catch and release cutthroat in summer and for wild steelhead in winter.

The Salmon River tends to be at its best for both chinook and winter steelhead after a spell of hard rain. The river usually clears quickly.

The riverbank between Otis and Hwy. 101 is privately owned, but some landowners grant permission to fish. Be sure to ask before you wet your line. There are two privately owned RV encampments on the river. The one near Hwy. 101 is operated by an RV membership organization without general public access. The camp near Rose Lodge is available for public use, though space is limited. Supplies are available at several service stations along the upper river. There are tackle stores on the lower river, and supplies and accommodations near Lincoln City.

SALMONBERRY RIVER. An important nursery for the Nehalem River's wild steelhead population. About 18 miles long, the Salmonberry enters the Nehalem about 11 miles south of Elsie on the Lower Nehalem River Road. Anglers can walk up from the mouth along the railroad tracks, but be aware that trains do make the run several times a week. Be wary of the tunnels in the upper river. The upper river can be reached by way of logging roads branching off Hwy. 26 in the vicinity of the big Sunset Wayside.

Salmonberry steelhead are particularly large and strong. The run peaks in February and March. All steelhead in the river are wild and must be released unharmed. The river is open for steelheading from November 1 to March 31. It is closed to salmon fishing and to all fishing from April 1 to October 31.

For a number of years, the Salmonberry has been the subject of intensive monitoring, study, and protection efforts by Ore-

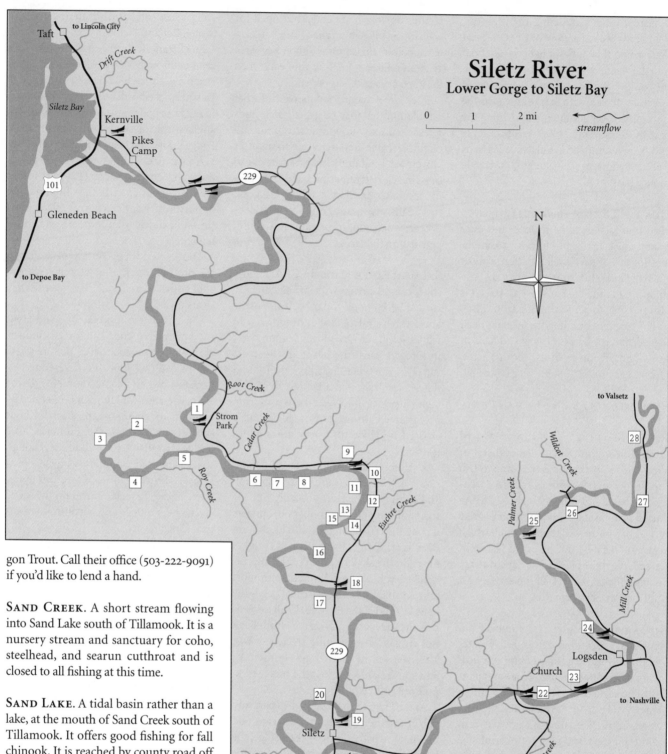

Siletz River
Lower Gorge to Siletz Bay

0   1   2 mi

streamflow

N

to Lincoln City
Taft

Drift Creek

Siletz Bay

Kernville

Pikes Camp

229

101

Gleneden Beach

to Depoe Bay

Root Creek

1
Strom Park
2
3
5
4
Roy Creek

Cedar Creek

9
6   7   8
10
11
12
13
15   14
Euchre Creek
16

18
17

229

20

19
Siletz

21

to Valsetz

28

Wildcat Creek

Palmer Creek

25   26

27

Mill Creek

24

Logsden

Church   23

22

to Nashville

Sams Creek

gon Trout. Call their office (503-222-9091) if you'd like to lend a hand.

SAND CREEK. A short stream flowing into Sand Lake south of Tillamook. It is a nursery stream and sanctuary for coho, steelhead, and searun cutthroat and is closed to all fishing at this time.

SAND LAKE. A tidal basin rather than a lake, at the mouth of Sand Creek south of Tillamook. It offers good fishing for fall chinook. It is reached by county road off Hwy. 101 at Hemlock. For an alternate route, follow the road north from Woods, a community on the Lower Nestucca Rd.

Fall chinook are present in good numbers in September. Smaller numbers of spring chinook are usually available in April and May. Sea-run cutthroat are present in July and August and may be fished catch and release. Chum salmon enter in November and December, but the fishery for them is closed. Steelhead enter in Feb-

ruary and March, but few are taken here. Most angling is from boats or by bank casting on the east side of the island. A bridge crosses to the island from the county road, and boats can be easily launched.

Flounder are occasionally caught between the south side of the island and the outlet. Blue prawns, which can be pur-

chased locally, make good flounder bait, as do mud shrimp and nightcrawlers. Surf perch can be fished on either side of the ocean outlet. Crabs are caught in the lake near the inlet.

There is a county park on the island and a campground on the northwest shore near the ocean.

1. *Strom Park.* Improved all-weather ramp but no other facilities; popular take-out after drifting from Morgan park; good lazy canoe water downstream; fall chinook, summer and winter steelhead, catch-and-release sea-run.

2. *Bull's Bag.* Walk in access to hole, or drift through.

3. *Cahill.* Good plunking hole.

4. *Butterfield Riffle.* River makes swing here; big eddy with gravel bottom.

5. *Big Eddy.* County boat launch across private property; huge eddy in tidewater; some good drifts on outgoing tide.

6. *Cedar Creek Drift.* Last drift; close to highway.

7. *Blackberry Hole.* Plunking; good drift at lower end.

8. *Gravel Hole.* Private; good drift from boat.

9. *Morgan Park.* County boat ramp.

10. *Bluff Hole.* Fish the head of this one; solid rock, but gets snaggy further down; about 300 yds. below Swinging Bridge.

11. *Swinging Bridge.* A few fishing shacks here.

12. *Hole Just Above Swinging Bridge.* Good boat hole; plunking at low water.

13. *Mitchell Hole.* Beautiful drift, best for boats.

14. *French Hole.* Nice fishing for drifters and plunkers; walk down from road 150 ft.

15. *Euchre Creek Hole.* Mouth of Euchre Cr.

16. *Kusydor Drift.* Nice spot; calm edges with swift center.

17. *Shock (Ojolla) Hole.* Fairly slow drift; fish both sides.

18. *First Steel Bridge.* Put-in just above bridge; you need a very long rope or cable to lower boat.

19. *Old Mill Park Boat Ramp.* Just north of Siletz town center.

20. *Second Steel Bridge.*

21. *Hee Hee Ilahee Park.* Put-in for 2-3 hr. drift; take out at Old Mill Park, just a 15 minute walk across town.

22. *Twin Bridges Boat Ramp.* Mouth of Sams Creek; nice 5 mile drift to Hee Hee Ilahee.

23. *Menonite Church.* Put-in across from church.

24. *Logsden Bridge.* Boat ramp above bridge; take road across from store.

25. *Moonshine County Park.* Popular put-in for winter steelhead; bank access; winter steelhead stocked in Palmer Creek show well here.

26. *Wildcat Bridge.* Georgia Pacific allows access above Wildcat Creek on weekends only when logging operations are in progress; contact Georgia Pacific in Toledo for update; good summer steelhead water.

27. *Lower Gorge.* Road follows river accessing several miles of good summer steelhead water through private property.

28. *Steel Bridge.*

SANDY ISLAND SLOUGH. A Columbia River slough north of Goble. It has a good population of black crappie but little public access. Ask permission to access across obviously private land.

SCHOONER CREEK. A tributary of Siletz Bay with wild cutthroat, chinook, and steelhead. It enters the north end of Siletz Bay near Taft and is crossed by Hwy. 101 at its mouth. A county road follows the stream for most of its 10 miles, but the river is open to fishing only up to Erickson Creek at about r.m. 4. The stream is pretty snaggy, varying in width from 25 to 50 feet with lots of deep pools and brushy banks.

Some chinook are taken in the creek in September and October, but most anglers fish chinook in the bay itself. The creek is closed to coho fishing. Wild steelhead are in the creek from December through February and may be fished catch and release. Best fishing for resident cutthroat is early

in the season. Sea-run are present in August and September and may be fished catch and release..

The closest overnight camping is at Devils Lake, about 4 miles south.

SEARS LAKE. A small wild cutthroat lake near Tierra Del Mar beach, between Sand Lake and Woods. This lake is privately owned and is not open to the public at this time.

SHAG LAKE (a.k.a. Burkes Lake). A 5-acre lake near Fort Stevens State Park, best in early season before heavy weed growth. It is very difficult to find, about ½ mile north of the gravel road from Warrenton to Fort Stevens Park, east of the paved road to Hammond. It is lightly fished for bass and panfish.

SILETZ BAY. Heavily fished for fall chinook and a pleasant place to clam or crab

if you're visiting Lincoln City. It extends about 5 miles from the jaws at Taft up to Kernville Bridge. The Siletz River enters the bay from the south at Kernville, while Drift Creek and Schooner Creek enter from the north. The bay is considerably silted up due to logging practices in bygone days.

From early spring to summer the chief angling attraction here is perch. Favorite baits are ghost or sand shrimp, kelp worms, and clam pieces. Perch to 3 pounds are caught up to the Kernville Bridge beginning in May. Perch leave well before the fall rains. In general, best catches are made on the flood tide from anchored boats, but casting from shore near the mouth can be productive.

Crabbing is best in September and October. Rings and bait are available locally and can be set adjacent to public docks on the bay.

Chinook enter the bay in early August, with peak presence here in September.

There are steelhead in the SILETZ RIVER year-round, good boating from Moonshine to Morgan Park. Photograph by Scott Richmond.

Many anglers cast from the banks between Taft and the jaws. Be prepared to lose lots of terminal gear, as the bottom is rocky. Spinners with feathered hooks or Kwik-fish-type lures are popular. Bait can be purchased locally, but gathering your own is not difficult. Shrimp are easily found at low water in the flats along the bay. Herring for bait (or eating) are taken intermittently throughout the summer.

Surf casters can do well on the ocean side of the jaws. The beach drops off rapidly, and at low water there's easy casting for redtail perch.

The tide flats between Cutler City and Kernville have good numbers of softshell clams during zero or minus tides.

Moorages with rental boats and ramps are available along the bay and upriver. On weekends, it's a good idea to make reservations. Be advised that the Siletz bar is more dangerous than most. It has no jetties, and lives have been lost in crossing. The lower bay can also be dangerous.

The nearest campground is at Devils Lake north of the Bay, and there are other campgrounds south on Hwy. 101. Siletz Bay State Park near Lincoln City offers opportunities for viewing brown pelicans in summer. Tackle shops, grocery stores, and motels are plentiful in the area.

Siletz River 🐟

A fine all around stream with opportunities to catch and keep fall chinook and summer and winter steelhead. It flows about 70 miles, entering the bay at Kernville at the junction of Hwy. 101 with Hwy. 229, which follows the lower part of the river. It's accessible from the Corvallis area by way of Hwy. 20 and county roads to the Logsden area, and from the Newport-Toledo area by Hwy. 229.

The Siletz is very fishable, with few snags. The main boating area is from Moonshine Park at r.m. 53 down to Morgan Park at r.m. 25. The town of Siletz has a good ramp with parking and picnic facilities at the Hwy. 229 bridge.

Fall chinook, both hatchery and wild, start moving through the bay in late July or August, and fishing holds up well until late fall. The Siletz muddies easily, and eggs work best when the water's turbid.

Steelhead are in the river and can be fished year-round. The river is stocked with summer and winter steelhead, and has wild runs of both. An estimated 80% of the current steelhead population is hatchery reared. All non-finclipped steelhead must be released unharmed. There are two summer steelhead peaks, in June and October. The winter run peaks in February and March. Hatchery steelhead are stocked between Moonshine Park and the Steel Bridge at r.m. 57, and these areas tend to attract concentrations of returning adult steelhead.

Sea-run cutthroat move up to tidewater in July. Fishing for them is catch and release at this time throughout Oregon.

The lower river and bay have many moorages where boats, bait, and tackle are available. Flood level on the Siletz is 16 ft. Optimum level for boating is 6.6, with acceptable levels from 4 to 6 ft. A river gauge reading is available. See Appendix.

Siltcoos Lake

One of Oregon's premier warmwater fisheries, which happens to also grow large trout, tucked a mile off Hwy. 101 in a beautiful wooded setting about 6 miles south of Florence. The community of Westlake is on its northwest shore. Canary Rd., about 6 miles south of Florence across from Honeyman State Park, accesses the lake's east shore after a very winding fifteen miles. This road has no outlet other than the lakeshore.

Siltcoos is connected to the ocean by the Siltcoos River, which flows 2 miles to the sea, offering a very pleasant canoe trip through sand dunes and old growth spruce. Take-out is in the Siltcoos estuary near Wax Myrtle Campground. Wild salmon and steelhead occasionally can be found in the river. The steelhead may be fished catch and release in season. Check the regulations.

Fishermen who have tasted the fabulous fishing offered by Siltcoos Lake have a singular dream—to orchestrate one great evening rise (participation mandatory) of what must be millions of brown bullhead, yellow perch, crappie, bass, bluegill, and trout.

The 3000-acre lake is considered to be one of the top warm water fisheries in the Northwest, cherished by dedicated bass anglers as well as generations of Oregon small fry who learned how to fish compliments of the lake's abundant yellow perch.

Largemouth bass fishing varies with the weather and the month, but can be very good here year-round. Five pounders are common, and bass to 8 pounds have been caught, particularly in late winter and early spring. Bass fishing is fine throughout the summer, though fewer large fish are taken. Bass angling is particularly good in the Booth arm, Fiddle Creek arm, Maple Creek arm, and Harmony Bay. Bass are also taken in good numbers along the west shore opposite Booth Island, and near the east shore of Booth Island. Plugs and plastic worms are effective year-round. Live bait is prohibited. A number of bass tournaments take place on the lake. Call any one of the resorts for information.

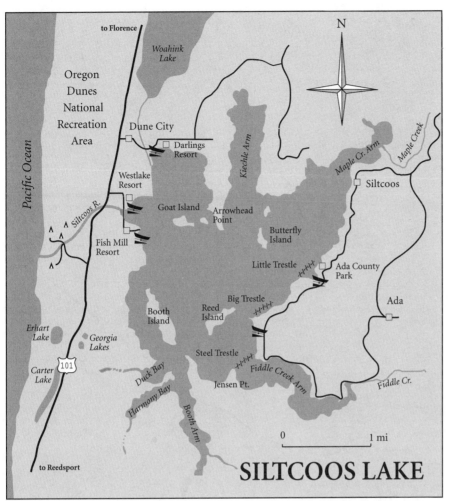

SILTCOOS LAKE

Perch, brown bullhead, crappie, and bluegill are best fished in summer when the water warms and other species are hard to catch. The brown bullhead fishery is often very good. Although generally fished at night, this popular cat can be caught in large numbers in the early morning. Most bullhead anglers fish the bottom with worms and stinky bait. Bullhead are caught near the east shore south of the little trestle, south of Goat Island, near the north shore at the west side of the Kiechle arm opposite Butterfly and Grass islands, and in uppermost Fiddle Creek arm. Perch can be caught throughout the lake. Try the area between Grass and Butterfly islands, just west of Goat Island, and just offshore from Ada. The big wooden trestle on the east shore is a good place for crappie.

Siltcoos is the best lake for wild cutthroat on the mid-coast. Be prepared for large fish, up to 20 inches and weighing 4 or 5 pounds. Limits of cutthroat are caught as early as April. In addition, the lake is stocked with legal rainbows each spring. Six- and 7-pound holdovers aren't un-common, and 9-pounders have been landed. Good catches are made in the Kiechle arm, near the mouth of the Maple Creek arm by Siltcoos, and northeast of Booth Island, among other places.

The lake is closed to coho fishing. Coho (juvenile or adult) hooked incidentally should be released unharmed.

Small runs of wild steelhead and searun cutthroat move through the lake heading for spawning grounds in the Siltcoos River. All steelhead in Siltcoos are wild and must be released unharmed.

There is a public boat ramp at Westlake with a wheelchair accessible fishing pier, and another ramp at the county park north of Ada. The nearest campground is at Honeyman State Park, and there are several forest service campgrounds on the Siltcoos River.

There are a number of resorts on the lake, including Darlings, Fish Mill Lodges and RV Park, and Westlake Resort, which offer cottage lodging, RV parks with hook-ups, boat and motor rentals, tackle, supplies, and lots of know-how on where the fish are biting and how to catch them. Supplies, good restaurants, and additional accommodations are available in Florence.

Siltcoos River. The outlet stream of Siltcoos Lake, closed to coho fishing but open for catch and release cutthroat and wild steelhead. Few, if any steelhead are caught here, as they tend to run quickly through the river, into the lake, and up to their spawning grounds in the creek inlets. The Siltcoos flows only about 2 miles before en-

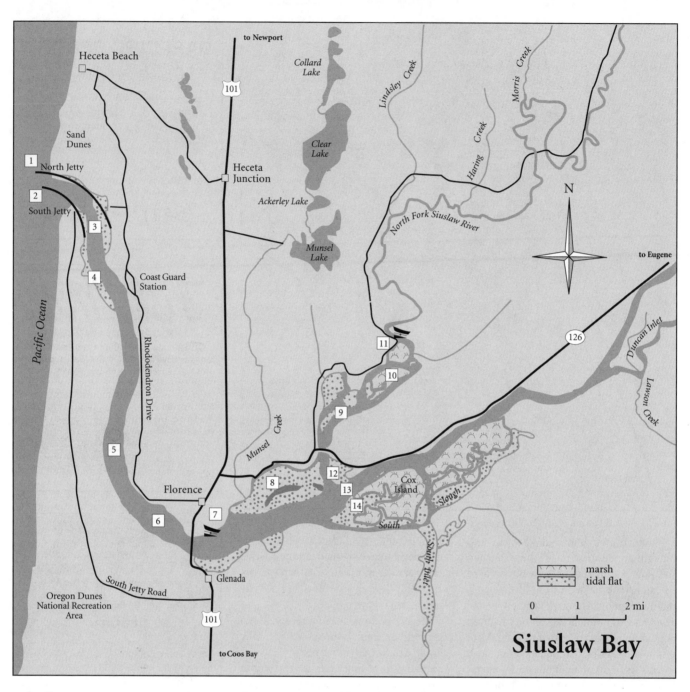

Siuslaw Bay

marsh
tidal flat

0   1   2 mi

tering the ocean.

There's good cutthroat fishing here in early spring and again in fall. Sea-run enter when the river is running high and fast enough to breach the bar, usually around October. Largemouth bass can be successfully fished in late summer.

Most anglers prefer to bank cast this stream, but you can float and fish. Canoeing from the public boat ramp at the lake to the campground beside the estuary offers a pleasant run through sand dunes and old growth spruce.

There is a public boat ramp north of Westlake. There is a large Forest Service campground complex along the river, with four separate campgrounds. The road into the campgrounds is a little over one mile south of the Westlake turnoff. These campgrounds generally support the dune buggy crowd. More camping is available at Honeyman State Park to the north.

Siuslaw Bay 🐟

A good variety bay west of Eugene, offering fine clamming, crabbing, and fishing from late spring through fall. Hwy. 126 provides direct access from I-5 in the Willamette Valley.

Salmon can be found outside the bar from mid-June to October. The Siuslaw bar used to be a tough one, and even the current jetties don't guarantee easy passage. When the bar is closed, some anglers troll the lower channel near the Coast Guard lookout, but only the rare salmon is taken there.

In July the bay and tidewater welcome searun cutthroat and jack salmon. These fish run to 18 inches, and the fishery for them holds up through August or September as the fish await the fall freshets. Eggs drifted under bobbers work well for the jacks. Sea-run must be released unharmed, so most anglers use spinners or big streamer flies. Look for searun at the mouths of the larger tributaries, such as Lawson

1. **North Jetty.** Fish for redtail perch, greenling in spring; best March to May, but rough seas may limit access.

2. **South Jetty.** Fish for redtail, greenling.

3. **Lower Channel.** Best crabbing in the bay on in-coming tide; some perch fishing; a rare salmon is taken.

4. **The Rock Dock.** Popular for crabbing, some perch; wheelchair accessible; good soft shells below.

5. **Flounder Hole.** Good hole for perch; good crabbing in vicinity.

6. **Upper Channel.** Fair late summer crabbing; anchor among pilings and fish redtail perch mid-May to July, striped perch and pile perch spring through fall.

7. **Holiday Harbor Docks and Boat Ramp.** Crab and fish for perch; RV park; handicap accessible.

8. **North Fork Clam Bed West.** Tremendous producer of soft-shell clams; access below bridge from gravel turn-outs.

9. **Mouth of North Fork.** Troll or cast lures to head of tide (3 miles to Portage) for salmon Aug. through Nov.; access from Bender Landing on North Fork.

10. **Bull Island.** ODFW owned access to wetlands (clam flats, bird watching).

11. **Benders Landing.** Access to Bull Island wetland.

12. **North Fork Clam Bed, East.** Dig for larger but less numerous softshell; access from turn-outs below bridge.

13. **Mouth of Siuslaw.** Troll to Mapleton for salmon, August and September.

14. **Cox Island.** Nature Conservancy marshland preserve; boat access only for good clam flats.

Creek on Duncan Inlet, and Karnowsky Creek a little farther up Duncan.

The bay is closed to coho fishing, but its fall chinook run is strong. In 1997, over 5,000 chinook were landed, rivaling the productive Tillamook Bay fishery. Chinook fishing in the bay is best in August, September and October from Cushman to Mapleton. Trolling with spinners and large cutbait herring (12 inches) is the most popular method. The bay has been closed to salmon fishing downstream of the Hwy. 101 bridge from July 1 to August 15.

A run of shad enters the bay in May and June. These are fished in the extreme upper tidewater area between Mapleton and Brickerville. Jigging with small darts is popular, but shad are a lot of fun on a fly rod, and tasty despite the bones.

This bay is the northernmost limit for striped bass. A few show up in February and March, following the smelt run.

Fishing from the rocks along shore or off the jetties can produce perch and greenling on shrimp or clam necks. Jetty fishing is best March through May, but rough seas may discourage access then. Angling from the jetties remains popular throughout the summer. A concrete pier east of the south jetty, locally called The Rock Dock, offers good crabbing and perch fishing. It is wheelchair accessible.

Crabbing is best after the spring freshets have passed through the bay. Crab are present up to Cushman (4 miles up-bay from Florence), though they get smaller upriver. Crabbing is best in the lower channel around the Coast Guard Station or off The Rock Dock. There is fair crabbing above and below the Hwy. 101 bridge from July through October.

For clam connoisseurs, Siuslaw Bay offers some of the best softshell flats on the coast. The flats to the west of the mouth of the North Fork are extremely productive. The flats to the east of the mouth produce fewer but larger softshells. Cox Island, at

the mouth of the Siuslaw, is a Nature Conservancy wildlife preserve, with good clam flats accessible only by boat. Large cockles and gapers are very plentiful in the lower bay below the Coast Guard Station, where they are gathered by divers.

There are three public boat ramps on the bay: near the Hwy. 101 Bridge at Florence, at Tiernan, and at Mapleton. Rough seas may cause extremely dangerous conditions on the lower bay as well as at the bar. Check with the Cost Guard for conditions and advisories.

Good accommodations are available in the area, with many motels and camp-

All searun cutthroat in Oregon are wild, and all fishing for them is catch-and-release. Photograph by Scott Richmond.

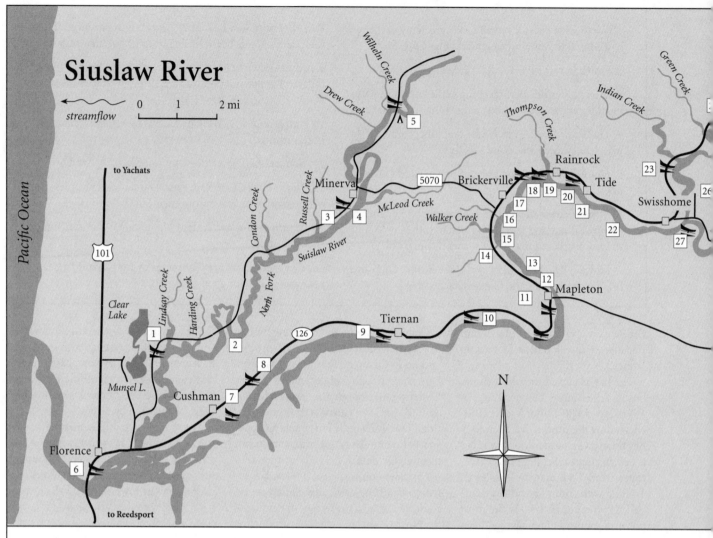

Siuslaw River

streamflow · 0 1 2 mi

Pacific Ocean

1. Bender Landing. County park with concrete boat ramp; good plunking from bank; wheelchair accessible.

2. Funke Bridge. Good plunking hole beneath second bridge on Portage Loop; room for 8 anglers on both sides of stream.; ask permission to fish.

3. Cedar Hole. Deep plunking hole by big cedar tree 9 miles up; get permission.

4. Houghton Landing. Good plunking hole with public boat access 9.6 miles up.

5. Campground. Good bank access from here on up.

6. Holiday Harbor. Paved boat ramp.

8. Cushman Marina. A gravel ramp 3 miles east of Florence.

7. Siuslaw Marina. Hoist facility 4 miles east of Florence.

9. Tiernan Boat Access. ODFW ramp.

10. C&D Dock. Hoist Facility.

11. Mapleton Landing. Paved ramp.

12. Mapleton Public Docks. Extensive facilities; handicap accessible.

13. Dollar Hole. Head of tide.

14. Farnam Riffle. Drift fish from boat or plunk below Farnam landing boat slide.

15. Walker Riffle. Good drift from boat 2½ miles above Mapleton.

16. Gauging Station Hole. Good deep plunking hole 3 miles above Mapleton.

17. Brickerville Hole. Primitive boat slide; trail is upstream from last house above Brickerville; good plunking hole; fish close to bank.

18. Thompson Creek. Four very good holes along edge of highway; includes good boat access site; good plunking in fast water.

19. Rainrock Hole. Extremely popular and productive plunking water; watch for long wide highway shoulder just below Thompson Creek; fair boat access.

20. Tide Wayside. At county park 6 miles above Mapleton across from market.

21. Red Hill Hole and Drift. Before railroad crossing 6½ miles above Mapleton.

22. Mill Hole and Drift. Walk through mill to river, about 7 miles above Mapleton.

23. Indian Creek. Hole just below creek; boat ramp.

24. Green Creek Hole. Good drift from boat and bank.

25. Deadwood Cr. Boat Access. Popular concrete ramp for drift boat launching; good holes for 5 miles upstream to Greenleaf Cr.

26. Konnie Memorial Fishing Access.

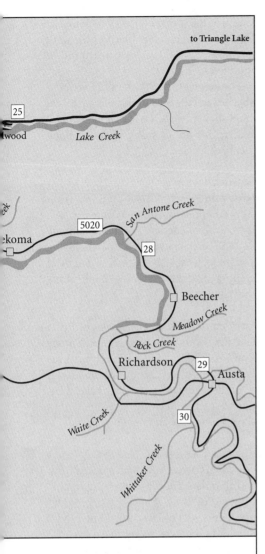

Concrete ramp with parking; bank access above mouth of Lake Cr. accesses The Horn; wheelchair accessible.

27. Church Access. Turn off highway at Evangelical Church in Swisshome, keep to right after railroad tracks; good drifts from boat and bank; unimproved boat access. Church hole below church, Sand Hole above Church.; ask permission to fish.

28. Swisshome to Richardson Bridge. 12 miles of beautiful water, accessible from boat or bank.

29. Austa. Unimproved put-in at covered bridge.

30. Whittaker Cr. Boat Ramp. Concrete BLM ramp.

grounds within a short distance. Marinas near the bridge provide boat rentals, gas, tackle, bait, and other supplies.

SIUSLAW RIVER. A good fall chinook stream, heading in the Coast Range west of Eugene and Cottage Grove and flowing over 100 miles to the ocean near Florence. The river also has winter steelhead and cutthroat. It is not heavily fished. A fish ladder at the falls on Lake Creek (a major tributary of the Siuslaw) allows salmon access to additional spawning grounds above Triangle Lake.

The Siuslaw is approached from the Willamette Valley by driving west from Eugene on Hwy. 126, which crosses the mainstem at Austa. From there one may turn downstream on a county road to Swisshome and the sea, upstream on a county road and a maze of logging roads that follow the river far into the hills, or continue on Hwy. 126 to its intersection with Hwy. 36 at Mapleton.

The entire Siuslaw and most of its tributaries are open for catch and release cutthroat fishing during the regular season. Sea-run usually return in several runs during August and September, though they occasionally hit the river all at once and scoot upriver. Angling for searun occurs mostly in the tidewater portion of the river (from Mapleton downstream).

The fall chinook run has been strong and steady. Chinook are in the river from September through December, but are dark and inedible after November. They are fished up into Lake Creek, but most are caught in tidewater between Cushman and Mapleton.

The winter steelhead run has been poor. Finclipped hatchery steelhead make up about half the annual catch. Unclipped steelhead must be released unharmed. Most hatchery steelhead are released in Whitaker Creek, so most angling pressure is from Whitaker downstream. The run enters the river in late January and holds strong through March.

This stream is often murky in winter. If you get to the river and find this to be so, you might try fishing Lake Creek. Lake Creek clears quickly after a rain and is a good steelhead producer.

A small run of shad appears in May and June. Most angling effort is concentrated between Mapleton and Brickerville, but some shad get as far up as Swisshome.

There are many boat ramps on the main river, including a public ramp at Tiernan. The Siuslaw is a wide, fast stream requiring skillful and cautious boating, especially in the upper areas. Guide service is available in Eugene, Swisshome, and Florence.

There are campgrounds at Honeyman State Park on the coast, Knowles Creek (USFS) about 3 miles east of Mapleton, Whittaker Creek (BLM) 1½ miles south of Austa, and Clay Creek (BLM) about 10 miles upstream from Whittaker Creek. Supplies are available at Mapleton and Florence, and at several marinas on the lower river. Accommodations are available in Florence. There is a wheelchair accessible dock with a decent fishery at Mapleton.

SIUSLAW RIVER, NORTH FORK. A bank fishery featuring cutthroat and a fair run of winter steelhead. This good size tributary of the Siuslaw River enters Siuslaw Bay east of Florence. The river is followed by a good paved road that runs north from Hwy. 126 about one mile east of Florence. The upper river can also be reached from Hwy. 36 at Firo on Forest Rd. 5070, which crosses the river at Minerva (Meadows Bridge).

About 25 miles long and 30 to 50 feet wide, it is not heavily fished. The bottom is primarily bedrock, sand, and gravel, and there is little cover for fish.

It offers fair catch and release fishing for wild resident cutthroat in early season and for searun in the fall. A wild winter steelhead run peaks in February and March and is fished primarily above Minerva and at the Forest Service campground about 13 miles upstream from Hwy. 126. Wild (non-finclipped) steelhead must be released unharmed.

The North Fork is exclusively a bank fishery as the river is too small for boats.

Camping facilities are available at Honeyman State Park south of Florence or at North Fork Siuslaw Campground about 3 miles upstream from Minerva. There is a wheelchair-accessible dock with accessible comfort facilities at Bender Landing.

SKOOKUM LAKE (Tillamook watershed). A small lake about 10 miles southwest of Tillamook at the head of Fawcett Creek. It is a reservoir for Tillamook City Water and is closed to public fishing.

SLUSHER LAKE. A good 20-acre bass and panfish lake at Camp Rilea, the National

There's good fishing for largemouth bass in many of Oregon's coastal lakes. Photograph by Bud Hartman.

Guard Camp southwest of Warrenton. Slusher is sometimes a player in Guard maneuvers that include helicopters and pontoon bridges, but most days the public is welcome to fish. The lake contains good size largemouth bass, yellow perch, and brown bullhead. The woody structure on the ocean side of the lake is a good place to poke around. This is a good lake for float tubes.

Check in at the gate or call ahead if you want to be sure of access. (See Appendix) In general, the public is welcome, and it's a pleasant place for a day's outing.

SMITH LAKE (Clatsop Co.). A long, narrow, shallow lake at the junction of the Hammond Rd. with Hwy. 101, about 2 miles south of Warrenton on the west side of Hwy. 101. It supports crappie, bluegill, brown bullhead, perch, and largemouth bass. Fish it early in the season, as it has a severe weed problem due to leaky septic systems in the vicinity. In fact, weeds have diminished a very good bass fishery here. There is no bank access, but you may be able to put a small boat in (or launch a float tube) at the north end. This is another lake to try while camping at Fort Stevens State Park. See Coffenbury.

SMITH LAKE (Tillamook Co.). A 35-acre trout lake near Rockaway, north of Tillamook Bay. It may be best known as the water

feature at Camp Magruder, a Methodist Church camp available to the public for group retreats.

Relatively weed free and 8 to 12 feet deep, the lake is stocked with legal rainbows in spring. Brown bullheads are plentiful but are only lightly fished. Largemouth bass have not thrived here.

The lake can be accessed from public land to the west as well as from the camp. There is no public boat ramp, but light craft can be launched with effort. There is a 5 mph speed limit on the lake.

SOAPSTONE LAKE. A small cutthroat lake in the North Fork Nehalem watershed whose outlet is Soapstone Creek. To reach it (good luck), drive to Necanicum Junction on Hwy. 26, southwest of Cannon Beach, then turn south on Hwy. 53. After about 8 miles and just before crossing the North Fork, turn northeast onto Coal Mountain Ridge Rd. At about 1½ miles you can spot the lake to the north. It's a 20-minute walk to the lake.

Soapstone covers 10 acres and is over 20 ft. deep. Full of brush and snags, it seems to have more salamanders than cutthroat. It's best fished in early season.

SOUTH LAKE. A 5-acre trout lake south of Hebo Lake, about ten miles from Hebo Ranger Station on the forest road west from the junction of highways 14 and 101.

Check at the sport shop at Hebo for exact location. It's generally inaccessible until mid-May, as the road is usually full of mudholes.

The lake is stocked with rainbow catchables several times in spring and has lots of crayfish, which are a good choice for bait fishing. It's full of snags, so bring along plenty of tackle.

SPRING LAKE (a.k.a. Ocean Lake). A fair bass fishery with legal rainbow trout stocked annually. About 13 acres, it is ½ mile north of Barview, north of Tillamook Bay and east of Hwy. 101 near Twin Rocks. You might be able to get a raft in, but most angling is done from the bank along the highway.

SPRUCE RUN LAKE. A small cutthroat lake formed by a beaver dam on Spruce Run Creek south of Elsie. To get there, see Lost Lake (Clatsop County). Spruce Run is a ½ mile hike southeast of Lost Lake. It has lots of small wild cutthroat trout. Only 3 acres, it is brushy and hard on tackle.

SUNSET LAKE (a.k.a. Neacoxie Lake). A very long, narrow lake, with stocked trout and abundant bullheads, as well as opportunities for bass, crappie, bluegill, and perch. It is west of Hwy. 101 about 4 miles north of Gearhart. To get there, take the road west from Hwy. 101 north of the Cullaby Lake junction. This road crosses over the north end of Sunset Lake.

Sunset is about 2 miles long and less than 500 ft. wide. It has about 110 surface acres with lots of water over 15 feet deep.

The lake offers good early-season fishing for stocked rainbow trout. Best fishing is mid-lake toward the south end, where the water is deepest.

Largemouth bass aren't thriving here, but some good catches are made below the narrows in the small pockets on the west shore. Crappie, perch, and bluegill are also present. Brown bullheads are particularly abundant.

Boats can be launched at the county ramp on the north side of the bridge. Speed limit on the lake is 10 mph. Bank fishing is confined to an area around the boat ramp.

SUTTON LAKE. Two fair size bodies of water connected by a narrow channel with a total area of about 100 acres. It is located

Not Road 2282
SP left at junction 2210

on the east side of Hwy. 101 about 6 miles north of Florence. Sutton has a few wild cutthroat and is stocked heavily in spring with legal rainbows. It's also a good panfish lake with strong populations of yellow perch and largemouth bass. This is a nice recreational area, and the lake is not fished hard.

Reeds and lily pads around the lake's perimeter limit shoreline fishing opportunities. Some catches are made from the bank next to the highway, but there's better bass and perch habitat around the private docks on the north side of the lake and near the channel connecting the two pools.

There's a parking area and small boat ramp near the creek outlet under Hwy. 101. The nearest camping facility is a Forest Service campground on Sutton Creek about ¼ mile west.

SWEET CREEK. A small stream with native cutthroat and steelhead, entering the Siuslaw River about 10 miles upstream from Florence. It can be reached by Hwy. 36 and a county road which follows it south. The creek is fair for cutthroat in early season, and a few return as searun in the fall. It is not stocked. It has a fair winter steelhead run for a creek this size, with fishing from December to March. Sweet Creek does not have good public access. Ask permission before you cross private land and be a considerate guest.

TAHKENITCH LAKE. A good, large coastal lake 5 miles south of Siltcoos Lake, potentially as productive as Siltcoos, but less popular. It has more than 1500 surface acres east of Hwy. 101, about 13 miles south of Florence.

Everyone in the family can catch fish here, but you'll need a boat since the shore is too brushy for bank angling. Best fishing is for crappie, bluegill, and yellow perch. Crappie are very plentiful, especially at the base of the trestles that cross the lake on the east side.

Bluegill, warmouth (like a bluegill but with a big mouth), and yellow perch are plentiful and provide a great fishery for youngsters with bobber and worm. Bluegill and warmouth run 5 to 7 inches. Yellow perch average 7 inches with some 10 to 12 inches. Fish for them along the shoreline, off the dock near the boat ramp, and near the bottom in deeper water.

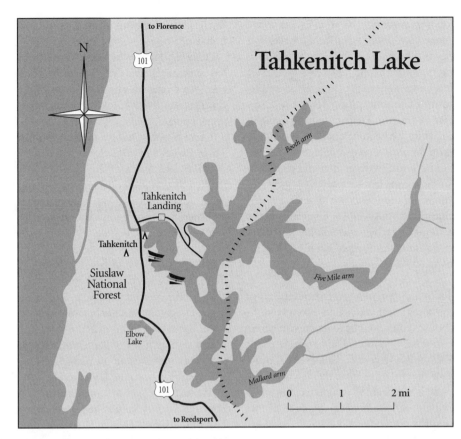

Largemouth bass in the 10 pound class have been taken from Tahkenitch. Look for bass in the arms, along the weedy shoreline, and near the trestles and other woody structure. Fivemile arm on the east side of the lake has especially good bass habitat. To reach it, head around the point to the east after launching. The arm is heavily vegetated with lots of downed wood. Bass are also caught near Weed Island, which is visible from the boat ramps. Though steepsided in most places, the island has two shallow sides that attracts spawners in spring. Catch and release on bass during spawning season, though not required, will help preserve the fishery.

There's a small wild cutthroat population in the lake, and legal rainbows are stocked each year.

One of the strongest runs of wild coho on the northern Oregon coast enters the lake in November, but the lake is closed to coho angling.

There are two public boat ramps off Hwy. 101, including one at Tahkenitch Landing Campground. An RV resort at the creek mouth provides rental boats and tackle. In addition to Tahkenitch Landing on the lake shore, there is a campground on the west side of Hwy. 101.

TAHOE LAKE. A 2-acre trout pond in the upper Trask River watershed east of Tillamook. From Hwy. 101 at Tillamook, follow Third Street east, then Trask River Rd. about 12½ miles to the end of pavement. Continue on the main gravel forest road about 6½ miles to a spur road on the right signed for the lake. Tahoe is stocked with legal rainbows in April and May. Excess adult hatchery steelhead may also be stocked if winter weather conditions allow access. There's good bank fishing from an unimproved trail around the lake.

TENMILE CREEK (Lane Co.). A real gem of a wild winter steelhead stream, 15 miles south of Waldport, crossed at its mouth by Hwy. 101. The creek is about 11 miles long and runs from 15 to 30 ft. wide. There is plenty of cover for fish, but it can be hard on tackle.

Wild winter steelhead are doing very well in this stream, protected both by catch and release regulations and by a closure on fishing during spring and summer when juvenile steelhead can be mistaken for trout. The creek opens for steelheading Nov. 1, with best fishing in February and March.

There's a lot of private land here, so ask permission before you fish. A good road follows the stream almost to its source and eventually ties in with Indian Creek Rd. heading north from the Hwy. 36. There's a campground 5 miles upstream from Hwy. 101, and a state park campground 4 miles south of the mouth on Hwy. 101. Use a Fire Protection District map to navigate roads in the headwaters since it's easy to drop into the wrong drainage up there.

The Tenmile watershed and its fishery are benefiting from considerable local care and restoration work. A 116-acre land purchase by the Audubon Society is being groomed as a fish and wildlife sanctuary and demonstration project for stream rehabilitation techniques.

THISSEL POND. A 3-acre trout fishery in the Alsea River watershed. From Hwy. 34 about 15 miles west of Alsea, turn north on Forest Rd. 62 toward Fall Creek Hatchery. Thissel is adjacent to Fall Creek about a mile downstream from the hatchery. The pond is in a peaceful wooded setting and is heavily stocked with legal rainbows in spring.

THREE RIVERS. A good salmon, steelhead, and cutthroat stream, tributary to the Big Nestucca. It is managed primarily as a salmon and steelhead brood stock stream with more limited angling opportunities than other north coast rivers.

Three Rivers enters the Nestucca about ½ mile north of Hebo. Only about 14 miles long, it nevertheless carries a lot of water. The mouth is near the junction of highways 101 and 22. Hwy. 22 follows it south towards Dolph. There is a hatchery about 1½ miles upstream from Hebo. The river is closed to all angling from the hatchery weir to the mouth from June 1 through September 30 to protect returning spring chinook and summer steelhead brood stock.

Wild cutthroat are plentiful here during the brief open season in spring (May 22 to June 1) and in October. Easily waded, it has all the attributes of good fly water, including boulders, gravel, and undercut banks. Spring chinook may also be fished during the brief spring trout window.

Fall chinook and coho reach Three Rivers in October, but angling for coho is prohibited. The river is stocked with both summer and winter steelhead, and there is a wild winter run. Peak winter steelheading is in late December and January, depending on water conditions. Wild (non-

finclipped) steelhead must be released unharmed.

Easily fished from the bank, Three Rivers has some nice gravel drifts where yarn and eggs are effective. The mouth of Three Rivers is an ideal hole for all species and is very popular.

There is public access at the mouth of Three Rivers and just below the hatchery deadline, but much of the lower river is flanked by private property. Supplies and accommodations are available at Hebo, and there is a campground about 5 miles south of Hebo on Hwy. 14.

THREEMILE LAKE. A fair size dune lake that features good perch and cutthroat angling for the determined angler. The lake is in the Oregon Dunes National Recreation Area about one mile northwest of the northernmost reach of Winchester Bay. It shows up quite well on the recreation area map available from the US Forest Service.

About 1½ miles north of Gardiner on Hwy. 101, County Rd. 247 heads west along Threemile Creek (which does not flow from or into the lake). Follow the road to within ½ mile of the ocean and hike north about .7 mile to the lake. Threemile has yellow perch which run to 14 inches and cutthroat over 14 inches, but it's a bear to fish without a boat. It's a good place for a raft or float tube.

TILLAMOOK BAY

Oregon's second largest bay and one of the state's premiere fisheries, featuring a large run of fall chinook as well as many other fishing opportunities. Exceeded in size only by Coos Bay, it is the estuary for five productive coast streams (from north to south), the Miami, Kilchis, Wilson, Trask, and Tillamook rivers. Its port city is Garibaldi.

The floods of '96 made some changes in the bay, including the deposit of millions of tons of silt which created some big new mud bars. The largest of these runs over a mile along Hwy. 101 from Kilchis Point to the mouth of the Miami, redefining the shape of the popular Ghost Hole. But gradually, the silt is moving out to sea, and the river's traditional holes and channels are reasserting themselves.

Halibut and bottom fish are the featured attractions of the off-shore charter fleet that operates out of Garibaldi. Spring and

fall chinook are fished inside and beyond the bar as regulations allow. Crab, perch, and clams are plentiful. Sturgeon move into the bay in numbers sufficient to encourage a popular fishery in winter and spring.

One of the closest bays to Portland, it is approached by good roads, and almost any spot on shore can be reached by car and a short walk. Tillamook Bay is also home to one of the Northwest's largest concentrations of waterfowl.

From the Willamette Valley, the bay is about 1½ hours. drive. From Portland, follow Hwy. 26 west to Banks, then Hwy. 6 to Tillamook. Turn south on Hwy. 101, which skirts the bay on its east and north shores. Bayocean Rd. follows the southwest shore. A gravel road closed to motor vehicles leads from the end of Bayocean Rd. to the south jetty.

Garibaldi is a major port for Oregon's offshore halibut and salmon fisheries. Offshore salmon and Pacific halibut fishing seasons and quotas are determined annually by the Pacific Fishery Management Council. General regulations are published in the spring of the year, but in-season changes are common. Get current information before planning a trip for either of these species. See Appendix.

Tillamook Bay's offshore salmon fishery is within the Cape Falcon to Humbug Mountain regulatory zone. Its halibut fishery is within the Cape Falcon to Florence North Jetty zone. The halibut season out of Tillamook Bay has been open intermittently from May to September. Offshore chinook seasons have recently been open from April 1 to October 1, and there have been selective offshore fishing opportunities for finclipped coho.

Plan on a full day's outing when fishing for halibut. The average catch weighs 30 lbs. with some fish to 90 lbs. When fishing for chinook, be prepared to fish deep. Unlike coho (which tend to travel close to the surface), offshore chinook are generally found at depths of 150 to 200 ft. Charter boats with commercial-grade downriggers can get your bait down to their level. If you're heading out on your own, trolling or mooching plug-cut herring using 2 to 3 ounces of lead can be effective. Fish the reefs, watch the birds (or your fish finder) for concentrations of bait fish, or follow the commercial boats to find schools of chinook.

The Tillamook bar can be quite dangerous to cross, so keep your eye on weather conditions, and be extremely careful. Small boats can only expect to get outside about 25 percent of the time, even in summer. The favorite salmon ground is south of the whistler buoy about a mile beyond the bar. A good destination for rockfish and lingcod is Three Arch Rocks off Cape Meares. Fish at 8 to 15 fathoms. Halibut are about 20 miles offshore due west of the bar. Most are caught in 9 fathoms and deeper. Charter boats head out regularly and are recommended for safe and successful offshore fishing.

The first fishing opportunity of the year in the bay itself is for sturgeon. Sturgeon are not full-time residents here, but begin moving into the bay in winter. The number of sturgeon in the bay gradually increases through spring. Best fishing is often a couple of days after a heavy storm. There are few giants in this migratory population. Most are 38 to 52 inches. In early season, most sturgeon are taken near Bay City. Later, they can be found in any of the deeper holes and channels. By May, sturgeon are caught as far up as Memaloose Point. The most popular sturgeon baits are mud shrimp, sand shrimp, and clams. Best fishing is during the slack following a low or minus tide. Sturgeon angling is holding steady, with best catches in the Ghost Hole, off the mouth of the Trask, and off the Bay Ocean Flats. These sturgeon are presumed to be migrants from the Columbia River.Though old timers say there are sturgeon in Tillamook Bay year-round, most sturgeon are caught in the bay from mid-February to mid-April.

Surf and bottom fish are also caught in Tillamook Bay as early as January and February. Cast from the jetties or from the rocks from the Barview area to Bay City for lingcod, rockfish, and perch. In recent years, the ling population has suffered a decline, and regulations reflect the effort to protect adult spawners. At this time, harvest is limited to one fish per day with a keeper slot length of 24-inch minimum and 34-inch maximum. Check current regulations.

The north jetty is the more protected of the two for early season outings. Later, perch and greenling are also fished from boats near the rock outcrops of the lower main channel, off the rocks at Barview Park near the mouth, and at the Old

Perch, greenling, and the occasional lingcod are caught off the rocks at Barview on TILLAMOOK BAY. *Photograph by Scott Richmond.*

Garibaldi Coast Guard Pier, which is open for public angling. It extends 700 feet into the bay and is also used for crabbing and, at the end, a chance for chinook. This pier is wheelchair accessible.

South jetty anglers take lingcod and chinook on bigger bait, or night fish for sea bass. Lingcod are also taken in the Barview area by boaters drifting herring. Common bottomfish baits include shrimp, clam necks, and kelp worms. Park-and-fish spots are available off Hwy. 101 from Bay City north to Hobsonville Point, an area that skirts the famous Ghost Hole, a popular salmon trolling area accessed by boats from public ramps in Bay City and downtown Garibaldi. The Bay City ramp is functional only at high tide.

A small run of spring chinook enters the bay beginning in late winter, with most catches made from April through June. The average springers weighs 18 to 20 pounds. Far more popular is the bay fishery for fall chinook, a large and healthy run with many more older and larger fish. The average Tillamook fall chinook weighs 25 to 27 pounds. Fall chinook enter the bay in

late August or early September, with peak catches in mid-October and good numbers often available till mid-November. Most fall chinook linger in the bay until the fall rains begin, at which point they head up into one of the bay's five major tributaries.

Boat anglers troll the lower main channel, in front and behind the south jetty, the Ghost Hole, and the upper channel as well as the mouth of the Tillamook River. Herring, either whole or plug cut, is favored as high up as the Bay City boat ramp. Upstream, spinners and Kwikfish type lures are used. Some anglers give the Kwickfish a herring or anchovy wrap. Spinners and lures also seem to be favored by anglers at the Sheep Corral, an area in the channel opposite Kilchis Pt.

The Ghost Hole, just south of Hobsonville Point, is a favorite spot for large chinook. Some successful bay anglers claim that fishing for chinook is best on the incoming tide through high slack.

Like all coastal waters, Tillamook Bay is subject to emergency salmon closures as well as extended season opportunities. See

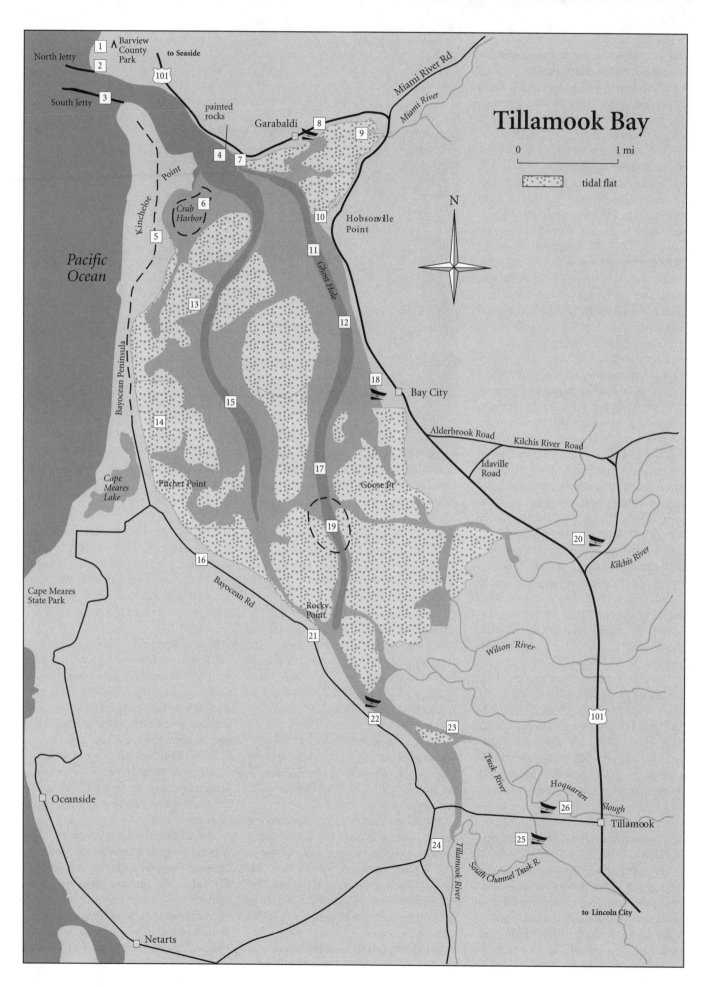

Tillamook Bay

0   1 mi

tidal flat

North Jetty

South Jetty

Barview County Park

to Seaside

painted rocks

Garabaldi

Miami River Rd

Miami River

Kincheloe Point

Crab Harbor

Pacific Ocean

Hobsonville Point

Ghost Hole

N

Bayocean Peninsula

Bay City

Alderbrook Road

Kilchis River Road

Idaville Road

Cape Meares Lake

Pitcher Point

Goose Pt

Kilchis River

Cape Meares State Park

Bayocean Rd

Rocky Point

Wilson River

Oceanside

Trask River

Hoquarten Slough

Tillamook

Netarts

Tillamook River

South Channel Trask R.

to Lincoln City

1. *Barview Park.* County park with camping, RV hook-ups; fish off the rock fill for perch.

2. *North Jetty.* Fish for rockfish, some perch, salmon off furthest point.

3. *South Jetty.* Less angling pressure, more wind, rougher sea; fish for perch, fall chinook, rockfish; use bigger bait for lingcod; night fish for sea bass.

4. *Painted Rocks.* fish for rockfish, perch; seaward, troll for salmon.

5. *Bay Ocean Trail.* 3 mile bike or hike on gravel road to South Jetty.

6. *Crab Harbor.* Well sheltered and popular for crabbing and clamming.

7. *Old Coast Guard Pier.* Dig flats for clams; fish for crab from pier; all facilities upgraded.

8. *Old Mill & Garibaldi.* 2 public boat ramps; pay to launch.

9. *Mouth of Miami.* Bank fishing below railroad bridge for fall chinook, chum salmon.

10. *Hobsonville Point.* Perch in May & June.

11. *Ghost Hole.* Popular for salmon; sturgeon at upper end; hole goes to 20 ft.

12. *Main Channel.* Use this channel to travel up or down bay.

13. *Clam Flats.* Boat access to clams.

14. *Mud Flats.* Hike across flats at low tide to fish for sturgeon; beware of rising tide and soft mud.

15. *Old Channel.* Fish here for sturgeon; channel gets very shallow seaward of this point at low tide; use main (east) channel to go down-bay.

16. *Bay Ocean Rd.* Bank fish for fall chinook.

17. *Mid-Bay.* Troll for salmon.

18. *Bay City Ramp.* Unimproved public ramp with poor access at low tide.

19. *Sheep Corral.* Troll for salmon among the pilings.

20. *Parks Landing.* Improved ramp is lowest take-out on Kilchis; provides bay access for car-top boats, but not at low water.

21. *Picket Fence at Rocky Point.* Popular for fall chinook; some springer activity.

22. *Memaloose Point* (Oyster House Hole). Improved county ramp accesses mouth of Tillamook salmon fishery; fee to launch.

23. *Mouth of Trask.* Sea-run and chinook.

24. *The Sturgeon Hole.* Fish for fall chinook & sturgeon, possible spring chinook or sea-run; limited parking.

25. *Carnahan Park Ramp.* Improved ramp at end of 5th St., City of Tillamook; accesses lower Trask tidewater and upper bay; heavily used; fee.

26. *Hoquarten Slough.* Boat ramp on First St., Tillamook; accesses Hoquarten & Doughterty sloughs & lower Trask; shallow at low tide; fish sloughs for fall chinook in low water years.

Appendix for information sources.

An occasional steelhead is picked up on lures trolled late in the season. There's a very good bank fishery for perch just off the Hobsonville Point. Park and fish from the rocks.

Crabbing is good year-round, with best catches in the winter. Most crabbers work Crab Harbor off the Bay Ocean Peninsula. Crab rings are available for rent at private marinas and bait shops, some of which also keep a crab cooker steaming.

For clamming, Tillamook Bay is hard to beat. Almost the entire perimeter of the bay has extensive clam beds. All the main species of clams can be gathered, although razors are getting scarce. Tidal flats throughout the bay produce large numbers of gapers, cockles, and softshells. Best access is on a zero or less tide. Littleneck clams and butter clams are most plentiful in the northern bay, softshells in the southern bay, and gapers (blue clams) are found everywhere. Check the regulations for the current harvest limit.

Herring sometimes enter the bay in spring through fall. Anglers use herring jigs to catch them for bait and eating. A shad run appears in June.

Moorages and supplies are plentiful around three sides of the bay. There are free public ramps at Bay City, Parks Landing on the Kilchis, and Hoquarten Slough. The Parks Landing ramp may only give access to open water during very high tides. There's a fee to launch at Carnahan Park in Tillamook, at Memaloose Pt. on the Bay Ocean Peninsula, and at private marinas on the bay. For campers, there is a big county park at Barview and another up the Kilchis River. About 12 miles south, Lookout State Park has an excellent campground with lots of space.

TILLAMOOK RIVER. A tributary of Tillamook Bay, flowing from the south and entering the bay near the mouth of the Trask River. Fall chinook provide the primary fishery here, with catch and release angling for wild winter steelhead and searun cutthroat, and some opportunities for sturgeon fishing in tidewater.

Fall chinook turn in from the bay in late September and October. Good numbers are caught in the lower river, including salmon "just visiting" in early season before heading to other Tillamook Bay tributaries. To fish the lower river, anglers launch at Carnahan Park Ramp on the Trask , at the county ramp at Memaloose Pt., or at Burton-Fraser boat ramp on the Tillamook River.

Bank anglers can fish at Tillamook Tidewater, a public access at the confluence of the Tillamook River and Trask River Slough, where there's a boardwalk and pier suitable for handicapped anglers. Tillamook Tidewater provides access to a good deep hole where chinook often hold as well as the occasional sturgeon. Bank anglers can also fish along Fraser Rd. between Tillamook Tidewater and the Burton-Fraser Bridge boat ramp.

Coho move into the river in October and November, but the river is closed to coho angling. Sea-run cutthroat trout are present from July through September and may be fished catch and release.

The Tillamook hosts a run of wild winter steelhead, which provide good fishing in late December and January.

The Tillamook gets very low and warm in summer.

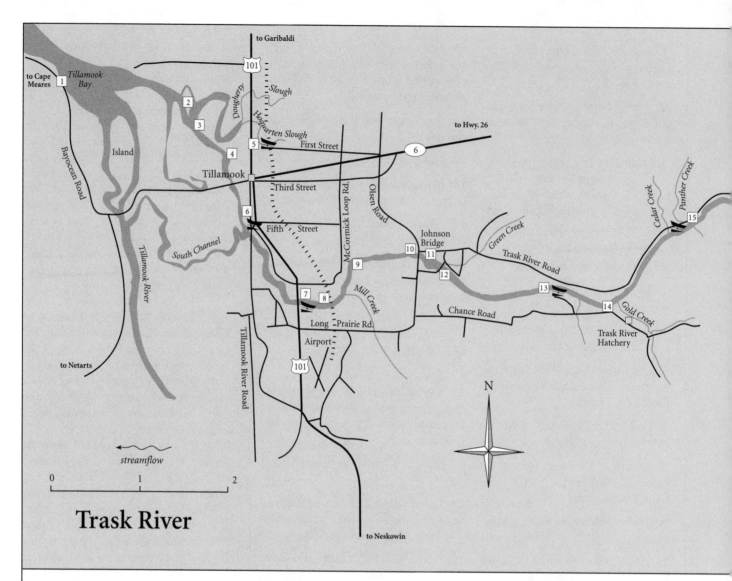

Trask River

1. **Memaloose Point.** Oyster House Hole. Improved county ramp accesses mouth of Tillamook salmon fishery; fee to launch.

2. **Piling Hole.** Good chinook hole downstream from Aufdermeyer's.

3. **Jack Salmon Point.** Walk downstream from Aufdermeyer Hole.

4. **Aufdermeyer (Hospital) Hole.** Most popular bank fishery on the river; pay a modest fee to fish.

5. **Hoquarten Slough.** Shallow at low tides; fish slough for fall chinook in low water years.

6. **Fifth St. Ramp.** City of Tillamook access to tidewater fisheries.

7. **Lower Trask Access.** Improved ramp to gravel bar; bank fishing at good salmon & steelhead hole; drive in off Long Prairie Rd.

8. **Slaughter Hole.** Pay to fish good salmon hole below railroad bridge in fall; park at slaughter house.

9. **Beeler Hole.** Boat fishery at big salmon hole.

10. **Holden Drift.** Walk down from Johnson Bridge; private property. Ask permission to fish.

11. **Johnson Bridge Drift.** Good salmon & steelhead drift just above bridge. Private property. Ask permission to fish from bank.

12. **Rock Hole.** Bedrock chute drops into good salmon hole; anchor on south side; steelhead drift. Private property; boat fishing only.

13. **Loren's Drift.** ODFW public access boat slide; ¼ mile bank access.

14. **Hannenkrat Drift .** Bank fish long stretch of good water off Chance Rd. just below fish hatchery; modest fee to launch; check regulations for hatchery deadline and closures.

15. **Wildlife Hole.** Steep bank, good holes; about ¼ mile of bank access.

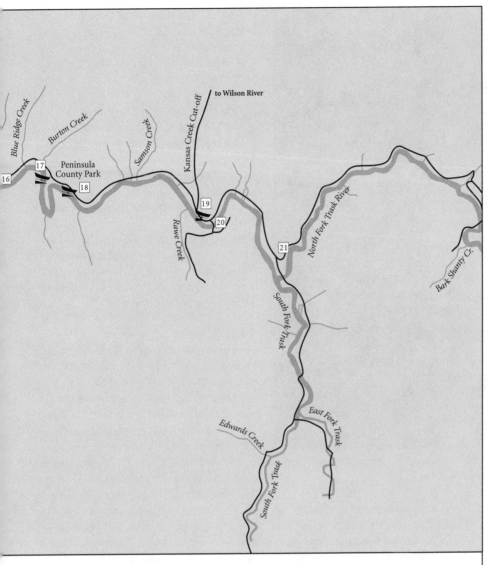

16. **Dam Hole.** Salmon and steelhead plunking; check regulations for deadline and closures.

17. **Last Chance.** Big curlers immediately below; most boaters play it safe and take-out at Upper Peninsula..

18. **Upper Peninsula Take-Out.**

19. **Stone Camp Slide.** Unimproved slide; drift down to Upper or Lower Peninsula; road leads in through camp opposite cut-off to Wilson River.

20. **Girl Scout Bridge.**

21. **Trask River Park.** Deadline for salmon fishing (confluence of north and south forks).

TOWN LAKE. A 9 acre impoundment near the community of Woods, with stocked trout and largemouth bass. From Hebo, travel south on Hwy. 101 to the Pacific City-Woods junction, and turn right towards Woods (Old Woods Rd.). Continue 3 miles to the community of Woods, turn right at the bridge, and continue one mile on the main road. The lake is on the right, just beyond a steep bank.

Most of the lake is surrounded by private land, but there is public access between the power transformers and the boat ramp. The bank is steep and brushy. An angling dock is accessible by steep, unimproved trails.

Legal size cutthroat and rainbows are stocked from mid-March through mid-April. Excess hatchery adult steelhead are released as available. Largemouth bass are also in residence, but anglers are encouraged to practice catch and release on the bass to preserve the fishery.

TRASK RIVER

A very good steelhead and salmon river, one of five tributaries to Tillamook Bay. It flows 50 miles out of the Coast Range, entering Tillamook Bay at the town of Tillamook south of the Wilson River. It is crossed by Hwy. 101 at the head of tidewater, and both its mainstem and forks are followed by good roads.

The Trask is fish-friendly, with lots of boulders and gravel stretches well suited to fly angling. The North Fork is especially pretty. The South Fork was ravaged by a forest fire in 1951 and was closed for a number of years. But The Tillamook Burn is now the Tillamook Forest, and the river reflects the forest's good health. Though the Trask still muddies, it clears quickly and is no longer quick to drop during dry spells.

The Trask is managed for wild winter steelhead, but some years, good numbers of finclipped hatchery steelhead stray into the river, mostly in summer. Finclipped steelhead are available to catch and keep. The winter run begins building in December and holds through April. The mainstem is open for steelhead year-round, and sections of both forks have steelheading seasons. Wild (finclipped) steelhead must be released unharmed.

There is a major fall chinook run on the Trask which peaks in October. Spring chinook appear in the river in April, with the run peaking in June. The Trask is also a very good wild cutthroat stream. Sea-run return as early as July and may be fished catch and release.

Juvenile shad have been appearing in the lower river in June, July, and early August. Most anglers jig for them off the pier at Tillamook Tidewater in Tillamook Bay rather than in the Trask itself.

The most popular bank fishery on the river is the ½-mile long Hospital Hole (also known as Aufdermeyer's) below the Third Street bridge in Tillamook. Access is through private property just west of the hospital. The landowner charges a modest

Good stretches of gravel provide spawning and rearing beds for TRASK RIVER *fall chinook. Photograph by Richard T. Grost.*

fee. Walk downstream to fish Jack Salmon Point and the Piling Hole. The Boat Ramp Hole at the head of tidewater above Hwy. 101 also attracts anglers. There are opportunities for bank fishing on the upper stream, including Loren's (also known as Hanenkrat Drift) below the fish hatchery off Chance Rd., and the Wildlife Hole (¼ mile access adjacent to Cedar Creek Boat Ramp on Trask River Rd).

Boaters primarily choose from among three possible drifts. Stone Camp to Upper Peninsula is for more experienced boaters. If you miss the take-out, there is another (but trickier) opportunity on the other side of the Peninsula. There is some very nasty water immediately after this take-out. The most popular drift is from Warrens (just below the hatchery) to the county landing at Hwy. 101. There is also an unimproved put-in at Cedar Creek, which anglers use to drift to Lorens.

Flood level on the Trask is similar to that of the Wilson at 11 ft., with best fishing at 6 ft., and acceptable levels between 5.3 ft. and 7 ft. Use the Wilson River readings as a gauge. See Appendix.

TRIANGLE LAKE. A large natural lake formed by an ancient landslide on Lake Creek in the Siuslaw watershed, very good for bass, panfish, kokanee, and trout. This 279-acre lake is west of Blachly on Hwy. 36. From Eugene, follow Hwy. 99 north, then Hwy. 36 west about 23 miles to the lake. From Florence, follow Hwy. 126 east to Mapleton, then pick up Hwy. 36 east.

Close to Eugene-Springfield, Triangle attracts many anglers and provides good catches of bluegill, as well as brown bullhead, perch, and largemouth.

There's lots of good bass habitat on the south and east sides of the lake, including overhanging brush and submerged wood. Fish the willows for nice size bluegill. Fishing small dark flies twitched just beneath the surface can be especially effective. A fish per cast is not uncommon in spring when male bluegills school up in the shadows near the brushy shoreline. The north side of the lake around the private homes and docks is less productive.

Triangle is 90 ft. deep in places, and depth-loving kokanee (landlocked sockeye salmon) are thriving here.

The lake has three small tributaries in addition to Lake Creek, which enters from the northeast and flows out at the south end of the lake. Wild cutthroat trout spawn in the tributaries and offer good fishing in the lake.

Lake Creek coho also move through Triangle, but fishing for them is prohibited. Coho smolts bear some resemblance to kokanee but are smaller; if in doubt about the identity of your catch, release it carefully.

Triangle is a multi-use recreational lake. Water skiers abound in summer, so best fishing is often early and late in the day, or in spring and fall. There's a fishing pier and a boat ramp with limited parking on the west shore. A small county park offers a limited number of camp sites.

TROJAN POND (a.k.a. Recreation Pond) A 27-acre lake adjacent to the decommissioned Trojan Nuclear Power Plant on Hwy. 30. Though still owned by PGE and used as a storage site for radioactive materials, the site is open to public use. The lake is stocked with legal trout and supports a variety of panfish.

This wetland setting is alluring but eerie, with a cooling tower and concrete reactor bunker as a back-drop. If thoughts about the by-products of the friendly atom don't disturb your sleep at night, DEQ assures us there's no reason not to enjoy this otherwise idyllic little fishery in rural Columbia County.

VERNONIA LAKE. A popular community fishing hole of 42 acres adjacent to the upper Nehalem River that grows large bluegill. It is at the south edge of the town of Vernonia, a community on Hwy. 47 between highways 26 and 30 northwest of Portland. The lake is a former mill pond with no inlets or outlets, its level maintained by means of a pump directly from the river.

There are lots of bluegills and crappie here as well as perch, largemouth bass and stocked legal rainbow trout. The bluegills grow to 12 inches. A path encircling the lake provides excellent bank access.

Light-weight boats can be launched but aren't necessary to reach good fishing, and only electric motors are allowed. There are areas on shore accessible to wheelchairs.

WEST LAKE. A good bass and panfish lake 3 miles north of Gearhart, east of Hwy. 101. The highway follows its western shore, and a county road accesses the eastern shore. About ½ mile long, it is similar in character and fishing opportunity to Sunset, Cullaby, and South. It contains good size perch and crappie, and fair size bluegill. Largemouth bass are available, with a few 2 pounds or better. Small boats can be launched off the road crossing. Fishing is best early in season before heavy weed growth.

WESTPORT SLOUGH. An extensive slough area on the lower Columbia with over 15 species of bass and panfish, northeast of Westport on Hwy. 30. A number of bridges and county roads provide good access. The slough mouth can be reached by going north on the Columbia from Woodson Boat Ramp, or from the public ramp at Westport.

It has lots of white and black crappie and fair numbers of bluegill, brown bullhead, and yellow perch. There is excellent largemouth bass water, with bass to 7 pounds taken on plugs and spinners.

WILSON RIVER

Traditionally one of the top ten producers of salmon and steelhead on the Oregon coast, a popular and accessible tributary of Tillamook Bay. It flows through Coast Range timberland then out across the bucolic Tillamook Valley, where black and white cows graze beside its banks. It is followed closely by Hwy. 6, also known as the Wilson River Rd., which runs west from Forest Grove.

Steelhead are in the Wilson year-round. Hatchery generated summer steelhead enter in May and run through August. The winter run begins with hatchery fish in late November. Wild winter steelhead join them from mid-February through March. Only adipose finclipped steelhead may be kept.

Spring chinook generally enter the Wilson in April. The run peaks in June and July, but the river has been closing to spring salmon fishing in mid-June. Check the regulations. A much larger fall chinook run can begin as early as mid-September (rains willing) with peak catches in November. Check the regulations for bait and hook restrictions.

VERNONIA LAKE has lots of bluegill as well as some good size largemouth bass. Photograph by Bob Judkins.

The Wilson has traditionally welcomed many searun cutthroat, usually starting mid-July. But searun returns are down here as in other Oregon coast streams. Fishing for them is catch and release.

The Wilson is very accessible for bank fishing along Hwy. 6. There are many pull-outs along the road. The river bank can be steep, with some bushwhacking necessary. There is excellent bank access at Fall Creek, Herd Hole, Kansas Creek Bridge, Lee's Bridge, Mining Creek, Siskeyville, and Zig Zag Creek. Most bank anglers use drift fishing techniques.

The Wilson is a good river for beginning drift boat operators. It has few hazards (most notable of which is The Minefield) and requires no more than the usual caution associated with operating a river boat. The Mine Field is between Siskeyville and Mills Bridge.

The Vanderzanden boat slide is the fur-

Except for The Mine Field, the WILSON RIVER has few boating hazards. Photograph by Scott Richmond.

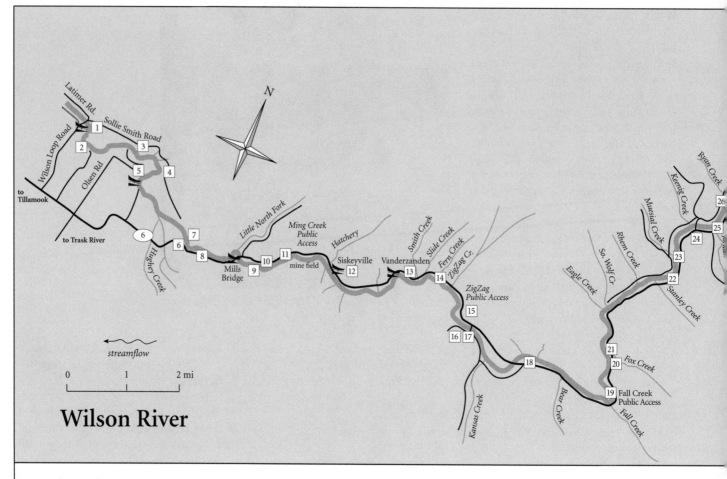

Wilson River

1. Solly Smith Boat Ramp. Improved ramp, lowest public access, just above Solly Smith Bridge; used as take-out; some bank fishing; user fee may be required (Tillamook County Parks).

2. Tittle Hole. Chinook only, no steelhead.

3. Lower Josi. Good drift near center of Josi Farm; long drift at low end of hole; pay to bank fish.

4. Upper Josi. Salmon hole; tail-out for steelhead; pay to fish from bank.

5. Donaldson Bar. Quarter mile steelhead drift; pay to put-in or take-out at gravel bar.

6. Guard Rail. Gravel bar and ½ mile drift; one of the popular spots on the river.

7. Trailer Park Hole. Bank access for paying guests only.

8. Mills Bridge Bar. County-owned access to put-in or take-out at gravel bar; good bank fishing for steelhead and salmon; handicapped anglers park on bar, others in lot.

9. Just Above the Bridge. Public access from south bank.

10. Slide Area . One-half mile of good steelhead drift water downstream and up to Blue Hole.

11. Ming Creek Public Access. Public bank angling for steelhead and salmon; no boat ramp.

12. Siskyville Slide. Improved ODFW boat slide, small parking area, about a quarter mile below Alice's Country House Restaurant.

13. Vanderzanden Slide (Herd Hole). Improved boat slide; quarter mile of north bank access on either side; good hole; some parking.

14. Yergen Access. Public access upstream about ¼ mile; watch for small turn-out at about road mile 13.5; trail to river starts 200 ft. downstream from parking area; good steelhead water and access to salmon holding hole; please use trail.

15. Zig Zag Public Access. Very steep bank access.

16. Kansas Creek Bridge. Access to ¾ mile south bank, ½ mile north bank downstream; good steelhead water.

17. Kansas Creek Bridge Hole. Right under bridge; good for salmon, steelhead.

18. Demolay Camp Hole. County park; rough water here to swinging bridge; put-in not recommended; good salmon hole; good steelhead drift upstream.

19. Fall Creek Public Access. Good winter steelhead water; drift fish above the creek, fish pocket water below; no angling within 200 ft. of fishway at mouth of Fall Creek.

20. Narrows. Walk in on trail from turn-out just upstream of mile post 14; good summer steelhead and salmon hole.

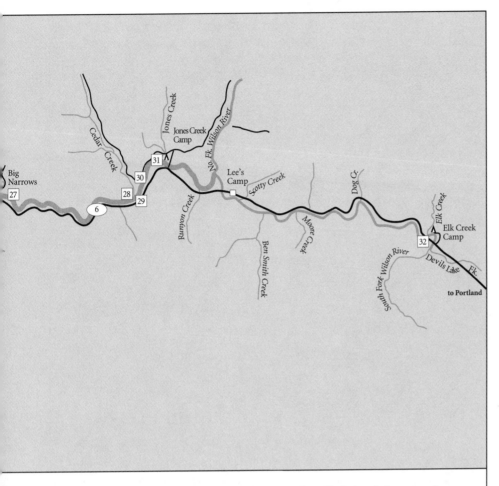

21. Fox Creek Hole. Salmon and summer steelhead hole just below mouth.

22. Overbank. Good sea-run cutthroat hole; steep bank.

23. Muesial Creek Hole. Good summer steelhead hole.

24. Cedar Butte Road (Keenig) Bridge Hole. Salmon holding hole and summer steelhead right under bridge; Oregon Department of Forestry camp on north bank has limited facilities.

25. Jordan Creek Bridge Hole. Good for both winter and summer steelhead; stay below bridge.

26. Harry Smith Hole. Good for salmon.

27. Turn-out Hole (a.k.a. Big Narrows). Turn-out on north side of Hwy. 6.

28. Cedar Creek Hole. Chinook holding area just below mouth of Cedar Creek.

29. Cedar Creek Drift. Good for summer steelhead.

30. Coyote Hole. Good for summer steelhead.

31. Jones Creek Bridge Hole. Fish right under bridge for salmon, steelhead; salmon and trout deadline; don't park on the road.

32. South Fork Confluence. Deadline for steelheading on the Wilson.

thest upstream put-in. There is also a slide put-in at Siskeyville and an opportunity to put-in or take-out at Mills Bridge gravel bar. The lowest public boat access on the river is Solly Smith. Motor boats can be launched at Solly Smith to fish the lower river. Few anglers attempt to thread their way through the maze of pilings from Tillamook bay up to Solly Smith.

A variety of methods are used to fish the Wilson, but plunking is discouraged due to the tendency to snag fish. Local anglers have been known to report snaggers and collect the $100 reward offered by the Tillamook Guides Association.

Accommodations are available in Tillamook. Supplies and shuttle services are available at tackle shops in Tillamook and at shops and markets along the river. Midway up the river, the Guide Shop currently operates a pleasant little cafe that serves fine clam chowder.

The South Fork Wilson River enters the mainstem 3 to 4 miles above Lee's Camp (on Hwy. 6). Above the South Fork confluence, the mainstem Wilson is popularly known as the Devils Lake Fork. Both South Fork and Devils Lake Fork are currently closed to all angling, as are all tributaries other than the Little North Fork, which is open for catch and release cutthroat fishing and for steelhead from December 1 through March 31.

Flood stage on the Wilson is 11 ft. Best fishing is between 6 and 3 feet. Fishing is generally better above Mills Bridge after a period of high water. Fish below Mills when the river has been holding steady for a time. A river gauge reading is available. See Appendix

WOAHINK LAKE. One of the deepest lakes on the Oregon coast. Its shoreline forms the eastern boundary of Honeyman State Park, 3 miles south of Florence. Woahink is very popular for water sports and recreation. It covers 350 acres and receives a stocking of legal rainbows each spring. It also has wild cutthroat, big yellow perch, and some largemouth bass.

The main body of the lake doesn't have great bass habitat, but there are some productive weedy areas and woody structure in the coves, especially at the south end and on the east side.

Large perch can be fished in winter and are especially partial to worms. Try a bobber and worm fished off the bottom in the

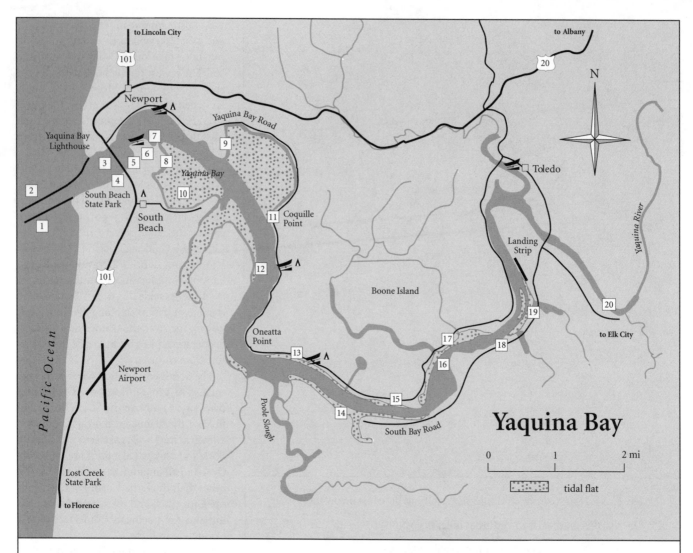

1. South Jetty. Fish for cabezon, greenling, striped perch; road goes directly to jetty.

2. North Jetty. Take long stairs at Park and rock-hop to jetty; fish for rockfish, greenling, cabezon, striped perch.

3. Lower Bay. Anchor or troll for salmon September to November.; also dungeness crab, lingcod, striped perch.

4. Bridge Flats South. Dig for cockle and gaper clams.

5. Public Dock. Set traps for dungeness crab.

6. Marina Breakwaters. Fish for perch, hatchery fall chinook; public access at Newport Marina.

7. Breakwater Flat. Dig on south side of flat only for gapers; boat access only.

8. Marine Science Center.

9. Gas Plant Dock. Wheelchair accessible dock; fish from dock and west bank for perch, spring through fall.

10. Up-Bay Flats. Dig for cockle, gaper clams; access from Science Center parking lot or Idaho Pt.

11. Coquille Pt. Fish rocky area from the bank for perch.

12. Mid-Bay. Troll for salmon, September to November.

13. Marker 25. Fish from bank for perch and sturgeon; intermittent bank access from marker upstream for perch, sturgeon; dig flats for softshell clams.

14. Softshell Flats South. Dig for softshells.

15. Softshell Flats North. Best digging for softshells.

16. Sturgeon Hole. Fish January to April.

17. Marker 37. Navigational marker on road; bank fish sturgeon hole.

18. Marker 38. Fish off South Bay Road for sturgeon winter and spring.

19. Creitser's Island. Boat to island for good softshell digging; access from Toledo public boat ramp.

20. Yaquina Tidewate. Launch at Toledo and troll for fall chinook September to October.

deep areas.

There are two excellent boat ramps at the north end of the lake, and campgrounds at Honeyman.

YACHATS RIVER (Pronounced ya-hots). A small coastal river entering the ocean south of the town of Yachats, crossed by Hwy. 101 near its mouth. Only about 15 miles long, it ranges from 30 to 50 feet wide. The Yachats River Rd. follows the mainstem to its forks, and other forest roads follow its tributaries.

Yachats offers catch and release fishing for resident cutthroat, searun, and wild winter steelhead. Steelhead enter the river in late November and can be fished through March. Most steelhead angling takes place in the lower few miles.

The river is closed to coho angling, but a small number of chinook enter the river and can be fished east of Hwy. 101. Nearby Beachside State Park, on the ocean about 4 miles north, used to host a unique surf smelt fishery in the late spring, but smelt haven't been seen in recent years.

There's a lot of posted land along the river. Ask permission of landowners before you approach the stream. There are campgrounds at state parks north and south on Hwy. 101 and in the Siuslaw National Forest near the headwaters.

YAQUINA BAY

Outlet for the Yaquina River system, one of the most popular and productive bays on the Oregon Coast. Newport, the bay's port city, hosts a large charter fleet that pursues bottom fish throughout the year, halibut and salmon as regulations allow. The bay has 1700 surface acres, and tidewater runs uprive r about 13 miles.

The Yaquina enters the ocean west of the community of Newport, about 110 miles from Portland, and it is easily reached by Hwy. 101 from north and south. From the Albany-Corvallis area, it's only an hour's drive on Hwy. 20 along the Elk and Yaquina rivers. The north bay shore is easily accessed by a road east to Toledo. Access on the south shore is limited to the stretch from Hwy. 101 east to Hinton Point. About half-way up the bay, Oysterville (on the south side) can be reached by a secondary road from Toledo.

The Yaquina bar is usually safe to cross, but checking with the Coast Guard is al-

Charter boats out of YAQUINA BAY target albacore tuna in August and September when warm currents bring the schools close to the Oregon coast. Photograph by Phil Simonski.

ways a good idea. Offshore salmon and Pacific halibut fishing seasons and quotas are determined annually by the Pacific Fishery Management Council. General regulations are published in the spring of the year, but in-season changes are common. Get current information before planning a trip for either of these species. See Appendix.

Yaquina Bay is within the Cape Falcon to Florence North Jetty halibut regulatory zone, and the Cape Falcon to Humbug Mountain offshore salmon fishing zone. In recent years, the halibut season out of Yaquina Bay has been open intermittently from May to September. Offshore chinook seasons have been open from April 1 to October 1, and there have been selective offshore fishing opportunities for finclipped coho.

Beyond the bar, halibut are caught from the whistler buoy to the lighthouse on Yaquina Head off Agate Beach. Halibut anglers drift herring on the bottom at around 30 fathoms. Bottom dwellers such as greenling, lingcod, cabezon, and rockfish are pursued over a series of reefs from the bay's south jetty to Waldport. Most of these fish can be found at 8 to 15 fathoms. Avoid the reef off the end of the south jetty and begin fishing at the airport (the beacon is visible). Whole herrings or leadhead jigs with plastic worms are favored for this fishery. Larger lingcod, red snapper, and halibut are fished at The Rockpile, about 13

miles west southwest of Newport. Fishing there is at 15 to 30 fathoms and deeper. In recent years, the ling population has suffered a decline, and regulations reflect the effort to protect adult spawners. At this time, harvest is limited to one fish per day with a keeper slot length of 24-inch minimum and 34-inch maximum. Check current regulations.

In some years, warm ocean currents bring schools of tuna close enough to the Oregon coast to allow a sport fishery for them. Unless you're an old salt and hooked into the local commercial fishing community, you'll probably want to book passage with a charter boat. The average tuna weighs between 15 and 25 pounds. Plan on a long day.

Bottom fish offer the most popular fishery within the bay itself. Cabezon and striped perch are taken from the south jetty, which is studded with rock breakwaters that offer prime rockfish habitat. Both rockfish and greenling are fished from the north jetty. Bank anglers catch perch from the Gas Plant dock, at the old La Paz Marina, and along the north shore around navigational marker 25. Boat anglers take perch in the lower bay and around the rocks off Coquille Pt.

Best salmon fishing in the bay is from September through early November. Most catches are made between the airport near Toledo and Elk City. Herring is the choice

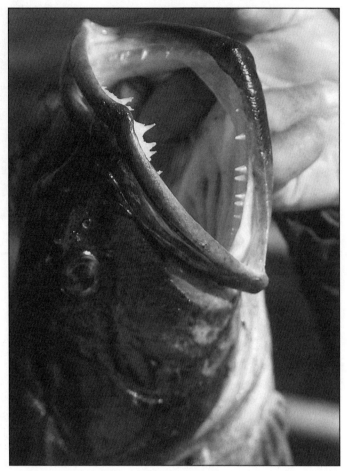

Lingcod can be caught in 15-30 fathoms at The Rockpile about 13 miles west southwest of YAQUINA BAY. Photograph by Scott Richmond.

Boats can be launched at the city-owned Newport Marina on Marine Science Drive in South Beach, or at several other public and privately owned ramps around the bay and in Yaquina River tidewater.

YAQUINA RIVER. The Yaquina is a medium-size stream entering Yaquina Bay at Newport, fished primarily for fall chinook. To reach the river from Hwy. 101, follow Hwy. 20 to Toledo, then follow signs to the Toledo Airport and Elk City Rd. Beyond Elk City, County Rd. 539 returns to Hwy. 20, which follows the Yaquina to Eddyville.

Most chinook angling takes place in the lower bay, but fish are taken up to the salmon and steelhead deadline at Eddyville.

Catch and release angling is fair for wild cutthroat in the upper river early in the season and for searun in the lower river in fall.

The confluence of Big Elk Creek and the Yaquina River at Elk City is a popular area for cutthroat as well as fall chinook. A small run of wild winter steelhead in the Yaquina draws few anglers.

YOUNGS BAY. A shallow freshwater bay near the mouth of the Columbia River adjacent to Astoria, formed by the confluence of Lewis and Clark, Young's, Klaskanine and Wallooski rivers. It offers sportfishing opportunities for hatchery reared spring and fall chinook, coho, and winter steelhead. All hatchery salmon are marked. Wild steelhead and searun cutthroat may also be present at times, but few if any wild salmon are present.

The Youngs Bay salmon hatchery program was established primarily to support the commercial fishing industry that was once the backbone of the local economy, but recreational anglers are welcome to take advantage of the program. Most sport anglers fish at the mouth of the bay, since Young's Bay is very shallow and requires different fishing techniques than anglers are used to employing. In the bay, sport anglers generally fish Friday through Sunday when commercial operations are closed. If you fish on weekdays during the commercial season, be careful to avoid the nets. Open seasons are set annually and are announced in *The Daily Astorian*, *The Oregonian*, and on the ODFW Web page. See Appendix.

Many returning salmon (both spring

bait, either mooched or trolled, and can be obtained locally or caught easily by jigging almost anywhere in the bay.

There is a growing sturgeon fishery in the bay beginning in January and continuing through May some years. Best fishing is often the last few hours of the ebb tide through the first hour of the flood. Good numbers of fish landed here are keeper length (42 to 60 inches). The favored bait is mud shrimp (less delicate than sand shrimp), but herring, anchovies, clam necks, squid, and combinations of the above also catch fish. A little extra scent can't hurt. Fresh and frozen bait is available at local shops.

There's good boat fishing for sturgeon from channel marker 25 to 45. Bank anglers fish for sturgeon off Yaquina Bay Road near markers 25 and 37. Other bank options are at markers 38 and 42 on South Bay Rd. and above Toledo on the Elk City Rd. at the Mill Creek confluence. Actively feeding sturgeon are most often found cruising the slopes and edges of troughs and holes rather than in the deepest channels.

Jigging for herring at South Beach Marina is a great way to harvest your own bait or to introduce youngsters to fishing. Two docks on either side of the boat ramp and the moorage dock farther north are open to the public. In years when herring are running, February and March often offer the best catches. Use a herring jig (a small bare hook with yarn). Tackle and instructions are available locally.

Crabs are taken year round. Pots are available for rent, and bait can be obtained at local bait and tackle shops. Pots are used rather than rings to discourage hungry seals. Check at the marina for current hot spots or try casting pots about ½ mile above the bridge on either side of the channel.

Newport is a delightful coast town with all the flavor of a working fishing port. Just being at dockside when a big charter boat starts unloading its catch is a thrill. If you have a chance, stop by the Oregon Coast Aquarium, a handsome facility on the bay's south shore.

and fall runs) linger in the bay, since their home water was the bay itself, where they grew to migrating size in a series of net pens upstream from Young's River Bridge by the Astoria Yacht Club boat ramp. Others eventually move through the bay and up the Klaskanine River to the Klaskanine Hatchery at milepost 12 on Hwy. 202.

Spring chinook enter the bay from early April through early June. The commercial season is generally limited to May. There are no wild chinook in the river at this time, though some wild steelhead and searun cutthroat may be present and must be released unharmed. Anglers should use larger gear appropriate to salmon to avoid accidentally catching these protected species.

The fall salmon fishery in the bay begins in July and continues through October. The first arrivals are fall chinook of Rogue River stock, followed by a run of tule chinook, then coho. The tules are a species native to the lower Columbia. They turn dark quickly after hitting fresh water, spawning within 15 to 20 days. Few, if any, wild salmon of any species are present.

The Young's Bay hatchery salmon programs have been in place for some time, but anglers are still experimenting with techniques for fishing this clear, shallow bay. Salmon have been caught on trolled herring (both whole and plug-cut), using long, light leader (12 to 14 ft. long, 10-pound test). Coho jacks are taken from the docks using small spoons and spinners, or on bobber and egg rigs. Creel checkers at the boat launches are a good source of information as to what's working, or stop by the marine supply store in Astoria.

For bank anglers, Youngs Bay offers little in the way of rocks or docks, and at high tides the bay creeps all the way up to Highway 202, which follows its east shore from the Highway 101 Bridge to Crosel Creek before continuing up the Klaskanine. If you

Perch, rockfish, and greenling are among the species that might be caught from the rocks below Yaquina Lighthouse. Photograph by Dennis Frates.

don't have a boat, the best place to fish the bay is from the Astoria Yacht Club docks.

Boats can be launched at Warrenton, at the East Mooring Basin in Astoria, or at the Astoria Yacht Club ramp. The Yacht Club ramp is suitable for larger boats only at high tide. All boats should avoid this ramp at minus tides. You can also launch in Klaskanine tidewater at the county ramp on the Youngs River Loop Road which heads south from Hwy. 202 at Olney.

The wind can pick up suddenly on the bay, especially in spring below the Highway 101 Bridge. If you launch at Warrenton, you

might not be able to make it back to the ramp until the wind dies down.

YOUNG'S RIVER. Tributary to Young's Bay near Astoria. A high falls about 9 miles up (½ mile above tidewater) is impassable to salmon and steelhead. A few are taken in tidewater, but the river is closed to all fishing from the first highway bridge below Youngs River Falls to the falls. Wild cutthroat are available for catch and release fishing in the upper river, which is accessed by logging roads. Use a current Protection District map to navigate in this stretch.

FISHING IN OREGON'S
SOUTHWEST ZONE

The Southwest Zone is defined by its two most important rivers, the Rogue and the Umpqua. These behemoths dwarf other coastal river systems, draining enormous watersheds that extend over 200 miles inland.

The Rogue River offers the state's best fishing for fin-clipped coho, and one of the Northwest's strongest populations of winter steelhead. It's famous for its run of *half-pounders*, immature summer steelhead who return to the river after less than a year at sea, adapting quickly to fresh water and feeding like trout. At various points along its flow it is accessed by private jet boats, commercial mail boats, drift boats, and rafts, by rough tracks, hiking trails, and paved roads. World class fishing, thrilling whitewater runs, a wild and scenic setting, and the added attraction of high quality backcountry lodges tucked into its remote canyons draw anglers from around the world.

The Umpqua is really three rivers: Umqpua, North Umpqua and South Umpqua. The mainstem and South Umpqua are nationally renowned for smallmouth bass. The North Umpqua is treasured for its summer steelhead, picturesque setting, and classic fly water.

Chetco, Coquille, Elk, Sixes, and Smith rivers have exceptional fisheries as well. The Elk is known for the size and strength of its wild winter steelhead, and appreciated for its capacity to clear quickly after a storm. The Sixes is a favorite for wild fall chinook, with earliest catches in the ocean surf. The *average* Chetco fall chinook weighs 30 pounds. The Smith offers Oregon's best opportunity to catch striped bass 35 pounds and larger.

Coos Bay, Chetco Bay, and Winchester Bay (mouth of the Umpqua) offer fall chinook, bottom fish, sturgeon, clamming, crabbing and access to excellent offshore fisheries. Chetco Bay is the state's top small craft port, with productive near-shore reefs and a unique opportunity to fish freely for Pacific halibut (a smaller halibut not subject to general halibut regulations at this time). The same rocky structure that contributes to the south coast's scenic charm also creates perfect conditions for surf fishing. Horsfall, Bastendorff, Whiskey Run, Seven Devils, and Bullards beaches offer the additional possibility of hooking striped bass in pursuit of the same redtail surf perch.

Small coastal lakes within the Oregon Dunes National Recreation Area and big Tenmile Lakes provide fishing for warmwater species and stocked trout in a salt air setting.

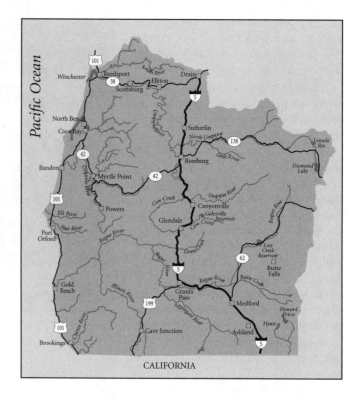

The Southwest Zone features many scenic resevoirs, created for irrigation and flood control but managed for sportfishing as well. Most receive a large annual stocking of trout and support additional fisheries. Applegate Reservoir has a reproducing population of landlocked chinook that can be fished like kokanee (landlocked sockeye salmon). Galesville has landlocked coho. Emigrant offers a fine smallmouth fishery and channel catfish to 26 pounds. Cooper Creek features exceptionally plump crappie.

Best trout stream trout fishing in the Southwest Zone is in the upper Rogue River above Lost Creek Reservoir and in the *holy water*, a productive tailrace fishery immediately below Lost Creek Dam, where the average catch is 16 inches. The North Umpqua above Soda Springs Dam also offers good trout harvest opportunities.

This zone encompasses portions of three mountain ranges (the Cascades, Coast Range, and Siskiyous), three national forests (Siskiyou, Umpqua, and Winema), and four federally designated wilderness areas (Wild Rogue, Rogue-Umpqua Divide, Sky Lakes, and Kalmiopsis).

The coastal climate here is subtly warmer than it is to the north. Inland, temperature extremes are greater, with cold-

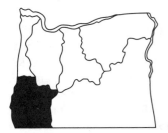

The Southwest Zone includes all waters draining directly to the Pacific Ocean south to the Oregon-California border, and including the Umpqua River drainage; and those portions of Klamath River drainage in Jackson County.

THE BEST FISHING IN OREGON'S SOUTHWEST ZONE

APPLEGATE RESERVOIR
One of the few Oregon reservoirs with good fishing for small-mouth bass, as well as good numbers of stocked trout and land-locked chinook.

APPLEGATE RIVER
Good fishing for both hatchery and wild winter steelhead.

CHETCO RIVER
A scenic stream flowing through myrtle groves, with a reputation for turning out unusually large fall chinook.

COOS BAY
Good bay fishing for fall chinook and finclipped coho in addition to rockfish and perch; some of the best crabbing in Oregon.

COQUILLE RIVER
Hosts one of the coast's healthiest runs of wild coho, with good fishing for fall chinook and both hatchery and wild winter steelhead.

ELK RIVER
Known for its large wild steelhead, fall chinook fishery in the surf, and capacity to clear quickly after a downpour.

EMIGRANT LAKE
Features channel catfish, large smallmouth bass, abundant crappie, and a waterslide for the youngsters.

LOST CREEK RESERVOIR
Smallmouth bass are the main pursuit, but landlocked chinook (fished like kokanee) are a growing attraction.

ROGUE RIVER
Wild, scenic, and a top producer of spring and fall chinook, fin-clipped coho, wild and hatchery steelhead, and a famous run of athletic half-pounders (juvenile steelhead).

ROGUE RIVER (Holy Water)
Immediately below Lost Creek Dam, a year-round tailrace fishery for large rainbow trout.

SMITH RIVER
Offers Oregon's best opportunity to hook a striped bass, and shelters one of the state's few healthy wild coho populations.

TENMILE LAKES
World-class largemouth bass fishery in a lovely coastal setting.

WINCHESTER BAY
Oregon's number 1 coastal sturgeon fishery,

UMPQUA RIVER
One of the finest smallmouth bass fisheries in America.

UMPQUA RIVER, NORTH
Treasured for its large run of wild summer steelhead, fished for winters as well, and for chinook and finclipped coho.

er winters and hotter summers. Annual rainfall varies from over 100 inches per year in the western Siskiyou Mts. to less than 20 inches at Medford.

The Southwest Zone is accessed by Hwy. 101 on the coast, and by I-5, which runs north-south from Portland into California between the Coast and Cascade mountain ranges. Routes inland from the coast are limited to Hwy. 38 (which leads from Reedsport on the lower Umpqua to Cottage Grove), Hwy. 42 (which follows the lower Coquille and emerges from the Coast Range at Roseburg), and Hwy. 199, (which heads northwest from Crescent City, CA to Grants Pass). There is no reliable through-road along the Rogue River between I-5 and the Coast.

Two highways access the zone's Cascade Mt. fisheries.

Hwy. 138 follows the North Umpqua upstream from Roseburg. Hwy. 62 follows the Rogue River upstream from Central Point. Secondary roads in all mountain areas are generally graded, but unpaved and unlighted.

Campgrounds are plentiful in the national forests , but are less available on the coast. Motels and private rv parks are plentiful on the coast, and are available inland near major communities. Many of the larger lakes and reservoirs offer "resort" facilities that lean toward rustic but comfortable. The Rogue River's backcountry lodges and Steamboat Inn on the North Umpqua are among Oregon's few upscale fishing resorts, with international repuations for dining and accomodations that match the world class fishing at their doorsteps.

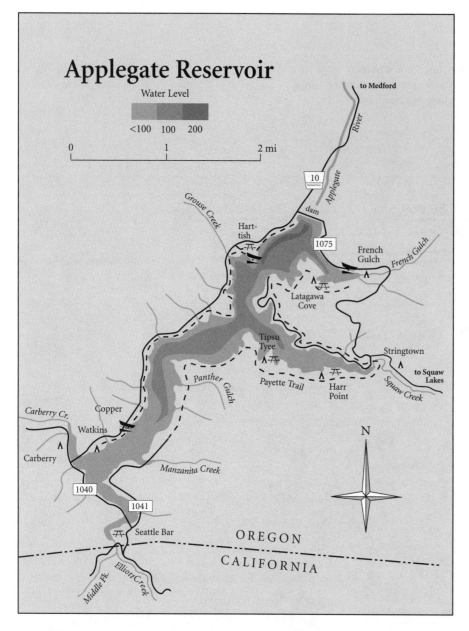

Applegate Reservoir

Water Level

<100 100 200

0   1   2 mi

to Medford

Applegate River

10

dam

1075

Hart-tish

Grouse Creek

French Gulch

French Gulch

Latagawa Cove

Tipsu Tyee

Stringtown

to Squaw Lakes

Squaw Creek

Panther Gulch

Payette Trail

Harr Point

N

Copper

Carberry Cr.

Watkins

Carberry

Manzanita Creek

1040

1041

Seattle Bar

OREGON

CALIFORNIA

Middle Fk.

Elliott Creek

AGATE RESERVOIR. An irrigation reservoir on Upper Dry Creek near White City, with fishing for bass and panfish. Follow Lake of the Woods Hwy. 140 east from White City, turn right on Antelope Rd., and follow the signs. Agate has 238 surface acres with a maximum depth of 55 ft., though depth fluctuates during the irrigation season.

The reservoir is open year-round, but fishing is best in spring. It is shallow with good brush structure opposite the dam. Fish the coves. Abundant yellow perch and good numbers of crappie, largemouth bass, brown bullhead, and bluegill are available. A canoe, float tube, raft, or rowboat is useful here. Only electric motors are allowed. There are boat ramps on the south side of the dam and a picnic area, but overnight camping is prohibited.

ALL SPORTSMAN'S PARK POND. A 3-acre former borrow pit in Grants Pass, now open for public recreational use. It is stocked with legal trout and has largemouth bass.

ALTA LAKE. A narrow 32-acre hike-in lake in the Seven Lakes Basin of the Sky Lakes Area, Rogue River National Forest. The basin is accessed by several trails from the west with trailheads on forest roads 3780, 3785, and 3790. The trailhead on Forest Rd. 3780, leading to Trail 980 then to Trail 979 is designated the Alta Lake Trail on the Sky Lakes Wilderness map.

Seven Lakes Basin is also approached by trails from the east, heading at Sevenmile

Marsh. At Ft. Klamath on Hwy. 62, turn west on County Rd. 1419. At about 4 miles, when the county road bears right, continue straight, then turn right onto Forest Rd. 3334 to Sevenmile Marsh Campground. Follow Trail 3703. At its junction with the Pacific Crest Trail, take the left fork. The trail west to Grass and Middle lakes is less than 3 miles from the junction. About ½ mile farther on the PCT, a trail leads west to Cliff Lake. To reach Alta, follow the Cliff Lake Trail past Cliff and South lakes. At the next trail junction, head north to Alta.

One of the last lakes in the area to thaw, Alta offers fair fishing for stocked brook trout. There is a natural campsite at the north end and good trail access to other fishable lakes east in the basin. See also Middle, Grass, and Cliff.

APPLEGATE RESERVOIR

A popular, deep multi-purpose reservoir on the upper Applegate river within view of the picturesque Siskiyou mountains. The pool varies from 990 to 360 surface acres, with a maximum depth of 225 ft. near the dam and an average depth of 83 ft. It offers good opportunities for stocked trout, landlocked chinook, large and smallmouth bass, and crappie. The reservoir's relatively low elevation provides a good growing season for warmwater fish. A 10-mph speed limit throughout the reservoir helps preserve the peaceful wilderness-like setting.

From Medford or Grants Pass, take Hwy. 238 south to the reservoir access road, which becomes Forest Rd. 10. At the reservoir, the left fork leads to French Gulch and Stringtown campgrounds on the upper northeast arm of the reservoir. The right fork leads to Watkins and Carberry camps at the southern end. A trail from French Gulch follows the east shore all the way to Manzanita Creek, about 4 miles. The entire shoreline, about 18 miles, can be hiked.

The reservoir is stocked annually with over 120,000 legal rainbows and 50,000 chinook fingerlings as well as some larger trout. The chinook grow to 16 inches and resemble kokanee. Try trolling for them deep, using a lead-core line.

Though not as productive for bass as shallower reservoirs, Applegate has some good bass water that has been enhanced by local bass clubs. The shallower Squaw Creek arm is especially productive. The addition of large root wads and bankside willow plantings have enhanced the Carberry and French Gulch arms. Bass are also attracted to Carberry's submerged forest. Bass to 10 pounds have been landed, and larger bass may be available.

Applegate is one of the few reservoirs with a good smallmouth bass population. Look for them around rocky structure (rip-rap) and drop-offs.

Both white and black crappie are available in the shallows at the heads of the arms and in the bays. Crappie are especially abundant in Carberry's flooded forest. Fishing is best in late spring, while the lake is still full and cool.

There are two year-round boat ramps, at Hart-tish Campground on the northwest shore and at Copper near Watkins Campground on the southwest shore. A ramp east of the dam near French Gulch Campground is usable only at low water. There is a speed limit in effect throughout the reservoir.

Latagawa, Tipsu Tyee, and Harr Point campgrounds are hike-in or boat-in only. There are additional campgrounds on the Applegate River Rd., including a group camp at Flumet Flat available by reservation. Campsites at nearby Squaw Lakes are available by reservation only. Wheelchair accessible restroom facilities are available at Carberry, Watkins, and Hart-tish campgrounds.

Reservoir level and water temperature are available by calling the Army Corp of Engineers information line. See Appendix.

APPLEGATE RIVER

A major tributary of the Rogue River, entering the mainstem 2 miles above Whitehorse Rapids, 5 miles west of Grants Pass. It offers fishing for both hatchery and wild winter steelhead.

Hwy. 199 and county roads access the lower river south of Grants Pass. A county road follows the south bank east from Wilderville, and another follows the north bank east from Jerome Prairie. There is a county park on the river about 5 miles south of Jerome. From Grants Pass, head south toward Murphy, and pick up Hwy. 238. From Medford, Hwy. 38 leads to the river road cut-off at the town of Ruch. The Applegate River Rd. follows the stream to Applegate Dam.

In addition to hatchery steelhead, which

The APPLEGATE RIVER offers fishing for both hatchery and wild winter steelhead. Photograph by Scott Richmond.

are present when the season opens January 1, the Applegate produces a good run of wild winter steelhead that arrive later in the season, peaking in March. Only finclipped steelhead may be kept. Best steelheading is downstream from the mouth of the Little Applegate, about 2.5 miles south of Ruch.

Catch and release fishing for wild rainbow trout is good from early season through late spring, especially in the upper river between the Little Applegate and the dam. In addition, a large number of finclipped juvenile steelhead (8 to 16 inches) typically fail to migrate and are available to catch and keep. In fact, keeping these interlopers is encouraged in order to reduce competition with the native residents. Trout fishing is allowed most of the year, except for a two-month closure in April and May to protect migrating coho and steelhead smolts.

Check the regulations for bait and hook restrictions. Angling from a floating device is prohibited, and though some may claim the river is boatable during high water, it isn't worth the risk (not to mention a few bridges above the town of Applegate that may be too low for safe passage when the river's above a certain height).

There are several camping and picnic areas on the upper river road before you get to the reservoir, including the Cantrall-Buckley Campground about 6 miles east of the community of Applegate a mile past the point where Hwy. 238 crosses the river.

BABYFOOT LAKE. A popular 4-acre lake in a designated botanical area just inside the Kalmiopsis Wilderness of the Siskiyou National Forest, accessible from the east. From Cave Junction, in the valley of the Illinois River, take Hwy. 199 north about 4 miles to Forest Rd. 4201, a gravel road, which you follow for roughly 10 miles. A dirt road near the end of Forest Rd. 4201 leads to the trailhead at Onion Camp. It's ½ mile to the lake.

Brook trout were plentiful here until someone illegally introduced largemouth bass. Fingerling trout are stocked in odd numbered years (which means there are generally larger trout in even numbered years). Best catches are made in spring and late fall. Since Babyfoot is a wilderness lake, there is no developed campground, and wilderness camping guidelines should be observed.

BEAL LAKE. A hike-in lake in the northern half of the Rogue River National Forest, northernmost of the Northern Blue Lake group east of Butte Falls Ranger Station. It's a 4-mile hike from the trailhead at the end of Forest Rd. 720, off Forest Rd. 37. A shorter trail, 982, leads into the basin from the summit of Blue Rock Mt.

Fishing is spotty but can be good for brook trout to 12 inches. This is a good lake to try in conjunction with other lakes in the area. See also Blue, Blue Canyon, Horseshoe.

BEALE LAKE. A hard to reach coastal lake with a good warmwater fishery about 7 miles north of North Bend, west of Hwy. 101. The lake has over 100 surface acres, cradled in the sand dunes of the Oregon Dunes National Recreation Area. It's about ½ mile from the highway by trail. Lightly fished, it has good largemouth bass, perch, and bluegill angling. It is not stocked due to its inaccessibility. There are two natural campsites near the southwest end of the lake.

BEN IRVING RESERVOIR. A 100-plus acre lake west of Roseburg, created by Berry Creek Dam. From Roseburg, take Hwy. 42 west, then County Rd. 365 about 2 miles south of the town of Tenmile.

Ben Irving is managed primarily for bass and panfish (including yellow perch), but legal rainbows are stocked at the rate of about a thousand a week from mid-March through Memorial Day. Largemouth bass and bluegill are thriving, though the largemouth tend to run small. The water is almost always turbid, so vibrating lures can be effective. Best bass habitat is at the upper end, where there is a lot of submerged wood.

There is a boat ramp and a variety of posted speed limits. Boating in the upper reservoir (above the "B" markers) is limited to electric motors only. Abundant waterfowl add character to the lake.

BIG BUTTE CREEK. A very nice 30-mile tributary of the upper Rogue, entering the river at McLeod near Lost Creek Lake. Big Butte is one of only a handful of Rogue tributaries open to fishing. Most are closed in an effort to protect juvenile steelhead and salmon which are too often mistaken for trout. The creek is closed below Cobleigh Rd.

To reach the lower stream from Medford, take Hwy. 62 north about 27 miles. To reach the upper waters, turn east off Hwy. 62 onto the Butte Falls Rd. Crowfoot, McNeil, and Cobleigh roads cross the creek. Butte Falls Rd. reaches the creek at about mile 16 and follows the south bank for about 2 miles. A dirt road crosses the creek and follows it another 2 miles to Big Butte Spring. The upper waters are accessible by taking the Butte Falls-Prospect Rd. to the Rancheria Rd. At about one mile, turn left off Rancheria. This road accesses the North Fork at about one mile and follows it for 4½ miles.

A good trout stream, Big Butte features catch and release fishing for cutthroat which can exceed 12 inches. Brook trout may also be present, and anglers are encouraged to catch and keep as many as possible in order to give the native cutthroat population a little more elbow room. North and South Fork headwaters and some tributaries are spring fed, so fishing holds up well through the summer. The creek is closed to salmon and steelhead angling.

BLUE CANYON LAKE. A small hike-in lake in the Blue Lake group of the Sky Lakes Wilderness Area, about a mile south of Blue Lake. See Blue Lake for directions. From Blue Lake, take the main Trail 982 for ¼ mile, then turn south and west on the Blue Canyon Trail. The lake is less than ½ mile from the fork, to the left of (and may not be visible from) the trail.

There's good fishing for brook trout here in spring and fall. September and October are the best months. Bait and spinners or lures will work anytime, but switch to flies in the evening for best results. The lake is stocked in odd number years, so larger trout are likely to present in even number years.

BLUE LAKE (Rogue watershed, a.k.a. South Blue). A 15-acre hike-in, in the south Sky Lakes Wilderness Area of the Rogue River National Forest. From Medford, take Hwy. 62 north to the Butte Falls Rd. From Butte Falls head east into Rogue River National Forest on Forest Rd. 30, then turn left on Forest Rd. 37. Just past the Parker Meadows cut-off on the left, make a hard right onto Forest Rd. 3770 to Blue Rock Mt. Bear left at the fork at about 4 miles and continue toward the summit. Trailhead 982, identified as the Blue Canyon Trail on the Wilderness map, is one mile past the fork, on the right. The hike to Blue Lake is less than 2 miles.

The summit of Blue Mt., about a mile further up the road, is the site of a former fire lookout tower and offers a grand view of the southern Oregon Cascades, including the rim of Crater Lake and Mt. McLoughlin. The Blue Canyon Trail continues through the basin, connecting with other trails, including the Pacific Crest Trail. The Blue Mt. Rd. is not recommended for trailers or RV's.

A deep lake with a good population of brook trout to 12 inches, Blue Lake can be fished by trolling or casting lures in the deep water on the west side. Fly fishing is excellent late in the day in the shoal areas on the east side, or by sinking wet flies off the rock point on the south shore. A float tube would come in handy. There are good campsites here, as at most lakes in the area. Other fishable lakes in the basin include Horseshoe, Pear, Blue Canyon. Check for early or late season conditions at Butte Falls Ranger Station.

BOLAN LAKE. A small lake near the California border in the Siskiyou Mountains. It can be reached by turning east from Hwy.199 onto County Rd. 5560 at O'Brien, 6 miles south of Cave Junction. Continue east on this road, which becomes County Rd. 5828 north of Takilma, to the boundary of the Siskiyou National Forest. Here the road becomes Forest Rd. 48. Follow this road for 10 twisting miles to Forest Rd. 4812, which leads 6 miles northeast to the lake. The last section of road is rough and winding. It is usually snowbound until late spring.

Only about 12 surface acres, Bolan has brook trout to 14 inches. Fishing holds up well throughout the season. Bait fishing is the most commonly used technique, but other methods work. There is a campground at the lake, and car-top boats can be launched. It is stocked with fingerlings in odd numbered years.

BRADLEY LAKE. A 30-acre coastal lake with trout and largemouth bass west of Hwy. 101, about 3 miles south of Bandon. Follow Bradley Lake Rd. about one mile west from the highway. China Creek flows into the lake and is crossed by Hwy. 101 east of the lake. Bradley provides good catches in early spring and summer for both stocked legal rainbows and trophy-size trout grown especially for this fishery. Wild cutthroat are also present, and there may be some largemouth bass. There is a 5 mph speed limit throughout the lake.

BRUSH CREEK. A classic little wild winter steelhead stream that flows through beautiful Humbug State Park. The lower end of the creek is about 5 miles south of Port Orford on Hwy. 101, and it's crossed by the highway a few times near the park. It's a rich stream with lots of gravel and boulders. The winter steelhead run here peaks in January.

The creek is currently closed to all angling throughout spring and summer, opening for steelhead November 1 and closing to all fishing after March 31. Searun cutthroat may be present during steelhead season and can be fished catch and release. The creek is closed for coho.

BUCKEYE LAKE. A fair, hike-in brook trout lake in the Umpqua Divide Scenic Area which offers ice fishing opportunities. It is 1½ miles south of Fish Lake, about 35 miles east of Tiller. Cliff Lake is up the trail from Buckeye. See Cliff Lake for road and trail directions.

Ten-acre Buckeye has good numbers of brook trout to 18 inches. Most of the catch is 7 to12 inches. It is stocked annually by volunteers on horseback. Bait, spinners, and flies are all effective. There are improved campsites at Buckeye and nearby Cliff Lake. Supplies are available at Tiller 35 miles west, or at Clearwater, 30 twisting miles north.

Anglers snowshoe in for brook trout in February and March, breaking through the ice. The road to the trailhead is often open.

BURMA POND. A 5-acre pond on BLM property near Wolf Creek, off Speaker Road. It is stocked with legal rainbow trout throughout the spring and has largemouth bass. There's easy bank access on the dike side. A float tube or light weight boat would be helpful.

BUTTERFIELD LAKE. A small lake about 16 miles south of Reedsport, ¼-mile west of Hwy. 101. Roughly 50 acres, the lake is bisected by the railroad right of way and has walk-in access only. Cutthroat trout and bass are reported, but success is unknown. It is not stocked, and there is no camping nearby.

CALAMUT LAKE. A good hike-in brook trout lake 4 miles northeast of Lemolo Lake south of the Douglas/Lane County line. The road to the lake has been closed, but a trail leads in from Linda Lake, one mile south of Calamut.

Linda Lake is not shown on the Umpqua National Forest map. From Inlet Campground, at the east end of Lemolo Lake, take Forest Rd. 999 east 2 miles to Forest Rd. 60. Turn left on Forest Rd. 60 and at about 2 miles, turn left on Forest Rd. 700. Signs will direct you to Linda Lake. Trailhead 1494 is on the right. The hike to Calamut is about a mile from Linda. The trail passes Lake Charlene on the way in.

Calamut covers 18 acres and offers fair fishing in spring and fall. No inlets or outlets support spawning, so it is stocked every two or three years with brook trout fingerlings. The brookies have been run-ning 6 to 12 inches. It usually can be reached in June. There are improved campsites at the lake.

CALAPOOYA CREEK. (Umpqua Watershed) A good size tributary of the Umpqua River, about 40 miles long, entering the mainstem at the community of Umpqua about 10 miles downstream from the forks, 20 road miles north of Roseburg. It is crossed by Hwy. 15 north of Sutherlin. Good roads follow the stream closely in both the lower and upper sections.

The creek has resident wild cutthroat and rainbow trout, fair runs of coho and steelhead, and a few fall chinook. There is a county park on the stream at Fair Oaks east of Sutherlin, but most property along the creek is privately owned.

At this time, Calapooya is closed to all angling due to concern for Umpqua basin cutthroat and in compliance with the Endangered Species Act. Umpqua basin cutthroat are scheduled for review. Check current regulations for a possible relaxation of restrictions.

CAMP CREEK (Umpqua Watershed). A fair size stream entering Mill Creek (outlet of Loon Lake) about 3 miles above its confluence with the Umpqua, 4 miles west of Scottsburg. It can be reached by Hwy. 38 from Reedsport or Drain. The Loon Lake Rd. crosses Camp Creek at its lower end. A paved road follows it east for 15 miles.

It is primarily a wild cutthroat stream with small runs of wild steelhead and salmon. At this time, Camp Creek is closed to all angling due to concern for Umpqua basin cutthroat and in compliance with the Endangered Species Act. Umpqua basin cutthroat are scheduled for review. Check current regulations for a possible relaxation of restrictions.

CANTON CREEK. A nice looking stream joining Steamboat Creek from the north, about a mile north of the junction of Steamboat and the North Umpqua. Canton is a sanctuary stream for adult summer steelhead and has long been closed to all angling.

CANYONVILLE POND. See **HERBERT LOG POND.**

CARBERRY CREEK. A nice wild trout stream, one of the inlet streams of Apple-gate Reservoir, entering the reservoir from the southwest. Forest Rd. 10 follows the western shore of the reservoir to Carberry Campground, then follows Carberry to its fork. Gravel roads parallel each of the forks, Sturgis and Steve.

Catch and release angling for wild cutthroat trout can be good at times.

CAREY LAKE. A 12-acre rainbow lake in the Blue Lake group. For directions, see Horseshoe Lake. Hike past Horseshoe to reach Carey.

CHETCO BAY. A small bay near the Oregon/California border whose good, safe bar contributes to its ranking as Oregon's top small craft port. The community of Brookings is its port city.

Chetco is remote for most Oregonians, but handy for Californians. From the Portland area it's about 340 miles on Hwy. 101, but it's only 24 miles from Crescent City, California.

The Chetco bar leads out into a sheltered cove that is shielded from summer winds. Twelve-foot boats and even canoes go to sea on good days. Charter boats out of Brookings offer bottom fishing trips year-round, and halibut and salmon trips in season.

Offshore anglers can fish for bottom fish over very productive reefs north and south of the bar. Black rockfish are especially abundant. In fall, California halibut are also available close to shore between the south jetty and the Winchuck River. After crossing the bar, head south, trolling within ¼-mile of the beach. These small halibut average 6 to 7 pounds and are considered to be bottomfish. Fishing for them is not restricted by Pacific halibut regulations at this time.

Chetco Bay also provides access to excellent offshore salmon and Pacific halibut waters. In recent years, the offshore chinook season out of Brookings has been open from about the end of May to mid-September with some mid-season closures. Pacific halibut fishing opportunities, generally scheduled between May and September, have been more limited recently.

Salmon and Pacific halibut fishing seasons and quotas are determined annually by the Pacific Fishery Management Council. General regulations are published in the spring of the year, but in-season changes are common. Always check before

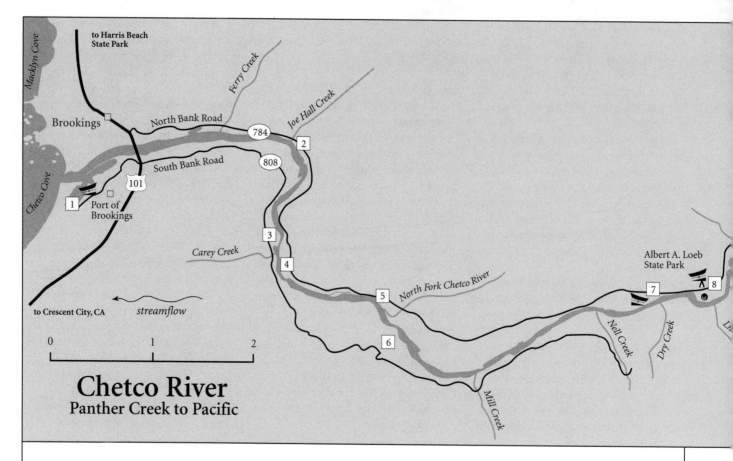

Chetco River
Panther Creek to Pacific

1. Port of Brookings. Paved boat ramp accesses tidewater fishery and Oregon's safest bar crossing.

2. Morris Hole. Bank fishing for chinook October and November.

3. Tide Rock. Bank fishing for chinook and steelhead October through April.

4. Social Security Ramp. Take-out and bank plunk for chinook and steelhead October through April.

5. Walk-in Access. Steelhead and chinook.

6. Piling Hole. Bank plunking for chinook and steelhead October through April.

7. Myrtle Grove (a.k.a. Willow Bar). Drift boat put-in and take-out from gravel bar; great bank plunking spot for good salmon and steelhead hole.

8. Loeb State Park. Take-out on gravel bar; bank fishing for salmon and steelhead October through April.

9. Ice Box. Private; launch with permission below Second Bridge; motors prohibited above this point.

10. Miller Bar. Launch from gravel; bank fishing; self-register to fish canyon stretch.

11. Nook Bar. Launch from gravel; bank fishing.

12. Redwood. Launch from gravel; bank fishing.

13. South Fork. Undeveloped launch; no bank fishing; day's drift to Loeb Park or points in between.

14. Low Water Bridge. Abandoned road bridge still a wade even in low water; accesses miles of west bank fishing along Chetco River Trail.

planning a trip to fish either of these species. See Appendix.

Fall chinook enter the bay mid-September to October. Trolling, bait fishing, and fly casting are all popular methods here. There is also a popular jetty fishery for early fall chinook during the 6 weeks before the rains hit.

Bottom fishing is productive in the bay year-round, as is perch fishing from adjacent beaches. Best perch catches are in May and June on the incoming tide. Jetty fishing for perch is only fair. The jetty is wheelchair accessible, as is a fishing pier on the south side of the bay. Crab and many other bay species are caught from the pier.

Accommodations are plentiful in Brookings, where marine and fishing supplies are also available. Harris Beach State Park 2 miles north of Brookings has a large campground. Sporthaven Trailer Park, run by the county, is south of town. Azalea State Park at Brookings does not allow overnight camping.

CHETCO RIVER

A very good winter steelhead and salmon stream at the extreme south end of the Oregon coast. Despite its modest size, the

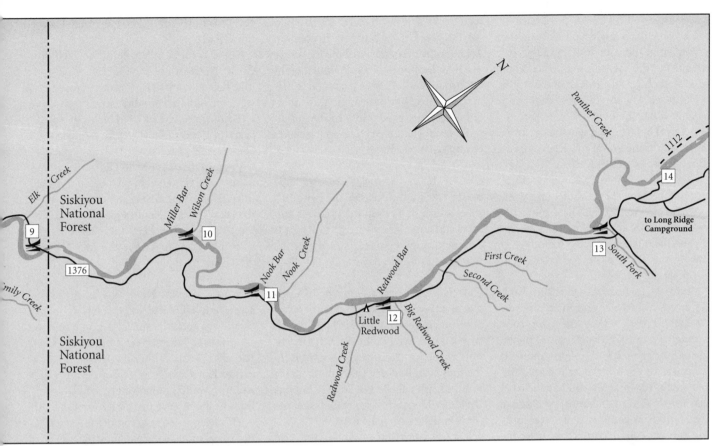

Chetco is known for growing big fish. Scenic, flanked by myrtle trees, the river enters the sea at Brookings after a 50-mile run. The best water is accessible to drift boats, and there are good bank fishing opportunities along both north and south bank roads. The North Bank Rd. follows the river about 10 miles into Siskiyou National Forest.

Fall chinook are available from September through December, with peak catches in October and November. The average catch is 30 pounds. A 64-pounder was landed here in 1998. Chinook move upstream when it rains, and best fishing usually follows a good rainstorm. During dry spells, the best chance for chinook is in tidewater. The river is closed to coho angling.

A good number of hatchery-reared winter steelhead are released into the Chetco system each year. Steelhead start showing well in December, and fishing holds up through March. Peak catches are generally made in January. The Chetco is consistently among the 10 best Oregon coastal streams for winter steelhead.

The river also offers limited catch and release fishing for wild cutthroat trout in early season, and for searun in late summer. Searun are primarily fished in the lower river around the Hwy. 101 bridge.

ODFW manages a number of fishing access areas on the river. From the South Bank Rd., anglers can approach popular bank fisheries at Tide Rock about two miles upstream from Hwy. 101, and the Pilling Hole, about two miles farther.

From the North Bank Rd., there is bank access at Morris Hole about 2 miles upstream, and at Social Security Boat Ramp another mile farther. Drift boats can be launched at Social Security, though a four-

The CHETCO RIVER turns out exceptionally large steelhead. Photograph by Scott Richmond.

wheel drive vehicle may be necessary in some years. Bank anglers plunk from the gravel bar at the launch site. Farther upstream there is walk-in public access to good water below the mouth of the North Fork Chetco. The Myrtle Grove boat ramp at Willow Bar (below Loeb State Park) is also a great bank fishing spot. Boats can be launched off the gravel bar. There are additional opportunities for launching and take-out at Loeb State Park and at several undeveloped gravel bars farther upstream.

Few anglers use jet sleds here due to the river's small size and shallow riffles; nevertheless, there is a designated motor deadline above Second Bridge (above Elk Creek) at the Ice Box Hole.

Above the Ice Box Hole, the North Bank Rd. crosses the Chetco and enters Siskiyou National Forest, where the river runs through a canyon. To keep track of public use of the canyon stretch, anglers are asked to register at a self-serve station at Miller Bar access. Above Redwood Bar, the road gets rough. Fishing the upper river above the South Fork confluence involves fording the river. A trail follows the Chetco for another 1½ miles.

A court ruling in 1995 verifying the Chetco's navigability at the time Oregon became a state insures angler access to the river bank below the high water mark. On the Chetco in particular, this means anglers can fish from side-channel and midstream gravel bars throughout the river without concern for landowner harassment, including a popular 10-mile stretch beginning one mile above the Chetco bar.

A gauge reading for the Chetco is available. See Appendix. The Chetco river gauge only came into service in 1999, so readings are only now being analyzed with regard to effect of river velocity and depth on fishing. In general, the Chetco clears within 24 hours of a storm and is fishable within 48 hours. A stable or dropping river level is a promising indicator of good fishing.

There are campgrounds at Harris Beach State Park 2 miles north of Brookings and at Loeb State Park.

CLEAR LAKE (Coos Co.). Don't confuse this with the large lake of the same name south of Reedsport in Douglas County. This Clear Lake is about 14 miles south of Reedsport on the west side of Hwy. 101, ½ mile north of Saunders Lake. To reach it, park along the highway and cross the railroad tracks. The north end of the lake is in the Oregon Dunes National Recreation Area. It offers very good fishing for yellow perch and supports a good population of cutthroat trout. About 15 acres , it is primarily fished by local anglers. Though quite deep, it comes close to drying up some years. There are no camping facilities or improvements here.

CLEAR LAKE (Douglas Co.). A large coastal lake on the east side of Hwy. 101, 7 miles south of Reedsport. It covers 290 acres andsupports cutthroat trout, but is closed to angling since it provides the water supply for Reedsport.

CLIFF LAKE (Umpqua watershed). A rich 7-acre hike-in brook trout lake in the South Umpqua watershed featuring the largest brook trout in the district, successfully fished by a knowing few. Cliff is up the trail from Buckeye Lake, about a mile south of Fish Lake in the Rogue-Umpqua Divide Wilderness north of Grasshopper Mt., Umpqua National Forest.

Skimmerhorn Trail 1578 offers the most direct approach to Cliff, though other trails access the lake basin. From Canyonville, follow the South Umpqua Rd. into the Umpqua National Forest, where it becomes Forest Rd. 28. About 4 miles past South Umpqua Falls Campground several roads branch off. Follow Forest Rd. 2830 for about 3 miles, then turn left on Forest Rd. 600 which leads to a trailhead. A short trail heading south interesects the Skimmerhorn Trail at a point about 1¾ miles from the lake. From this point, the trail reaches Buckeye at about 1½ miles, and Cliff ¼-mile farther. Trail 1578 actually begins at the junction of roads 2830 and 2840. Starting the hike at that point adds about 1½ miles to the walk.

Cliff Lake holds fish that exceed 4 pounds, but they can be cagey. Best fishing is in spring and fall. Trolling with spinner and bait produces well in spring. Ice fishing is a possibility in February and March if you're willing to snowshoe in. The road to the trailhead is often open in winter. There are campsites at Cliff and Buckeye.

CLIFF LAKE (Seven Lakes Basin). A good hike-in brook trout lake in the Sky Lakes Wilderness, at the summit between the headwaters of the Middle Fork of the Rogue and Seven Mile Creek. The basin is about 10 miles south of Crater Lake National Park.

Cliff Lake is ¼ mile west of the Pacific Crest Trail north of Devil's Peak. It's a 5-mile hike to the lake by trails from east or west. See Alta Lake for directions.

There are nice brook trout in this 10-acre lake and plenty of shoal area for fly anglers. Dark wet fly patterns weighted and fished with slow retrieve, do well. The trout population is maintained by air stocking with fingerlings. There are natural campsites at the lake. This is a picturesque area, and if the fishing is slow here, there are other lakes in the area to try. See also Alta, Middle, Grass.

COOPER CREEK RESERVOIR. A 140-acre multiple-use reservoir that offers good fishing for stocked trout, largemouth bass, and panfish. The reservoir is 2 miles east of Sutherlin. From Sutherlin, take the road east to Fair Oaks, 2 miles from Hwy. 99, and turn south onto a county road which leads to the reservoir in a bit over a mile.

This steep-sided reservoir in a forest setting offers some of the plumpest bluegill in Western Oregon, with lots of fish between 8 and 10 inches. Largemouth bass are also of good size, though not abundant. Voluntary catch and release of largemouth will help sustain this fishery. Crappie are plentiful in the arms of the lake during spring and early summer. Yellow, purple, or white jigs trolled through the shallows produce well. Brown bullhead catfish are also available. Legal-size rainbow trout are stocked each spring.

Algae sets in early here, encircling the lake by May. Consider using surface lures to deal with the algae, or fish in deeper water beyond the algae band. Submerged stumps provide the primary structure, with best warmwater fishing at the upper end away from the dam. In winter, though, good numbers of crappie are taken in the deep water near the dam.

There is good bank access, but anglers should be wary of steep drop-offs. An easy hiking trail encircles the lake.

Douglas County maintains two nice picnic areas, each with its own concrete boat ramp. The reservoir is popular with water skiers, but there are speed limits associated with the inlet arms. Overnight camping is prohibited.

Recommended for youngsters (but beware of the drop-offs). The local bass club sponsors an annual kids' derby here, providing equipment, boats, and expert guides for the youngsters. For more information, contact the district ODFW office. There is a wheelchair accessible fishing dock.

COOS BAY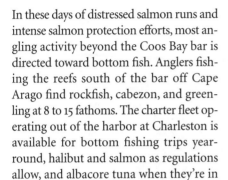

In these days of distressed salmon runs and intense salmon protection efforts, most angling activity beyond the Coos Bay bar is directed toward bottom fish. Anglers fishing the reefs south of the bar off Cape Arago find rockfish, cabezon, and greenling at 8 to 15 fathoms. The charter fleet operating out of the harbor at Charleston is available for bottom fishing trips year-round, halibut and salmon as regulations allow, and albacore tuna when they're in the area.

Chinook and coho salmon are outside the bay from May through September. Offshore salmon and Pacific halibut fishing seasons and quotas are determined annually by the Pacific Fishery Management Council. General regulations are published in the spring of the year, but in-season changes are common. Get current information before planning a trip for either of these species. See Appendix.

Coos Bay's offshore salmon fishery is within the Cape Falcon to Humbug Mountain regulatory zone. Its halibut fishery is within the Florence North Jetty to California zone. The halibut season out of Coos Bay has been open intermittently from May to September. Offshore chinook seasons have recently been open from April 1 to October 31, and there have been selective offshore fishing opportunities for finclipped coho.

Two popular spots for chinook fishing outside the bay are about one mile west and 1 to 2 miles north of the north jetty, and between the bar and whistle buoy. The Coos Bay bar is more easily negotiated than most, but beware of heavy wind or fog conditions.

Inside the bay, greenling, lingcod, and several species of perch are fished from north and south jetties, and perch are caught from many docks and bridges, including the boat docks in Charleston and the Charleston, Hwy. 101, and Haynes Inlet bridges. Boaters catch perch around the submerged rock jetty in the lower bay (look for the hazard markers), and both boat and bank anglers fish from Fossil

Striped bass and the perch they pursue can be fished in the surf along Coos County beaches. Photograph by Scott Richmond.

Point to Pony Point. This area has many submerged rock structures that make good perch habitat. Bank anglers in this area should avoid trespassing on private property. Perch start schooling in the bay in March. Best catches are on the incoming tide. In recent years, the ling population has suffered a decline, and regulations reflect the effort to protect adult spawners. At this time, harvest is limited to one fish per day with a keeper slot length of 24-inch minimum and 34-inch maximum. Check current regulations.

There's good fishing in the bay for fall chinook, as well as a growing fishery for hatchery-reared coho in Isthmus Slough. In 1998, 13,000 hatchery-reared coho and chinook returned to the Isthmus. Fishing begins in the slough in mid-August and continues through November. Anglers fish from the tide gate at the head of the slough down to the bay. Boats can be launched from a ramp at the head of Isthmus Slough off Hwy. 42 or at the new Eastside Boat Basin ramp on the lower slough. Bank anglers can fish at the boat ramps or at several points along Hwy. 42. Fishing is good throughout the narrow 15-mile tongue of tidewater.

As regulations allow, salmon anglers also pursue an exciting fishery between the jetties, mooching herring on the incoming tide. Their quarry is migrating salmon that move briefly into the bay in pursuit of bait

fish. Most recently, this area has been closed to salmon fishing from July 1 to mid-August but has been open the rest of the year.

Striped bass are still caught in Coos Bay, though the fishery continues in decline. Southern Oregon is the northern extreme of this fish's range, and conditions for successful spawning are seldom met in Coos Bay. Better opportunities for striped bass can be found in Winchester Bay and the lower Smith River. Nor are there plans for additional stocking since stripers prey on threatened salmon. However, at this time you may still find stripers in Coos Bay's sloughs and in the upper tidewater from autumn through March, especially in the South Fork of the Coos River. From mid-June through mid-August, stripers may be found mid-bay around the Hwy. 101 bridge, though few are seen these days. Stripers may be tempted by a big plug or by bait and have been known to take a fly. The minimum keeper size is 30 inches.

There are also opportunities to catch striped bass in the surf along Coos County beaches in January and February. Best striper surf fishing is within a couple of hours either side of high tide. Horsfall, Bastendorff, Whiskey Run, Seven Devils, and Bullards beaches offer good surf-fishing opportunities. Fish for stripers as you would surf perch, which are also available from these beaches.

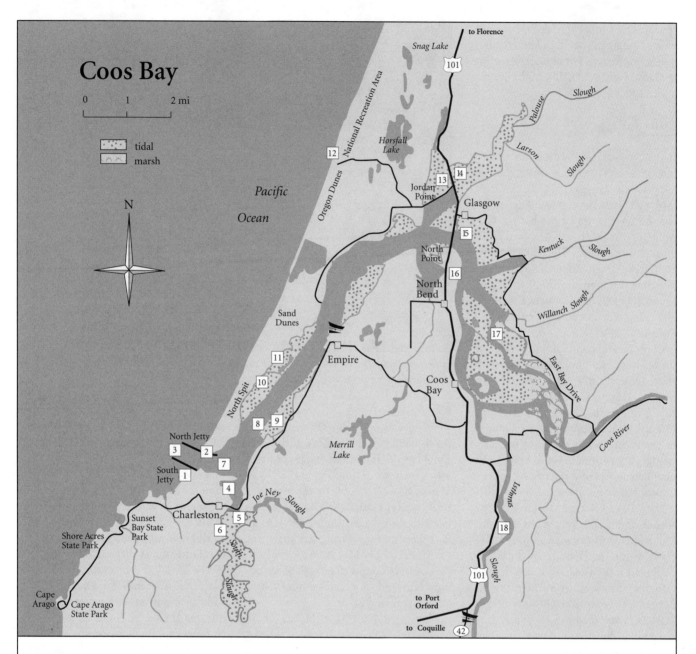

Coos Bay

0   1   2 mi

tidal
marsh

N

Pacific
Ocean

1. South Jetty. Park at Bastendorf County Park; fish for red-tail perch, greenling, ling cod, occasional salmon.

2. North Jetty. Fish for redtail perch, greenling, lingcod.

3. Lower Bay. Troll and mooch herring for salmon.

4. Charleston Waterfront. Public access to extensive boat docks for perch February through summer, smelt and herring jigged June-September; dungeness and rock crab; gapers & cockles.

5. Charleston Bridge. Park near bridge to dig Charleston Flats for cockles, gapers, some butter clams.

6. South Slough Flat. Fair digging for cockles, gapers, some butter clams; park along primitive Port Access Road (watch for potholes).

7. Submerged Rock Jetty. Good fishing at high tide for perch, rockfish, greenling, occasional lingcod.

8. Fossil Point. Natural rock structures provide good perch habitat; fish from boat and bank; best on incoming tide; bank anglers, respect private property.

9. Pigeon Pt. Flats. Popular digging for gapers, butter clams; limited parking but accessible.

10 North Spit. Best digging on the bay for gapers, cockles, softshell; walk out at low tide along entire bay side of spit.

11. Clam Island. Fish for dungeness and some red rock crab off island; also gapers & cockles.

12. Horsfall Beach. Fish for surf perch and in January and February, for stripers pursuing them.

13. Menasha Dike Flats. Closed due to toxic substance found in clams.

14. Haynes Inlet Bridge. Fish from bridge for perch.

15. Sturgeon Hole.

16. Hwy. 101 Bridge. Fish from bridge for perch.

17. Coos Channel. Fish for shad and remnant striped bass.

18. Isthmus Slough. Good bank access to coho; boat ramp upstream.

Fishing for sturgeon, both white and green, has been fair to good in Coos Bay. Anglers use big gobs of bait and fish the deep holes. A favorite spot is above the Hwy. 101 bridge off North Point in winter and early spring. Sturgeon are also caught in the lower Coos River in late spring and summer.

Coos Bay has a very productive crab fishery. In fact, there are so many crabs in the bay that anglers pursuing other quarry usually prefer to use artificial bait rather than feed the crabs. Dungeness and rock crab are fished from Charleston docks and off Clam Island, among other places. Anglers jig for herring and smelt from the Charleston boat docks from June to September. Sardines and Pacific mackerel sometimes put in an appearance. Large schools entered the bay for the first time in the summer of 1998. Anglers had great success jigging for them off the public and boat docks in Charleston.

The best clam flats in the bay run the length of the North Spit. Walk out at low tide and dig for gapers, cockles, and softshell clams. Menasha Dike Flats also offer good digging on either side of the causeway from Hwy. 101 to Horsfall Beach. South Slough Flat offers fair digging for cockles, gapers, and some butter clams. Park along the Port Access Rd., but keep a sharp eye out for potholes.

South Slough, a natural nursery for Dungeness crab and important bait fish area south of Charleston, has been designated a National Estuarine Reserve and is a good place to explore by canoe. Check at the interpretive center four miles south of Charleston on Seven Devils Road for important information about canoe safety in the slough.

When on the main bay, boaters should be wary of prevailing northwest winds in summer, which can turn the bay very rough when the winds meet an incoming tide. Always wear a life jacket.

Supplies and accommodations are available in Charleston, the city of Coos Bay, and at North Bend. Charleston has extensive, welcoming public docks and marinas, and is the gateway to two magnificent state parks, Shore Acres (for day use only) and Sunset Bay (which has a full service campground, including showers). Bastendorff County Park south of Charleston also has excellent camping facilities.

COOS RIVER. The Coos River flows only a little over 4 miles from the confluence of its major tributaries, the Millicoma River and the South Fork Coos west of Coos Bay. It is accessible from Hwy. 101. With the fading of the striped bass fishery, shad and salmon are the primary fisheries.

The fall salmon runs continue to benefit from the efforts of local volunteers. The earliest fall chinook arrive in August. Coho follow in November, but the river is closed for coho fishing.

Steelhead (both wild and finclipped hatchery) move through the river from December through March. Searun cutthroat appear in late fall and may be fished catch and release.

Shad angling is very popular, though primarily a boat fishery due to limited bank access. Anglers use light tackle, and the shad put up a good fight. Extremely small spinners, small wobblers, darts, and weighted streamer flies are all successful for shad to 3 pounds. This fishery usually takes off in May and June.

Tackle, supplies, and advice are available in Coos Bay. Boats can be launched at Doras and Rooke Higgins on the Millicoma, and at the Myrtle Tree Boat Ramp on the South Coos River.

COOS RIVER, SOUTH FORK. A good south coast stream with a variety of fishing opportunities. It meets the Millicoma to form Coos River about 4 miles above the bay, 6 miles east of the city of Coos Bay. County roads follow the stream throughout its length.

South Coos has good populations of cutthroat, fall chinook, coho, steelhead, and a large shad run, as well as a few striped bass.

Fall chinook show well in September and October. The fishery is concentrated in the area of Myrtle Tree Boat Ramp due to releases from an ODFW STEP facility on nearby Morgan Creek. The coho run peaks in late November and December but is closed to angling.

Steelhead are available from December through March with plunking very popular. The river is planted with finclipped steelhead descended from the native Coos River strain in an effort to produce more reliable returns.

Both resident and searun cutthroat are present. Occasional striped bass are caught in July.

In May and June shad move into the South Fork, and anglers turn out in droves to cast or troll for them, using small spinners or weighted flies. Bank angling access is limited to the mouth of Daniels Creek across from the Myrtle Tree ramp. Boaters take shad throughout the river.

COQUILLE RIVER

A very productive south coast stream with limited bank access but excellent boat access, entering the ocean at a small bay near Bandon after a 30-mile run through the Siskiyou Mountains. It is crossed by Hwy. 42S at Coquille, about 20 miles up from the mouth. Highway 42 from Roseburg follows the river downstream from the forks at Myrtle Point. The river hosts both wild and finclipped steelhead, a small number of spring chinook, a strong population of fall chinook, and one of the coast's healthier runs of wild coho.

Coquille Bay is fished for salmon, various perch, Dungeness crab, and smelt. Both north and south jetties are well used by anglers, as are the Bandon City Docks, where good numbers of perch and crab are taken from April through October. Smelt are jigged from the docks between July and September. Softshell clams are dug primarily in the flats adjacent to the Bandon Treatment Plant.

A few spring chinook move into the river during summer, but salmon fishing begins in earnest with fall chinook in September. Many anglers troll for chinook in the lower river, with herring and lures equally popular. Coho arrive in October. Angling for wild coho is prohibited, but the river may be open for finclipped coho from September to mid-October. Check current regulations.

Efforts to build up the Coquille's wild salmon runs through riparian and in-

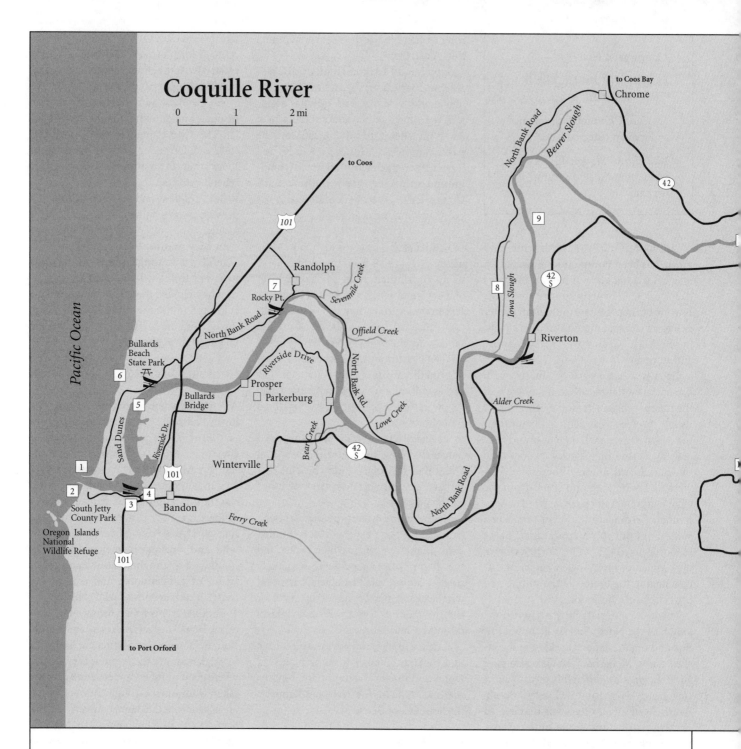

Coquille River

0   1   2 mi

1. North Jetty. Fish for perch, rockfish.

2. South Jetty. Fish for perch.

3. Bandon Boat Basin. Public ramp; fish from docks for perch & crab April through October, smelt July through September.

4. Mouth of Ferry Creek. Returning hatchery chinook September to October, coho October to November); dig flats at Bandon Treatment Plant upstream for softshell clams.

5. Crabbing. best from Bullards downstream.

6. Bullards Beach. prime surf fishing for perch.

7. Rocky Pt. Boat Ramp. troll from here up to Sevenmile Creek for salmon.

8. Sloughs. Fish for brown bullhead, largemouth bass.

9. Riverton to Myrtle Point. fish for brown bullheads in open water, July to September.

10. Sturdivant Park. fish from float for salmon, steelhead, and cutthroat.

11. Myrtle Pt. to Coquille. Plunk for winter steelhead January-February; troll for fall chinook September through October, for searun cutthroat late summer and fall.

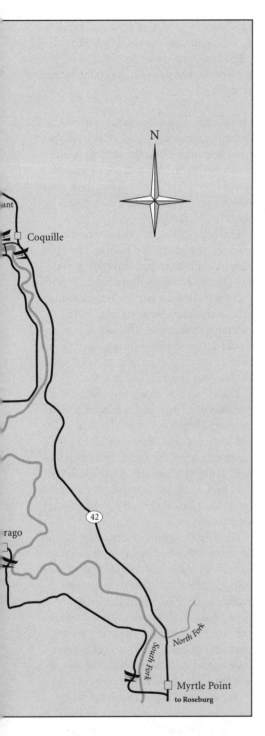

"Shrimp cocktail" (salmon eggs and sand shrimp) is a popular chinook bait on the south coast. Photograph by Richard T. Grost.

stream restoration have shown good results. Hatchery programs and acclimation ponds are providing additional fishing opportunities. A popular fishery for fall chinook near Rocky Point Boat Ramp is sustained by hatchery releases in nearby Sevenmile Creek.

Steelhead move into the river beginning in late November, with peak returns in January and February in both tidewater and the forks. Both wild and hatchery fish are present. Boat and bank plunking are popular in the upper tidewater from Coquille Boat Ramp to the forks from late November into March. Only finclipped steelhead may be kept.

Searun cutthroat may be fished catch and release in late summer and fall. The sloughs and lower river from Riverton to Myrtleare home to bullheads and largemouth bass. Striped bass are very occasionally seen here.

Salmon and steelhead fishing in the Coquille is primarily a boat show, with developed ramps at Bullards Beach State Park, Bandon Boat Basin, Rocky Point near Randolph, and at Riverton, Coquille, Arago, and Myrtle Point.

Non-boating anglers can fish for salmon and steelhead from a sturdy fishing float at Sturdivant Park, and from the banks at the mouth of Ferry Creek in Bandon.

COQUILLE RIVER, EAST FORK. A good trout and steelhead stream meeting the North Fork of the Coquille at Gravelford, about 5 miles east of Myrtle Point on Hwy. 42. A good road follows it throughout its 30-mile length.

The upper river has good trout water, with plenty of pools and boulder areas that shelter cutthroat trout. Fishing for cutthroat is catch and release.

The first steelhead show here in November after rains raise the river level. Best steelhead angling is in January and February. A steelhead acclimation pond constructed at a site on Hantz Creek at Fronas Park near Dora attracts a concentration of returning steelhead to that area. Only finclipped steelhead may be kept.

Fall chinook are present in good numbers in October, and coho in November, but most of these fish enter the East Fork ripe for spawning and should be left undisturbed. The East Fork is closed to fishing for coho.

COQUILLE RIVER, MIDDLE FORK. A large fork of the Coquille, joining the South Fork south of Myrtle Point, fished primarily for wild cutthroat. About 40 miles long, it is followed closely by Hwy. 42 throughout most of its length.

Angling for native cutthroat trout can be productive. All trout must be released unharmed. The Middle Fork's salmon and steelhead runs are fairly small and lightly fished. The steelhead run usually peaks in January. Only finclipped steelhead may be kept. The river is closed to angling above Myrtle Creek from September 15 through November 30 to protect spawning salmon.

COQUILLE RIVER, NORTH FORK. A good steelhead and cutthroat stream, joining the mainstem west of Myrtle Point after a 40-mile run. A county road follows the North Fork northeast from Myrtle Pt. on Hwy. 42. The upper river can be reached by the Fairview Rd. from Coquille.

This fork of the Coquille offers very good catch and release angling for wild cutthroat trout in early spring and for returning searun in late fall.

Fall chinook appear here in October. Best steelheading is in January and February. Drift fishing is the most popular steelheading technique here. All non-finclipped steelhead must be released unharmed.

Much of the fishing occurs around Laverne County Park.

COQUILLE RIVER, SOUTH FORK. A very productive fork of the Coquille River, featuring the most consistent steelheading in the area. Over 50 miles long, it is followed closely by a paved road from Myrtle Point on Hwy. 42 to Powers, about 20 miles upstream.

Once offering some of the best trout fishing on the south coast, the South Fork is now managed primarily for winter steelhead, both wild and hatchery. January and February are the prime steelheading months. The river still offers good fishing for wild cutthroat in early season. A few fall chinook are caught in the lower river in early October.

A 12-mile section of the river from the Forest Service boundary above Powers to Coquille River Falls is an important salmon and steelhead spawning and rearing area and is closed to all angling.

COW CREEK. An important tributary of the South Umpqua, entering the river from the west about 8 miles south of Myrtle Creek. Over 80 miles long, it joins the South Umpqua between Riddle and Canyonville. Cow Creek can be fished for winter steelhead and smallmouth bass but is closed to fishing for wild cutthroat trout at this time. Check current regulations.

There are smallmouth bass in the lower creek up to Glendale. Access is limited due to private property. There are several BLM picnic areas on the creek south of Riddle and a small campground on Cow Creek Rd. 18 miles upstream from Azalea at Devil's Flat.

CROOKS LAKE. A cutthroat lake 10 miles south of Bandon on Hwy. 101. About 50 acres, 1½ miles west of the highway, it is privately owned, with no public access.

DAVIDSON LAKE. Prominent on some maps, this 25-acre lake is about 7 miles south of Bandon on Hwy. 101. It is between the ocean and highway, near the sand dunes. It supports black bass and good size trout, but is privately owned and without public access.

DENMAN MANAGEMENT AREA. An ODFW angling and waterfowl development 6 miles north of Medford. The 20 small ponds are managed for bass, panfish, and waterfowl. Legal rainbows are occasionally stocked in spring. The tract of land covers several thousand acres.

These ponds offer good bank fishing in spring before they get slimy. Best fishing is in the six ponds near the headquarters. Most of the ponds are only an acre or two. Whetstone Pond No.1, a 10-acre pond near the management headquarters, is very popular for largemouth bass, bluegill, crappie and catfish. Bass have been taken up to 7 lbs. Early spring fishing produces brown bullhead to 2 pounds. Check with the resident manager for the best spots and for special regulations. Get a map of the area at the ODFW office, open weekdays.

You'll have plenty of feathered company here. Keep an eye out for Canada geese, cinnamon teals, and mallards in summer.

Egrets can be spotted in winter and spring, as well as redtail hawks, black shoulder kites, and barn owls. Recommended for youngsters. The ponds are open for fishing year-round.

DIAMOND LAKE (Umpqua watershed). A large, extremely productive rainbow trout lake in an attractive setting, 15 miles north of Crater Lake in the Umpqua National Forest. The lake is at elevation 5100 ft. with an eastern skyline dominated by 9000 ft. Mt. Thielsen.

Historically one of the best trout fisheries in the state, the lake is currently plagued with a rampant tui chub population. If concerns regarding chemical treatment are satisfactorily addressed, the tui (and everything else in the lake) will be eradicated in fall 2001. The lake will be restocked the following spring. Given Diamond's capacity to grow large trout, good fishing could resume within a year.

Under normal conditions, as many as 342,000 trout are caught here in a single year, including many of good size. In recent years, the average fish has weighed a little more than a pound. But in years past, before thoughtless saboteurs introduced the tui chub as illegal live bait, the average catch was much larger, and 6 to 8-pounders were common.

Diamond is at the eastern edge of the Umpqua watershed and is most easily approached from eastern Oregon. From Hwy. 97, Hwy. 138 leads 20 miles west directly to the lake. From Roseburg, Diamond Lake is about 90 miles east. From the south, Diamond Lake is 108 miles northeast of Medford by way of highways 62, 230, and 138. Roads to the lake are usually open by late May.

At over 2800 acres, Diamond is one of the larger natural lakes in the state. It is rich in natural food, and fish put on weight fast. The trout fishery is sustained primarily by the introduction of rainbow fingerlings right after ice out. These fish reach legal size by fall and are of good size by ice-out the following year.

Angling holds up throughout the season, but the most exciting time to be here is the first month after ice-out, when the inlets swarm with spawning trout. Smaller fish follow the large spawners in pursuit of eggs. Adding to the excitement at that time of year is a very heavy midge hatch that gives an edge to fly anglers with a supply of

At elevation 5183 ft., Diamond Lake is often just beginning to thaw by opening day. Photograph by Richard T. Grost.

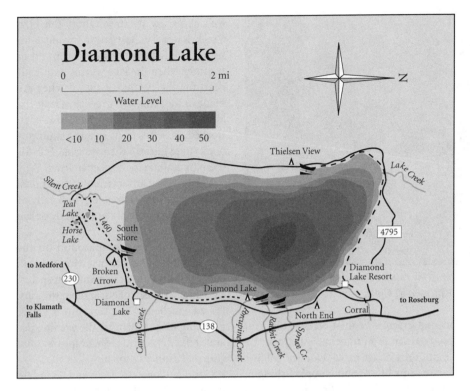

Diamond Lake

0   1   2 mi

Water Level

<10 10   20   30   40   50

Silent Creek
Teal Lake
Horse Lake
1460
South Shore
to Medford
230
Broken Arrow
to Klamath Falls
Diamond Lake
138
Camp Creek
Diamond Lake
Porcupine Creek
Rabbit Creek
Spruce Cr.
North End
Corral
Diamond Lake Resort
to Roseburg
Thielsen View
Lake Creek
4795
N

---

gives an edge to fly anglers with a supply of tiny chironomid nymph imitations. Ice-out usually occurs in early May, but can vary from spring to spring. Call the Forest Service Information Station at the lake for an update on the condition of the fishery. See Appendix.

At this time, trolling is the only way to avoid hooking the tui in summer. Trolling in the deep areas near the center of the lake and parallel to the west and east shores near drop-offs can be profitable. Fly anglers also have success trolling nymphs and streamers along the west shore, in 10 to 20 feet of water.

Under normal conditions, all methods of angling are successfully used here. Bait takes fish in the shoal areas at depths of 10 to 30 ft.. Single eggs and worms work well, and cheese bait or Power Bait on size 16 or 18 treble hooks is very popular. The north end of the lake is heavily worked by bait anglers and still bears the outdated name "Velveeta Hole." Drifting worms through the weed beds at the south end usually produces the largest fish. Diamond Lake trout have a reputation for leader shyness, so use the lightest line you can handle. Four-pound test can be too heavy for still-fishing here.

Fly anglers working small dark nymphs will almost always take fish. Small dry flies work well early and late in the day. When the lake warms in late summer, trout seek

Creek) is at the southwest end of the lake near the bottom of the "U."

Eel provides good fishing for wild and stocked trout. Bank access is limited, but nice catches are made off the public dock. Fly-fishing can be good and saves on tackle. Bait fishing also produces consistently.

Largemouth bass fishing attract a growing number of anglers. Good numbers are caught throughout the summer. Look for them near the inlet and outlet, along the shoreline, near the docks, in the shallows of the arms. A timber blow-down in the southeast provides especially good bass habitat. Crayfish imitations can be productive since the lake has a good population of the real thing.

A hatchery coho program here has been discontinued, but steelhead acclimated in Tenmile Creek often enter the lake and are available for harvest from December through March. The lake's outlet, Eel Creek, is closed to fishing, but steelhead can also be intercepted below the Eel Creek Confluence with Tenmile.

There is a campground and boat ramp in the state park at the southwest end of the lake, and a 10 mph speed limit is in effect. Shoreline access is limited to the park, as the rest of the lakeshore is steep and inaccessible. Supplies are available in Lakeside. The Lakeside airstrip is a half-hour hike from the State Park camp.

ELK CREEK (Umpqua watershed). A tributary of the mainstem Umpqua River, entering the river at Elkton. It is currently closed to all angling due to concern for Umpqua basin cutthroat and in compliance with the Endangered Species Act. Umpqua basin cutthroat are scheduled for review. Check current regulations for a possible relaxation of restrictions.

ELK RIVER

A south coast stream known for its large wild steelhead, popular chinook hatchery program, and its capacity to clear within 24 hours of heavy rain.

The river flows west about 30 miles, entering the ocean north of Port Orford, south of Camp Blanco. It's crossed by Hwy. 101 about 3 miles north of Port Orford. A paved road follows its south bank to the steelhead deadline at Bald Mt. Creek above Elk River Hatchery.

Fall chinook enter the Elk as soon as the rain-swollen river breaches the sand dune at the mouth, usually in October. The earliest fishing possible is actually a surf fishery on the beach. Walk south to the river's mouth, about a mile along the beach from Cape Blanco State Park,. Fishing here can be fantastic, with big fish hooked through December. This surf fishery is governed by regulations set by the Pacific Fishery Management Council and may be subject to in-season changes. See Appendix.

Though small, the Elk is a good steelhead river, known for the size and strength of its wild fish. You'll find only an occasional hatchery stray here, and all wild steelhead must be released unharmed. Bring a camera to record your "trophy" catch. January and February are the best steelheading months.

Most steelhead and salmon angling takes place in the lower river below the hatchery. Unfortunately, access is a problem here, as most of the river flows through private property. Ask permission. There is public bank access at the Hwy. 101 bridge, at the hatchery (note the hatchery area closure), at the 5-mile marker on Elk River Rd., and near the 7-mile marker (The Culvert Hole). Anglers staying at Elk River Campground (a privately owned RV park) can fish about a mile of good bank water, including the RV Park Hole.

Boating anglers have few options. Put in at Elk River Hatchery for a 9-mile drift to

Fall chinook enter the ELK *as soon as the rain-swollen river breaches the sand dune at its mouth. Photograph by Richard T. Grost.*

the only public take-out (Ironhead, ½ mile above Hwy. 101). You'll need 4-wheel drive to pull a boat up the steep bank at Ironhead. Another option is to take out after 6 miles at the RV park, for a small fee. The park also offers car shuttle service.

The river is fishable between 7 and 3½ ft., but under 4 ft. it is a little low for consistent success, and over 6 ft. it is too fast. For a river gauge reading, call the Elk River Hatchery. See Appendix.

There are native cutthroat available for catch and release fishing in the upper river, which flows through the Siskiyou National Forest. The roads are steep, narrow, unpaved, and poorly marked. Carry a current Siskiyou Forest map if you venture far. Forest Road 5325 follows the mainstem Elk a good ways into the forest. There are a number of public campgrounds along the river road.

EMIGRANT LAKE 🐟

A big irrigation reservoir in Jackson County near Ashland, offering a variety of excellent fishing opportunities close to town, including large and smallmouth bass, channel cats, panfish, stocked rainbow trout, and landlocked chinook. The reservoir is north of Hwy. 66 about 5 miles southeast of Ashland. It can have up to 800 surface acres, but fluctuates considerably due to withdrawals.

Smallmouth bass fishing is popular here with catches to 12 inches, especially around the rock dam face. There's also good fishing for crappie, largemouth bass, bluegill, and brown bullhead catfish. An experi-

mental crappie regulation instituted in 1999 (8 inch minimum) may increase the size of the average catch. Flooded willows in the arms offer good crappie fishing in spring, especially in the Emigrant and Hill Creek arms. Largemouth bass to 5 pounds are found among the willows in spring.

Channel cats to 26 pounds have been landed. Brown bullhead are plentiful and of good size (to 15 inches). Bullhead are eager biters—as swimmers here can attest!

Legal rainbows are stocked in spring, as

well as excess steelhead from the Lost Creek hatchery. Best trout fishing is in spring and fall. Trout fishing drops off in summer when the lake warms and trout head for the bottom. Good catches are made in the Emigrant Creek arm near the inlet. Fingerling chinook have also been stocked, as well as trout-size and adult chinook (to 14 inches) when available. Fish for them by trolling in the deeper water.

The reservoir attracts many recreational users, including water-skiers. Fish early or late for undisturbed waters, or early or late in the season.

The county run campground on the lake is comfortably situated within an oak grove and provides trailer and tent spaces, a boat ramp, flush toilets, and hot showers. It's an excellent place to camp if you're planning to spiff up after the evening rise and take in a little Shakespeare or a gourmet dinner in town.

Good bank access, eager and abundant crappie, and the attraction of a water slide for cooling down when the bite is off make this a good place to bring youngsters.

EMPIRE LAKES. Three artificial lakes that offer opportunities to catch very large stocked trout as well as warmwater species. The lakes (Lower, Middle & Upper Em-

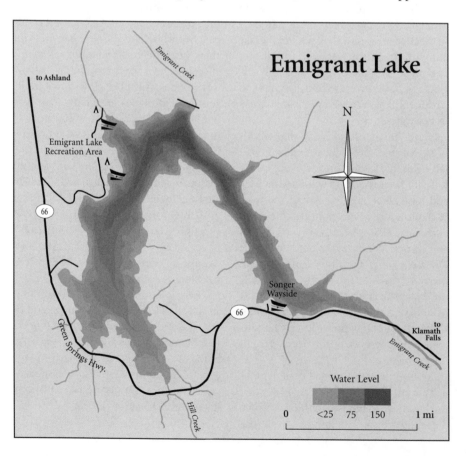

pire) are north of the road that runs from Coos Bay to Empire. They fluctuate with water use from a maximum of 50 acres.

The lakes are stocked with rainbow trout several times throughout the year and with a large number of trophy-size trout and surplus hatchery steelhead. The steelhead may be counted as trout in the daily limit. A steelhead tag is not required. There are also self-sustaining populations of largemouth bass, bluegill, and perch.

A paved trail encircles the lakes, which are easily fished from the bank. There is a picnic area and boat ramp on the upper lake. Only electric motors are allowed. Recommended for youngsters. Wheelchair accessible facilities.

EUCHRE CREEK (Curry Co.). A small coastal stream with wild cutthroat and wild winter steelhead, entering the ocean about 20 miles south of Port Orford at Ophir. It is crossed by Hwy. 101 near the mouth. A fair road follows the stream for about 7 miles. Road easements provide some public access. All fishing on the stream is catch and release.

The salmon runs on Euchre have not responded to enhancement efforts during the past ten years, and the run is thought to be extinct. Restoration efforts continue.

EVANS CREEK. A fair size tributary of the Rogue River, entering from the north about 20 miles east of Grants Pass at the town of Rogue River. About 20 miles long, it is currently closed to all angling to protect juvenile steelhead and salmon.

EXPO PONDS. Five ponds at the Jackson County Expo Center off I-5 at the Central Point Interchange. The ponds are open year-round and are stocked with legal trout throughout the spring. Largemouth bass, bluegill, crappie, and brown bullhead are available. Recommended for youngsters.

FISH CREEK (Umpqua watershed). A wonderful trout fishery high up the North Umpqua River above an impassable barrier to salmon and steelhead. It enters the North Umpqua from the south one mile below Toketee Falls, about 40 miles upstream from Glide on the North Umpqua Highway. Two logging roads hit the upper stream, one heading south from Toketee Generator Plant, and the other following Copelands Creek near Eagle Rock.

The stream offers good early fishing for wild trout. Follow Watson Creek Rd. to the Fish Cr. forebay for rainbows to 17 inches.

There are forest campgrounds at Fish Creek and at Camas Creek, about 5 miles south of the highway.

FISH LAKE (Umpqua watershed). A big, beautiful trout lake beneath Grasshopper Mt. in the Umpqua-Rogue Divide Wilderness. This 95-acre hike-in rainbow and brook trout lake is at elevation 3500 ft., 1½ miles (and 800 ft.) below Buckeye and Cliff Lakes.

Follow the South Umpqua River Rd. (County Rd. 1) from Canyonville. At Tiller follow County Rd. 46 into the forest, where it becomes Forest Rd. 28. Continue about 4 miles past South Umpqua Falls Camp to 2830, which forks to the right. At about 5 miles, near the Skimmerhorn Trailhead, bear left onto Forest Rd. 2840. Fish Lake Trail 1570 begins at the first hairpin turn on this road. The trail follows Fish Lake Creek, reaching the lake in a little more than 3 miles. Or follow Forest Rd. 2840 about 4½ miles farther to access The Beaver Swamp Trail, which reaches the lake in just 1½ miles. Use the Umpqua National Forest map to navigate.

Fish Lake rainbow and brook trout reproduce naturally and grow to 20 inches. The lake can be fished from shore, but a raft or float tube will increase your chances. All methods will take fish. There's an undeveloped camp at the lake and developed campgrounds on Forest Rd. 28. Trail bikes are not allowed in the wilderness.

FISH LAKE (Rogue watershed). A large, very popular lake about 37 miles northeast of Medford on Hwy. 140. It is headwaters of the North Fork of Little Butte Creek. Take Hwy. 62 north from Medford, to its junction with Hwy. 140. From Ashland, take Dead Indian Memorial Rd. (east of the municipal airport) about 4 miles past Howard Prairie Lake to Big Elk Rd., a northbound paved road which joins Hwy. 140 near Fish Lake. From Klamath Falls, take Hwy. 140 north past Lake of the Woods.

With 440 surface acres in a setting of old growth Douglas fir, the lake provides good fishing for stocked legal rainbows. Brook trout are also present. Trout 5 to 8 pounds are caught regularly.

Fish lake is a natural lake that has been augmented by a dam to increase its size for irrigation purposes. More than 30 springs keep the lake cool year-round. Best fishing is in the old lake channel west of the resort.

There is good bank access, except on the southwest shore where a lava flow meets the lake. The bank between the two campgrounds (with a gradually sloping lake bottom) offers safe and productive fishing for youngsters.

The campgrounds, Doe Point and Fish Lake, are at the east end of the lake. Fish Lake is a popular stopover for hikers on the Pacific Crest Trail, which comes to within ½ mile of lake.

There is a boat launch at Fish Lake Campground. Fish Lake Resort on the west shore is in the style of a 1950s vintage fishing camp. Its cabins are rustic but clean and suitable for families. There is also an RV park, boat rentals, restaurant, tackle, and general supplies. A 10 mph speed limit throughout the lake keeps the atmosphere peaceful and is good for fishing.

FLORAS CREEK. A short south coast stream fished for wild cutthroat, winter steelhead, and chinook. The creek is closed to coho angling. Hwy. 101 crosses it about 15 miles south of Bandon. The upper stream is followed by a road for about 5 miles, but the stream is usually in a gorge well below the road and bordered by mostly private property. The stream below Hwy. 101 can be reached in several spots by car, but the area is swampy.

Cutthroat fishing is catch and release only and is best in early season. Chinook show up in October or later, depending on the breaching of the outlet dune by high water. Steelhead enter in December and are available through March. The creek is lightly fished due to difficulty of access. Except for the occasional hatchery stray, all steelhead in the creek are wild. Only finclipped steelhead may be kept.

FLORAS LAKE. A large, lake west of Hwy. 101, about 17 miles south of Bandon. A good road south of Langlois runs 2 miles west from Hwy. 101 to the lake. The lake covers 250 acres and in places reaches a depth of 50 ft..

Rainbow trout are lightly stocked, and searun cutthroat are sometimes available for catch and release angling.

The lake has a few largemouth bass 7 to 8 pounds, but fishing is slow. Try plugging into the open water near the beds.

Chinook, coho, and steelhead all move through the lake into the upper tributaries. Both steelhead and chinook are caught here. The lake is closed to coho fishing.

Boice Cope County Park provides camping and a boat ramp on the lake. The lake is best fished from a boat, but keep a weather eye out, since it can get very windy here. In fact, the lake is heavily used by wind surfers.

FORDS MILL POND. A hundred-acre pond with bass and panfish on Hwy. 225 near Sutherlin, about one mile west of the junction of highways. 225 and 99. The current owners have closed the pond to public access.

GARRISON LAKE. A 134-acre lake that offers fishing for stocked rainbows, wild cutthroat, a good population of bass, and abundant yellow perch. It is west of Port Orford off Hwy. 101. Up to 30 ft. deep in places, the lake is typical for the coast area, with partly sandy shores and a severe weed problem. The lake may have been breached by high tides in 1999, which may have some effect on the fishery.

Garrison is stocked with hatchery rainbows and has some wild cutthroat. Yellow perch run to good size. The largemouth population is currently depleted, as the fish are slow to reproduce here and budget constraints have not allowed stocking on a regular basis. Check the regulations for catch limits.

The lake is best fished by boat. There is a state-owned boat ramp and parking area at the south end of the lake, and another county ramp at the north end. The nearest public campground is at Battle Rock State Park in Port Orford. There is a private RV park at the lake.

GALESVILLE RESERVOIR. An attractive 640-acre impoundment in a timbered valley on Cow Creek, tributary to the South Umpqua. It features trophy-size largemouth bass, other warmwater species, abundant trout, and a unique fishery for landlocked coho. To reach it, take the Azalea Exit No. 88 off I-5 onto County Rd. 36.

The reservoir was developed with warmwater fishing in mind, so most trees and brush were left intact to serve as fish habitat. Fish the submerged trees along the northwest edge for good size largemouth

bass. There is a slot limit on the largemouth bass to increase the average size and provide more spawners. There are also bluegill of good size, crappie, and some smallmouth. A small boat or canoe will let you weave among the partially submerged timber.

The lake is amply stocked with trout and offers opportunities for coho to 15 inches. Troll the deeper areas for coho.

There is bank access along the south side road, a good boat ramp on the north side, and a natural launch area on the Cow Creek Arm, where only electric motors are allowed. There's also a 5 mph area in the north, though motorized water sports are popular on the main body of the lake.

There is no camping allowed at Galesville, but it has an attractive picnic area.

GOLD RAY FOREBAY. The 80-acre forebay to Gold Ray Dam on the Rogue River. Access is a problem due to the railroad tracks. There is no official boat access due to the danger of boats going over the dam (some have). A popular warmwater fishery here has diminished due to releases of cold water to benefit Rogue River salmon, steelhead, and trout.

GRASS LAKE. A rich, self-sustaining brook trout lake in the Seven Lakes Basin of the northern Sky Lakes Wilderness, headwaters of the Rogue River Middle Fork, offering very good fly-fishing opportunities. It is accessible from both east and west. See Alta Lake for detailed directions.

Trail 981 accesses the basin from Forest Rd. 344, continuing past the cut-off to Alta, to the cut-off to Middle then Grass Lake. Trail 3703 approaches the basin from Forest Rd. 3334 on the east at Sevenmile Marsh Campground, joining the Pacific Crest Trail after about 2 miles. The trail to Grass cuts off the PCT after about 2 miles.

With 30 surface acres, Grass supports wild brook trout and is stocked with brook trout in odd number years. Trout run to 15 inches, averaging 9 to 12 inches. Usually the most productive of the Seven Lakes group, it is quite shallow, and fly fishing is effective. There are natural campsites at Grass and at other nearby lakes. For trail information, check with the Butte Falls Ranger Station. See also Cliff, Middle, Alta.

GRAVE CREEK. A fairly large tributary of the Rogue River, entering from the east,

about 6 miles north of Galice. A spawning stream for Rogue River salmon and steelhead, the creek is closed to all angling.

HALL LAKE. A small lake about 10 miles south of Reedsport on Hwy. 101, which is gradually being filled in by sand dunes. Private property surrounds the lake. It has a largemouth bass and a good population of cutthroat.

HERBERT LOG POND (a.k.a. Canyonville Pond). A nice 10-acre mill pond purchased by the state for angling. It is located on Hwy. 227 in a county park about one mile east of I-5 at Canyonville.

The pond produces good numbers of largemouth bass, black crappie, and brown bullhead. Bank fishing is ideal for youngsters. Motorboats are prohibited, but a float tube, canoe, or raft will help you reach the larger bass. Supplies and accommodations are available at Canyonville. Recommended for youngsters.

HOOVER PONDS. A series of four artificial ponds visible from Hwy. 140 north of Medford. They have naturally reproducing populations of largemouth bass, bluegill, crappie and brown bullhead. The ponds are small, 4 to 10 acres each, and most fishing is from the bank. They are generally turbid due to heavy use of the surrounding area by off-road vehicles. Jackson Pond, at the County Sports Park, is just east of the Hoover complex and offers fishing for bass and bluegill.

HORSESHOE LAKE (Blue Lake Basin). A good hike-in brook and rainbow trout lake in the Sky Lakes Wilderness, Rogue River National Forest. See Blue Lake (Rogue watershed) for road and trail directions. Horseshoe is about ½ mile southeast of Blue Lake. Bear left at the trail fork. Other good lakes nearby include Blue Canyon, Pear, and Carey.

Horseshoe Lake is about 20 acres with good shoal areas and cover for fish. The lake has good numbers of brook trout to 18 inches and a smaller population of rainbows about the same size. The big brookies can be hard to catch. Fly fishing seems to be most productive here, though casting small lures from shore with a slow retrieve can be effective.

There are good natural campsites at the lake. Improved sites are available at nearby lakes. The Blue Rock Mt. Rd. usually opens in June.

HORSFALL LAKE. An extremely shallow but sometimes large lake within the National Dunes Recreation Area north of North Bend offering pretty good fishing for largemouth some years. Like all dune lakes, Horsfall can vary dramatically in size from year to year depending on the water table. Fishing is best after several years of good rainfall.

From Hwy. 101, cross the Haynes Inlet of Coos Bay, turning onto the Bluebill Lake Rd. about half-way across the inlet. Horsfall Lake is northwest of Little Bluebill, part of a complex that includes adjacent Spirit Lake and Sandpoint Lake to the north. Horsfall supports yellow perch, largemouth bass, and brown bullhead. Though hard to reach, the largemouth make it worth the effort.

HOWARD PRAIRIE LAKE. One of southern Oregon's most popular lakes, a large irrigation reservoir in an alpine setting east of Ashland. It has a large trout population and grows fish very well. Depending on irrigation needs and rainfall, the reservoir varies from 2000 to 1500 acres.

From Ashland, take Hwy. 66 to Dead Indian Memorial Rd. past the municipal airport. Follow this paved road 22 miles to the reservoir. The route from Medford is circuitous but possible. Take Hwy. 62 to Hwy. 140, the Lake of the Woods Hwy. Turn south at Lake Creek, following Little Butte Rd. to Soda Creek Rd., then Conde Creek Rd. to Dead Indian Memorial Rd., emerging west of Howard Prairie.

The reservoir is stocked annually with 350,000 rainbow fingerlings which grow to 10 to 15 inches and average over a pound. Four and 5 pounders are not uncommon.

Most anglers still-fish using Power Bait, though worms and eggs fished just off the bottom take fish in early season, and trolling with spinner/bait combinations works well. Good trout spots include the area south of the island, and the far north arm. Best trolling is in the deep water in the east inside channel. Fly anglers might try streamers on a slow troll or cast to the shallows. A lot of the larger rainbows are taken late in the day on flies slowly trolled just under the surface.

While trolling is very popular, the lake can successfully be fished from its banks.

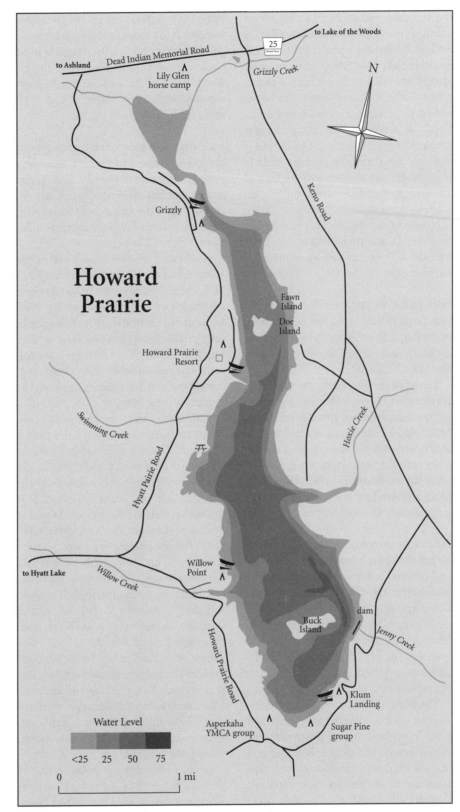

The most popular area is between Klum Landing and the Dam.

Largemouth bass were introduced illegally some time ago and are now an established and growing fishery. If you enjoy brown bullhead, there are plenty of them here, too. The bullheads average 8 inches and run to 11 inches. Worms are the favored bait. Pumpkinseed sunfish are also present. Smallmouth have also been illegally introduced and may have some effect on the trout fishery in coming years.

There is a campground at Howard Prairie Resort, as well as at Willow Point on the west shore and at Klum Landing on the south shore. A horse camp, Lily Glen, is well back from the water at the far north end of the lake. Two group camps are available by reservation. Sugar Pine, a campground with drinking water, may be reserved by calling Jackson County Parks Dept. See Appendix. Camp Asperkaha is managed by the Medford YMCA and is available for rental. Its facilities include covered sleeping shelters with bunks and an open air but fully equipped kitchen shelter.

Howard Prairie Resort offers supplies, boat rentals, and trailer rentals. It is open only during trout season. Recommended for youngsters.

HUNTER CREEK. A small coast stream that flows directly into the ocean south of the Rogue River Estuary. Hwy. 101 crosses its mouth about 2 miles south of Gold Beach.

Restoration efforts have resulted in an increased fall chinook run, and a fishery for them has opened downstream from Mateer Bridge. Season dates may vary, so check current regulations. Hunter also offers an excellent opportunity to experience small stream fishing for wild winter steelhead. Steelhead are generally in the creek from January through March.

HYATT RESERVOIR. A big reservoir with largemouth bass, brown bullhead catfish, and nice size rainbow trout. It has about 950 surface acres. Hyatt is north of the Green Springs summit on Hwy. 66, which leads from Ashland to Klamath Falls. The lake is 5 miles from Green Springs, which is about 13 miles east of Ashland. Dead Indian Memorial Rd. accesses the reservoir from the north.

The lake is stocked annually with about 250,000 rainbow fingerlings, which tend to grow larger here than at nearby Howard Prairie Reservoir. Since the bullhead population was dealt a blow several years ago, trout to 20 inches are now available, though the bullhead will inevitably make a comeback. Troll the west shore and the northeast cove for trout.

Best largemouth fishing is on the east side of the reservoir and in the coves where there is submerged and standing timber. Good water is accessible from the bank.

There is a large BLM campground with

boat ramp at the south end of the reservoir, but it is a considerable distance from good water. Camp on the east side to be close to good fishing. Float tube anglers won't have far to kick to reach good warmwater habitat. There is a 10 mph speed limit throughout the lake.

ILLINOIS RIVER. A major tributary of the lower Rogue River with a legendary run of wild winter steelhead prized for size and vitality, but currently dangerously depleted. It joins the Rogue from the south at the community of Agness, about 25 miles upriver from Gold Beach.

Headwaters of the Illinois are in the Siskiyou National Forest east of Cave Junction, where there is good catch and release angling for wild trout in early spring. Winter steelhead are fished catch and release in the 25 miles from Pomeroy Dam at Cave Junction to Oak Flat, and there is a small catch and release fishery for fall chinook, during the first fall freshets, between the mouth and Oak Flat .

The Illinois can get very low and warm. Despite danger signals for more than a decade, this river and its fish populations continue to be abused. Conditions brought on by heavy irrigation withdrawals, intensive mining in past years, and overzealous timber harvests are further aggravated in periods of drought. To protect what is left of the fishery, angling is limited to catch and release, and only artificial flies and lures may be used. All tributaries are closed to fishing, and the mainstem itself is closed to fishing above Pomeroy Dam. Winter steelhead are generally in the Illinois from December through March.

Boat access is limited to the extreme lower river near Agness, and the 5-mile section between Kerby Bridge and Pomeroy Dam. Some boaters in this upper reach use small sleds. But the Illinois is extremely treacherous, and most reasonable anglers fish it from the bank.

To access the most popular section of the river, follow Hwy. 199 north from Cave Junction to Selma, then turn left on County Rd. 5070, which becomes Forest Rd. 4203. This road leads to Kerby Flat, then follows the river to Oak Flat, ending at Briggs Creek. Watch for roadside turn-outs indicating popular river access points. At Briggs Creek, a Forest Service trail leads down to the river and follows it for about 5 miles to the Weaver Ranch, just beyond

Pine Creek. This portion of the river is designated Wild and Scenic and is included in the Kalmiopsis Wilderness.

JOHNSON MILL POND. A 90-acre former mill pond beside the Coquille River, with fishing for stocked trout, largemouth bass, and lots of bluegill in a pleasant, peaceful setting.

About 2½ miles from Coquille on Hwy. 42, turn west on Johnson Mill Rd. A sign welcomes you to the Mill Pond area. The gravel road leads first to a main parking lot with a little dock and picnic area, then continues on to several smaller parking areas before ending at a locked gate, beyond which only foot traffic is allowed.

A dike separates the pond from the Coquille River, and in some years, the pond is incorporated into the Coquille. Coho and steelhead may be recruited into the resident pond population when the river water recedes. These may be caught as trout, with no additional tag required.

Light-weight boats can easily be launched, but this is a great float tube lake. There's lots of submerged structure (old logs) and weed beds to attract fish. Locals say best fishing is at the south end (not surprisingly, the farthest from vehicle access). The lake is open for year-round fishing.

A level trail encircles the lake, including the top of the dike. Facilities include picnic tables and restrooms, but there is no water or trash pick-up. The pond is open for day use only.

JORDAN LAKE. A pond near the Weyerhaeuser paper mill west of Jordan Point on Coos Bay. It is severely affected during drought, but has been known to rebuild a good size population of yellow perch, and small numbers of good-size largemouth bass and brown bullhead.

JUMP OFF JOE CREEK. A 20-mile tributary of the Middle Rogue River, entering the Rogue in the Merlin area northwest of Grants Pass. It is crossed by Hwy. 99 about 10 miles north of Grants Pass and followed east by paved road for a good distance. At this time it is closed to all fishing.

LAKE CREEK (Umpqua watershed). The outlet stream of Diamond Lake, headwaters of the North Umpqua. The creek runs lo miles north from the lake to Lemolo Reservoir. Roads follow within a mile throughout its length. Hwy. 138 crosses about 5 miles downstream from the lake at Thielsen Campground. The Umpqua National Forest map shows a rough track (Forest Rd. 4792) leading south from the Forest Rd. 60 junction with 138 near Thielsen, following the creek for almost 4 miles. North from Thielsen Camp, Forest Rd. 2610 to Lemolo Lake stays within a mile of the creek, though the creek runs through a deep canyon there.

The upper end of the creek near Diamond Lake has been known to support good size rainbows to 2 pounds in the years before the tui chub population explosion. The beaver flats below yield more brown and brook trout in a series of pools. Hardy anglers might like to try a 2-day hike-and-fish along the creek from Diamond Lake to Lemolo for the chance of a catch worth bragging about, especially in fall.

There are camping facilities and supplies at Diamond and Lemolo lakes, with additional camping at Thielsen Campground.

LAKE IN THE WOODS.
A small, accessible lake in the Umpqua National Forest due east of Roseburg. Take the North Umpqua Rd. to Glide, and the Little River Rd., Forest Rd. 27, to the lake. It's about 24 miles from Glide.

At elevation 3000 ft., Lake in the Woods is snow-free early in the season. Only about 4 acres, it provides fine fishing for rainbows averaging 10 inches, but trout to 19 inches have been caught. The biggest fish respond to bait, but fly casting can be effective. It is easily fished from shore. Motor boats are not allowed.

Camp sites on the lakeshore are nice for those who get the view spots, but the round-up of RV's on the bank detracts somewhat from the overall aesthetics of the place.

LAKE MARIE.
A 5-acre rainbow lake within Umpqua Lighthouse State Park, about 2 miles south of Winchester Bay off Hwy. 101. There's fair fishing for cutthroat early in the season, and fly anglers do well. The lake is stocked with hatchery trout. Largemouth bass and yellow perch are also present.

There is no boat ramp, and motor boats are prohibited. The state park has picnic and camping facilities.

LEMOLO LAKE.
The largest reservoir in the upper North Umpqua power development, with 415 surface acres when full. Lemolo is lightly fished, probably because it is positioned between popular Diamond Lake and Toketee Reservoir. It's a scenic spot, situated among the pines with Mt. Thielsen looming above and lots of browns and kokanee below.

From Diamond Lake, take Hwy. 138 north about 7 miles to Forest Rd. 2610, which leads north about 5 miles to the reservoir. From Roseburg, Forest Rd. 2610 is about 80 miles east by way of Hwy. 138.

There's fair angling for brown trout from opening day through fall. Angling success usually falls off during midsummer. Draw-down in the fall reduces the pool to about 140 acres and severely limits angler success.

This reservoir is currently managed for wild brown trout. The typical catch averages 12 inches, and much larger fish are present. A few monster browns to 15 lbs. have been taken, and there are rumors of much larger fish. It takes a substantial lure to interest these big old carnivores. Look for browns in the North Umpqua and Lake Creek arms in early season, and off East Lemolo Campground.

Kokanee are also present, but few anglers seem to take advantage of the availability of these tasty landlocked salmon. There's a good opportunity to view them in their spawning colors mid-September to mid-October in crystal clear Spring River. Brook trout to 12 inches and a few rainbows are found near the dam and inlet.

Boat and bank anglers do equally well till June, when boats are needed to get to the best fishing. Float tubes are handy in the inlet areas, and fly fishing is very popular here. There are boat ramps at Poole Creek Campground and at the resort, and boats can be slid into the lake at East Lemolo Campground. There are speed restrictions associated with Poole Creek Inlet. Check the current boating regulations for specifics.

There are four campgrounds on the Lake, and the Forest Service maintains a group campsite at Poole Creek, which is available by reservation. A resort at the northwest end of the lake south of the dam includes a lodge, groceries, tackle shop, dining room, cabins, boat and motor rentals, and a service station. Lemolo is not open for ice fishing as it is heavily drawn down in winter.

LIBBY POND.
A 10-acre trout pond with opportunities for trophy fish, about 7 miles east of Gold Beach near the south bank of the Rogue River off County Rd. 595.

The lake is stocked with legal trout in spring as well as a good number of over-size trout grown especially for this fishery. An annual Free Fishing Day Derby is a popular family attraction. Brown bullhead are also available, but most fishing is for the trout.

Libby offers good bank access, but small boats and float tubes are handy. Best fishing is earlier in season, since the lake warms in summer. Recommended for youngsters.

LITTLE APPLEGATE RIVER. An important tributary of the Applegate River, entering the river about 3 miles south of Ruch. It is closed to all angling at this time.

LITTLE BUTTE CREEK. One of the few tributaries of the Rogue River open to trout fishing. It enters the Rogue from the east about a mile upstream of Tou Velle State Park. To reach the creek from Medford, follow Hwy. 62 north, then Hwy. 140 (Lake of the Woods Hwy.) east. Hwy. 140 crosses the creek near Brownsboro and follows it about 6 miles. Turn right on Lake Creek Loop Rd. to reach the South Fork Little Butte Rd which follows the fork into its headwaters. Continue east on Hwy. 140 to access North Fork Little Butte Creek.

North Fork Little Butte drains Fish Lake, and best public access is just downstream from the lake's outlet, where there are lots of brook trout. There's good hike-in access to the headwaters of South Fork Little Butte in the National Forest off Dead Indian Memorial Rd. Fishing is catch and release only for rainbows and cutthroat, but there is no limit on brook trout.

LITTLE HYATT LAKE. A pretty little 5-acre lake on BLM property south of Hyatt Prairie Reservoir. From the reservoir, head south on Old Hyatt Prairie Rd., or drive north on Greensprings Hwy. 66. Meadows on the east and north shores allow good bank access. The west bank is forested. The lake is stocked with fingerling rainbows and has largemouth bass, brown bullhead, and crappie. There are no developed camps at the lake.

LITTLE RIVER. A tributary of the North Umpqua, joining the North Umpqua at Glide, about 20 miles east of Roseburg on Hwy. 138. It is followed east from Glide by paved road for about 15 miles, and by grav-

el road another 15 miles to the headwaters.

The river has resident cutthroat as well as runs of summer steelhead and fall chinook. At this time, the river is closed to all angling due to Endangered Species Act concerns. Check current regulations.

LOON LAKE. A large, deep lake draining into the lower Umpqua River. Loon Lake offers good angling for trout in spring and fall, and fair angling for largemouth bass throughout the season. From Hwy. 38 (Reedsport to Darwin), a county road leads south about 6 miles to the lake. The turn onto this road is about 3 miles west of Scottsburg. Driving south on I-5, take the Drain Exit. The lake can also be reached from Coos Bay by very poor roads up the Millicoma River.

Loon Lake is 2 miles long with 275 surface acres and is very deep with little shoal area. Stocked rainbow trout may be kept for the pan, but wild cutthroat, present in good numbers, must be released unharmed. Rainbow trout are generally available for several months into the season, with catches to 18 inches.

Largemouth black bass provide fair angling. Look for them along the south shore's rocky cliff and among the boulders and root wads at the west end in about 8 feet of water. Bass to 8 pounds are caught by anglers casting lures, plugs and bait. The average bass is 2 to 4 pounds. Crappie to 12 inches and brown bullhead to 16 inches are available in fair numbers. Nice size bluegill

are also present. If you see a large shadow slip beneath your boat, or feel like you've hooked a freight train, it's probably one of the large sturgeon that have startled more than one unsuspecting angler.

There are two resorts on the lake where angling information and supplies can be obtained. Boats and motors are available. Loon Lake Recreation Site, an excellent BLM campground and boat ramp, is at the north end of the lake south of the outlet crossing. The area is well protected from the wind, with pleasant sandy beaches and a wheelchair accessible dock. Camping and overnight accommodations are available at Loon Lake Resort. There are several picnic areas nearby on Hwy. 38. Recommended for youngsters. Wheelchair accessible.

LOST CREEK Reservoir

A 3,500-acre reservoir on the Rogue River, fished primarily for smallmouth bass and stocked trout. Lost Creek is at r.m. 157 just upstream from Cole Rivers Hatchery. Bluegill, bullhead, crappie, and sunfish are also available, as well as landlocked chinook. The reservoir is open year-round.

Located about 30 miles northwest of Medford on Hwy. 62, it was built for flood control and to enhance downstream water flow for salmon and steelhead. First filled in 1977, it has a maximum depth of 322 ft. with very little shallows.

Smallmouth bass are a big fishery here. Fish for them along the dam and in rocky

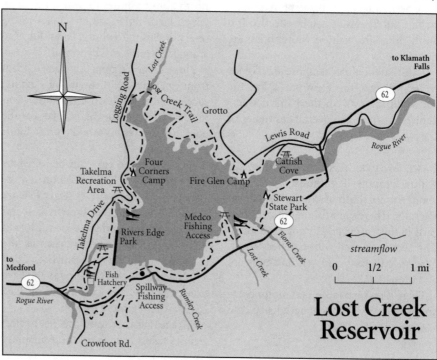

Lost Creek Reservoir

areas, such as the outcrops near the resort swimming area and in the shallows among the willows along the southwest shore.

Largemouth to 5 pounds are fewer in number than in days gone by due to competition from the smallmouth. Still, those that remain tend to be big. In the spring, anglers work the shoal areas on the south side of the reservoir, and the willowy areas of the north shore's shallow coves. The north shore warms first, attracting bait fish that draw the attention of larger bass. Later in the season when the reservoir warms, the mouths of tributary streams on the south shore are productive. Good catches are also made above the highway bridge where there is a lot of submerged structure and off the dam face. Bass fishing has been best when the reservoir is holding maximum water.

Lost Creek is stocked annually with 90,000 legal and fingerling rainbow trout, which grow to 16 inches. It also has wild populations of cutthroat and brown trout. A 24-inch brown was caught here in 1999.

Still-fishing is limited to a few shoal areas. Trolling with spinner and worm or lures works most consistently, particularly at the upper end at the junction of north and south forks. Other good trolling areas are along the dam and around the point of the island. Bank anglers fish beside the spillway, along the dam face, and in the cove off Takelma Drive. Cold sunny days in December, January, and February can produce surprisingly good catches on a troll here.

Chinook fingerlings are also stocked and reach 16 inches. Troll deep for the chinook. Bluegill, crappie, pumpkinseed sunfish, and bullhead also provide good fishing.

There's camping at Stewart State Park on the south shore, and boat ramps in Stewart Park and near the north abutment of the dam. There is a 5 mph speed limit in the Rogue River Arm above Peyton Bridge, and in the Lost Creek arm above the narrows. A privately run moorage within the state park rents boats and has some supplies. Supplies are also available in Prospect, Shady Cove, and Trail on Hwy. 62.

LOST LAKE (Umpqua watershed). An 8 to 10 acre beaver pond in the Callahan Mountains near the town of Umpqua, with fine fly fishing for wild cutthroat. Take the Hubbard Creek Rd. from Umpqua into the mountains, following the ridge crest.

Take the first road on the right, and at about 100 yds., turn left to the creek. As you cross the creek, a trail leads off to the left about 300 yds. to the lake. Good luck!

LOST LAKE (Rogue watershed). A 10-acre lake at the head of Little Butte Creek, stocked by air with rainbow and brook trout. The lake is in the vicinity of the Lake Creek Rd., off un-named Medco and BLM roads. Check with the district ODFW office in Central Point for directions.

LUCILLE LAKE. An 8-acre hike-in lake in the Umpqua National Forest about 8 miles west of Lemolo Lake, ½ mile due west of Maidu Lake. The lake has very little cover and has consistently winterkilled. It is no longer stocked.

MAIDU LAKE. A good brook trout lake in the headwaters of the North Umpqua off the Pacific Crest Trail. It's an 8-mile hike from Forest Rd. 958 west of the Bradley Creek Arm of Lemolo. A shorter hike begins at Miller Lake in the Winema National Forest. Take Trail 1446 (which follows the north shore of Miller) up to the Pacific Crest Trail. It's about one mile to this junction, and less then a mile farther northwest to Maidu.

At 20 acres, Maidu has good size brook trout to 16 inches, with a few larger. Any method takes fish, but fly fishing really pays off in the evening. The resident population is supplemented by fingerlings brought in annually by volunteers on horseback. The lake is usually accessible in late June.

MATSON CREEK. A good little trout stream with wild cutthroat, about 10 miles long, tributary to the East Fork Millicoma River. Matson joins the east fork about 10 miles east of Allegany, which is about 10 miles east of Coos Bay. Roads here are primitive logging tracks. This is Weyerhaeuser timber country and access is limited. There are several high falls in the upper stream and real rough going.

The upper stream offers good catch and release fishing for small wild cutthroat. This is a good beginner's stream, with the opportunity to catch and release 30 to 40 small fish per day. Some 11- and 12-inchers are also available.

MEDCO POND. An old 70-acre log pond between Prospect and Butte Falls, on the

Prospect-Butte Falls Hwy. northeast of Medford. From Medford, follow Hwy. 62 east to the Butte Falls Hwy. Follow this past Butte Falls to the junction with Prospect Road. Head north 15 miles. The lake is on the east side of the road.

Medco is owned by a private timber company which allows public use. It is stocked with legal rainbows and has a good population of bass and bluegill. The bass run to 5 pounds and bluegill to 8 inches. A popular Free Fishing Day event takes place here annually.

MIDDLE LAKE. (Seven Lakes Basin) A good fly fishing lake in the Sky Lakes Wilderness, accessible from east or west. For directions, see Grass Lake, Alta Lake. Middle Lake is between Grass and Cliff lakes, less than ¼-mile from each.

Middle Lake is stocked in odd years with fingerlings and has wild brook trout. The fish run to 16 inches and better, and angling holds up well all season. The west end seems to offer best fishing. Try wet bucktails and streamers in the morning and evening. There are good campsites here, as at other lakes in the basin.

MILLICOMA RIVER (North Fork of Coos River). A major tributary of the Coos River, with a large run of shad, good angling for fall chinook, and substantial numbers of both hatchery and wild winter steelhead. The main river is only about 7 or 8 miles long from Allegany to its confluence with the Coos. Above Allegany (which is head of tide) the river splits into East and West Forks. Access is by paved county roads off Hwy. 101 near Coos Bay.

Shad fishing is excellent at times, with best fishing in May and June. Best shad catches seem to be around the mid-section of the river near the tavern, especially on hot, sunny afternoons. It's a pretty stream and a nice place to spend a summer day.

Anglers troll for fall chinook in September, October and November. The average year sees a couple-hundred salmon landed. The river is closed to coho fishing. Most of the good steelhead angling takes place in the upper forks from December through March, with peak hook-ups from late December to mid-February. Good numbers of finclipped hatchery steelhead are available for harvest.

Searun cutthroat are present from August through October and may be fished catch and release.

Boats can be launched at Doras Ramp, ¼ mile upstream from the confluence and at Rooke Higgins, a facility with plenty of parking about 3 miles farther upstream.

MILLICOMA RIVER, EAST FORK.
A nice size stream with a good run of fin-clipped winter steelhead and plentiful cutthroat trout. About 25 miles long, it joins the main river at Allegany, about 10 miles east of Coos Bay. A road follows the East Fork another 10 miles, with logging roads branching off to follow its tributaries.

In these times of dwindling cutthroat numbers, the East Fork Millicoma maintains a healthy resident cutthroat population. Best fishing (catch and release only at this time) is in early season. Glen Creek, joining from the east about 6 miles upstream, is also productive for cutthroat.

Winter steelhead, primarily finclipped, are picked up in good numbers from December through February. The East Fork receives the largest number of steelhead smolts in the Coos watershed.

MILLICOMA RIVER, WEST FORK.
A very good hatchery steelhead stream with good catch and release fishing for cutthroat in its headwaters. About 30 miles long, it joins the mainstem Millicoma at head of tidewater at Allegany. Allegany is about 10 miles east of Coos Bay on the Coos River Hwy. east from Hwy. 101. The West Fork Millicoma Rd. follows the fork north out of Allegany to Stalls Falls. A network of logging roads approach its headwaters in Elliot State Forest.

The upper stream flowing through Elliott State Forest can offer very good catch and release fishing for wild cutthroat, especially in the vicinity of Elkhorn Ranch, an old homestead incorporated within state lands. This is a beautiful reach of the river, with deep pools that offer year-round shelter for resident cutts when the Millicoma gets low in summer. The Elkhorn reach is accessible to motor vehicles by way of a network of rough roads. Use an Elliott State Forest map (available at State Forest Headquarters in Coos Bay) to make your way through the maze. There are no signs identifying the Elkhorn area, so you'll need to ask around or do some exploring. Best fishing is in May and June before the river gets low.

About 35,000 steelhead smolts are re-

leased annually from the hatchery near Mile Post 9, providing good returns in the vicinity of the hatchery. The run hits its stride in December and holds through February. The West Fork has a high steelheader success rate for a small stream.

Bank access is limited along the lower river due to private property, but only a few experienced boaters float the river. Boats can be launched at the county bridge, 5½ miles upstream from the confluence, but this is definitely not novice water. There are many rapids between the put-in and Rooke Higgins, the nearest public take-out on the mainstem. Most anglers get permission to take-out on private property mid-way through the drift.

The steelhead hatchery about 9 miles above Allegany is the site of a popular steelheading bank fishery from December through February. An interpretive center at the hatchery is open to the public. It includes a rearing pond with an underwater viewing window. Best viewing is October through May. Educational programs for groups can be arranged by calling the ODFW office in Charleston. This facility is recommended for youngsters.

MYRTLE CREEK (Umpqua watershed).
A tributary of the South Umpqua, actually two forks, each about 20 miles long, entering the South Umpqua at the town of Myrtle Creek on Hwy. 99. At this time the stream is closed to all angling due to Endangered Species Act concerns. Check current regulations for a possible relaxation of trout fishing restrictions.

Salmon and steelhead enter Myrtle Creek for spawning and may be observed but should not be disturbed.

MUD LAKE.
A 3-acre lake in the Blue Lake Group, situated between Blue and Beale. Though it is not stocked, it has a naturally reproducing population of brook trout.

NATIONAL CREEK.
A small but scenic tributary of the upper Rogue with stocked trout available for harvest. It enters the Rogue west of Crater Lake National Park about 4 miles north of the junction of highways 62 and 230. About 5 miles north of the junction on Hwy. 230, take Forest Rd. 6530 to the right. This road follows the stream for most of its 5-mile length. National offers fair early season fishing for brook trout and rainbows, with best fish-

ing in June. Union Creek Campground, south of the Hwy. 62/230 junction, is a popularcamping spot beside the Rogue Gorge.

NEW RIVER.
The short but interesting outlet stream for Floras Lake, with fishing for wild chinook and catch and release opportunities for steelhead and cutthroat. The stream runs north about 8 miles from Floras Lake, parallel to the Pacific and separated from the surf by dunes. New River has been known to breach the dunes in different places from year to year, changing the location of its mouth. The outlet appears to be moving north, and at this time there is public access to the river mouth through a site purchased by BLM at Storm Ranch. The Storm Ranch access is off Croft Rd. north of the Curry/Coos County line between Langlois and Bandon.

New River offers pretty good chinook bank angling from September through October. A fair run of wild winter steelhead enters in December and may be fished catch and release. Searun cutthroat are in the river from July through fall, also available for catch and release angling. The river is closed to coho angling.There's excellent surfperch fishing adjacent to the mouth.

Boats can be launched at the Floras Lake outlet for a pleasant float to the BLM access site. Be warned that it can get windy, turning this into a longer drift than anticipated. Motors are not allowed.

The BLM has large holdings along the stream and is trying to preserve the natural scenic values of the sand dunes as well as protect the nesting sites of snowy plovers. Be particularly careful to avoid plover nests in the vicinity of Storm Ranch.

PEAR LAKE.
A good brook trout lake in the Blue Lake group of the southern Sky Lakes Wilderness. A long narrow lake, it is just east of Horseshoe Lake on Trail 982. See Blue Lake for complete directions from the west. It's a 4-mile hike, past Blue and Horseshoe lakes, to Pear.

To access the basin from the east, take Hwy. 140 (Lake of the Woods Rd.) to Forest Rd. 3651. The junction is about 6 miles northeast of Lake of the Woods and 4 miles west of the junction of highways 140 and 62 near Upper Klamath Lake. Turn left on Forest Rd. 3659 toward Big Meadows about 1½ miles north of the junction of forest roads 3651 and 3458. Trailhead 3712 is at the apex of the hairpin curve on Forest Rd. 3659. Follow Trail 3712, which crosses over the Pacific Crest Trail after about a mile, and continues to the basin. At the next fork, follow Trail 982 southwest around the south end of Island Lake to Pear. It's less than a 4-mile hike to Pear.

Stocked with fingerlings in odd-number years (suggesting best catches in even-numbers), this 25-acre lake supports a good population of brook trout to 14 inches. Catches are good in spring and fall. During the day, fish the deep water in the north end. In the evening the fish school and feed in the shallower southern end of the lake. A float tube or rubber raft would come in handy. Pear is usually accessible in early June.

PISTOL RIVER. A short south coast stream, with fall chinook and a small winter steelhead run. It flows into the Pacific about 15 miles south of Gold Beach and is crossed near the mouth by Hwy. 101. Only 20 miles long, it is followed east by a good road about 8 miles upstream from its mouth. Above that the only access is by logging roads or trails. Most of the river is bordered by private timber land. Get permission before you cross private land.

The Pistol's chinook population has been modestly increasing in recent years, and fishing has resumed on a limited basis downstream from Deep Creek. Check the regulations. Steelhead in the river are all wild and must be fished catch and release.

Very little trout fishing takes place here, but searun cutthroat enter when the bar is breached in September or October. The Pistol mouth is bar-bound in the summer, and returning cutthroat are held out until late August or September most years. Check with the ODFW office at Gold Beach for an update.

Fish habitat in the Pistol has been hard hit by logging operations in the watershed. The river flows through an area of unstable gravel that is particularly vulnerable. Spawning gravel has been badly scoured, and holding areas have filled in. Rehabilitation work continues.

PLAT I RESERVOIR. A very productive 140-acre lake, 4 miles east of Sutherlin off the Plat I (as in "eye") Rd. Built for flood control and irrigation in the late '60s, it supports good populations of rainbows, crappies, bluegills, largemouth bass, and lots of brown bullheads.

Flooded willows on the upper end of the reservoir away from the dam offer good warmwater habitat accessible to boat anglers. Anglers can walk to the end of the road to the pasture fence and launch a float tube at that point to reach brushy habitat on the north side. A shallow bay and peninsula at the upper end are also productive.

Water levels drop during the summer, and the reservoir is heavily drawn down in winter, calling a halt to bass fishing from November through February. Spring and early summer are the best times to fish. Bass to 6 pounds are common. Plastic worms, nightcrawlers, and streamer flies are all effective. The reservoir is stocked with catchable rainbows through Free Fishing Day in June.

There is a good boat ramp, but you'll need a light boat with a short shaft motor to get into the shallows where the bass tend to lurk. There are no campsites at the lake. There's a 10 mph speed limit on the lake before 11 a.m. and after 6 p.m. Recommended for youngsters.

POWERS POND. An old mill pond at the edge of the Coquille River near the community of Powers, about 21 miles upstream from Myrtle Point. It was purchased by the county for fishing and recreation.

Surrounded by manicured grounds, it has about 10 surface acres. During high water winters, it can be incorporated into the river.

The lake is heavily stocked with legal rainbows and trophy-size trout (about 16,000 in 1999) and has largemouth bass, black crappie, and brown bullhead. Best fishing is in spring before the water warms and the park gets crowded.

The pond offers good swimming, and the park has RV facilities, showers, and a picnic area. Recommended for youngsters.

ROCK CREEK (Umpqua watershed). A wild cutthroat stream, flowing 20 miles to the North Umpqua. The creek enters the river from the north about 27 miles east of Roseburg. It is closed to all angling due to concern for Umpqua basin cutthroat in compliance with the Endangered Species Act. Umpqua basin cutthroat are scheduled for review by the National Marine Fisheries Service. Check current regulations for a possible relaxation of restrictions.

Rogue River

ROGUE RIVER: Bay. A narrow estuary with a difficult bar crossing that serves primarily as a point of access to the lower Rogue River's outstanding chinook and steelhead fisheries. Gold Beach is the major port town. Questionable secondary roads connect I-5 with the lower Rogue valley at Agness. Best direct routes are Hwy. 42 west from Roseburg and Hwy. 199 from Grants Pass. A dramatic but somewhat slower approach can be made by following Hwy. 101 from north or south. From Portland, it's a little more than 300 miles to Gold Beach. Allow at least 6 hours for the trip.

The Rogue River bar is not an easy one to cross and is only occasionally safe for small boats. Check with the local Coast Guard substation at Doyle Point. When the bar is calm, it provides access to good bottom fishing associated with the Rogue River Reef 2 to 3 miles out.

Spring chinook enter the bay in late March, but the major fishery for them begins up-bay, from Elephant Rock to head of tide at The Clay Banks. Peak catches are in May. By July, all the springers have moved through the bay and into the river.

Fall chinook first enter the bay in July, and fishing for them usually picks up in August. Anglers troll or mooch herring and anchovies above and below the Hwy. 101 bridge. A few are caught off the north jetty, and there is a good bank fishery for them on the sand spit near the south jetty. Popular spots are below Elephant Rock, at Johns Hole in the lower river, and at the Ferry Hole above The Clay Banks. The Clay Bank is a popular gravel bar access. Boat anglers form hog lines (boats anchored side by side) to fish for chinook at the upper end just below the riffle. Fly anglers fish the lower end.

Summer steelhead hit the bay in good numbers in late July, and winter steelhead in November, but angling for them takes place upriver.

Perch and the occasional lingcod are caught off the north jetty in spring, and crab are available. Best crab catches are downstream from Doyle Point. Avoid setting pots in the channel.

Boats can be launched on the south side of the bay at the Port Commission Ramp in Gold Beach below the Hwy. 101 bridge. Boats and equipment are available for rent nearby. About 3½ miles upstream, small

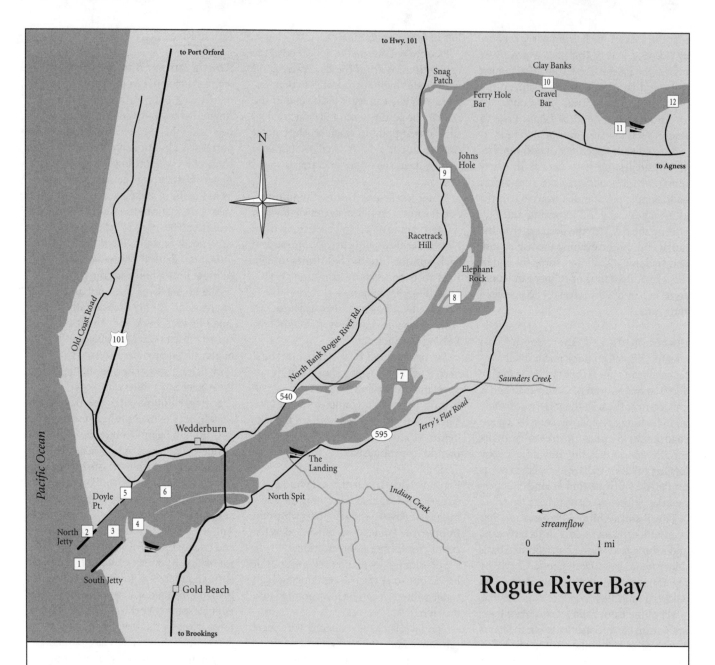

Rogue River Bay

1. Rogue Reef Access. Calm days only; excellent bottom fishing 2-3 miles out.

2. North Jetty. Preferred to south jetty for lingcod, perch in spring, chinook July through Sept.

3. Crab. productive crabbing; avoiding setting pots in channel.

4. Sand Spit. Bank fishery for fall chinook July through Sept.; use spinners, herring, anchovy.

5. Doyle Point. Best Dungeness crabbing in bay.

6. North Side of Channel. Troll up to The Landing for fall chinook.

7. Woodruff Riffle. First riffle heading upstream; troll for fall chinook.

8. Elephant Rock. Chinook hole three quarters of a mile down-bay from rock.

9. Johns Hole. Rocky point creates chinook hole; spring and fall.

10. Clay Banks. Gravel bar access to fly fish for chinook at lower end; hog line plunkers at upper bar just below riffle.

11. Ferry Hole. Drive onto gravel bar to launch drift boats and prams for chinook.

12. Willows. Bank fishery for winter steelhead and spring chinook; unsigned gravel access road.

boats can be slipped into the river at the Mill gravel bar on the south bank directly across from Ferry Hole. There is a developed ramp on the north bank at the Ferry Hole, but it has limited parking space. Larger boats can be launched at Canfield Riffle, 15 miles further up County Rd. 540. Private ramps with public access are numerous in the Gold Beach area, including Huntley Park about 6 miles upstream on the south bank. The lower river is broad and provides easy boating.

Restaurants, motels, RV parks, and full-service resorts are plentiful in the Gold Beach/Wedderburn area. The nearest public coastal campground is about 20 miles north at Humbug Mt. State Park, but there's a large campground at Huntley Park, and there are Forest Service campgrounds upstream at Lobster Creek and Quosatana (pronounced *kwo-sate-na*).

ROGUE RIVER: Grave Creek to Head of Tide. An extremely productive 60-mile segment of the Rogue, more than half of which is designated Wild and Scenic and accessible only by boat or foot trail. Anglers fish this portion of the Rogue primarily for spring and fall chinook, summer and winter steelhead, half-pounders (immature summer steelhead), and finclipped coho. Challenging terrain helps maintain outstanding angling here year-round. Road access is limited to the stretch from tidewater up to Foster Bar, just above the settlement of Ilahee, about 27 river miles.

The Rogue hosts several distinct populations of chinook, including a run bound for the Applegate, one that heads for lower river tributaries, and one that continues into the upper river. Best fishing for chinook is from April through October. Peak catches in this portion of the river are in April and May (with good fishing through June if the water stays cool) and again in August and September. Most anglers plunk bait (anchovies or herring), or fish spinners, or spinner and bait combinations.

These runs have been declining since the early 1980s, and special regulations are in effect. In 1999, there was a fishery for wild chinook below the Illinois confluence for the first time in many years. Above the Illinois, the river has remained open to chinook fishing year-round. Check the regulations for current harvest opportunities and be aware that fishing opportunities can change mid-season. A call to the dis-

Chinook are in the ROGUE from April through October. Photograph by Scott Richmond.

trict ODFW office in Gold Beach is a good idea before planning a trip.

The Rogue River coho population is stable, though diminished from historical numbers, and fishing for finclipped coho has been permitted here when other coho fisheries throughout Oregon have been closed. Check for emergency closures before fishing, however. Coho enter the river in August with peak catches in October.

Rogue River steelhead are doing fairly well at this time in comparison with their north coast cousins, perhaps because of localized ocean conditions or good habitat. Steelhead of one population or another are in the river throughout the year, but most catches are made from September through February, with greatest numbers hooked in January and February. In 1999, this section of the Rogue was one of the few flowing waters in Oregon where anglers were allowed to harvest wild steelhead (winter run only). In other years, depending on returns, all steelhead may be restricted to finclipped fish. Check current regulations.

Half-pounders (immature summer steelhead that return to the river after less than a year at sea) are one of the Rogue's unique sportfishing delights. In late summer and early fall, these small steelhead enter the Rogue from the ocean by the tens of thousands. Traveling in schools, they move relatively quickly through the river below Agness. By September and October, half-pounders are behaving more like resident trout, lingering in one spot longer and making themselves at home in their

wintering grounds. A good number remain throughout the winter from the Illinois confluence upstream to Foster Bar. Others move in the canyon or upstream as far as Galice (most years) or the Applegate (some years).

For regulatory purposes, half-pounders are considered to be trout, and no steelhead tag is required to fish for them. Wild half-pounders must be released unharmed, but 30 to 50 per cent of the run is usually finclipped and available for harvest. Half-pounders are known for their aggressive spirit and are caught using many techniques. Check regulations for hook and bait restrictions. Though not required at this time, single-point barbless hooks make release of these large wild fish less stressful for both the catcher and the caught. This is a wonderful fishery for fly angling, since half-pounders feed like residents. Try nymph imitations on either a sink-tip or floating line. Half-pounders will even take dry flies when a hatch is on.

In recent years there has been an increase in the number of pike minnows (squawfish) throughout the river. Pike minnows compete for limited forage and habitat with juvenile steelhead and salmon. Though there is no "cash redemption" program for them here, as in the Columbia River, anglers are urged to catch and destroy as many as possible.

From Grave Creek down to Foster Bar, the Rogue is bounded on all sides by the Wild Rogue Wilderness. This section contains a string of superior riffles and bars,

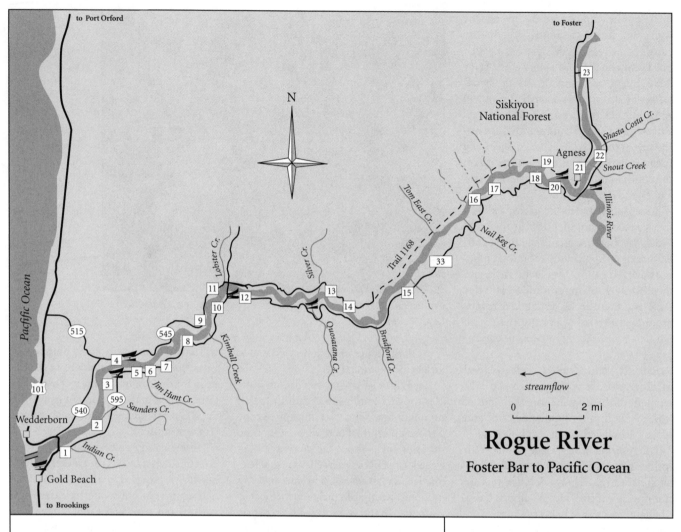

to Port Orford

to Foster

N

Pacific Ocean

Siskiyou
National Forest

Agness

23
22
19
21
17
16
18
20
33
15
14
13
11
12
10
9
8
4
7
5 **6**
3
515
545
101
540
595
2
1

Shasta Costa Cr.
Snout Creek
Illinois River
Tom East Cr.
Nail Keg Cr.
Bradford Cr.
Quosatana Cr.
Silver Cr.
Lobster Cr.
Kimball Creek
Jim Hunt Cr.
Saunders Cr.
Indian Cr.

Wedderborn

Gold Beach

to Brookings

streamflow

0   1   2 mi

Rogue River
Foster Bar to Pacific Ocean

1. *Indian Creek Park.*

2. *Elephant Rock.* .

3. *Champion Mill.*

4. *Claybanks.*

5. *Ferry Hole.*

6. *The Willows.*

7. *Coyote Riffle.*

8. *Huntley Bar and Park.*

9. *Kimball Riffle.*

10. *Orchard Bar.*

11. *Jim Davis Riffle.*

12. *Lobster Creek Boat Ramp.*

13. *Quosatana Campground.*

14. *Big Fish Riffle.*

15. *Rachel's Delight.*

16. *Bear Riffle.*

17. *Copper Canyon.*

18. *Crooked Riffle.*

19. *Hotel Riffle.*

20. *Hog Eddy.*

21. *Shasta Costa Riffle.*

22. *Coon Rock.*

23. *Walker Riffle.*

most of which are popularly named. A riffle on the Rogue is a place where the river drops, usually in the presence of big boulders. The result is water that is both fast and white. Below a riffle, the tail-out offers good holding water for salmon and steel-head as they pause before the upstream challenge. Above the riffle is the head and pool, where salmon and steelhead linger for a little R&R before their next effort. Some anglers use an anchor on a quick-release pulley to stop mid-stream in order to fish the waters at the head of a riffle. Experienced rowers can hold a driftboat in the water at the head of a riffle while passengers fish the head and pool.

Some anglers reach this stretch of the Rogue by jet boat from the lower river, but jet sleds are only allowed as far as Blossom Bar, about 15 miles above Foster Bar. This provides access to a handful of back-country lodges, including those at Marial, Paradise Bar, Half Moon Bar, and Clay Hill. A five-day drift from Grave Creek to Foster Bar often includes a stop at Black Bar Lodge, about half-way between Grave Creek and Marial. These lodges primarily support guided steelhead trips from August through October. Summer steelhead are the most popular fishery in this stretch.

A hiking trail on the north bank from Grave Creek downstream to Illahe offers many angling opportunities, climbing high above the river in the canyons, but dropping down to riverside at the bars. The section most popular with anglers is the 2-mile trek from Grave Creek to Rainie Falls, where salmon and steelhead hold for long periods. Many anglers also hike the additional mile to Whiskey Creek. There is an unmaintained trail on the south bank from Grave Creek to Rainie. At Rainie Falls, anglers can find spring chinook, steelhead, fall chinook and shad. Rainie is the end of the line for shad, which reach the falls about July 4.

To reach Grave Creek from I-5 north of Grants Pass, take the Merlin Exit to the Merlin-Galice Rd. Grave Creek is about 7 miles north of Galice.

Access to the other end of the wilderness trail and to the lower Rogue begins at Gold Beach on the coast. Follow County Rd. 595 from the south end of the Hwy. 101 bridge across the estuary. This road becomes Forest Rd. 33. It parallels the river's south bank closely for about 17 miles, then pulls back from the river through a deep canyon stretch known as Copper Canyon, crossing the mainstem Rogue about 3 miles above the confluence of the Illinois River. This bridge is known locally as Coon Rock Bridge. The trailhead at Illahe is about 7 miles further upstream at Illahe Campground. The little community of Agness is on the north bank, back downstream at the Illinois confluence.

Between tidewater and the bridge, the south bank road offers a number of access points. Indian Creek Park a mile upstream from Hwy. 101, has a campground but doesn't access good fishing water. The first good fishing access is at the popular Ferry Hole about 3 miles upstream. You can fish from the gravel bar at Ferry Hole, or launch a boat at the developed ramp there. You can also launch a boat off the Old Mill gravel bar across from the Ferry Hole, or at Huntley Park, about 2 miles above tidewater. From these points, anglers drift down to fish Coyote Riffle or the Ferry Hole. Huntley also provides a half-mile gravel bar from which bank casters fish for chinook and steelhead.

There's an improved ramp at Lobster Creek, about 3 miles farther upstream off the south bank road, which also offers excellent bank access to good water.

Quosatana Campground (pronounced Kwo-sate-na) offers good bank fishing and has a paved ramp popular as a jet boat access to the Copper Canyon fisheries halfway to Agness. Steep, rough tracks lead down to the water both upstream and down from Quosatana. Look for pull-outs

(little more than wide spots in the road). Cole Riffle, about 3 miles above Quosatana, has excellent fly fishing water. A trail leads down to the Cole Riffle at mile post 17. About seven miles above Quosatana the road is carved out of the canyon wall, and there is no further bank access until the Illinois crossing.

About ¼ mile below the Illinois confluence, the Hotel Riffle offers good bank fishing and especially good fly water. Above, you can launch a boat from the camp at Hog Eddy, with permission from Cougar Lane Store. Both the Hotel Riffle and Hog Eddy are especially good steelhead spots. About two miles above the Illinois, Shasta Costa Riffles offer a challenge. Shasta Costa (upper and lower) is just above Cougar Lane Lodge. There is a pull-off and a short (steep) trail down to the riffles. Upper Shasta Costa is considerably more challenging than Lower.

About ½ mile above Coon Rock Bridge, Walker Riffle generally holds steelhead during the prime season (August, September, and October). Walker is ribbonned with bedrock and offers treacherous wading. Use a cut pole or wading staff to avoid slipping into the river.

Foster Bar is about three miles above Walker. It has an improved boat ramp and access to very good steelhead water. Boats with small motors drift down to the next riffle, then fish their way back up to Foster several times in a day. Foster Bar to Quosatana is a popular long day drift for winter steelhead. At low water, be advised that

Two-mile Riffle (about 2½ miles below Foster Bar) is Class 4 whitewater, for experienced boaters only.

Below Agness, access to the north bank of the Rogue (except by boat) is pretty much restricted to the lower 10 miles. County Rd. 540 heads up the north bank from the north end of the Hwy. 101 bridge at Wedderburn. Pull-outs along the road generally indicate popular fishing spots. The north bank accesses some good water, including the Ferry Hole, Kimball Riffle, and Coyote. You can launch a boat from the old concrete ferry ramp (at high water only) or off the gravel bar at Coyote.

A bridge across the river at Lobster Creek (about 10 miles upstream) connects north and south bank roads. The north bank road continues across Lobster Creek, though it has been known to wash out after a hard winter. Dunkelburger Bar Access is off the north bank road about 3 miles upstream from Lobster Creek. There is good bank access at Dunkelburger for spring chinook and steelhead.

About 7 miles beyond Dunkelburger, the north bank road ends near Trailhead 1168 which leads to Agness, a 10-mile hike upstream. Unlike the upriver trail from Graves Creek to Illahe, this trail is suited more to scenic enjoyment than to angling. Though well maintained, it remains high above the river and is cursed with rampant poison oak off-trail.

Below Agness, the Rogue is suitable for novice river boaters. Above, even experienced boaters would benefit from follow-

Most Rogue River steelhead are caught from September through February. Photograph by Scott Richmond

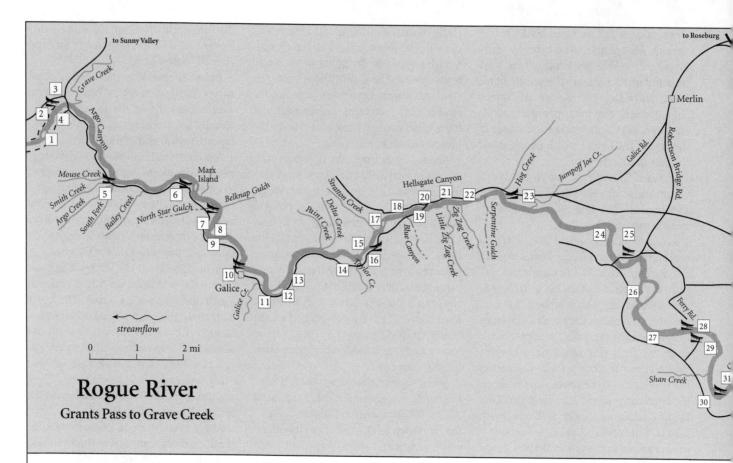

Rogue River

Grants Pass to Grave Creek

1. Pierce Riffle. (not Tom Pierce Park). Paved ramp; nature trail; good salmon and steelhead water upstream.

2. Chinook Park. Paved boat ramp with handicapped fishing dock and amenities; access to good steelhead water; walk up to fish Green Cr. Riffle.

3. Baker Park. Gravel bar launch; chinook and steelhead hole under bridge.

4. Tussy Park. Bank fishing at county park.

5. Schroeder Park. Paved boat ramp, camping, handicapped fishing platform and bank access to salmon and steelhead.

6. White Rocks. Undeveloped access; fish from the rocks.

7. Lathrop Landing. Paved ramp, a few rocks to fish from.

8. Whitehorse Riffle. Upper boundary for Wild and Scenic Rogue.

9. Whitehorse Park. Gravel bar launch; walk up and fish mouth of Applegate; also good water downstream 1 mile.

10. Matson Park. Gravel bar launch; good bank fishing for steelhead and salmon.

11. Finley Bend. Hike down from the road to fish from rocks.

12. Griffin Park. Paved boat ramp, camping; fish the bend ¾ miles; very good bank access to good steelhead water.

13. Ferry Hole Park. Paved boat ramp, bank fishing; popu-

lar put-in and take-out.

14. Flanagan Slough. Old mine site, now BLM property; walk in on old road to fish salmon and steelhead.

15. Brushy Chutes.

16. Robertson Bridge. Paved boat ramp; popular steelhead bank fishery upstream.

17. Hussy Hole. Bank fishing.

18. Hog Creek Landing. Paved boat ramp, popular with rafters; good for fall chinook.

19. Hellsgate Access. Bank fishing.

20. Dunn Riffle. Bank fishing.

21. Hellsgate Bridge. Bank fishing.

22. South Access. Bank fishing.

23. Hellsgate Park. Bank fishing.

24. Stratton Creek. Follow the river downstream to the fish the creek mouth; popular bank fishery for winter steelhead.

25. Taylor Creek Gorge.

26. Indian Mary Park. Pay to use paved boat ramp, campground; gravel bar launch; some bank fishing for steelhead.

27. Rainbow Access. Bank fishing.

28. Ennis Park. Paved boat ramp; long gravel bar access to Ennis Riffle; good for steelhead.

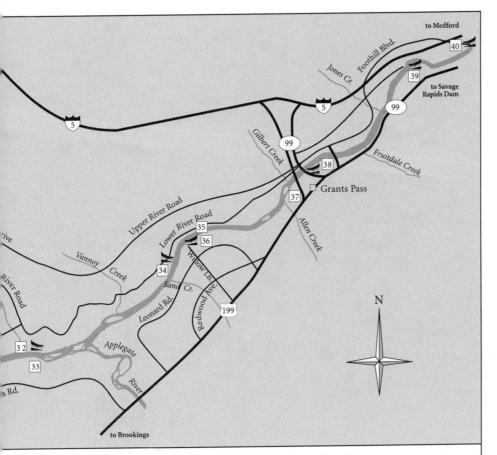

29. *Carpenters Island.* Bank fishing.

30. *Galice Riffle.*

31. *Galice Ramp.* Paved boat ramp, bank fishing.

32. *BLM Access.* Fish anywhere along Merlin-Galice Rd.

33. *Rocky Riffle.*

34. *Rand Access.* Gravel bar launch, bank fishing.

35. *Almeda Park.* Paved boat ramp, bank fishing.

36. *Argo Access.* Gravel bar launch, bank fishing, access to Argo Riffle.

37. *South Access Trail.*

38. *Grave Creek Landing.* Paved boat ramp, bank fishing.

39. *Rogue River Trail.*

40. *Rainie Falls.*

ROGUE RIVER: Grants Pass to Grave Creek. From Grave Creek downstream for about 35 miles there is no road access to the Rogue. At Grave Creek, anglers can launch a boat or pick up the Rogue River Trail on the north bank. A south bank trail at Grave Creek goes as far as Rainie Falls. From Grave Creek upstream, however, the river is very accessible. Roads follow and cross it all the way to Lost Creek Reservoir and beyond. This portion of the river offers many good angling opportunities.

The summer run steelhead fishery gathers steam here in September, with peak catches in October. The winter run overtakes the summer run in January, peaking in February, with good catches into March. The majority of summer steelhead are wild, and fishing for them continues to be catch and release only. A greater percentage of the winter run is finclipped, and in 1999 there was also an opportunity to harvest wild winter steelhead in this stretch (February 1 to April 30). Check the regulations. Half-pounders are in this section of the river from late fall through January and may be fished as trout (currently, catch and release on wild trout). Fall chinook provide good fishing in late August and September.

One of the most popular boat fisheries in this section is at Galice, where there's an improved boat ramp and a store with fishing supplies. Steelhead anglers drift to Rand or Almeda, a day's trip. Rocky Riffle immediately below Galice, and Galice Riffle immediately above, are very popular steelhead and half-pounder fisheries. This is usually the upper limit for half-pounders, though in some years they're caught up to the Applegate. The river from Almeda to Grave Creek is lightly fished for summer and winter steelhead.

To reach Galice from I-5 north of Grants Pass, take the Merlin Exit and follow the Merlin-Galice Rd. west. At Merlin, a county road heads southwest to Robertson Bridge.

Robertson Bridge to Galice is a long day's drift (about 11 river miles), accessing some good gravel bars and steelhead drift-fishing water. The trip includes a float through Hellgate Canyon. Some anglers do shorter trips from the bridge, mounting small kicker motors on their drift boats to enable them to motor up to a favorite water and drift down again. This is a practical technique in the slower, quieter stretches of the river above and below the bridge (between Ferry Park on the east

ing a lead boat familiar with the river's hazards and temperament.

Most drift trips from Grave Creek are 3 to 4 days. Anglers wishing to book guides and rooms at the back-country lodges would be well advised to make reservations early in the year. Fishing guides can be located through local fly and tackle shops and lodges. TuTuTun Lodge and several private RV parks provide the only overnight facilities on the North Bank Rogue River Rd. Camping is available on the south bank road at Huntley Park, Lobster Creek, and Quosatana below Foster Bar, and at Brushy Bar within the Wild Rogue Wilderness. Unimproved sites are

plentiful all along the trail to Grave Creek, which passes through a forested terrain of mixed Douglas fir, madrone, and maple.

All tributaries of the Rogue are closed to fishing in this stretch, except for the Illinois River.

Rogue River gauge readings are available. See Appendix. The Rogue can fish well, using one technique or another, within a vast range of flows (from 800 to 15,000 cfs). Plunkers catch salmon and steelhead at very high flows. In general, the river is fishable for salmon and steelhead within 36 hours after it begins to drop. Good fishing usually resumes within two to three days.

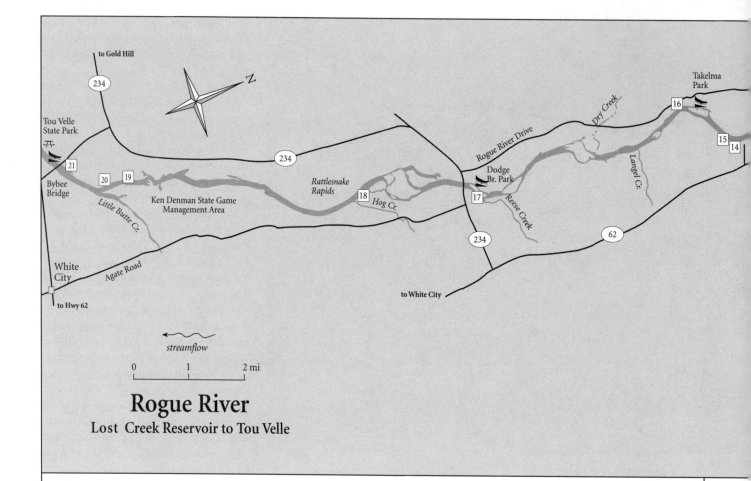

Rogue River
Lost Creek Reservoir to Tou Velle

1. Touvelle. Fish both banks 1½ miles upstream; good steelhead water, occasional chinook; last take-out for 6 miles; boat ramp.

2. Modoc Ponds Hole. Popular for steelhead, salmon; follow access road; locked gate (key available at ODFW headquarters, Game Management. Area).

3. Padegans Hole. Salmon

4. Jackson Falls. Good salmon just above Rattlesnake Rapids.

5. Dodge Bridge Park. Steelhead hole with occasional salmon; bank fishing and wheelchair accessible platform; boat ramp.

6. Takelma Park. Bank fishing; good steelhead hole.

7. Betts Hole. Salmon; boat only.

8. Brophy Road. Public acccess to a half mile of bank fishing; good steelhead water.

9. Shady Cove Park. Bank fishing for steelhead; wheelchair accessible.

10. Shady Cove Hole. Above bridge; popular spot for salmon, occasional steelhead; boat and bank access.

11. Trail Creek. Steelhead hole below rapids.

12. Cable Hole. Salmon and steelhead from boat and bank.

13. Mouth of Elk Creek. Popular steelhead and salmon access from boat and bank.

14. Rogue Elk Park. Bank access to Elk Creek bar, good for steelhead; boat ramp.

15. Peter Pan Hole. Salmon and steelhead; bank access above park; park on road.

16. Owl Hoot & Robbers Roost. Boat and bank accesss to good steelhead holes; bank anglers park along road; Robbers Roost is upstream, Owl Hoot downstream.

17. Pump Hole. Good for salmon; boat access.

18. Slide Hole. Access to high steep bank popular for chinook, right below Casey State Park.

19. Casey State Park. Good bank access to salmon and steelhead water; boat ramp; wheelchair accessible.

20. Macgregor Park. Boat ramp; wheelchair accessible platform; bank access (north and south) to several good salmon holes and steelhead water.

21. Holy Water. Rainbows to 18" in tailrace fishery between Lost Creek and Barrier dams; ¾ mile of classic fly-fishing water accessible from both banks; Corp of Engineers park on south bank, gravel road on north.

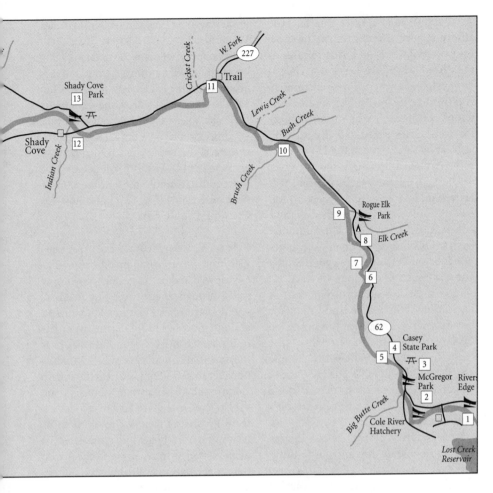

river, forming a small reservoir (Gold Ray Pool). Above Shady Cove, the valley narrows and confines the river for 10 to 12 miles up to Lost Creek Dam, the end of the mainstem Rogue.

There are major fisheries for spring and fall chinook in this reach, a good size run of finclipped hatchery coho, summer and winter steelhead, and an exciting fly-only tailrace fishery for large resident rainbows.

Most spring chinook in this stretch are caught above Gold Ray Dam from May through July, but there are some opportunities to catch them closer to Grants Pass. The first fishery for springers east of the city is at Pierce Riffle, about ¾ mile below Savage Rapids Dam. Boats launch at Pierce Riffle County Park off Foothill Blvd. on the north bank. Jet sleds motor up through the riffle to fish the deadline below the dam. Drift boat anglers row up to Pierce Riffle. There is a bank fishery for springers at the Savage Rapids deadline, accessed through the viewing area at the dam.

Fall chinook are also a popular fishery, particularly in the Grants Pass area in August and September. Finclipped coho heading for Cole Rivers Hatchery reach this section in late October and November.

Summer steelhead are plentiful in September and October between Gold Ray Dam and Cole Rivers Hatchery. To protect spawning salmon in the reach at this time, the fishery is restricted to the use of artificial flies and barbless hooks. Anglers use both standard fly fishing gear, and spinning rods and reels rigged with bubble floats. Currently, only finclipped steelhead may be kept during this time period. Winter steelhead are in this stretch of the river from January through April. Peak catches are in January and February. Recently, this stretch of the river has been open to harvest of both finclipped and wild winter steelhead. Check current regulations.

There is a lot of private riverfront property in this stretch, but there are bank fishing opportunities at several parks, boat ramps, and easements adjacent to Hwy. 62.

A boat ramp at Valley of the Rogue State Park, about 5 miles east of Grants Pass, is the put-in for an easy 2½ mile drift through good steelhead water to Coyote Evans County Wayside. There's also bank fishing at Valley of the Rogue for steelhead and resident trout.

About 4 miles upstream, there's bank angling at Rock Point Bridge on Hwy. 99

bank and Griffin Park on the west). From Grants Pass, the Lower River Rd. offers a pretty drive to Robertson Bridge.

Whitehorse Riffle, below the mouth of the Applegate, is a good steelhead producer with bedrock shelves and channels that hold fish. There's an unimproved ramp at Whitehorse Park on the north bank. Whitehorse to Ferry Park is a short but productive drift.

Anglers fish off the mouth of the Applegate for steelhead and for fall chinook returning to the Applegate to spawn in late August and early September. These salmon are not in prime condition, but are still palatable. The Applegate marks the end of heavy recreational activity on the Rogue west of Grants Pass.

There's a lot of good bank access between Grave Creek and the Applegate. Anglers park and fish along the Merlin-Galice Rd. between Galice and Grave Creek. Argo Riffle is a popular bank fishery about 2 miles above Grave Creek. A mile above Argo Riffle, Almeda Park offers ½ mile of good beach fishing with plentiful parking. Anglers also fish at Rand, and at the Chair Riffle just above. Rock Riffle above Galice

is accessible to bank anglers, but there is little access at Galice itself. Ennis Riffle, about 2 miles above Galice, includes two gravel bars. Indian Mary Park, just below Taylor Creek. Gorge, offers quiet water for trout fishing. Bank anglers fish above and below Hellgate Bridge for steelhead, and there is bank access at Ferry and Griffin parks.

Camping in this stretch is limited to Indian Mary Park, a popular tourist spot in a pleasant setting.

All tributaries of the Rogue in this stretch are closed to fishing, except the Applegate River.

ROGUE RIVER: Lost Creek Dam to Grants Pass. This stretch of the Rogue is characterized by private property, irrigation impoundments, and limited public access; yet it continues to offer excellent fishing—testament to the incredible vitality of this river and its fish. East of Grants Pass, above the wretched Savage Rapids Dam (a fish killer with little justification for its existence), the Rogue flows through a broad valley, its banks lined with cottonwoods and willows. East of the town of Gold Hill, Gold Ray Dam backs up the and at Sardine Creek near the junction of Gold Hill and Sardine Creek roads. At Gold Hill on Hwy. 234, there's an improved boat ramp at Gold Nugget Park. Gold Ray Dam is a popular spot for spring chinook and summer steelhead. Boaters launch sleds and drift boats with motors at an unimproved boat ramp off a dirt road between the dam and Gold Hill on the south bank, then motor up to the deadline. This road offers about 1½ miles of bank access.

The water above Gold Ray Pool is especially productive for spring chinook (though the popular Salmon Rock Hole disappeared in the flood of '96). Boaters launch jet sleds at Tou Velle State Park on the south bank north of Medford. Anglers also bank fish for trout at Tou Velle. High Banks, just below Tou Velle, is a popular fly fishing spot for summer steelhead (boat access only).

Dodge Bridge Park, near the Hwy. 234 crossing of the Rogue, offers a nice long day's drift to Tou Velle, about 8 miles. There's good still-water fishing for spring chinook and summer steelhead in this stretch, but there are rapids that should be scouted and attempted only by experienced boaters. An occasional chinook and steelhead are hooked from the bank at Dodge Bridge, where there is also a wheelchair accessible fishing ramp that actually accesses good salmon and steelhead water.

Above Dodge Bridge on the west bank road to Shady Cove, Takelma Park offers a boat ramp and good bank access for spring chinook, steelhead, and trout. There's also a boat ramp at Shady Cove County Park, but bank access is limited to the area above Shady Cove Bridge (where there happens to be a good salmon hole). From Shady Cove to Lost Creek Dam, Hwy. 62 runs close to the river with good access for bank anglers.

The mouth of Trail Creek is a popular bank access area. Anglers pull off and fish near the junction of highways 62 and 227. Rogue Elk County Park on Hwy. 62 is popular with boaters in pursuit of spring chinook and early summer steelhead. There's also a bank fishery for trout. Casey State Park, just west of the dam, has a boat ramp and excellent bank access for spring chinook, summer steelhead, and trout. Between Casey State Park and Lost Creek Dam, the river runs through public land where bank access is plentiful.

Immediately below Lost Creek Dam is "The Holy Water," a three-quarter mile tailrace fishery where resident rainbow trout thrive on the cool, rich releases of water from Lost Creek Reservoir. The average catch is 16 inches, and encounters with trout 20 inches and larger are commonplace. Open for year-round angling, this stretch is restricted to fly fishing with barbless hooks. To reach the Holy Water from Hwy. 62, follow signs to Cole River Hatchery. To fish the west bank, bear left at the weir and park along the road. To fish the east bank, turn right at the weir and park at Rivers Edge Park. The salmonfly hatch from late May through June draws crowds of anglers, but there's good fishing here year-round throughout the reach.

There are also wild cutthroat trout in this section of the Rogue, and fishing for them is catch and release at this time.

Campgrounds in this stretch of the Rogue are limited to Valley of the Rogue State Park on Hwy. 99, Rogue Elk County Park on Hwy. 62 east of the dam, and the vast Stewart State Park on the reservoir's south bank off Hwy. 62.

All tributaries of the Rogue in this stretch, other than Big and Little Butte creeks, are closed to all angling at this time.

There are river gauge readings available at several points along this stretch of the Rogue. In general, however, water clarity is more important than stream flow. Water releases from Lost Creek Dam can raise the river level without increasing turbidity. Rogue River turbidity is included in the fish report in local newspapers. When the river is turbid, the half-mile flow between the Big Butte Creek confluence and Cole Rivers Hatchery is almost always clear enough for good fishing. River temperature and the fish count at Lost Creek Dam are available by calling the Army Corp of Engineers. See Appendix.

ROGUE RIVER, MIDDLE FORK. A fair wild trout stream with harvest opportunities, flowing into the upper Rogue above Lost Creek Reservoir. From Medford take Hwy. 62 north to Prospect, about 45 miles, then follow Forest Rd. 37 from Prospect to the Middle Fork. Or follow the Butte Falls Rd. to its junction with the Middle Fork at Forest Rd. 37. About 3 miles after Forest Rd. 37 crosses the Middle Fork, a forest road on the left (before Imnaha Campground) leads to Trail 978, which follows the upper Middle Fork into its headwaters in the Seven Lakes Basin of the Sky Lakes Wilderness.

The upper portion of the stream is lightly fished for wild cutthroat trout and migrants from the high lakes. See also Alta, Middle Grass, Cliff. Check the regulations for limits. There is no limit on brook trout.

Campgrounds near the Middle Fork include a large campground at Joseph Stewart State Park on Lost Creek Reservoir, and three campgrounds south of the Middle Fork on Forest Rd. 37 (Imnaha, Sumpter Creek, and South Fork).

ROGUE RIVER, NORTH FORK. A popular trout stream with harvest opportunities for wild and hatchery stock, flowing 47 miles through Rogue River National Forest into Lost Creek Reservoir. Highways 62 and 230 more or less follow the river to its headwaters south of Diamond Lake, near the northern boundary of Crater Lake National Park. Forest roads access the stream at the mouths of many fine tributaries, and the Upper Rogue River Trail 1034 follows it from Prospect through the forest to its headwaters. Early season road access is often limited by heavy snow, so check with the ranger station at Prospect. Roads are usually open by late May.

The North Fork supports good populations of wild rainbows, cutthroat, a few browns, and lots of brook trout. There is no limit on the number or size of brook trout that may be kept. Rainbow and cutthroat average 6 to 12 inches, with an infrequent brown taken in the 5 to 10 pound range. Legal rainbows are stocked weekly from Memorial Day till Labor Day between Natural Bridge Campground and Hamaker Meadows. Fish are released near all public access points, including the campgrounds at Union Creek, Farewell Bend, and Hamaker Meadows, and near the Jackson/Douglas County Rd.

There's good fishing near the mouths of the North Fork's many tributaries, including Mill, Abbot, Union, Wizard, National, Foster, and Minnehaha. Most tributaries are best in early season before they get low, but Union and Mill are good all summer.

ROGUE RIVER, SOUTH FORK. A nice trout stream with harvest opportunities for wild trout, flowing into Lost Creek Reservoir. It is best fished in mid-summer. From Medford take Hwy. 62 north to the Butte Falls Rd. Head north on the Butte Falls-

Prospect Rd., turning onto Forest Rd. 34 toward Lodgepole, crossing the upper stream at South Fork Campground. Trail 988 follows the stream to Rogue Head Camp in the Blue Lake Group of the Sky Lakes Area. The upper stream is also accessed by forest roads from Prospect.

The upper portion is lightly fished and supports wild rainbows, cutthroat, and brook trout. A number of beaver ponds in the headwaters contain surprisingly big trout. There is no limit on the number or size or quantity of brook trout that may be kept. Campgrounds near the South Fork include a large camp at Joseph Stewart State Park on Lost Creek Reservoir, Imnaha and South Fork camps off Forest Rd. 37, Parker Meadows, and Upper South Fork.

ROUND LAKE. A five-acre lake in the south Sky Lakes Wilderness, Rogue River National Forest. Round Lake is off Trail 982 just before Blue Lake. See Blue Lake for directions. Round Lake is stocked with brook trout.

SAUNDERS LAKE. An attractive, relatively deep coastal lake of about 55 acres west of Hwy. 101, about 15 miles south of Reedsport. It offers fishing for stocked trout, largemouth bass, and panfish.

The lake is stocked several times in spring with legal rainbow trout (which are usually fished out in early summer) and with trophy-size trout that may reach 8 to 10 pounds by fall. Bait fishing takes most of the trout, but mayfly hatches in spring provide an opportunity for good fly fishing.

Yellow perch, crappie, bluegill, and bass are available year-round, with especially good bass fishing in fall.

There is a county park with boat ramp and bank fishing at the south end of the lake, but the rest of the lake shore is private, and no camping is allowed. Campgrounds, accommodations, and supplies are available at Lakeside, 4 miles north.

SELMAC LAKE. A producer of trophy-size largemouth bass, 23 miles southwest of Grants Pass, with large numbers of stocked rainbows and excellent facilities for family outings. Take Hwy. 199 to Selmac, and turn east. It's 4 miles to the lake. With about 160 surface acres, this artificial lake provides lots of angling opportunity.

Selmac is managed for trophy bass, and two state record bass have been produced

Driftboats are just right for fishing the SIXES, a small river known for its fine run of wild fall chinook. Photograph by Scott Richmond.

here, including an 11 lb. 7.4 oz. fish caught in 1991. Anglers are restricted to catching one bass per day. Rainbow trout are stocked in early spring, and there are many crappie, bluegill, and brown bullhead. Look for largemouth around the stumps and overhanging brush. The shallow coves on the south side are almost wall-to-wall with brown bullheads and are productive for bass in spring.

There is a county park here with boat rentals and ramp, tent sites, drinking water, picnic facilities, and a swimming area. A lot of good water is accessible to float tubes. Finger-like dikes projecting into the lake provide excellent bank access. Recommended for youngsters.

SHUTTPELZ LAKE. A perfect little wild cutthroat fishery is the Oregon Dunes National Recreation Area. The lake is off Wildwood Drive west of Hwy. 101 at the Eel Lake turn-off.

Shuttpelz is deep with a lot of the submerged structure that trout appreciate. It grows fish to very good size. Angling is catch and release, restricted to barbless artificial lures and flies. This is an excellent float tube lake.

SIXES RIVER. To reach the Sixes below Hwy. 101, head west on Cape Blanco Hwy., following signs to the historic Hughes House. A trail near the boat ramp and picnic area at the house leads to the Sixes. Sixes River Rd. follows the river upstream from Hwy. 101.

The Sixes has a good run of wild winter steelhead that enter the river beginning in November, with fish available into March. Steelheading is catch and release. Resident cutthroat and searun in fall may also be fished catch and release.

But the Sixes is best known for its fine run of wild fall chinook. Salmon move into the river after the first fall rains breach the bar at the river's mouth (as late as November some years). The peak of the run is generally in mid-December. Earliest catches are off the beach near the mouth at the state park. This surf fishery is governed by regulations set by the Pacific Fishery Management Council and may be subject to in-season changes. See Appendix.

The Orchard Hole, a popular tidewater fishery two miles up from the mouth, was once accessible through private property. To reach it, park at the State Park and walk upstream along the river. Squaw Bluff, another good spot, is about three-quarters of a mile above Orchard.

Above tidewater, bank anglers can access the river behind the store at the Hwy. 101 takeout, at Mid-Drift (an ODFW gravel bar access about three miles farther upstream), and at many points along Sixes River Rd. Look for pull-outs with trails down to the river. Respect private property and obey No Trespassing signs.

Drift boats are the right size for this small river. Put in at Edson Creek Park and take out at the Hwy. 101 bridge, or cut the trip short at Mid-Drift. Boats can also be launched near Hughes House within the state park.

There are campgrounds at Cape Blanco State Park and at Sixes River Campground (about six miles above Edson Creek).

Smith River

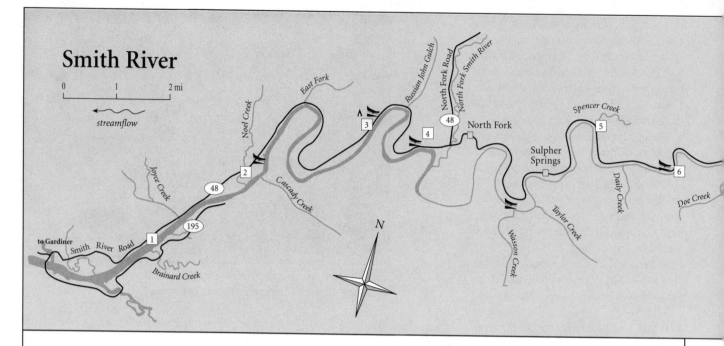

0   1   2 mi

streamflow

1. Sandy Beach. Easy undeveloped put-in; good bank fishing.

2. Smith River Marina. Private facility; modest fee to use ramp; accesses good salmon and striper water; RV and tent sites.

3. Noel Ranch. Paved public ramp; good bank fishing; popular spot for shad in May and June.

4. Riverside County Park. Paved ramps; good bank fishing, picnic area.

5. Spencer Creek. Head of tide; chinook deadline.

6. Dailey Ranch. Pole slide take-out at upper end of ranch.

7. Fawn Creek. Campground with river access.

8. Smith River Falls. Highest developed put-in; popular drift to Dailey Pole Slide; campsites.

9. Vincent Creek. Campsites, river access.

10. Sisters Creek. Deadline for all fishing; campground with river access.

SKOOKUM LAKE (Umpqua watershed). A three-quarter mile hike-in for brook trout in the Skookum Prairie area, about 10 miles west of Diamond Lake. From Hwy. 230, south of Diamond, take Forest Rd. 3703 about 2½ miles, then Forest Rd. 200 (an unimproved track) to the right. Skookum is less than ¼ mile from road's end.

With about 15 surface acres, Skookum provides good catches of brook trout to 10 inches, and a few to 18. The outlet, Skookum Creek, produces small (but mature) rainbow and brook trout. The lake is usually inaccessible until late June. There are natural campsites available.

SKOOKUM POND. An artificial pond in the Umpqua National Forest that has been overrun by illegally introduced bullheads. There's no limit on the catch, and they taste pretty good, so help yourself. A few rainbows may still be present as well, and there's an excellent population of crayfish.

From the South Umpqua road (46) take Forest Rd. 29 (Jackson Creek Rd.) east. about 14 miles to Forest Rd. 2924. After a hairpin turn, continue due east (on Forest Rd. 200) to the pond. It is about 2½ miles from the hairpin to Skookum. There is no sign on the road indicating that the pond is here, so watch your odometer. The pond has a lot of submerged snags and stumps that provide good habitat. Aquatic vegetation is heavy, but there is room for a small boat. Largemouth bass were illegally introduced but didn't seem to take.

SMITH RIVER

A major tributary of the Umpqua River system, joining the Umpqua in Winchester Bay (the Umpqua's estuary). It has fair runs of wild fall chinook and steelhead, a good population of cutthroat trout, and Oregon's best opportunity to hook a striped bass. In addition, it is a refuge for the region's endangered coho, maintaining one of the Northwest's few healthy wild coho populations. At this time, the Smith is closed to fishing for both coho and trout due to Endangered Species Act concerns. Trout fishing restrictions may be eased following a review of the basin's cutthroat status. Check the regulations.

After a 75-mile tumble through the Coast Range, the Smith enters the bay at Gardiner, 9 miles from the Pacific. From Gardiner on Hwy. 101, County Rd. 48 heads east to the river and follows it closely for 30 miles. A variety of gravel roads access its headwaters, but the river is closed to all angling above North Sister Creek at this time.

To reach the Smith by back roads from Roseburg or the Willamette Valley, follow Hwy. 38 west. County roads cut north to the Smith about 8 miles west of Elkton (upstream of Sawyers Rapids on the Umpqua), and from the Wells Creek Guard Station (about 3½ miles upstream from Scottsburg).

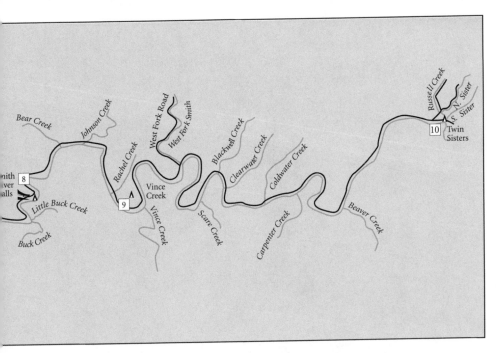

Wild chinook provide an early fall fishery in tidewater below Spencer Creek. The river is closed to chinook fishing above Spencer to protect salmon on their spawning grounds. The river is open for steelheading to Sisters Creek. Both wild and hatchery steelhead may still be available at this time, though the hatchery program was phased out after stocking in 1998, and few will be available after 2001. Most finclipped steelhead will be found below Spencer Creek. Wild steelhead must be released unharmed.

Striped bass are reproducing modestly in the lower Smith, migrating seasonally between the river and Winchester Bay, following the food supply. In March, April, and May, stripers can be found in the river's tidewater stretch. They return to the bay in late spring and summer to feed on marine fish, then return to the river to spawn in September and October. Best angling is upriver in spring and fall. Most anglers fish big plugs at night, either rowing or using electric motors. Most catches are in the 16 to 20 inch class and must be released unharmed, but some adults 35 pounds and larger are hooked here. The smaller fish are generally found in schools, while the larger fish are loners. Minimum length for catch-and-keep is 30 inches.

The Smith has a good shad run May through June. The run extends up to head of tide at Spencer Creek. Shad are available to both boat and bank anglers, caught on troll and cast. A favorite shad spot is the Noel Ranch Boat Ramp at about r.m. 8.

The Smith is very accessible to boat and bank anglers, primarily from the north bank road. The farthest upstream official put-in is at Smith River Falls (r.m. 26), with a popular drift down to Dailey Pole Slide (r.m. 11), a take-out at the upper end of Dailey Ranch. There is a boat ramp and bank fishery at Riverside County Park about 11 miles up Smith River Rd., and another at Noel Ranch, about 2½ miles below Riverside. Sandy Beach, the lowest access on the river, has a good bank fishery, and boats can be launched from the beach.

Camping facilities are available at Fawn Creek, a BLM facility a mile downstream from Smith River Falls, and also at Smith River Falls, Vincent Creek, and Twin Sisters. There are bank fishing opportunities at all the campgrounds. Above the falls, boats can be launched from several access roads that were once low water crossings for logging operations. The old crossings are also good bank fishing sites.

SMITH RIVER, NORTH FORK. A large, productive tributary of the Smith River with a good run of wild winter steelhead. It joins the Smith 13 miles above Winchester Bay. The North Fork Rd. follows the river north from the Smith River Rd. near the community of North Fork, about 15 miles from Gardiner.

Wild winter steelhead may be fished upstream to Bridge 10 (about 20 miles upriver). The run usually peaks in December and January. Most anglers use drift fishing techniques. Bank access is very good, with many landowners granting permission to fish when asked. (Be sure to ask.) When the mainstem Smith is turbid, the North Fork is often clear.

The North Fork is closed to trout angling at this time to protect Umpqua watershed cutthroat, but check the regulations for a possible easing of restrictions.

Drift boats can be launched adjacent to the bridge crossings. There is an unimproved take-out right above the Culvert Hole, 5 miles upstream from the mouth at the first rapids above tidewater. Warning: Don't boat Culvert Hole.

SMITH RIVER, WEST FORK. A beautiful wild trout stream, about 10 miles long, joining the mainstem Smith about 5 miles above Smith River Falls. A BLM road follows the north bank almost to the headwaters. At this time, it is closed to protect endangered Umpqua watershed cutthroat, Check current regulations.

SNAG LAKE. A 30-acre warmwater fishery 5½ miles north of North Bend. Turn west off Hwy. 101 ontoHauser Depot Rd. Snag supports largemouth bass, yellow perch, and brown bullhead. Access is limited to hike-in or off-road vehicles. The lake has been known to go dry.

SODA SPRING RESERVOIR. A small reservoir on the North Umpqua with fishing for rainbow trout. It is 7 miles downstream from Toketee Lake on the north side of Hwy. 138, about 40 miles east of Glide. From Roseburg, take Hwy. 138, or take County Rd. 200 from Hwy. 99 at Wilbur. No longer stocked, it has rainbows to 20 inches, browns, and brook trout. It is lightly fished and has a winter boat closure due to danger from the spillway.

SOUTH UMPQUA RIVER. See **UMPQUA RIVER, SOUTH.**

SPAULDING POND. A 4-acre mill pond, 30 ft. deep, located about 20 miles northwest of Grants Pass. It is just off the Onion Mt. Lookout Rd. in Siskiyou National Forest. Spaulding is stocked with legal rainbows in spring.

SQUAW LAKE (Coquille watershed). A 2-acre lake in an isolated spot off the South

Fork Coquille River road, about 22 miles south of Powers. The River Rd. leaves Hwy. 42 about 3 miles south of Myrtle Point and is paved to the lake.

Squaw is stocked with legal rainbows each season. The Forest Service maintains a nice little primitive campground at the lake.

SQUAW LAKES (Rogue watershed). A good family recreation area in the upper Applegate drainage, about 4 miles east of Applegate Reservoir, 3 miles north of the California border.

From I-5 or Hwy. 99 take Hwy. 238 south to Ruch; then follow the Applegate River Rd. south to Applegate Reservoir. Cross the dam face to Forest Rd. 1075, which follows Squaw Creek to the lakes.

Big Squaw has about 50 surface acres. Little (or Upper) Squaw Lake is about ¼ as big, located about a mile southeast of the large lake. This is a good fishery for float tubes since it's ¼ mile from the parking lot to the lower lake. The road in can be rough in early spring.

Both lakes have good populations of wild cutthroat averaging 9 inches as well as lots of crappie, bluegill, and brown bullhead to 10 inches. Largemouth bass of fair size are well established.

The lakes are very popular and are heavily fished with good results, especially in fall and early spring. Good shoreline cover and rocky ledges on the east side of the lower lake attract crappie.

Camping is by reservation only. Contact the Star Ranger District at the town of McKee on the Applegate River. Additional camping is available at Applegate Reservoir. Recommended for youngsters.

STEAMBOAT CREEK. A scenic tributary of the North Umpqua River, entering the mainstem at Steamboat Ranger Station about 21 miles east of Glide. Closed to all fishing, it is a designated sanctuary for summer steelhead.

STUMP LAKE. A 30-acre reservoir on Clearwater Creek in the vicinity of Diamond Lake. The lake is on Hwy. 138, 11 miles northwest of Diamond Lake Resort.

Stump isn't much to look at, but it has plump brook rainbow trout to 15 inches. Snags and stumps make trolling or spin-fishing difficult. Still-fishing with bait saves tackle, and there's good fly action in fall.

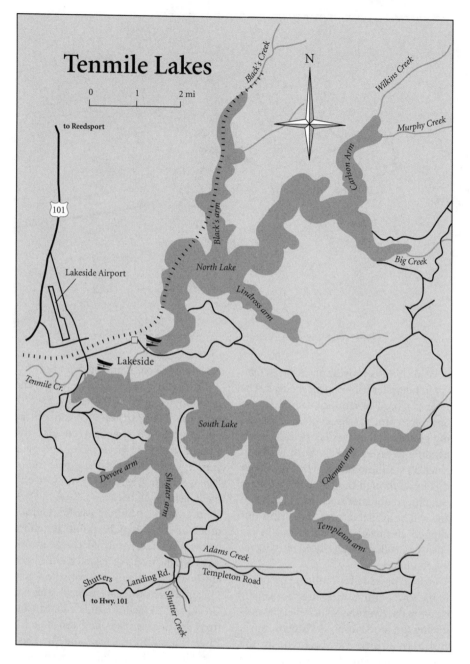

Tenmile Lakes

There are improved campgrounds at Clearwater Falls about 3 miles east, and at Whitehorse Falls 1½ miles west.

SUCKER CREEK. A tributary of the beleaguered Illinois River. Like all tributaries of the Illinois, it is closed to all angling.

TANNEN LAKES. Two hike-in lakes in the Siskiyou Mountains near the California border, usually accessible by early June. They are northwest of Tannen Mountain and can be reached by hiking ¼ mile by trail from Forest Rd. 041 south and east of Bolan Lake. From Cave Junction it's about 21 miles to Bolan Lake following Hwy. 46 to Holland, and Forest Rd. 4703 to a grav-

el road access to Bolan. The Tannens can also be reached by heading north from Happy Camp, California. The hike is less than one mile.

The Tannens are stocked with brook trout in odd number years. Fishing holds up well all season, with catches to 15 inches. Tannen is 8 acres and 28 ft. deep. East Tannen is smaller, brushy on three sides, and only 7 ft. deep. A one-mile trail leads up to East Tannen. There are natural campsites at Tannen.

TEAL LAKE. A one-acre lake 8 miles south of Reedsport, several hundred yards south of Clear Lake. Teal has cutthroat trout, but is closed to public access.

TENMILE CREEK. A 3-mile long steelhead fishery, the outlet to Tenmile Lakes. It can be accessed at Spinreel Campground off Hwy. 101, from the Oregon Dunes National Recreation Area (by hike-in or off-road vehicle), or by drifting down from South Tenmile.

Hatchery steelhead are acclimated in Tenmile and in its tributary Saunders Creek at the lower end of Spinreel Campground. Best fishing is December through March, though steelhead are seen in the creek year-round. The spawning run peaks in mid-December. Tenmile can be counted on to run clear when other coastal streams are off-color following heavy rains.

Spinreel Campground is a nice Forest Service facility that attracts a noisy dune buggy crowd in summer. The campground is open year-round, and late season camping here can be pleasant.

TENMILE LAKES

A premier largemouth bass fishery, world class for quantity of catch, if not for size. Big, rich, and productive, North and South Tenmile nestle in gorgeous coastal foothills. They offer miles of intricate shoreline with shallow bays, arms, and enticing fingers to explore for bass, brown bullheads, bluegills, crappies, rainbows, cutthroat, and the occasional steelhead. There are even rumors of a landlocked behemoth of undetermined species whom the locals have affectionately named "Tillie," and while the lakes lack the depth generally associated with land-locked sea monsters, it isn't that hard to imagine such a presence on a fog-draped morning at Tenmile. (The occasional 5 ft. green sturgeon has been hooked here.)

The two lakes are tucked off to the east of Hwy. 101 at Lakeside, about 12 miles south of Reedsport. North Lake is a bit under 1,000 acres, and South Lake is several hundred acres larger. Their average depth is about 15 ft., and neither lake has any really deep holes.

Many bass tournaments take place here, and the pros catch 20 to 50 largemouth per day in the 2 to 5 pound range. Bass to 8 pounds are common in late spring, and bass to 10 pounds are available.

Tenmile bass are catchable year-round, but best fishing is May through September or once the water warms to 70 degrees. In May and June when the bass spawn, spin-

Look for bluegills in TENMILE'*s calm coves and around downed trees. Photograph by Dennis Frates.*

nerbaits are effective around the willows and docks (dark at night, chartreuse during the day). The shallow shoreline (over 170 miles of it) is always productive, with abundant aquatic weeds as well as the willows, docks, and other structures that bass favor. Plastic worms, weedless spoons, and topwater lures are popular. Favorite areas in South Lake are the Coleman and Templeton arms. In North Lake, a lot of bass are caught near the railroad trestles and in Lindross and Black's arms.

Hybrid bass, introduced in an effort to control a burgeoning bluegill population, are about gone. The program was discontinued because the bass had a tendency to stray beyond the Tenmile system. A few may still be available after 2000. The state record hybrid (18 lbs. 8 oz.) was taken from Ana Reservoir, but bass to 16 lbs. 14 oz. have been caught at Tenmile.

Bluegill aren't as abundant as they once were, but there are still enough to keep the youngsters interested. Try any calm cove, or around downed trees. Black crappie showed up here a few years ago and now provide another focus for anglers with limited patience. Docks or structure in 6 to 12 ft. of water should produce consistent action. Catches of up to 50 crappie per day are not uncommon. Brown bullhead are numerous off the points. Look for them in areas that are deeper and less weedy.

Tenmile Lakes were once primarily cold water fisheries, with a large population of cutthroat and good runs of coho and steelhead. As logging and development around the lake took their toll, the lake filled and warmed, and the traditional fisheries have declined. Nevertheless, trout are stocked annually, and there are plenty of fish in the

2 to 4 lb. class with some to 20 inches. For larger trout, try fishing deep off the points, or drag a lake troll. These days, rainbows are more abundant than cutthroat.

Coho are holding their own in the Tenmile system, but the fishery for wild coho is closed here as elsewhere in the state. Coho generally enter as the water rises, some years as early as late October. November and early December see the greatest numbers.

Steelhead are occasionally hooked in the lakes in spring. Most are hatchery reared and may be kept, but some are wild. All non-finclipped steelhead must be released unharmed. There is a good fishery for hatchery steelhead in the lakes' outlet, Tenmile Creek.

There are no public campgrounds on the lakes, but there are a few private resorts and RV parks. The nearest campground is Spinreel, a Forest Service camp on Tenmile Creek on the west side of Hwy. 101. A marina at Lakeside has boat rentals and supplies. Flying fishermen will appreciate the airstrip at Lakeside, a 10-minute walk from South Lake. A nice public fishing dock at a county park in Lakeside on South Lake accesses very productive water. All species are caught from the dock, which is wheelchair accessible. Recommended for youngsters.

TOKETEE RESERVOIR. One of several power system reservoirs on the upper North Umpqua, with several hundred surface acres. It is successfully managed for brown trout. Located about 60 miles east of Roseburg, 40 miles east of Glide, it can be approached from both east and west on the North Umpqua River Rd., Hwy. 138. From the east, take Hwy. 97 to the Hwy. 138

Most sturgeon caught in WINCHESTER BAY are within the slot limit.
Photograph courtesy of Randy Sampson.

1. South Jetty. Fish for salmon, perch, rockfish.

2. Lower Bay. Fish from boat and bank for salmon, perch, rockfish.

3. Training Jetty and Extension. Public access for salmon, perch, rockfish, crab.

4. Social Security Bay. Shore access for perch, striped bass.

5. Crabbing.

6. Coast Guard Dock. Public access for perch, rockfish, dungeness crab

7. Winchester Point. Gravel fill access to bank fishery for rockfish, perch.

8. Net Pens.

9. Public Docks. Charter boats, public moorage, and dock fishing for tomcod, perch, rockperch.

(Diamond Lake) cut-off. Toketee is about 23 miles west of Diamond Lake.

The reservoir has good numbers of browns and a few brook trout. The browns run to 11 to 13 inches and are taken on bait, Kwikfish-type lures, and flies. Fishing nymphs in the shallows can also be effective, and the browns do rise to take mayfly imitations on warm afternoons when a hatch is coming off the lake. Float tube anglers do very well here.

Fishing is good in spring, tapers off in summer, and picks up again in fall. Some of the best fishing is often February through April. Toketee is open and accessible year-round.

There are two Forest Service campgrounds at the north and south ends of the lake and a boat ramp on the eastern shore. Good forest campsites are also available up and down river on North Umpqua Rd.

TWIN LAKES (Umpqua watershed). Two nice brook trout lakes between North and South Umpqua drainages, a half-mile hike from the road. Take North Umpqua Hwy. 138 about 32 miles east of Glide to the Wilson Creek Rd., Forest Rd. 4770. Bear right at the forks. The trailhead is on the west side of the road, about 7 miles in. The lakes are also approachable by trail from Twin Lakes Mountain, by way of Little River Rd.

The larger, lower lake is about 12 acres, and the smaller twin is half that size. Both have brook trout to 15 inches and are

stocked annually with fingerlings. Bait or spinners should work well in early season, with flies good in late summer and fall.

The Twins are among the last lakes to thaw in the Umpqua watershed, and the smaller Twin sometimes winterkills. They are usually accessible by late June.

UMPQUA RIVER

UMPQUA RIVER: Winchester Bay (Scottsburg Park to Winchester Bar). Oregon's number one coastal sturgeon fishery, with limited offshore opportunities for halibut and bottom fish, and bay fishing for fall chinook, finclipped coho, striped bass, perch, crabs, and softshell clams. There are three port towns on the bay, Winchester Bay (closest to the bar), Reedsport, and Gardiner.

From the east, the bay is approached by Hwy. 38, which cuts through the Coast Range south of Cottage Grove. From Florence on the coast, it's 15 miles south by Hwy. 101.

The charter fleet out of Winchester Bay is considerably reduced in size since the decline of the coho fishery that was its mainstay. Charter boats are still available for halibut and chinook trips as ocean regulations allow, and for bottom fishing year-round. The Winchester Bay reefs are farther offshore than those associated with other Oregon bays, so be prepared for a long day.

The bay itself offers good fishing

throughout the year for a variety of species. In spring, anglers dig clams, trap crabs, and fish for striped bass, white sturgeon, and perch. Spring chinook are only lightly fished in the estuary as they move quickly through the bay to the lower mainstem.

In summer, there are green sturgeon, stripers in the lower bay, and a chance to catch migrating chinook (bound for points north) who turn into Winchester briefly in pursuit of bait fish. This particular chinook fishery is limited by a closure below Salmon Harbor from July 1 to August 16.

Sturgeon attract a lot of anglers to Winchester Bay. White sturgeon are in the bay year-round with peak catches in January, February and March. Green sturgeon enter the bay in summer and are available through early July. Unlike the Columbia River sturgeon fishery, the majority of sturgeon caught in Winchester Bay are within the keeper size slot (42 to 60 inches). Earliest catches are in the Big Bend area just below Gardiner, followed by a fishery at Reedsport beneath the Hwy. 101 Bridge and at the bluff about 1½ miles above Reedsport. The fishery then moves upstream toward Mill Creek at Scottsburg Park, where sturgeon are fished from boat and bank. Bank anglers access the river from turn-outs on Hwy. 38, at the junction

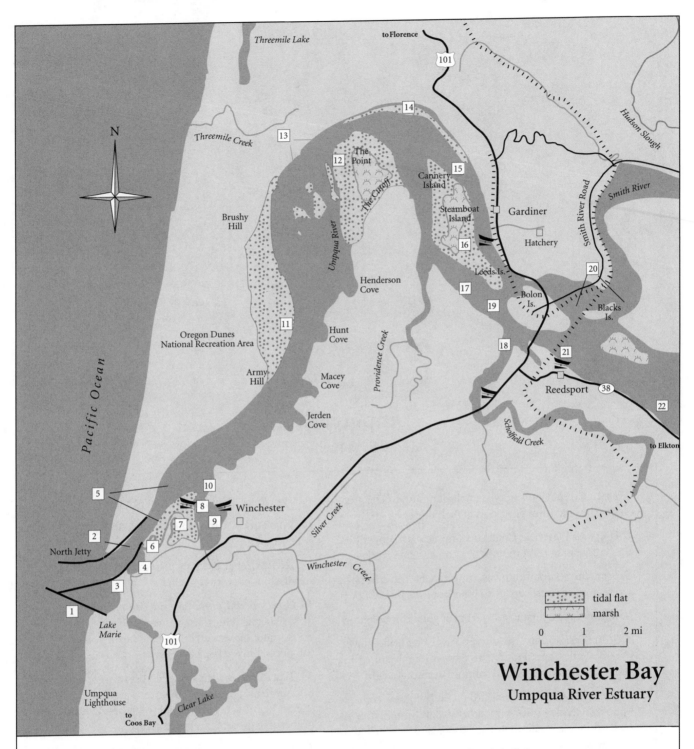

Winchester Bay
Umpqua River Estuary

tidal flat

marsh

0   1   2 mi

10. Coast Guard Park. Bank fishing from rock crib for perch and rockfish.

11. North Spit. Softshells; shad in channel May–June.

12. The Point. Softshells.

13. Channel. Salmon, striped bass, sturgeon, pinkfin perch July–August, shad May–June.

14. Three Mile Flats. Softshell clams.

15. Sturgeon.

16. Steamboat Island. Softshell clams.

17. Striped Bass.

18. Sea-run Cutthroat.

19. Bolon Island. Most popular softshell digging.

20. Mouth of the Smith. Striped bass, salmon.

21. Reedsport. Public boat ramp and docks; fish for striped bass, sturgeon, salmon.

22. Mouth of the Umpqua. Striped bass, salmon, sturgeon.

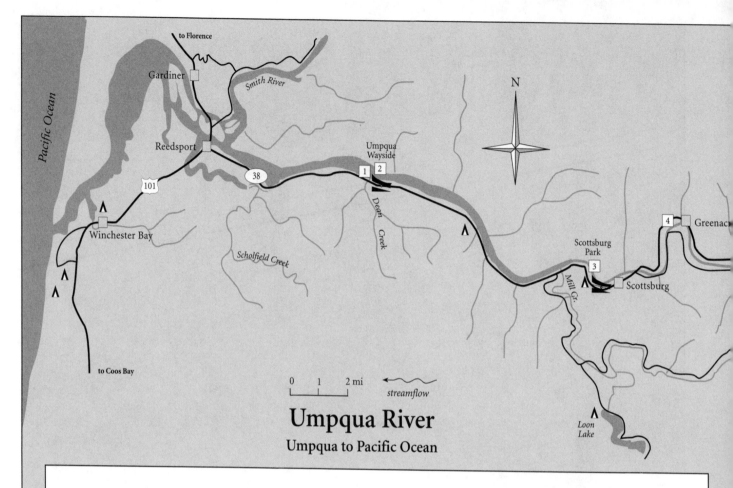

Umpqua River
Umpqua to Pacific Ocean

1. Dean Creek. Good sturgeon hole at mouth of Dean, accessible by boat from Reedsport at high tide only.

2. Umpqua Waywide. Concrete ramp; access to upper tidal area, sturgeon holes at mouths of Dean and Mill creeks.

3. Scottsburg Park. Improved ramp suitable for drift boats and motorized riverboats; good fisheries upstream and down.

4. Jimmy Creek. First in a sequence of good chinook holes.

5. Scott Creek Ramp. Use to access Low Water Bridge downstream 4 miles, and pools below Sawyer Rapids, for spring and fall chinook, winter and summer steelhead, shad.

6. Paradise Creek Ramp. Little used but good concrete ramp off Henderer Rd. 9 mi. downstream from Elkton accesses chinook, smallmouth, and coho; hard to launch during low water.

7. Sawyer Rapids. A series of rapids with pools below, and a 1200 ft. pool above accessed by Fee Pay Ramp a half mile above on Hwy. 38.

8. Bunch Bar. Day-use park with primitive ramp and bank fishing on first riffle above Sawyer Rapids upper pool; excellent for winter steelhead.

9. Elkton Bridge. Fish from bridge and both banks for spring chinook, winter steelhead. Smallmouth bass here to the forks.

10. Tyee Road. Drift boat slide at Myrtle Grove.

11. Tyee Park. Quarter mile of bank access to good winter steelhead slot.

12. Yellow Creek Boat Ramp. Improved ramp accesses shad, spring chinook, winter steelhead.

13. Osprey Boat Ramp. Take-out from James Wood (12-mile drift) for smallmouth bass, winter steelhead, fall & spring chinook, coho; motorized boats can launch at higher flows to fish pools; limited bank access.

14. Tyee Access Bridge. Bridge across mainstem offers access to both banks; deep slots upstream a quarter mile, downstream ¾ mile; stay below high water mark; respect private property to protect continued access.

15. James Wood Boat Ramp. Concrete ramp at mile marker 7.5; limited bank access (fish below high water mark) for winter steelhead, smallmouth, spring and fall chinook; put-in for driftboats to Osprey (long day's drift).

16. Mack Brown County Park. Primitive boat ramp accesses all Umpqua fisheries.

17. Umpqua Boat Ramp. Improved ramp; access for spring chinook, summer & winter steelhead, shad.

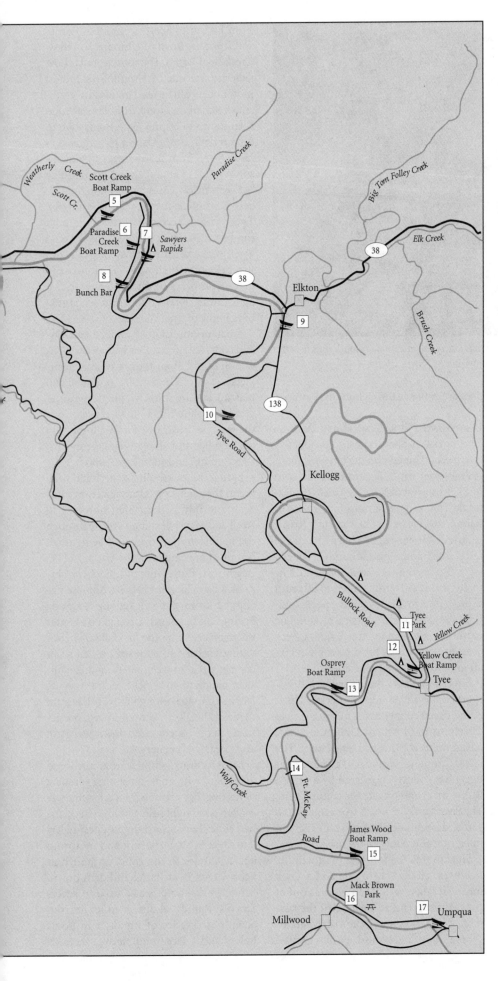

of the road to Loon Lake (second highway bridge), and downstream from Mill Creek. Anglers fish the bottom with mud shrimp, smelt, herring, and sand shrimp.

Coho were once a major fishery in the bay. Today, anglers can fish for finclipped coho early in the season. Coho move quickly upstream with the first good rains. Wild coho must be released unharmed.

Fall chinook, once a minor fishery here, are present in growing numbers in response to a program in which hatchery-reared juveniles are acclimated to the bay in net pens on the west side of Salmon Harbor (a STEPP volunteer project). Adult fall chinook enter the bay from late July through September. Both wild and hatchery runs tend to linger in the estuary and are available for harvest, providing good fall fishing. Fall chinook average 14 to 18 pounds, while coho are generally 8 to 9 pounds. Boat anglers fish between the jetties below the town of Winchester Bay as well as up-bay in the main channel north of Steamboat Island between Gardiner and The Point. There are also salmon fisheries off the mouths of the Smith and Umpqua. Bank fisheries for salmon include the south jetty, training jetty and extension, and the public docks in Reedsport.

There are good numbers of jack salmon in the estuary in fall, especially in the vicinity of Scholfield Creek. Scholfield itself is closed to salmon angling.

A population of striped bass reproduces modestly in the lower Smith River, migrating between the Smith and Winchester Bay, following the food source. These large bass live and grow a long time (up to 27 years), and thrillers to 45 pounds have been taken. In the bay, stripers are primarily caught on trolled plugs or bait. Popular baits include herring, anchovies, sea and mud worms, and fresh or frozen smelt. A smelt wrap on a large Kwikfish-type lure can also be effective. In late summer, try surface plugs or fly fishing for a heart-stopping thrill.

Stripers are fished by boat anglers in Social Security Bay south of the town of Winchester Bay, in the main channel below Gardiner, from the docks at Reedsport, at the mouths of the Smith and Umpqua, and below the mouth of Scholfield Creek. Anglers also fish in Scholfield Creek itself, which is open for striper fishing only, and only up to the first railroad bridge. Stripers are fished in the bay from June to October.

The UMPQUA has one of the finest smallmouth bass fisheries in the U.S. Photograph by Scott Richmond.

In general, stripers move into the Smith tidewater in March, April, and May (in pursuit of bait fish), and again in September and October to spawn.

Perch and rockfish are available to anglers boating the lower bay, and there are good bank fisheries for them at South Jetty, the Training Jetty and extension, the Coast Guard Dock south of Winchester Bay, Winchester Point gravel fill, and the public docks and Coast Guard Park in Winchester Bay.

Softshell clams can be dug in many of the coves and flats on both sides of the bay. The flats off Bolon Island are most popular, but good numbers are also dug in the North Spit Flats, off The Point, and above Steamboat Island. Crabs are available in good numbers, with best catches in spring off Winchester Point.

There are public boat ramps in Gardiner, in Reedsport at the mouth of the Umpqua as well as on Scholfield Creek, at the docks in Winchester Bay, and at Scottsburg Park about 12 miles above Reedsport.

Campgrounds are available at Windy Cove in Winchester Bay, at Lake Marie south of the lighthouse, at William Tugman State Park south at Eel Lake, and at forest service campgrounds on Eel Creek south of Tugman Park on Hwy. 101. There are additional campgrounds seven miles north of Gardiner at Tahkenitch Lake and at Siltcoos Lake. RV parks, motels, moorages and other accommodations and supplies are available throughout the bay area.

UMPQUA RIVER: Scottsburg Park to The Forks.

A handsome and productive river, second longest on the Oregon Coast. It flows over 100 miles from its forks, 10 miles northwest of Roseburg, to Winchester Bay. Once most famous for its runs of salmon, steelhead, and searun cutthroat, it is now acknowledged to have one of the finest smallmouth bass fisheries in America. It also hosts a very large shad run. The mainstem is currently closed to all trout fishing due to Endangered Species Act (ESA) restrictions. The status of Umpqua cutthroat is scheduled for review. Check current regulations for a possible relaxation of trout fishing restrictions.

Hwy. 38 follows the river from Reedsport east about 36 miles to Elkton. Gravel and paved county roads follow the river closely to the town of Umpqua, where paved roads continue to The Forks. The lower Umpqua meanders through relatively flat country, bordered by a mix of BLM timber and private agricultural land. The river varies in width from 100 to 200 yards, dropping only 400 ft. in the 100 miles from Roseburg to the bay.

Smallmouth are found throughout the mainstem all the way to The Forks. Look for them wherever there are pools out of the main current, at the edge of the current, or in slackwater off the main channel.

Smallmouth are most easily accessed from Elkton to Scott Creek Boat Ramp, and from the town of Umpqua to Yellow Creek Boat Ramp. The most popular boat fisheries are out of Umpqua (standard motor boats can be used in this low-gradient stretch of the river), from James Wood Boat Ramp to Osprey Boat Ramp (a 6 to 8-hour drift), from Osprey to Ferguson (3 hours), and from Yellow Creek to Hutchison Wayside (3 hours). There's good fishing between Yellow Creek and Elkton, but access is limited due to private property. There's bank access at each of the boat ramps and at two bridges (Elkton and Tyee) that cross the mainstem. Walk and fish below the high water mark to avoid private property conflicts. There are also bank fishing opportunities between Scottsburg and Umpqua Wayside.

Smallmouth fishing begins in late May and continues to October with peak catches in July and August. In early season, anglers use worms and grubs (both real and plastic), adding spinners, plugs, topwater crankbaits, and flies to their repertoire as the water warms. Look for smallmouth in back eddies and along ledges, drop-offs, rocky points, and submerged wood.

Spring chinook, both hatchery and wild, are in the mainstem Umpqua from mid-March to July, with greatest numbers in April and May. Fall chinook move through the mainstem in August and September, but most are caught in the estuary up to Reedsport. Both wild and hatchery chinook are available for harvest. Adipose fin-clipped coho are stocked up to Soda Springs on the North Umpqua and enter the mainstem after the first fall rains, providing a fishery until the season closes December 31. Coho are fished from the mainstem mouth up to Winchester Dam on the North Umpqua, though most catches are made in the North Umpqua itself, particularly in the Narrows and Swiftwater Park areas near the hatchery.

Most salmon fishing is from anchored driftboats, with anglers running spinners or herring. Early season fishing for chinook is often good right below Jimmy Creek, the first riffle above Scottsburg Bridge. Anglers launch at Scottsburg Park and motor up about 3 miles to the riffle, or launch at Scott Creek Boat Ramp and drift down. Scott Creek Ramp is also used to access Sawyer Rapids about a mile upriver. Sawyer is a series of rapids with pools below and a large pool above, accessed from a ramp ½ mile farther up Hwy. 38. Bank anglers can fish the Sawyer Rapids upper pool from Bunch Bar, a day-use park about 5 miles west of Elkton, or at Sawyer Rapids RV Park (for a small fee). Other popular spring chinook bank access points are at Elkton Bridge, Yellow Creek Boat Ramp, and Umpqua Boat Ramp.

Steelhead are enthusiastically fished on the mainstem, though without the intensity and religious fervor of the North Fork fishery. Mainstem summer steelhead are all finclipped hatchery stock. The winter run is considerably larger than the summer and includes good numbers of both hatchery and wild fish. Only finclipped steelhead may be kept. Check the regulations for bait and hook restrictions.

Summer steelhead are fished in from May through August, with peak catches in June and July. The most popular boat ramps for summer steelhead are Yellow Creek, Umpqua, and The Forks. Bank anglers find best access above Yellow Creek, where there is some BLM land along the river. Look for turn-outs on Bullock Rd. downstream from Tyee.

Anglers begin fishing for winter steelhead in mid-November, but the action is generally slow until late December. Peak fishing is in February and March. The earliest winter steelhead catches are made between Scottsburg and Elkton. Below Sawyer Rapids there's a good bank fishery at the RV park. The Elkton area offers good bank access off Mehl Canyon Rd., and there is good drift boat fishing throughout that stretch. The most popular day drifts are from Elkton RV Park to Sawyer Rapids (both charge a small fee to launch and take out), Yellow Creek Boat Ramp to Hutchison Wayside (a.k.a. The Nine Hole, an undeveloped ramp at mile post 9 on Hwy. 138w), Umpqua to James Wood Boat Ramp, and The Forks to Umpqua. The standard method is to run plugs in front of the drift boat. These same floats can be used to fish summer steelhead.

Shad enter the river in May and June from Scottsburg to the forks. Shad to 4 pounds are ho-hum, and there are many 5-pounders. Sawyer Rapids, Yellow Creek Boat Ramp, Umpqua, and The Forks are good shad spots. Yellow Creek attracts the largest number of bank anglers, but any of the winter steelhead drifts can be fished for shad in season. Shad anglers use light tackle with shad darts, shad flies, or jigs.

The only public campground on the mainstem is Tyee County Park on Bullock Rd., directly across from Yellow Creek There are private RV parks on Hwy. 138.

Umpqua river levels are available. See Appendix. For chinook and steelhead fishing, consider the river to be blown out of shape when the gauge at Elkton reads 15 ft. or higher.

UMPQUA RIVER, NORTH

One of Oregon's most treasured streams, beloved for its pristine quality and picturesque setting, and for its large run of summer steelhead. Spring chinook and winter steelhead also return to the river to spawn, and there are finclipped hatchery runs of summer and winter steelhead, spring chinook, and coho. A productive stretch of the North Umpqua is restricted to fly fishing only.

The North Umpqua is open for trout fishing above Soda Springs Reservoir, where rainbows and browns (rather than cutthroat) are the resident species. Elsewhere in the river (as throughout the Umpqua watershed), trout fishing is closed due to Endangered Species Act (ESA) restrictions. Reclassification of Umpqua cutthroat is scheduled for review by Federal agencies. Check current regulations for a possible relaxation of restrictions.

The North Umpqua, originating high in the Cascade Mountains at Maidu Lake, is fed by the outflow of big Diamond Lake and by snow melt and springs on a tumultuous 100-mile journey through a steep forested canyon. It joins the South Umpqua northwest of Roseburg to form the mainstem Umpqua.

The North Umpqua offers a pleasant lesson in how big fish navigate their home stream, where they pause before attempting a chute, where they rest after they've made it to the upper pool. Here, historically, anglers have been able to find fish where the books say they should be. And each riffle, tail-out, chute, and pool seems to have been lovingly (or ruefully) named by local anglers.

For the past several seasons, after a long slump, summer steelhead returns to the North Umpqua have been good. The mixed run of wild and hatchery stock enters the North Umpqua in June. Most angler effort is in July and August, then again in October and November after the water cools. (The bite is usually off in September when the water reaches peak temperatures.) At this time, only finclipped summer steelhead are available for harvest. Check the regulations for hook restrictions.

The river is open to fly fishing only for 31 miles from the boundary markers above Rock Creek to Soda Springs Dam. Anglers may cast flies using either standard fly fishing or spinning gear. Consult the regulations for specifics.

The NORTH UMPQUA *is fished for both wild and hatchery spring chinook. Photograph by Richard T. Grost.*

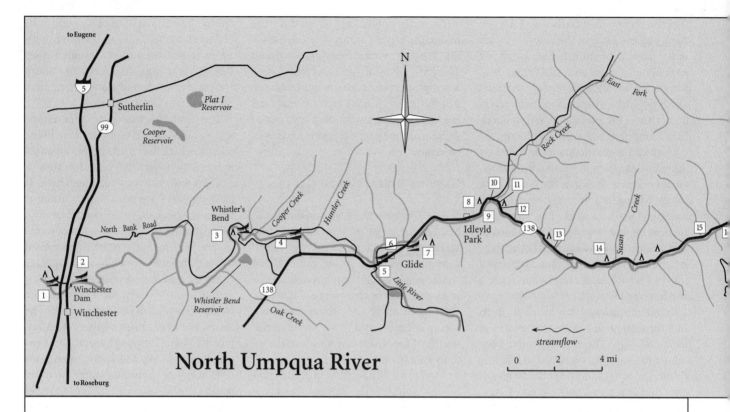

North Umpqua River

1. Amacher Park. To just below Winchester Dam, most popular fishing on the river; productive bank access for a quarter mile above boat ramp.

2. Page Road Take-Out. Pole slide above dam.

3. Whistler's Bend. County park with boat ramp, camping; one mile of good bank fishing.

4. Rock Pit Boat Access. Drift boats only, just east of Whislter's Lane off Hwy. 138.

5. Colliding Rivers. Boat ramp; good steelhead holes downstream.

6. Barn Hole. One major hole in two miles of good water accessed by Old Glide Rd. off Hwy. 138; bank fishing along road.

7. Lone Rock. Pole slide boat ramp; deadline for boat angling.

8. Narrows. One of the best holes on the river for coho, winter steelhead, chinook; bank access upstream and down; private property below wayside; unlimited public access upstream.

9. Max's Place. One of the better drifts for spring chinook, summer and winter steelhead, coho; classic tailout for fly fishing.

10. Swiftwater Bridge. Fish 200 yds. of good water on north and south banks.

11. Rock Creek. Huge pool where finclipped coho congregate prior to running up to hatchery; fly-only water begins 700 ft. upstream from markers.

12. Famous. Bedrock tail-out.

13. Lower Honey. Pocket water and some gravel.

14. Susan Creek. Long classic steelhead run; tail-out, riffle, bedrock, shelf; BLM campground.

15. Fairview. Dead drift through a deep chute and around big boulders.

16. Wright Creek. Wide tail-out of bedrock ledges where steelhead rest above major rapids.

17. Lower & Upper Archie. Two 20 ft. deep pools between major rapids.

18. Williams Creek. Half-mile classic run.

19. The Ledges. Shallow water featuring series of ledge slots where steelhead lie.

20. Steamboat Creek (Camp Water). At least 25 named holes where steelheaders and summer steelhead congregate bridge accesses south bank; Steamboat Creek is closed to angling.

21. Redman Creek. Gravel tail-out above major rapids.

22. Calf Creek. Pocket water.

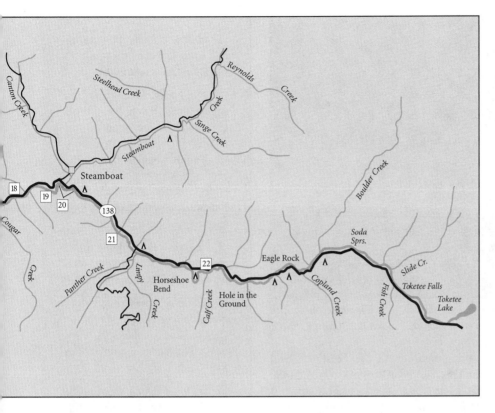

brook trout and browns to 1½ pounds.

The lower 35 miles of the North Umpqua are fished primarily from boats since most of the surrounding land is privately owned. From The Forks County Park, about 6 miles north of Roseburg, anglers can motor about ½ mile upstream. Jet sleds can navigate the 5 miles up to Winchester Dam; few jet the river above the dam. There is also a productive bank fishery at The Forks for salmon, steelhead, smallmouth bass, and shad. The most popular stretch on the lower river is from Amacher Park to just below Winchester Dam for steelhead and salmon. There is ¼ mile of good bank access at Amacher.

Above Winchester, Whistler's Bend County Park offers a mile of good bank fishing for salmon and steelhead in a fine stretch of classic water, including tail-out, riffle, bedrock chutes, and pockets.

Boat and bank access picks up from Glide east, with a boat ramp at the confluence of Little River (a.k.a. Colliding Rivers) accessing a string of good steelhead holes downstream. Anglers bank fish along the Old Glide Rd. off Hwy. 138, with the Barn Hole just one of many in a 2-mile stretch of good water. The deadline for boats on the North Umpqua is at Lone Rock Boat Ramp, about 3 miles west of the community of Idleyld Park. There's a lot of good water in the Idleyld area, but not a lot of bank access. A 200 yd. stretch is accessible from the north and south banks at Bridge

Steelhead anglers generally fish through November, take a break in December, then return to the river in January to fish the North Fork's winter run. At this time, wild winter steelhead as well as finclipped fish are available for harvest after January 1 below the fly fishing boundary. Above the boundary, only finclipped steelhead may be kept.

Spring chinook are in the river from April through October. At this time, they may be fished from the mouth to the fly fishing boundary, from January through July. Both wild and hatchery chinook are available for harvest. Peak catches are made in May, June, and July. The fly-only stretch is closed to chinook angling.

Finclipped coho from Rock Creek Hatchery are released from Soda Springs to the mouth, providing a fishery from October into early December. Greatest concentrations of coho (and anglers) are in the Narrows and Swiftwater Bridge areas near the town of Idleyld (pronounced *Idel-id*).

The North Umpqua is closed to all trout fishing below Soda Springs Dam to protect endangered cutthroat trout. Above Soda Springs, the season is open from late April through October. Here the resident species are rainbows and browns, and introduced brook trout may caught in unlimited numbers.

Roads follow the river closely all the way

from the forks to Lemolo Lake. Above Lemolo, as the highway swings south toward Diamond Lake, Forest Rd. 60 leads to the Kelsay Valley Trailhead, which tracks the North Umpqua to its headwaters at Maidu. West of the trailhead, forest roads follow the North Umpqua inlet of Lemolo Lake, including a stretch between Crystal Springs and Lemolo that offers excellent opportunities for late season fishing for

The mouth of Susan Creek is a popular spot for steelheading on the NORTH UMPQUA. *Photograph by Richard T. Grost.*

Below Soda Springs Power House on the NORTH UMPQUA, anglers can use bait to fish for summer steelhead. Photograph by Richard T. Grost.

to Nowhere, off Hwy. 138. Rock Creek joins the river about one mile east of Idleyld. There is a hatchery about ¾ mile up the Rock Creek Rd., and fish congregate in a huge pool at the confluence prior to running up.

From just above Rock Creek to Soda Springs Power House, only fly-fishing is permitted. Fly anglers in pursuit of steelhead use heavy gear in order to make long casts, and to break through the canyon winds. Named holes follow closely upon one another, many of them associated with the North Umpqua's plentiful tributaries. Among them are Susan Creek, Fairview, Wright Creek, Lower & Upper Archie, Williams Creek, The Ledges, and Steamboat.

Steamboat Creek itself is a steelhead spawning ground closed to angling. But the bend of river that includes the Steamboat confluence attracts anglers from throughout the world. Called the Camp Water by familiars, this 400 yard stretch of pocket water includes at least 25 named holes where summer steelhead and steelheaders gather under the protective eye of an organization of fly anglers called the Steamboaters. Steamboat Inn is a popular gathering place for out-of-town anglers who can afford high class lodging or a splurge on gourmet dining. It has also served as the unofficial information center and high command post for planning river protection and restoration strategies.

Whistler's Bend County Park offers the only campground on the lower river, but campgrounds are plentiful east of Idleyld on Hwy. 138 and at the reservoirs. At Susan Creek there is a full-service BLM camp as well as a long, classic steelhead run—tailout, riffle, bedrock, shelf. Other large facilities are at Bogus Creek and Island. There are two small camps on Steamboat Creek (Canton Creek and Steamboat Falls). There are large camps at Apple Creek, Horseshoe Bend, and Eagle Rock, a small camp at Boulder Flat, and large camps at Toketee and Lemolo. There are also two BLM campgrounds on the Rock Creek Rd. (County Rd. 78) about 5 miles above the hatchery.

North Umpqua river levels are available. See Appendix. Gauges are below Winchester Dam and below Steamboat near Glide. In general, the river is unfishable using any method at readings above 8000 cfs. The fly only section is hard to fish at readings above 3000.

UMPQUA RIVER, SOUTH. A big river, flowing over 95 miles from headwaters in the Rogue-Umpqua Divide Wilderness, joining the North Umpqua at The Forks about 10 miles northwest of Roseburg to form the mainstem Umpqua. The South Umpqua is fished primarily for small mouth bass and winter steelhead. Only finclipped steelhead may be kept at this time. The river is closed to all salmon angling. There are shad opportunities in the lower mile. Brief closures on the river in spring and fall protect spawning salmon.

South of Roseburg the South Umpqua is

1. Hestness Park. Boat ramp and limited bank fishing for all but shad and smallmouth.

2. The Forks. Access to a half mile of excellent water for all Umpqua species; year 'round fishing for salmon, steelhead, smallmouth; bank fish for summer and winter steelhead, finclipped coho, and shad; good hardware water; mainstem regs apply up to South Umpqua.

3. Singleton Park. Bank access to lower half mile of good fork water for all Umpqua species.

4. Mouth of Deer Creek. Urban bank fishing bank fishing for steelhead at Stephens St. Park near Chamber of Commerce in Roseburg.

5. Templin Beach. Boat ramp off Mosher Avenue in Roseburg; boat and bank access to winter steelhead, smallmouth bass; both drift and motor boats.

6. Foot of Lane St. Urban bank fishing; Roseburg up from Oak St. Bridge.

7. Fairgrounds. Improved ramp at end of Portland Ave., Roseburg; fish for spring chinook, winter and summer steelhead, shad, smallmouth; camping.

8. Hult Saw Mill. Primitive ramp handles drift boats only at low water; good fishing for winter steelhead, smallmouth.

9. Happy Valley. Improved boat ramp on Happy Valley Rd. accesses winter steelhead and smallmouth bass water.

10. Mouth of Lookingglass. Bank access only to a good winter steelhead hole.

flanked by I-5 and accessed by county roads from Winston to Canyonville. From Canyonville upstream, it is followed by Hwy. 227 to Tiller, then by County Rd. 46 into the Umpqua National Forest. Forest Rd. 28 continues along the stream past

11. Coon Hollow. Primitive boat ramp accesses winter steelhead, smallmouth.

12. Boomer Hill. Primitive boat ramp accesses winter steelhead, smallmouth.

13. Mouth of Myrtle Creek. Bank access for drift-fishing in county park just off I-5 exit; unimproved gravel put-in off 4th Avenue.

14. Lawson's Bar. Gravel bar launch accesses winter steelhead, smallmouth bass.

15. Stanton County Park. Unimproved soft gravel boat ramp sometimes requires 4-wheel drive; bank access for winter steelhead and smallmouth.

16. Canyonvile County Park. Improved ramp accesses winter steelhead, smallmouth, some shad; tent campsites.

17. Days Creek Bridge. Primitive ramp accesses winter steelhead, some smallmouth; no bank access.

18. Lavadoure Creek Boat Access. At MP 13.4, primitive ramp used for winter steelhead.

19. Milo Public Access. Primitive boat ramp for winter steelhead.

20. Coffee Creek Ramp. Primitive boat ramp for winter steelhead.

21. C'S Rock. At MP 28.1, bank access for winter steelhead.

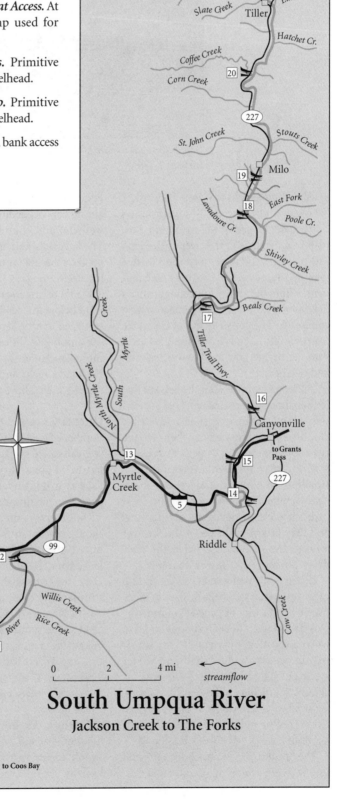

South Umpqua River
Jackson Creek to The Forks

Blue herons get a share of the UMPQUA's bounty. Photograph by Richard T. Grost.

South Umpqua Falls to Camp Comfort.

Forest land along the South Umpqua was heavily logged in the 1950s and '60s, with maintenance of the river's fisheries a low priority. Today, reforestation, better logging practices, and sensitive management within the several impacting agencies have allowed the South Umpqua to stage a comeback. The construction of Galesville Dam has also helped, providing a better summer stream flow for the river's salmon and steelhead.

The lower 30 miles offer the best angling for smallmouth bass, though bass are present up to Days Creek east of Canyonville. Good bass angling begins whenever the river temperature hits 65 degrees, generally from May through September. The smallmouth population decreases above Canyonville. Anglers access the best bedrock pockets from driftboats in spring; and they fish from the banks and bridges around the boat ramps when the river drops too low for drifting in summer.

Urban bank anglers can fish the mouth of Deer Creek at Stephens St. Park in Roseburg or at the foot of Lane St. up from the Oak St. Bridge. The Fairgrounds south of town also offers opportunity for smallmouth bass as well as shad and winter steelhead. The area around Winston, including the vicinity of Lookingglass Creek, is popular with smallmouth bass anglers. Coon Hollow and Round Prairie, off Hwy. 99, both have good bedrock bass pools.

The South Umpqua has both early and late arriving winter steelhead runs. The first run usually appears in the river in late November (depending on the arrival of fall freshets) and continues into December. The late run shows in late December with good catches till tax time. The river is open for steelhead up to Jackson Creek Bridge, and a lot of angling takes place in the area right below the deadline. Only finclipped steelhead may be kept.

Camping facilities are available at Dumont Creek about 7 miles above Tiller, at Boulder Creek, and at Camp Comfort about 7 miles above South Umpqua Falls.

UNION CREEK. One of the dwindling number of western Oregon streams where you can catch and keep wild trout. Tributary to the upper Rogue River in the Crater Lake area, it is understandably a popular attraction for summer vacationers.

Union enters the Rogue from the east about 10 miles north of Prospect, upstream from Natural Bridge. From Medford, follow Hwy. 62 about 58 miles north and east. Hwy. 62 crosses the lower end of the stream about one mile south of the junction of Hwy. 62 (to Crater Lake) and Hwy. 230 (to Diamond Lake). Forest Rd. 6230 follows the creek for about 7 miles from Rt. 230, and Forest Rd. 900 continues to its headwaters. There is a trail along the creek for several miles upstream from Union Creek Resort.

Fishing is best from late spring through July, but the creek holds up well all season. Brook trout, cutthroat, rainbows, and browns are all available. Browns to 10 pounds are rare but not unknown. From late May through the end of August, the stream is heavily stocked with rainbow trout off campgrounds near the mouth. Access to the stream is sometimes blocked by snow until after opening day.

There are Forest Service campgrounds at Union Creek, Farewell Bend and Natural Bridge.

VINCENT CREEK. A very good wild trout stream, tributary of the Smith River. The upper end can be reached by road from Hwy. 38, 1½ miles east of Scottsburg. Take the road leading north from Wells Creek Guard Station and follow it over the ridge to the Vincent Creek watershed. The lower end of the creek is reached by the Vincent Creek Rd., about 4 miles above Smith River Falls.

Like many Umpqua basin streams, it is closed to all fishing at this time to comply with Endangered Species Act (ESA) restrictions concerning the basin's cutthroat. Cutthroat status is scheduled for review. Check current regulations for a possible relaxation of restrictions.

WASSON LAKE. A rarity among lakes in the region, supporting its own population of wild cutthroat. Small and remote (though accessible by road), it is in western Douglas County north of the lower Umpqua River and south of Smith River. The lake is on public land and is the source of Wasson Creek, a tributary of the Smith. The lake is best reached from the Vincent Creek Rd. (See Vincent Creek.) This road is seldom passable until mid-summer.

Only about 5 acres, Wasson grows wild cutthroat that average 8 inches and run to l5 inches. At this time, the lake is closed to fishing due to general cutthroat protection in the basin. A review of cutthroat status may result in a relaxation of restrictions. Check current regulations.

WILLOW CREEK RESERVOIR (Rogue River watershed). A very popular reservoir with rainbow trout, largemouth bass, and crappie. From Medford, head north on Hwy. 62, turning east onto Butte Falls-Fish Lake Rd. About 10 miles east of Butte Falls, turn south on Willow Lake Rd.

Rainbow trout reproduce naturally in the reservoir and grow to 18 inches and larger. Additional legal rainbow are stocked annually. Fishing holds up well throughout the season, with May and September the best months. Trolling is common, but bait fishing accounts for most of the catch. Fly fishing in the upper shoal areas can produce some nice rainbow. Try a nymph with a sunken line, using a slow, jerky retrieve.

Black crappie to 10 inches are also available. Look for them along the dam face and under the docks at the marina. There are good number of largemouth bass. Because of the reservoir's high elevation, the bass rarely surpass 4 pounds, but the catch rate is good. Fish for them beneath the overhanging brush in the coves.

Boats can be easily launched. Only electric motors are allowed on the Balm Fork arm, and there is a 5 mph speed limit on portions of the Willow Creek arm. A resort at the lake is now closed, but there are some nice new cabins available for rent through the Jackson County Roads and Parks Dept. There are also several pleasant picnic areas along the lakeshore.

WINCHESTER BAY. See **UMPQUA RIVER, WINCHESTER BAY.**)

WINCHUCK RIVER. Oregon's southernmost river, actually dipping down to the California border about a mile above its mouth, 7 miles south of Bandon. In addition to fall chinook and winter steelhead, it offers excellent catch and release fishing for cutthroat trout.

The Winchuck River Rd. follows the river from its mouth up to Fourth of July Creek in the Siskiyou National Forest. The river is closed to fishing above Wheeler, about 10 miles from the mouth.

Fall chinook enter the Winchuck in November and are present through January. There is no spring chinook run here. Winter steelhead are generally fished from December through March. Except for an occasional finclipped hatchery stray, all are wild and must be released unharmed.

Like the Elk River, the Winchuck clears quickly after a storm. Except for residential development along the lower stream, it flows through pristine forested habitat. Its exceptional clarity can make it a difficult river to fish.

The Winchuck is closed to fishing from any floating device, but it can be accessed by bank anglers at a few public fishing sites along the river road, at a campground near Wheeler Creek, as well as from easements where the road swings close to the river's edge. There is a lot of private property below the national forest and a lot of "No Trespassing" signs. After all, at this point you're almost in California.

WOLF LAKE. An 8-acre hike-in brook trout lake in the headwaters of the South Umpqua River. Following the South Umpqua River within Umpqua National Forest on Forest Rd. 28, continue past Camp Comfort and the Boze Ranger Station, then take the left fork at the junction with Forest Rd. 2823. At French Junction, turn east on Forest Rd. 960 toward Black Rock. The trail to the lake (1478) is on the right at about 3½ miles.

Wolf offers good angling for brook trout to 16 inches. It is stocked annually by volunteers on horseback. Fishing can be great in early spring if you can get in. The roads are usually accessible in mid-June.

YANKEE RESERVOIR. Prominent on maps of the area, a privately owned 3½-acre impoundment on Yankee Creek, closed to public access. It is one mile upstream from Antelope Creek Rd. about 6 miles from White City.

FISHING IN OREGON'S
WILLAMETTE RIVER ZONE

Four out of five Oregon anglers live within the Willamette River Zone. This region is defined by the reach of the Willamette River and its tributaries, which drain the east slope of the Coast Range and the west slope of the Cascades for 150 miles north to south.

The Willamette Zone is blessed with an abundance of water, in the form of rain at lower elevations and snow at higher. The result is plentiful and varied fishing.

Though it flows through the state's most dense urban areas, heaviest concentration of industry, and most intensive farming—the Willamette River itself offers some of the zone's best fishing. In the Portland area, it is local tradition to hit the river at sun-up and be at work by 9 when the spring chinook season is open. Sturgeon are another popular fishery, especially in winter in the Willamette below Oregon City Falls. Bass and panfish are abundant throughout the river, sheltering near submerged bridge footings, docks, pilings, and log rafts in the urbanized reaches—and in the many sloughs and backwaters characteristic of the river's rural flow. The largest and most productive of these sloughs is Multnomah Channel, offering outstanding fishing for largemouth and smallmouth bass, catfish, crappie, perch and crayfish as well as walleye and spring chinook.

Salmon and steelhead are the primary fisheries of the zone's other big rivers: Clackamas, Sandy, North Santiam, South Santiam, Middle Fork Willamette.

The McKenzie River, closed to fishing for its wild chinook, is open for finclipped winter steelhead and for trout. McKenzie River rainbows, known as *redbands*, offer a quality trout fishing experience within easy reach of major Willamette Valley population centers. Other good trout streams include the North Fork of the Middle Fork Willamette, Salmon River (Sandy watershed), and the Oak Grove Fork of the Clackamas.

Much of the power of the Willamette has been tamed by flood control and irrigation reservoirs. West-side reservoirs are most productive for warmwater species. Cottage Grove, Dorena, Fern Ridge, and Henry Hagg grow trophy-size largemouth and smallmouth bass. East-side reservoirs (Detroit, Green Peter, Harriet, and Timothy) are more productive for cold water fisheries such as trout and kokanee.

Streams flowing into the Willamette from the east originate in the glaciers and lake basins of the Cascade Mountains. These basins are accessed by a well-maintained net-

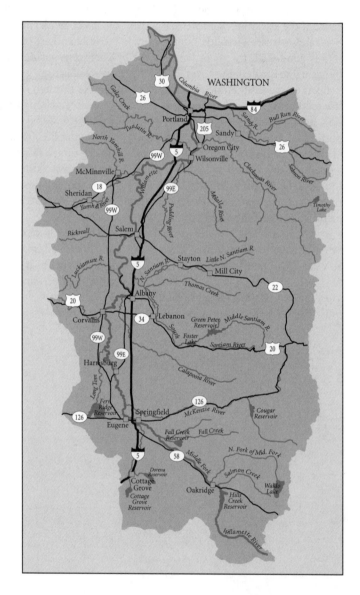

work of trails, including the Pacific Crest Scenic Trail which runs along the continent's mountainous spine from Canada to Mexico. Many of Oregon's basin lakes are stocked with brook trout and are among the most charming fisheries in the world. Eight Lakes Basin, Jefferson Park, Olallie Lakes Scenic Area, Mink Lakes Basin, Taylor Burn, and Waldo Lake Basin offer the greatest concentration of high lakes in the Willamette Zone. Refer to Mt. Hood and Willamette National Forest maps for a complete array of backcountry opportunities.

Aside from the rain, the Willamette Zone has an idyllic

The Willamette River Zone includes all waters draining to the Columbia River between the city of St. Helens and Bonneville Dam, except for those portions of tributaries east of the Sandy River that are downstream from the Union Pacific Railroad line. It includes all waters on Sauvie Island except the Columbia River.

THE BEST FISHING IN OREGON'S WILLAMETTE RIVER ZONE

CLACKAMAS RIVER (below Rivermill Dam)
For spring chinook and year-round steelhead, both hatchery and wild.

CLACKAMAS RIVER, OAK GROVE FORK
Good trout fishing with opportunities for harvest.

DETROIT LAKE
Fishing for a huge stocking of catchable trout as well as koka-nee, landlocked chinook, and catfish.

DORENA RESERVOIR
Known for its big largemouth bass and steady breeze.

EIGHT LAKES BASIN
Take your pick of Alforja, Bowerman, Blue, Chiquito, Duffy, Jorn, Mowich, or Red Butte for trout fishing in a grand mountain setting.

GREEN PETER RESERVOIR
Could use some help thinning out the kokanee population.

HAGG LAKE
Record-breaking smallmouth bass are the main feature, but perch, bluegill, crappie, and stocked trout are also plentiful.

HARRIET LAKE
Consistently good for rainbow and brown trout, with trophy trout opportunities.

HILLS CREEK RESERVOIR
Offers quite a few rainbow trout over 20 inches, as well as good fishing for crappie.

LOST LAKE
A stopover fishery off the Santiam Highway, offering catch and release fishing for plump brook and rainbow trout.

MARION LAKE
One of Oregon's best hike-in trout lakes.

McKENZIE RIVER
One of the finest trout streams in Oregon, for quality and quantity of wild fish close to civilization.

MULTNOMAH CHANNEL
Spring chinook are still king here, but there are tremendous numbers of bass and panfish as well as walleye.

SALMON RIVER (Sandy watershed)
Quality catch-and-release trout fishing in a wilderness-like setting close to Portland.

SANDY RIVER
Excellent salmon and steelhead fishing close to Oregon's largest metropolitan area.

SANTIAM RIVER, NORTH
A favorite of fly fishing steelheaders, with popular fisheries for finclipped summer steelhead, wild winter steelhead, and spring chinook.

SANTIAM RIVER, SOUTH
Hatchery steelhead are the most popular quarry, including many in the 15-pound class.

WILLAMETTE RIVER (Oregon City to Columbia River)
Offering some of Oregon's best fishing for spring chinook and sturgeon in a unique setting of soaring bridges, handsome skyscrapers, and industrial bustle.

WILLAMETTE RIVER (Eugene to Oregon City)
Explore its many sloughs and backwaters for largemouth and smallmouth bass and panfish.

WILLAMETTE RIVER, MIDDLE FORK
Hills Creek to Lookout Point Reservoir, offers good year-round (catch-and-release) fishing for wild trout.

climate. At lower elevations, temperatures rarely reach the freezing point in winter, or above 90°F in summer. The air is cooled and freshened by marine breezes. By mid-June, most trails in the Cascades are cleared of snow, and eager brook trout rise to any offering.

I-5 provides easy north-south access throughout the zone, and paved two-lane roads follow each river and many of the major tributaries. Some forest roads are also paved, though most are gravel (and some are ungraded).

Campgrounds are abundant in the national forests. Accomodations are available in the I-5 corridor, but are sparse along the river roads and near lakes and reservoirs.

ABERNETHY CREEK. A wild cutthroat stream that joins the Willamette River on the east side of Oregon City. About 12 miles long, it flows from the Highland Butte area. In Oregon City the creek is crossed by several bridges in town and is followed and crossed by county roads throughout its mid-section. The upper waters can be approached by way of Hwy. 213 east through Beaver Creek.

Except for road easements and bridges, the creek flows through private property. Fishing is strictly catch and release for the trout, using artificial flies and lures. Abernethy has small runs of coho and winter steelhead but is closed to fishing for those species.

ABERNETHY LAKES. A couple of hike-in brook trout lakes with a lot of little fish. The trail to the lakes is about a mile long. Take Forest Rd. 5899 northwest from West Bay, at the west end of Odell Lake. This road follows the railroad track to a derail station called Abernethy, a little over 2 miles from Odell. Follow Deer Creek Trail 3670 south and watch for the sign to the lakes. The trail is well blazed. The upper lake is northwest of the lower.

Both lakes have naturally reproducing brook trout. The lower lake has about 2 surface acres and is fairly shallow. It loses fish during hard winters. The upper lake is about 16 acres and 20 feet deep. Its brookies run to 13 inches. Both lakes are at elevation 4950 ft. There are natural campsites at the lakes. Campgrounds and supplies are available at Odell Lake.

ABIQUA CREEK. A very nice wild cutthroat trout stream with a fair run of wild winter steelhead. The stream heads in the Cascades east of Silverton and flows into the Pudding River. It is crossed by Hwy. 213 about 24 miles south of Oregon City, just 2 miles north of Silverton. Its mouth is about 3 miles farther west.

Abiqua flows through private land throughout its run, with public access at road crossings only. A good road follows the stream east for 9 miles, then leaves the stream, staying on the ridges. Abiqua flows about 30 miles and gets low in summer.

The creek opens for trout fishing at the end of May to protect spawning wild winter steelhead. Its wild cutthroat generally run 6 to 12 inches. Trout fishing is catch and release with artificial flies and lures. At this time, the creek is closed to both salmon and steelhead angling.

ADAIR POND. A 6-acre pond south of Adair Village on Hwy. 99W, chock full of good size bluegill, bass, and channel catfish. Red ear sunfish are also present, but they rarely bite. Bass to 8 pounds are taken, and channel cats are currently in the 4-pound range. The pond is immediately behind the ODFW regional office. Park in the ODFW parking lot. Stop by the office if you have any questions. Enthusiastically recommended for youngsters.

AERIAL LAKE. A hike-in trout lake in the Horse Lake area west of Elk Lake off Century Drive. The trailhead is across from Elk Lake Ranger Station at the north end of Elk Lake, 35 miles from Bend. From the ranger station, follow the trail west to Horse Lakes. After about 4 miles, turn south at the trail junction. In less than a quarter mile, two side trails join the main trail. Take the right fork to Aeriel, less than a mile farther. The left trail leads to Sunset Lake.

Aerial Lake is only about 3 acres, but fairly deep and lightly fished. It is stocked with both rainbow and brook trout, and they have been known to show some size. The lake is usually accessible in July. Bring mosquito repellent.

AGENCY CREEK. A fair size trout stream, tributary to the South Yamhill River, offering catch and release angling for wild cutthroat trout. It flows into the Yamhill at Grande Ronde Agency, about 3 miles northwest of Valley Junction on Hwy. 18. A BLM road parallels the creek upstream from Grande Ronde Agency and provides good access. It can also be reached by way of Hwy. 22.

It's a good early-season stream and can be fished at several bridges, but it gets low quickly in summer.

ALDER CREEK. A wild cutthroat and rainbow stream open for catch and release angling with artificial flies and lures. Flowing 5 miles between brushy banks, Alder is a tributary of the Sandy River, joining it from the south at the community of Alder Creek, 9 miles east of the city of Sandy. It is crossed by Hwy. 26 at its mouth. Only about 5 miles long, it doesn't produce very long in the spring. Several dirt roads from the Cherryville area access the upper reaches of the stream.

The trout here run 6 to 10 inches, averaging 8. It is closed to salmon and steelhead angling.

ALFORJA LAKE. A consistent producer of fair size brook trout in the headwaters of the North Santiam near Duffy Butte, Mt. Jefferson Wilderness. A 4-acre lake, not very well known, it is off the trail and lightly fished. See Duffy Lake for directions into the basin. Alforja is about three quarters of a mile southwest of Duffy. Cincha Lake is north of Alforja.

The naturally reproducing brook trout here run to 13 inches and will usually hit anything in early season. In late summer and fall, flies work best in morning and evening. The lake is brushy, but not hard to fish.

ALICE LAKE. A tiny lake of about an acre, right on Trail 3422, 1½ miles north of Duffy Lake just south of Red Butte. See Duffy Lake for directions. There are usually lots of fair size brook trout and cutthroat here in early season, but fishing tapers off in fall because the lake's so small. There are good campsites along this part of the trail.

ALTON BAKER CANAL. A pleasant little diversion of the Willamette, created especially for canoeing in Springfield and Eugene. It offers limited fishing for stocked rainbow trout.

The canal has very little current and can be comfortably paddled both upstream and down. There are opportunities to launch at the upstream end at the foot of Aspen St. (off Centennial Blvd. in Springfield, upstream from the I-5 bridge), and at the downstream end from Day island Rd. (off Country Club Rd. near Autzen Stadium). There are paths on either side of the canal, and much of the riparian area is manicured. A culvert and two small dams are easily portaged.

Legal rainbows are stocked several times and in several locations from February through June, but they tend to follow the current back to the river pretty quickly. It may be best to follow the fish truck if you're bringing youngsters here to fish and want to insure success. A 4-acre pond near the canal's mid-point has more natural vegetation that may encourage some trout to linger a bit.

AMOS AND ANDY LAKES. Two small high lakes in the southeast corner of the Willamette National Forest, a bushwhack from Indigo Lake. See Indigo Lake for directions. From Indigo, hike cross country 1¼ miles northeast, skirting a butte which projects northwest from Sawtooth Mt. and divides the Indigo basin from the basin holding Amos and Andy. Hold your elevation, as Amos and Andy are just slightly higher than Indigo.

Is it worth it? The lakes are stocked by air from time to time, but at 6,000 ft. and only 10 ft. deep, they frequently winterkill. On the other hand, a lot of 6 to 10 inch brook trout might just be hungrily awaiting you.

ANN LAKE. A good brook trout lake of about 20 acres just north of Marion Lake. See Marion Lake for road and trail directions. Ann is on the Marion Lake Trail about one mile in, on the left.

It provides excellent angling in early season for brook trout to 15 inches. A good fly lake, it usually holds up well throughout the season, though it may be slow in late summer. There's a lot of vegetation around the shore, so a float tube would be very handy. It is usually accessible by late May.

AVERILL LAKE. A good 11½ acre brook trout lake in the western portion of the Olallie Lakes group about 95 miles southeast of Portland. Quickest route is by trail from the west.

Follow the Breitenbush River Rd., Forest Rd. 46, from Detroit Reservoir to the Mt. Hood National Forest boundary. Turn east onto the Breitenbush Lake Rd., Forest Rd. 42, then go left at the fork onto Forest Rd. 380 about a half-mile farther. About a quarter mile from where 380 passes under the power transmission lines, pick up Trail 719, which leads east about 1½ miles to the lake. The trail first passes Red Lake. Averill can also be reached by way of trails leading into the basin from Olallie Lake on the east.

Averill is an excellent fly fishing lake, but other methods will work. Brook trout here run 6 to 12 inches. There are fair natural campsites at the lake. It's usually not accessible until late June. Come prepared for mosquitoes.

BAKER CREEK. A small trout stream, about 9 miles long, north of McMinnville. It flows into the North Yamhill River from

Fishing creeks in the Willamette Zone is primarily catch-and-release for wild trout using artifiicial flies and lures. Photograph by Dennis Frates.

the west. Baker Creek is crossed just above its mouth by the paved Carlton-McMinnville Rd. Several good roads follow and cross the creek. These are reached by going west from the north end of McMinnville.

Baker contains wild cutthroat to 12 inches. At this time, it is catch and release only. Rainbow Lake Education Center is on the creek. An old water supply dam currently blocks fish passage to the upper stream. Above the dam, the creek flows through BLM land, and hiking is permitted.

BAYS LAKE. A 9-acre brook trout lake in the picturesque and popular Jefferson Park of the Mt. Jefferson Wilderness. This natural alpine parkland of wildflower meadows and wooded hummocks is on a saddle dominated by Mt. Jefferson to the south.

There are several approaches to Jefferson Park, all at least a 5-mile hike. One approach is from the north by way of the Pacific Crest Trail from Breitenbush Lake, arduous, but with great views all the way in. Another popular approach is from the west by a trail that follows Woodpecker Ridge to the PCT, and the PCT north to the Park.

Take North Santiam Hwy. 22 to Pamelia Creek Rd. 2246, about 7 miles south of Idanha. At the first fork, bear left onto Forest Rd. 040 and follow it about 4 miles to its end. A trail leads east 1½ miles to

the Pacific Crest Trail. Follow the PCT north to Bays.

Bays Lake is quite deep and easy to fish, with a rocky shoreline and many bays. It offers good fly angling, particularly along the western shore. The lake is stocked by air with brook trout every two years. This area is high, and the fish don't put on much growth, but by August they bite readily enough. Scout Lake to the east holds some good size brook trout, but you'll work harder for them.

Unfortunately, the beauty and accessibility of this area has led to heavy use, especially on weekends. To help keep track of users, there are self-issuing camping permits at the trailheads. This is a wilderness area, and campers are urged to use no-trace methods and to camp well back from the water in order to assist in the regeneration of fragile plant life. Open fires are prohibited.

BEAR CREEK (Lane Co.). A wild cutthroat stream, open for harvest at this time. About 8 miles long, it joins the Long Tom River about 3 miles west of Junction City at Hwy. 99. It is followed and crossed by Hwy. 360 as well as by several county roads. Bear Creek is not stocked but offers fair spring angling. It is usually fished down by June. It is primarily a local fishery, and there is not much public access.

BEAR LAKE (Mt. Hood National Forest). A nice little 2-acre hike-in brook trout lake in the Mt. Hood Forest southwest of Hood River. The lake is about 2 miles northeast of Rainy Lake.

From the community of Dee, drive north about 2 miles towards Punchbowl Falls, and pick up Forest Rd. 2820, which twists and winds its way west. The trailhead is on the north side of the road about 2 miles beyond the intersection of Forest Rd. 2821. If you get to Rainy Lake, you've missed the trail by about a mile. Bear is on a spur trail off the Defiance Mt. Trail 413. The trailhead described here leads north less than a quarter mile to Trail 413, which you take to the east. About a quarter mile farther brings you to the Bear Lake Trail, cutting off to the north and leading ½ mile to the lake.

Though small, Bear Lake is fairly deep and hardly ever winterkills. At elevation 3800 ft., it is stocked by air with fingerling brook trout. The catch ranges in size from 8 to 12 inches. The road to the trailhead usually opens by late June.

BEAR LAKE. (Willamette National Forest) Across the ridge from Firecamp Lakes, one mile south of Slideout. See Slideout Lake for directions. Bear has 9 surface acres and is 24 ft. deep, tucked within a thick stand of alder. It is stocked every other year with brook trout. You might need orienteering skills to find it.

BENSON LAKE (McKenzie River watershed). A nice trout lake of about 25 acres, 1½ miles by trail from Scott Lake on McKenzie Pass Hwy. 242. The McKenzie Hwy. is usually the last Cascade crossing to open each spring. The trailhead is at Scott Lake Campground, and the trail leads northwest to Benson, then on to Tenas Lake and Mt. Scott.

There's a mixed bag of trout here (rainbows, cutthroat, and brook trout), with some to 18 inches. Best fishing is in early season as soon as the road is open. There are no improved campsites at the lake, but there are campgrounds at Scott Lake and along the highway close by.

This is a great introductory hike-in lake for youngsters. The trail is easy, the scenery is pretty, and the fish are plentiful.

BENSON LAKE (Columbia Gorge). A 23-acre lake in Benson State Park, adjacent to the Columbia River on the south side of I-84 just before Multnomah Falls. The lake has populations of brown bullhead, white crappie, pumpkinseed sunfish, and largemouth bass. It is stocked from April through June with 14,000 catchable rainbows and with trophy-size trout when they are available.

There is no boat ramp, but anglers can launch rafts, light-weight boats, and float tubes. The banks are quite flat, offering unimproved access for less-abled anglers. The lake itself is open for year-round fishing, but the park closes after Labor Day. Off-season, park on the access road and hike in. Unimproved wheelchair access when the park is open.

BERLEY LAKES. Two small trout lakes north of the Santiam Hwy. near the summit. Take the Pacific Crest Trail north from Santiam Pass at Hwy. 20, and hike 1½ miles north to its junction with Trail 3491, which ultimately leads to Duffy Lake. Follow 3491 two miles north to Lower Berley Lake. Upper Berley is off the trail about an eighth mile northwest of Lower.

The lakes are both about 7 acres. They are air stocked with either cutthroat or brook trout at least every other year. Any method will take fish here.

BETH LAKE. An interesting lake to find and to fish. It's located near the upper Collawash River in the Bull of the Woods area, some 50 miles southeast of Portland. Five acres and 35 ft. deep, it sits at an elevation of 4450 ft.

Follow the Clackamas River Hwy. 224 to Ripplebrook Ranger Station; then take Forest Rd. 63 south along the Collawash River. About 10 miles south, in the Toms Meadow area, take Forest Rd. 6340 southwest to where Forest Rd. 6341 forks to the right. Take 6341 about 5 miles south. Look for a trail sign where the road crosses Pansy Creek and switches back to the north. Follow Trail 551 about ½ mile to Trail 549, which intersects from the left (east). Follow 549 to its junction with 550, then cross over 550 and head up the ridge. Keep bearing northeast, and you'll hit the small stream that flows into the lake.

There are wild brook trout to 13 inches here, and the lake is easy to fish from the bank. There's one good campsite on the northwest shore.

BETHANY LAKE. A warmwater impoundment on a tributary of Rock Creek in Washington County north of Aloha. It offers fishing for largemouth bass, bluegill, bullheads, and stocked trout. From Hwy. 26, take the 185th St. Exit, and follow 185th north. This busy (though semi-rural) street crosses the lake at its upper end and provides the lake's best parking opportunity (on the road easement). There is limited neighborhood parking at another access off Columbia Blvd. (not the same as the street of that name in North Portland!). From 185th St., turn west on Rock Creek Blvd., then right on Columbia Blvd. Park on the street near the barricade. A path leads to the dam area.

Bethany is about 500 ft. wide and ½ mile long. It was dredged from 185th St. halfway to the dam, so that end currently offers the deepest, coolest refuge for trout. The lake gets very warm in summer. Trout fishing is limited to early spring. Bluegill, largemouth bass, and large brown bullhead are available year-round. The bass grow to respectable size, with some to five pounds.

Bethany is managed as an open space by Tualatin Hills Parks and Recreation.

BETTY LAKE. An easy to reach, 40-acre hike-in lake that grows big trout high in the Cascades. The lake is at an elevation of 5500 ft., one mile southeast of the south end of Waldo Lake.

Take Hwy. 58 from Oakridge about 20 miles to Waldo Lake Rd. 5897. After about five miles, look for the sign for Betty Lake Trail 3664 on the west side of the road. It's an easy ½ mile hike to the lake.

The rainbows average 10 inches, and fish to 23 inches are available. A float tube or raft is useful here. Bait or lures work well anytime, and flies will take large fish early in the day and near dusk. Remember the slogan, "Waldo Lake, Famous Mosquitoes." There are several other small lakes within a mile of Betty that may hold fish.

BIG CLIFF RESERVOIR. About 150 acres on the North Santiam River, built about the same time as Detroit Reservoir. The dam is located several miles below Detroit Dam.

Eclipsed by the popularity of Detroit, Big Cliff is lightly fished but offers good catches of rainbows and very large whitefish (up to 33 inches). There is a poor boat ramp near Detroit Reservoir Dam. Keep in mind that this is a re-regulation reservoir, subject to extreme and rapid water level fluctuations (up to 6 ft.). After launching a boat, be careful to park well away from the shore, or you may be inundated. Nearest campgrounds are upriver off Hwy. 22.

BIG LAKE. Over 225 acres, south of Santiam Hwy. 20 near the summit of the Cascades. It is about 8 miles southeast of the junction of North and South Santiam highways. The lake is 4 miles down Forest Rd. 2690, which leads south from Hwy. 20 near Santiam Lodge. Continue south past Hoodoo Ski Bowl.

Speed boaters and water-skiers offer fisher folk plenty of competition here, but Big Lake has some large brook trout, as well as stocked kokanee, rainbows, and cutthroat. The lake can get rough in the afternoon, so plan to fish early or late.

There are several nice campgrounds on the lake and good boat ramps. Open year-round, it is a available for ice fishing.

SLIDE LAKES. Two pretty little hike-ins with brook trout in the headwaters of the Collawash River. Located in the Bull of the Woods area at about 4300 ft., the lakes are about 3 miles from the nearest road, less than ½ mile northeast of Bull of the Woods Lookout.

From Estacada, follow the Clackamas River upstream on Hwy. 224 to Ripplebrook Ranger Station, then take Forest Rd. 63 south along the Collawash River. After about 10 miles, in the Toms Meadow area, take Forest Rd. 6340 southwest several miles to Trailhead 550 near the end of the road. Three miles south on this trail south brings you to Bull of the Woods Lookout. Upper Big Slide Lake is ½ mile northeast on Trail 555. Big Slide is about a mile farther north on the opposite side of the trail.

Stocked by air (in odd number years), the brook trout here average 9 inches with a range from 6 to 11 inches. Just an acre each and shallow, the lakes occasionally winterkill. They're easy to fish, and any method can be effective. Try fly angling evenings in late summer. Upper Big Slide is in a setting of tall timber with some talus slopes. There are three nice natural campsites at the lake.

Supplies are available at Estacada or at Detroit if you come in from the south. Other lakes nearby are stocked with brook trout. See Welcome, Pansy, and Lenore.

BINGHAM LAKE (Linn Co.). A small cutthroat lake in the Mt. Jefferson Wilderness Area ½ mile west of the Pacific Crest Trail in the Bingham Basin, south of Mt. Jefferson. It is about a 6-mile hike from Marion Lake and about 5 miles south from Pamelia. There is no blazed trail. The lake is the source of Minto Creek, a tributary of the North Santiam River.

Bingham is about 4 acres and has cutthroat that exceed 15 inches. It is lightly fished (rarely found?) and can provide good fly fishing for the pathfinding angler.

BINGO LAKE. A shallow lake ½ mile west of the southern tip of Waldo Lake at the head of Black Creek, reached best by boat from Shadow Bay Campground on Waldo. It can also be approached by trails leading from Waldo Lake, and from the north from Black Creek or Salmon Creek roads out of Oakridge.

About 4 acres and shallow, it frequently winterkills. Nevertheless, it is stocked periodically with cutthroat. Neighboring Bongo Lake is a bushwhack three quarters of a mile northwest. Bongo covers 9 acres and has naturally reproducing brook trout. This here's 'skeeter country from late spring to early summer, so be prepared.

BIRTHDAY LAKE. A small hike-in brook trout lake 3 miles south of Waldo in the Island Lakes Basin. See Island Lakes for the best route into the basin. Birthday Lake is less than ½ mile south of Lower Island Lake, reached by Trail 3674.

Birthday is about 3 acres, just north of the trail. Its brook trout are small, from 6 to 10 inches, but they're usually aggressive in spring and fall. Fly angling can be good. An occasional lunker is taken. There are natural campsites here, in addition to established campgrounds at Gold and Waldo lakes. The roads in are usually accessible by late June. Other lakes within ½ mile of Birthday are stocked.

BLAIR LAKE. A 35-acre brook trout lake in the Willamette National Forest at the head of Salmon Creek, northeast of Oakridge on Hwy. 58. From Oakridge, take the Salmon Creek Rd., Forest Rd. 24 (look for the salmon hatchery signs) about 9 miles northeast to the signed Blair Lake turnoff. Follow Forest Rd. 1934 north about 8 miles to the lake.

The naturally reproducing brook trout at Blair run 6 to 16 inches, averaging 10 inches, and there are plenty of them. There are several nice campsites near the lake outlet, a very short hike from the road. Evening fly angling is generally excellent, with mosquitoes, blue uprights, caddis and gray hackles good bets. Motorboats are prohibited.

About 1½ miles east is Devil's Lake, which has no trail access. It is only about 5 acres but has nice brook trout to 14 inches.

The Blair Lake Rd. takes you past the small but pleasant Wall Creek Warm Springs, suitable for a soak on a summer day. (The pool isn't hot enough for cold weather comfort.) The springs are shown on the Forest Service map, about a quarter mile on a trail that follows Wall Creek. The trailhead is on the first hairpin turn, about ½ mile from the junction of Forest Rd. 1934 with the Salmon Creek Rd. There are good camps along the Salmon Creek Rd.

BLOWOUT CREEK. A good trout stream with harvest opportunities in the North Santiam area of Willamette National Forest. Take Hwy. 22 to Forest Rd. 10, about 3 miles south of the community of Detroit. Forest Rd. 10 crosses the North Fork of the Santiam River and follows the south shore of the reservoir to Blowout Creek, then follows the creek to its headwaters.

Blowout has a population of wild rainbows and cutthroat. Bait and spinner work best in early season, and fly angling is productive when the water warms in late spring. There are no camps on the upper stream, but there is a good campground at Stahlman Point on Detroit Reservoir, and there are other camps on the north shore along Hwy. 22.

BLUE LAKE (Willamette watershed). A productive little brook trout lake on the western border of Diamond Peak Wilderness Area, recommended as an introductory hike-in experience for youngsters.

From Oakridge, drive south on Hwy. 58 a mile or so to the Hills Creek Reservoir turn-off. Follow Forest Rd. 21 around the west shore of the reservoir and up the upper Middle Fork of the Willamette, about 26 miles (from the dam) to where Forest Rd. 2145 forks northeast. Take 2145 about 5 miles to a fork where Forest Rd. 2149 turns east, then south. Follow 2149 about 4 miles to the Blue Lake Trailhead. It's an easy ½ mile hike east to the lake on a well marked trail. The roads usually open in late June.

Blue Lake covers 20 acres and is 33 ft. deep. It has naturally reproducing brook trout that run 6 to 16 inches, with a few larger taken at times. Bait and lures are best during the day, and fly angling is effective mornings and evenings. This is a good lake for a float tube. Don't forget the mosquito repellent.

BLUE LAKE (Santiam watershed). A 12-acre brook trout lake in the Eight Lakes Basin of Mt. Jefferson Wilderness. Blue Lake is a quarter mile northeast of Jorn Lake in the northern part of the basin, south of Marion Lake.

Blue Lake is over 40 ft. deep, and though its fish tend to be short, they are usually deep bodied. They average 6 to 11 inches, with most on the small side. Any method will take fish. Several other lakes are close by, and all are fishable. See Jorn, Bowerman, Teto and Chiquito.

BLUE LAKE (Bull Run watershed). About 50 acres at the head of the Bull Run River in Portland's water supply reserve. Closed to all recreational use.

BLUE LAKE (Sandy River watershed). A 62-acre trout and warmwater fishery east of Portland, 3 miles west of Troutdale. The lake is north of Hwy. 30, ½ mile south of the Columbia River. A paved road leads to the north end, where there is a county park. The rest of the lakeshore is privately owned and closed to public use.

Blue Lake is stocked annually with about 6000 legal rainbow trout and has some good size largemouth bass that are taken on bait and lures. Best bass habitat is at the west end where there is submerged wood and vegetation. Angling for crappie, green sunfish, and bluegill can be very good.

The park is large and has extensive picnic facilities, but no camping. Rental boats are available in summer, with private boats allowed only in winter and restricted to no larger than 14 ft. in length (17 ft. for canoes), and maximum 3 hp motors. Facilities include a wheelchair accessible with submerged structure to attract fish to the area.

BLUE RIVER. A good size tributary of the McKenzie River in the Willamette National Forest, flowing into Blue River Reservoir

about 43 miles east of Eugene off Hwy.126. Forest Rd. 15, leaves the highway about 5 miles east of the community of Blue River and follows the middle and upper stream more than 10 miles.

The main catch consists of stocked rainbow trout in the first 5 miles above the reservoir, although wild cutthroat and rainbows are present in small numbers. Only finclipped trout may be kept. The catch rate for bank angling is on a par with the main McKenzie. The fish usually run 8 to 12 inches, but a few larger are taken. Bait is best in early season. Later there is fair fly angling.

Camping is available at Blue River Reservoir, and there are numerous camps near McKenzie Bridge to the east.

BLUE RIVER RESERVOIR. A 935-acre flood control lake on a major tributary of the McKenzie River, offering fair to good angling for stocked rainbows. Non-finclipped trout must be released unharmed.

Blue River Reservoir is north of Hwy. 126, about 45 miles east of Eugene in the heart of the McKenzie Recreational Area. The dam is about 2 miles above the mouth of Blue River. To get there from Springfield, follow Hwy. 126 east about 3 miles past Blue River Ranger Station. Turn left on Forest Rd. 15.

By mid-August the reservoir is drawn way down, driving trout to sulk in the depths and limiting boat ramp accessibility. (Few things are uglier than a drawn-down reservoir). There are two boat ramps, one mid-way down the lake (where the road first reaches the reservoir), and the other at the northeast end near Mona Campground.

BLUEGILL LAKE. A lightly fished 7-acre bass and panfish pond on the eastern edge of Salem. It is located in Cascade Park, across the creek from Walter Wirth Lake, which is also in the park. Bluegill is just west of I-5, between the airport road and Turner Rd.

It has good populations of crappie and bluegill, and a fair number of largemouth bass and carp. Bait fishing is the most popular method.

BOND BUTTE POND. A 35-acre pond south of Albany. The lake is east of I-5 at Bond Butte Overpass, 15 miles south of the town of Bond Butte. Take the Harrisburg

exit off I-5. The pond contains channel cats, white crappie, and a few largemouth bass.

BONGO LAKE. A 9-acre brook trout lake near Waldo Lake. See Bingo Lake for road and trail directions.

BOOT LAKE. A generally productive brook trout lake in the Mink Lake Basin of Three Sisters Wilderness, about ½ mile due east of Cliff Lake. See Cliff Lake for directions from the Bend area by way of Elk Lake. From Cliff Lake you can test your compass skills on this 5-acre target.

Boot Lake is quite deep for its size, a good lake for lures, spinners, or bait, as the bottom drops off quickly in most spots. Fly fishing can be good at dusk. There are nice campsites at the lake. Early summer mosquitoes up here are legendary.

BOWERMAN LAKE. Usually a good producer of brook trout, at the north end of Eight Lakes Basin. It is reached by 6 miles of trail from the Duffy Lake Trailhead, 3 miles off Hwy. 22. Bowerman is east of Jorn Lake. It can also be approached from Marion Lake by a 5-mile hike.

Bowerman is shallow and covers only about 6 acres. The lake is a consistent producer of brook trout 6 to 12 inches. The outlet runs into Little Bowerman Lake, which is only a few acres and isn't stocked, since it winterkills. Fly fishing is usually good, though bait and lures will take fish, too. There are good campsites throughout the area. This is a scenic spot, and there are many other lakes to explore.

BREITENBUSH LAKE (Confederated Tribes Warm Springs). A fine lake of 65 acres at the southern end of the Olallie Lake area north of Mt. Jefferson, about 105 miles from Portland. Take Hwy. 26 about 8 miles south of the Hwy. 35 junction to Forest Rd. 42, which cuts south. Stay on 42 until you reach Forest Rd. 4220, following signs to Olallie Lake. Continue past Olallie to Breitenbush Lake, about 3 miles south.

It can also be reached from Detroit Reservoir by following Forest Rd. 46 up the North Fork of the Breitenbush River to Forest Rd. 4220. Watch for signs to the lake. Neither road is usually open before late June, so check with the Forest Service for conditions. Both approach roads are rough, with the way in from the north either muddy or dusty, and from the west, rocky.

Breitenbush is on a plateau, partially within Warm Springs Reservation. Tribal permits are generally required to fish waters on tribal land, but one is not needed to fish Breitenbush. Other good lakes off the road to the north, not on tribal land, include Olallie, Monon, and Horseshoe.

Breitenbush is a nice family lake and has excellent fishing at times. The lake is stocked from time to time, and has natural reproduction of brook trout and rainbows. About 75 acres with quite a bit of shoal area, it offers good fly fishing in fall. August and September are the best months. The fish usually run 6 to 12 inches with a few larger. There is a campground at the north end of the lake. Boats can be easily launched, but motors are prohibited.

BREITENBUSH RIVER. A tributary to the Santiam system, with catch and release opportunities for wild trout and catch and some stocked trout in the lower reach. It flows 30 miles down the slopes of Mt. Jefferson in Willamette National Forest to Detroit Reservoir.

The lower stream is crossed by Santiam Pass Hwy. 22 at the point where it enters the reservoir. A good road, Forest Rd. 46 follows the stream northeast to the Mt. Hood Forest boundary. A poor road, Forest Rd. 42 follows the North Fork to its source at Breitenbush Lake.

The river is stocked from the reservoir up to the confluence of the South Fork Breitenbush. Wild cutthroat and rainbows are available throughout the river but must be released unharmed. The rainbows run 7 to 12 inches, though larger rainbows can be found in the lower river late in the season. Whitefish are also present.

The lower end of the stream in the Breitenbush arm of Detroit Reservoir can be fished by boat until the water drops. Upstream of the reservoir, the river runs through a gorge but is accessible from the road above in some places. In most areas the bank is steep and brushy. There is some good fly water available. There are four nice campgrounds between the reservoir and Breitenbush Hot Springs, about 12 miles upstream. The hot springs are privately owned and managed as a wildlife sanctuary and holistic retreat center. Cabins are available by reservation.

BRICE CREEK. A tributary of Row River of the Coast Fork Willamette, joining the Row about 5 miles east of Dorena Reservoir. From Cottage Grove, follow Row River Rd. past Dorena Reservoir to Disston, where a gravel road (Brice River Rd.) follows Brice to its headwaters.

The creek is not stocked, but wild cutthroat are present. Most angling is confined to the lower 8 miles, but some fish are taken in the upper stretch. There are several campgrounds along the creek southeast of Disston.

BRIDAL VEIL CREEK. A nice little stream for catch and release wild cutthroat in the Columbia Gorge area. Only 7 miles long, it enters the Columbia following a scenic fall 29 miles east of Portland. Angling is confined to the stream above the waterfall. A poor dirt road follows the creek upstream from the community of Bridal Veil, and the upper end is accessed by branch roads from the Larch Mountain Rd. To reach Bridal Veil, follow I-84 east to Exit 28, or take the scenic Crown Pt. Highway.

A 10-inch fish is a whopper in this little stream, but Bridal Veil has some feisty little wild cutthroat. Fly fishing works well in late summer and fall using sneak tactics. Bridal Veil Falls State Park offers day use facilities only.

BRITTANY LAKE. A small but deep hike-in brook trout lake north of Waldo Lake. It is one of several lakes within the 1996 Moolack Burn. From North Waldo Campground at the northeast end of Waldo, take Trail 3590 west. At slightly over one mile, a trail cuts north and reaches Rigdon Lakes in one mile. Brittany is a quarter-mile bushwhack northeast of Lower Rigdon.

Though only about 4 acres, Brittany is almost 30 feet deep. It is at elevation 5,600 ft., a lightly fished, good little lake. Any method works, but flies are always productive. Though it no longer offers pleasant camping due to the complete lack of shade, the regenerating burn is interesting to see, and the lake continues to be stocked.

BROOK LAKE (Confederated Tribes Warm Springs). A small brook trout lake east of Olallie Meadows Campground, 3 miles north of Olallie Lake. See Breitenbush Lake for road directions. One of a group of three good lakes, including Jude and Russ, in a line ½ mile southeast of the

campground by easy trail.

About 4 acres, Brook has brook trout from 7 to 16 inches. It's pretty brushy for bank fishing. A rubber boat or float tube comes in handy here. Bait or bait and spinner will usually take fish. Fly angling is good in evenings, especially in the fall.

Brook and its two neighbors are on reservation land, but tribal fishing permits are not required at this time. It is usually inaccessible before early June. Camping at the lakes is prohibited due to fire danger.

BROWN-MINTO ISLAND COMPLEX. On the Willamette River south of Salem, a network of borrow pits and sloughs accessed by boat from the river, or from the east bank. It is home to largemouth bass, white crappie, bluegill, brown bullhead, and channel cats. Minto-Brown Island is operated as a public park by the City of Salem and includes picnic facilities and trails. There are two fishing platforms on the big slough below the main parking area. The park is off River Rd. south of the Hwy. 22 bridge across the Willamette. The closest public boat ramp is at Wallace Marine Park in Salem on the west bank, just north of the Hwy. 22 bridge. Two fishing platforms on the big slough are accessible to handicapped anglers. Recommended for youngsters.

BUCK LAKE. A 9-acre brook trout lake off the upper Clackamas Rd. west of Timothy Lake, about 42 miles south of Estacada. It can be reached from the Shellrock Creek Rd., Forest Rd. 58, by turning right onto Forest Rd. 5810 about one mile north of Shellrock Campground. Drive 5 miles to Forest Rd. 210. Trailhead 728 is about one mile up this road on the left. It's a quarter-mile hike south to the lake. If you are at Timothy Lake, head west on Trail 5810 to reach the spur.

Buck is stocked in odd number years with brook trout that grow to 10 inches, with some to 12 inches. All methods are used, but fly angling produces consistently after the first month or two. At 4000 ft., there may still be some snow here when the lake is first accessible in early June. Supplies are available in Estacada or Government Camp.

BULL RUN RIVER. Best known as the water supply for the city of Portland, a large tributary of the lower Sandy River entering it from the east about 16 miles upstream from the Sandy's confluence with the Columbia. It is crossed by the east side Sandy River Rd. about 1½ miles above the Bull Run confluence with the Sandy. Its headwaters are in the Bull Run watershed reserve and are closed to public access.

The lower 1½ miles can be fished for hatchery spring chinook and for finclipped summer and winter steelhead who stray up the Bull Run, mistaking it for the Sandy. Wild trout are available for catch and release angling up to the fenced off reserve, though not much fishing takes place due to water level fluctuations.

BUMP LAKE. A 3-acre drive-in lake at 4300 ft. in the Olallie Lakes group. The lake is accessed by a series of spur roads off Forest Rd. 46 north of Breitenbush. It is stocked with brook trout. Check the Mt. Hood National Forest Map for directions.

BURNT LAKE. This is a favorite of many hiking anglers as it is fairly accessible and close to Portland. The lake is about 8 acres and supports brook trout. Take Hwy. 26 east from Zigzag to an unnumbered forest road heading north about one mile east of Tollgate Campground. At about 4 miles, the road ends at Trailhead 772. Burnt Lake is 3 miles northeast by trail, to the east of East Zigzag Mountain. The trail passes 2-acre Devil's Lake about half-way. There are also brook trout in Devil's.

The brookies in Burnt average about 9 inches, with a size range 6 to 14 inches. Some years the fish run larger than others. All methods are used, with flies working well in summer and fall. This is a pretty place, in alpine country at 4100 ft., usually inaccessible until early June. There are pleasant campsites at the lake.

BURNT TOP LAKE (a.k.a. Top Lake). A fairly good 20-acre trout lake in the Three Sisters Wilderness, north of the Horse Lake area on the west side of the Cascade summit. It's a long hike from the west side McKenzie drainage. Best way in is from the east. From Bend, take the Cascade Lakes Hwy. south toward Bachelor Butte. About 5 miles past the ski resort and just past the Devil's Lake Campground, a well-signed trail leads west to Sister's Mirror Lake. Burnt Top is 1½ miles farther west. Follow Trail 3527. The lake is a quarter mile south of the trail northeast of Burnt Top Peak.

There is no trail to the lake.

Fly fishing is good here, though lures and bait can be worked easily from shore as well. Angling is consistently good due to light pressure, with trout 8 to 11 inches. There are pretty campsites here and one mile east at Sisters Mirror Lake. It is usually accessible by early July.

BUTTE CREEK (Molalla watershed). A fair wild cutthroat stream with a small run of wild winter steelhead. Roads follow both sides of the stream, but in the upper reaches the roads are not close to the creek.

Butte Creek forms the boundary between Clackamas and Marion counties, about 20 miles from the Salem area and 40 miles south of Portland. It flows northwest over 30 miles from the lower Cascade range into the Pudding River near Woodburn. Hwy. 213 crosses it about 5 miles north of Silverton.

Fishing is pretty much confined to the area above Scott's Mills, 2 miles east of the highway. Trout fishing is catch and release, and the creek is closed to steelheading.

BYBEE LAKE. A 200-acre warmwater lake in a large bottomland complex that also includes Smith Lake as well as smaller ponds, sloughs, swamps, and marshes. The complex, which is on a peninsula between Columbia Slough at Oregon Slough near the confluence of Willamette and Columbia rivers, has been designated a Metropolitan Greenspace. More a wetland than a lake, Bybee supports largemouth bass, crappie, bluegill, and bullhead catfish. Bass to 4 pounds have been taken here. The lake is best fished in spring when the water is higher.

Access to Bybee is either by canoe or foot trail. Trailheads are on Marine Drive west of Heron Lakes Golf Course near the Multnomah County Expo Center, and on Columbia Blvd. on the north side of the bridge that crosses Columbia Slough near Kelley Point Park.

Canoe access to Bybee is by way of Columbia Slough, Smith Lake, or the small pond complex off Marine Drive between Smith and Bybee lakes. Canoes can be launched into the Columbia Slough off Columbia Blvd. at the Columbia Slough crossing near Kelley Point (paddle east to reach Bybee), or near the former St. Johns Landfill(paddle west). Some portaging between the slough and Bybee is required.

Bybee is a gem of a little wilderness in the heart of Portland's industrial sector. Wildlife is abundant, including mosquitoes in season. Dress appropriately for blackberry brambles and nettles.

CALAPOOIA RIVER. Offering good catch and release fishing for wild rainbows and cutthroat trout, and some warmwater opportunities. A tributary of the mid-Willamette, it flows 65 miles to its confluence near Albany from headwaters in the Cascade range between South Santiam and McKenzie rivers. Trout fishing is confined to the upper half of the stream. Largemouth and smallmouth bass and panfish can be found near its mouth. The river is closed to steelhead and salmon angling.

Trout run 7 to 12 inches. The upper stretch is usually a good bet in late season, with fewer, but larger fish, available. From Holley, which is south of Sweet Home on Hwy. 228, a good road follows the stream for 9 miles to Dollar, and a fair road continues upstream another 12 miles to the North Fork. The lower river is followed and crossed by many roads from Holley to Albany.

CAMP CREEK (Sandy watershed). A tributary of the upper Sandy River in the Mt. Hood National Forest. Though only 7 miles long, it provides fair fishing for wild cutthroat. Camp Creek joins the Zig Zag River one mile east of Rhododendron. Hwy. 26 follows the creek north from Rhododendron to Government Camp, but access is good only in the lower stretch.

Bright spinners and lures are best early in the year, when the stream is silty from glacial run-off. Fly anglers can do well in summer and fall. Fishing is catch and release only and is restricted to the use of artificial flies and lures only.

There are two campgrounds along the stream, Tollgate east of Rhododendron, and Camp Creek 2½ miles farther east. Both are off Hwy. 26.

CAMPERS LAKE. A fairly consistent producer of cutthroat to 14 inches, east of the McKenzie Pass Highway 242, about a mile north of the Scott Lake turnoff. Campers has about 13 surface acres and is mostly shallow, with the deepest area (the north end) about 15 feet. It's a good fly fishing lake if you can get out beyond the shoal area—a good lake for float tubes. It is best fished earlier in the season, and has been known to dry up.

There are no improved campsites at the lake, but there are campgrounds on the highway south.

CANBY POND. About one acre, in Canby City Park at the western edge of the town off Hwy. 99E. It can be fished year-round for largemouth bass, crappie, and bluegill. It is stocked with legal trout from fall through April..

CANIM LAKE. An easy to find brook trout lake north of Waldo Lake. Canim is 2 miles west of North Waldo Campground on Trail 3590. It is within 1996 Moolack Burn. The lake winterkills easily and is only occasionally stocked.

CARMEN RESERVOIR (a.k.a. Beaver Marsh Reservoir). On the upper McKenzie River, built by the Eugene Electric and Water Board. Unlike a lot of power reservoirs, this one provides good fishing. It has about 65 surface acres.

In a scenic area, it is about 2 miles south of Clear Lake on Hwy. 126, 21 miles north of the McKenzie Hwy.

Fishing is primarily for rainbows 7 to 12 inches, but larger rainbows are available. A few brook trout and cutthroat are also caught. Trolling takes most fish, but any method will work. Plan to row, since motorboats are prohibited. There is a nice campsite near the north end of the lake.

CAST CREEK. A small wild trout stream in the Sandy River watershed, Mt. Hood National Forest, about 5 miles northeast of Zigzag. It flows north from Cast Lake into Lost Creek. To reach it, take the Lost Creek Rd., Forest Rd. 18, north from Zigzag (on Hwy. 26) about 5 miles to the Riley and McNeil campgrounds turn-off. Cast Creek is crossed by Forest Rd. 382 about ½ mile past Riley Campground.

It provides fair fishing for wild cutthroat and brook trout from 6 to 10 inches. There are three forest camps nearby—Riley, McNeil, and Lost Creek. Fishing is catch and release only, restricted to artificial flies and lures.

CAST LAKE. A good hike-in brook trout lake on the west slope of Mt. Hood within Mt. Hood Wilderness. From Hwy. 26 about 1½ miles east of Rhododendron,

take the Devil Canyon Rd. north about 5 miles to Trailhead 772. Hike to Devil's Lake, about 1½ miles, then take Trail 774 north ½ mile then west another half mile to the lake. Burnt Lake is 1½ miles east. Cast can also be approached from the north by Cast Creek Trail 773, which heads at Riley Campground on the Lolo Pass highway.

Dumbell shaped, this 7-acre lake is 17 ft. deep at elevation 4450 ft. From time to time it produces very good catches of trout, but it can be slow. Brook trout run 6 to 13 inches. The lake is stocked in even number years, so other things being equal, larger fish are often available in odd number years. All angling methods can be used as the lake is easy to fish. Spinner and bait combinations do well in early season, and fly anglers take large fish in late fall. There are no campsites at the lake, but Devil's Meadow has a good camp. The lake is usually accessible in early June.

CEDAR CREEK. A tributary of the middle Sandy River entering from the east north of the town of Sandy, about 27 miles from Portland. The upper stream is crossed by Hwy. 26 near Cherryville, and the lower section is followed for a way by county roads.

There is a salmon hatchery near the mouth, and no angling is allowed on hatchery grounds or from the dam downstream to the mouth. There is a false outlet at the head of an island in the vicinity of the mouth, so make sure you're not in the closed area. Watch for signs. Many unhappy anglers have been given tickets catching coho in what they thought was the Sandy River.

Cedar Creek isn't stocked, but wild cutthroat and rainbow 6 to 10 inches are available for catch and release angling in the upper stream (artificial flies and lures only). There is some private property along the creek, so be wary of trespassing.

CERVUS LAKE. A shallow 12-acre lake in the Taylor Burn area, 2 miles north of Waldo Lake. One of 10 lakes within the 1996 Moolack Burn, it was never a viable trout fishery (frequent winterkills) and is no longer being stocked.

CHAMPOEG CREEK. A small wild trout stream about 12 miles long, flowing through agricultural land into the

Willamette near Champoeg State Park. The creek has been severely degraded by development in the area and is not stocked. There remains a small population of wild cutthroat that may be fished catch and release. Access is limited to the state park.

CHEHALEM CREEK. A small trout stream that heads in the Chehalem Mts. north of Newberg in Yamhill County. Tributary to the Willamette, it is crossed just above its mouth by Hwy. 99W at the east end of Newberg. Land development in the area has taken its toll on this small stream, though a few small wild cutthroat are present and may be fished catch and release. Adjacent property is all private, except for road crossings.

CHETLO LAKE. A large, good brook trout lake one mile west of the north end of Waldo Lake. It was not affected by the 1996 fire. Chetlo is a 4-mile hike from North Waldo Lake Campground. Take Trail 3590 west 2½ miles to the outlet stream, which is headwaters of the Middle Fork of the Willamette. Some anglers take boats across the north end of Waldo Lake to this point. Pick up Trail 3583 and follow it south 1½ miles to Chetlo.

Chetlo is about 19 acres and can be finicky about producing at times. Brook trout are stocked by air, and the catch generally runs 6 to 16 inches, but a few larger have been reported. A rubber boat or float tube would be handy. Best angling is in August and September. Try a double blade spinner with a worm trailer fished slowly for the larger trout during the day.

In late spring mosquitoes in this area are awesome. Be prepared. There are natural campsites here, and other good lakes are within a mile or two. The area is usually inaccessible until late June.

CHIQUITO LAKE. A fair size trout lake at the north end of the Eight Lakes Basin, southwest of Mt. Jefferson. Chiquito is a quarter mile northeast of Bowerman Lake. It has a naturally sustained brook trout population, with catches ranging from 6 to 11 inches. All methods are generally productive. There are good campsites near Jorn Lake, and there are other good lakes to the south.

CINCHA LAKE. A small brook trout lake south of the Duffy Lake trail in Mt. Jeffer-

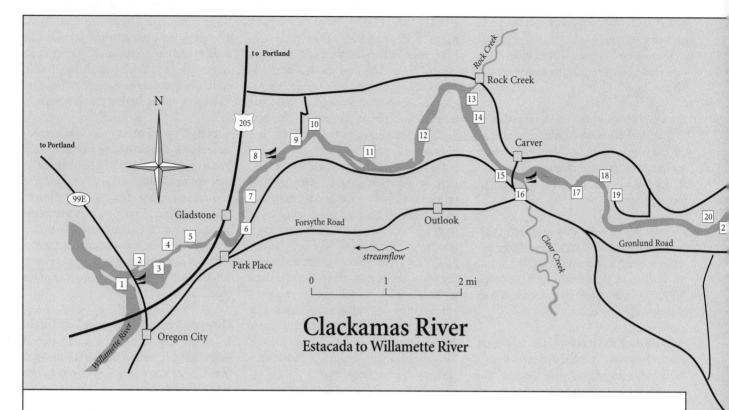

Clackamas River
Estacada to Willamette River

1. Clackamette Park. Popular plunking for spring chinook, steelhead, smallmouth where the Clackamas enters the Willamette.

2. First Riffle. Popular spot for coho jacks.

3. Old Street Car Bridge. Popular summer steelhead and jack salmon drift.

4. Cross Park. Good bank angling access for jack salmon and steelhead (winter and summer).

5. Old Clackamas River Road. Pull-out at water intake plant; fish for spring chinook.

6. High Rocks. A popular swimming hole and good place to catch spring chinook.

7. Brett's Drift. Just below Riverside Park and around the corner.

8. Riverside Park. Good boat launch; plunk for salmon.

9. Erickson's Eddy. A half mile above Riverside park, a popular salmon role.

10. Cape Horn Drift. Around the corner and against the high bank.

11. Coffey's Drift. Another popular bank area down over a short riffle from Steven's.

12. Stevens. A popular bank area one mile below Rock Creek at the highway.

13. Rock Creek Drift. Long and good for salmon and steelhead.

14. Smith's Drift. Shallow, but a good producer.

15. Carver Bridge Drift. Just downstream from bridge; good steelhead drift up against the clay bank.

16. Carver Boat Ramp. On south shore, just upstream from Carver Bridge; good bank angling at mouth of Clear Creek.

17. Big Fish Hole. Just around the corner from Larry's; cast toward high bank.

18. Larry's. Fast and shallow

19. Dog Hole. Long and good for salmon, steelhead.

20. Grant's Park Drift. Private property, once a park, with good bank fishing. Ask permission to fish.

21. Red Barn Drift. Several hundred yards long, a popular drift; cast towards south shore.

22. Latourette Drift. Best for steelhead and coho, about ½ mile below Barton.

23. Barton Park. Just upstream of bridge; has good boat launch; good steelhead drift under bridge and downstream several hundred yards.

24. Clark's Eddy. A deep salmon hole, 2 miles below Power Line Hole.

25. Power Line Hole. Several sets of power lines here; cast toward high clay bank.

26. Bonnie Lure. County park at mouth of Eagle Creek with good run of salmon and steelhead headin' for home at Eagle Creek Hatchery.

27. Swinging Bridge. No bridge here, but good fishing about a mile below Eddy.

28. Fish with Eddy. A mile below Feldheimer's, a long drift against a high clay bank.

29. Feldheimer's. Gravel boat ramp; Old Barlow Trail used to cross here on ferry.

30. Paradise Park. Below Eagle's Nest river splits into several channels; these come together against high clay bank, forming this popular drift.

31. Eagle's Nest Drift. Good bank drift at lower end of McIver Park.

32. McIver Park. Two boat ramps, one beside hatchery intake, one just below dangerous rapids; good salmon, steelhead drift just off second ramp.

33. Green Gauge. Good bank angling between hatchery intake and dam deadline.

son Wilderness. Hard to find, it is lightly fished and has been known to put out some big fish. From North Santiam Hwy. 22 about 5 miles north of Santiam Junction, take Forest Rd. 2267 to the Duffy Lake trailhead. At about 1¾ miles, a trail intersects from the north. Cincha is due south of the trail intersection about a quarter mile. (Sounds easy, but it's not).

Cincha is small and has a little sister just to the west. Cincha is about 2 acres and shallow, while Little Cincha is smaller but deeper. Both lakes are stocked by air every few years. There are good campsites at the larger lakes in the basin. See Duffy, Mowich, Jorn, and Red Butte lakes.

CLACKAMAS RIVER

A favorite of anglers in the greater Portland area, offering year-round fishing opportunities for steelhead and an excellent fishery for finclipped coho. Hatchery produced summer steelhead, both hatchery and wild winter steelhead, spring chinook, and coho all come home to this major tributary of the lower Willamette. Wild trout are also available for catch and release angling.

The Clackamas heads in the Olallie Lake Basin between Mt. Hood and Mt. Jefferson, and flows 83 miles through Mt. Hood National Forest to enter the Willamette north of the I-205 Bridge at Oregon City. A beautiful high-gradient stream throughout most of its run, the Clackamas has carved handsome canyons out of the steep Douglas fir forest, rushing past giant boulders, its shoreline a tumble of smooth river rock. The river has three major tributary streams, the North and Oak Grove forks, and the Collawash River.

Hwy. 224 follows the Clackamas closely for 40 miles, from one mile north of Carv-

The CLACKAMAS RIVER is a favorite with Portland anglers for year-round steelheading. Courtesy of John Ramsour.

er near Oregon City to Ripplebrook Ranger Station in Mt. Hood National Forest. From there upstream, the river can be accessed from Forest Rd. 46 all the way to its headwaters in the Olallie Lake basin.

There are three hydroelectric dams on the river managed by Portland General Electric (PGE), at river miles 23, 28, and 30. The lowest, River Mill, is considered to be the dividing line between the upper and lower river. Reservoirs behind River Mill and North Fork dams are stocked and open for fishing. (See Estacada Lake and North Fork Reservoir.)

Coho and winter steelhead for the Clackamas are reared at a hatchery on Eagle Creek, a tributary of the Clackamas about 8 river miles downstream from Estacada. Spring chinook released in the lower Clackamas and at Clackamette Park on the Willamette are reared at McIver Fish Hatchery.

Spring chinook offer a popular fishery from late March through June, with peak catches in April and May. Hatchery-reared coho appear with the first big rains of September and are available through October. A small number of wild coho enter the Clackamas from late October through November. The fishery closes October 31 to protect this wild run. Hatchery coho returns were excellent 1999, following several years of high water. Finclipped coho may be kept.

The river's several different populations of steelhead return in overlapping runs throughout the year. Winter steelhead

begin arriving around Thanksgiving, with peak catches of bright fish (still fresh from the ocean) through January. By February, many of these have darkened (matured) and are less suitable for harvest. In March, late arriving (wild) winter steelhead join the spring chinook, along with the beginnings of the summer-run steelhead (all hatchery produced). Summer steelhead continue to run strong through early June, with catches made through early fall. Finclipped steelhead may be kept.

Trout fishing throughout the Clackamas is catch and release. Above June creek, where a pristine reach of the river has been managed for wild trout on a catch and release basis for years, the trout population is thriving. Increased numbers of wild trout should soon be available lower in the system as well.

The good thing about the Clackamas is that is offers superior angling for large fish in a beautiful setting within an hour's drive of Portland. The bad thing is that, just an hour's drive from Portland, most of the land adjacent to the lower river is privately owned. Consequently, the lower Clackamas is primarily a boater's show.

The river is suited to riverboats only (rafts, drift boat, and jet sleds) except near the mouth and in the big pool at McIver Park near Estacada. From the mouth, anglers in standard motorboats can fish good water up to the first riffle above the Hwy. 99 bridge.

Be aware that spring chinook season typically brings on hoglines at the mouth,

with boats anchored and tied in tight formation. Upriver at McIver, small motor boats can launch to fish the Big Flats, a half-mile pool of relatively slow water below a major rapid, The Minefield. The most popular drifts on the Clackamas are below this rapid, named for the sharp protruding rocks that stud the riverbed there. Even experienced driftboat handlers as well as jet boat operators who value their hulls avoid this stretch. From McIver to the mouth, the Clackamas offers fairly easy drifting, interspersed with rapids that are real enough, but not overwhelming for beginning driftboat operators. It is very popular with rafters.

There are five improved boat ramps on the lower river, and one natural gravel put-in. McIver Park, about 21 miles above the mouth, offers the last two improved boat ramps upstream. To reach McIver, take I-205 to Hwy. 224 north of Gladstone. Follow 224 east to Carver, turning right at Carver Store and crossing the bridge over the river. Turn left onto Springwater Rd., and drive about 7 miles to the park. Feldheimer's, the gravel bar launch, is off Springwater Rd. 2 miles before you reach McIver (If you pass the tavern, you've missed Feldheimer's). The next ramp downriver is at Barton Park. Follow Hwy. 224 toward Estacada to Barton Store, then turn right onto Baker's Ferry Rd., which leads to the river. Carver Boat Ramp is across the bridge from Carver store, a quarter mile past the first blocked driveway. The gate to the ramp is locked each night.

The last ramp above the mouth is at Riverside Park in Clackamas. Follow the merged highways 212/224 east, one stoplight past the 82nd St. junction, turning right onto Evelyn St. (Watch for the green ODFW sign.) ODFW's Northwest Regional Headquarters is on this road, with some river frontage for bank angling. Follow Evelyn through an industrial warehouse district to the park.

At the mouth of the Clackamas, Clackamette Park offers a huge boat ramp and access to both the Willamette and the Clackamas. The park is off Hwy. 99E at the north end of Oregon City.

Bank angling on the lower river is restricted primarily to parks and bridges. There's some bank angling at Clackamette Park, and good bank opportunities at Cross Park and High Rocks. To reach High

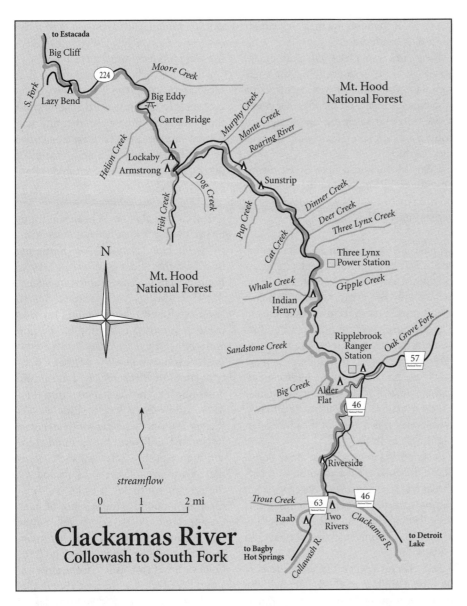

Clackamas River
Collowash to South Fork

Rocks, a popular salmon and swimming hole, take the Gladstone exit off I-205, turn left, and continue past the DMV office to High Rocks on the east bank. The bridge across the river to Cross Park on the west bank is open to foot traffic only. Riverside Park also offers a strip of bank for salmon and steelhead angling, and there is bank access on the south bank River Rd. above the river gauging station downstream from Carver.

ODFW owns a strip of bank from Carver Bridge up to Clear Creek (purchased especially for bank angling), and there is bank angling at Barton Park, and at Bonnie Lure Park (off Hwy. 224 about 6 miles below River Mill Dam). Bonnie Lure, an undeveloped county park, accesses the fishery at the mouth of Eagle Creek. Park at the gate and walk in along a path to the river. This is a great spot for coho, though

it can get crowded. Be prepared to wade out on the gravel. The river bank is also accessible from McIver Park to below River Mill Dam. From the dam up to Mt. Hood Forest most bank access is owned by Portland General Electric and is open to public use, but the river is closed to salmon and steelhead angling.

River levels for the Clackamas are available. See Appendix. The best reading for salmon and steelhead fishing is considered by many to be 4½ ft., with readings as low as 3.6 and as high as 5.4 still worth the trip. Flood level on the Clackamas is 18 ft.

Camping facilities are available below the national forest at Barton and McIver parks. Within Mt. Hood National Forest, there are camps along Forest Rd. 46.

Supplies are available at Barton and Carver stores and in Estacada. There are no motels along the river.

CLACKAMAS RIVER, NORTH FORK. A good size stream offering catch and release fishing for wild cutthroat. It enters the Clackamas from the east about 15 miles southeast of Estacada. Forest Rd. 4610 follows the fork from the east end of North Fork Reservoir upstream, rarely straying more than a quarter to ½ mile from the fork. Forest Rd. 4613 crosses the stream near Whiskey Creek. There are many falls on the North Fork. Boyer and Winslow creeks, both good size tributaries, join the North Fork at North Campground, about 9 miles upstream.

Cutthroat here run 6 to 11 inches. The North Fork road is usually open by late April. For information about fishing the reservoir, see North Fork Reservoir. River gauge readings and fish counts at the dam are available. See Appendix.

CLACKAMAS RIVER OAK GROVE FORK

A major tributary of the upper Clackamas, affording good trout fishing and opportunities for harvest. About 25 miles long, it heads in the Big Meadows area in the northwest corner of Warm Springs Reservation. It flows 7 miles to Timothy Lake, then into much smaller Lake Harriet (both reservoirs), to its confluence with the Clackamas above Ripplebrook Ranger Station, about 31 miles east of Estacada.

Both banks of the lower 5 miles are followed by forest roads east from Ripplebrook to Lake Harriet. The roads meet upstream of Harriet, and Forest Rd. 57 continues upstream about a mile beyond Timothy. Shortly thereafter, the river enters the reservation, where a tribal fishing permit is required.

The Oak Grove Fork is open for harvesting trout from the bridge on Forest Rd. 57 upstream to Timothy Lake. Above Harriet there are good populations of wild cutthroat that may be fished catch and release. A few brown trout, spawners from Lake Harriet, are occasionally hooked. Brook trout are most abundant in the river's highest reaches. Size range of all fish is 6 to 14 inches, with the larger fish hooked within a few miles above the reservoirs.

Fishing is restricted to artificial flies and lures throughout the Oak Grove Fork.

There are campgrounds at Ripplebrook, Rainbow, Lake Harriet, Shellrock Creek and in the Timothy Lake area. Supplies are available at Estacada and North Fork Reservoir.

CLACKAMAS RIVER, SOUTH FORK. A nice stream, entering the main river near Memaloose log scaling station at the east end of North Fork Reservoir. A long-time water source for Oregon City and closed to all angling, the South Fork is now open for catch and release trout fishing, offering some exciting sport for energetic anglers.

Most of the river flows through deep canyon, with a number of natural barriers. Best trout fishing is above these barriers. Memaloose Creek joins the South Fork just above its confluence with the mainstem Clackamas.

One way to approach the South Fork is by way of Trail 516. In Estacada, turn off Hwy. 224 and cross the Clackamas, heading south along DuBois Creek toward Dodge. Forest Rd. 45, the Hillockburn Rd., approaches and follows the South Fork canyon. About 2 miles past the spur road to Hillockburn Spring (about 2¼ miles east of Dodge), Trail 516 leads down to the river.

CLAGGET LAKE. See **FIRECAMP LAKES.**

CLEAR CREEK (Clackamas watershed). A major tributary of the lower Clackamas River, flowing from the south into the mainstem at Carver, about 6 miles east of Clackamas. The creek is about 24 miles long and heads in the low hills west of the Clackamas River south of Viola. It is followed by county roads south of Hwy. 211. The upper end can be reached by going east from Hwy. 213 in the Mulino area.

It's primarily a wild cutthroat trout stream, though a few wild steelhead and coho enter in January and February. The creek is closed to salmon and steelhead angling, and trout fishing is catch and release with artificial flies and lures.

CLEAR FORK. A tributary of the upper Sandy River above Brightwood Bridge which provides good catch and release trout fishing in late spring and summer in its lower stretch. From Portland, take Hwy. 26 east to Zigzag, a distance of 43 miles. Turn north on Forest Rd. 18, the Lolo Pass Rd., which follows Clear Fork about a quarter mile to the north of the stream. Five miles north of Zigzag, at McNeil Campground, the road comes very close to

the creek. It then follows the creek closely toward its headwaters.

Clear Fork is very cold, and its abundant small wild cutthroat are reluctant biters until late May. Sandy River steelhead are sometimes present, but the stream is closed to salmon and steelhead angling. Trout fishing is catch and release with artificial flies and lures.

Riley, McNeil, and Lost Creek campgrounds are all located near the midsection of the stream. Supplies are available in Zigzag and Welches.

CLEAR LAKE (McKenzie River watershed). The very scenic and geologically fascinating headwaters of the McKenzie River, created only 3000 years ago by a lava flow that formed a natural dam on the stream. The impoundment inundated a standing Douglas fir forest, which the lake's cold waters have preserved. The Underwater Forest, as it is named on Forest Service maps, can be viewed by boaters through Clear Lake's crystalline lens. The lake is off Hwy. 126, about 3 miles south of the junction of highways 126 and 20.

It supports a large self-sustaining population of brook trout and some wild cutthroat and is stocked with easier-to-catch rainbow trout. It covers 148 acres and is deep throughout, reaching 175 ft. near the south end. The only shallows are near Cold Water Cove.

Still-fishing and trolling are the predominant angling methods here, with fly fishing near shore. There is a campground at Cold Water Cove on the east shore, and a resort with rustic cabins, docks, and rental row boats on the west shore. The resort is run by the Santiam Fish and Game Association, a mid-valley club, and is open to public use. There is a pole slide boat ramp at Cold Water Cove. Motor boats are prohibited on the lake.

CLEARY POND. A 4-acre pond with largemouth bass in Fern Ridge Wildlife Management Area. It is west of Neilson Rd. about ½ mile south of Hwy. 126.

CLIFF LAKE (Mink Lake Basin). A popular 40-acre rainbow trout lake in Three Sisters Wilderness. It is off the Pacific Crest Trail 1½ miles east of Mink Lake (There is a trail between the two). The trail up to the PCT heads on Hwy. 46 at a turn-around between Elk Lake and Hosmer Lake. The

stocked trout in Cliff average 9 to 10 inches and run to 15 inches. Fished rather heavily, it still produces using all techniques.

There is a shelter at the lake as well as nice natural campsites. The area is usually accessible in late June, with angling good then and again in late summer and fall. Closest supplies are at Elk Lake Resort and at McKenzie Bridge. There are a lot of other good lakes close by. See Porky, Mink, Moody, Vogel.

COLLAWASH RIVER. A beautiful tributary of the Clackamas River, flowing within the Mt. Hood National Forest, entering the Clackamas about 35 miles southeast of Estacada. The Collawash and its tributary, the Hot Springs Fork, feature fair to good catch and release angling for wild trout. It is closed to fishing for salmon and steelhead.

The Collawash heads in Marion County north of the Breitenbush drainage and flows north to the Clackamas. From Estacada, follow Hwy. 224 to Ripplebrook Ranger Station, then head south on Forest Rd. 46 to Two Rivers Campground at the confluence of the Collawash and Clackamas. A good road, Forest Rd. 63, follows the stream south for 9 miles to Tom's Meadow. About 2½ miles south of Raab Campground, Forest Rd. 70, follows the Hot Springs Fork west for about 7 miles. Trails access the upper reaches of both the Collawash and Hot Springs forks, as well as a number of lakes in the area. (See Bull of The Woods, Big Slide, and Welcome lakes.)

Rainbow trout are the main catch near the road. Further upstream, the catch consists of rainbow and an occasional brook trout, with bull trout scarce but occasionally hooked in all sections.

Plentiful trout of good size are hooked by anglers hiking up the Hot Springs Fork to Bagby Guard Station and above. Trail 544 to Bagby Hot Springs and beyond heads about one mile south of Pegleg Campground. The stream is frequently within sight of the trail, which crosses the fork twice. A large parking area at the trailhead is well signed.

The hot springs are a treat. Facilities include both open-air communal tubs and hollowed log tubs in private compartments within a rough-hewn bath house. Friends of Bagby Hot Springs helped restore the facilities after a fire some years ago and continue to provide year-round caretakers, but weekend evenings can still get rowdy. The safest time to visit is weekdays during daylight hours. The Forest Service recommends leaving your car unlocked (with no valuables, of course) to prevent damage from break-ins. Camping is not allowed at the hot spring.

The mainstem Collowash upstream from Tom's Meadow to the confluence of Elk Lake Creek can be accessed by trail or bushwhack and offers good fishing. The average catch is 9 inches , with the occasional 15-incher. Fishing is restricted to artificial flies and lures throughout. There's beautiful fly water in both the mainstem and Hot Springs Fork. Light leader and small dry flies work well in late summer and fall.

There are four campgrounds in the lower 4 miles between the Hot Springs Fork and the Clackamas River, and two campgrounds on the Hot Springs Fork.

COLLINS LAKE. A tiny rainbow and brook trout lake of about one acre, south of the old highway at the west end of Government Camp on Hwy. 26. The lake is formed by a block on one fork of Camp Creek. Though privately owned, it is open to public use and is stocked with legal rainbow through August. It also has naturally reproducing populations of rainbow and brook trout. Camping is not permitted at the lake.

COLORADO LAKE. A 30-acre private lake 2 miles east of Corvallis, open to public use for a fee. The lake contains largemouth bass, white and black crappie, bluegill, and brown bullhead catfish.

COLUMBIA SLOUGH. A long back eddy of the Columbia River which borders North Portland from Kelley Point to east of Parkrose. Deceptively innocent-looking with its cottonwood fringe, plentiful wildlife, and good population of warmwater fish, it is considered by some to be one of the most polluted waters in the west. Mercury, PCBs and other industrial poisons are present, as well as raw sewage. Signs throughout the slough warn visitors not to swim or eat any fish taken from the water. Clean-up efforts begun in 1994 continue.

The slough provides habitat for largemouth bass, crappie, bullhead, bluegill, perch, crawfish, and many species of rough

There's a time to fish and a time to reconsider your tactics. Photograph by Dennis Frates.

fish that provide food for the bass. Occasional sturgeon and steelhead are also spotted, as well as salmon smolts. Catch and release angling for all species is recommended.

Access to the slough is best from northeast 17th Ave. west to the Willamette. Canoes can be slipped into the water here, or at other points all the way to Parkrose. Columbia and Sandy boulevards parallel the slough, and many roads cross it, providing right-of-way access to its narrow shore. The Four Corners area between NE 158th and 185th avenues features a narrow channel with overhanging trees, shrubs, and submerged structures that are attractive to bass. This upper area may be less contaminated than the lower slough.

Remember, industrial pollution can be very poisonous. Don't even wade in the water.

COMMONWEALTH LAKE. A stocked trout and warmwater fishery in a neighborhood park on the outskirts of Beaverton, managed by Tualatin Hills Park and Recreation District. The lake was built by developers and captures the waters of

Johnson Creek (Tualatin River watershed).

From Hwy. 26, take Cedar Hills Blvd. south to Butner Rd., the first right-hand turn (west). Follow Butner for ½ mile to Commonwealth Lake Park's tiny parking lot at the north end of the lake. Additional parking is available on neighborhood streets.

The lake is stocked with legal rainbow trout in spring, and fishing holds up into the summer with some holdovers through the winter. Bass, bluegill, and crappie are also available. This is a delightful and convenient fishery for youngsters, complete with resident waterfowl , grassy picnic areas, and playground equipment. Fishing platforms are wheelchair accessible.

COPEPOD LAKE. A good trout lake in the Mink Lake Basin at the head of the South Fork of the McKenzie River. The lake is north of the Goose Lake/Corner Lake Trail, ½ mile west of the junction of that trail with the Pacific Crest Trail. See Cliff Lake for directions into the basin.

About 20 acres, Copecod has plump brook trout from 6 to 16 inches and some rainbows. Fly angling is good here, with wet flies working well most of the time. Bucktail coachman or caddis and most streamer flies will take fish. There are good natural campsites here and at other lakes in the basin. There is a shelter at Cliff Lake, a little over a mile south by trail. Copepod is usually accessible in late June, but the mosquitoes can be fierce. Best angling is in the fall.

CORNER LAKE. A 60-acre brook trout lake in the northern Mink Lake Basin, at the head of the South Fork McKenzie. It is about 2 trail miles north of Mink Lake and just north of Goose Lake, which flows into it. See Cliff Lake for directions into the basin.

Corner usually produces fair to good fishing for wild brook trout through most of the season. The fish range from 6 to 18 inches, with the average catch 10 inches. All methods will take fish. Goose Lake, actually more a wetland than a lake southeast of Corner, can be fished early in the season. There are many fine natural campsites throughout the basin.

COTTAGE GROVE PONDS. Six bass and panfish ponds with stocked rainbow trout available in spring. Follow Row River Rd. to the truck scale, where the road crosses the Row River across from the car lot. Signs point toward Dorena Dam. A paved bicycle path leads to the first pond. Park near, but do not block the scales. The area is managed as South Lane Regional Park.

COTTAGE GROVE RESERVOIR. A large flood control reservoir on the Coast Fork of the Willamette River whose trophy-size bass draw a lot of attention. It is managed primarily for bass and panfish, with catch-and-release regulations on bass over 15 inches to encourage a large average catch.

From I-5 near Cottage Grove, take exit 170, and follow London Rd. to the reservoir's west shore and the boat ramp near the dam. To reach Pine Meadows Campground or the Wilson Creek Park boat ramp on the east shore (usable only at full pool), turn left onto Cottage Grove Reservoir Rd. before reaching the lake. The reservoir has up to 1300 surface acres at full pool (in spring and summer) and is drained beginning the day after Labor Day.

Recreational boating is the primary activity here in summer, but trophy-size largemouth bass are also a big draw. In

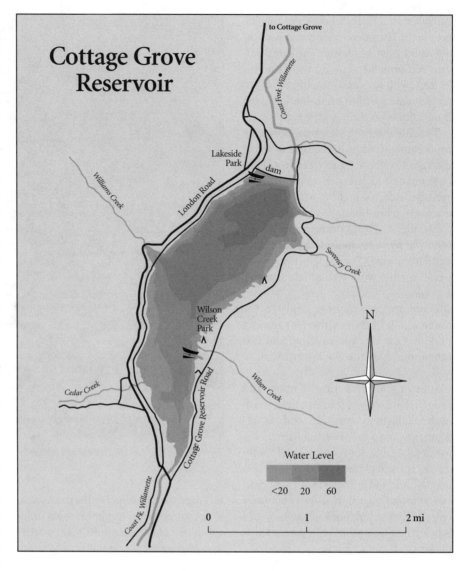

spring and early summer, look for bass among the weed beds at the south end. As the water warms, bass move to the mouths of tributary streams, along the dam spillway, and into the old creek and river channels. A depth finder will help you locate the channels after the water grows murky in summer.

Bank anglers fish from the spillway for catfish, crappie, bluegill, and the occasional bass. Look for bass at the upper end among the reed canary grass in spring, and in the channels and off rocky shorelines in summer. Bluegill and crappie are fished from the dam in fall and winter. Legal rainbow trout are stocked.

There is a health advisory on fish taken from this reservoir. Be aware they may contain poisonous levels of mercury. The longer a fish lives in the reservoir, the more likely it is to absorb and retain mercury. To play it safe, eat only the catchable trout, and the earlier in the season the better. See

the regulations for details.

There are three picnic areas here as well as the campground, and lots of parking. Accommodations and supplies are available in Cottage Grove.

COTTONWOOD MEADOWS LAKE. A small lake in the High Rock lakes area of the Mt. Hood National Forest, north of the Oak Grove Fork of the Clackamas River. From Estacada take Hwy. 224 to Ripplebrook Ranger Station, about 30 miles, then follow the Oak Grove Fork Rd. (Forest Rd. 57) to the Shellrock Creek Rd. (Forest Rd. 58). About 2½ miles north of Shellrock Campground, turn west onto Forest Rd. 5830, and drive to Hideaway Lake. About 1½ miles beyond Hideway, the road crosses a creek (near a trail crossing). Follow the creek to the lake.

Cottonwood Meadows Lake is about 8 acres and shallow, ideal for fly angling if it doesn't get too low, and capable of growing good size fish. It has a lot of shoal area and deeper channels, and though it has its ups and downs, it's usually consistent for cutthroat 8 to 12 inches. In some years, fish to 16 inches have been taken in good numbers. Natural campsites are available. It's usually accessible in early June.

COUGAR LAKE (Molalla watershed). A small brook trout lake near the headwaters of the North Fork Molalla River. Privately owned by a timber company, it is closed to public use.

COUGAR RESERVOIR (McKenzie watershed). A large reservoir on the South Fork of the McKenzie River, 50 miles east of Eugene. Used both for power and flood control, it fluctuates considerably but provides fair fishing for stocked rainbow trout. To reach it, take Hwy. 126 east from Eugene. Four miles past the community of Blue River, turn south on South Fork Rd., and follow it 3 miles to the lake.

Cougar has about 1200 surface acres when full and is 6 miles long. The primary catch is rainbow trout, and best fishing is in winter. The lake is seldom fished in summer. Bull trout are also present, but fishing for them is prohibited. Boat anglers have success fishing the coves, where there are usually large concentrations of trout. Bank anglers have good success at the upper end near the bridge.

Cougar Hot Springs is an added treat for visitors here. It's on Rider Creek about a quarter mile west of the reservoir. About 4 miles south of the dam, the west shore road bisects an embayment at the mouth of Rider Creek. There you will find a small parking area. Follow the trail along the north shore of the creek to the hot springs. There is a small fee to access the springs.

There are several forest campgrounds in the vicinity. Echo is on the East Fork Rd. (Forest Rd. 1993) near the lower end of the reservoir; Slide Creek is on the east shore near the southern end; and French Pete is one mile south on Forest Rd. 19. There are additional campgrounds along the South Fork McKenzie.

CRABTREE CREEK. A wild trout stream east of Albany, flowing from the Cascade foothills south of the North Santiam River into the South Santiam River near Scio. The lower end is crossed by Hwy. 226 about 9 miles north of Lebanon. Both paved and gravel roads follow and cross the lower end, and from Lacomb upstream a fair road follows it to the headwaters. The extreme upper portion is sometimes closed to access by a logging concern during fire season.

Crabtree is no longer stocked with trout, but it has some wild cutthroat available for catch and release angling. It is closed to steelheading.

CRAIG LAKE. A hard to find brook trout lake in the Santiam watershed. Though not a long hike, it sits atop Craig Butte at elevation 5300 ft and is easily missed. It is across the canyon and west of the head of Lost Lake Creek, three quarters of a mile due south of Lower Berley Lake.

Take the Pacific Crest Trail north 1½ miles from the Santiam Pass area (½ mile west of the Hoodoo Ski Bowl turn-off) to the junction of Trail 3491. Follow 3491 about a mile north, and look for a fair trail up the northeast side of Craig Butte. It is about ½ mile to the lake by this trail.

Craig Lake is about 5 acres and 14 ft. deep. Fly fishing is usually the most productive technique. There are good natural campsites at the lake.

CRESWELL PONDS. Freeway ponds east of Creswell, containing largemouth bass, bluegill, brown bullhead, and black crappie. The ponds are shallow and weedy. From I-5, take the Creswell exit south along the east side of the freeway.

CRIPPLE CREEK LAKE. A very good 15-acre hike-in brook trout lake at the south end of the High Rock Lakes group in Mt. Hood National Forest. The lake is at elevation 4300 ft.

From Estacada, follow Hwy. 224 past Ripplebrook Ranger Station, then turn northeast on Forest Rd. 4631 toward Silvertip. About 4 miles from Ripplebrook, Forest Rd. 4635 cuts sharply back to the northwest. Follow it 10 miles. After crossing Cripple Creek, the head of Trail 702 to Cache Meadow is on the east side of the road. (The road dead ends a mile or so beyond the trailhead.) Follow the creek upstream about a mile to the lake, an elevation gain of 300 ft.

By late June the High Rock Rd. is usually open, and the lake can also be reached by a 2-mile hike southwest from Frazier Mt. From Frazier turn-around, take Trail. 517 to Cache Meadow, and follow the stream south ½ mile.

Brook trout in the lake run 7 to 13 inches. All methods can be used. Stocked in odd number years, it gets very heavy pressure in even number years when the fish have grown to good size. There are natural campsites at the lake.

CUNNINGHAM LAKE. A 200-acre bass and panfish lake near the north end of Sauvie Island, northwest of Portland. The lake is at the head of Cunningham Slough near the narrow neck of the island. Subjected to flood waters in the spring and affected by tides, it has a good selection of the warm water fish found in the Willamette and mid-Columbia.

The lake can be reached by way of Cunningham Slough, which is on the east bank of Multnomah Channel across from the Crown Paper Mill south of St. Helens. Launch at Scappoose Bay Marina. An alternate route is to boat south 3 miles from the mouth of Scappoose Bay to the east side of Multnomah Channel at a point opposite Jackson or Santosh Slough. Tie up and walk several hundred yards to the shore of the lake.

Brown bullhead angling is very good at times if you have a boat to get to them. Largemouth bass, crappie and perch move in and out of the lake with the tidal action. Best angling is in June and July when the water is up.

Tackle and supplies are available at marinas on Multnomah Channel.

CUNNINGHAM SLOUGH. A good bass and panfish fishery south of St. Helens at the north end of Sauvie Island. A boat is required to fish it. The slough is about 5 miles long and serpentines out of Cunningham Lake, flowing into Multnomah Channel across from the mouth of Scappoose Bay. Enter the slough on either side of Long Island at its mouth. By boat from St. Helens, it's about a 2-mile run upstream. From the public ramp on Scappoose Bay it's 1½ miles down the bay and across the channel. Scappoose Bay is about 25 miles north of Portland and also offers good warm water angling.

The main catch in the slough is brown bullhead, which are very plentiful at times. These catfish run 8 to 12 inches with an occasional larger one. A number of good size perch are picked up in the lower slough, and crappie respond to cut bait, jig flies, and spinners. Best spots to fish are at the mouths of the smaller sloughs. Angling is best on the ebb tide, according to the experts, but fish can be caught any time.

Angling can be very good for bass to 5 pounds. Areas near the mouth and at the outlets of the smaller streams produce best results. This is a good spot to test everything in your tackle box. Bass seem to hit best at the tide changes.

Sauvie Island fisheries are open from April 16 through the end of waterfowl hunting season in October. Tackle, and supplies are available at marinas on Multnomah Channel and Scappoose Bay.

CYGNET LAKE. Adjacent to Swan Lake, not far from Gander in a lake basin northwest of Waldo Lake. See Gander Lake for directions. From Gander, continue east on Trail 3568 to Swan. Cygnet, at 6 acres, is immediately west of Swan, about mid-way along Swan's west shore. It is stocked with rainbow and brook trout fingerlings. See also Gosling Lakes.

DAIRY CREEK, EAST FORK (Tualatin watershed). A tributary of the Tualatin River about 25 miles west of Portland, crossed by Hwy. 26. The stream flows from the north and joins West Dairy Creek, entering the Tualatin River near Cornelius.

Trout angling is largely confined to the area north of Hwy. 26. A good road turns north off the highway toward Mountain-

dale just before Hwy. 26 crosses the stream. A paved and gravel road follows the stream up about 10 miles. The lower creek has a lot of private property, so don't trespass. Fishing is for wild cutthroat trout, catch and release with artificial flies and lures. The stream is closed to fishing for salmon and steelhead angling.

DAIRY CREEK, WEST FORK (Tualatin watershed). A good wild cutthroat stream in Washington County, tributary to the Tualatin River, with headwaters north of Hwy. 26. It flows south along Hwy. 47, through Manning and Banks, joining East Dairy Creek near Cornelius.

This is an excellent wild cutthroat stream with brushy banks and lots of cover for fish. Fishing is catch and release with artificial flies and lures. There's some private property along the stream, so avoid trespassing. The stream is closed to salmon and steelhead angling.

DALY LAKE. Cupped in the headwaters of the Middle Fork of the Santiam River, 11 acres, not too remote, with excellent angling for brook trout and cutthroat. From Hwy. 22, the North Santiam Rd., turn west on Scar Mt. Road (Forest Rd. 2266) about 22 miles southeast of Idanha. Don't take the wrong turn and get onto Forest Rd. 1164, which will take you too far north. About 4 miles from Hwy. 22, Forest Rd. 2266 passes between Daly and Parrish Lakes. Daly is on the north side.

Vast numbers of catchable trout, kokanee, landlocked chinook, and brown bullheads draw anglers to DETROIT RESERVOIR. *Photograph by Jerry Korson.*

Daly Lake has a lot of cutthroat 6 to 10 inches, with a few larger, as well as brook trout 6 to 12 inches. Both trout populations are sustained by natural reproduction. All methods will take fish, with fly fishing especially good in late summer and fall. The east side of the lake has the best fly water. There are good natural campsites here. Riggs Lake, also good for brook and cutthroat, is west along the same road. Parrish is close by. The road may still be snowbound in early June.

DARK LAKE (Confederated Tribes Warm Springs). The middle lake in a chain of five, which also includes Trout, Island, Long, and Olallie. It is accessible only by unimproved trail from either Olallie Lake on the east or Trout Lake on the west. From Trout Lake Campground, it's about a 1½ mile hike. The first quarter mile of trail is a fairly steep uphill grind, but the remaining distance is more easily traveled, passing Island Lake on the way in. The trail from Olallie Lake begins at the southeast end of Olallie and is most easily reached from Olallie Peninsula Campground.

With a maximum depth of 52 feet, Dark Lake is the deepest lake in the chain. It occupies a glacial cirque, its west and south shores abutting a steep talus slope 200 feet high. The shadow of this cliff over the lake and the lake's depth are responsible for its name. Dark Lake is at 4690 ft. and has a surface area of about 22 acres. There isn't a lot of shoal area around the lake. It supports brook trout. A CTWS permit is required to fish. Daily and annual permits are sold at stores on the reservation, at G.I. Joe's throughout the state, and at many fly shops. No overnight camping is allowed due to fire danger.

DAVIS LAKE (Santiam watershed). A lightly fished (hard to find) 3 acre brook trout lake between Marion Lake and the old Santiam Rd. within the Mt. Jefferson Wilderness. It is 4 miles south of Marion Falls Ranger Station on North Santiam Hwy. 22. Forest Rd. 2261 leads east to the Pine Ridge Scout Camp. From the camp, take Trail 3443 southeast about 2 miles. The trail stays a quarter mile south of the lake, crossing an inlet stream that can be followed to Davis.

The lake is very shallow and good for fly fishing, but it sometimes loses fish to winterkill. When it gets by for a few years without winter loss, it grows some good size brook trout. Fair natural campsites are available.

DEEP CREEK (Clackamas watershed). A wild cutthroat stream, tributary to the lower Clackamas River. The stream is about 15 miles southeast of Portland and enters the Clackamas River near Barton. The upper North Fork is crossed by Hwy. 26 south of Orient, and the mainstem is crossed by Hwy. 211 southwest of Sandy. Other county roads cross and follow the stream from the mouth eastward.

The creek is open to trout angling above the fish ladder at Sizemore Dam. Fishing is good in May and June, but the stream gets low in summer. Fishing is catch and release only, with artificial flies and lures.

Wild winter steelhead and coho may be present, but the creek is closed to fishing for them.

There's private property along the creek, but some owners will allow you to fish if you ask permission.

DEER CREEK (Yamhill watershed). A wild cutthroat stream flowing into the South Yamhill River about 3 miles east of Sheridan off Hwy. 18. The creek is crossed by the highway east of Sheridan and followed north by good roads for about 11 miles up Gopher Valley.

Fishing is best in the portion north of the highway. As in all west valley streams, best fishing is in spring. The average trout is around 9 inches with few larger. Fishing is catch and release only, with artificial flies and lures. There's a lot of private land along the stream.

DELTA PARK PONDS. Offering bass and panfish opportunities in the Portland metropolitan area. From I-5 North take the Delta Park Exit after crossing Columbia Slough. The city-owned park is west of the freeway.

Unfortunately, fishing seems to be losing ground to other park activities. The golf course ponds are closed to angling. However, there are a half dozen lakes and sloughs here, many of which are still accessible when the race horses and race cars aren't running! The four largest lakes contain bass, perch, catfish, and bluegill. All can be easily fished from the bank.

DELTA PONDS. A network of ponds in a

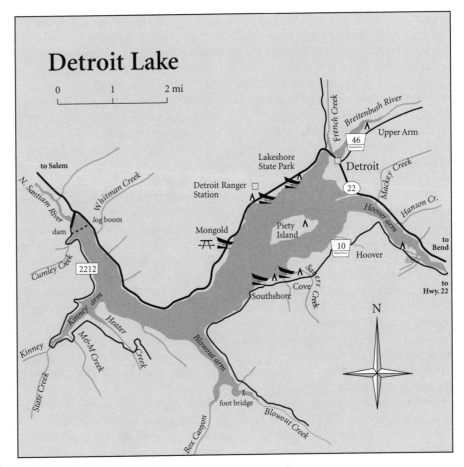

former gravel pit, offering 200 acres of bass and panfish water east of Delta Hwy., north of Valley River Center in North Eugene. There's good bank fishing, though it does get brushy. Fish for largemouth bass, white crappie, brown bullhead, and bluegill. There are plenty of blackberries to nibble in August. Recommended for introducing youngsters to fishing..

DENUDE LAKE. A scenic 9-acre brook trout lake in the Sisters Mirror Lakes Basin of the Three Sisters Wilderness, northwest of Elk Lake near the Cascade summit.

The Pacific Crest Trail crosses the basin, which is about 5 miles northwest of Elk Lake. One of several approaches begins at Elk Lake Resort, about 35 miles southwest of Bend on the Cascade Lakes Hwy. 46. Take the Horse Lake Trail 1½ miles west to its intersection with the PCT, and turn north onto the PCT. Hike 4½ miles north to the Sisters Mirror area. Another route, about 3 miles to the lake, is by Trail 20, which leads northwest from Hwy. 46 ½ mile north of Sink Creek, which is about 2 miles north of the Elk Lake Resort turn-off. Denude is the western-most lake in the basin.

The Mirror Lakes are on a picturesque plateau in an alpine setting. Most are quite shallow and don't provide much fishing. The brook trout in Denude average 9 inches, ranging 6 to 14 inches. They are easily fished from shore by all methods. Good natural campsites are available. This is designated wilderness, so no-trace camping guidelines should be followed.

DETROIT LAKE

A large popular reservoir on the North Fork Santiam River that provides good angling for trout and other species. No other lake in Oregon receives as many catchable trout annually.

Detroit is about a hundred miles from Portland, 50 miles east of Salem, off Hwy. 22. The town of Detroit is near the upper (east) end of the lake.

Detroit Dam is used for flood control and power, so water level in the reservoir fluctuates during the year, though it's usually full in spring and summer, with over 3000 surface acres. In fall the water is lowered, but fishing can still be good in the pools and near the dam. Power boats and water-skiers can be disruptive to angling in summer. Fish early to avoid conflicts.

About 120,000 catchable trout are stocked throughout the season. Rainbows, kokanee, and chinook fingerlings are added in late spring, and some chinook make their way down from the hatchery at Marion Forks to take up residence in the reservoir. Detroit also has a few wild brook trout and cutthroat that drift in from Breitenbush and North Santiam rivers and from Blowout and Kinney creeks.

Most anglers catch the stocked rainbows, which range from 12 to 16 inches. Large holdover trout are also available. Best trout fishing is in the arms and shoal areas in spring and after Labor Day, but good catches are made throughout the summer. Try the northeast end of Piety Island, south of the motel on either side of the peninsula, and near the northeast shore below Hoover Arm. The tributary arms are also good producers.

Still-fishing with bait is the most popular trout technique here, but trolling catches the big guys. One popular trout set-up is a rudder-flasher with 2 ft. leader, followed by a small Kwikfish-type lure or worm. A small Spin-n-glo behind a large flashers also work well, but remember to troll very slowly. Brown bullhead, though not stocked by the state, have increased in number and provide quite a fishery. They run to 14 inches and are taken with nightcrawlers on the bottom.

Kokanee anglers use downriggers to fish as deep as 80 to 100 ft. in July and August, or troll deep around the island and towards the dam. Kokanee grow well in Detroit, but few anglers pursue them here.

Landlocked chinook are gaining popularity with anglers. Fish deep in summer (near the bottom in 60 to 80 feet of water), shallower in spring and fall (20 to 50 feet). Most are caught by trolling. Blowout Creek and Kinney Creek arms are productive, as is trolling near the dam in spring. The chinook can reach 5 to 7 pounds.

There are three boat ramps off Hwy. 22 toward the east end of the reservoir at Mongold campground and Lakeshore State Park. On the south shore, there are boat ramps on the south bank of Hoover Arm, on Sauers Creek at Cove Campground, and at Southshore Campground. Cove is a group camp, available by reservation through the Detroit Ranger Station, Willamette National Forest. There is also a boat-in campground on Piety Knob, an island in the main pool at the east end of the reservoir.

Bank angling opportunities vary depending on water level. Bank fishing can be good in the North Santiam and Breitenbush arms, and around Tumble and French creeks (or associated with any of the inlets). It is always possible to fish from the fishing pier at the dam for trout and (sometimes) kokanee. The lake is generally shallower near the campgrounds, so fishing opportunities there are best in early season before the water warms.

Supplies are available in Dtroit.

DEXTER RESERVOIR. A fair size reservoir on the lower Middle Fork Willamette with opportunities for trout and bass. It is about 20 miles east of Eugene, downstream from Lookout Reservoir. The community of Lowell is on the north shore.

Dexter is heavily infested with northern pike minnow, but good numbers of legal rainbows are stocked annually, and there's a good fall and winter fishery for 12 to 15 inch trout that fatten in the productive tailwaters of Look-out Point Reservoir (which is adjacent to Dexter). Largemouth and smallmouth bass are available at the lower end and on either side of the causeway (the road to Lowell), where bass appreciate the submerged rocky road foundation.

Lowell encourages the catching of northern pike minnow through an annual jamboree in July in conjunction with their Blackberry Jam Festival. Prizes are awarded for most pike-minnow caught and for catching specially tagged fish. There are camping, boating, and picnic facilities on the north and south shores.

DINGER LAKE. A good little trout lake at 4000 ft. elevation, 2½ miles northwest of Timothy Lake in the Mt. Hood National Forest. It is about 77 miles from Portland.

From Pine Point Campground on the southwest arm of Timothy Lake, drive northwest on Forest Rd. 5820 toward Black Wolf Meadows Trailhead. About 3 miles from the campground, a short spur road cuts back to the northeast. If you see the trailhead for Trail 724, you've gone ½ mile too far. Take the spur road to its end. From there, Dinger is a third of a mile bushwhack northwest.

Dinger is stocked with rainbows and cutthroat. It is very shallow and in some years loses fish to winterkill. This shallowness also makes it an excellent fly lake for trout 7 to 14 inches. There are good natural campsites and a spring at the lake. It is usually accessible in late May.

DIXIE LAKES. A couple of small brook trout lakes at the southern end of the Eight Lakes Basin in Mt. Jefferson Wilderness. Easy to find, they're fished lightly by anglers passing through on the way to more popular spots. See Duffy Lake for directions. From Duffy, take the trail leading southeast toward Santiam Lake. At the meadow trail intersection about ½ mile down the trail, turn north toward Jorn

In spring, look for largemouth bass among the channels at the upper end of DORENA RESERVOIR. *Photograph by Richard T. Grost.*

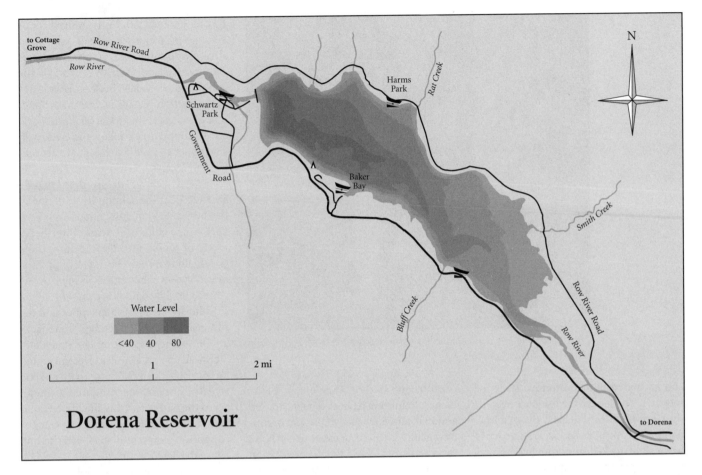

Dorena Reservoir

Lake. The Dixies are about three-quarters of a mile from this junction on the west side of the trail.

North Dixie has about 3 surface acres and is 8 ft. deep. It has brook trout to 12 inches. The South lake is smaller, shallower, and is not stocked. It may or may not have fish. There are lots of adequate campsites nearby.

DON LAKES. These trout lakes are hard to find. In fact, the Forest Service map doesn't show their location correctly, which doesn't make finding them easier. Upper Don Lake is about ½ mile due north of Parrish Lake and ½ mile northwest of Daly Lake. See Daly Lake for road directions. From Daly, it's about a half-mile bushwhack to the Don Lakes, bearing northwest and descending slightly. The maps show them closer, but you'll have to cross two stream beds on your way.

Lower Don Lake is about 3 acres and over 20 ft. deep. Upper Don is a quarter mile or so up the stream bed and is smaller but also deep. Brook trout in both lakes grow to 12 inches, and there are lots of them. The lower lake also has quite a few cutthroat. There are good campsites in the

area. A float tube would be handy but isn't necessary.

DORENA RESERVOIR

A pretty, peaceful reservoir on the Row River east of Cottage Grove, known for big largemouth bass and consistent winds. It attracts both anglers and sailors. Used mainly for flood control, it has about 1800 surface acres when full and holds its water level pretty well throughout spring and summer. It is drawn down beginning the day after Labor Day but can be fished year-round.

From I-5, take Exit 174 at Cottage Grove, and follow Row River Rd. east about 5 miles. To reach Baker Bay, bear right onto Government Rd., and follow the reservoir's south shore. Row River Rd. skirts the north shore, rejoining Government Rd. southeast of Dorena.

In spring and summer, bass to 8 pounds can be found in the Row River inlet and among the reed canary grass and channels at the upper end. Submerged stumps generally shelter a couple of bass. Rootwads also provide good habitat (Fish around the edges). Once draw-down is well under way,

most bass are caught near the dam. Only bass under 15 inches. may be kept.

Dorena also offers fishing for stocked rainbows trout, wild cutthroat, brown bullhead, bluegill, and black crappie. The trout run 6 to 14 inches. Trolling hardware accounts for most of the catch, but bait fishing is also productive. Bank anglers fish from the dam, along the north shore and Row River inlet, and at a few points on the south shore. Crappie and bluegill seek the deeper water near the dam in winter.

Harms Park boat ramp on the north shore can be used when the reservoir is full in spring and summer. Baker Bay ramp on the south shore is usable year-round, though even it can get muddy when the reservoir is low. Rental boats and motors and a limited selection of supplies are available at Baker Bay.

There are camping facilities at Baker Bay and at Schwartz Park on Row River immediately downstream from the reservoir. Campsites at Baker Bay are in a wooded area next to the lake.

There is a health advisory on fish taken from Dorena. As with Cottage Grove Reservoir nearby, Dorena's fish may be

Finclipped coho are available for harvest in EAGLE CREEK. *Photograph courtesy of Randy Sampson.*

contaminated with poisonous levels of mercury. The longer the fish have been in the reservoir, the more likely the contamination. The most conservative approach is to eat only stocked trout caught here, and the earlier in the season the better. Bullhead are particularly vulnerable to mercury contamination. See the regulations for official recommendations.

DORMAN POND. A 12-acre pond west of Forest Grove at the junction of highways 8 and 6, on the south side of the road. Legal rainbows stocked in spring attract a lot of early attention. Later in the season, you'll find more solitude to fish good populations of largemouth bass, bluegill, brown bullhead, and black crappie.

Dorman is an old, high borrow pit, privately owned but open to the public. With little oversight by either landowners or public agencies, it has been over-used and abused.

DUFFY LAKE

One of the best lakes in the Eight Lakes Basin of Mt. Jefferson Wilderness. From North Santiam Hwy. 22 about 8 miles south of Marion Forks (look for the sign to Big Meadow Horse Camp), drive 3 miles east on Forest Rd. 2267 to Duffy Lake Trailhead. Hike 3 miles east on the Duffy Lake Trail 3427.

Heavily used, Duffy is 30 acres and a consistent producer of brook trout 6 to 15 inches. Rainbows have also been stocked and make up a quarter of the catch, running a little smaller, but easier to catch. It's easy to fish from shore, but the brook trout are most easily taken while trolling, especially in early season. Pack in a float tube. Fly angling is good in fall from late afternoon till dark.

There are nice campsites at Duffy and at other good lakes in the area. See Cinca, Alforja, and Mowich. The basin is usually accessible by June, but it has a short season due to early snow.

DUMBELL LAKE. One of the northernmost lakes of the Mink Lake Basin. From Elk Lake Resort, take Trail 3517 west 2½ miles to the Pacific Crest Trail, then hike south about 3½ miles to Dumbell. An alternate approach is from the south by the Six Lakes Trail, which begins one mile south of Elk Lake. This route will take you past Davis and Blow lakes. The Pacific Crest Trail touches the eastern shore of Dumbell, and the lake gets pressure from a lot of hikers weary of freeze-dried fare.

Dumbell covers 6 acres and doesn't hold up well under the angling pressure. Its brook trout run 6 to 14 inches. There are several unnamed lakes west of Dumbell that might provide surprises for the adventurous. Supplies are available at Elk Lake Resort.

EAGLE CREEK (Clackamas watershed). A very good winter steelhead and coho stream with some wild cutthroat. It enters the lower Clackamas River west of the community of Eagle Creek on Hwy. 211, 5 miles north of Estacada. From Portland, take Hwy. 224 through Carver. From Eagle Creek, county roads follow the creek east. The upper 10 miles of stream are accessible only by trail.

Eagle Creek heads in the Cascade foothills near the Salmon River divide. A hatchery operation upstream of Eagle Fern Park rears coho and winter steelhead, many of which are released into Eagle Creek. Returns have been good (an estimated 15,000 coho returns in 1998). A few spring and fall chinook are present .

Coho appear in late September, and the run peaks around November. Coho jacks are present in good numbers in late fall. Steelhead enter the creek in December and are available through March, with angling activity from the Scout Camp at the mouth up to the hatchery. Only finclipped coho and steelhead may be kept. The creek is closed to salmon and steelhead angling above the hatchery intake.

Wild cutthroat are available for catch and release angling with artificial flies and lures, and there's lots of good fly water here. Young steelhead that fail to go to sea, about 10 inches long, may also be present. Mostly males, they are already mature and will put up a good scrap, but they are dark like spawners.

Check the regulations for hook and bait restrictions. There are no overnight campsites on the creek, but Eagle Fern Park has a nice picnic area.

EAST McFARLAND LAKE. A lightly fished trout lake 2 miles north of Irish Mt. about 6 trail miles north of Irish Lake. About 10 acres and over 30 ft. deep, it's very difficult to get to. The best route is to hike north 6 miles on the Pacific Crest Trail from Irish Lake, passing Dennis and Lindick lakes. About a quarter mile north of Lindick, bushwhack about ½ mile west to reach East McFarland. The road to Irish is very rough. Watch your oil pan.

East McFarland is stocked by air with rainbows and cutthroat, and there is usually some carry-over each year. It is usually inaccessible until late June.

EASTERN BROOK LAKE. An 11-acre lake in the Taylor Burn area, very close to Taylor Burn Forest Camp, north of Waldo Lake. From Oakridge on Hwy. 58, drive 20 miles east, turning north on the Waldo Lake Rd., Forest Rd. 5897. When you get to North Waldo Campground, head north on the old road that meets the Taylor Burn Rd. in about 4 miles. From Bend, take the Cascade Lakes Hwy. to Little Cultus, or cut west off Hwy. 97 onto any of the roads to Crane Prairie or Wickiup Reservoir, and follow the signs to Taylor Burn. From Taylor Burn Camp, head south ½ mile on the Wahana Trail, then west down a side trail a quarter mile through a meadow to the lake. There are good campsites and water at Taylor Burn Camp.

Eastern Brook Lake is deep and usually holds a lot of fish, but it has its slack periods. Alternate your methods for better luck. Spinner and bait fished slowly will usually produce. The brook trout run 6 to 18 inches, with most around 10 inches. The road to the trailhead usually opens near the end of June.

The south end of Eastern Brook was burned over in the 1996 Moolack fire.

E.E. WILSON POND. An 8-acre pond heavily stocked with legal rainbows and larger trout. Brood trout, trophy-size trout (to 1½ pounds) and hatchery steelhead are also added when available from the hatchery. Red-ear sunfish are also present, but generally elusive.

The pond is in the E.E. Wilson Wildlife Management Area of Camp Adair, off Hwy. 99W. The management area also provides habitat for deer, waterfowl, and pheasant. Anglers are urged to show consideration for nesting waterfowl in spring by staying on the path to the pond and confining activity to the angling area only. The management area is closed from October 1 through January 31 for waterfowl hunting season. Anglers are asked to register at a self-serve permit station to help monitor public use of this fishery.

The half-mile trail leading from the parking lot to the pond is not paved, but it is wheelchair accessible. Recommendedfor introducing youngsters to fishing.

EDDEELEO LAKE, LOWER. A large brook trout lake in the Taylor Burn area of the Central Cascades, about ½ mile north of Upper Eddeeleo Lake. See Upper Eddeeleo for directions. Lower Eddeeleo has 160 surface acres and is productive.

It's a good deep lake suited to any angling method. It can be fished from shore, but a float tube would be very useful. Angling is for naturally reproducing brook trout from 6 to 14 inches. Rainbows have not been stocked for some time, but a remnant might be present.

Fly angling is good early and late in the day. Bucktails fished wet with a slow retrieve have been successful on larger fish. Other good flies are the blue upright, mosquito, black gnat, spruce fly and gray and brown hackles. If things get dull, try Long Lake to the north of Upper Eddeeleo and Round Lake to the south. There are lots of good campsites in the area, usually accessible by late June.

EDDEELEO LAKE, UPPER. A good brook trout lake 2 miles northwest of Waldo Lake in the headwaters of the North Willamette River. About 63 acres, the lake is approached from Taylor Burn Campground, 7 rough road miles north of the North Waldo Lake Campground. The area is usually accessible in late June. The Indian-sounding name for this lake is actually a combination of the first names of Ed Clark, Dee Wright, and Leo McMahon, three forest service workers who first stocked the lake.

From Taylor Burn, take Trail 3553 west from camp, down through the Willamette canyon, and up to the Quinn Lakes Trail junction. Head south on Trail 3597 for 3 miles past Long and Lower Eddeeleo lakes.

Upper Eddeeleo can also be reached from the Wehanna Trail 3590, which skirts the northwest shore of Waldo Lake. Some anglers camp at North Waldo and boat across to the outlet at the northwest corner of Waldo. From there it's only a 1½ mile hike into the Eddeeleos.

The brook trout average run 6 to 14 inches. The lake holds up well all season. The shore is quite brushy, making fly angling difficult from the bank, but flies work well early and late in the day. Bait and lures are effective any time. Other lakes close by are Lower Eddeeleo and Round Lake. Chetlo Lake is about a mile south.

EDNA LAKE. A small trout lake just a few hundred yards west of Taylor Burn Campground, 7 miles by rough road north of North Waldo Lake Campground. Take the Olallie Trail (leading to the Erma Bell Lakes) west out of Taylor Burn. In about a quarter mile, the trail passes Edna Lake.

Edna is only 3 acres, but is lightly fished and holds up well. The trout range 6 to 10 inches. It's easy to fish from shore or from logs extending into the water.

ELBOW LAKE (Middle Fork Willamette watershed). A 10-acre trout lake near the northwest edge of Waldo Lake, about ½ mile south of Chetlo Lake. It's about 5½ trail miles from Taylor Burn or North Waldo Lake campgrounds. The easiest way in is by boat from Waldo Lake. See Chetlo Lake for directions.

Different trout species are stocked from year to year, but the size of the catch is generally 6-13 inches. Elbow can be fished from shore, and all methods can be effective, but the lake has its ups and downs.

ELK LAKE (Clackamas watershed). A lightly fished 60-acre trout and kokanee lake at the head of Elk Creek, a major tributary of the upper Collawash River. It can't be reached by road from the Mt. Hood Forest. Best approach is from Detroit on Hwy. 22. Take Forest Rd. 46 four miles northeast from Detroit to Forest Rd. 4696, which intersects from the north. Follow 4696 one mile, then take Forest Rd. 4697 left 6 ferociously rough, steep miles to the lake. This road is usually impassable until late June.

Elk Lake usually provides good fishing for brook trout and cutthroat 7 to 10 inches. A population of kokanee reproduces naturally here, with the average catch 8 to 9 inches. Though it's easy to fish from shore, a boat or float tube would be handy. All methods are used, but bait angling and trolling are best in early season. Fly angling picks up in late August and September. There's a good size campground, but no room for trailers. This is a good base camp for pack trips to lakes north. See Twin Lakes, Pansy, Big Slide.

EMERALD LAKE. A privately owned 4-acre trout lake 19 miles east of Molalla on the North Fork Molalla River. Owned by a logging company, the lake is closed to public use.

ERMA BELL LAKES. A series of three very good rainbow lakes in the northern part of the Taylor Burn area. The lakes are along the Olallie Trail 3563. The northernmost is Lower Erma Bell.

According to Lewis McArthur, these lakes are named for what must have been one of Oregon's earliest automobile victims. Miss Erma Bell, employed by

the Forest Service as a statistician, died in an automobile accident in April of 1918, and the Forest Service named these lakes for her.

The Ermabells can be approached from the north by driving to Skookum Creek Campground in the headwaters of the North Fork of the Middle Fork of the Willamette, by way of North Fork Rd. Take Trail 3563 south 2 miles to Lower Erma Bell. An alternative approach is from Taylor Burn Campground, 7 miles by rough road north of North Waldo Lake Campground. Take Trail 3563 north about 2 miles to Upper Erma Bell.

Upper Erma Bell is the smallest of the three, with 25 surface acres. Middle and Lower are each around 60 acres. Each of the lakes is fairly deep.

Lower and Middle have wild rainbows. Lower's rainbows run 6 to 15 inches. They can be fished from shore. All methods will take fish, with fly angling good in mornings and evenings. Nymph patterns and deep fished wet flies should do well.

Middle Erma Bell is a quarter mile south and slightly higher. It is a little larger and is very consistent for rainbows to 14 inches. All methods will work, and an occasional larger trout is taken.

The upper lake is ½ mile farther south and west of the trail. It has brook trout that average 10 inches.

In order to regenerate fragile lakeside vegetation, much of the land adjacent to the lakes is currently roped off to discourage camping. The Ermabells are easily accessed as a day hike from developed campgrounds at Skookum Creek or Kiahane on the North Fork Rd. The lakes are usually accessible near the end of June, depending on depth of snow pack.

ESTACADA LAKE (Rivermill Reservoir).The pool behind River Mill Dam on the Clackamas River. It is about 3 miles east of Estacada along Hwy. 224. Stocked with finclipped trout through September, it receives a total of 21,000 trout and is popular with local anglers. Only finclipped trout may be kept. Wild juvenile steelhead are present and must be released unharmed.

Spring chinook, steelhead, and coho pass through the lake on their way upriver. Chinook and steelhead may be fished during trout season (April 24 to October 31), though only finclipped steelhead may be kept. There is currently a brief open season for finclipped coho as well. check the current regulations.

The reservoir is in a steep-sided canyon with no access from the banks. A dock and log boom at the lower end near the boat ramp provides the only fishery for non-boating anglers. Trout can be found near the log booms, but most steelhead and spring chinoiok are farther out. The boat ramp is at the lower end of the reservoir near River Mill Dam.

EUGENE REST AREA PONDS. A series of ponds on the west side of Hwy. 99W between Eugene and Junction City, north of Clear Lake Rd. The ponds were contaminated by chemicals from a plant across the road. Do not fish here.

FAIRVIEW CREEK. A 5-acre urban stream, fed by springs southeast of Grant Butte in Gresham and flowing five miles across East Multnomah County before entering Fairview Lake. The creek once provided habitat for cutthroat trout and steelhead. Much degraded by development and pollution, it is presently in the care of the Fairview Creek Watershed Conservation Group, among whose goals is the restoration of the creek's fish population.

For more information about Fairview Creek, or to participate in the restoration project, call the Fairview Creek Watershed Conservation Group at 503-231-2270.

FAIRVIEW LAKE. A bass and panfish lake of more than 200 acres, north of Hwy. 30 and west of Troutdale. Adjacent to Blue Lake, it has a mixed population that includes a lot of rough fish. The lake is completely surrounded by private lands and is currently closed to the public.

FALL CREEK (Middle Fork Willamette watershed). A beautiful stream with angling for chinook, stocked rainbow trout, and wild cutthroat. Quite popular with residents of the Eugene-Springfield area, it flows 30 miles from the Cascades into Fall Creek Reservoir, before joining the Middle Fork Willamette.

From 1-5 south of Springfield, take Hwy.

58 east to Dexter Reservoir, crossing Dexter on the Lowell Rd. and continuing north to Unity. Follow County Rd. 6204 to Fall Creek Reservoir Dam, the reservoir's north shore, and Fall Creek flowing in from the east. Fall Creek National Recreation Trail follows the stream for 10 miles beginning at Dolly Varden Campground. Forest Rd. 18 follows the creek to its headwaters.

Fall Creek is heavily stocked with rainbow trout in the first 13 miles above the reservoir (from the reservoir to Sunshine Creek above Puma Campground). Wild cutthroat are also available. The average catch is about 9 inches with some trout to 12 inches. Bait and spinner are most effective in early season, with fly angling picking up in summer and through the fall.

Spring chinook have been stocked in the stream below the reservoir. The first returns are expected in 2002. Finclipped summer steelhead are also available, as well as naturally reproducing winter steelhead. Below the dam, the creek is currently open for trout fishing year-round, and for salmon and steelhead from November 1 to April 23. Check current regulations.

There's a lot of private land in the lower section, but the upper stream flows through the Willamette National Forest. This is a fine recreational area, with several good swimming holes and four National Forest campgrounds in a 7-mile stretch.

FALL CREEK RESERVOIR. A flood control reservoir about 12 miles southeast of the Eugene-Springfield area, fished for largemouth bass and crappie. About 1800 acres when full, it is drawn down low beginning the day after Labor Day. From Hwy. 58, cross Dexter Reservoir toward Lowell, continuing north to Unity. Turn right, and continue east to fish the Winberry arm of the reservoir, or turn left onto Big Fall Creek Rd. to reach the reservoir's north shore and the Big Fall Creek arm. The dam is just below the junction of the two creeks.

This reservoir is coming on as a largemouth bass fishery, with fish to 3 pounds common, and some to 5 pounds. Look for them near drop-offs, in the channels, and around submerged stumps. Crappie and bluegills are also available. Some legal rainbows are stocked, offering good fishing early in the season and in late fall. Most anglers choose to troll.

There are several boat ramps and picnic

areas on the reservoir, with campgrounds on the Fall Creek Rd.

FALL CREEK, LITTLE. The only completely free-flowing tributary of the Middle Fork Willamette, supporting both winter and summer steelhead as well as healthy populations of wild cutthroat, rainbow trout, big Willamette River migrants, and a small run of chinook.

About 20 miles long, Little Fall Creek flows into lower (big) Fall Creek near the community of Fall Creek, east of Springfield. From Springfield, follow South 42nd St. to Jasper Rd., turning left onto Jasper and continuing through the community of Jasper. Little Fall Creek joins Fall creek downstream of the second bridge. Don't cross the bridge. Continue northeast on County Rd. 6230, which follows Little Fall Creek into its headwaters. The creek is open for fishing from its mouth upstream to the concrete fish ladder at stream mile 12. The ladder allows migrant fish access to good spawning gravel above a formerly impassable waterfall.

Summer steelhead return to Little Fall from March through October, with peak numbers moving through the lower stream from mid-May through July. Though full-size, they are months away from spawning (February to April), so they are bright silver and full of energy. Winter steelhead arrive in March and spawn from April to June. Only finclipped steelhead may be retained. Chinook are generally found here in September.

Little Fall Creek offers several trout fishing opportunities. Wild resident cutthroat and rainbows may be fished and harvested from late April through October. Most are 6 to 9 inches. Considerably larger Willamette River redsides and cutthroat move into Little Fall Creek in late winter and early spring to spawn in the gravel beds above the falls. Fishing for trout at this time of year is catch and release only. Check the regulations for dates. Willamette River spawners range from 12 to 14 inches, with the occasional fish to 19 inches. Large trout in small streams are especially wary. Light line and tackle are recommended for best success. Barbless hooks and artificial flies and lures are encouraged, though not required.

Individual landowners along the first few miles of the creek have been known to give permission to access the stream. Ask

More hatchery-reared trout than ever are being stocked in lakes throughout the Willamette Zone. Photograph by Terry Hines.

politely, and pack out everything you pack in. Above mile post 12, most of the land along the creek is industrial timberland (Weyerhauser at this time). A gate across the road at mile post 12 is often open during the day during logging operations. Don't get locked in. The public is welcome to park at the gate and walk or bicycle in to the creek at all times. The gate is kept open for two months during hunting season in October and November. Keep an ear tuned for logging trucks. There are no campgrounds along the creek.

FANNO CREEK. An urban trout stream meandering 14 miles through residential, commercial, and industrial lands in west Multnomah and Washington counties. It flows into the Tualatin River at the city of Durham, downstream from Cook Park.

A network of little parks, private woodlots, and urban wetlands have helped keep the creek alive. There is a nice population of wild cutthroat trout eking out a living here, available for catch and release fishing by neighborhood kids (artificial flies and lures only). If you're one of them, you know how to find the creek. Fanno may be fished for trout from the late May opener to October 31. It is closed to fishing for salmon and steelhead.

The creek is being cared for by Fans of Fanno Creek, a citizen watershed protection group dedicated to preserving the creek and its fish and wildlife. For more information about Fanno Creek or to participate in restoration efforts, write Fans of Fanno, PO Box 25835, Portland, OR 97225 or Call Watershed Partners, United Sewerage Agency.

FARADAY LAKE. A popular and accessible 25-acre reservoir off the mainstem Clackamas River near Estacada. It is used for power purposes, but provides fair angling. To reach it, follow Hwy. 224 southeast from Estacada, to a bridge that crosses the river about 2 miles from town.

Faraday is stocked with a large number of legal rainbows (26,000 per year) and recycled hatchery steelhead. Only finclipped trout and steelhead may be retained. Migrating salmon and steelhead occasionally enter the lake through the diversion canal. All salmon and finclipped steelhead may be caught as trout (no salmon and steelhead tag necessary). For information about the availability of recycled steelhead and salmon in Faraday, call the PGE Fish Line. See Appendix.

Faraday is fairly shallow due to siltation, especially at the upstream end. Deep holes near the downstream dam structure can hold larger fish. Most anglers use bait, but spinners and other lures will produce from the bank. The lake is open year-round.

FAY LAKE. A fairly good brook trout lake off North Santiam Hwy. 22, in the Big Meadows area about 8 miles south of Marion Forks. From Hwy. 22, follow Forest Rd. 2267 southeast for about a mile, turning left on 2257 for 2 miles into Big Meadows. Bear right onto 2257. Fay is on the right side of the road. There may be more roads in this area than show on the current maps, but if you find Big Meadows, you'll find the lake.

Fay Lake is only about 7 acres but holds up well even with heavy pressure. Brook trout run 6 to 15 inches. Stocked rainbows about the same size make up half the catch. It's a hard lake to fish, shallow and clear, and if there is no wind on the surface the fish spook easily. The Forest Service has felled and submerged a number of big trees to enhance fish cover. The lake is brushy and hard to fish from shore, but it is easily waded. A float tube or rubber boat would be useful. There are good campsites at Big Meadows.

FERN RIDGE RESERVOIR. The largest lake in the Willamette Valley, a huge flood control reservoir on the Long Tom River, 12 miles west of Eugene. Known for its consistent wind, it attracts a large flotilla of sailboats and sail boards, but also offers good fishing for largemouth bass. Largemouth bass, bluegill, crappie, and cutthroat trout are also available. Fern Ridge has 9000 surface acres at full pool.

From Eugene, follow Hwy. 126 west about 12 miles, then turn north towards Elmira on the Territorial Highway. The dam is at the north end of the reservoir, about five miles beyond Elmira.

At full pool, look for bass in the reservoir's many little fingers. Bass can be found prowling the weedy slopes of the reservoir mornings and evenings. East of Perkins Peninsula Park, the Coyote Creek bypass leads to a lightly fished slough area that looks very promising for bass and panfish, with submerged trees and overhanging brush. To reach it, turn left downstream of the highway bridge. Flooded timber stands, riprap, weed beds and submerged creek channels throughout the reservoir offer excellent bass habitat. When the reservoir is low, fish near the dam. Crappie are particularly plentiful in spring along Hwy. 126, off Perkins Peninsula Park, and along the dam.

If you don't have a boat, the dam offers fishing opportunities year-round. Crappie are plentiful in the cement spillway structures below the dam (this area is especially good in winter) and at the inflow of the Long Tom River in the southwest arm. Bluegill are available in the shallows and the weedy areas. Bank anglers can also fish Kirk Pond, a long finger of water that parallels the dam north of Clear Lake Rd.

Fern Ridge is very popular for general water recreation. There are boat ramps on either side of the dam (at Richardson Park on the west and Orchard Point Park on the east), and at Perkins Peninsula Park off

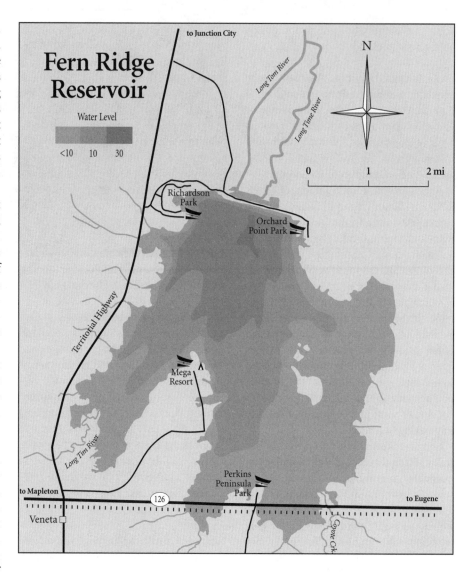

Hwy. 126 on the south shore. Boats can be rented at Orchard Pt. The parks also have docks, swimming areas, and picnic facilities. Kirk Park (on Kirk Pond) has picnic facilities only.

FIR LAKE. Once a real sleeper, difficult to reach, with anglers in the know making terrific catches and keeping mum. It's not a big lake, only about 6 acres, but it's quite deep and puts out some really good brook trout. Most of the fish run 10 to 12 inches, but there are larger ones to 18 inches.

It used to be a brushy hike by compass to the lake, but there is now a blazed trail. To get there, first drive to Fay Lake. See Fay Lake for directions. Go north past Fay about a quarter mile to a turn-out. A blazed trail takes off to the east from here, and it's about one mile to Fir (past Pika Lake, which has brook trout). Fir is fairly brushy but can be fished easily from logs if you don't have a rubber boat or float tube.

FIRECAMP LAKES. A group of three lakes northwest of Mt. Jefferson, near the head of the South Fork of the Breitenbush River. From Detroit on Hwy. 22, take Breitenbush Forest Rd. 46 for 10 miles (one mile past the Hot Springs), then take Forest Rd. 4685 to road's end. Crown Lake, the largest of the group, is 2 miles east on Trail 3361, at elevation 4852 ft.

Crown is about 16 acres and quite shallow. It is no longer stocked due to a tendency to winterkill and out of concern for its amphibian population. The next lake, just a few hundred yards southeast, is Clagget Lake. This is a small but deep lake of several acres and is the most reliable lake of the three. The third lake, Sheep, is brushy, shallow, and hard to fish, but it produces larger trout.

This is an old burned-off area, great for huckleberries in late fall. Just over the ridge to the east are three other lakes which have good fishing at times. See Slideout Lake.

FIRST LAKE. A 3-acre trout lake accessed by road north of Olallie Lake. It is the first lake south of Lower Lake Campground. The Olallie Lake Basin is about 100 miles from Portland by way of highways 26 or 224 and a network of forest roads. First Lake is west of the road. See Olallie Lake for directions.

First Lake is stocked with cutthroat or rainbow fingerlings in odd number years. It doesn't have a large trout population, but fish 8 to 13 inches are available, and the lake is lightly fished. Spinner and bait and small lures cast from shore are effective. There are campsites at Lower Lake Campground to the north and around Olallie Lake to the south. Other drive-to lakes in the area include Monon and Horseshoe. For hike-in lakes, see Gifford Lakes.

FIRST AND SECOND LAKES. Two ox-bows off the Willamette in the city of Albany, fished primarily for crappie and largemouth bass. Theses are former industrial waste ponds, and though tested for safety, it is unofficially recommended that you not eat what you catch here.

The city is developing the lake area into a park (Simpson Park) at the south end of First lake. The park will provide access between the Willamette and the lakes. First Lake is the most accessible of the two. Light weight (hand carried) boats can be launched on First and paddled to Second. Bank access is best in spring. Second Lake (the deeper of the two) is connected to First by a narrow channel.

White crappie, black crappie, and largemouth bass predominate, though in high water years when the Willamette flows through the oxbows, a variety of species may take up temporary residence.

FISH CREEK (Clackamas watershed) Once responsible for more than a third of the steelhead smolts in the Upper Clackamas River system. The Fish Creek watershed suffered more than 230 landslides, several road washouts, and loss of a bridge during the 1996 floods, attributed to heavy logging and road building on unstable slopes. The watershed is closed to public access at this time. The creek and its tributaries are closed to all fishing. Work is underway to obliterate all but a few of the lower roads in the watershed (5410, 5411, and 5412). Upon completion of the project (October, 2000), the old road beds may be used for hiking, bicycling, and horseback riding. Three lakes in the watershed will be a long trek for the adventuring angler, but possibly worth the effort. See High, Surprise, and Skookum.

FISH LAKE (Clackamas Co.). A 20-acre lake northwest of Olallie Lake, featuring small stocked cutthroat and a few brook trout. From Lower Lake Campground on Olallie Lake Rd. (Forest Rd. 4220), follow Trail 717 northwest over a mile to the lake.

Though the trout only run 6 to 11 inches, good catches are made using all techniques. Bait, small lures, and spinners work well, with wet flies effective in the evening. This is a very deep lake, and a float tube would be useful. There are primitive campsites at the lake, but a power transmission line mars the scenery. There's a good camp at Lower Lake.

FISH LAKE (Hood River watershed). A small brook trout lake in Mt. Hood National Forest about a mile by trail north of Wahtum Lake, 25 miles southwest of Hood River. Trail 408 leads north from the Wahtum Lake parking area about 2 miles to the lake. When road conditions are suitable, you can follow a primitive road just over one mile around the east side of Wahtum then northwest. This road intersects the trail and saves a mile of hiking.

Fish Lake is just 2 acres and shallow with a history of winterkills. It has been stocked with brook trout, but at this time it isn't scheduled for restocking.

FISH LAKE (Santiam watershed) A shallow cutthroat lake north of Clear Lake, off the South Santiam Hwy. 20. It's about 72 miles from Albany, 3 miles west of Santiam Junction.

About 50 acres, Fish Lake drains into Clear Lake. It has an unusually short open season (late April through May) because it tends to dry up, making its fish too vulnerable to be sporting. Cutthroat from 6 to 14 inches are present, and fly fishing is very effective. There's a small campground here, and supplies can be obtained at Clear Lake Resort. Motorboats are prohibited.

FISHER LAKES. Two small, lightly fished trout lakes in the Horse Lake area of the Upper McKenzie watershed. See Horse Lake for directions. From Upper Horse Lake, take the McBee Trail southwest 1½ miles. The trail goes right by Fisher Lakes. Brook trout and cutthroat are present, with the average catch 8 to 10 inches.

East Fisher is about 2 acres and 20 feet deep. It's shaped like a dumbell and is easily fished from shore by standing on the logs that line its bank. There are many good campsites in the Horse Lake area.

FOSTER RESERVOIR. A 1200 acre reservoir on the Santiam River near the town of Foster, about 3 miles east of Sweet Home, north of Hwy. 20. It backs up the South and Middle Forks of the Santiam River, offering fishing for trout, bass, and bluegills.

Foster is stocked with catchable rainbows in April and May. Unauthorized plants of largemouth bass and bluegills are established, but the bass run small due to fluctuations in the reservoir's pool. The reservoir is lowered in April and May to allow young steelhead to escape. Smallmouth bass have also been unofficially introduced. Look for warmwater fish in association with natural variations in the reservoir bed, old channels, and submerged stumps.

Bank anglers fish from the dam face off the rip rap, from flat areas in the South Fork arm, and along the north shore. The Little Fork arm can be a little steep for comfortable bank fishing.

There are boat ramps at Gedney Creek Access, Sunnyside Park, and Calkins Park. Most boat angling takes place here from April 1 to mid-June, after which other water recreation sports take over the place.

Campgrounds are available at Sunnyside Park and at Meare Bend upstream of the reservoir. Sunnyside has lots of amenities for a public campground in this area, including flush toilets and showers. Recommended for youngsters.

FRAZIER LAKE (Clackamas watershed). A 3-acre lake in the High Rock Lakes area, one mile northeast of Shellrock Lake. From High Rocks Lookout, reached by the Squaw Mt. Rd. (Forest Rd. 4610) or by the Shellrock Creek Rd. (Forest Rd. 58) from the Clackamas River on the south, head west on Forest Rd. 240 toward Frazier Mt. About 2½ miles west there is a switchback from which the lake can be seen.. It's a half-mile hike from the road to the lake. There are other approaches to the lake as well. Check the Mt. Hood National Forest map.

Frazier is about 8 ft. deep, at an elevation

Carp are one of many warmwater fish you might find at the end of your line in the GILBERT RIVER. Photograph by Mark Van Duser

of 4100 ft. It contains brook trout 6 to 11 inches. All methods seem effective, with bait best early in the season and flies in summer and fall. The road in is usually snowbound until late June.

FREEWAY PONDS. Trout ponds along I-5 about 3 miles south of Albany. Take the State Police exit and follow the frontage road south. The ponds are stocked with legal rainbows in spring. Later, they offer pretty good fishing for bluegill, crappie, and largemouth bass. Crappie are especially plentiful, with good numbers close to shore in spring. A boat can be useful. Recommended for youngsters.

FROG LAKE RESERVOIR. Given the redundant name to distinguish it from another Frog Lake in the Clackamas River drainage. This Frog Lake is associated with the Three Lynx Power Station on the Oak Grove Fork of the Clackamas, and is notable for its population of large rainbow and brown trout, both of which migrate to the reservoir through a pipeline from Harriet Lake. About 16 acres, it can be reached from the Three Lynx Rd., off Hwy. 224. Frog Lake Reservoir is on the right. Boats are prohibited. Parking is plentiful.

This is an undeveloped recreation site, without camping or picnicking facilities, but Harriet Lake fish grow to nice size in this relatively non-competitive environment. There's not much shoal here, so plan to fish deep. There's a good chance the big trout stick around to feast on Frog Lake's

plentiful sculpin population, so choose your fly or lure accordingly.

GALES CREEK. A winter steelhead and wild cutthroat stream flowing through private agricultural and timber land in Washington County west of Portland. It is a major tributary of the Tualatin River, which it joins just south of Forest Grove.

Gales Creek heads in the coast range near the headwaters of the Wilson River. The upper creek is followed by Hwy. 6, and the lower water by Hwy. 8. From Portland take Hwy. 26 west to the junction of Hwy. 6, then follow the highway to the stream.

Gales Creek is open for steelheading November 1 through March 31. Only fin-clipped steelhead may be retained. The run usually peaks December through February. Wild cutthroat trout are also present and may be fished catch and release.

GANDER LAKE. A fair size rainbow and brook trout lake at 5000 ft. elevation, northwest of Waldo Lake. Forest roads have crept up on this lake and cut the hiking distance from 9 miles to a little over one, increasing the pressure and reducing the catch. Better have your forest map in hand when you set out for Gander, as you must navigate through a maze of roads to get to the trailhead.

From the south end of Oakridge on Hwy. 58, take the Salmon Creek road east (Forest Rd. 24). Watch for hatchery signs to locate the road. At about 11 miles, take Forest Rd. 2417 east. At roughly 12 miles

(within about 4 miles of road's end), 2417 makes a tight S-turn. At the second curve, continue straight onto a road (unnumbered on Forest Service maps) that leads to Trail 3568 to Gander. It is about 1½ miles to the lake. A fork to the south right before reaching Gander leads to Gosling lake. Trail 3568 continues past the north end of Gander to Swan lake.

Gander covers 58 acres and is stocked with rainbow and brook trout. The average fish is around 10 to 11 inches, and they have been known to run to 16 inches. It's a good fly fishing lake and can be fished from shore, but you'll do better if you get out on the lake. Good natural campsites are available. Cygnet, Swan, and Gosling (three little lakes from 6 to 12 acres) offer additional trout opportunities nearby.

GIFFORD LAKES. Two beautiful little stocked rainbow lakes in the Olallie area about one mile west of the Skyline Rd. north of Olallie Lake. They are most easily reached by hiking from Lower Lake Campground, around the north shore of Lower Lake to the junction of Trail 706, then directly south ½ mile. Upper Gifford is east of the trail.

The upper lake has about 8 surface acres and is quite deep. It is easily fished from shore, with plenty of casting room. All methods are effective. The rainbows run to 14 inches, averaging 10. Lower Gifford, to the north, has some good size brook trout. A float tube would be useful.

Finley Lake perches on a rock cliff above the talus slope at the east shore of Upper Gifford. Though no longer stocked, it makes a very scenic campsite. There's also a prime campsite on the peninsula at Upper Gifford and other undeveloped sites between upper and lower lakes. The area is not accessible until late June.

GILBERT RIVER. A warmwater fishery winding 4 slender miles through Sauvie Island, about 10 miles northwest of Portland off Hwy. 30. Sauvie Island offers a welcome respite from urban life for both wildlife and humans. See Sturgeon Lake, McNary Lake, Pete's Slough, and Cunningham Slough and Lake for other fishing opportunities nearby.

The property surrounding the Gilbert is managed by ODFW for wildlife refuge and hunting, with a focus on the waterfowl that take advantage of the island's extensive wetland habitats. Almost incidentally, the Gilbert provides pretty good fishing for walleye, largemouth bass, crappie, bluegill, yellow perch, and brown bullhead. Canoes or small motor boats are appropriate for this quiet backwater in its bucolic setting. Like all fisheries within the island complex, it is open from April 16 through September 30. The truncated season protects wintering waterfowl.

More a slough than a river, the Gilbert heads in Sturgeon Lake and flows into Multnomah Channel. To reach the gravel boat ramp at the Gilbert mouth after crossing Multnomah Channel on Sauvie Island Bridge, follow Sauvie Island Rd. north (straight ahead) about 2 miles, then turn right on Reeder Rd. Reeder crosses over to the Columbia River side of the island and follows the Columbia to within a few miles of the island's northernmost point. After about 15 miles on Reeder, look for a sign on the left for Gilbert River Boat Ramp.

To reach the handicapped angler accessible fishing platform at The Big Eddy on the Gilbert, continue north on Sauvie Island Rd., about 5 miles from the bridge. Look for The Big Eddy sign on the right.

The Gilbert is also accessible to hike-in anglers at many points along its meander by way of a network of trails, dikes, footbridges, and dirt roads open to public use during the open season. Park at any of the designated sites within the refuge. Maps of the Wildlife Area are available at the Management Headquarters on Sauvie Island Rd. north of the Reeder Rd. junction.

You will need to purchase a recreation permit to park on the island. Day use and annual passes are available at the market on the island immediately north of the bridge. Aside from one or two seasonal establishments offering local produce (and a number of U-Pick opportunities), this market is the only retail operation on the island. There are no gas stations.

GNAT LAKE. A good 3-acre brook trout lake in the Mink Lakes Basin. Gnat is about 1½ miles west of the Pacific Crest Trail near the Goose and Corner lakes trail. It is stocked with fingerling cutthroat trout every few years and provides good catches of 10-inch trout. You can fish from shore, but a float tube wouldn't hurt.

GOLD LAKE. A very good trout lake north of the Willamette Pass summit off Hwy. 58., with rainbows and book trout to 20 inches. Fishing is restricted to fly angling with barbless hooks

From Oakridge, follow Hwy. 58 southeast 23 miles. Look for the Gold Lake sign about 2 miles south of the Waldo Lake turn-off. Forest Rd. 500 reaches the Gold Lake campground at the southwest corner of the lake in about 2 miles. The road is often snow-bound till June, and may be rough and muddy in early season.

The catch is at least 5 to 1 brook trout to rainbow, and anglers are encouraged to catch and keep any quantity of brookies. Rainbows must be released unharmed. Fishing holds up well due to the short season and restricted tackle. Fish range from 6 to 20 inches.

Gold is about ½ mile long and has slightly more than 100 surface acres. Although it can be fished from shore, it's pretty brushy, and a boat (hand-powered only) is strongly recommended. A trail on the west side is not very helpful for fishing. Use the trail at the end of the east-side campground to launch a float tube or wade.

The shallower water at the northeast end of the lake always seems to be liveliest, though catches are made throughout the lake. Trying to match the hatch here can be a challenge. Midges, caddis, mayflies, dragonflies, and damselflies are all available to the trout. Use long thin leaders, and bring plenty of fine tippet material. Slowly trolling a wet fly or nymph may stir up action when the hatch is off.

There's a nice campground here, with a boat ramp (though no motors are allowed), and a rustic shelter. Closest sources of supplies are the Odell Lake resorts. The trailhead for Marilyn Lakes (less than a mile distant) is on the Gold Lake access road.

All tributaries to Gold Lake are closed to fishing, and Salt Creek, the outlet stream, is closed 100 yds. below the boat ramp to protect rainbow trout spawning areas.

GOODFELLOW LAKES. A series of three lakes in the closed area of the Bull Run Watershed, water supply for the city of Portland. Gates on the roads leading to the area are locked. The lakes are closed to fishing.

GOOSE LAKE. A 9-acre bass and panfish lake 7 miles north of Salem. Access is through Willamette Mission Park off the Wheatland Ferry Rd. Largemouth bass and white crappie are available.

GORDON CREEK. A small tributary of the Sandy River providing interesting fishing for wild cutthroat and rainbow trout. The stream is about 12 miles long and joins the lower Sandy from the east. Sandy River Rd. crosses the mouth of Gordon about 7 miles south of Hwy. 30. No road follows the creek, but the upper reaches are accessible from several dirt roads that cut south off the Larch Mt. Rd.

Rainbow trout predominate, averaging 9 inches with a few fish larger. Beaver ponds in the upper tributaries have been known to hold fair size cutthroat. All trout fishing is catch and release with artificial flies and lures. The creek is closed to fishing for salmon and steelhead.

GORDON LAKES. Two small cutthroat lakes south of South Santiam Hwy. 20, about 15 miles east of Cascadia. Take Forest Rd. 2044 south from Hwy. 20 at House Rock Campground. At about 3 miles, follow Forest Rd. 230 southwest about 2 miles to road's end. The lakes are a quarter mile northwest. The area is usually accessible in June.

These are wild cutthroat lakes, each about 7 acres and fairly deep with fish 6 to 15 inches. Bait fishing with eggs or worms is effective in early season, and spinner and bait combinations should attract some large fish. Fly angling is good later in the season.

The lakes are connected by stream and trail, with the further lake larger and slightly lower in elevation deeper, and with a brushy shore that makes casting difficult. An old growth log extending into the lake serves as a natural pier. Both lakes offer pleasant swimming in late summer.

GOSLING LAKE. A 6½ acre lake in Waldo Lake Wilderness northwest of Waldo Lake. For directions see Gander lake. Gosling is stocked with rainbow or brook trout every other year, depending on what's available. Swan Lake is nearby.

GOVERNMENT ISLAND LAKE (a.k.a. Beer Can Lake). At the west end of state-owned Government Island, in the Columbia River east of Portland. It supports a portion of the I-205 Bridge across the river but can only be reached by boat. Landing on the island is prohibited, but when the river is high you can take a boat up Beer Can Slough on the north side of the island. At low water, it may also be possible to fish the lake within the high water zone around the lake's perimeter.

The 40-acre lake contains crappie, brown bullhead, perch and a few largemouth bass. Angling is usually fair before spring high water and again for a few months after. Bait, spinners, and plugs are all used with success, with bait most popular. The island is owned by the Port of Portland, which has eliminated public access following repeated acts of vandalism.

GREEN PEAK LAKE. A lightly fished, hard to find, brook trout lake near the Eight Lakes Basin in Mt. Jefferson Wilderness Area. Best approach is from Blue Lake. See Blue Lake for directions. Green Peak is a steep bushwhack one mile due west of Blue. The lake is about 6 acres and 12 ft. deep. It puts out fair numbers of 10 to 12 inch brook trout, but some large ones show up from time to time. There are good natural campsites.

GREEN PETER RESERVOIR

A flood control reservoir on the Middle Santiam River with a very good kokanee fishery, as well as rainbow trout and largemouth bass. The reservoir is east of Sweet Home and Foster, north of Hwy. 20. Quartzville Creek and the Middle Santiam form a pool of over 3700 acres when full.

Kokanee are the primary focus of angler attention, and they could apparently stand even more. At present there is a bonus bag of 25 fish in addition to the regular 5 to encourage anglers to help thin the population. The kokanee are of good size, 12 to 13 inches, and are usually closer to the surface than at Detroit Reservoir or Odell. Anglers jig Buzz Bombs at about 40 ft., going deeper later in the year.

Largemouth bass are well established (though hard to locate), and catchable rainbow trout are stocked in April.

There are boat ramps at Thistle Creek and Whitcomb Creek parks. Thistle Creek ramp is usable at low water. There are overnight camping facilities at Whitcomb Creek Park upstream on the reservoir.

GREEN POINT CREEK. A small wild trout stream tributary to the West Fork Hood River. It heads near Wahtum Lake and flows into the West Fork Hood River near Dee. To reach Green Point, cross the

West Fork downstream from Dee off Hwy. 281 (Hood River Hwy.) and turn right on Punchbowl Rd. After the next creek crossing, turn onto Forest Rd. 2810, bearing right at the next fork to follow Green Point to its headwaters.

The creek offers fair catch and release angling for wild trout. Tackle is restricted to artificial flies and lures.

GROSSMAN POND. A privately owned 2-acre pond with a good warmwater fish populations near Independence, open to public fishing by permission of the owner. Follow Monmouth St. to Talmadge Rd. Turn south at 0.6 mile. Bluegill and largemouth bass are available.

The owner of the pond is especially protective of the largemouth bass, and continued use of this nice little fishery is contingent on anglers voluntarily releasing all bass caught.

HAGG LAKE, HENRY

A destination fishery for smallmouth bass anglers, source of the current state record smallmouth, and a popular fishery for trout and panfish. Henry Hagg Lake is a flood control and water supply reservoir in the Tualatin watershed 7 miles southwest of Forest Grove in Washington County. It is fed by 11 creeks, each of which forms an arm or smaller cove. Its main sources are Scoggins, Tanner, and Sain creeks.

From Hwy. 47 south of Dilley near Forest Grove, a paved road runs about 3 miles west to the reservoir. A second road from Gaston also reaches the lake. The reservoir has 1100 surface acres when full. Unlike most other reservoirs in the state, it is closed to recreational use in winter. It is managed by Washington County Parks and Recreation, which charges for day use.

Open from the third Saturday in April through October, Hagg is at its best in spring and fall, since it is drawn down in summer to accommodate winter run-off. Though the reservoir has a maximum depth of 110 ft., there is little oxygen to sustain fish below 30 ft.

Two record smallmouth bass have been caught here, the most recent in 1997, weighing 7 pounds, 4 ounces. Smallmouth in the 4- to 6-pound range are fairly common. When the lake temperature reaches 60 to 65 degrees, smallmouth move into the shallows to spawn. Look for them in

Perch fishing is at its best when HAGG LAKE is drawn down in summer. Photograph by Bob Judkins.

the grassy areas of the Tanner Creek arm to the north, along the north shore, in the Sain Creek Arm to the west, and in the coves north and south of Boat Ramp A.

When the water temperature climbs above 65 degrees, smallmouth move into the cooler water of the deep south end near the dam and the Scoggins Creek outlet. Smallmouth are also picked up along the riprap near the boat ramps.

In spring, lures imitating perch, crayfish, and trout fingerlings are effective bass attractors. Later in the season, try topwater plugs in the morning, and deep water plugs when the sun is high. Plastic worms, grubs, and jigs can be productive year-round. Best fishing for smallmouth is generally in spring and fall.

Largemouth bass are present in smaller numbers, though 7-pounders are hooked every year. Look for them in the shallows after the smallmouth have returned to deeper water. Later, they can be found near the dam.

Hagg Lake was originally intended as a trout lake. Today, warmwater species are far more plentiful, but there's still good trout fishing. ODFW plants about 40,000 legal trout in spring, as well as 60,000 fingerlings. Holdover rainbow trout can reach 4 to 7 pounds. Tens of thousands of excess steelhead fingerlings are added to the pool in some years, and there are wild cutthroat in the inlet arms.

Best trout fishing is in spring and early summer before the water warms, and again in fall. Early in the season, the newly introduced catchable trout tend to move around the reservoir in large schools, following the shoreline. Fishing from the banks or trolling the edges can be very productive. In mid-summer, or any time the sun is bright, troll the deeper water. Big holdover trout are generally found in the old creek channel down the middle of the lake. When trout fishing is slow in the main reservoir, consider turning your attention to the aggressive wild cutthroat in arms.

Yellow perch provide a popular fishery throughout the summer. The Tanner Creek arm and the little cove north of A-Ramp (east shore at the end of Herr Rd.) are especially productive. Bluegill and crappie are plentiful in the coves. Focus on submerged structure such as trees and root wads. Bullhead catfish, 12 to 14 inches and weighing 1 to 3 pounds, can be found on the bottom in holes and troughs. The Tan-

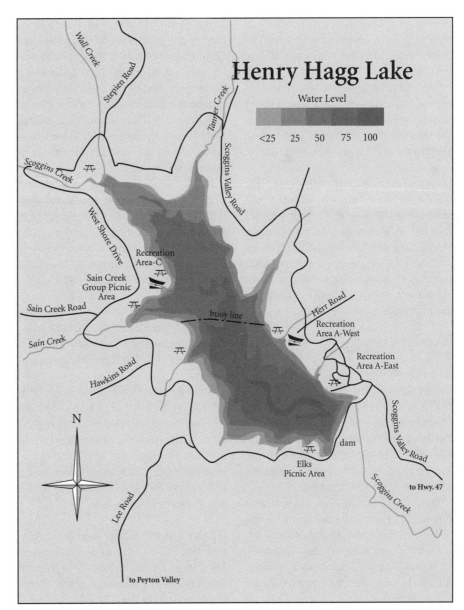

Henry Hagg Lake

Water Level

<25   25   50   75   100

ner Creek arm is especially productive for bullhead catfish.

There are two boat ramps on the lake, in Recreation Area A off Herr Rd., and in Recreation Area C off West Shore Drive north of the Sain Creek arm. Anglers will appreciate the "slow, no wake" requirement within 200 ft. of shore (to minimize shoreline erosion and the resulting turbidity) and in the entire north half of the reservoir. Don't come here expecting a wilderness experience. This place can be very busy in summer. In fact, boats are required to move in a counter-clockwise pattern in the south half of the lake to minimize the possibility of collisions.

There's fair bank fishing at many points around the lake, from a dike near C-Ramp, and from the dam. There are fishing piers near the Elk Point Picnic Area at the south end of the lake and near C-Ramp on the west shore. Both piers are accessible to wheelchairs. There is no camping allowed at Hagg, but there are several picnic areas, including a group shelter available by reservation. See Appendix.

HALDEMAN POND. A 4-acre pond on Sauvie Island within the Sauvie Island Wildlife Recreation Area. The pond is on Oak Island in Sturgeon Lake. After crossing the Sauvie Island Bridge from Hwy. 30, continue straight on Sauvie Island Rd., turning right onto Reeder Rd. then left on Oak Island Rd.

Legal trout are stocked annually until June, when the water begins to grow to warm to sustain them. Bluegill and largemouth bass are available throughout the open season, from April 16 through September 30. Sauvie Island fisheries close early to protect wintering waterfowl. The trout average 10 inches with some as large as 15 inches.

You will need to purchase a recreation permit to park on Sauvie Island. Day or seasonal passes are sold at the market on the island north of the bridge. There are no gas stations or other services on the island.

HANKS LAKE. A small scenic trout lake high in the Mt. Jefferson Wilderness south of Mt. Jefferson, west of Cathedral Rocks. Located in a cove-like meadow beside Hunts Lake. It is best reached by a short, steep trail from Pamelia. For directions, see Hunts Lake. Hanks offers consistent fishing for brook trout. There are beautiful natural campsites at both lakes.

HARRIET LAKE

A hydropower reservoir with a good trout fishery, including trophy trout opportunities. It is on the Oak Grove Fork of the Clackamas River, about 60 miles from Portland. Narrow and deep, this 23-acre reservoir supports three varieties of trout. Rainbows predominate, but lunker brown and brook trout also lurk here.

From Estacada, take Hwy. 224 southeast into the Mt. Hood National Forest to Ripplebrook Ranger Station. About a mile beyond the ranger station, follow Forest Rd. 57 toward Timothy Lake. At about 6 miles, this road crosses the Oak Grove Fork, and Forest Rd. 4630 cuts back west a mile to Harriet Lake.

Harriet receives as many as 24,000 catchable rainbow trout through August each year, as well as 1000 trophy-size rainbows, stocked in September to give them time to grow fat and wily in time for spring fishing.

Best fishing is at the upper end of the reservoir, where large rainbows and browns to 4 pounds are taken each spring. Most of the catch consists of rainbows 8 to 15 inches. The action usually slows in summer and fall. Most fish are taken by trolling large spinners and worms. Lures and spinners cast from shore are also effective.

The campground and picnic area at the head of the lake were expanded and upgraded in 1998.

HARVEY LAKE (Middle Fork Willamette watershed). A rainbow trout lake in the Taylor Burn area north of Waldo Lake. Harvey is 1½ miles south of Taylor Burn Campground off Olallie Trail 3583, a quarter mile south of Wahanna Lake and a bushwhack west of the trail. Taylor Burn campground is reached by 7 miles of rough road leading north from North Waldo Lake Campground. Harvey was burnt over in the Moolack Fire but continues to be stocked.

Harvey is 22 acres and up to 24 feet deep. It is stocked regularly with rainbow fingerlings. The fish do well and range in size from 6 to 18 inches. Harvey can be fished from shore, and any method will take fish when they're hitting. Other lakes in the area include Kiwa and the Rigdons.

HEAD LAKE. A 2-acre cutthroat trout lake off the Skyline Rd. north of Olallie Lake. Head Lake is west of the road, about a quarter mile south of Lower Lake Campground.

It can be fished from shore and is fairly productive for fish 7 to 14 inches. Spinner and bait are usually best, with fly angling good in late summer evenings. There is no camp at the lake, but there are campgrounds at Olallie. Other good lakes in the area include Fish and Monon. The road is rarely open before late June.

HEART LAKE (Santiam watershed). A 13-acre trout lake south of South Santiam Hwy. 20, about 7 miles west of the Santiam Junction. About 3 miles west of Lost Prairie Campground on Hwy. 20, take Forest Rd. 60, which cuts back sharply to the east. After 2 miles the road crosses Indian Creek and turns north. Stay on 60 and proceed east a little over a mile to where the road dips to cross a stream. This stream is the outlet of Heart Lake, and the lake is upstream an excruciatingly steep half mile.

Heart Lake is stocked with cutthroat and brook trout. Fishing usually holds up well into the season with catches 6 to 12 inches. Heart is 13 acres and fairly deep. All methods of angling will take fish, with flies especially good in fall.

HELEN LAKE. A 6-acre lake in the Taylor Burn area north of Waldo Lake, offering good rainbow trout fishing at times. A quarter-mile trail leads north to the lake from the very rough Taylor Burn Rd., Forest Rd. 517. Watch your oil pan on this one. The trailhead is at Taylor Butte, about one mile east of the Taylor Burn Campground.

Helen can be easily fished from shore. It's deep throughout, and lures or spinners cast and retrieved slowly bring up the fish. Flies work nicely in the evening. The average catch is 8 to 10 inches with a few to 14 inches. Helen is usually accessible in late June.

HIDEAWAY LAKE. A 12-acre lake stocked with either cutthroat or rainbows, in the upper Clackamas River watershed near the head of the South Fork of Shellrock Creek. Once a dandy hike-in lake, it is now accessed by road and is heavily fished. From Estacada follow Hwy. 224 to the Timothy Lake Rd., turning north at Shellrock Creek. At about 3 miles, follow Forest Rd. 5830 to the left. In 4 miles you'll be at the lake.

There's some natural reproduction of trout here, and the lake is stocked in odd number years, but pressure is high. It's shallow enough to provide good fly fishing. The trout are 7 to 13 inches with most around 10 inches. A nice campground has been provided courtesy of an Isaak Walton League chapter. Anglers can show their appreciation by helping to keep the grounds and facilities clean. The lake is usually snowbound until late May.

HIDDEN LAKE (McKenzie watershed). A good 11-acre wild cutthroat lake, 3 miles south of Cougar Reservoir. Not as well hidden as it was before the roads came in, it will still take your attention to find it.

From McKenzie Hwy. 126, take the South Fork of the McKenzie Rd. past Cougar Reservoir to Forest Rd. 1980, ½ mile past French Pete Campground. Drive west on 1980 about 3 miles, crossing Buoy Creek to a right angle intersection with Forest Rd. 231. Stay on 1980, which is the hard left, and you will again cross Buoy Creek, the outlet from Hidden Lake. There is no trail, and the lake is difficult to spot from the road, about 300 yards west, but you can always follow the stream. The snow usually melts by early June.

The cutthroat here are all wild and run 6 to 16 inches. Bait or spinner combinations are best early in the season, and wet flies are effective.

Supplies are available at Blue River or McKenzie Bridge on Hwy. 126. All tributaries of the lake are closed to angling.

High Lake (Clackamas watershed). A little pocket near the top of Fish Creek Mt. in the Fish Creek drainage south of the upper Clackamas River. From Estacada drive southeast on Hwy. 224 to Fish Creek Campground. Turn right on Forest Rd. 54 and follow it to the end.

All roads into the Fish Creek watershed are currently closed to public access while work proceeds to partially obliterate all but a few of the lower roads (5410, 5411, and 5412) following a series of devastating landslides in 1996. Upon completion of this work (October, 2000), the old road beds will be open to hiking, bicycling, and horse back riding. Check with the Mt. Hood National Forest office in Estacada or at Ripplebrook for trail information. See Appendix.

High Lake will be a long trek in. According to the current Mt. Hood National Forest map, the trail should follow the old road 5420 about 10 miles south, old road 290 about a mile north, and Trail 541 a steep 1½ miles to High Lake. After this long a closure, it may be worth the effort.

High Lake has a lot of brook trout 6 to 11 inches. The lake is about 3 acres and 12 feet deep. There are some nice natural campsites here. It is usually accessible in early June. See Skookum Lake.

Hills Creek (Middle Fork Willamette watershed). A tributary of the upper Middle Fork of the Willamette River, with stocked rainbow trout. It flows into Hills Creek Reservoir about 4 miles southeast of Oakridge. About 18 miles long, the creek heads in Diamond Peak Wilderness. Forest Rd. 23 follows it from the reservoir upstream.

The lower 3 to 4 miles are stocked with legal rainbow trout till early summer. A few wild cutthroat are present, but rainbows predominate, running 10 to 12 inches. There are campgrounds at the reservoir.

Hills Creek Reservoir

A multi-purpose reservoir 3 miles south of Oakridge, offering lots of crappie and consistently good fishing in fall, winter, and early spring for stocked rainbow trout and wild cutthroat. The reservoir was created by the damming of Hills Creek and the Middle Fork of the Willamette. To get there take Hwy. 58 southeast from Eugene to Oakridge. About one mile beyond Oakridge, follow the signs. The reservoir is about 8 miles long and has 2735 surface acres. It is heavily fished due to easy access.

It is kept well stocked with rainbows and picks up cutthroat from its tributaries. Most of the rainbows are 8 to 12 inches, but quite a few grow larger, with some to 20 inches. All methods can produce, though trolling is most popular. The crappie fishery is concentrated in the Hills Creek Arm at the upper end of the reservoir. Best warmwater fishing occurs in years when the reservoir has been low, and vegetation has grown thick and is later submerged. During high water years, the warmwater fish population can get a little thin.

The Forest Service and Corps of Engineers have provided good recreational facilities here. Packard Creek Campground, on the west bank about 3½ miles upstream from the dam, has a paved boat ramp and RV and picnic facilities. There is another ramp at the C.T. Beach Picnic area, about 2 miles from the dam on the Hills Creek arm. Supplies and accommodations are available in Oakridge.

Honey Lakes A couple of nice cutthroat lakes in the Three Sisters Wilderness Area, 6 miles due west of South Sister and 6 miles south of Linton Lake. The lake basin is about 6-miles from the nearest road.

Just east of McKenzie Bridge Ranger Station on Hwy. 126, take the Foley Ridge Rd., Forest Rd. 2643, about 12 miles to the end where it meets the Substitute Point Trail 3511. A 5-mile hike takes you past Substitute Point to the intersection of Trail 3520. Follow 3520 south 1½ miles to the basin. It's also possible to approach from the east by a side trail leading from the Pacific Crest Scenic Trail.

There are two main lakes in this group. Honey is the larger at about 12 acres. Its trout range 6 to 15 inches. Kidney Lake is the other good lake in the basin. It's ½ mile to the west of Honey and is good for trout to 16 inches. Kidney Lake is about half the size of Honey. Both lakes are exceptionally cold. There are several smaller pothole lakes in the area, but they produce little but mosquitoes. There are good natural campsites in the basin. Users are urged to follow no-trace camping guidelines.

Horse Creek. A tributary of the upper McKenzie River with wild cutthroat, open for catch and release angling using artificial flies and lures. About 24 miles long, the stream heads in the Horse Lake area north of the Mink Lake Basin and flows northwest to its confluence near McKenzie Bridge on Hwy. 126. Forest Rd. 2638 follows the lower 10 miles of the stream to the boundary of Three Sisters Wilderness.

Horse Creek is clear, swift, and cold, and fishing can be slow. The average trout is 9 to 12 inches. Horse Creek Campground, about a mile above McKenzie Bridge, is a group site available by reservation. The nearest general use campground is at McKenzie Bridge.

Horse Lakes. Several good hike-in trout lakes in the Three Sisters Wilderness Area at the head of Horse Creek, a tributary of the McKenzie River. Trails coming into the area from the west are all very long. Best access is from Elk Lake on the Cascade Lakes Hwy. 35 miles southwest of Bend. Trail 3517 heads at the Elk Lake Guard Station and leads 4 miles west to Upper Horse Lake.

The upper lake covers 60 acres and contains naturally reproducing brook trout, including some of good size. It can be fished from shore, but more water can be covered from a raft or float tube. It offers good fly angling in late summer and fall.

Middle Horse Lake is about ½ mile west, but a little longer by the Horse Creek Trail (which is easier than beating brush). Middle Lake is about 5 acres, with small brook and cutthroat trout 6 to 10 inches.

Lower Horse Lake, northwest of Middle Lake, is shallow and about 25 acres. It has a population of wild cutthroat and some brook trout. The cutthroat are small but eager and are a lot of fun on light fly tackle. It really takes a rubber raft or float tube to fish this area decently.

There are many other smaller lakes in the area, such as Sunset, Moonlight, Herb, Marten, Fisher, Aerial, and Mile lakes. Most are stocked with brook trout or rainbows.

Horseshoe Lake (Mink Lake Basin). A good hike-in rainbow lake on the Pacific Crest Trail in the Mink Lake Basin west of Elk Lake. For trail directions, see Cliff Lake. The Lake is about a mile south of Cliff. The first lake you pass on the west side of the trail is Moody Lake. It has cutthroat and rainbows. Horseshoe is a quarter mile farther south, on the east side of the trail.

Horseshoe is 60 acres, fairly shallow, and grows exceptionally large trout for a high mountain lake. Its rainbows average 6 to 20 inches. All methods can produce, with fly fishing good in the evenings. There are good campsites nearby, and a shelter at Cliff Lake. Some of the many nearby fishable lakes include Mink, Mac, Cliff, Porky, and Merrill.

HORSESHOE LAKE (Willamette watershed). A classic oxbow lake formed when the Willamette river punched through a bend and shifted course. The lake is about 40 miles southwest of Portland between Dayton and St. Paul. It has good populations of crappie, bluegill, perch, brown bullhead and largemouth bass but is surrounded by private land and is closed to public access at this time.

HORSESHOE LAKE (Olallie Lake basin). A pretty, 14-acre brook trout and rainbow lake between Olallie and Breitenbush lakes on Forest Rd. 4220. You can drive right to this scenic beauty, and there is a campground here. A spit of land juts into the lake from the west shore giving the lake its characteristic shape. It's easy to fish from shore.

HUNTS LAKE. A small scenic trout lake in the Mt. Jefferson Wilderness south of Mt. Jefferson, west of Cathedral Rocks. The Pacific Crest Trail passes above the lake a third of a mile to the east. Best approach is from Pamelia Lake by taking the trail that follows Hunts Creek upstream (south) for 3 miles to the junction of Trail 3430. Follow this trail east past Hanks Lake and north to Hunts Lake, a total distance of about a mile.

Hunts Lake is 6 acres and offers both rainbow and cutthroat. The cutthroat average 9 inches with a few to 12 inches. All methods of angling can be effective.

Hanks Lake, a quarter mile south, is slightly larger and contains brook trout about the same size as those in Hunts. It's a beautiful alpine area with attractive natural campsites. Both lakes are consistent and easy to fish.

INDIAN PRAIRIE LAKE. A good rainbow lake just outside the Willamette National Forest in the headwaters of Thomas Creek, south of the North Santiam Hwy. The lake is between the head of Neal Creek and Indian Prairie Creek. The quality of roads in this area depends on logging status. There are no signs to the lake. Contact the State Forestry Department or the Linn County Fire Patrol District map for help in locating it. Indian Prairie lake is owned by a an industrial timber company that allows public access. There are two gates. The first is about 3 miles from the lake and may be locked. Foot access is permitted. Motor boats are prohibited.

INDIGO LAKE. A pretty hike-in trout lake with good fishing in the southeast corner of Willamette National Forest, 5 miles south of Summit Lake. This is a fine getaway, though mosquitoes can be fierce. An easy trail begins at the south end of Timpanogas Lake Campground and climbs 700 feet in 1½ miles directly to the lake. See Timpanogas for directions.

Indigo is at 6000 feet in a basin directly below Sawtooth Mountain, which dominates the view when you reach the lake. The south end is a talus slope that offers plenty of backcasting room for fly anglers at the deepest end, over 30 feet just 100 feet from shore. The forest runs right up to the lake along the rest of the shore except at the extreme north end. The north half of the lake is under 10 feet deep.

Trout run 8 to 10 inches with some to 14 inches. Rainbow, cutthroat, and brook trout are often in residence. The lake isn't heavily fished, and almost any method will take fish when they're feeding. There are improved campsites at the south end of the lake. Timpanogas Lake has a fully developed campground. The road to Timpanogas usually opens in late June.

ISLAND LAKE (Mink Lake basin). A 3-acre lake offering fair fishing for rainbow trout. It's at the north end of the basin, east of Elk Lake. For trail directions, see Dumbell Lake. Island is ½ mile south of Dumbell on the west side of the Pacific Crest Scenic Trail.

The lake is stocked by air. Trout average 9 inches and run to 11 inches. Best fishing is early in the season and again in late fall. Though a little too accessible for great angling, it usually produces a few fish. There are natural campsites in the area.

ISLAND LAKE (Confederated Tribes of Warm Springs). Fourth in the chain of lakes from Olallie to Trout Lake. This oval lake's name is derived from a one acre island located in the middle. It is accessible only by unimproved trail from either Olallie Lake east or Trout Lake west. See Dark Lake for directions.

Island has about 26 surface acres at elevation 4650 ft. It is the shallowest lake of the chain, with a maximum depth of only 10 feet. Most of the lake is 3 feet deep or less. Brook trout are stocked here. The lake is difficult to fish without a raft or float tube. A CTWS permit is required to fish. Daily and annual permits are sold at stores on the reservation, at G.I. Joe's throughout the state, and at many fly shops. No overnight camping is allowed due to fire danger.

ISLAND LAKES (Island Lakes basin). Two small brook trout lakes in a basin west of Gold Lake. They provide good fishing for a few months in early summer and fall.

From Oakridge, follow Hwy. 58 about 14 miles southeast. Just past the railroad trestle crossing over the highway, turn north on Forest Rd. 5883, and follow it about 9 miles to its end. The trailhead for Fuji Mt. and Island Lakes begins at road's end. Hike a little less than a mile on Trail 3674, then turn north (left) on Trail 3586. Island Lakes are about ½ mile northwest of the junction. Lower Island, on the south side of the trail, is about 7 acres. Upper Island Lake, on the north side of the trail, is about 9 acres.

The trout average 10 inches, with a few to 13 inches and better. All methods will work, with fly angling especially good in the evening. There are nice natural campsites at the lakes and a developed campground at Gold Lake. Lorin Lake is three quarters of a mile bushwhack due east and slightly lower than Island Lakes. Birthday Lake is about a third of a mile east of the junction of trails 3674 and 3586.

JOHNSON CREEK (Multnomah Co.). An urban trout stream with wild cutthroat and fragile runs of coho, winter steelhead, and fall chinook. It flows 24 miles from Boring, past Gresham and through southeast Portland, entering the Willamette River north of Milwaukie. Roads follow and cross the creek in many places.

Johnson Creek is one of the region's last free-flowing urban streams, and though severely degraded by development and by agricultural and industrial pollution, it still supports fish. It is closed to salmon and steelhead angling, but open for catch and release trout fishing using artificial flies and lures.

Access is difficult because of private homes along the stream, but there is open water in the upper creek, and angling is possible throughout at public road crossings. If you live in the neighborhood, you know where these crossings are. Other access points are Tideman Johnson Park off southeast Berkeley Way in Eastmoreland, and Johnson Creek Park between Sherrett and Marion in Sellwood. The city of Milwaukie owns land along the bank from the mouth upstream one mile, open to public access from Hwy. 99E.

From summer through fall, bass and panfish are taken in the lower few miles of the stream. Waterfront Park Boat Ramp on the Willamette at the Johnson Creek confluence offers some access to good bass water.

JORN LAKE. A heavily fished lake in the Eight Lakes Basin of Mt. Jefferson Wilderness. Take Trail 3422 four miles south from the western shore of Marion Lake to Jorn. This is beautiful hiking country.

The brook trout here average 10 to 12 inches with a few to 15 inches. Rainbow trout are also available and may be easier to catch. All methods of angling will work at times, and the lake can be easily fished from shore. This 35-acre lake is hit hard because of its central location in the basin and pretty campsites. Fly fishing in the late afternoon and evenings usually pays off.

There are many good lakes in the basin. See Bowerman, Teto, Chiquito, Blue, Duffy, and Mowich lakes. The area can also be reached from Duffy Lake to the south. It is usually accessible in early June depending on snow pack.

JUDE LAKE (Confederated Tribes Warm Springs). One of a group of three hike-in brook trout lakes east of the Skyline Rd. and north of Olallie Lake. The trail begins at Olallie Meadow Campground, 3 miles north of Olallie Lake. It's ½ mile hike to Jude.

Jude is about 2 acres and quite brushy. Bait or spinner and bait combinations are effective early in the season, and fly angling works well later. The fish run 8 to 12 inches. A tribal permit is not required to fish Jude or nearby Russ and Brook lakes.

Overnight camping is prohibited. The nearest campground is at Olallie Lake.

JUNCTION CITY POND. An 8-acre pond on the west side of Hwy. 99 about 3 miles south of Junction City, 0.9 miles south of the Hwy. 36 junction. The pond is heavily stocked with rainbow trout, brood fish, and surplus steelhead. It also supports crappie, brown bullhead, and largemouth bass. A former gravel pit, and not at all picturesque, it can nevertheless offer lively fishing in spring.

JUNCTION LAKE. A pretty 50-acre hike-in lake amongst old trees at a trail junction in the Mink Lake Basin west of Elk Lake. It is ½ mile northwest of Mink Lake and at least 6 miles by trail from the nearest road. See Mink Lake for directions.

Junction supports rainbow and cutthroat from 8 to 11 inches, with a few to 15 inches. A float tube would be helpful. This is an on again, off again lake. Inquire at the Elk Lake Guard Station for current conditions. Good natural campsites are plentiful throughout the basin. Other good lakes in the basin include Mink, Porky, Corner, and Cliff.

KELLOGG CREEK. An urban stream flowing through southeast Portland from Johnson City near Milwaukie to the Willamette River. It originates in a little wetland upstream from Lake Lenore. Near the Willamette, it enters Kellogg Lake, which can be seen from Dogwood Park. Though flowing through intensely developed, primarily residential land, the creek is shaded by what urban planners call a linear forest and supports a small population of wild cutthroat trout and fragile runs of coho and winter steelhead. It is closed to salmon and steelhead angling. The creek is open for catch and release trout fishing with artificial flies and lures from late May through October.

KIRK POND. A 10-acre fishery on the north side of Clear Lake Rd. north of Fern Ridge Dam. See Fern Ridge Reservoir for directions. Kirk Pond supports white crappie, largemouth bass, bluegill, and brown bullhead. There is a BLM park adjacent to the pond, available for day use. See Fern Ridge Reservoir for additional fishing and camping opportunities.

KIWA LAKE. A good rainbow and brook trout lake in the heart of the Taylor Burn area north of Waldo Lake. Kiwa was burned over in the 1996 Moolack fire, but will continue to be stocked and may be worth the hike.

Kiwa is 2 miles south of Taylor Burn Campground by way of Olallie Trail 3583, on the east side of the trail. To reach Taylor Burn Campground, follow a rough road 7 miles north from North Waldo Lake Campground. An easier drive, but slightly longer hike, begins at North Waldo Lake Campground. Hike west along the northern shore of Waldo Lake on Trail 3590, then north on Trail 3583 past the Rigdon lakes to Kiwa.

Deservedly popular, Kiwa is consistent year after year for good size rainbow and brook trout. It covers about 40 acres and reaches a depth of 25 ft. The trout average 10 inches and run to 16. All methods of angling work, and you can easily fish from shore. Bait angling is always good. Lures trolled or cast from shore work well. Fly fishing with wet patterns produces mornings and evenings. Be warned that mosquitoes are fierce here in summer until the first frost. There are campgrounds at Taylor Burn and North Waldo Lake.

LAKE OF THE WOODS (Marion Lake Basin). A 5-acre rainbow lake 2 miles northeast of Marion Lake. Take the trail running north from the northeast shore of Marion. It's about 2 miles to Lake of the Woods.

The lake is stocked by air with rainbow trout, and the average catch is 8 to 10 inches, but a few get larger. All methods work well, with spinner and bait preferred early in the season. The lake is lightly fished and holds up well. It is usually accessible by mid-June.

LAMBERT SLOUGH. Longest slough on the Willamette, offering very good fishing for bass and panfish 19 miles downstream from Salem. Most anglers reach it from the boat ramp at San Salvadore Park near St. Paul, or from Wheatland. There is no public bank access.

Lambert is 3 miles long and 30 to 50 yards wide. It supports a variety of panfish and offers some of the best largemouth bass fishing in this stretch of the Willamette, though the bass tend to run small (average size 10 inches). A fish find-

Submerged stumps and snags shelter largemouth bass in LAMBERT SLOUGH. *Photograph by Richard T. Grost.*

er can come in handy for locating the submerged structure that bass use for cover, or fish overhanging brush and partially submerged logs. Gravel bars can be a problem moving through the slough for all but jet-powered boats when the river gets low.

LAYING CREEK. A wild cutthroat stream, tributary of Row River (of the coast Fork Willamette) southeast of Cottage Grove. It joins Brice Creek at Disston, 22 miles from Cottage Grove. From Cottage Grove, follow Row River Rd. 9 (County Rd. 2400) east past Dorena Reservoir to the community of Disston. From Disston, Forest Primary Rt. 17 follows Layng Creek upstream into Umpqua National Forest.

Unlike most other streams in the Willamette Zone, streams within the Coast Fork Willamette watershed are not restricted to artificial flies and lures at this time. Bait is legal and effective for taking trout on Laying. Rujada Campground is on the creek just inside the National Forest boundary, about 2½ miles from Disston.

LENORE LAKE. Shown on some maps as Leone Lake, a good hike-in brook trout lake tucked away in the Pansy Lake Basin, in the Bull of the Woods area of the upper Collawash River. A beautiful spot, Lenore offers good fishing for wild 7-inch overcrowded and hungry brookies. It's about a 5-mile hike by trail from any road. The area is accessed by several trails, and there are other lakes worth visiting in the area. See Big Slide, Welcome, and West lakes.

Hike in to Bull of the Woods Lookout (See Big Slide Lake for one approach), then take Trail 554 (Battle Creek and Welcome Lake) southeast ½ mile to its intersection with Trail 555, which comes in from the northeast. Follow 555 about 2 miles to Big Slide Mt. A short, steep spur trail leads from the northeast side of the mountain to Lenore, which is due north of the mountain. Check at Ripplebrook Ranger Station for latest road and trail information.

Brook trout 7 to 10 inches are thick here. The lake is about 5 acres, shallow with a rocky shore, and can be easily bank fished. Flies will work best.

LEONE LAKE. This is a good but difficult to find brook trout lake in the North Santiam area northeast of Detroit Reservoir. Take Forest Rd. 46 northeast from Detroit to the Boulder Ridge Rd., Forest Rd. 2231 at Breitenbush Hot Springs. Follow 2231 about 3 miles to a short spur road, Forest Rd. 916, entering from the south a third of a mile west of the Hill Creek crossing. Trail 3367 leads from the end of the spur west about ½ mile to the lake. Bring your forest map.

Leone's brook trout average 9 to 12 inches with a few larger. An occasional brown trout is taken. Spinner and bait and still-fishing both work well, and flies are good mornings and evenings. There are good natural campsites in the vicinity.

LINTON LAKE. A 75-acre brown trout lake off the old McKenzie Pass Hwy., easi-

ly reached, yet holds up well. Rainbow or brook trout may also be present. The lake was formed when a wall of lava flowed across Linton Creek, perhaps as recently as 3000 years ago. The trail to the lake leads through a classic lava field before diving into the forest.

To reach Linton drive 15 miles east from McKenzie Bridge on McKenzie Pass Hwy. 242 to Alder Springs Campground. The trailhead is on the south side of the highway just before the campground.

Linton has 70 surface acres and reaches a depth of 82 ft. It is one of the few lakes in the Oregon Cascades that has a reproducing population of brown trout. These fish are thriving and range 10 to 16 inches and larger. Small flatfish-type lures or flashing lures from one to two inches may fool them. A rubber raft or float tube is advisable for effective fishing.

Rainbow and brook trout are generally 10 to 14 inches. Bait is effective, and flies are especially good in the evening. The catch rate isn't high at Linton, but the fish are worth the effort. There are nice natural campsites at the lake and a campground at Alder Spring.

LITTLE FALL CREEK. See FALL CREEK, LITTLE.

LITTLE LUCKIAMUTE RIVER. See LUCKIAMUTE RIVER, LITTLE.

LITTLE NORTH SANTIAM RIVER. See SANTIAM RIVER, LITTLE NORTH.

LONG LAKE (Confederated Tribes Warm Springs). One of four trout lakes on tribal land in a chain east of Olallie Lake. See also Dark, Island, and Trout. Long is closest to Olallie, accessible by trail from the southeast end of the lake. Fishing here, as for other lakes in the chain, requires a CTWS permit. Daily and annual permits are sold at stores on the reservation, at G.I. Joe's throughout the state, and at many fly shops. Camping is not allowed.

LONG LAKE (N. Fk. Willamette watershed). Consistently good for naturally reproducing brook trout and cutthroat, 3 miles northwest of Waldo Lake in the headwaters of the North Fork of the Willamette. From Taylor Burn Campground take Trail 3553 west about 2 miles to Fisher Creek, where you pick up Trail

3597 heading south to the Quinn Lakes. Long Lake is a bit over ½ mile from the trail junction, about a quarter mile south of middle Quinn Lake.

True to its name, Long Lake is three-quarters of a mile long and only a few hundred yards wide, with a total of 50 surface acres. It can be fished from shore. The trout range 6 to16 inches, averaging 10 inches, and fishing holds up well through the season. There are good lakes north and south along the trail. The area is generally inaccessible until late June.

LONG TOM RIVER. A long stream originating west of Eugene near Siuslaw Hwy. 36, and flowing south into Fern Ridge Reservoir. It offers very good trout fishing as well as bass and panfish opportunities. Downstream from the reservoir, it flows north past Junction City and along Hwy. 99W to join the Willamette about half-way between Corvallis and Monroe.

Above the reservoir, Long Tom is primarily a trout stream, with a good population of wild cutthroat. Below, the reservoir, trout, bass, and panfish are caught. Some nice size cutthroat, which fatten in Fern Ridge Reservoir and the Willamette, are taken above and below the reservoir on spinner and bait. Long Tom is one of the few river systems in the Willamette Zone where trout may be harvested, though fishing is catch and release from November 1 through late April when migrants from the Willamette and the Reservoir move into the lower Long Tom to spawn. Barbless hooks and use of artificial flies and lures is encouraged for this fishery, though the regulations don't require it (since bait is used to fish for the bullhead that attract many anglers to the river during this season).

Below Fern Ridge, largemouth bass, smallmouth bass, white crappie, and brown bullhead catfish offer a popular fishery. There is a good spring fishery for white crappie below Fern Ridge Reservoir. Best crappie catches are in March. Bullhead are abundant and continue to offer good fishing after the river gets too warm for other species. Look for them in slack water.

There are bank fishing opportunities in Monroe City Park. Boating is limited due to structures in the river below Fern Ridge Dam. These structures, called "drop structures," provide gradient control, creating a series of little lakes in the river. Canoes can be launched off the lowest road crossing for a two-mile drift to the mouth and on down the Willamette to Peoria (the nearest take-out), a nice day trip.

Sturgeon congregate in a hole at the mouth of the Long Tom, part of a sturgeon stocking program in this section of the river. A good number should be approaching legal size about this time. Oversize fish are also present.

There is a large sucker population in the river, particularly below the dam in Monroe. Nightcrawlers fished on the bottom with a sliding egg sinker will take both suckers and carp.

There is a State Park picnic area on the upper stream, and many facilities are available at Fern Ridge Reservoir. There are no campgrounds on the river itself.

A river gauge reading is available. See Appendix.

LOOKOUT POINT RESERVOIR. One of the largest artificial impoundments in the state, stretching 14 miles along Hwy. 58 from 21 miles east of Eugene to within 6 miles of Oakridge. Created by a dam on the Middle Willamette, with over 4300 acres when full, it is only lightly used by anglers due to heavy wind and big waves. The reservoir is heavily infested with suckers and northern pike minnow (squawfish) but still can produce good bank and troll catches of rainbows and landlocked chinook. Illegally introduced crappie are also present, as well as a small population of largemouth bass.

The reservoir is heavily drawn down from late July until early May, but boat ramps on the north shore near Lowell and at the dam remain functional year-round. Black Canyon Campground at the southwest end has good camping facilities and a boat ramp, though the ramp is above the water line in winter.

LORIN LAKE. A bushwhack rainbow trout lake in the Island Lakes basin. See Island Lakes for directions. Lorin Lake is three quarters of a mile due east and slightly lower than the Island Lakes.

Ten acres and 17 feet deep, Lorin is at about 6,000 ft. and rarely thaws before late June. It can be fished from shore, but a rubber raft or float tube would be handy. Natural campsites are available. Jo Ann Lake (which is stocked with cutthroat) is below Lorin ½ mile to the southeast. Both Joann and Lorin can be tricky to find.

LOST CREEK (Sandy watershed). A tributary of the upper Sandy, joining it about 4 miles northeast of Zigzag. Lost Creek is closed to salmon and steelhead angling, but offers catch and release fishing for wild trout and unlimited catch of brook trout.

From Zigzag on Hwy. 26, turn north on Lolo Pass Rd. and continue about 4½ miles to McNeil Campground. Take Forest Rd. 1825, which begins following Lost Creek within ½ mile. About a mile upstream, at Lost Creek Campground, Forest Rd. 109 branches south and continues along the

Oregon law requires all boaters to wear life jackets. Photograph by Jerry Korson.

Pull off Hwy. 22 and fish the evening rise beneath Mt. Washington at LOST LAKE. Photograph by Dennis Frates.

creek another 2 miles upstream.

Lost Creek has some nice wild cutthroat and a few brook trout (probably migrants from Cast Lake in the headwaters). The lake is restricted to the use of artificial flies and lures.

Lost Creek Campground has a wheelchair accessible fishing structure. Riley and McNeil campgrounds are on the Sandy within ½ mile of the confluence.

LOST CREEK (Middle Willamette watershed). A wild cutthroat stream about 15 miles long, joining the Middle Willamette below Dexter Reservoir. A paved road cuts southeast off Hwy. 58 at Dexter and follows the stream 10 miles. The stream flows through primarily private property, with no public angling access or campgrounds.

LOST LAKE

(Santiam watershed) A good place to stop and catch (and release) a few plump trout during the evening rise, on your way to or from other more distinctive fisheries. Lost Lake is on the north side of Santiam Hwy. 20, visible from the road, and the sound of the highway is always in the background (though not really intrusive when you've got a feisty rainbows on the line). It is two miles east of Santiam Junction, near mile post 77.

Lost Lake is fed by several streams, and though it has no visible outlet, it leaks through lava cracks and can get very low. It has about 50 surface acres at ice-out most years.

Wild brook trout 6 to 15 inches are available, but rainbows 9 to 11 inches are the primary catch. Trolling works well early in the year (though motors are prohibited on the lake), and fly fishing is effective in summer and fall. Fall fishing can be particularly good. Angling is restricted to catch and release with artificial flies or lures.

Good catches can be made from shore, but a car-top boat or float tube will allow you to reach the productive holes where the fish tend to concentrate. When the water level gets too low, fish tend to pile up in the holes and are too vulnerable for good sportsmanship.

Lost Lake is open year-round, but situated near the summit of the Santiam Pass, it usually builds up a solid ice pack (though it never winterkills). There is a campground on the west shore of the lake.

LOWER LAKE. A good trout lake, very accessible, west of the Skyline Rd., Forest Rd. 4220, about one mile north of Olallie Lake. Take Hwy. 26 east, then Forest Rd. 4220 south to the area, about 100 miles from Portland.

Lower Lake is 14 acres and very deep. A lot of water can be covered from shore, and all angling methods can be effective. Trolling with small lures or spinner and bait works well.

Stocked cutthroat or rainbows range 7 to 14 inches. Fly anglers will find good water along the north shore. Evening angling in late spring and fall is especially productive.

There is a good size campground at the east end of the lake. The road in is usually inaccessible until late June.

LUCKIAMUTE RIVER. Pronounced *Lucky-mute*, a tributary of the mainstem Willamette, flowing from the Coast Range near Valsetz, with opportunities for smallmouth bass, and catch and release trout fishing. It is closed to steelheading at this time to protect its diminished steelhead run.

The Big Lucky flows into the Willamette River at a point south of Independence. To reach the lower Luckiamute from Monmouth or Independence, follow Monmouth St. east to Buena Vista Rd. Turn south on Buena Vista. To fish the upper river, take Hwy. 223 (the Kings Valley Hwy.) north from Hwy. 20 west of Corvallis, or south from Dallas. Turn west on Luckiamute River Rd. Beyond the community of Hoskins, the river flows through private timberland where anglers can access the river, though the road is sometimes gated during fire season.

There is a healthy population of wild cutthroat throughout the river, with best fishing in the upper stretch. The Luckiamute is a good trout stream in early season and again late in fall after the water cools. At this time, the river opens for trout fishing in late May.

The lower Luckiamute offers fair fishing for smallmouth bass, with some larger fish available. If you don't mind a hike with a bushwhack at the end, park at Luckiamute Landing (off Buena Vista Rd.) and walk to the river, being careful to skirt the cropland. In spring when the water's still high enough, the best way to fish this stretch is by motoring up the Luckiamute from Buena Vista Park on the Willamette (near Buena Vista Ferry). Canoes can be launched at the Buena Vista Rd. crossing for a 3-mile drift to the landing, but there's no place to park on Buena Vista Rd. Nice size largemouth bass and bluegill are available in the finger sloughs at the mouth of the Luckiamute.

LUCKIAMUTE RIVER, LITTLE. Often a very good trout stream for the first 3 months of the season, offering catch and release angling for wild cutthroat at this time. It flows from the coast range near Valsetz and joins the Big Luckiamute about 2½ miles west of Sara Helmick State Park (south of Monmouth, off Hwy. 99W).

Good roads follow and cross the stream west through Falls City, but there is very limited access due to private property. A 4-mile stretch from Falls City upstream is easily reached from the highway. Above this point, anglers can hike to the river from a logging road that follows within a mile of the stream. This road is open except during fire season. Wild cutthroat 6 to 13 inches are available in the upper waters. Fishing is catch and release only, with artificial flies and lures.

MAC LAKE. A rainbow trout lake near the Pacific Crest Trail in the southern portion of the Mink Lake Basin, west of Elk Lake. Mac Lake is ½ mile southeast of Mink Lake and 1½ miles south of Cliff Lake and the Pacific Crest Trail. It is one mile east of Packsaddle Mt. For a good overview of the basin, climb Packsaddle. You'll be able to pick out the various lakes from your map.

Mac Lake covers 70 acres and is stocked by air with fingerling rainbows. Average size is 10 inches, with some to 15 inches. The lake can be effe ctively fished from shore, with flies best mornings and evenings. There are good natural campsites.

MARIE LAKE (Diamond Peak Wilderness). A trout lake northwest of Summit Lake, north of what is known as the Diamond Rockpile south of Diamond Peak. Take the Pacific Crest Trail north from where it crosses the road west of Summit Lake Campground. About 2 miles north, the PCT intersects Trail 3672. Follow this trail west about ½ mile to Marie.

Marie is easy to fish from shore. Stocked with both rainbows and cutthroat, it yields fish 6 to 14 inches. In some years, larger fish have been taken. Spinner and bait usually work well any time, and fly fishing is effective in the evenings. There are good natural campsites available. The area is usually inaccessible until late June.

MARILYN LAKES. Two good hike-in brook trout lakes near Gold Lake in the Willamette Pass area. These lakes are tailor-made for fly fishing. They are about one mile north of Hwy. 58, 23 miles southeast of Oakridge. See Gold Lake for directions. The Marilyn Lakes Trailhead is off the Gold Lake access road, and the lakes themselves can be reached in an easy 20-minute walk south.

The Marilyns are each about 25 acres and drain into Salt Creek. Brook trout here run 6 to 16 inches. The upper lake has smaller but more plentiful fish. The lower has larger fish in small numbers. They are lightly fished, as most fly anglers in the area focus on Gold Lake's feisty rainbows. Late fall fly anglers can take some real lunkers here. Ice fishing is also a possibility. Drive to the Sno-Park on Waldo Lake Road and ski or snowshoe in. There are no campsites near the lakes.

MARION CREEK. Also known as the Marion Fork of the North Santiam, a cold, fast trout stream. Lightly fished and open for catch and release only at this time, it flows from Marion Lake in Mt. Jefferson Wilderness. A good road, Forest Rd. 2255, leaves Santiam Pass Hwy. 22 at the Marion Forks Ranger Station (about 15 miles south of Detroit at Detroit Reservoir) and follows the stream to Marion Falls, about 2 miles downstream from Marion Lake.

Cold and clear, Marion is difficult to fish, though fly fishing can be effective late in the season. The stream is seldom productive early in the year. If you are in the area, pay a visit to the salmon hatchery on the south side of the stream near Hwy. 22. There's a good forest campground at the creek mouth.

MARION LAKE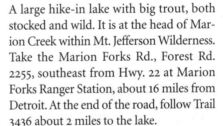

A large hike-in lake with big trout, both stocked and wild. It is at the head of Marion Creek within Mt. Jefferson Wilderness. Take the Marion Forks Rd., Forest Rd. 2255, southeast from Hwy. 22 at Marion Forks Ranger Station, about 16 miles from Detroit. At the end of the road, follow Trail 3436 about 2 miles to the lake.

Marion is about 350 acres and holds some nice fish. The catch rate is variable, but size makes up for it. Brook trout and rainbows are equally plentiful, averaging 11 to 14 inches, with a good number of 3 to 4 pounders taken each season. A rubber boat or float tube is useful here, although the lake can be fished from shore. Bait angling and lures will take fish throughout the season. Cutthroat are also present and will put up a good fight on light gear. Other smaller lakes nearby offer good angling. See Ann, Jorn, and Mowich.

MARY'S RIVER A fair trout stream flowing into the Willamette River at Corvallis, with opportunities for bass and crappie near the mouth. It heads on Mary's peak, highest point in the Coast Range, and flows over 30 miles to the Willamette. Hwy. 20 follows the river from Corvallis to Blodgett, where a good forest road heads north, accessing the upper forks. Private property restricts access in the lower river. It is closed to steelheading.

Mary's River has a good population of wild cutthroat, typically from 7 to 12 inches, and a small winter steelhead run. Whitefish are abundant and reach 2 lbs. They will take a fly, offer good sport on light tackle, and are good eating. Smallmouth can be fished near the mouth. Best access is in Corvallis at Downtown Waterfront Park. Crappie and largemouth are also present. Fishing for all species is restricted to artificial flies and lures at this time. Check current regulations for a possible easing of tackle restrictions.

A river gauge reading is available. See Appendix.

McDOWELL CREEK. A small wild cutthroat stream entering the South Santiam River about 9 miles southeast of Lebanon. Take Hwy. 20 south from Lebanon to McDowell Creek Rd., about 3 miles south of Hamilton Creek. A road follows the stream closely for about 5 miles, but only a mile of this lower stretch is open to public access. The upper stream is in private forest land, which may be accessible.

Wild cutthroat 6 to 12 inches are available for catch and release. There is also a small wild winter steelhead run. McDowell Creek Park (which features some pretty waterfalls) offers trails along the creek. There is no camping along the stream.

McFARLAND LAKE. A 39-acre trout lake north of Irish Mt. about a mile west of the Pacific Crest Trail. You'll work to get here, but the hike sure does thin out the crowd. Take Trail 3307 west from Forest Rd. 1958, a 4- to 5-mile hike.

Stocked with rainbows, McFarland is a good, deep lake for lure fishing, and all methods of angling will take trout when they're hitting. Some lunkers are taken

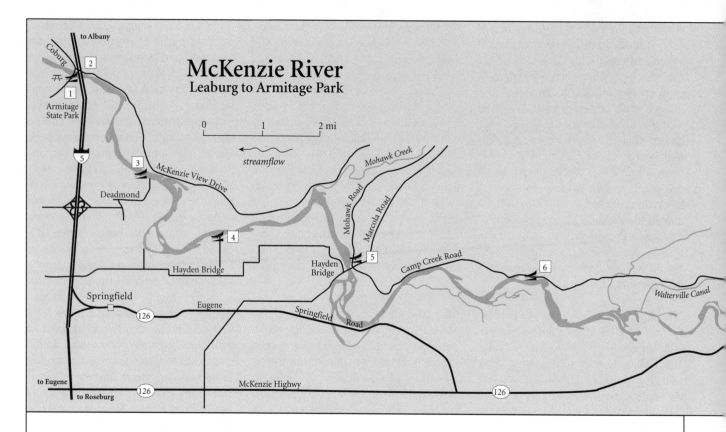

McKenzie River
Leaburg to Armitage Park

0   1   2 mi

streamflow

to Albany

Coburg

Armitage State Park

to Eugene

to Roseburg

McKenzie View Drive

Deadmond

Hayden Bridge

Springfield

Eugene

Springfield Road

Mohawk Creek

Mohawk Road

Marcola Road

Hayden Bridge

Camp Creek Road

Walterville Canal

McKenzie Highwy

---

1. Armitage Park. Take-out for pleasant drift from Deadmond Ferry; good bank fishing.

2. McKenzie View. Public access to 200 yds of good water upstream and down from I-5 bridge; park on road and scramble down to river.

3. Deadmond Ferry. Boat slide too steep for good take-out; pleasant evening's drift to Armitage; access to good fishing on both banks.

4. Rodakowski Boat Ramp. On Harvest lane; paved ramp with some bank access.

5. Hayden Bridge. Steep paved ramp; bank fishing on both sides of bridge.

6. Bellinger Landing. Paved ramp with limited bank access; better fishing on opposite shore.

7. Hendricks Bridge Wayside. Paved ramp with good bank access.

8. Partridge Lane. Put-in only; steep dirt slide on Partridge Lane off Hwy. 126

9. Walterville Landing. Near Walterville school; paved ramp near canal entrance.

10. Deerhorn Boat Ramp. Put-in and take-out.

11. Deerhorn County Park. Paved ramp with some bank access; good fishing below the bridge.

12. Leaburg Landing. Put-in or take-out; some bank angling for trout, summer steelhead, chinook.

---

each season. The catch runs 6 to 16 inches, averaging 13 inches. There are good natural campsites available and several other small fishable lakes nearby. See East McFarland, Piper, and Smith. McFarland is usually inaccessible until late June.

McKAY CREEK (Tualatin watershed). A good early-season trout stream only 20 miles west of Portland, crossed by Hwy. 26. The creek flows into the Tualatin River south of Hillsboro, heading in the West Hills, north of North Plains near the Multnomah County line. From North Plains,

the stream is followed north by gravel roads for about 9 miles. Most anglers fish the stretch north of the highway. Fishing is catch and release with artificial flies and lures.

Angling is good for a few weeks after opening, but slows up early. Some warmwater species are taken near the mouth. Watch for private property,

McKENZIE RIVER

One of the finest trout streams in Oregon—not for huge fish, but for quality and

quantity of wild fish, proximity to population centers, and beauty of the river. It's the river for which the McKenzie River drift boat was named, the boat that draws so little water it can float on dew and slide over rocky rapids.

The McKenzie River features catch and release fishing for plump and spunky wild rainbow trout, recognized as a unique strain called "McKenzie Redside." Wild cutthroat, a few brook trout from Clear Lake in the upper waters, hatchery rainbows available for harvest, and a good hatchery run of summer steelhead provide

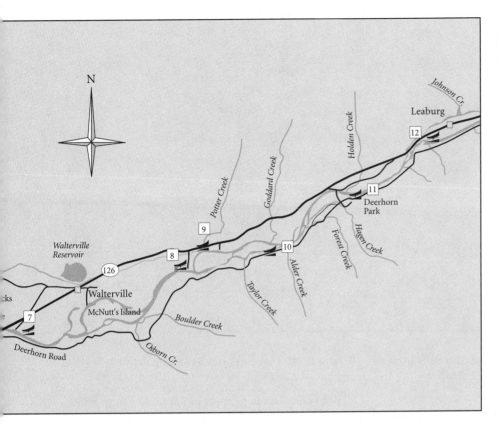

Leaburg Dam, the river is essentially a dam pool. Premier boat fishing begins again at Greenwood Landing and continues un-abated to the mouth.

Reaching the best water can be a chore without a boat, as the McKenzie runs through primarily private land in the lower 50 river miles. Most bank access is at boat ramps and parks.

To reach Armitage State Park, drive north from Eugene on Coburg Rd., or take I-5 south to the Coburg Exit, south of the McKenzie crossing. Most of the park stretches west of I-5. Anglers can also cross the McKenzie on Coburg Rd. and fish the north bank about 200 yds. upstream and down from the I-5 Bridge. Park on McKenzie View Drive and make your way down to the river, keeping an eye out for stinging nettles. Despite its proximity to urban centers, not to mention the interstate, this is a rural spot, and it's easy to lose youself in the world of the river.

There is also bank access at Deadmond Ferry Slide on the south bank at the end of Deadmond Ferry Rd. To get there take the Belt Line Hwy. east to Game Farm Rd. Turn left then right onto Deadmond. Rodakowski Boat Ramp off Hayden Bridge Rd. has bank access downstream from the ramp.

Hayden Bridge in Springfield, Hendricks Bridge State Park north of Cedar Flat on Hwy. 126, and Greenwood Drive Ramp

additional angling opportunities. There is no fishery for the river's precious population of spring chinook, recognized as the last significant wild spring chinook run in the Willamette watershed.

The McKenzie flows past giant boulders and through forested canyons at a grade that delights rafters and with an iridescence that inspires poetry. It has only one major (Class 4) rapids in its boatable stretch, and is a good river for less experienced riverboat anglers.

It flows 89 miles in all, from Clear Lake in Willamette National Forest south 14 miles to Belknap Springs, then west to the Willamette River. The upper reach is very cold and swift, and the fishing is slow. By Blue River, the valley begins to open up and the gradient is moderated. From there downstream to its confluence with the Willamette north of Eugene, conditions for trout fishing are excellent. It is accessible by side roads off Hwy. 126 throughout most of its length.

Finding good trout water is easy if you have a boat. There are almost 3-dozen public boat ramps on the McKenzie, with the lowest at Armitage State Park north of Eugene and the highest at Olallie Campground in Willamette National Forest, about 12 miles east of the town of McKenzie Bridge. For fishing purposes, the most

important boat ramps are from Forest Glen Landing (near Blue River) downstream to Armitage Park.

Consult the legend accompanying the maps for information about the various boat ramps. Of particular note are the ramps at Ben and Kay Dorris State Park (last take-out before Martin Rapids) and Helfrich Landing (first put-in after Martin

The McKenzie River, *one of Oregon's most beloved streams, is treasured for its classic beauty and plentiful wild trout. Photograph by Dennis Frates.*

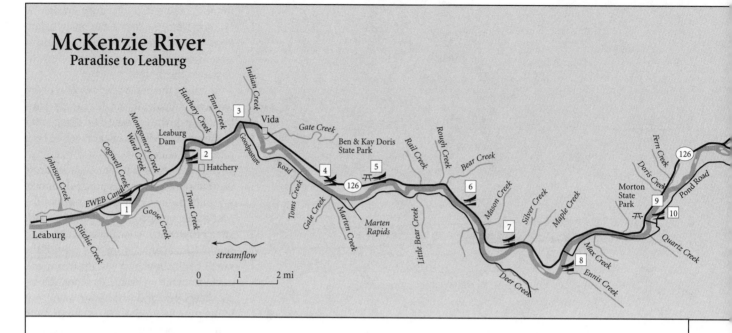

McKenzie River
Paradise to Leaburg

streamflow

0   1   2 mi

1. Greenwood Landing. Popular take-out for drift from Leaburg Dam; access to Curry Holes for salmon & steelhead just upstream.

2. Waterboard Park. Good boat and bank access for stocked trout.

3. Goodpasture Covered Bridge. Bank fishing.

4. Helfrich Landing. Off Thompson Lane; county park take-out below Martin Rapids; put-in for about 5 miles of good water without bank access.

5. Ben & Kay Dorris State Park. Popular take-out to avoid Martin Rapids (Class 3-4); bank fishing.

6. Rennie Landing. Paved ramp; some bank access; good drift includes Browns Hole (white water pocket near south bank).

7. Silver Creek Landing. Paved ramp with bank access; nice water between here and Rennie.

8. Rosboro Landing. Unimproved put-in; several rapids here to Silver Creek (1½ miles) but offers access to good boat fishing; with some bank access.

9. Howard J. Morton State Park. Limited fishing access, but pretty picnic spot.

10. Finn Rock. Major raft put-in for popular drift to Helfrich; good flat take-out.

11. Forest Glen Landing. Upper limit of heavy trout stocking.

12. Bad Road. Four-wheel drive only 1½ miles either side of this point..

13. Hamlin Landing. Lightly stocked; fish mostly for catch-and-release-wild redsides.

14. Delta Campground. Bank fishing

15. Brukhart Bridge Landing. Steep paved ramp, best for launching.

16. McKenzie Bridge Campground. Unimproved dirt ramp at west end of campground; some bank access.

17. McKenzie River Trail. Popular hiking trail along fast water; fish pocket water for wild redsides with some brook trout near Clear Lake.

18. Paradise Campground. Unimproved ramp; popular take-out for advanced river runners who launch at Whitewater Slide or Olallie Campground; water above Paradise is shallow and fast with many rapids.

east of Leaburg all offer access to good bank-fishable water, as does Deerhorn Co. Park on the south bank. To reach Deerhorn, turn right onto Deerhorn Rd. before crossing Hendricks Bridge on Hwy. 126. Helfrich Landing on the north bank right below Martin Rapids offers interesting trout fishing, as does Ben and Kay Dorris State Park (right above the rapids). Silver Creek, Finn Rock, and Forest Glen Boat Ramps (all off Hwy. 126) are good bank fisheries. Above Forest Glen (at Blue River), the river picks up speed, and bank fishing is more difficult.

The McKenzie is a particular favorite of fly anglers. It has a rich and varied insect population, featuring year-round caddis hatches (including its own McKenzie Caddis, a bright green critter that makes it appearance in spring). Other hatches of note are March Brown mayflies (on overcast days in March and April) and Little Yellow Stoneflies (in July). From Hayden Bridge to the mouth, the river is restricted to using artificial flies and lures and is open for year-round catch and release angling. Check the current regulations for other

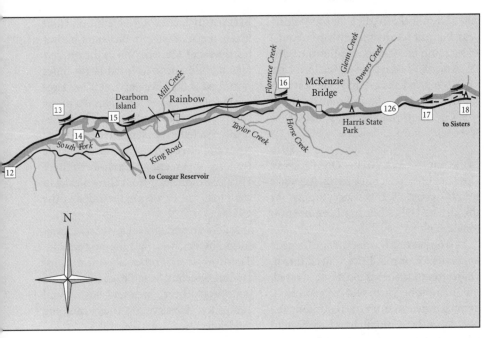

opportunities and restrictions.

Trout are plentiful throughout the river and the calendar year. The river's prize catch is the native rainbow (redside). Redsides are distinguished by their bright orange spots and large size (both length and girth). Most trout over 10 inches are wild redsides. The average catch is 12 inches, with many larger fish (to 15 inches) and some as big as steelhead (20 inches). The river's wild cutthroat are generally smaller and are found in slower water, such as the stretch from Harvest Lane to the mouth. Bull trout are also present. Fishing for wild trout in the McKenzie is catch and release at all times of year throughout the river.

Hatchery rainbows are stocked in abundance from early spring through summer, from Hayden Bridge upstream to Forest Glen. Over 150,000 are released at intervals. Hatchery trout can be distinguished by their adipose finclip. Few are found in the river by fall, since those that aren't caught succumb to the rigors of life in a wild stream. If you use bait to fish for them, be prepared to cut the line if your offering is taken by a wild trout. Use of a barbless hook is a good idea (though not required) in all fisheries where catch and release may be necessary. Whitefish are plentiful below Leaburg Dam and can grow to good size.

A good-size run of hatchery-reared summer steelhead begins returning to the McKenzie in May, with best catches from July on. In most years, over a thousand steelhead are caught. These fish move quickly through the lower river, heading for the hatchery at Leaburg Dam. Fishing for them is concentrated from the town of Leaburg up to the dam, but there are good fishing opportunities from Hendricks Bridge to the dam. Best bank access for this fishery is at Greenwood Landing, east of the town of Leaburg.

There is no longer a fishery for McKenzie River spring chinook, which have been particularly vulnerable to changes in water temperature resulting from flood control dams on the river. In 1999 they were listed as threatened under the Endangered Species Act, and efforts to protect them drive chinook fishing restrictions on the lower Willamette. You may see chinook in the McKenzie in May and June, but don't disturb them.

Developed camping and picnic sites are limited along the river below the National Forest. Armitage State Park north of Eugene offers picnic facilities only. Ben and Kay Doris State Park east of Vida has a campground. Above Blue River the McKenzie flows through Willamette National Forest, where there are streamside campgrounds roughly every 5 miles. Delta, McKenzie Bridge, and Paradise are right on the McKenzie. Limberlost is about 2 miles up the Lost Creek Rd. just before Belknap Springs. Additional camps are available in the headwaters area from Trail Bridge to Clear Lake. There is a wheelchair-accessible fishing platform and comfort facilities at Silver Creek Landing.

McKenzie River, South Fork. A popular trout stream flowing into the upper McKenzie between the towns of Blue River and McKenzie Bridge. It joins the mainstem McKenzie about 3 miles upstream from Blue River. The river is dammed to create Cougar Reservoir about 3 miles above the confluence. Cougar is about 5 miles long. A good forest road, Forest Rd. 19, follows the river upstream for 12 miles, then the river splits into two forks, Elk Creek and Roaring River.

Elk Creek can be followed upstream 3 miles on Forest Rd. 1964 to Trailhead 3510, which leads into the Mink Lake Basin. Forest Rd. 19 follows Roaring River Creek then McBee Creek over a divide to the southwest before dropping into the headwaters of the North Fork of the Willamette.

Wild redsides, cutthroat, and bull trout are available for catch and release angling. The catch rate is high for such a popular stream, but the fish don't run large. Average size is 8 to 11 inches. There's good fly water, especially above the reservoir.

There are six campgrounds on the upper stream. Tributaries enter the fork at several of these camps, providing additional catch and release angling opportunities. Use light leader and stealth tactics to fool these wild cutthroat. French Pete Creek, which enters from the east at French Pete Campground, offers many miles of hiking through old growth timber. The water in the creek is cold, swift, and clear. Augusta Creek, which drains a considerable area, enters the river from the south at Dutch Oven Campground.

When studying a map of the South Fork, you will probably notice reference to Cougar Hot Springs. These are located about a quarter mile west of the reservoir near Rider Creek. There is a parking area on the reservoir side, and a short trail follows Rider to the hot springs. These are the most beautiful hot springs in Oregon, cascading through a fern-y forest glen into rock pools. Problems associated with visitors to the springs seem to have been reduced by requiring a fee for admission to the hot springs area.

McNary Lakes. Two warm-water lakes at the north end of Sauvie Island. You can drive to them when the roads dry out. The lakes are about 2 miles north of Sturgeon Lake and are connected to it by Pete's Slough. Take Hwy. 30 NW from Portland

10 miles, then cross to Sauvie Island by the bridge. Follow Reeder Road (which crosses the island to the Columbia side) for about 11 miles to the waterfowl area checking station. Turn left onto a gravel road, and drive about one mile to a parking area. After July, and before the May high water, you can drive over the dike then follow dirt roads one mile north to the lakes. If the gate is locked you'll have to walk, as it's kept closed for your protection. The area is flooded each spring for several months.

There's lots of room to fish, either from bank or small boat. Brown bullhead are taken on worms. Bass anglers do well for a month or so once the water starts dropping, but will do better in moving water after that. Plugs, Kwikfish-type lures, and spinning lures all work at times. The crappie take small flashing lures, pork rind, and even maribou flies if retrieved very slowly.

For other waters close by, see Pete's Slough, Gilbert River, Haldeman Pond, Sturgeon Lake. No overnight camping is allowed. Fishing on Sauvie Island is restricted during waterfowl season. You will need to purchase a recreation permit to park on the island. Day or seasonal passes are sold at the market on the island north of the bridge.

MCNULTY CREEK. Flowing about 7 miles long through Columbia County into Scappoose Bay south of St. Helens. Bordered by private property, it is crossed by Hwy. 30 in St. Helens and is accessible primarily at road crossings.

The creek provides fair early season catch and release trout fishing for wild cutthroat and the occasional rainbow. It is not stocked, and the fish are mostly under 10 inches. Trout fishing is restricted to artificial flies and lures only. The creek gets very warm and low after the first month or two. At its confluence with the bay, there is fair fishing for bass, perch, and brown bullhead.

MELAKWA LAKE. A 35-acre rainbow and cutthroat lake in Willamette National Forest west of the McKenzie Pass, off Hwy. 242 southwest of Scott Lake. There is a Scout camp here, and the boys fish it hard. The trout run 6 to 12 inches. Motor boats are prohibited on the lake.

MELIS LAKE. A small brook trout lake mid-way between the Eight Lakes Basin and Marion Lake in Mt. Jefferson Wilderness. It is just south of Jenny Lake, about 2 miles south of Marion, and the same distance north of Jorn Lake on the Jorn Lake Trail. See Jorn Lake for trail directions.

Not a very rich lake, its brook trout run small. It's only 5 acres, but it does have some fair natural campsites.

MERCER RESERVOIR. On Rickreall Creek, 10 miles west of Dallas on Allendale Rd. It serves as the water supply for the city of Dallas but has been open to public angling.

This 60-acre reservoir on Boise Cascade land is fished primarily for wild cutthroat, which run to 12 inches. Boats are allowed, but no motors. There's lots of good bank angling available from the road along the west shore. Largemouth bass have been illegally introduced and are thriving, though the average size is small.

The gate on the road to the reservoir is locked at this time, though anglers may walk or bicycle in. Best fishing is in spring.

MERRILL LAKE. A small trout lake in the south end of the Mink Lake Basin. Merrill is south of the Pacific Crest Trail, a quarter mile west of Horseshoe Lake and east of Mac Lake. See Cliff Lake for trail directions.

Though only 7 acres, Merrill is consistent for cutthroat 9 to 10 inches with some to 15, though not many. All methods will take fish when they're hitting. The area is usually accessible in late June.

MICKEY LAKE. A lightly fished hike-in cutthroat lake in the Taylor Burn area, managed for large trout. Like other lakes within the 1996 Moolack Burn, Mikey will continues to be stocked. To reach it, head south from Taylor Burn on Olallie Trail 3583, or north from Waldo Lake on the same trail. Mickey is a quarter mile northeast of Lower Rigdon. See Rigdon Lakes for trail directions. Mickey Lake is northwest of Brittany, another good lake.

About 5 acres and deep, over 40 ft. in places, it has turned out some lunkers. The trout don't spawn here, so it is stocked every few years. A good rocky shoal in the center of the lake is a consistent producer on flies. There were no good campsites here even before the fire.

MILDRED LAKE. A 3-acre brook trout lake in the headwaters of Breitenbush River northwest of Mt. Jefferson in the Mt. Jefferson Wilderness. Mildred is 1½ miles northeast of the Firecamp Lakes. See Firecamp Lakes for directions. This is a pretty spot, but tough to reach—a little basin beneath Mt. Jefferson, separated by a ridge from the Firecamps. There is no visible trail, so orienteering skills are required. Hike east-northeast from Crown Lake in the Firecamps, crossing the ridge at the saddle.

Mildred reportedly contains brook trout to 12 inches, with fall the best season. There are several other lakes nearby, including Slideout, Swindle, and Bear. It's a good huckleberry area and has natural campsites. Observe no-trace camping guidelines.

MILE LAKE. A 7-acre rainbow and cutthroat lake in the Horse Lake group northwest of Elk Lake in the Three Sisters Wilderness. It is between Horse Mt. and Horse Lake Guard Station. A trail due west from Horse Lake reaches Mile in one mile, then continues on to Park Lake.

The rainbows here are 6 to 13 inches. This lake has its ups and downs, hot one year and cold the next, but there are other lakes in the area to try if you catch this one on an off year.

MILK CREEK. A fair trout stream for catch and release angling in early season, flowing into the Molalla River southeast of Canby. It is crossed by Hwy. 213 at Mulino, about 11 miles south of Oregon City. From Mulino a county road follows the creek east to Hwy. 211, which follows the stream toward its headwaters in the Colton area. It is only accessible at road crossings due to private ownership throughout.

Milk Creek has a fair population of wild cutthroat. The best section to fish is west and east of Colton. It is closed to salmon and steelhead fishing.

MILL CREEK. (mid-Willamette watershed) A long stream with catch and release trout fishing and opportunities for viewing (but not fishing) a sizable fall chinook run in the heart of Salem. The creek flows from the east near Stayton and joins the Willamette River at the capital. Pringle Park, behind Salem Hospital, is a popular viewing area during the spawning migration in September and October.

The creek is closely followed by Hwy. 22 and the paved road from Aumsville to Salem. Private land throughout makes access difficult, though it can be fished at road crossings. Mill Creek supports a small wild trout population. The lower end of the creek below Turner offers some fishing for bluegill and crappie. It is closed to salmon and steelhead fishing.

MILL CREEK (Yamhill watershed). A catch and release wild cutthroat stream, joining the Yamhill from the south halfway between Willamina and Sheridan. Hwy. 18 crosses the creek shortly above the mouth, and Hwy. 22 crosses it about 5 miles above that. Harmony Rd. follows the lower end, and Mill Creek Rd. follows the creek south of Hwy. 22. About 20 miles long, its lower 10 miles pass through agricultural lands with limited access.

The upper end is on Willamette Industries property, which is open to the public. Here the creek runs through a wooded canyon, where most of the wild cutthroat are concentrated. The cutthroat run 9 to 12 inches. Best fishing is before late June.

The creek supports a small run of wild winter steelhead, but it is closed to fishing for steelhead.

Willamette Industries has provided several day use facilities and a campground on the upper creek.

MILTON CREEK. A wild cutthroat trout stream entering the Columbia near St. Helens, about 30 miles northwest of Portland. It provides early season catch and release angling in its upper reaches and supports a very small number of wild winter steelhead and coho.

Eighteen miles long, Milton heads in the Nehalem Mts. west of St. Helens and meanders through town and into Scappoose Bay near the bay's mouth. The only public access to the upper waters is at county road crossings. The creek is very shallow and generally warm in its flow through McCormick Park in St. Helens during trout season, but there are some good riffles and pools in the upper area. Angling usually falls off in late June when the water gets low and warm throughout. Milton is closed to fishing for salmon and steelhead.

There is fair bass angling in the late spring near the mouth.

MINK LAKE. The largest lake in the Mink Lake Basin, 180 acres at 6000 ft. elevation. Mink Lake is at the head of the South Fork of the McKenzie River. Less alpine and more heavily forested than other lakes in the vicinity, it is more attractive to backcountry hikers interested in fishing than to those whose main focus is scenic vistas.

Trails enter the area from all directions. To approach from the west, drive into the headwaters of the South Fork on Forest Rd. 19. At Frissel Crossing Campground, head east on Forest Rd. 1964 about 2½ miles to a short northern spur which accesses Trail 3510. This trail leads about 7 miles to Mink Lake. Two popular eastern approaches are from Elk Lake on the Pacific Crest Trail, about 11 miles, or on the Six Lakes Trail by way of Blow Lake, about 8 miles. Trails surround the lake, and there are other good lakes in every direction.

Mink Lake is stocked with lots of rainbows and cutthroat, and it usually produces fair catches. The fish run from 6 to 20 inches. A float tube would be handy, as the lake is large, and the fish are sometimes hard to find. All methods of angling are used. There are good natural campsites all around the lake. Mosquitoes are very fierce in spring. See also Cliff, Moody, Porky.

MIRROR LAKE (Sandy watershed). A popular lake with a spectacular view of Mt. Hood, reached by a short hike from Hwy. 26. It offers good trout angling despite heavy pressure. Most visitors are sightseers and hikers. The trailhead is about 53 miles from Portland, west of Government Camp. Trail 664, the Tom, Dick, and Harry Mountain Trail, reaches the lake in a little over a mile. The trailhead is on the south side of Hwy. 26 at Yocum Falls, about one mile west of Multipor Ski area. It's fairly steep, gaining 650 ft. between the highway and lake.

Mirror Lake is stocked with rainbows or brook trout (depending on availability). Most of the catch runs 6 to 9 inches. Some larger fish remain each year, and good anglers can do well, especially on flies. Best fishing is early in June and again in fall, when the crowd thins out. The lake is 8 acres with some improved campsites. A boat or float tube is not necessary.

MIRROR POND (Columbia Gorge). One of the I-84 ponds adjacent to the Columbia River, featuring bass and panfish. It is about 8 miles east of Troutdale, south of I-84 across from Rooster Rock State Park. The pond is directly under Crown Point State Park.

Mirror Pond is fed by several small streams and receives water from the Columbia during the freshet in May and June. It is almost a mile long and a quarter mile wide in spots. Largemouth bass 3 to 4 pounds have been taken on plugs or spinning lures. Weedless lures fished in the shallows in June are effective. There's a large population of crappie, and brown bullhead, perch, and bluegill are available. Bullhead fishing is best when the water drops.

There is limited parking at the pond off a dirt access road immediately west of Rooster Rock. Camping is available at the state park.

MISSION CREEK RESERVOIR. A 130-acre reservoir with good populations of bass and panfish north of St. Paul, 5 miles south of Newburg. Public access is limited to the south end of the reservoir, which can be reached by Hwy. 219 from Newburg. There is limited parking on the road shoulder, and car-top boats can be launched.

Most anglers fish from the highway shoulder. Good catches of bluegill to 8 inches are made in early spring, though weeds become a problem later in the season. After June you'll need a boat to get to open water. There's good bass water here if you can get to it.

MISSION LAKE. A 19-acre oxbow lake along the Willamette River in Willamette Mission County Park, one mile south of Wheatland, about 8 miles north of Salem. Take the Brooks exit off I-5, and drive towards Wheatland, or take the ferry from Wheatland to the east bank of the Willamette.

The lake has a good population of bass and panfish, including largemouth bass, white crappie, brown bullhead, and bluegill, though weed growth makes it difficult to fish in summer. Park facilities include fishing platforms and a boat ramp (electric motors only). A trail within the park leads to Goose Lake, a 9-acre oxbow offering the same species as Mission Lake.

MOHAWK RIVER. An important tributary of the lower McKenzie River, joining the main stream at Springfield. It is the pri-

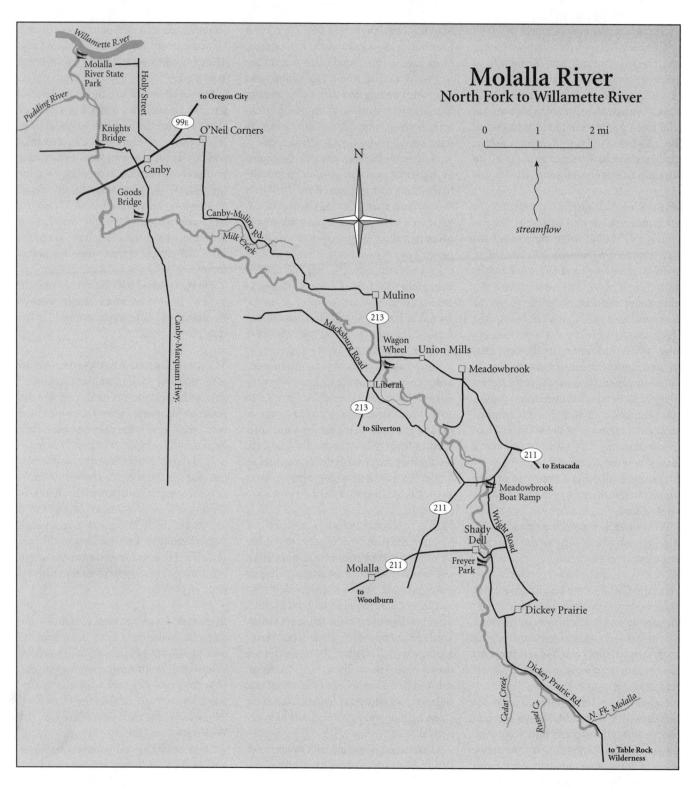

Molalla River
North Fork to Willamette River

0   1   2 mi

N

streamflow

Willamette River

Molalla River State Park

Pudding River

Knights Bridge

Holly Street

to Oregon City

99E

O'Neil Corners

Canby

Goods Bridge

Canby-Mulino Rd.

Milk Creek

Canby-Marquam Hwy.

Mulino

213

Macksburg Road

Wagon Wheel

Union Mills

Meadowbrook

Liberal

213

to Silverton

211

to Estacada

Meadowbrook Boat Ramp

211

Shady Dell

Wright Road

Freyer Park

Molalla

211

to Woodburn

Dickey Prairie

Cedar Creek

Russel Cr.

Dickey Prairie Rd.

N. Fk. Molalla

to Table Rock Wilderness

mary nursery for McKenzie's cutthroat population and provides fair fishing for wild cutthroat early in the season.

The river is followed northeast from Springfield by a paved road to Marcola, which is about half-way up the stream. From there, gravel roads access the upper river. Mill Creek, a fair tributary, comes in from the east, just north of Marcola. Most angling takes place in this area. The lower

stream has much private land and almost no access. It is best fished early in the season as the river gets pretty low by July

MOLALLA RIVER. A 45-mile tributary of the Willamette, with an excellent population of smallmouth bass at its mouth, harvest opportunities for spring chinook, catch and release fishing for wild winter steelhead, and harvest of the river's rem-

nant hatchery steelhead runs (both winter and summer, last stocked in 1996 and 1997). The Mollala heads in the Cascades within Mt. Hood National Forest and flows into the Willamette near Canby.

The lower stream is followed and crossed by paved backroads in the vicinities of Canby, Liberal, Union Mills, and Molalla. Above Molalla, a paved road closely follows the river through BLM property where bank access is open to the public.

The Molalla has a late wild winter steelhead run. Surprised trout anglers occasionally hook up with a mint bright steelhead after trout season opens at the end of May. Wild steelhead turn into the Willamette beginning in February and generally run through April. Remnants of the winter hatchery run arrive earlier (in December). Remnants of the hatchery summer steelhead run are in the river from May through early July. Non-finclipped steelhead must be released unharmed. Few finclipped steelhead will be available after the year 2000.

Spring chinook, both hatchery and wild, begin turning into the Molalla in April, with the run peaking in May and June. The hatchery chinook are finclipped, though there is no restriction on harvesting wild chinook at this time. The fishery closes August 15. Most Molalla chinook are taken in the Willamette just before they turn up their home stream. Fall chinook are no longer stocked, and the wild run returns after the August closure.

There are wild cutthroat in the river and its tributaries, available for catch and release angling. The lower 10 miles, west of Hwy. 213, are generally less productive than the upper waters. Trout fishing is catch and release only. Check the regulations for tackle restrictions.

Smallmouth bass can be found in good numbers in the slack water at the river's confluence with the Willamette. Park at Molalla River State Park and hike parallel to the Willamette about 1½ miles, or boat in, anchoring on the gravel bar at the mouth and wading to access the best water. This fishery is open year-round with best catches in June. Check the regulations for bait and hook restrictions.

The river is most accessible from drift boats, with the best run from Molalla down to Canby. Keep your eyes open for sweepers (partially submerged fallen trees). From Canby downstream the river can be handled by novice boaters. The stretch from Liberal to the state park provides a long day's drift, with a few steelhead holes and some classic slicks before the Pudding River muddies the water. If you take out at the state park, take time to enjoy the long easy trail along the river and the extensive heron rookery in the trees just back from water's edge. The take-out here is steep and often silted, so four-wheel drive with plenty of horse power is advisable.

A number of boat ramps on the Molalla have closed in recent years, including the Logging Bridge, Goods Bridge, and Knights Bridge. At this time, boats can be launched at Feyrer Park east of Molalla (gravel ramp), the Hwy. 211 Bridge (pole slide), Hwy. 213 Bridge at Liberal (a gravel bar, also known as Wagonwheel Park), City Park off 99E at the west end of Canby (gravel ramp), and Molalla State Park on the Willamette about ½ mile below the Molalla mouth (paved ramp). Popular drifts are from Freyer Park to Meadowbrook pole slide (2 miles), Meadow Brook to Wagonwheel (4 miles), Waggonwheel to Canby Park (12 miles) and Canby to the mouth (4 miles).

There's a lot of private land along the Molalla, but paved and gravel roads access the stream in many places. There are no campgrounds on the river.

MOODY LAKE. A 5-acre brook trout lake west of the Pacific Crest Trail in the Mink Lake Basin. See Cliff Lake for directions. Moody is one mile south of Cliff Lake. There are fish here, but they're hard to catch. They will take flies late in the day. (Mosquito imitations are always a good bet in the Mink Lake Basin). The average catch is 8 to 9 inches with a few to 12 inches.

MOOLACK LAKE. A good hike-in brook trout lake 2 miles southeast of Moolack Mt. and west of the Taylor Burn area. Moolack was a Chinook jargon word for elk. Shortest way in to this lake is from Taylor Burn Campground, which is best approached by the road from North Waldo Lake Campground. Hike west on the Blair Lake Trail 3553 about 2 miles, then take the Moolack Trail north ½ mile to the lake. This last trail is poorly marked, so keep a sharp eye. It's also possible to hike in from the west, starting on Trail 3594 east of Etta Prairie on Forest Rd. 2417 in the headwaters of Furnish Creek, a tributary of Salmon Creek. Bring your map.

About 14 acres, Moolack puts out some nice rainbows and cutthroat averaging 11 to 12 inches. All methods of fishing produce, and fly angling can be excellent in the fall. There are a few good natural campsites. The area is usually accessible by late June.

MOONLIGHT LAKE. A very productive small lake with lots of rainbow trout, just under 2 miles northwest of Horse Lake. It is lightly fished due to its location. The best route is by way of Bend and the Cascade Lakes Hwy. to Elk Lake. Take the Horse Lakes Trail 3517 west to Upper Horse Lake. From there, head northwest on trail 3514, the Horse Cr. Trail, and continue 2 miles. Keep watch to the left, and you'll spot the lake.

Moonlight Lake covers 8 acres and reaches a maximum depth of 14 feet. There's a lot of brush along the edges, so a rubber boat or float tube will help. The trout average 8 to 10 inches, but a few to 16 inches are caught. Any method usually works here. There are no good campsites at the lake.

MOSBY CREEK. A tributary of Row River in southern Lane County, offering catch and release fishing for wild trout. It flows over 20 miles to its confluence east of Cottage Grove from headwaters in the hills west of the northwest corner of the Umpqua National Forest.

From Hwy. 99 at Cottage Grove, turn east towards Dorena Reservoir, then south. A gravel road follows the stream closely for about 15 miles, then a dirt road takes over. A private timber company gate prevents vehicle access to several miles of the upper river, but anglers can continue on foot.

The creek has a fair catch rate for rainbow and cutthroat trout, though there's a lot of inaccessible private land. There is no camping along the stream.

MOTHER LODE LAKES. In the Pansy Basin area of the Collawash River headwaters, hard to reach but worth the effort for fine scenery and good fishing. The lakes are about half-way between Pansy Lake and the Twin Lakes. See Pansy Lake for trail directions. The Mother Lodes are west of the trail, on the east side of Mother Lode Mountain. Trail No. 558 will get you closest.

These are a series of 3 small lakes, each about an acre or two at an elevation of about 4000 ft. Currently only Ercrama Lake, the largest, is stocked (usually with cutthroat, sometimes with rainbows). It can easily be fished from shore.

MT. HOOD COMMUNITY COLLEGE PONDS. Trout ponds on the Stark St. campus in Gresham, east of Portland. The ponds are stocked with legal rainbows in early season, but the water quality is poor due to run-off from nearby golf courses. Fishing falls off when the water warms .

MOWICH LAKE A large and very good rainbow and brook trout lake in the Eight Lakes Basin of Mt. Jefferson Wilderness. Mowich is the Chinook word for deer. The largest lake in the basin, it covers 54 acres and reaches a depth of 45 ft. It is ½ mile north of Duffy Lake by Trail 3422 and can be reached from Marion Lake by good trail.

Its brook trout run 8 to 16 inches. Bait fishing with worms, or eggs and lures will take fish almost any time, and fly fishing is effective early and late in the day. The lake is usually accessible by June.

MUDDY CREEK (Mary's watershed). A tributary of Mary's River that lives up to its name in spring. It is south of Corvallis, west of 99W, with headwaters in the hills west of Monroe. It flows over 20 miles north to join the Mary's at Corvallis. Many roads follow and cross the creek.

Muddy is a slow moving creek with a mud bottom. The stream is not stocked but offers angling for bass, crappie, and a good population of wild cutthroat averaging 8 to 11 inches. Angling is good in early season and after the fall rains begin. Access is a problem due to private land holdings.

MUDDY FORK. A small fork of the upper Sandy River which offers catch and release fishing for wild cutthroat. It joins the main Sandy and the Clear Fork about 5 miles northeast of Zigzag north of McNeil Campground. To reach it, drive north from Zigzag on Forest Rd. 18, the Lolo Pass Rd. Follow Forest Rd. 100 from Lost Creek Campground about 2 miles to its end. There Trail 797 leads north about ½ mile to cross Muddy Fork. There is no road access to Muddy Fork.

Muddy Fork has some wild cutthroat of fair size, and anglers can do well in spring after the water warms and before the glacial silt starts flowing. There are several forest campgrounds in the vicinity. Tackle is restricted to artificial flies and lures. The Fork is closed to fishing for salmon and steelhead.

MULTNOMAH CHANNEL

A long, natural channel near the mouth of the Willamette, carrying a significant flow of the main river to the Columbia. It features a very popular fishery for spring chinook, with opportunities for sturgeon, walleye, bass, and panfish. It forms the southern shore of Sauvie Island, a large delta island about 9 miles northwest of Portland, and flows into the Columbia River at St. Helens. See Columbia River (St. Helens to Bonneville) for a map showing the channel's relationship to the Columbia and Willamette.

A growing number of anglers are successfully pursuing walleye in MULTNOMAH CHANNEL. *Photograph by Bud Hartman.*

Hwy. 30 follows the channel's west bank for most of its length, with plentiful bank access on Sauvie Island. Cross the Sauvie Island Bridge and follow Sauvie Island Rd. north to access the Channel's east bank. Much of the land along the Channel on the island is publicly owned (Sauvie Island Wildlife Area). Private land is well marked.

The spring chinook season varies from year to year, depending on estimates of run size. In recent years, opportunities have been restricted. Finclipping hatchery chinook will allow selective harvest and should increase fishing opportunities.

Chinook enter the Channel as early as mid-February, with the pace picking up from late March through May. The last week in April and the first week in May are often especially productive. The average chinook weighs 18 pounds, but a few fish over 40 pounds are landed each spring.

Most chinook anglers troll the Channel, although you'll find anchored boats at hot spots when the tide is running. Trollers move very slowly and fish the bottom, except in deep water, where they troll at 10 to 15 ft. Herring bait takes the overwhelming number of chinook, but lures also prove worthy. When the water is murky, hardware trollers use good size spinners or wobblers (copper finishes are especially effective at this time), changing to smaller lures as the water clears. Plugs and Kwik-fish-type lures in silver, gold, and other light finishes are generally effective.

Favorite spots include the mouth of Scappoose Bay, the Santosh Slough area, Coon Island, the Tank Hole, Rocky Point, and the head of the channel at the Willamette. Remember to keep an eye out for tow boats, whose vision is often impaired by barge loads.

Walleye are now well established in the Channel. Rocky Point, Brown's Landing, and Coon Island to the Gilbert River are popular walleye spots. See Columbia River, St. Helens to Bonneville Dam, for a discussion of this fishery.

From July through September, many channel anglers bring home a mess of catfish, largemouth and smallmouth bass, perch, and crappie. A tremendous number of panfish are taken around the log rafts, pilings, and abandoned docks, and at the mouths of streams. Boat angling is easiest, but a number of these areas can be reached from the bank on both sides of the channel.

The channel also offers western Oregon's

greatest sport catch of crayfish. Try baiting these with shad, which are available near Coon Island in June. A few sturgeon are picked up in the lower and upper channel.

There are boat ramps at Burlington Ferry off Hwy. 30 across from Sauvie Island, Brown's Landing 3 miles east of Scappoose on Dike Rd., Gilbert River mouth on Sauvie Island, and at Scappoose Bay Marina north of Scappoose. Look for boat ramp signs on Hwy. 30. Channel boaters also put in at Cathedral Park on the Willamette and at St. Helens.

MULTNOMAH CREEK. A 7-mile stream flowing into the Columbia Gorge, forming the spectacular Multnomah Falls east of Portland. It drains into Benson Lake at Hwy. 30. The only trout fishing is in the upper stream. Cut south off the scenic road at Bridal Veil, and drive 6 miles to the creek. A trail follows the creek both ways from the road's end. Wild cutthroat 6 to 9 inches with a few to 12 inches are available for catch and release angling.

NASH LAKE. naturally reproducing brook trout lake in the Three Sisters Wilderness, 6 air miles northwest of Elk Lake. Best access is from the east side of the Cascades. Take the Cascade Lakes Hwy. to Sisters Mirror Lake Trailhead, a quarter mile north of Sink Creek, which is midway between Devil and Elk lakes. Follow Trail 20 to the Sisters Mirror Lake group, then continue west 3 more miles.

Nash Lake has 33 surface acres at 4900 ft. elevation. The lake is heavily fished for an isolated lake, but still produces consistently. The trout average 10 inches and get as large as 15. A few cutthroat are also present. Fly fishing is exceptional here late in the year. There are good natural campsites.

NIGHTSHADE LAKES. Two little brook trout lakes off the beaten path in the Mink Lake Basin, offering rather poor fishing. The west lake usually has the larger fish. There are no campsites available. If you still want to give it a try, bushwhack northwest from the north end of Dumbell Lake. A half mile will get you to Krag Lake, and the Nightshades are a quarter mile farther west.

NORTH FORK RESERVOIR. A large, accessible power reservoir on the Clackamas River, with 350 surface acres when full. It is

7 miles south of Estacada off Hwy. 224, about 35 miles southeast of Portland. The reservoir is formed by a PGE dam on the mainstem at the confluence of the North Fork and Clackamas rivers.

The pool is 4 miles long, quite narrow and deep. It isn't very productive for wild fish, but it is heavily stocked with legal rainbows every few weeks during the season and attracts a lot of anglers. In 1999, 66,000 catchable trout were stocked. Wild cutthroat, bull, brook and brown trout occasionally drop in from the river. Fishing for them is catch and release. Only fin-clipped trout may be harvested.

Best fishing is at the upper end where trout are stocked near the in-flow and the resort. Best angling is with bait or troll and spinner combinations. Bank angling is possible in quite a few places. A flat bank area near the mouth is an especially good place for youngsters.

PGE has provided three boat ramps, picnic, and camping facilities. There is a concession with supplies, tackle and boats at the upper end of the pool. A portion of the reservoir 2.3 miles above the dam has a 10-mph speed restriction to protect angling in the resort and park area.

NOTCH LAKE. A 4-acre trout lake in the headwaters of Hills Creek west of Diamond Peak Wilderness. Follow the Hills Creek road, Forest Rd. 23, to Forest Rd. 2145, continuing 2 miles to Trail 3662, which follows the north bank of upper Hills Creek one mile to the lake. Cutthroat and rainbows here run 6 to 11 inches. In most years the lake is accessible by early June. There are no improvements.

OAK GROVE FORK. See **CLACKAMAS RIVER, OAK GROVE FORK.**

ONEONTA CREEK. A small stream entering the Columbia River in the picturesque Columbia Gorge, dropping from the cliff between Benson State Park and Dodson several miles east of Multnomah Falls. Only 5 miles long, it is followed by trail through its own scenic gorge, and offers catch and release fishing for small rainbow and cutthroat trout in spring and summer. Tackle is limited to artificial flies and lures.

OPAL LAKE. (Middle Fork Willamette watershed). A fairly good trout lake in the Willamette National Forest west of the

southern boundary of Diamond Peak Wilderness. Follow Forest Rd. 211 from the southwest end of Crescent Lake, then turn left on Forest Rd. 398. Opal is about 13 miles from Crescent Lake.

About 15 acres, the lake supports both rainbow and brook trout. The rainbows average 8 inches and run to 13 inches. Brook trout are generally a little smaller. All methods can be used. The lake is fishable from shore. There's a small campground here and another at Timpanogas Lake, a mile south.

OPAL LAKE. (North Santiam watershed). A brook trout lake 6 miles north of Detroit Reservoir at the head of Opal Creek. Take the Little North Santiam River Rd. past the Pearl Creek Guard Station on Forest Rd. 2207 to Shady Cove Campground. Cross the bridge on Cedar Creek Rd., taking the left fork uphill and switching back at the next right. Opal Lake is a half-mile bushwhack at the bottom of the ridge.

It is at elevation 3476 ft. with 11 surface acres and 40 ft. deep. Opal has a naturally reproducing population of brook trout.

OSWEGO CREEK. Once known as Sucker Creek, it flows out of Lake Oswego south of Portland and is crossed by Hwy. 43 near the mouth. There is only about a mile of stream between the lake and the Willamette.

An occasional cutthroat is spotted here in winter, but most fishing is for warmwater fish in the lower half mile. A lot of crappie are picked up near the mouth. Small runs of winter steelhead and coho return to the creek each year, but the creek is closed to salmon and steelhead fishing. Minimal parking is available at Oswego City Park near the mouth.

OSWEGO, LAKE. A large private lake south of Portland, whose outlet at the town of Lake Oswego drains into the Willamette River. The lake is about 3 miles long and a third mile wide. Its shores are completely developed, and almost exclusively residential. A private corporation controls access and polices the lake against trespassers. There is no public access. It is fed by the Tualatin River and is privately stocked. The lake was originally called Sucker Lake, but the name offended the residents of this posh district, so they renamed it. There are probably warmwater fish here, but it is not stocked. You can fish the outlet stream, Oswego Creek, as long as you don't trespass.

OTTER LAKE. (Middle Fork Wilamette watershed). A very productive 17-acre trout lake at the north end of the Taylor Burn area, one mile northeast of Erma Bell Lakes. Approach the lake from the north, from Skookum Creek Campground at the end of the Box Canyon Rd. (Forest Rd. 1957). The campground can be reached from the North Fork of the Willamette or the South Fork of the McKenzie. Head south ½ mile from Skookum Campground, then take Trail 3558 to the lake.

To approach from the south, take the Williams Lake Trail north from Taylor Burn Campground 3 miles to the lake. The Williams Lake Trail parallels the Olallie Trail, but is on the east side of Erma Bell Lakes.

Otter Lake is a consistent producer of rainbow and brook trout, with sizable fish available. Late fall is the best time for success. The lake is very brushy around the shore, so carry in a rubber boat or float tube. There are good natural campsites at Otter Lake and a small camp at Skookum Creek. It is usually accessible in late June.

PALMER LAKE. A 15-acre lake northeast of Larch Mt. on the Latourell Prairie Rd. It is in the closed area of the Bull Run watershed and is not open for angling.

PAMELIA LAKE. A large lake with small cutthroat in the Mt. Jefferson Wilderness directly below the southwest flank of the mountain. About 7 miles south of Idanha, take Pamelia Rd., Forest Rd. 2246, east 4 miles to Trail 3439. The lake is 2 miles down the trail over easy terrain.

Pamelia has about 50 surface acres but gets low in late summer and fall. It has excellent spawning habitat and can suffer from overpopulation, reducing the average size. All methods will take fish here. The road is accessible during winter, and the lake is open for angling, so anglers could do a little snowshoe ice fishing here.

There are several good natural campsites at the lake, and there are other good lakes in the neighborhood. See Hanks and Hunts. Supplies are available at Idanha or Detroit. The lake is often ice-free by late May, but there is usually lots of snow left.

PANSY LAKE. In the Pansy Basin near the head of the Hot Springs Fork of the Collawash River. Take Hwy. 224 past Estacada 34 miles to the mouth of the Collawash. From there, follow Forest Rd. 63 up the Collawash to Tom Meadows, then Forest Rd. 6340 and Forest Rd. 6341 to the Pansy Trail 551. Hike south for one mile to Pansy Basin. Bear right, and cross the meadow to the rock slide. Hike ½ mile up the ridge by trail. The lake is west of Bull of the Woods Lookout, The trails are well signed.

Pansy covers about 6 acres and is very shallow. It is stocked with brook trout in odd number years and supports some natural reproduction as well, offering consistent catches of 8 to 9 inch fish, with some to 12 inches. Fly angling or small lures work best due to the lake's shallow depth. Fall is the best season to fish here.

PANTHER CREEK. A small wild trout stream flowing into the North Yamhill River north of McMinnville off Hwy. 18. The lower end of the stream is crossed by the paved road north from McMinnville to Carlton. A paved road west from Carlton accesses the upper stream. Panther provides good catch and release angling the first few months of trout season, but gets low in the summer. A few fair size cutthroat are occasionally hooked.

The creek flows entirely through private agricultural land, with public access only at road crossings.

PARRISH LAKE. A good brook trout lake west of the North Santiam River, about 9 miles northwest of Santiam Junction. From Hwy. 22, turn west 7 miles south of the Marion Forks Ranger Station onto Forest Rd. 2266. Follow this road west about 5 miles. The road runs between Daly Lake on the north and Parrish Lake on the south.

Parrish is about 7 acres and produces brook trout 6 to 13 inches. Fishing is usually good early and late in the season. All methods can be effective. There are good natural campsites available. It is usually accessible in late May.

PATJENS LAKES. A group of three small lakes south of Big Lake along the Cascade Summit, southwest of Santiam Pass Hwy. 20. At Hoodoo Ski Bowl, turn onto Forest Rd. 2690. It's 4 miles to Big Lake, and the

Patjens are 2 miles south by Trail 3395. The upper and deepest lake covers about 3 acres and has brook trout 6 to 12 inches. The middle lake covers 6 acres and has rainbow trout. The lower lake is just a shallow pot hole and doesn't hold fish. The lakes are lightly fished. The best campsites are at Big Lake.

PENN LAKE. A trout lake in the north Mink Lake Basin, at the head of the South Fork McKenzie, west of Elk Lake. See Corner Lake for directions. Penn Lake is lightly fished due to its position in the basin. It is about a quarter mile northwest of Corner Lake by a good trail.

It contains naturally reproducing cutthroat and brook trout. About 26 acres and very shallow, it occasionally winterkills. Best fishing for brook trout is early in the year and again in fall.

PETE'S SLOUGH. A Columbia River backwater on Sauvie Island at the north end of Sturgeon Lake, fished for bass and panfish. After crossing Sauvie Island Bridge 10 miles west of Portland off Hwy. 30, follow Sauvie Island Rd. north, turn right on Reeder Rd., and follow Reeder Rd. 11 miles to the checking station. Drive left about a mile and cross the dike, where several dirt roads head west to the slough. The dike crossing is closed from late May through June, as the area is flooded.

Pete's Slough connects McNary and Sturgeon lakes and is fishable all along the shore. See McNary Lake. A footbridge crosses the slough and provides fishing access. Crappie, brown bullhead, and other panfish are available in good numbers. Bait is most popular, but small lures and streamer flies take large crappie. An occasional largemouth bass is caught, but they're not numerous. Try plugging the few shallow oxbows. The entrances to the many duck lakes are also frequent bass hang-outs. Overnight camping is not permitted on the island. Minimal supplies are available at the island store near the bridge. There are no gas stations or restaurants on the island. A recreation permit is required to park on Sauvie Island. Day and seasonal passes are sold at the market.

PIKA LAKE. A small brook trout lake, lightly fished but not too hard to reach. It's in the Big Meadows area off the North Santiam. See Fay Lake for directions. Continue past Fay for a quarter mile, then follow a blazed trail south. It's ½ mile to the lake. Though only 3 acres, Pika is very brushy and hard to fish, so a rubber boat or float tube is helpful. Its fish bite well on almost anything once you get out to them. Brook trout here run 8 to 10 inches. There are no good campsites at the lake.

PINE RIDGE LAKE. Also known as Pine Lake, adjacent to a heavily-used Scout camp. It can be reached from Marion Forks on Hwy. 22 by turning east onto Twin Meadows Rd. (Forest Rd. 2261) about 4 miles south of Marion Forks. From this point it's five miles to the lake. Pine Ridge is a fine lake for youngsters. Cutthroat and rainbows run to 13 inches, and some brook trout may grow larger. Trails lead to other lakes in the area. See Temple, Davis. Public camping is prohibited. Recommended for introducing youngsters to fishing.

PIPER LAKE. A lightly fished 5-acre brook trout lake in the Irish Mt. area north of Irish and Taylor lakes. See McFarland Lake for directions. Piper is a few hundred yards west of McFarland. Although small, the lake has a maximum depth of 24 ft. It's not very productive, but some nice brook trout catches have been reported. It's a good lake to try while in the Irish Mountain area.

PLATT LAKE. An 8-acre trout lake in the Horse Lake area west of Elk Lake. See Horse Lake for directions. Platt Lake is 2 miles southwest of Upper Horse Lake. Take Horse Mt. Trail 3530, which goes right to the lake. Platt has some nice brook trout around 10 inches. All methods of angling will take fish at times, and the lake is easily fished from shore. There are good natural campsites at the lake. Other small lakes to the south are also stocked. See Mile Lake.

PLAZA LAKE. A 5-acre hike-in brook trout lake east of Hwy. 224 near Squaw Mt., in a setting of rare old growth forest. The lake drains into the South Fork of the Salmon River (Sandy watershed) from elevation 3650 ft. The hike in is about 20 minutes.

From Estacada follow Hwy. 224 about 6 miles to the North Fork Rd. (Forest Rd. 4610). At about 6 miles, Forest Rd. 4610 crosses Winslow Creek then cuts right sharply, while Forest Rd. 4613 continues straight ahead to North Fork Crossing Campground. Stay on 4610 (known as the Squaw Mt. Rd.) 11 miles to Twin Springs Campground. About one mile past the camp, Trail 788 to Plaza Lake heads east. The trail is three quarters of a mile downhill, although the lake is only ½ mile or less from the road.

Though small, Plaza produces a fair number of pan-size brook trout 6 to 10 inches. It is stocked in odd number years. All methods of angling will take fish here. It's usually not accessible until late June.

PLUMB LAKE. A brook trout lake in the Mink Lake Basin, ½ mile northeast of Junction Lake on the trail to Corner Lake. See Mink Lake and Junction Lake for directions. One of the smaller lakes in the Mink Lake Basin, it covers 15 acres and reaches a maximum depth of 17 ft. Brook trout reproduce naturally here, and fishing for them is generally good. It's a good fly fishing lake, with best catches late in the day.

POPE LAKE. A Sauvie Island lake containing brown bullhead, crappie, bass, some carp, and chubs. To reach the lake, take Hwy. 30 north from Portland to the Sauvie Island Bridge. Cross to the island, continuing north on Sauvie Island Road. Turn right on Reeder Rd. and follow Reeder about 10 miles to a slough with moorage on the right. The lake is about 300 yards directly west. The surest way to find the lake is to proceed to the waterfowl checking station, then walk due south for ½ mile. This is part of the Sauvie Island Wildlife Area. A piece of land at the south end of Pope Lake is private property, so watch the signs.

Pope has about 10 surface acres and is easily fished from shore. Fair size bass are taken on plugs and spinners, and crappie will hit smaller lures. Angling for brown bullhead is fair throughout the summer. There is no camping in this area. Like all Sauvie Island fisheries, Pope is open from April 16 through September 30.

You will need to purchase a recreation permit to park on Sauvie Island. Day use and seasonal passes are sold at the market on the island just north of the bridge. There are no gas stations or restaurants on the island.

PORKY LAKE. One of the most productive and consistent lakes in the Mink Lake Basin. See Cliff Lake and Mink Lake for directions. It has about 38 surface acres, located ½ mile east of Mink Lake, half-way to Cliff Lake.

Porky is a very rich body of water with lots of naturally reproducing brook trout. It usually holds up throughout the season. All methods will catch fish, with fly fishing especially good in late summer. There are good natural campsites at the lake.

PRESLEY LAKE. A 3-acre, shallow, drive-in lake 3 miles northwest of Marion Lake. About ½ mile south of Marion Forks Ranger Station, turn east onto Forest Rd. 2257. Follow this road about 2 miles to Forest Rd. 515, a left fork which goes to Horn Creek Unit 2. At about ½ mile, you can see the Presley to the north. A rugged spur road runs down to the lake. Though shallow, and with little winter survival, Presley is stocked with fingerling rainbows, so best fishing is towards the end of the season. There are no camping facilities.

PRILL LAKE. A small brook trout lake in the Marion Lake Basin. See Marion Lake for directions. From Marion, follow the trail around the east bank to Mist Creek. Prill is about one mile east by very steep trail. It covers 8 acres and is 20 feet deep. Brook trout 8 to 14 inches will hit anything. There are a few natural campsites.

PUDDING RIVER. A tributary of the Molalla River with headwaters east of Salem, offering catch and release angling for wild trout. It flows through the center of Marion County north into Clackamas County, where it joins the Mollala River near Canby. It is crossed by Hwy. 99E outside Aurora. A number of paved and gravel roads in the Silverton, Mt. Angel, and Woodburn areas cross the stream. Most bank angling takes place at the road crossings.

The Pudding isn't stocked, but its main tributaries (Drift, Butte, Silver, and Abiqua creeks) keep the upper waters fairly populated with trout. Cutthroat dominate the catch, with a few rainbows taken. The lower river has fair populations of bass and panfish, but at this time, all fishing in the Pudding is restricted to artificial flies and lures.

The river is closed to fishing for the winter steelhead that spawn and rear in its tributary streams. The extreme lower river can be drifted in small boats, and some anglers motor up from the Willamette when the water is high. The lower river is sometimes navigable into June.

PYRAMID LAKE. (Clackamas watershed) An accessible hike-in cutthroat lake in the High Rocks area of the Clackamas drainage. At elevation 4000 ft., this 4-acre lake is usually accessible earlier than other lakes in Mt. Hood National Forest.

From Estacada, take Hwy. 224 about 30 miles southeast to Ripplebrook Ranger Station, and continue another 8 miles to the Shellrock Rd. (Forest Rd. 58). A little over 4 miles north past Shellrock Campground, Forest Rd. 140 branches off to the left. Follow Forest Rd. 140 about 2 miles to road's end at Pyramid Lake Trailhead. The trail to Pyramid is just ½ mile.

The lake is stocked with cutthroat trout, and fishing holds up well, producing catches 6 to 13 inches. Bait and spinner work best in early season, with good fly angling later on. There are natural campsites at the lake.

PYRAMID LAKE. (Olallie Lake Area). An up and down lake for brook trout, with occasional winterkills. Some years have produced fine, plump brookies. The lake is 1½ miles west of Breitenbush Lake. See Breitenbush Lake for directions. The trail to Pyramid takes off south at the bridge over the Breitenbush Lake outlet, following the creek upstream ½ mile, then traversing a steep slope. Pyramid is on a flat, ½ mile west of Pyramid Butte.

The lake is about 5 acres and shallow. When the fish are there, fly fishing is excellent. There are some pretty, natural campsites at the lake..

QUARTZVILLE CREEK. An excellent trout stream, also known as the Quartzville Fork of the Santiam, with harvest opportunities for stocked trout. It enters Green Peter Reservoir from the north about 12 miles east of Sweet Home., forming the northeast arm of the reservoir.

From Hwy. 20 at Sweet Home, continue east to the upstream end of Foster Reservoir, then turn north (left) toward Sunnyside Campground crossing the northeast arm of Foster. Turn right on the Quartzville Rd., which follows the northern shore of Green Peter Reservoir, including the Quartsville Arm. This paved road

follows Quartzville Creek upstream more than 25 miles into Willamette National Forest (Forest Rd. 11).

The creek has lots of productive water, most on BLM or National Forest land and is one of the few streams in the Willamette Zone that continue to be stocked (catchable rainbow trout in spring and early summer). Some nice wild cutthroat are also present, though only finclipped trout may be kept. Light gear is usually best. Fly fishing can be good when the water warms. Best catches are from Canal Creek down to the Forks Canal.

Camping is available on Green Peter at Whitcomb Creek Campground west of the creek mouth, and at Yellowbottom BLM Campground about 6 miles upstream from the reservoir.

QUESTION MARK LAKE. A good trout lake in the Mink Lake Basin. It receives a lot of pressure but still produces well. The lake takes its name from its unique shape and not from puzzled fly anglers trying to match the hatch. The lake is on the east edge of the basin. From the junction of the Six Lakes Trail and the Pacific Crest Trail, which meet at Ledge Lake Meadow, it's a quarter mile northwest through the trees to Question Mark.

The lake is about 10 acres and deep in spots, but with lots of shoal area for easy fly fishing. It's a very easy lake to fish. The rainbow and cutthroat trout run 7 to 12 inches, with a few larger. There are excellent campsites here. Snow often obscures the trail until late June.

QUINN LAKES. Two popular trout lakes west of Taylor Burn Campground across a canyon carved by the North Fork of the Willamette. It's about a 2-mile hike on Blair Lake Trail 3553. Lower Quinn Lake is south of the trail at the head of Fisher Creek. The Quinns can also be reached from North Waldo Camp or from the Oakridge area by the Salmon Creek Rd. and Forest Rd. 2417. See Eddeeleo Lakes for trail details.

Lower Quinn is 12 acres and has rainbow trout. The shore is a little brushy, but it can be fished in places. A raft or float tube would be handy. Upper Quinn Lake is a quarter mile south, with 17 surface acres. Upper has brook trout and, like most brook trout lakes, it slows up for periods during the season.

RED BUTTE LAKE. A scenic 6-acre lake in the Eight Lakes Basin of the Mt. Jefferson Wilderness. It is west of the trail running south from Jorn Lake, about ½ mile south of Jorn, 2 miles north of Duffy. See Jorn and Duffy for directions.

Red Butte is long, narrow, and fairly deep for its size. Being on the trail, it's fished frequently. Stocked by the state every other year, the brook trout average 8 to 9 inches, with a few to 12 inches. It's easily fished from shore. There are good natural campsites near the lake, and additional sites at Jorn. There are other good lakes north and south.

This is a heavily used wilderness area. Camp well back from the lake to help preserve the fragile vegetation.

RIGDON LAKES. A pair of inconsistent trout lakes in the Taylor Burn area north of Waldo Lake, with both rainbow and cutthroat trout. These lakes were burnt over in the 1996 Charlton Burn, but continue to be stocked.

From Taylor Burn Campground, 7 miles north of the North Waldo Lake Campground by poor road, take the Olallie Trail 3583 south to Kiwa Lake, and turn east off the trail south of Kiwa. The Rigdons are ½ mile east of the trail, east of Rigdon Butte. From North Waldo, take the trail along the north end of Waldo Lake about 2 miles, then head north by trail about ½ mile to the Rigdons.

Upper Rigdon offers fair brook trout angling on its 50 acres. The fish run 6 to 13 inches. Lower Rigdon is a few hundred yards to the south. About the same size as Upper, it sometimes holds rainbow and brook trout to 15 inches. Both lakes can be fished from shore. Bait, lures, and flies can all work here depending on conditions. These lakes are at their best in late summer and fall.

ROARING RIVER. (Clackamas watershed). A tributary of the upper Clackamas, offering good catch and release, hike-in angling for wild trout. About 15 miles long, it heads in the High Rock area of Mt. Hood National Forest about 4 miles northwest of Timothy Lake. It joins the Clackamas upstream from Fish Creek at Roaring River Campground on Hwy. 224.

Anglers must hike to reach the stream. Bring your forest map. The canyon is very deep, and the hiking tough. Some anglers hike up from the forest camp at the mouth. The central creek can be reached by a 3-mile hike on a trail south from Lookout Spring Camp on the Squaw Mt. Rd. A dirt road, Forest Rd. 4611, can be followed from about one mile south of North Fork Crossing Campground to a trailhead which takes at least 2 miles off this hike.

For rugged hikers, the upper river can be reached by a trek into the canyon about 2 miles by trail from Twin Springs Camp, which is several miles further east on Squaw Mt. Rd. Cutthroat run 6 to 12 inches. If you like fishing in solitude, this is the spot. Summer steelhead are found in the lower 3 miles of river below the falls (there's a nice pool below the falls that often holds steelhead), but the river is closed to steelhead fishing.

There are several camps on the Squaw Mt. Rd. and near the mouth on Hwy. 224, and there are natural sites in the canyon.

ROARING RIVER. (South Santiam watershed). A small wild trout stream, tributary to Crabtree Creek east of Albany. It offers catch and release angling for cutthroat. From Hwy. 99E, turn east at Jefferson, continue through Scio, then follow the Crabtree Creek Rd. Roaring River is only about 8 miles long, and most of it runs close to the road.

The river's cutthroat are generally small, though larger fish are occasionally caught near the mouth. A trout and steelhead hatchery near the mouth is a nice spot to visit. There are no campgrounds on the river, but there is a nice little day-use park near the fish hatchery which includes a tiny pond stocked with legal trout, recommended for youngsters only.

ROARING RIVER PARK POND. A tiny pond on the grounds of the fish hatchery on Roraring River. See above.

ROBINSON LAKE. A good cutthroat lake on the western border of Mt. Washington Wilderness, accessible and popular. To reach the lake, take Robinson Rd. (Forest Rd. 2664) east from Hwy. 126, the McKenzie River Hwy. The turn-off is about 4 miles south of Clear Lake. Follow this road about 4 miles to the end, where a trail leads a quarter mile east to the lake.

Robinson is only 5 acres and mostly shallow, but runs to 20 ft. deep in spots. It offers good trout angling using any method, with most fish averaging 12 inches and some beauties to 16 inches. Campsites are available to the north of Hwy. 126 at Carmen Reservoir and Clear Lake.

ROCK CREEK. (Molalla River watershed). A tributary of Butte Creek in the Pudding River drainage, offering fair early-season catch and release fishing for wild cutthroat. Its confluence with Butte is about 5 miles south of Canby. The head of the creek is about 10 miles south of Molalla. The stream is crossed by Hwy. 213 a few miles south of Molalla, and by paved and gravel roads throughout its length.

Rock Creek cutthroat run 6 to 12 inches. Bear Creek, flowing into Rock Creek near Marks Prairie, has some fair cutthroat angling, too. Best fishing is in May and June. Most land along the creek is privately owned with access by permission only.

ROCK LAKES. (Clackamas watershed). Three good lakes in the High Rock area, north of Hwy. 224, offering a variety of trout for the hiking angler. Upper Rock and Middle Rock feature rainbows, and Lower supports brook trout.

The lakes are over 50 miles from Portland. The shortest hike in is by Trail 512, which heads between Frazier Fork and Frazier Turnaround campgrounds. Follow Hwy. 224 from Estacada to the Shellrock Rd., Forest Rd. 58, and drive 7 miles to High Rock Springs Campground. Just north of the campground, take Forest Rd. 240 five miles west to Frazier Forks Campground. The lakes are one mile west on Serene Lake Trail 512. Lower Rock Lake is to the north. Signs mark the trail junctions.

The lower lake is about 9 acres and 13 ft. deep. Middle Rock is 15 acres and 34 ft. deep. Upper Rock is only 3 acres, but 22 ft. deep. All the lakes have reproducing populations of brook trout as well as stocked fish. Average catch in all the lakes is 8 to 9 inches, though some brook trout over 12 inches have been hooked.

The lakes are fished rather heavily since they are so close to the road. One or more of the three is usually putting out catches. All methods of angling can be used, from boat or bank. Spinner and bait are usually good in early season, fly fishing in late summer and fall.

There are good campsites at the two larger lakes. They are usually inaccessible until early June, except by hiking west from Shellrock Lake. The road to Frazier Mt. is sometimes snowed in until late June.

ROCKPILE LAKE. A scenic cutthroat trout lake in Diamond Peak Wilderness at 6100 ft., east of a peak called Diamond Rockpile. It is a few hundred yards southeast of Marie Lake. See Marie Lake for directions.

This 6-acre lake is fished heavily, but it produces some nice cutthroat. The fish average 10 inches and run to 14 inches. The lake is easily fished from shore, and all methods can be used. There are good natural campsites here, and a full-service campground at Summit Lake. It is usually snowbound until late June.

ROOSTER ROCK SLOUGH. A neat Columbia River backwater that offers fishing for smallmouth and crappie as well as walleye within Rooster Rock State Park. Adjacent to the north lane of the freeway, it has about 5 surface acres.

There is a deep hole at the base of a sheer rock wall at the west end of the slough where walleye can be caught. Be very careful if you park on the west-bound shoulder of I-84 to access the walleye hole.

Fish for smallmouth and crappie along the riprap that lines the boat channel leading to the Columbia.

ROSLYN LAKE. A 160-acre impoundment near the town of Sandy, filled with water diverted from the Little Sandy and Sandy rivers. At this time, it is owned and managed by PGE for hydropower water storage, and used for general recreation, including fishing for catchable trout. At this time, the future of Roslyn is in dispute. PGE intends to remove Little Sandy and Marmot dams, which divert river water for the lake. Possible alternatives include pumping water from natural springs in the area or from the Bull Run River, with a reduction in lake size to about 50 acres.

From Hwy. 26 at the east end of Sandy, turn north onto Dodge Park Rd. It's about 4 miles to the lake.

Catchable rainbow trout are stocked from March through August (about 20,000 annually). Recycled winter and summer steelhead from the fish trap at Marmot Dam are released in Roslyn. Best fishing is on the east side, near the inlet source.

The lake is surrounded by a pleasant,

tree-lined park with an old fashioned summer camp atmosphere, including a picnic area with barbecue facilities, snack bar, and paddleboat rentals. No motorboats are allowed, but car-top or rubber boats and canoes can be launched. A naturally flat bank permits wheelchair access. There is a fee for admission to the park on weekends.

For information about the stocking of recycled hatchery steelhead, call the PGE Fish Line. See Appendix.

ROUND LAKE. (Middle Fork Willamette watershed). A good brook trout and rainbow lake in the Eddeeleo group south of Taylor Burn, northwest of Waldo Lake. See Eddeeleo Lakes for directions. Round Lake is east of Upper Eddeeleo, 100 yards from the trail that leads to North Waldo.

The catch averages 8 to 11 inches, with some fish to 16 inches. All methods of angling are used with good results. Trout reproduce naturally here. The lake covers 20 acres and is easily fished from shore. There are good natural campsites available, and excellent fishing in other lakes north and south.

ROUND LAKE. (Clackamas watershed). A productive brown trout lake high in the southern Mt. Hood National Forest, popular with float tube anglers and restricted to artificial flies and lures.

The route to Round Lake (on Forest Rd. 6370) has been complicated by a landslide closing a portion of that road north of the lake. The slide will not be cleared. Round Lake must now be approached from the south. One possible route is from Hwy. 22 (the North Santiam Hwy.). About 5½ miles after crossing the Breitenbush arm of Detroit Lake, look for Forest Rd. 4696 on the left. Follow it beyond the hairpin turn (the hairpin cut-off is a very b ad road), then make a sharp right onto 850, which leads to 6370, which leads to Round Lake. Another option is to follow Hwy. 224 east from Estacada to Ripplebrook Ranger Station, turning south on Forest Rd. 46 and following it about 28 miles to Forest Rd. 6350. After 5 miles on 6350, the road splits into 3 forks. Take the left fork (6355) and go about 200 yards before making a sharp left onto 220, which leads to 6370 (a right turn), which leads to the lake. The current Mt. Hood National Forest map does not show the road closure. Good luck.

Round Lake is 9 acres and about 20 ft.

deep. It has naturally reproducing brown trout, supplemented by stocked brook trout. The brook trout have been running 8 to 14 inches, and the browns 8 to 16 inches. It's a tough lake to fish from shore because of weeds along the shoals. Bring a float tube for best results. All methods will produce, but the browns are wary, so use light gear. There is a small campground above the lake, with an easy trail to the lake itself.

ROW RIVER. (Rhymes with "cow") A wild cutthroat stream northeast of Cottage Grove, with opportunities to keep your catch, a major tributary of the Coast Fork of the Willamette River. It is dammed at river mile 8½ to form Dorena Reservoir.

Access to the Row is limited to road crossings and to Schwarts Park below the dam. See Dorena for directions to the river. Row River Rd. follows the river to its forks, Brice and Sharps creeks.

Fishing for cutthroat is best above the reservoir. A spinner will work best in early season, with good fly fishing later. At this time, the Row is open for trout fishing year-round, with opportunities for harvest from late April through October, and catch and release fishing with artificial flies and lures throughout the rest of the year. There are campgrounds at Schwartz Park, on Dorena, and in Umpqua National Forest along Brice and Scharps creeks.

RUSS LAKE. (Confederated Tribes Warm Springs) A 6-acre brook trout lake east of Olallie Meadows Campground on the Skyline Rd. An easygoing trail reaches the lake in less than 1½ miles after passing two other small, good lakes. See Jude and Brook.

The fish run 6 to 15 inches. The bank is brushy, so a float tube would be helpful. Angling with wet flies is usually good in the morning and late in the day. Spinner and bait will work well almost anytime.

Although the lake is on Warm Springs Reservation, tribal permits are not required. Overnight camping is prohibited due to fire danger.

ST. LOUIS PONDS. A group of seven constructed ponds offering an interesting variety of panfish near the community of Gervais, south of Woodburn. From I-5 take the Woodburn Exit west to Gervais Rd. Head south, then west on Jenson Rd. The

ponds are in an attractive setting of natural undergrowth. They are located to the left of the railroad. A large parking area is provided. The area can be very muddy and almost inaccessible in spring and early summer.

The ponds have been open to angling since 1980, and there is a little of everything in them, including largemouth bass, channel cats, bluegill, fewer black and white crappie than in past years, and red-ear sunfish. Aquatic weed growth has been a problem, but efforts are underway to keep the water open. In recent years, fish have been plentiful but small. A decision to stock predator-size bass starting in 1999 may result in larger average catches. Pond No. 3 is stocked with legal trout in spring.

The seven ponds have a combined area of 55 acres. They were excavated by the State Highway Dept. in a maze design and offer an impressive 7 miles of bank fishing. This is strictly a bank fishery, as floating devices are prohibited. The path to Pond No. 3 is wheelchair accessible and a fishing float there has wheelchair guard rails.

The ponds are open (for day use only) from late January till mid-October. The autumn closure protects wintering waterfowl. There is a small picnic area. The ponds are closed to use after dark. Recommended for youngsters.

SALMON CREEK. A good trout stream, tributary of the Middle Fork Willamette, flowing 26 miles from headwaters in Waldo Meadows to its confluence with the Middle Fork at Oakridge. It offers fishing for both wild cutthroat and stocked rainbows, with harvest opportunities.

To reach Salmon Creek, follow Hwy. 58 east from Springfield through Oakridge. The road to the Salmon Creek Fish Hatchery, one mile east of town, joins Forest Rd. 24, which follows the creek for about 10 miles. Logging roads access the upper stream and many of the tributaries.

Salmon Creek is heavily stocked with rainbow hatchery trout, and offers an opportunity to catch and keep wild trout as well. It originates in Upper and Lower Salmon Lakes in the high lakes area west of Waldo Lake and is fed by many small tributaries and two good size creeks (Furnish and Black), all of which have wild cutthroat. It has better trout habitat than nearby Salt Creek (less gradient, more pools), and consequently has a better population of wild fish.

The name Salmon Creek derives from a run of spring chinook that once spawned here. The run was destroyed when the Army Corps of Engineers failed to construct fishways over Dexter and Lookout Point dams on the Middle Fork Willamette. To mitigate for the loss, the Corps has built a fish trap at Dexter Dam, where ODFW collects salmon eggs for rearing in a hatchery on the creek. The creek is closed to salmon angling. There is a campground at Salmon Creek Falls.

SALMON RIVER

(Sandy River watershed). A beautiful tributary of the upper Sandy River with a good population of wild cutthroat, and small runs of winter steelhead, chinook, and coho. Fishing at this time is limited to catch and release for wild cutthroat, using artificial flies and lures. The Salmon joins the Sandy from the south at Brightwood, a community on Hwy. 26 about 4 miles west of Zigzag.

At Wildwood on Hwy. 26, a road leads south to a BLM recreation area on the Salmon, about 3 miles upstream from the mouth. Roads due south from Wemme and Zigzag Ranger Station join the Salmon about 6 miles from the mouth and continue south as Forest Rd. 2618, which follows the river about 5 miles upstream to Trail 742. The trail keeps pace with the river for 11 miles in a wilderness-like setting. This charming wooded stretch, dotted with deep pools, offers a quality angling experience. The upper river can be reached by trails which head from forest roads south of Trillium Lake. Refer to the Mt. Hood National Forest map.

The Salmon River heads on the upper slopes of Mt. Hood, carrying snow melt down from Palmer Glacier. It flows 31 miles, 24 through national forest. Thirteen miles above the mouth a series of scenic waterfalls form a barrier to salmon and steelhead passage. Above the falls there is a good population of wild cutthroat.

There are camping facilities at the Wildwood Recreation Site on Hwy. 26 and at Green Canyon Campground on Forest Rd. 2618, about 5 miles south of Zigzag. The Fly Fishing Shop in the shopping center at Welches is information central for fishing the Salmon and the Sandy.

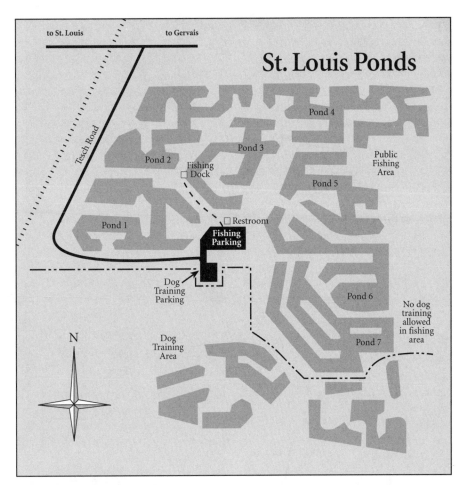

SALMONBERRY LAKE. A 3-acre stocked rainbow fishery near St. Helens, formerly a city water supply. From Hwy. 30 at St. Helens, head west on the Pittsburgh-St. Helens Rd. about 9 miles, turning left onto Salmonberry Rd. soon after the main road itself turns to gravel. The access road leads to a gate. Park and walk in to the lake. Salmonberry is stocked with about 4000 catchable rainbow trout in April and May.

SALT CREEK. An important tributary of the Middle Fork Willamette River, flowing 28 miles through Willamette Pass from its source at Gold Lake to its confluence with the Middle Fork at Oakridge. It is closely followed by Hwy. 58 to the Gold Lake cut-off and is a popular tourist fishery, due more to its proximity to the highway than to its productivity.

Steep and tumultuous throughout much of its run, it offers limited trout habitat and, consequently, has only a small wild trout population. Habitat in the lower 10 miles was improved by the floods in the late '90's.

The most productive stretch for small but feisty wild trout is the few miles from Hwy. 58 Bridge down to Salt Creek Falls. Here the creek flows at a diminished gradient, meandering prettily through meadows. It is brushy and hard to fish, but wild rainbow and brook trout are plentiful. Rainbow trout are stocked from the mouth to South Fork Bridge (about 7 miles above Blue Pool Campground). Salt Creek Falls is a handsome 286 ft. falls which can be viewed from a paved trail on the south side of Hwy. 58, 20 miles east of Oakridge.

There are campgrounds on the creek within Willamette National Forest at Blue Pool (a nice swimming hole) about 8 miles east of Oakridge, and at Salt Creek Falls.

McCredie Hot Springs, an undeveloped natural hot spring pool beside the creek, is less than one mile from Blue Pool. There is a large gravel parking area above the springs, but no sign. Nude bathing is the common practice. There are no facilities of any kind here, so users are urged to carry out all trash and respect the delicate sanitation situation. The nearest outhouses are at Blue Pool. As with all hot springs in Oregon within easy reach of population centers (this one is right below busy Hwy. 58), users are urged to be wary. Daylight soaks

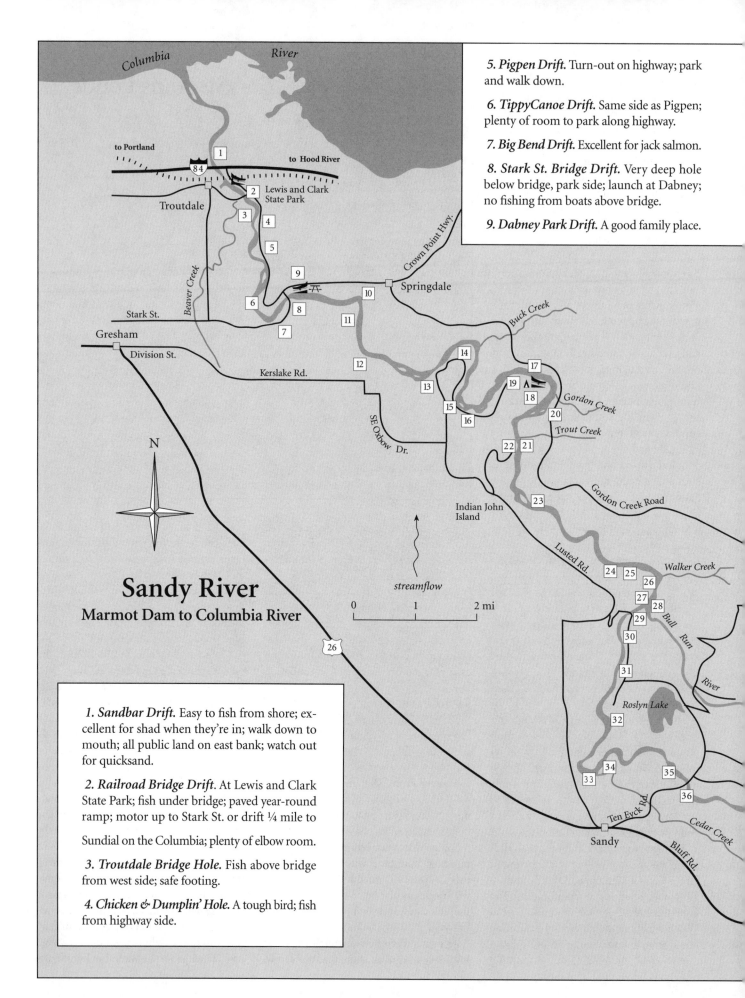

Sandy River

Marmot Dam to Columbia River

N

streamflow

0   1   2 mi

5. Pigpen Drift. Turn-out on highway; park and walk down.

6. TippyCanoe Drift. Same side as Pigpen; plenty of room to park along highway.

7. Big Bend Drift. Excellent for jack salmon.

8. Stark St. Bridge Drift. Very deep hole below bridge, park side; launch at Dabney; no fishing from boats above bridge.

9. Dabney Park Drift. A good family place.

1. Sandbar Drift. Easy to fish from shore; excellent for shad when they're in; walk down to mouth; all public land on east bank; watch out for quicksand.

2. Railroad Bridge Drift. At Lewis and Clark State Park; fish under bridge; paved year-round ramp; motor up to Stark St. or drift ¼ mile to Sundial on the Columbia; plenty of elbow room.

3. Troutdale Bridge Hole. Fish above bridge from west side; safe footing.

4. Chicken & Dumplin' Hole. A tough bird; fish from highway side.

Columbia River

to Portland

to Hood River

Troutdale

Lewis and Clark State Park

Beaver Creek

Stark St.

Gresham

Division St.

Kerslake Rd.

Crown Point Hwy.

Springdale

Buck Creek

SE Oxbow Dr.

Gordon Creek

Trout Creek

Indian John Island

Gordon Creek Road

Lusted Rd.

Walker Creek

Bull Run River

Roslyn Lake

Ten Eyck Rd.

Cedar Creek

Bluff Rd.

Sandy

10. Fill Your Waders Drift. A long cast, hard to fish; boats only.

11. Good Plunking Hole.

12. Springdale Hole. Fish from north bank at leaning log; boats only.

13. Collins Hole. Good plunking; drift fish tailout; boats only.

14. YMCA Drift. Big long slick.

15. Hossner Drift. Deep plunking hole; tailout and 300 yds. of good drift water below.

16. Upper Hossner Drift. Good drift-fishing.

17. Sawmill Drift. Also known as Stump Hole; real good drift water; the tackle snatcher on the river; fish from north side.

18. Oxbow Launch. Park extends almost to Gordon Creek.

19. Turnaround Hole. Long drift, good boat access; watch for quicksand below Buck Creek.

20. Gordon Creek Drift. Long, deep riffle; drift it with floating lure; easy access.

21. Trout Creek Drift. This one can be waded at low water.

22. Big Rock Hole. Deep drift, good in low water; long walk in.

23. Indian John Island Drift. Good water above island, Oxbow side; walk up from Oxbow Park.

24. Butler's Eddy. Walk here from Gauge Hole; fish bottom of rough water.

25. Blue Hole. Below Gauge hole; good for spring chinook; fish tailout for steelhead.

26. Gauge Hole. Walk from Pipeline Hole (rough road); fish deep water close to bank on pipeline side.

27. Swimming Hole. Girl Scout Camp; upper end is good.

28. Pipeline Hole. Downstream from mouth of Bull Run; big deep hole, excellent for plunking or drifting.

29. Dodge Park Bridge Hole. Downstream from bridge.

30. Garbage Pit Hole. Plunking and drifting; fairly easy access and good parking.

31. Alders Hole. Long and deep; hard to get into.

32. Soapstone Drift. Fairly deep hole drifts down to gravel bar; walk up from Alders.

33. Mouth of Cedar Creek. Plunking hole on Cedar Cr. side, drift-fishing on opposite side; accessible from Cedar Cr.

34. Okie Drift. Long fast drift, good for floating lures; just above mouth of Cedar Cr.

35. Revenue Bridge. Fish south side of stream below bridge.

36. Lower Canyon Hike. Park at bridge and hike up lower canyon.

37. Airport Hole. Park on road and walk downstream into canyon.

38. Power Line Hole. Long walk in.

39. Upper Canyon Hike. Walk into canyon and fish to below dam; road parallels stream to dam.

40. Marmot Dam. Excellent bank angling access for winter steelhead; good for summer steelhead and spring chinook.

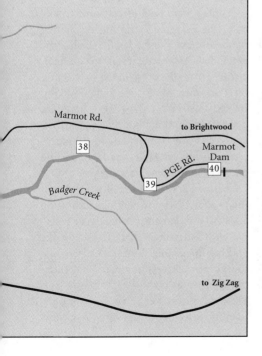

are probably safest. Weekend evenings can get rowdy here. Don't leave valuables in your car.

SANDY RIVER

An excellent steelhead and salmon river, conveniently close to Portland. Most fish are caught within an hour's drive of the city. The Sandy heads in the glaciers of Mt. Hood and flows 50 miles west to join the Columbia River at Troutdale.

At this time, the river is open to salmon and steelhead fishing from the river mouth east of Troutdale, to Marmot Dam (about 4 miles east of the town of Sandy). PGE has announced plans to remove the dam by 2005. Removal of Marmot will affect fish concentrations, influence hatchery management decisions, and change an-

gling opportunities. Stay tuned.

The river can be approached from I-84 (Lewis & Clark State Park exit), from Gresham by way of Stark Street (the Stark Street Bridge crosses the Sandy), and from the town of Sandy by way of Ten Eyck Rd. off Hwy. 26.

The Sandy has three species of salmon. The spring chinook run is the strongest, a wild population supplemented by a large hatchery component. Springers enter the river in April, and fishing holds up through June. All returning hatchery spring chinook will be finclipped by 2002, and regulations will undoubtedly change at that point to require selected harvest of finclipped chinook only. The river is closed to salmon fishing from July 15 through August 31 to protect spawning chinook.

Fall chinook appear in late August, and

the run peaks in October. These fish spawn in the lower river and are rarely seen above the town of Sandy. An annual Salmon Festival celebrating the return of fall chinook to the river takes place the third weekend in October at Oxbow Park. The Festival offers educational programs and guided tours of salmon spawning areas.

The wild coho population is very low, but finclipped hatchery coho are doing well and are available for harvest from September 1 through October 31.

Popular salmon lures used on the Sandy include small spinners, fluorescent wobblers, and Hotshots. Check current regulations for special hook and bait restrictions.

Steelhead are in the river year-round and not a month passes without a catch. Winter steelhead provide the biggest fishery by far. Fishing picks up in late November and remains very good through April. The wild run is still in decline, but hatchery returns have been good. Summer steelhead are present in force from late May through August. Only finclipped steelhead may be kept.

Sandy River steelhead average 6 pounds, but 15 pounders have been taken. Eggs, yarn, sand shrimp, and lures are all used, and in significant quantities, since this boulder-strewn river tends to be a real tackle-grabber.

Boat fishing is permitted below the powerline crossing about a mile below Oxbow Park. Above this point, plenty of good water is accessible from the bank. If you use boats as a means of transportation above the deadline, disconnect tackle while in transit.

The most popular boat drifts on the river are from Oxbow County Park to Dabney State Park, and from Dabney to Lewis and Clark State Park near the mouth, each a good day's run. The Sandy is only navigable by riverboats.

Excellent steelhead and salmon water is accessible to bank anglers throughout much of the river. From the bank at Lewis and Clark, anglers can fish the Sandbar and Railroad Bridge drifts. To reach Lewis and Clark, follow I-84 to the Lewis and Clark Exit east of Troutdale. There is also a good hole above Troutdale Bridge (off Crown Point Hwy.) that can be fished from the west bank. Crown Point Hwy. crosses the river and follows the Sandy's east bank to Springdale, providing access to Chicken & Dumplin' Hole, Pigpen Drift, Tippycanoe Drift, and Big Bend Drift. Anglers can park along the road. At Springdale, follow Hurlburt Rd. east to the road junction near Big Creek, and turn onto Gordon Creek Rd., which follows the Sandy's north bank. Gordon Creek and Trout Creek drifts can be reached off this road.

The term drift, by the way, is used in several different ways when discussing steelhead fishing in the northwest. It is used to refer to the distance covered by a day's float downstream in a riverboat (a good day's drift), or to a stretch of the river favored by steelhead (Pigpen Drift), sometimes interchangeable with the term hole. It is also used to distinguish the steelhead angler who moves from place to place on the river (drift fisherman) from the angler who fishes one spot hour after hour (plunker).

Dabney State Park offers bank access, and is a good place for non-fishing family members to play and relax. To reach Dabney, follow Stark Street east from Gresham, crossing from the south to the north bank on the Stark St. Bridge (a.k.a. Viking Bridge) just below the park. There is a good deep plunking hole below Stark St. Bridge. Above Dabney, Fill Your Waders Drift, Springdale Hole, and Collins Hole are accessible only to boat anglers.

Oxbow Park offers excellent access to many good holes and drifts, including the YMCA Drift, Hossner Drift, Upper Hossner Drift, Sawmill Drift, the Crusher Hole, and Big Rock Hole. To reach Oxbow, follow Division St. east from Gresham, turning right onto Oxbow Dr., then left on Oxbow Parkway. Keep an eye out for signs identifying a chinook spawning area with-

Steelhead can be fished in the SANDY RIVER year-round. Photograph by Mach Bachman.

in the park. This section is closed to fishing September 16 through November 15.

Dodge Park also provides outstanding bank angling opportunities. To reach the park, follow Division St. east beyond Gresham, turning right onto Oxbow Drive, then right onto Lusted Rd. at the Oxbow Parkway junction. Lusted Rd. follows the river along a high bluff, dropping down at Dodge and crossing to the Sandy's north bank. Buttler's Eddy, Blue Hole, Gauge Hole, Swimming Hole, and Pipeline Hole are all accessible from the bank at Dodge. Across the river from Dodge by way of Dodge Park Bridge, Lusted Rd. provides additional access.

There is also excellent steelhead water in the Revenue Bridge area north of the community of Sandy. From Hwy. 26 turn north onto Ten Eyck Rd., crossing Cedar Creek and following signs to the ODFW Hatchery. Park in the lot and walk down to the river to fish a good hole at the mouth of Cedar Creek. Fishing is prohibited in Cedar Creek itself. Okie Drift is just above the creek mouth, and there is often good fishing below the bridge.

Upstream there is a lot of good water available for bank fishing off a private PGE road on the north bank. Cross Revenue Bridge, turnright onto Marmot Rd. and climb Devil's Backbone, then drop down onto the PGE road, which is usually open to public use.

Shad occasionally enter the Sandy from the Columbia, usually in June if the Columbia is high. Most anglers fish for them from boats below I-84. Smelt enter the Sandy when they feel like it. Only the smelt seem to know exactly which years and when, and they aren't talking. Anglers can call the ODFW Columbia Regional Office for a smelt update in March or April. When smelt do enter the Sandy, they are caught by dipping hand nets from the bank in the area from Stark St. Bridge to the mouth, with heaviest concentration around the old Troutdale Bridge.

Trout are not stocked in the Sandy, and the river is generally too turbid for good trout fishing.

The only campground on the lower Sandy is at Oxbow County Park. Other parks along the river have picnic facilities only. Additional campgrounds are available in Mt. Hood National Forest off Hwy. 26.

River gauge readings are available. For

The SANDY RIVER is an hour's drive, and a world away, from Portland. Photograph by Mark Bachman.

fish counts over Marmot Dam, call the PGE Fish Line. See Appendix.

SANTIAM RIVER. A 12-mile flow from the confluence of the North Santiam and South Santiam rivers east of the town of Jefferson, to the Willamette River a mile upstream from Buena Vista. It is fished for spring chinook, summer steelhead, and smallmouth bass.

Summer steelhead (a finclipped all-hatchery run) begin move through the mainstem from mid-April through June or mid-July, with peak catches in June and July. Winter steelhead (all wild) are present from March through May. Only finclipped steelhead may be kept. Chinook are in the river from May through October, with peak catches in May and June. The mouth of the Santiam is an outstanding spot for spring chinook.

Smallmouth bass are fished from Crabtree Creek on the South Santiam to the mainstem mouth. Look for them in pockets where they can hold out of the main current, such as slots in the riprap.

This is primarily a boating river, though anglers do fish from the bridge at the Jefferson Boat Ramp (for chinook and steelhead) and at the I-5 crossing (steelhead and chinook plunking).

Boaters launch at Jefferson and at the I-5 Rest Area ramp. Jet boats are popular for the fishery between the I-5 ramp and Buena Vista. The fish count over

Willamette Falls can be informative for fishing the Santiam. See Appendix. It takes about 12 days for salmon and steelhead to reach the Santiam after passing the falls.

SANTIAM RIVER, MIDDLE. A fine trout stream whose access is severely limited by the whim of industrial timberland owners in the lower reach, and by landslide damaged forest roads in the upper. This major tributary of the South Santiam flows 30 miles to the Foster Dam pool, where it forms the northeast arm of the reservoir. Only a few miles above Foster, its flow is obstructed by Green Peter Dam to form Green Peter Lake with Quartzville Creek.

Above Green Peter, the Middle Santiam flows free for about 20 miles, where it currently serves as a virtual wild trout sanctuary. Rainbows and cutthroat average 6 to 9 inches, with fish to 15 inches present. Most of the larger fish are in the lower reach of this section.

Access to the lower river is restricted by the current owners of the timberland through which it flows (Giustina Resources of Eugene). At this writing, the Giustina road leading to upper Green Peter and following the Middle Santiam upstream is closed to both vehicle and foot traffic except on weekends during hunting season (which generally overlaps a couple of weeks with trout season) the last two weeks of October. Check state hunting regulations and call Giustina for verification

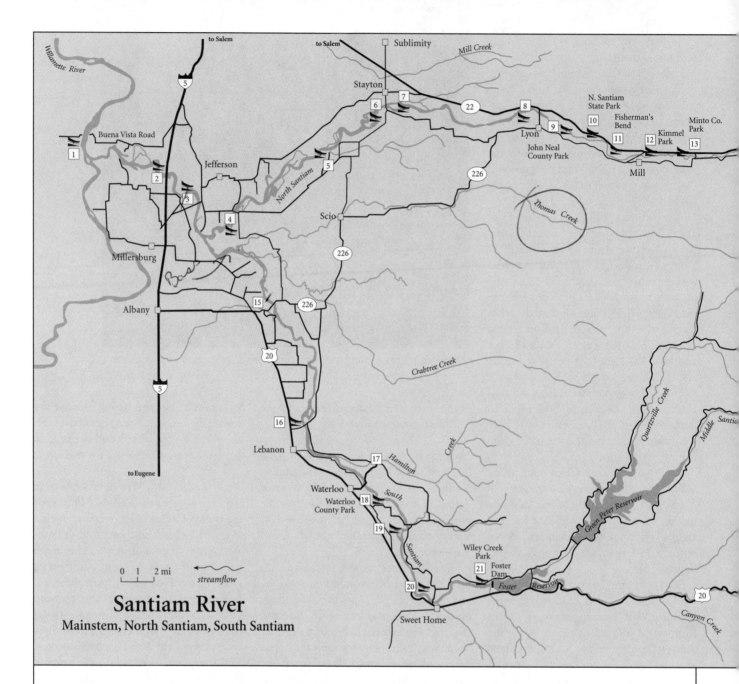

Santiam River
Mainstem, North Santiam, South Santiam

0 1 2 mi   ← *streamflow*

1. Buena Vista Ferry. Improved ramp, popular take-out for drift from I-5 ramp; beware of strong current immediately downstream.

2. I-5 Ramp. Access through freeway rest area; good smallmouth water here to mouth; take out at Buena Vista.

3. Jefferson Boat Ramp. Improved ramp with good bank angling from bridge for chinook and steelhead among rock ledges.

4. Green's Bridge. Public boat and bank access from gravel bar; popular drift for winter steelhead in March and April to confluence with So.

5. Buell Miller Boat Ramp (Shelburn). Improved ramp, limited parking; beware of impassable log jams in main channel; channel braiding; 7 miles to next take-out.

6. Stayton Bridge. Improved public ramp at south end of bridge for easy 5 mile drift to next take-out; good chinook holding water; some bank angling on north side.

7. Stayton Island. Tricky take-out; in high flows use wooden slide to portage over upper and lower Bennet dams; otherwise, check with City of Stayton Police for key to old water supply bridge access from right channel.

8. Mehama Bridge. Fish above bridge on south bank and good water upstream a half mile; paved ramp on south side accesses 7 mile drift to Stayton Is. with many holes and drifts; verify accessibility of next take-out.

9. John Neal County Park. Easy one-mile drift from improved ramp to Mehama; good holes with bedrock ledges near mouth of Little North. Santiam; good bank access for all fisheries.

10. Unimproved launch. From gravel road west of parking lot; drift 1+ miles to Neal Park or 2+ miles to Mehama Bridge (intermediate boaters); good bank access for summer steelhead, spring chinook, stocked rainbows.

11. Fisherman's Bend. BLM park, campground, good ramp; prior to park opening, launch boats off bank west of park entrance; drift 4 miles to next take-out (moderately experienced boaters); good bank access for summer steelhead, spring chinook.

12. Kimmel Park. Pole slide put-in and winch take-out; falls below boatable in high water only; old dam hole attracts chinook, steelhead, trout.

13. Minto County Park. Take-out only suitable for rafts; good bank access for salmon and steelhead

14. Packsaddle County Park. Concrete slab launch; rough rapids for experienced boaters only; next take-out 4½ miles at Kimmel on south side; bank angling at lower end of park for summer steelhead, chinook in June and July.

15. Sanderson's Bridge. Gravel bar access at end of old highway right-of-way; get key to gate from Linn Co. Road Dept.; bank angling above and below bridge; drift 10 mi. to Jefferson beyond North Santiam confluence.

16. Gill Landing. Seldom used ramp above Grant. St. Bridge; shallow drift over gravel bars.

17. Lebanon Dam. Popular bank angling for spring chinook mid-May to mid-June.

18. Waterloo County Park. Last developed take-out before Lebanon Dam; good bank fishing above bridge where fish hold below cascade upstream from ramp.

19. McDowell Creek. Private fee-pay access to unimproved gravel bar upstream of bridge; next take-out 4 miles at Waterloo.

20. Sweet Home Boat Ramp. Steep improved ramp at south end of Pleasant Valley Bridge; next take-out a slow 6 miles to McDowell Creek; good bank fishing chinook hole downstream of bridge; park along highway.

21. Wiley Creek Park. Intensive bank fishery for heavy concentrations of summer steelhead below Foster Dam April to August; winter steelhead March-April; spring chinook May to August; improved ramp accesses most popular drift on river.

before setting out.

To reach this private road head north off Hwy. 20 at a spot designated Cascadia Dam site on the Willamette National Forest map (about 1½ miles west of Cascadia State Park). This road leads to the south bank of Green Peter. Turn east at the reservoir and continue about 7 miles before crossing to the north bank at the upper end of the dam pool. The private road closely follows the Middle Santiam about 6 miles upstream, providing access to good trout water.

At other times of the year, the only way to access this section of the river is to boat in from Green Peter. Tie up at the upper end of the reservoir, check in at the care-

taker's trailer at the head of the lake, and obtain a permit to hike along the stream. The caretaker is generally on duty during trout fishing season and during hunting season. To make arrangements in advance, call Giustina Resources. See Appendix.

Above the Giustina property, the river flows through a 7-mile roadless area, a wooded canyon that beckons adventurous anglers. The river heads in the Three Pyramids area southwest of Mt. Jefferson Wilderness, Willamette National Forest.

Near its headwaters, the river is again accessible. Forest Rd. 2041, which heads north from Hwy. 20 at Upper Soda (a mile past Fernview Campground) used to cross the river, but was closed about 2 miles from the river after a massive landslide in 1996. The Forest Service has established a trail to the river which begins 200 yards back from

the road closure, bypassing a steep portion of the blown road. There is some very nice fly fishing water near the old road crossing, with broad flat banks and good gravel. Forest Rd. 2047 heads north from Hwy. 20 at House Rock Camp, following Sheep Creek and meeting the river below Iron Mt. Lookout. This road follows the Middle Santiam about 3 miles downstream. These roads are snowbound until May or June.

The only developed campground on the Middle Santiam is on the north bank of Green Peter, but there are natural campsites in the Willamette National Forest along the upper river.

SANTIAM RIVER, LITTLE NORTH. An accessible little fork of the North Santiam, with a good run of wild winter steelhead for its size, finclipped summer steelhead,

The NORTH SANTIAM is a favorite of fly fishing steelheaders. Photograph by Dan Reynolds

and wild rainbow and cutthroat trout.

It enters the North Santiam at Mehama, about 30 miles east of Salem off Hwy. 22. A paved road up Little North soon turns to gravel, following the river into Willamette National Forest, where it becomes Forest Rd. 2207. Road access ends at a locked gate about 4 miles above Shady Cove. The area above the gate is known as "Jaw Bone Flats." Best trout fishing is in the upper reaches of the stream. Trout fishing is catch and release.

The Little North wild winter steelhead run arrives in November and provides catch and fishing through March. Finclipped strays from the North Santiam hatchery program (now discontinued) may be available through 2001. There is no summer steelhead hatchery program on the Little North but there are usually a good number of strays from the North Santiam, especially in June and July. All non-finclipped steelhead must be released unharmed. The river is closed for chinook.

There is a campground at Shady Cove on the river road. There are also undeveloped sites along the stream within the National Forest.

SANTIAM RIVER, NORTH

One of two equally productive forks of the Santiam River, with popular fisheries for summer steelhead, spring chinook, and wild trout. Wild winter steelhead may be fished catch and release, and the remnants of a hatchery stocking program will be available for harvest through 2001. Over 60 miles long, this major tributary of the Willamette River is easily accessible from boat or bank, providing good angling the year-round.

North and South Santiam meet near Jefferson, east of Hwy. 99E about 5 miles north of Albany, 12 miles from the Willamette confluence. Salmon and steelhead are confined to the river below Big Cliff Dam, which forms Detroit Reservoir. The lower river is followed east by the Jefferson-Stayton Rd. Upstream from Stayton, Hwy. 22 follows the river to within 8 miles of its headwaters at Santiam Lake in the southern Marion Lake Basin of Mt. Jefferson Wilderness, Willamette National Forest.

Steelhead are in the river between the mouth and Big Cliff Dam year-round. There are no steelhead above Detroit Reservoir. The summer run is totally hatchery generated and finclipped. Good numbers are present from May through October, with peak presence in June and July. A hatchery program for winter steelhead has been discontinued, but finclipped winter fish will return through 2001. The hatchery run enters the river in November. Wild winter steelhead begin entering the river in December, with peak numbers moving through the system from February through May. The river is open for steelheading year-round, but non-finclipped steelhead must be released unharmed.

The North Santiam is a favorite river for fly fishing steelheaders. Summer steelhead feed like trout once they've made themselves at home, and anglers often can tempt them using a floating greased line, skating steelhead flies on the surface. Naturals on the river include stoneflies, caddis, green drakes, and mayflies. Popular steelhead flies include the Purple Matuka, Green-Butted Skunk, Macks Canyon, and Golden Demon. Bait anglers use small clusters of salmon eggs, sand shrimp, crayfish, and nightcrawlers. Popular lures include cork drifters (pink pearl, red, and chartreuse), blue and green finish spoons, and French blades. Lighter gear is appropriate for the summer fishery here, as the river is usually low and clear.

Despite a lengthy open fishing season, spring chinook generally reach the North Santiam in mid-May, with peak catches through June. Most fishing takes place in the area from Stayton upstream to Mill City. Most are of hatchery origin and are finclipped. The average catch is 15 pounds, with many considerably larger. Look for them in deep pools and eddies near suitable (low gradient) spawning areas, and in deeper riffles. Large gobs of eggs, Steelies, and Hotshots can all be effective under different conditions. Good fishing can occur both as the river is rising and when it begins to drop after a rain. The best indicator of chinook availability is the fish count at Willamette Falls. Large numbers over the falls mean large numbers moving into the Santiam about 12 days later.

Trout are no longer stocked in the North Santiam, but there's fair fishing for wild rainbows and cutthroat below Detroit Reservoir, and better fishing above it, particularly in the area above the community of Elkhorn. At this time, all trout fishing from the mouth to Big Cliff Dam is catch and release. Above Detroit Reservoir, where there are no wild juvenile steelhead that might be taken mistakenly as trout, anglers can keep a few for the pan, and there are some fish of good size here. The water above Marion Forks is especially productive for fly fishing. Above the last highway bridge in the Big Meadows area, small wild cutthroat are available, as well as brook trout that migrated from the lakes above. ODFW encourages anglers to catch and keep as many brook trout as possible. Late season angling in this section is usually productive.

The North Santiam is boatable from Big Cliff Dam to the mouth, but the river is laced with formidable rapids, and boating experience and advance scouting are recommended. See the accompanying map for public boat ramps. Popular one-day drifts include Packsaddle County Park to Kimmel (rough rapids below Packsaddle), Fishermen's Bend to North Santiam State Park, State Park to John Neal Park or Mehama Bridge, Stayton Bridge to Buell Miller, and Green's Bridge to Jefferson.

Bank anglers have good access to salmon and steelhead at Packsaddle Park, Minto Park, Kimmel Park, Mill City Bridge (check regulations for special closures there), Fishermen's Bend, North Santiam State Park, John Neal Park, Mehama Bridge, Stayton Bridge, and Green's Bridge.

Below Detroit Reservoir, camping facilities are available at Fishermen's Bend BLM Recreation Area west of Mill City. There are Willamette National Forest campgrounds at Detroit Lake, and off Hwy. 22 east of Idanha at Whispering Forks and Marion Falls. River gauge readings are available. The fish count over Willamette Falls can be informative for fishing here. See Appendix. It takes about 12 days for salmon and steelhead to travel between the falls and the Santiam.

SANTIAM RIVER, SOUTH

One of two equally popular and productive forks of the Santiam River, with strong runs of hatchery summer steelhead and hatchery spring chinook. The South Santiam joins the North Santiam near Jeffer-

son, about 5 miles north of Albany, 12 miles from the Willamette confluence. It flows about 80 miles from its headwaters in Willamette National Forest, interrupted by a dam east of Sweet Home that creates Foster Reservoir.

Hwy. 20 roughly follows the river from Albany to Sweet Home, with river crossings on Hwy. 226 east of Albany, at Lebanon on the Grant St. Bridge, and at Sweet Home on the Pleasant Valley Bridge. Above Foster Reservoir, Hwy. 20 follows the river very closely to its headwaters.

Summer steelhead offer the most popular sport on the South Santiam. A hatchery fishery (virtually all finclipped and available to keep), summers are in the river year-round, with heavy catches made from April through October or until the water level gets too high for successful fishing. The run peaks in June and July, but ODFW operates a steelhead "recycling" program that traps fish at Foster Dam and releases them as far downstream as Pleasant Valley boat ramp to allow anglers a second

chance. The river's winter steelhead are a wild run, present from January through May. All non-finclipped steelhead must be released unharmed.

Both summer and winter steelhead returning from sea after two years average 8 pounds, while three year salt steelhead weigh in at about 12 pounds. Steelhead to 15 pounds are not uncommon. Sand shrimp and salmon eggs are the most common bait, with drift fishing techniques effective when the river is low. Fly fishing for steelhead is popular on the South Santiam. Favorite flies include the Green Butted Skunk and Muddler Minnow.

Most steelhead angling takes place in the Sweet Home and Foster Dam areas. The most popular bank fishery is at Wiley Creek Park below Foster, where heavy concentrations of anglers fish heavy concentrations of steelhead from March to August.

The South Santiam's hatchery chinook program continues to thrive (there are no wild chinook in the river). Chinook are

Virtually all summer steelhead on the SOUTH SANTIAM are finclipped and available for harvest. Photograph by Dan Reynolds.

The SOUTH SANTIAM is a good choice for novice river boaters. Photograph by Jerry Korson.

present from April through October, with peak catches in May and June. The season closes August 15. The most popular chinook fisheries (with access from bank and boat) are at the Cable and Waterfall holes below Foster Dam from May through August, downstream from the Pleasant Valley Bridge at Sweet Home, and below Lebanon Dam from mid-May to Mid-June. The chinook average 13 to 17 pounds, with fish to 30 pounds available.

Favorite angling techniques include bobbers and jigs, and back-bouncing eggs or egg and shrimp combinations. When back-bouncing, Corkies or Spin-N-Glos are used to float the set-up, which usually includes 4 to 5 ounces of weight on about 8 inches of leader. Smaller baits are usually best when the water is running fast. Boat anglers pull Hot Shots for steelhead and Kwikfish-type lures for chinook.

The South Santiam is a popular river for drift boats and jet sleds. Its less challenging whitewater makes it especially good for beginning boaters. Boat ramps are available at Wiley Creek Park (accessing the most popular drift on the river), and at Sweet Home on the south end of Pleasant Valley Bridge. There are fee-pay gravel bar access sites at Sanderson's Bridge 10 miles south of Jefferson and at McDowell Creek. Boaters can take out at Waterloo-Linn County Park right before Lebanon Dam.

Wild cutthroat are available for catch and release fishing above Foster Dam. Fly fishing is very good up here, with light gear a necessity for all angling later in the season.

Smallmouth bass are in the river from Thomas Creek downstream about 4 miles. Look for them along rocky banks in light current. Bank angling in this stretch of the river is restricted due to private land holdings, but boat anglers reach the fishery in jet sleds or by putting in at Sanderson's and drifting to Jefferson. The average smallmouth weighs a pound.

Camping facilities are available at Foster Reservoir, at Cascadia 5 miles east of Foster, and at four campgrounds on Hwy. 20 in the Willamette National Forest (Trout Creek, Fernview, House Rock, and Yukwah). There are wheelchair accessible piers at Yukwah and downstream from Fern View Camp.

River gauge readings are available. The fish count over Willamette Falls can be informative. See Appendix. It takes about 12 days for salmon and steelhead to reach the Santiam after passing the falls.

SANTOSH SLOUGH. A Columbia River Slough off Multnomah Channel, offering good fishing for bass and panfish. Take Hwy. 30 through Scappoose, turn right at the airport sign, then left onto Honeyman Rd. The slough access is beyond the airport and the gravel operation. Park at the metal dike gate, and walk in along the dirt road. Vehicle access has been closed due to abuse of the site. A 2000 ft. bank area is open to the public.

There are crappie, bass, perch, and bullhead catfish here, with some crappie to three quarters of a pound and bass to 2 pounds. Rafts and canoes are best suited to the narrow slough, though boats occasionally squeeze in from Multnomah Channel.

SCAPPOOSE BAY. A popular access to Multnomah Channel and the Columbia River, lightly fished for bass and panfish. The bay is near the Channel's confluence with the Columbia, mid-way between the towns of Scappoose and St. Helens. It is fed by several Columbia County creeks, including Scappoose, Honeyman, Milton, and McNulty.

Follow Hwy. 30 west of Portland and north toward St. Helens. About 7 miles north of Scappoose, look for the green public boat ramp sign, cross the railroad tracks, and turn left onto Old Portland Rd. Scappoose Bay Marina is on the right, a large paved facility with plenty of parking.

The bay is home to a good number of warmwater fish, including largemouth bass, crappie, bluegills, brown bullheads, perch, and lots and lots of carp. Heading down-bay from the boat ramp, there is good structure to explore on the way to the Channel, including docks, pilings, and old log rafts along the bay's western shore. The mouths of McNulty and Milton creeks are also good spots. Bluegills and crappie are most frequently found around the marina docks and pilings and by the burnt log dump downstream from the marina. Smallmouth can be found near the brushy shore. Catfish are everywhere. If your line hits bottom, you'll probably catch a catfish.

Impressive schools of carp cruise throughout the bay, moving into the shallows to spawn. They make good bait for the bay's large population of crayfish. Perch school up in spring and mid-summer. Look for them around log rafts and *dolphins* (pilings wired together, traditionally used to tie-up log rafts). There is a sturgeon hole at the bay's mouth.

Scappoose Bay is tidally influenced, which becomes very apparent when the water's low. Some anglers claim bass fishing is best on the high slack tide. Bass are most active when the water temperature is between 65 and 72 degrees. Though the boat channel is dredged regularly, the rest of the bay can get very shallow and warm. Crayfish are large and plentiful and are a favorite bass bait. A number of bass tournaments take place here each year, but most contestants do their fishing in Multnomah Channel or the Columbia.

Upstream of the marina, the bay is too shallow for motor boats but offers pleasant canoe and kayak cruising in the company of blue herons, bald eagles, otters, and muskrats. The shoreline is rural bucolic and includes a piece of state-owned oak bottomland on the east shore.

A little bank fishery off the short nature trail downstream from the marina can accommodate a dozen anglers, and a generous landowner up-bay and adjacent to the marina property allows fishing from the banks along his pasture. (Be a considerate guest; clean up after yourself and less considerate others.) A public fishing dock is under consideration. Fishing from the marina docks is prohibited at this time.

A store and deli at the marina has been an on-again, off-again concession. Don't count on it. Supplies are available in Scappoose and St. Helens.

SCAPPOOSE CREEK. A six-mile flow from the confluence of North and South Scappoose creeks, through private property and into Scappoose Bay. The creek and its tributaries support wild cutthroat and very small numbers of winter steelhead, coho, and chinook. The creek and its tributaries are closed to all salmon and steelhead angling, but offer catch and release fishing for wild cutthroat using artificial flies and lures.

North Scappoose Creek is a pretty, high-gradient stream flowing southeast through industrial and BLM timberland from the Nehalem Mountains near Vernonia. It is followed closely by the Scappoose-Vernonia Rd. A fish ladder at Bonney Falls about 4½ miles northwest of Scappoose allows salmon and steelhead access to spawning grounds in the upper stream. South Scappoose Creek, the most productive of the two forks, is followed west by Dutch Canyon Rd. It is a low-gradient stream flowing through agricultural land. The only way to reach good fishing water is through private property. Ask permission to gain access.

SCOGGINS CREEK. A fair early-season trout stream in the Tualatin River watershed south of Forest Grove. It heads in the coast range near the Tillamook Co. line and flows east 13 miles, one drainage south of Gales Creek. It's a major inlet for Hagg Lake and is the reservoir's outlet stream.

Scoggins supports wild cutthroat, which may be fished catch and release using artificial flies and lures. A gravel logging road follows it upstream quite a ways. Angling usually slows by June, and the creek gets quite low in late summer.

The lower section is crossed near the mouth by Hwy. 47 about 4 miles south of Forest Grove and is followed upstream by a good road. Trout run 6 to 11 inches.

SCOTT LAKE. Two connected lakes (18 and 26 acres) off McKenzie Hwy. 242, offering good trout fishing and a beautiful view of the Three Sisters. Stocked cutthroat average 10 to 12 inches, with some larger. There is a primitive campground here and some good walk-in campsites. Scott makes a good base camp for day hikes to Benson and Tenas lakes. Campers Lake is just up the road.

SCOUT LAKE. (Jefferson Park).A good lake in a beautiful natural alpine park at the base of Mt. Jefferson. See Bays Lake for trail directions into the park. Scout Lake is a quarter mile east of Bays Lake.

Seven acres and 30 ft. deep, it is stocked by air with fingerling brook trout. These fish are not easily caught, but they run to 3 pounds. Try a grasshopper in late August. Heavy use has impacted the land along the lakeshore, and camping is discouraged within 100 feet of the shore to allow regeneration of fragile vegetation.

SEPARATION LAKE. A relatively isolated 5-acre brook trout lake in Three Sisters Wilderness. From McKenzie Bridge on Hwy. 126 east of Eugene, take the Horse Creek Rd. Forest Rd. 2638 southeast 8 miles to Roney Creek. A trail from there leads about 7 miles to the lake.

Separation Lake had good angling for 10 to 14 inch brook trout. A few trout 18 inches or more have been taken. It can be easily fished from shore. Natural campsites are available.

SERENE LAKE. A 20-acre hike-in brook trout and rainbow lake at 4350 ft. in the western part of the High Rock area of the upper Clackamas watershed. Trail 512 begins at Frazier Forks Campground and winds past the Rock Lakes. For detailed directions to the trailhead see Rock Lakes.

Signs point the way for the easy 3 mile hike west to Serene.

Serene is stocked with brook or rainbow trout, which are usually present in good numbers. Fish run 6 to 15 inches. All methods can be effective depending on the season. Bait or lure fishing is best in early season, and fly fishing is best in late summer and fall. There are good natural campsites. Some pasture is available if you're on horseback. The road is snowbound until late June.

SHARPS CREEK. A small trout stream flowing into the Row River at Culp Creek, about 5 miles upstream from Dorena Reservoir. It's about 12 miles long. To reach it, turn east on the Row River Rd. from 99W at Cottage Grove. At the creek crossing, a gravel road follows the stream south to its head. Sharps has a good population of wild cutthroat, available for catch and keep angling. Check the regulations for season and limits.

SHEEP LAKE. One of the three Firecamp Lakes northwest of Mt. Jefferson near the head of the South Fork of the Breitenbush River. See Firecamp Lakes for directions. Only Sheep and Claggett are stocked with brook trout by air. There are good huckleberries up here.

SHELLROCK CREEK. A small accessible trout stream in the upper Clackamas drainage. Shellrock flows south from the High Rock area and enters the Oak Grove Fork several miles above Harriet Lake.

From Estacada, follow Hwy. 224 to Ripplebrook Ranger Station. From there take Forest Rd. 57 up the Oak Grove Fork. About 2 miles east of Harriet Lake, this road crosses the mouth of Shellrock Creek and turns north to follow it upstream. At this point the road becomes Forest Rd. 58, and you'll almost immediately pass Shellrock Creek Campground. It's 38 miles from Estacada to this point. Shellrock Rd. follows the creek's east bank up to High Rock.

The stream has wild cutthroat 6 to 10 inches, as well as a few brook trout that drift down from the lakes above. There are campgrounds at both ends of the creek. Trout fishing is catch and release.

SHELLROCK LAKE. A very pretty, popular 20-acre brook trout lake in the High

Rock lakes area. It can be accessed by a good but steep trail one mile south of Frazier Forks Campground or (easier) from Hideaway Lake to the south. See Hideaway Lake for directions. Shellrock is ½ mile north of Hideaway by Trail 700, which circles Hideaway Lake.

Rainbow, cutthroat, and brook trout are stocked. The lake is fished hard but manages to produce a lot of fish 6 to 13 inches. Shellrock is a shallow lake, and fly fishing is very good mornings and evenings. Wet flies retrieved slowly often work well. Bait angling is good at the start of the season. The lake is at 4200 ft., and snow usually limits access until mid- to late June. There are good natural campsites at the lake.

SHINING LAKE. A productive 12-acre rainbow trout lake in the High Rock area of the upper Clackamas watershed, about 55 miles from Portland.

The trailhead is a little over 3 miles west of Frazier Forks Campground on Indian Ridge Rd. The trail takes off from the north side of the road, about ½ mile before the dead-end. The lake is an easy 15-minute hike. For road directions to Frazier Forks, see Rock Lakes.

Shining is stocked with rainbow trout that grow to good size, averaging 6 to 13 inches, and there are usually plenty of them. The lake is 24 ft. deep, and all angling methods take fish. A lot of crayfish are present, and the tails attract big trout. This is a good fly lake in late fall, in fact, it is often a hot spot in general near the end of the season.

There is a campsite and spring at the lake, and a campground on the road above. This area is excellent for huckleberries.

SHORT LAKE. A small but deep brook trout lake one mile north of Breitenbush Hot Springs. To reach it, follow the Breitenbush River Rd. from Detroit to Breitenbush Campground. Take the first road to the left, then the next right. This is Forest Rd. 46-040. It heads north up the west side of Short Creek and reaches Short lake in 2 miles. You can see the lake south of the road. There used to be big brook trout to 18 inches here, but since the road came in, the size has dropped.

SILVER CREEK. (Molalla watershed) Best known for its falls, which are the featured attraction of Silver Falls State Park south-east of Silverton. It offers catch and release fishing for wild cutthroat and rainbow trout. A major tributary of the Pudding River, it flows about 25 miles from the confluence of its forks to the Pudding River west of Silverton. It is dammed near town to form Silverton Reservoir.

Silver Creek is most popularly fished within the state park, which covers almost 9,000 acres and offers many recreational opportunities as well as access to the creek and its tributaries. To reach the park from Silverton, head south on Hwy. 214 (Silver Creek Falls Hwy.).

A fair number of wild cutthroat trout are taken in both the forks and mainstem. The average catch is between 6 and 11 inches. There is also public access to the creek at Silverton City Park. Both cutthroat and rainbows are available downstream of the reservoir.

SILVERTON RESERVOIR. A 65-acre water supply reservoir on Silver Creek, source of drinking water for the town of Silverton. It is stocked with legal size trout early each season and has wild cutthroat and brown bullhead. Bank access is very limited, but non-motorized boats (and float tubes) can launch at the city park on the reservoir.

SILVER KING LAKE. A nice brook trout lake, still fairly isolated, in the upper Collawash River headwaters west of Silver King Mountain. Shortest way in is by Trail 544 from Elk Lake. It's about 4 miles by ridge walk north to the lake. See Elk Lake for road directions.

A longer but interesting approach is by trail up the Hot Springs Fork of the Collawash River. Take Hwy. 224 to the Collawash River Rd. (Forest Rd. 63). Follow this to the Bagby Hot Springs Trailhead (Trail 544). The route to the lake via the Hot Springs Fork is 8½ miles. A soak at Bagby Hot Springs (followed by an icy shower in the little falls a little further along the trail) should invigorate you for the hike, or you might fish your way along the stream. After 8 miles on Trail 544 south, you will reach a sign reading Silver King Mt. A quarter mile further, watch for a trail leading up to the lake.

The lake is only 4 acres and 8 feet deep, at about 4100 ft. There's good angling for brook trout 7 to 14 inches. All methods are effective here.

SKOOKUM LAKE. (Clackamas River watershed). A small trout lake in the headwaters of Fish Creek, southeast of Estacada. Skookum is at elevation 3800 ft. The lake has only 4 surface acres but is fairly deep.

All roads into the Fish Creek watershed are currently closed to public access while work proceeds to obliterate all but a few of the lower roads (5410, 5411, and 5412) following a series of devastating landslides in 1996. Upon completion of this work (October, 2000), the old road beds will be open to hiking, bicycling, and horseback riding. Call the Mt. Hood National Forest, Clackamas River Ranger District in Estacada or Ripplebrook Guard Station for trail information. See Appendix.

From Estacada, follow Hwy. 224 southeast to Fish Creek Campground. Turn right on Forest Rd. 54 and follow it to the end. Based on the current Mt. Hood National Forest map, the new trail will follow old Forest Rd. 54 about 1½ miles to old Forest Rd. 5420. Skookum is 20 miles farther on 5420.

The lake will continue to be stocked in odd number years, and has traditionally supported a good population of brook trout 6 to 12 inches. With its increased isolation, the lake may well offer anglers either increased quantity of fish available, or increased size of the catch. Fly fishing can be very good in late fall.

SKOOKUM LAKE. (Mid-Willamette River watershed). A private bass and panfish lake, open to the public for a fee. It is west of Champoeg State Park, 3 miles south of Newberg. From I-5, follow signs to Champoeg Park and continue west on Champoeg road. The road to the lake is on the left, about 3 miles west of the park. About 25 acres and lightly fished, it maintains the usual assortment of panfish, including bluegill, crappie, and brown bullhead. There are a few boats for rent.

SLIDEOUT LAKE. A fair brook trout lake high in the headwaters of the Breitenbush River, east of Firecamp Lakes. See Firecamp Lakes for trail directions. Slideout is a hard mile's bushwhack over the ridge to the east of the Firecamp area. It is downstream and north about ½ mile from Swindle Lake.

A fairly deep lake, Slideout is about 10 acres and lightly fished. The brook trout run 6 to 11 inches, but there may be a few sleepers. It can be fished from shore.

SMITH LAKE. (McKenzie watershed). An 8-acre brook trout lake one mile north of Irish Mt. Smith Lake is about a quarter mile southwest of McFarland Lake. See McFarland for directions. Any method will take fish here almost any time. Natural campsites are available. McFarland Lake offers more exciting fishing.

SMITH LAKE. (lower Columbia River). A 60-acre lake between Marine Drive and North Portland Rd. west of Heron Lakes Golf Course and the Multnomah County Expo Center. It is part of a wetland complex that includes the Columbia Slough, Bybee Lake, and several smaller ponds and marshes.

More a wetland itself than a lake, Smith does offer fishing for white crappie, brown bullhead, bluegill, yellow perch, and largemouth bass. Canoes can be launched from a site at the north end of the lake off Marine Drive. The wetland complex is being developed as an urban wilderness by the Portland Bureau of Parks and Recreation.

SMITH RIVER RESERVOIR. A narrow, deep reservoir in the upper McKenzie. Follow Hwy. 126 (the McKenzie) 71 miles to Carmen Bridge at Trail Bridge Reservoir. From there, turn north on Forest Rd. 730, which ends at Smith Dam.

The reservoir is stocked with legal rainbows, and fishing is usually good. Most are taken by trolling or still-fishing. They run 9 to 13 inches, though a few good size cutthroat show up in the catch, and brook trout to 12 inches are occasionally hooked.

There is a good boat ramp at the dam (speed limit 10 mph). Camping facilities are at the north end of the reservoir. Additional campsites are available at Trail Bridge Reservoir.

SPINNING LAKE. A good brook trout lake just off the road in the Breitenbush Lake area. The quarter-mile trail to Spinning begins about 1½ miles west of Breitenbush Lake, where the Pyramid Lake outlet crosses Forest Rd. 4220. See Breitenbush Lake for road directions.

Spinning Lake is only 3 acres and shallow, but it's lightly fished and holds up well. Brook trout run big, with most from 10 to 18 inches and larger. The lake loses fish in severe winters, but there are almost always some survivors. There are no campsites at the lake.

SPIRIT LAKE. A good 12-acre brook trout lake in the headwaters of Salmon Creek about 5 miles west of Waldo Lake. From Oakridge, take the Salmon Creek Rd., Forest Rd. 24, all the way up to the Black Creek Branch Rd. (Forest Rd. 2421). About ½ mile up Forest Rd. 2421, turn north on Forest Rd. 2422, and proceed 7 twisting miles to the Spirit Lake Trailhead. Trail 3584 offers an easy quarter-mile hike to the lake.

The brook trout in Spirit Lake are in good shape and average about 10 inches, with some to 15 inches. All methods can be used effectively. Recommended for introducing youngsters to fishing.

SPY LAKE. A small trout lake north of the Mink Lake Basin, well off the beaten track. See Corner Lake for directions. From Corner Lake, take Trail 3517 north one mile. Spy Lake is a quarter mile east of the trail. Only 3 acres but 20 feet deep, the lake is lightly fished, with a population of cutthroat in the 6- to 9-inch range. Nice natural campsites are available.

SQUAW LAKES. (Clackamas watershed) A series of small brook trout lakes east of the Clackamas River near Squaw Mt. The three main lakes total only about 7 acres, and all are quite shallow, at elevation 3550 ft.

From Estacada, take Hwy. 224 southeast 6 miles to North Fork Reservoir, then head east on Forest Rd. 4610, the North Fork Rd. about 14 miles. The lakes are north of the road. Twin Springs Campground is about 2 miles farther along the road, so if you miss the lakes, backtrack from there. Private property in the area may be fenced, but the western shores of the lakes are in the Mt. Hood National Forest.

All three lakes offer good fishing for naturally reproducing brook trout, 6 to 14 inches. Things can get slow here in midsummer, but fall angling is usually good. Squaw Lakes only run about 5 feet deep, so fly fishing can be effective. Weighted wet flies have hooked some big fish. There are a few natural campsites at the lakes and a campground at Twin Springs.

STILL CREEK. A very clear wild cutthroat stream in Mt. Hood National Forest, open for catch and release trout fishing with artificial flies and lures. It flows into the Zigzag River about 2 miles east of the community of Zigzag. The creek heads near Hwy. 26 in the Government Camp area and loops south of the highway to meet the Zigzag. Forest Rd. 2612 follows the creek quite closely throughout its length. The upper road is usually snowbound until late May.

The creek is not stocked with trout, but it offers fair fishing in a pristine mountain setting. Hatchery-reared summer steelhead are released near the lower end, but the creek itself isn't open to fishing for steelhead.

STURGEON LAKE. A 3500-acre bass and panfish lake in the center of Sauvie Island which was once thought to be a sturgeon spawning ground. Actually, very few sturgeon are found in the lake and surrounding water, and most are too small to keep. Roads almost encircle the lake, but you cannot drive around it because of the Gilbert River outlet at the north end. In recent years the lake has begun to silt in, and efforts to flush it with a channel from the Columbia River have been only marginally successful.

From Portland drive northwest 10 miles on Hwy. 30 to the Sauvie Island Bridge. Follow Sauvie Island Rd. north after crossing to the island. Turn right on Reeder Rd. to reach the Oak Island access to the lake, or continue on Reeder about 1½ miles past the Oak Island Junction to Coon Pt., where there is a parking area beside the road. The Point, just over the dike, offers good bank angling opportunities. Reeder Rd. continues east to the junction with Gillihan Loop Rd., then turns north, following the Columbia River toward the north end of Sauvie Island.

The west bank of Sturgeon Lake can be accessed through Game Management land at several points along Reeder. Anglers can also boat into the lake from the Gilbert River. There is a public boat ramp on Sauvie Island at the Gilbert River confluence with Multnomah Channel. From the mainland, boaters can launch at Brown's Landing (off Hwy. 30 south of Scappoose) and head downstream to the Gilbert mouth. It is about 5 miles from the Gilbert River mouth to Sturgeon Lake.

Crappie are the most abundant species in the lake, which also supports brown bullhead, perch, bluegill, and largemouth bass. Fishing off Oak Island has been especially good in recent years. Some fairly large bass are available in the shoal areas in

June and July. Anglers seem to prefer using surface plugs. Other species are primarily taken on bait, with fishing best on the incoming tide, especially near the sloughs and streams. Crappie get big here and will hit spinner and bait, or pork rind and feathered jigs.

The lake is closed to angling October 1 to April 15 to protect wintering waterfowl. You'll need a recreation permit to park on the island. Day use and seasonal permits are sold at the market north of the bridge. See also Haldeman Pond, Gilbert River, and McNary.

SUNSET LAKE. (Horse Lakes Basin). A good trout lake west of Elk Lake in Three Sisters Wilderness. The easiest route to the lake is by the Island Meadow Trail from Elk Lake Lodge. The junction with the Pacific Crest Trail is about one mile west. Follow the PCT west one mile to a side trail cutting to the north. This trail leads to Sunset Lake in about a mile, then continues to Horse Lake.

Sunset is about 40 acres and fairly shallow. It can be fished from shore using all methods. Rainbow and brook trout here average 9 to 12 inches. The lake has slow periods but is usually good. There are good natural campsites here and at other lakes to the west. Other lakes in the basin include Horse, Moonlight, Herb, Marten, Fisher, Aerial, and Mile.

SURPRISE LAKE. (Clackamas Watershed). Mt. Hood National Forest has a few Surprise Lakes. This one is south of the Clackamas River on the west side of the Fish Creek divide. The lake is about 5 acres and supports a good number of very nice rainbows. It is at elevation 4050 ft.

All roads into the Fish Creek watershed are currently closed to public access while work proceeds to obliterate all but a few of the lower roads (5410, 5411, and 5412) following a series of devastating landslides in 1996. Upon completion of this work (October, 2000), the old road beds will be open to hiking, bicycling, and horseback riding. Call the Mt. Hood National Forest in Estacada or Ripplebrook Guard Station for trail information.

From Estacada, take Hwy. 224, southeast 16 miles to Fish Creek Campground. Follow Forest Rd. 54 to its end. According to the current Mt. Hood National Forest map, the new trail should follow the old

Forest Rd. 54 about 6 miles, turning left onto old Forest Rd. 5440. Follow 5440 about 7 miles to the Surprise. Distinctive Camelback Mountain is visible north of the lake across the canyon.

The fish here run 8 to 16 inches. This is a very shallow lake with little cover, so stealth is in order. On the other hand, given the long trek to get here, you may be the first human these fish have ever seen, and they may leap into the net out of curiosity.

Surprise occasionally loses fish to winterkill, but it will continue to be restocked in odd number years. There are fair natural campsites at the lake.

SURPRISE LAKE. (Olallie Area). A hike-in cutthroat lake west of the Skyline Rd. in Mt. Hood National Forest. The 2-mile trail to Surprise heads at Lower Lake Campground ½ mile north of Olallie Lake. Trail 717 reaches Surprise a quarter mile beyond Fish Lake.

Cutthroat here range 6 to 12 inches and are feisty, but there aren't a lot of them There are some fair natural campsites here, and a developed campground at Lower Lake. Skyline Road is usually snowbound until the end of June.

SWAN LAKE. A 11.8 acre hike-in lake in the Waldo Lake Wilderness northwest of Waldo Lake. It is stocked with rainbow or brook trout in alternate years, depending on what's available. It can be fished in conjunction with nearby Gander and Gosling Lakes. See Gander for Directions. To hike directly to Swan, continue on Forest Rd. 2417 past the Gander cut-off. At road's end, Trail 3570 leads about 1½ mile to Swan.

TANNER CREEK. Best known as an access point for bank anglers fishing the Columbia below Bonneville. About 8 miles long, it flows directly into the Columbia about 41 miles east of Portland off I-84. A dirt road follows it upstream several miles, and a trail continues beyond that point.

The mouth of Tanner Creek offers one of the few bank access points for the Columbia system's shad fishery. Anglers walk down to the creek from the Bonneville Dam access road. Shad usually appear in May.

Tanner is open for steelheading below the railroad bridge. Check Columbia River Regulations for season dates. The creek has small runs of both summer and winter

steelhead, which peak in July and December. Finclipped steelhead may be kept.

The upper creek has a few wild cutthroat which can be fished catch and release with artificial flies and lures.

TEMPLE LAKE. A good hike-in trout lake in the upper North Santiam watershed west of Marion Lake. Best access is from Pine Ridge Lake by Forest Rd. 2261, the Twin Meadows Rd. south of Marion Forks. If the road is snowbound early in the season, you may have to hike up to the Scout Camp at Pine Ridge. Follow Trail 3443 east about 2 miles to a spur trail that leads north a quarter of a mile to the lake.

Temple covers 7 acres and is quite shallow. It is stocked by air with rainbow or brook trout, and fishing generally hold up well. Most catches are 9 to 11 inches, with some over 15 inches. Almost any method works, with flies a good bet early or late in the day.

TENAS LAKES. Three heavily-fished trout lakes 2 miles northwest of Scott Lake Campground on the McKenzie Pass Highway. These are especially good lakes for a family outing, only a 2-mile hike from Scott Lake Camp. Take Trail 3502 and head north from Benson Lake.

One lake has brook trout, one cutthroat, and one rainbow. Damifino which is which. They all seem to produce lots of small fish. The first or Lower Tenas is about 3 acres and quite deep. The middle and upper lakes (a bit north) are only an acre or so but are 15 to 20 ft. deep. They are usually inaccessible until late June. Recommended for youngsters.

TETO LAKE. A fair, self-sustaining brook trout lake at the northern end of the Eight Lakes Basin southwest of Mt. Jefferson. Teto is west of Chiquito, about ½ mile northeast and several hundred feet below Jorn Lake. See Jorn for trail directions.

Teto has 12 surface acres and lots of little brook trout. It's a fairly deep lake, and all methods are used with success.

THOMAS CREEK. (South Santiam watershed). A good size tributary of the South Santiam with opportunities for smallmouth bass and catch and release trout fishing. It joins the South Santiam near Scio. Thomas flows about 35 miles from the east slope of the Cascades near Mill

City. Hwy. 226 follows it from Scio to Jordan, and a gravel road continues upstream about 10 miles farther. A hiking trail follows the extreme upper end. Access is somewhat restricted.

Smallmouth bass are well established in the lower 8 miles below Scio. Wild cutthroat are fairly plentiful, and there's good fly fishing when the water warms and clears. Check the regulations for bait and tackle restrictions.

Thomas has a remnant run of fall chinook and a wild winter steelhead run that peaks in March and April, but the creek is closed to both salmon and steelhead fishing at this time.

TIMBER LAKE. A 15-acre lake in the compound of the Timber Lake Job Corps Center, open to public fishing for stocked legal rainbows and small brown bullhead. To reach it, take Hwy. 224 east from Estacada. The compound is just west of Ripplebrook Ranger Station.

TIMBER LINN LAKE. A one-acre pond in Albany City Park, stocked with legal rainbows in spring. It may have largemouth and other warmwater fish.

TIMOTHY LAKE. (a.k.a. Timothy Meadows Reservoir). A productive 1400 acre hydropower reservoir on the Oak Grove fork of the Clackamas, featuring three varieties of trout, kokanee, and quantities of crayfish. It's about 80 miles to Timothy from Portland by way of Hwy. 26 and Forest Rd. 42 (the Skyline Rd.). It can also be reached from Estacada by Hwy. 224 along the Clackamas River, a route which appears to be shorter, but is slower.

For the Skyline route, follow Hwy. 26 about 11 miles east of Government Camp, and turn west onto Forest Rd. 42 about 2 miles past the Clear Lake turn-off. Seven miles south at Joe Graham Campground, take Forest Rd. 57 about 2 miles west to the reservoir.

Timothy supports brook, rainbow, and cutthroat trout. Brook trout are very plentiful, with some over 5 pounds and challenging to catch. Catchable rainbows are stocked by the thousands beginning in May (30,000 in 1999). Kokanee provide good sport from spring through early summer. When the water warms they move down to the thermocline, and the success rate drops off. The kokanee are 8 to

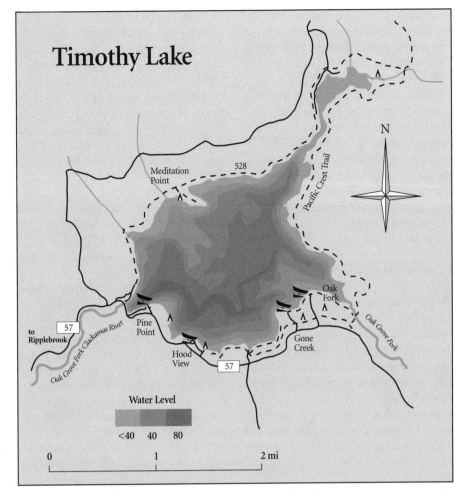

11 inches. Most angling is from boats, with bait fishing and trolling both effective. Bank anglers favor spinning gear and small lures. Fly angling can be excellent near the mouths of the tributaries in late summer and fall. Toward the end of the summer, the lake can get quite warm, and few people launch a boat in August.

The reservoir supports a large population of crayfish, which are found in all the shallows, including right off the campgrounds. Fish for them with traps baited with pieces of fish or chicken. Crayfish tails can be very tempting to the lake's big brookies.

There are 5 large campgrounds around the lake, each within sight of a boat ramp. The Pine Point ramp is usable even when the reservoir is drawn down. Meditation Point Campground on the north side can be reached only by boat or trail. Several smaller lakes are within easy hiking distance. See Dinger and Buck. Timothy has wheelchair accessible fishing facilities.

TIMPANOGAS LAKE. A very nice drive-to brook trout lake in the headwaters of the

Middle Willamette. It can be reached by road from Oakridge or Crescent Lake. Neither of these approaches is open until late June in most years. The Crescent Lake approach is a bit rougher, but quicker if you can tolerate it.

From Oakridge, drive south on Hwy. 58 a mile or so to the Hills Creek Reservoir turnoff. Follow Forest Rd. 21 around the west shore of the reservoir and up the upper Middle Willamette about 33 miles (from the dam) to Forest Rd. 2154. Take Forest Rd. 2154 about 5 miles to its junction with Forest Rd. 398/399. Follow Forest Rd. 399 ½ mile south to Timpanogas.

From the town of Crescent Lake on Hwy. 58, follow Forest Rd. 244 around the northwest shore of the lake 6 miles, turning northwest on Forest Rd. 211 (Summit Lake Rd.) and following it 6 miles to Summit Lake Campground. From the campground, follow Forest Rd. 398 about 4 miles to Timpanogas

Timpanogas is a pretty 40-acre lake at elevation 5300 ft., in a setting of thick fir forest and abundant huckleberries. It's a little over 100 feet deep near the center, with most of its shoal water near the northwest shore. It supports brook trout and is easily fished. Trolling is quite popular, but motors are prohibited, and only light-weight boats can be launched.

There's a small but pleasant campground on the southwest shore close to Lower (or Little) Timpanogas Lake, but mosquitoes can be awesome throughout much of the summer. Little Timpanogas, west of the large lake, is 7 acres and offers fair fishing for brook trout. There are several hike-in lakes to the south, and Opal Lake is a mile north and a bit off the road. See Indigo, June.

TORREY LAKE. A large lake with fair angling for rainbow and cutthroat trout in the Taylor Burn area north of Waldo Lake. To reach it, follow a one mile trail from a trailhead on the awful Taylor Burn Rd., 2 miles north of North Waldo Campground.

Torrey has 70 surface acres and can be fished from shore, but a rubber boat or float tube would help. The average catch is 11 inches. All methods are effective here, with fly angling good in the evenings. The nearest campground is Taylor Burn. It is usually accessible in late June.

TRAIL BRIDGE RESERVOIR. A 90-acre reservoir on the upper McKenzie with fishing for stocked rainbow trout. The reservoir is about 14 miles northeast of McKenzie Bridge off Hwy. 126.

Rainbow trout are the primary catch here, ranging in size 8 to 16 inches. Only finclipped trout may be kept. Most anglers still-fish or troll very slowly along the shoal areas.

A few (non-finclipped) wild cutthroat and brook trout are present, but the focus of this selective fishery regulation is the reservoir's bull trout population. Bull trout are a protected species in most Oregon waters.

There is a boat launch and wheelchair accessible fishing facilities at the north end of the reservoir adjacent to a large campground.

TRILLIUM LAKE. A very scenic trout lake on the south slope of Mt. Hood, 3 miles from Government Camp. From Hwy. 26, head south on Forest Rd. 2656 opposite the road to Snow Bunny Lodge.

Trillium is formed by the damming of the headwaters of Mud Creek. It has about 60 surface acres, lots of shoal area, and is encircled by a path. Pressure is very heavy on this drive-in lake so close to Portland.

The lake is stocked with impressive numbers of fingerling and legal rainbows for a lake of this size (16,000 catchables in 1999). The average catch is 6-14 inches. Trophy-size trout are stocked in September to winter-over and provide additional fishing enjoyment in the spring. Fly fishing is quite good in late summer and fall.

A large campground accommodates trailers. There is a boat ramp, but motors are prohibited. Youngsters can fish from the dam, and there is a fishing float at the campground that is wheelchair accessible.

TROUT LAKE. (Confederated Tribes Warm Springs). See Central Zone.

TUALATIN RIVER. A meandering valley stream, flowing east about 75 miles out of the coast range and across populous Washington County. It enters the Willamette River several miles upstream of Oregon City. The Tualatin is fed by a number of good tributaries, including Gales, Dairy, and Scoggins creeks. At this time, it offers fishing for bass and panfish, catch and release fishing for trout, and opportunities to harvest a final stocking of finclipped steelhead and coho.

The river is crossed and followed by many roads southwest of Portland and in the Hillsboro-Forest Grove area.

Best fishing opportunities are for bass and panfish in the low, slow valley reaches. Fish from road and bridge easements, and at city parks in Tigard and Tualatin. Best trout fishing is in the upper river above Gaston, which is on Hwy. 47 south of Forest Grove, but this part of the river is almost inaccessible due to private land holdings. Fishing for trout is catch and release with artificial flies and lures.

The Tualatin has a small run of wild winter steelhead. A steelhead hatchery program has been discontinued. The last stocking was in 1998 in the vicinity of Cherry Grove Bridge and in Gales Creek below Hagg Lake. Finclipped coho are also available. Best fishing for both species is in November and December.

The Tualatin is increasingly popular as a flat water canoe route through a rural and semi-rural landscape, including the Tualatin River National Wildlife Refuge. Put-ins and take-outs are mostly unofficial (bridges and parks) or with landowner permission. Popular canoe access points include Rood Bridge Park at the mouth of Rock Creek (off Rood Bridge Rd. south of TV-Hwy. 8), Scholls Bridge (Hwy. 210 south of Scholls Ferry Rd.), Schamburg Bridge (Elsner Rd. south of Scholls-Sherwood Rd.), Hwy. 99W bridge, Cook Park in Tualatin (off 92nd St.), Tualatin Community Park (off Tualatin Rd. via Upper Boones Ferry Rd.), Browns Ferry Park (Nyberg Lane), Rivergrove Boat Ramp (Dogwood Dr. via SW Childs and SW Marlin), Shipley Bridge (Shadow Wood Dr. off Stafford Rd.), Fields Bridge in West Linn (Borland Rd. via Dollar St. off Hwy. 212)) and Willamette Park in West Linn (12th St.).

A paddler's guide to the river is available from Tualatin Riverkeepers. See Appendix. Popular paddles are Rood to Scholls (6 hrs.), Scholls to Schamburg (5 hrs.), Schamburg to 99W (2½ hrs.), 99W to Cook Park (1 hr.) Cook Park to Tualatin Community Park (30 minutes), Tualatin to Brown's Ferry (45 minutes), and Brown's Ferry to Shipley (1 hr.) It is usually possible to easily paddle both upstream and down.

Long-suffering from the effects of intense agricultural and residential development along its banks, the Tualatin is being closely monitored by volunteer groups, including Tualatin Riverkeepers which has pioneered restoration efforts in the watershed.

TUMBLE LAKE. A fairly good 20-acre hike-in brook trout lake about 3 miles north of Detroit Reservoir at the head of Tumble Creek. Best approach is by the French Creek Rd. (Forest Rd. 2223) leading north from Hwy. 22 at Detroit. Follow it 8 miles to the Dome Rock Trail, which heads east then south to the lake.

Tumble has naturally spawning brook trout that range 6 to 11 inches. Trout are usually plentiful and can be caught using all methods. There are a few natural campsites around the lake. The outlet stream drops off a sheer cliff to the stream bed below.

TWIN LAKES. (Clackamas watershed). Two good brook trout lakes in southern Mt. Hood National Forest near the head of the Collawash River. Best approach is by trail from Elk Lake north of Detroit. See

Elk Lake for directions. The road is generally snowbound until June.

Twin Lakes are a pleasant 4-mile hike north from Elk Lake by Trail 544. The two 12-acre lakes lie in an east/west line south of Mother Lode Mt. and are connected by a stream flowing east.

They have excellent natural reproduction, with fish from 6 to 13 inches. Both lakes are deep, and all methods of angling can be effective. A float tube would be helpful. Fly angling is excellent late in the year, mornings and evenings. West Twin, which is fished most heavily, has three campsites. East Twin has one campsite. The lakes can also be approached from the north by way of Bagby Hot Springs, a 12-mile trek. See Mother Lode Lakes for trail details.

VEDA LAKE. A 3-acre hike-in lake which is very good for small brook trout. On the south slope of Mt. Hood about 5 miles south of Government Camp, it produces consistently despite its small size and accessibility. From Hwy. 26 turn south onto Forest Rd. 2613 about a quarter of a mile east of the Timberline Lodge turnoff. From Fir Tree Campground about 5 miles south, follow Trail 673 directly to the lake, an easy mile downhill.

Brook trout are stocked by helicopter, and there are a few wild trout. The catch is generally 6 to 13 inches. All methods can be used, and the lake is easily fished from shore. Bait angling is best early in the season, with fly fishing good in the fall, mornings and evenings. Wet flies or nymph patterns retrieved slowly are especially effective. There is a natural campsite at the lake. Roads usually open about the end of June.

VIVIAN LAKE. A 20-acre brook trout lake on the northwest slope of Mt. Yoran in Diamond Peak Wilderness. To reach it, hike south on Trail 3662 from Salt Creek Falls, about 4 miles.

The lake is fairly deep, at elevation 5500 ft. A float tube would be handy. It is stocked by air every few years. There are several good natural campsites. Bushwhacking ½ mile north along the lake's outlet creek will bring you to Lopez Lake, which also has brook trout and doesn't see a lot of traffic.

VOGEL LAKE. A 25-acre brook trout lake in the Mink Lake Basin west of Elk Lake.

For trail directions, see Cliff Lake and Mink Lake. Vogel is a quarter of a mile southeast of Cliff Lake, east of the Pacific Crest Trail. Quite shallow, it frequently winterkills. There is an island in the lake with the remnants of an old trapper's cabin, and there are good natural campsites around the shore.

WAHANNA LAKE. A rainbow lake within short hiking distance of Taylor Burn Campground, north of Waldo Lake. Taylor Burn Camp is 7 miles north of Waldo Lake by rough road. To reach Wahanna, follow Trail 3583 about 1½ miles south from Taylor Burn.

About 60 acres, it generally offers good fishing for rainbow averaging 10 inches and up to 4 pounds. It can be fished from shore in places, but a float tube is helpful. All methods are effective at times. Try trolling a red and white flash bait for the large fish during the day. Fly fishing is good in the evenings, especially late in the year.

WAHKEENA POND. An ODFW salmon rearing pond adjoining Benson Lake in Benson State Park adjacent to the Columbia River. It offers fishing for stocked trout and a large variety of warmwater fish. Wahkeena is the first lake on the right approaching the park. Park in the large parking lot.

First opened to public fishing in 1998, the pond supports large and smallmouth bass, black crappie, bluegills, and yellow perch. ODFW and the Oregon Bass and Panfish Club worked together to install submerged structure at the east end of the pond within casting distance of the docks. There's good natural habitat along the north shore, but little along the railroad grade. Consider releasing all warmwater fish caught here for a few more years till the populations are well established. Legal rainbows are stocked from April through June.

There are two docks (one wheelchair accessible) and an unimproved boat ramp.

WALDO LAKE. A sparkling blue gem of distilled water in an exquisite alpine setting, ranking among the purist (and least productive) waters in the world. It covers almost 10 square miles and is over 400 feet deep in places. The water is so clean that the bottom can still be seen at depths well over a 100 ft.

Waldo is usually Oregon's second largest natural lake, following Upper Klamath. Source of the North Fork of the Middle Fork of the Willamette River, it stretches along the backbone of the Cascades at the mid-point of the Oregon range. To reach it, drive about 23 miles southeast of Oakridge on Hwy. 58. At a well signed intersection, Forest Rd. 5897 forks to the northeast and follows the east side of Waldo about one mile from the lake, with three spur roads leading west to the lake. The spurs at the south and north ends have lakeside campgrounds (though the north campground is closed at this time due to fire damage). From the east, Forest Rd. 5897 leads to North Waldo Camp by way of various connecting roads from Crane Prairie, Wickiup and Davis Lakes. Trails lead into Waldo Lake from all directions.

The Oregon Bass and Panfish Club built and submerged channel cat "condos" to attract fish to the dock area at WAHKEENA POND. Photograph by Bob Judkins.

Waldo has very little natural forage to sustain the fish ODFW has stocked here since 1938, including kokanee and several species of trout. At this time, there are supposed to be a fair number of brook trout in the lake (including some to 5 pounds) and some leftover kokanee. But in a lake of over 6400 acres, it's a job finding them. Fall is definitely the best time to try, and you'll beat the mosquitoes as well.

Waldo can be fished from shore, but most angling is done from boats. Speed limit is 10 mph. Trolling is probably the most productive method, but bait angling and fly fishing are profitable when feeding fish are located. Productive areas include the shoal areas at the north and south ends. The lake is very deep, so be careful not to get below the fish. Catching is usually confined to morning and evening hours. When the wind comes up, this water gets really rough. Small boats should stay near the shoreline.

The 1996 Moolack fire reached Waldo's north shore, and camping there is restricted at this time. There are additional campgrounds on the south shore, including picturesque natural campsites on rocky promontories. But Waldo's mosquitoes are legendary, and throughout much of the season, campgrounds are almost deserted. In spring and early summer, persistent campers often take to their boats to escape the blood thirsty hordes, as mosquitoes seldom attack beyond about 100 ft. offshore. Bring lots of repellent.

WALL LAKE. A fairly good brook trout lake at the west end of the Olallie Lake group, about 100 miles from Portland by way of Hwy. 26 and the Skyline Rd. From Lower Lake Campground one mile north of Olallie Lake, take Trail 706 southwest one mile to Trail 719. Follow 719 west ½ mile to Wall Lake. Averill and Red Lakes are further west on Trail 719. Easy to fish, Wall Lake brook trout run 6 to 13 inches. Small lures or spinners usually work well, and evening fly fishing can be effective. There are good natural campsites here.

WALLING POND. An old gravel pit that is open for largemouth bass year-round and is well stocked with legal rainbows in spring and fall. It is within Salem city limits west of I-5. To reach it, follow Turner Rd. or Mission St. The lake is south of Hines St. Public access is on 16th St. north

of McGilchrist. The larger pond is private. Most anglers use bait to catch the pond's 10 to 12 inch trout. There are no facilities of any kind.

WALTER WIRTH LAKE. A trout, bass and panfish lake on the east edge of Salem. It is fed by Mill Creek and is within Cascade Gateway Park, west of I-5 at its junction with Hwy. 22. The lake can be reached from the airport road or Turner Rd. Largemouth bass, white crappie, brown bullhead, and bluegill are available as well as stocked legal rainbows and an occasional brood trout. Recommended for youngsters. Wheelchair accessible.

WALTERVILLE POND. A shallow 66-acre diversion pond for power generation east of Springfield. It supports largemouth bass, black crappie, and brown bullhead. Trout stocking, attempted one season, was discontinued when angler enthusiasm caused a local traffic jam.

WARREN LAKE. A 5-acre brook trout lake at the head of Warren Creek. The creek flows north 3 miles into the Columbia River about 9 miles west of the community of Hood River. Warren is a quarter of a mile by trail from the end of a rough road southeast of Mt. Defiance. You might want to walk the last mile of road.

To reach the trailhead, follow the directions to Bear Lake, but take Forest Rd. 2821 (to the left) at the fork, heading northeast on Forest Rd. 2820. This is where you might begin to consider the capabilities of your vehicle. At the next T-intersection, turn right, away from Mt. Defiance. The road ends in a third of a mile, and the trail heads west to Warren Lake.

Warren Lake is about 5 acres and only 8 ft. deep at elevation of 3750 ft. It is fished quite heavily, yielding good catches of small brook trout. Most of the fish are 8 to 10 inches with a few to 12 inches. All methods can be used effectively, with flies working well in late summer and fall.

There is no camp at the lake. The nearest developed campground is at Rainy Lake, 3 miles west of the Forest Rd. 2821 turnoff on Forest Rd. 2820. It is normally accessible in June.

WAVERLY LAKE. A beautiful little urban lake with an excellent bluegill population, north of Albany along Hwy. 99E. Look for

the giant wood duck (there's probably good fishing under the duck!). About 10 acres, it offers good catches but is only lightly fished. In addition to bluegill, there are largemouth bass, some crappie, catfish, and a few stocked trout in spring. The lake is easily fished from shore.

WELCOME LAKES. Two brook trout lakes in the headwaters of the Collawash River east of Bull of the Woods Lookout. Several trails lead into this area. The most direct route is by way of Elk Lake Creek Trail 559 to Trail 554, which follows Welcome Creek to the lakes. This is a hike of 3 ½ miles. To reach the trailhead, follow the Collawash Rd., Forest Rd. 63, south a twisty four or five miles past Toms Meadow to Forest Rd. 6380. Follow Forest Rd.. 6380 about 2 miles to a T-intersection where a short spur road leads in from the south. Trail 559 begins at the end of this spur.

The largest lake, Lower Welcome, is about 6 acres, and West Welcome is about 3 acres. Both are shallow and rich. Upper Welcome is only one acre and has no fish, campsites, or trail directly to it. Lower and West Welcome both have some natural reproduction, and Lower Welcome is stocked each year.

Brook trout in Lower and West run to 12 inches, averaging 8 or 9 inches. There are good populations of fish in both lakes. Fly fishing is the best method after early season. There are no campsites at West Welcome, but good campsites at Lower Welcome. The lakes are accessible in early June from the north, if you don't mind hiking through snow. However, don't underestimate the challenge of keeping track of the trail (through dense forest) when it is intermittently covered by snow.

WHIG LAKE. A brook trout lake in an area well sprinkled with good lakes. Whig is located in the Taylor Burn area north of Waldo Lake. It is ½ mile south of Taylor Butte, a prominent landmark along Forest Rd. 517 leading to Taylor Burn Campground. To reach the campground, head north from North Waldo Campground on Forest Rd. 514 to its intersection with Forest Rd. 517, then turn west on Forest Rd. 517. Both roads are rough. If you park at Taylor Butte, circle the Butte and you'll come to long, narrow Whig Lake at the west end of Torrey Lake.

Its shape makes it easy to fish from

shore. The lake covers about 17 acres and is 10 feet deep. The catch ranges 10 to 16 inches. Lures and bait are usually effective, but fly fishing mornings and evenings, especially in the fall, will really take fish. Bucktail coachman, caddis fly, mosquito, blue upright, and March brown are all good pattern choices. There's a good camp at Taylor Burn.

WIDGEON LAKE. A good 3-acre brook trout lake in the Big Meadows area east of Hwy. 22. See Fay Lake for directions. Go north past Fay a quarter of a mile, and take the blazed trail east about ½ mile past Fir Lake. Widgeon is small, but fairly deep and lightly fished. The brook trout run 8 to 13 inches. The shore is pretty brushy, so a float tube is useful. It is a good late season lake.

WILEY CREEK. A tributary of the South Santiam joining the river at Foster, east of Sweet Home. The creek is followed throughout its length by a gravel road. Wild cutthroat are present in the upper creek, but most trout-size fish in lower Wiley are juvenile steelhead. The creek is closed to steelhead angling at this time.

WILLAMETTE RIVER

WILLAMETEE RIVER: Oregon City to Columbia River. One of the few rivers in the world that offers salmon and steelhead angling in the midst of a major metropolitan area. The Willamette is the number one producer of spring chinook in Oregon. Bass and panfish are also available near islands, log rafts, and the many structures in this section of the river (bridges, sea walls, docks, pilings), as well as in the sloughs. The largest slough in this portion of the river, Willamette Slough (a.k.a. Multnomah Channel), adds 33 additional river miles to the spring chinook fishery in addition to opportunities for bass and panfish. It is treated separately in this book. See Multnomah Channel.

If the Columbia is an interstate for salmon and steelhead, the lower Willamette River is like a good four-lane highway. Most salmon and steelhead are just passing through on their way home to tributary spawning grounds or hatchery nurseries. The Clackamas River is the primary tributary of the lower Willamette, joining the Willamette north of Oregon City. The mouth of the Clackamas is a

Black crappie are attracted to the pilings along the WILLAMETTE RIVER in North Portland. Photograph by Marcia Hartman.

popular fishery for both spring chinook and steelhead. Willamette Falls, an impressive cataract spanning the river at Oregon City, creates another concentration of migratory fish and fishing activity. Acclimation pens for hatchery chinook juveniles encourage additional concentrations of returning adult salmon in the Portland metropolitan area.

In this section, the Willamette flows a quarter-mile wide and quietly powerful. Its current is fed by six major tributaries—the Coast Fork, Middle Fork, North Middle Fork, McKenzie, North and South Santiams, and Clackamas (each a major river system in itself) and by many smaller rivers and streams. These drain snow-melt from two major mountain ranges, the Coast Range on the west and the Cascades on the east (including two glacial peaks Mt. Hood and Mt. Jefferson), as well as the smaller Callapooya Mts. of Southern Oregon. The Willamette flows more than 200 miles to its meeting with the Columbia River 4 miles north of Portland.

Salmon. Spring chinook are the most highly prized fishery in this 25-mile stretch

of the river. The average weight of a 3-year old Willamette springer is 15 pounds. The earlier arriving 5-year olds average 21 pounds. Wild Willamette River spring chinook have been known to reach 53 pounds, though fish of that size have not been seen in recent years.

The majority of the Willamette's wild chinook were sacrificed to hydro-electric and flood control projects years ago. The current spring chinook population is estimated to be as much as 90% of hatchery origin. Only the McKenzie River's wild spring chinook run is still considered to be viable. To protect this valuable chinook gene pool, the spring chinook fishery throughout the Willamette is carefully monitored, and fishing has been restricted in years with estimated low returns. Once all hatchery chinook are finclipped (by 2002 if the program continues on schedule), anglers will be able to fish selectively for hatchery chinook. At that point the season may more closely resemble that of days gone by—beginning when the first fish show up and water conditions are right, and ending when the last tail turns up the

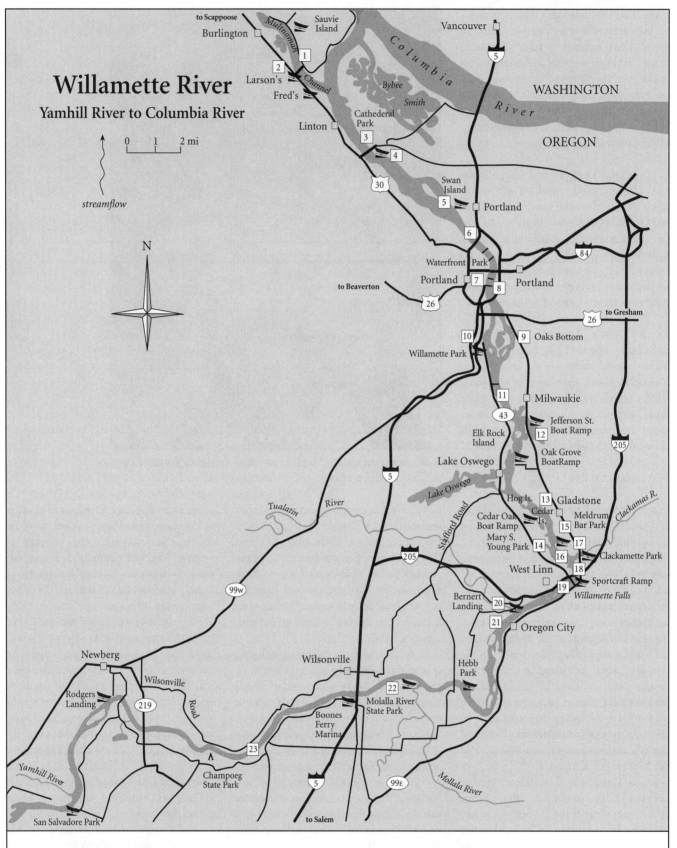

Willamette River
Yamhill River to Columbia River

0   1   2 mi

streamflow

N

to Scappoose
Burlington

Sauvie Island

Multnomah Channel

1

2

Larson's
Fred's

Columbia River

Vancouver

5

WASHINGTON

Bybee

Smith

Cathedral Park

3

Linton

4

30

Swan Island

5

Portland

6

Waterfront Park

Portland

7

8

Portland

84

to Beaverton

26

26 **to Gresham**

10

9 Oaks Bottom

Willamette Park

11

43

Milwaukie

Jefferson St. Boat Ramp

12

Elk Rock Island

Oak Grove BoatRamp

Lake Oswego

5

Tualatin   River

Lake Oswego

Hog Is.

13 Gladstone

Clackamas R.

Cedar Is.

Cedar Oak Boat Ramp

Meldrum Bar Park

15

Mary S. Young Park

14

17

16

Clackamette Park

West Linn

18

Stafford Road

205

19

Sportcraft Ramp

Willamette Falls

Bernert Landing

20

21 Oregon City

99w

Newberg

Wilsonville

Road

Wilsonville

Hebb Park

Rodgers Landing

219

Boones Ferry Marina

Molalla River State Park

22

23

Champoeg State Park

Yamhill River

5

to Salem

99E

Mollala River

San Salvadore Park

---

1. Multnomah Channel. Troll for spring chinook in less high-pressure environment; bass and panfish near submerged and floating strucures.

2. Larson's Marina. Chinook acclimation net pens attract

returning finclipped spring chinook.

3. Cathedral Park. Improved public ramps, floats, bank access for all species.

4. St. Johns Bridge Boat Ramp. Popular access to chinook

Clackamas or the ladders at Oregon City.

The first chinook appear in the Willamette in February. In March the run comes on steadily, and catching is good if the water isn't too murky. April is usually the hottest month at the Clackamas mouth, with peak numbers at Oregon City in late April and early May. Smaller numbers of chinook are often still present during the June shad run.

Most chinook anglers in this stretch fish from boats. The most popular boat fishery is from Meldrum Bar to Willamette Falls. This area includes two major chinook gathering spots—the mouth of the Clackamas, and the pool below Willamette Falls. Always an imposition to salmon and steelhead, the falls became an obstruction when a concrete lip and power turbines were installed. A large fishway on the west side of the river enables fish passage. Fish are ob-

served and counted as they swim up the fishway. A daily count of fish over the falls is available. See Appendix.

The schooling of fish at the base of the falls has resulted in the most competitive chinook fishery on the river. When chi-

nook are in, boaters at the Clackamas mouth and at Willamette Falls traditionally anchor side by side to form a "hogline." Near the falls, the water is swift and turbulent. Anglers must use caution and observe posted boat deadlines. The turbulence of

---

fisheries at mouth of Willamette and in Multnomah Channel; troll from bridge to mouth; fish pilings and log rafts for largemouth bass and panfish.

5. Swan Island. Fish current break for sturgeon; fish lagoon for panfish; best fishing downstream from cross street between Basin and Lagoon avenues and in main Willamette from Channel Ave.; floats and improved ramp on east shore of lagoon.

6. Fremont Bridge. Fish east side for sturgeon; productive hole downstream opposite Shenanigan's; best January through March.

7. Portland Waterfront. Plunk the length of the harbor wall in downtown Portland (Waterfront Park) and the sea walls on the east shore beneath freeway ramps for all species.

8. OMSI. Acclimation ponds attracts hatchery chinook; no fishing from dock.

9. Oaks Bottom. Fish from bank for plentiful bass, crappie, perch, crawfish; fish water below log booms but do not venture onto logs.

10. Willamette Park (Portland). Fish weekdays and early to avoid conflict with motor-craft enthusiasts; plunk shallow water south of ramp for bass and panfish; use float to access deeper holes; popular launch for spring chinook trolling beneath Sellwood Bridge.

11. Milwaukie to Sellwood Bridge. Productive and popular trolling for spring chinook.

12. Jefferson Street Boat Ramp. City-run ramp with some bank access for bass and panfish; cast to submerged pilings, logs, and stumps; wade to mouth of Johnson Creek during

low water for smallmouth and crappie.

13. Cedar Oak Boat Ramp to Oregon City. Productive trolling for spring chinook in less competetive atmosphere.

14. Mary S. Young Park. Bank fish for sturgeon.

15. Meldrum Bar. Most popular bank fishery on lower river for summer steelhead, spring chinook; park on gravel bar.

16. Oregon City to Meldrum Bar. Three miles of intensive trolling for summer and winter steelhead, spring chinook, and sturgeon; bank fishing in Oregon City from 99E sea wall and platform a half mile below falls.

17. Dahl Park. Access to north bank of Clackamas; productive bank fishery for summer steelhead, spring chinook.

18. Clackamette Park. Clackamas mouth very productive for summer steelhead, spring chinook, shad; don't be intimidated by the hoglines (it's your river, too).

19. Willamette Falls. Pool attracts concentrations of migrating fish and anglers; most competetive fishery on the river.

20. Bernert Landing. Adjacent to Willamette Park, West Linn; fish for sturgeon, spring chinook.

21. Rock Island Sloughs. Landing but no boat ramp; good submerged and floating structure for bass and panfish.

22. Molalla River Mouth. Steep boat ramps into Willamette; fish for winter steelhead late January through March, chinook in April; fish lower Molalla for bass, crappie, catfish.

23. Newberg to Wilsonville. Fish deep holes for sturgeon.

the water, the roaring of the falls, as well as the intense concentration of fish and anglers create a charged atmosphere here that may be unnerving to some. If you can't find a place in the line-up, or prefer a less pressurized environment, there are many other options, including the stretch between Cedar Oaks Park and Oregon City, and between Milwaukie and Sellwood Bridge.

Portland Harbor, which has been dredged to 50 feet from bank to bank to permit passage of commercial freighters, has little to offer weary salmon in search of a resting place from strong currents, but acclimation ponds at OMSI (on the east bank downstream from the Marquam I-5 Bridge) may succeed in attracting salmon back to their old nursery area. Other acclimation ponds are off Clackamas Cove on the east bank and near Larson's Marina in upper Multnomah Channel.

The best chinook bank fisheries are on the river's east bank. Clackamette and Meldrum Bar parks, respectively south and north of the Clackamas confluence with the Willamette in Oregon City, are premiere spots. To reach Meldrum Bar, turn west off Hwy. 99E onto River Rd., then head north on River Rd. to the park entrance. Anglers fish right off the parking area, from and in the vicinity of the bulkhead that extends into the Willamette, along the flats north of the bulkhead, and from the peninsula that forms the lagoon in which the boat ramp is located. To reach Clackamette Park, take Exit 9 off Hwy. 205, turning right off the exit ramp, left onto Dunes Dr. at the light, then right onto Clackamette Dr. Chinook are also taken at Dahl Park on the north bank immediately adjacent to the Clackamas mouth, from the catwalk behind the West Linn Municipal Building, from the sea wall and fishing platform at Oregon City, at the Swan Island Lagoon float in North Portland, and at Cathedral Park in North Portland. Chinook are caught at all times of the day, but many "regulars" are off the water by early afternoon.

A boat load of sturgeon for a boat load of lower WILLAMETTE anglers. Limit is one per day per angler. Photograph courtesy of John Ramsour.

Chinook boat anglers prefer to use herring and prawns as bait in early season, both fishing at anchor and trolling. Most bank anglers seem to prefer prawns or Spin-N-Glos, frequently using double hook-ups with 4 to 6 ounces of weight. Both bank and boat anglers switch to hardware later in the season. Common lures include wobblers, plugs, Clamshell Spinners, and Kwikfish-type lures.

Chinook follow the shoreline during their run upriver, generally staying within 20 ft. of the surface in the deeply dredged portion of the channel. On cloudy days, they are often found as shallow as 10 ft. Effective trollers troll s-l-o-w-l-y. Some use a spinner to gauge speed. In deep water, fish at 15 to 20 ft., just above cruising chinook. When the water is turbid, fish at 6 to 8 ft. In addition to Multnomah Channel, the most popular trolls in this section are from Milwaukie to the Sellwood Bridge, and from the St. Johns Bridge to the mouth.

Salmon follow fairly definite current movements. Anglers try to locate these routes and troll through them, or troll an S-curve through water whose current is broken by tied up ships, log rafts, and bridge abutments. Salmon sometimes lie in the slack water pocket beside or just downstream from these obstructions.

The Willamette is strongly affected by tidal flows. Best fishing is on the flood tide (toward high) and one hour on either side of low and high slack. It is possible to motor down to catch high slack, then chase it back up the river. Adjust Astoria tide readings (printed in the daily newspaper) for the lower Willamette by adding 6 hours to the Astoria time for a correct Oregon City reading, 4 hours for Sellwood Bridge angling, and 2 hours for Multnomah Channel angling.

Best chinook fishing on the Willamette is generally when the river stage level is at about 6½ ft., with clarity between 3½ and 5.2. A river clarity reading is available. See Appendix.

Sturgeon. Sturgeon provide a year-round fishery in this stretch of the Willamette, though the greatest concentration of sturgeon is found here in winter. Sturgeon of all size classes may be present, attracted to the Willamette (from the Columbia) by its relatively warmer, calmer flow and by its abundant supply of resident forage (crayfish and freshwater clams). January through March is considered to be

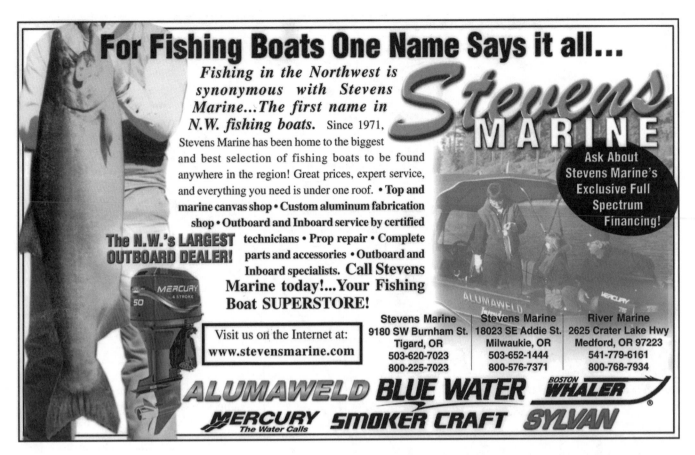
prime time.

Look for sturgeon in the river's deep holes and troughs, which serve as food caches for these bottom cruisers. A depth finder is helpful for identifying likely spots. Keep your bait on the bottom.

There are popular sturgeon bank fisheries at Mary Young Park and the West Linn Cat Walk on the west bank, at Meldrum Bar and Sellwood on the east bank. Some catches are made by anglers fishing from the OMSI dock adjacent to the Steel Bridge in Northeast Portland.

Boaters can prowl a wider range, including the area from the falls down to Meldrum Bar. The ledges and current breaks associated with the bridges can often be productive, especially after a heavy rain. Try the east side of the Fremont Bridge, the Railroad Bridge, and upstream from the St. John's Bridge. Fish ledges and troughs from 30 to 45 ft. deep. Other sturgeon haunts include an 85-ft. hole in front of Shenanigan's Restaurant on the east bank downstream from the Fremont Bridge, the current break adjacent to Swan Island, the dredged holes adjacent to the coal docks midway between St. Johns Bridge and Multnomah Channel, and along Sauvie Island's south shore upstream from the mouth of Columbia Slough.

Smelt are the most popular bait here as in the Columbia, but crayfish, herring, lamprey eel, and nightcrawlers can all be fished effective.

This section of the Willamette is strongly influenced by the tides. You'll need more weight to keep your bait on the bottom during the outgoing tide.

Shad. The lower Willamette shad fishery is primarily a boat show, beginning in early May and extending through the July 4 weekend, with a peak in June. Thousands of shad are taken in the main channel from the mouth of the Clackamas to Willamette Falls, and in the Coon Island vicinity of Multnomah Channel. There is some bank angling for shad at Clackamette Park.

Steelhead. Modest numbers of winter and summer steelhead are hooked in this stretch of the river from late December through June, primarily in the vicinity of the Clackamas mouth and near the falls. Finclipped steelhead may be kept.

Bass and Panfish. In addition to islands and sloughs, this reach of the Willamette has many structures that attract concentrations of warmwater fish. Look for them near bridges, sea walls, docks, pilings, and log rafts.

There is good bank fishing for bass, crappie, perch, and crayfish at Oaks Bottom in Sellwood, particularly below the log booms (though standing on the booms themselves is extremely dangerous). Other good bank fisheries are at Ross Island, with its blue heron rookery mid-river in south Portland, Swan Island in north Portland; Elk Rock Island near Milwaukie; and Cedar Island north of Gladstone. Swan Island Lagoon can be fished from floats, with best catches downstream from the cross street between Basin and Lagoon Avenue. Bass and panfish are also fished at Cathedral Park, Willamette Park (plunk the shallow water south of the ramp), the harbor wall at Waterfront Park, and Milwaukie Boat Ramp. The mouth of Johnson Creek offers excellent crappie fishing and smallmouth bass. It can be reached from the Milwaukie Boat Ramp by wading during low water. At Mary S. Young Park in West Linn, a footbridge to Cedar Island is installed annually in May or June after the river drops. Fishing platforms on the island provide access to a lagoon with excellent fishing for smallmouth and crappie.

There is a health advisory on resident fish in this section of the Willamette (See current regulations). Limit or avoid con-

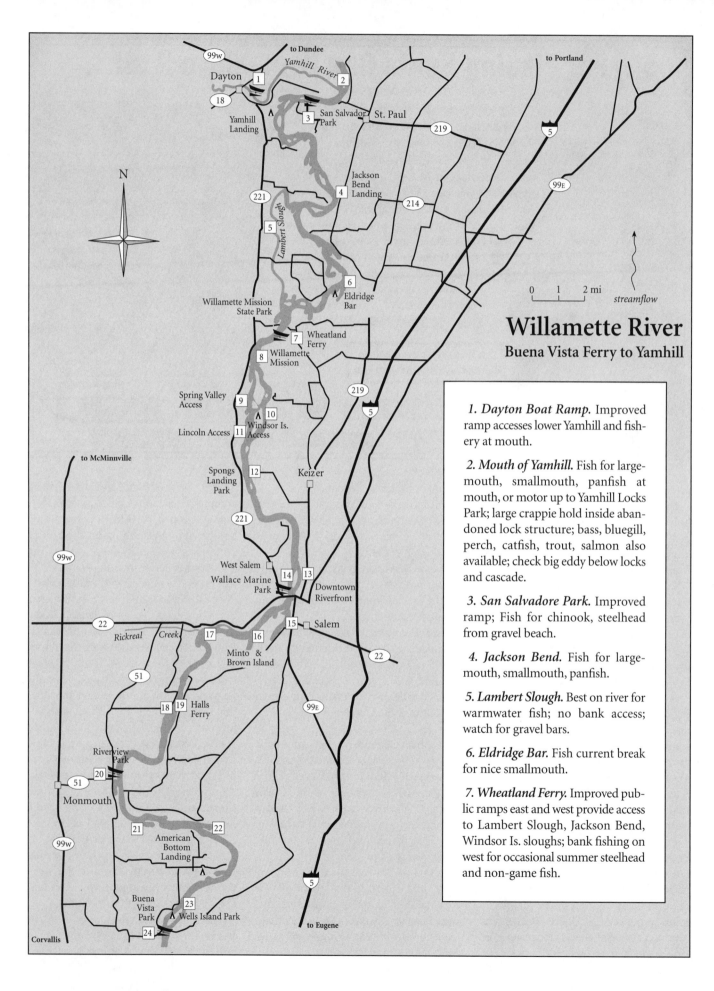

Willamette River
Buena Vista Ferry to Yamhill

0   1   2 mi

streamflow

1. Dayton Boat Ramp. Improved ramp accesses lower Yamhill and fishery at mouth.

2. Mouth of Yamhill. Fish for largemouth, smallmouth, panfish at mouth, or motor up to Yamhill Locks Park; large crappie hold inside abandoned lock structure; bass, bluegill, perch, catfish, trout, salmon also available; check big eddy below locks and cascade.

3. San Salvadore Park. Improved ramp; Fish for chinook, steelhead from gravel beach.

4. Jackson Bend. Fish for largemouth, smallmouth, panfish.

5. Lambert Slough. Best on river for warmwater fish; no bank access; watch for gravel bars.

6. Eldridge Bar. Fish current break for nice smallmouth.

7. Wheatland Ferry. Improved public ramps east and west provide access to Lambert Slough, Jackson Bend, Windsor Is. sloughs; bank fishing on west for occasional summer steelhead and non-game fish.

8. Willamette Mission State Park. Improved boat ramp next to Wheatland Ferry slip accesses several warmwater sloughs; cut-off oxbow lake in park refills with Willamette fish following high water; fish from boat or bank.

9. Pumphouse Slough. Fair to good for bass, bluegill; good cover along west side; bank access at Spring Valley (a.k.a. Mennonite Hole).

10. Lone Tree Bar. Fish for bass, panfish.

11. Lincoln Access. Bank fish for smallmouth.

12. Spong's Landing. Bank fishing at public park.

13. Salem Public Dock. Upstream from Hwy. 22 overpass; tie up to fish for largemouth bass and steelhead; if you dash into town for a latte, leave someone behind to watch the boat.

14. Wallace Marine Park. Improved ramp above bridge accesses Willamette Slough; bank angling in main river for spring and fall chinook below bridge.

15. Willamette Slough. Fish for bass and panfish.

16. Minto & Brown Island. Public park on River Rd. South, not accessible by river; fish several sloughs for bass and panfish.

17. Mouth of Rickreall Creek. Good spot to fish for smallmouth (boat access only); launch at Wallace Park.

18. Emil Mark/Lloyd Strange Hole. Polk County park; plunk for spring chinook and steelhead off end of Green Village Rd. off Hwy. 51 (across and downstream from Halls Ferry Access).

19. Halls Ferry Access. Limited bank angling from Greenway, or launch cartop boat to access slough for bass, panfish; neat float tube spot for fly fishing smallmouth at mouth of Roberts Slough.

20. Riverview Park (Independence). Some bank fishing; improved ramp accessing good bass, panfish sloughs from here to Salem.

21. Murphy Slough. Good depth and cover for largemouth and crappie.

22. Judson Slough. Good bluegill, crappie, some largemouth.

23. Wells Island Park. Camp mid-river; no drinking water.

24. Buena Vista. County park and ferry; improved boat ramp provides downstream take-out for floating the Santiam from I-5 bridge; motor upstream for smallmouth bass, largemouth, crappie, bluegill; good holding water for chinook and steelhead at mouth of Santiam; beware of strong currents downriver of ferry.

---

sumption. Especially avoid eating bullhead and larger bass (which live a long time in the Willamette's chemical soup). Enjoy this fishery as a chance to practice technique, enjoy a day on the river, and experience fast catch-and-release action close to home.

Facilities. Two of the best resources for fishing supplies and Willamette River expertise in the Portland metropolitan area are Fisherman's Marine Supply and G.I. Joe's. There are public boat ramps at Sauvie Island on Multnomah Channel, Cathedral Park in North Portland, Swan Island, Willamette Park in southwest Portland, Milwaukie off Hwy. 99E, Meldrum Bar Park, and Clackamette Park. There are numerous private moorages and boat ramps throughout this stretch, open to public use for a modest fee. Rental boats are available at some of these facilities.

The locks at Willamette Falls are operated by the Army Corps of Engineers and are open to public use for free from 7 a.m. to 11 p.m. daily. Boaters should tie up at the Corps dock on the west bank, and pull the signal cord to alert the operator. Vessels should have fenders to protect their hulls from the lock walls. Allow about 35 minutes for passage through the 5 chambers.

WILLAMETTE RIVER: Eugene to Oregon City. This 100-mile portion of the Willamette serves as a highway for thousands of migrating spring chinook and summer and winter steelhead bound for their spawning grounds in the Molalla, Yamhill, Luckiamute, McKenzie, North and South Santiams, and the forks of the Willamette. The river is also year-round home to largemouth bass, smallmouth bass, panfish, channel catfish, and sturgeon. Trout and whitefish grow more numerous from Harrisburg upstream.

The Willamette can be reached by secondary roads off Hwy. 99E and Hwy. 99W. It can be boated by all manner of craft launched from many improved, primitive, and natural sites on both banks of the river. Anglers commonly motor upstream from a ramp, and fish and drift their way back. Boat ramps popularly used by Willamette anglers in this section are located at Willamette Park and Bernert Landing in West Linn, Molalla River State Park off Hwy. 99E north of Canby, Hebb Park ½ mile north of Canby Ferry Rd.,

Rodgers Landing just outside of Newberg, San Salvador Park two miles south of the Yamhill confluence, Willamette Mission State Park next to the Wheatland Ferry off Hwy. 221 between Dayton and Keizer, Wallace Marine Park off Hwy. 221 in West Salem, Independence Riverview Park off Hwy. 51 at Independence, Buena Vista Ferry south of Monmouth, Bryant Park in Albany, Hyak Park on Hwy. 20 west of Albany, Pioneer Boat Basin off 99W at Corvallis, Willamette Park off Hwy. 99W south of Corvallis, Peoria Park in Peoria, McCartney Park north of Harrisburg, Hileman and Whitely landings off River Rd. north of Eugene, Alton Baker Park in Eugene, and Island Park in Springfield. The river is used heavily by pleasure boaters.

Salmon. Chinook angling activity in this stretch of the Willamette has traditionally been light despite the fact that tens of thousands of adult chinook make it over the falls. Anglers in this stretch must be willing to learn some new tactics and to locate the holes and slots where salmon linger.

From the Yamhill River confluence to Willamette Falls, the Willamette is moder-

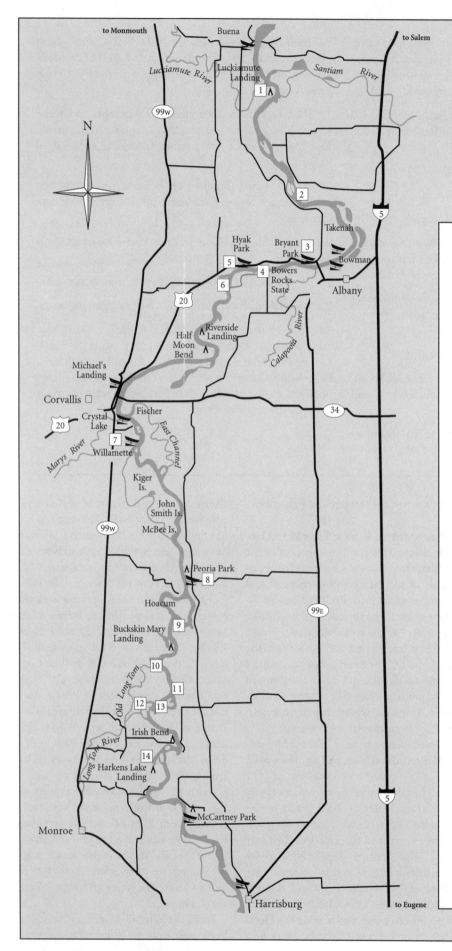

Willamette River

Harrisburg to Buena Vista

0   1   2 mi

streamflow

1. Luckiamute Slough. Good boat fishing until June for largemouth, crappie, bluegill.

2. Black Dog Slough. Bluegill, largemouth, crappie.

3. Bryant Park. Improved ramp offers high water access to large pool at mouth of Calapooia (ramp is difficult in low water); fish from the dock for smallmouth.

4. Bowers Rock. Large slough with good bank cover; good for crappie and largemouth in spring; shallow in summer.

5. Hyak Park. Improved ramp accesses nearby sloughs for bass and panfish.

6. Collins Bay. Nearly circular slough with shallow neck holds abundant crappie, bluegill.

7. Willamette Park/Crystal Boat Ramp. Improved ramps access East Channel and mouth of Mary's River for bass and panfish.

8. Peoria Park. Improved ramp accesses many sloughs and holes here to Corvallis, a 12-mile drift; try waters around McBee, John Smith, Kiger, and Fischer islands for bass and panfish.

9. Slough. Good bass and panfish cover at head of Hoacum Island.

10. Mouth of Old Long Tom Channel. Sturgeon hole; old channel forms productive slough for bass toward upper end.

11. Sturgeon. Good water here to Old Long Tom mouth.

12. Mouth of Long Tom. Sturgeon hole at mouth; good small-mouth and largemouth bass in lower river accessible by 2-mile canoe drift from last downstream road crossing; take-out at Peoria.

13. Slough. Deep slough with good cover offers bass and panfish opportunities.

14. Harkens Lake. Boat-in campground; fish adjacent slough for largemouth bass.

The WILLAMETTE at Irish Bend. Photograph by Dennis Frates.

ately slack, and trolling is the most effective chinook tactic. Wobblers (such as an Alvin) trolled in a zig-zag pattern work well. Brass/chrome or silver are the most popular colors. The most popular anchor fishery is at the mouth of the Molalla, where spinners are generally effective. There are bank fishing opportunities at Green Villa Park north of Independence and at Spring Valley Park. Bank anglers have good success with Spin-N-Glo's.

Above the Yamhill, the current is generally too strong for trolling, though some anglers backtroll Kwikfish-type lures. Use of bait is currently restricted to sturgeon fishing only, but bait always was useless here for chinook fishing anyway due to the large population of non-game fish looking for an easy hand-out. Mid-stream current edges and drop-offs can be productive places to anchor and fish, but you must keep a sharp eye out for large drifting debris and be prepared to disengage quickly from your anchor. For safety, boating anglers in this section should use a bow slide with chocks, cleats, and an anchor buoy. A 25-pound rocking chair-type anchor on 200 ft. of stout rope is best for dealing with the shallowness of the river in this section and its hard-pan bottom.

Most anglers prefer to anchor close to the bank, fishing spinners in 4 to 6 ft. deep slots. Keep the spinner in the slot until a salmon wanders in. Anglers generally use a 17 to 21 inch lead dropper line with a slightly longer leader. Amount of lead can vary from 1 to 8 ounces, depending on current and depth. You'll need to experiment.

The most effective spinner sizes are numbers. 3, 4, or 5. Vary the color according to the light and clarity of the water.

The greatest chinook presence in this reach is often the first 20 days in May. If you follow the fish counts over Willamette Falls, calculate that the fish will reach the Yamhill in about 7 days.

Steelhead. Summer steelhead are moving upstream during this time as well and can be fished with the same lures as salmon. All summer steelhead here are of hatchery origin and should be finclipped and available for harvest. Summer steelheading has occasionally been restricted when spring chinook emergency regulations were implemented. Check with ODFW. See Appendix. Few anglers fish the upper Willamette for winter steelhead. Winter steelhead in this stretch are all wild.

Bass and Panfish. This section of the river beckons the adventurous bass and panfish angler for whom exploration is part of the fun. Numerous sloughs offer quiet refuge for largemouth and smallmouth bass, crappie, bluegill, and catfish. The main channel is broken by islands mid-stream that divide and slow the flow to either side. Look for largemouth in the sloughs under logs and brush piles, casting plugs or spinning lures along the shore where there's lots of cover to draw them out. Smallmouth are present in good numbers from Salem to Corvallis, found primarily at the mouths of the sloughs and at the edges of the main current. The largest fish are taken in early spring (March

and April.

Rock Island Sloughs (two sloughs off 99E near West Linn) offers good habitat among submerged rocks, log booms and sunken trees. Lambert Slough, about 4 miles long and 6 to 7 miles from boat ramps upstream or down, offers some of the best smallmouth fishing in the Willamette. There is no bank access here, and boaters should be wary of gravel bars. Best access is from Wheatland Ferry Boat Ramp, which is also used to reach Jackson Bend and Windsor Island sloughs. Launch at Wallace Marine Park or Independence to fish the mouth of Rickreall Creek, good for both largemouth and smallmouth bass.

There's a lot of good boatable bass and panfish water between Independence and Salem, including Murphy and Judson sloughs. Luckiamute Slough, in the Luckiamute upstream from the Luckiamute River confluence, offers good early season boat fishing for largemouth, crappie, and bluegill (best before June). The 12-mile drift from Peoria Park to Corvallis offers many promising sloughs and holes, including the waters around McBee, John Smith, Kiger, and Fischer islands.

One of the few slough areas in this section with bank access is Minto & Brown Slough south of Salem, in Minto Brown Park off River Rd. The park has both wheelchair accessible docks and bank access. Float tubes and cartop boats can be launched. Fishing is in the slough and an old borrow pit pond for large carp, largemouth bass, bluegill, and bullhead. Another bank fishing opportunity in this stretch of the Willamette is the Lincoln Access off Hwy. 221 north of Salem, especially good for smallmouth bass. Halls Ferry Access on the east bank south of Salem is a nice place to launch a float tube and fly fish for smallmouth at the mouth of Roberts Slough.

Sturgeon. Sturgeon are available in this stretch, though they don't make it over the falls on their own. Sturgeon have been stocked here since the early 1950s, and a good number should be approaching legal size. Sturgeon probably don't spawn naturally above the falls.

Fish the deep holes and eddies using large gobs of nightcrawlers, crawfish tails, or pieces of scrap fish. ODFW encourages anglers to help monitor the sturgeon fishery here by reporting catches to the district office in Corvallis. See Appendix. Log books are available for anglers who would like to participate in the sturgeon study program.

Trout. There is some fishing for rainbow and cutthroat trout in the Corvallis area, but trout fishing is best from Peoria upstream, where there are more gravel bars, channels, and other structure that provide good trout habitat. Upstream of Albany, the river is open for trout fishing year-round. Check the regulations for gear restrictions and harvest restrictions and opportunities.

Cutthroat grow to good size in the mainstem Willamette, head up the tributaries each winter, and return in early spring. The areas near the mouths of good cutthroat tributary streams can be excellent in April. Cutthroat are scattered throughout the river in summer.

Trout fishing drops off in this stretch as the water warms, and whitefish predominate by June. Whitefish actually present a year-round angling opportunity here. Look for them in the same places as trout. In winter, whitefish are often quite active.

Facilities. Natural campsites are available on many of the islands in the river, and there is a developed campground on Wells Island below Buena Vista Ferry. Most of the parks that have boat ramps or fishing access do not have camping facilities, but there are campgrounds at Spring Valley Access on the west bank upstream from Wheatland Ferry, Sidney Landing on the east bank about 5 miles below Independence, American Bottom Landing on the west bank 2 miles above Sidney, Luckia-

mute Landing at the Luckiamute confluence, Riverside Landing on the east bank southwest of Albany, Half Moon Bend Landing downstream about 4 miles from Corvallis on the west bank, Buckskin Mary Landing 4 miles above Peoria Park on the west bank, and Harkens Lake Landing 3 miles below McCartney Park on the west bank.

Health Advisory. There is a mercury contamination alert for Willamette River fish. See the regulations for details. In general, resident fish are more likely to contain dangerous levels of mercury than migrants such as salmon and steelhead, and the older (larger) the fish, the greater the opportunity for contamination.

WILLAMETTE RIVER: Coast Fork to McKenzie River. This 12-mile stretch (unique in character and with its own regulations) offers year-round trout fishing in the heart of one of Oregon's population centers, the Eugene-Springfield area. Wild cutthroat 9 to 12 inches and plump rainbows in the 14 to 17 inch range are present, as well as smaller hatchery rainbows that drop out of Alton Baker Canal. The fishery is open for harvest of finclipped trout from late April through October.

Beautiful riffles characterize this stretch of the river, including a nice set as the river makes a sweep around Alton Baker Park and behind Valley River Shopping Center. There are 6 miles of good bank fishing and wading between Day Island Park in Springfield and Beltline Rd. In addition to the parks, there is access from bike paths in both Eugene and Springfield, at Beltline Bridge, and Valley River Center.

There are boat ramps at Day Island Park, "D" Street, Valley River Center, and on Beltline Rd. (an unimproved launch).

Spring chinook heading for the Middle Fork of the Willamette are also lightly fished in this stretch. Popular spots include the Washington/Jefferson St. bridge hole, and good hole near the middle of the flow through Alton Baker Park. Almost all these chinook are hatchery fish.

WILLAMETTE RIVER, COAST FORK. Least productive of the major Willamette tributaries. It heads in the vicinity of Black Butte in the Calapooya Mts., flowing 7 miles to Cottage Grove Reservoir, closely followed by a road. The upper portion supports wild cutthroat trout. There is

some good fishing near the dam. The lower river is stocked with rainbow trout in the town park in Cottage Grove in early season.

There is a mercury alert for this tributary of the Willamette. See the Regulations booklet for details.

WILLAMETTE RIVER, MIDDLE FORK

The largest tributary to the upper Willamette, open for year-round trout fishing, spring chinook, and finclipped summer steelhead. It joins the Coast Fork to form the mainstem Willamette south of Springfield.

Highways 58, 99, and 126 meet near its mouth. From Springfield to Lowell (at Dexter Reservoir) a paved county road follows the river's lower 18 miles. Hwy. 58 then follows it past Lookout Point Reservoir to just above Oakridge. About 3 miles southeast of Oakridge, Forest Rd. 21 cuts to the south, follows the river past Hills Creek Reservoir, and continues into the headwaters.

The Middle Fork offers a variety of water and fishing opportunities. From Dexter Reservoir downstream the river resembles the mainstem Willamette, flowing through mostly flat agricultural lands. Most anglers fish this stretch for summer steelhead and spring chinook, though some trout are present.

Best fishing for spring chinook is between Springfield and Dexter Dam. The run generally peaks from late May through June. Most anglers use spinners or Kwikfish-type lures.

There's a boat ramp at Clearwater Lane in Springfield, a gravel bar access at Jasper Bridge, and two ramps below Dexter Dam on each bank of the river. Pengra Greenway Boat Ramp is about 3 miles below the dam. Between Pengra and Jasper, the river breaks into small channels that are easily obstructed by woody debris. Check with the local Sheriff's office before drifting this portion of the river.

Between Hills Creek Reservoir and Lookout Point, the Middle Fork is a wild trout stream—big, lively, and inviting. Since the late '90s, this stretch has been managed for wild trout only, and populations of both rainbows and cutthroat have been steadily increasing. Trout are plentiful, though few lunkers are present. The average rainbow runs 9 to 14 inches, with cutthroat slightly smaller. Larger trout occasionally make their way into the river from Lookout Point Reservoir. There are no salmon or steelhead above the dams.

Trout fishing is best in May and June when caddis hatch throughout the day. In summer, most hatches take place in the evening. Cold releases from Hills Creek Reservoir can occasionally slow the summer catch rate, but dam releases support a nice winter trout fishery, especially righ† below the dam. Though this is not one of Oregon's premium tailrace fisheries, there are active insect hatches throughout the winter.

This stretch of the river is approachable from frequent turn-outs off Hwy. 58 (north bank road) and Forest Rd. 5852 (south bank). There is excellent south bank access from Black Canyon campground to Deception creek. On the north bank, anglers can hike and fish along a developed trail from Ferrin Campground almost to Oak Ridge. There is fishable water at Greenwater City Park in Oakridge and very good water right below Hills Creek Dam accessible from Corps property.

The river between Hills Creek and Lookout Point reservoirs can be drifted, though boaters should scout the water, which includes at least one Class III rapid. The only developed ramps are a steep pole slide at Greenwater Park in Oakridge and a paved ramp at Black Canyon Campground. You may have to drag your boat across gravel to reach the pavement at Black Canyon when the river's low. Undeveloped put-ins and take-outs include a site below the bridge downstream from Hills Creek Reservoir (scout the boulder garden just below the put in) and a gravel bar at the mouth of the North Fork of the Middle Fork (scout the significant rapid just above the mouth if you're drifting down).

Middle Fork is open for trout fishing throughout the year, with catch and release restrictions year-round in some stretches and at some times of year in others. Check the regulations for dates and tackle requirements.

Above Hills Creek Reservoir, both rainbow and cutthroat trout are present in fair numbers, and trout are stocked from Campers Flat downstream to the reservoir. Fin-clipped trout may be kept. Continuation of this stocking program depends on

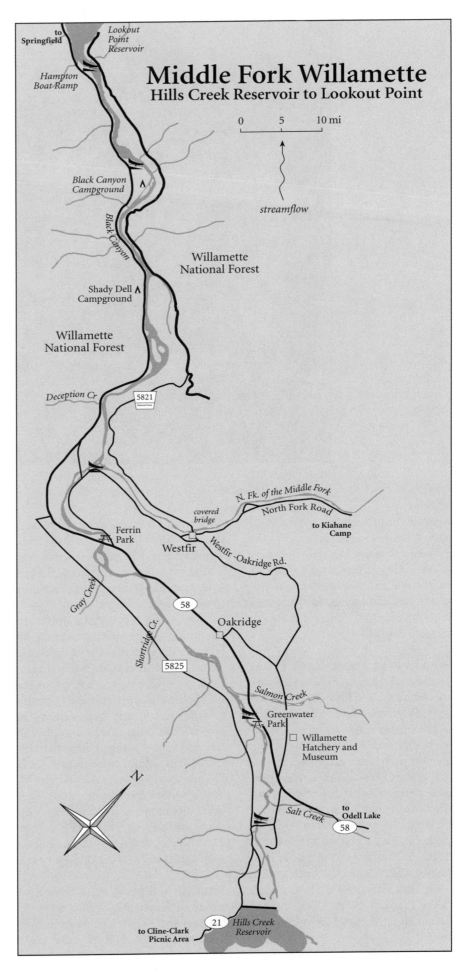

Middle Fork Willamette
Hills Creek Reservoir to Lookout Point

Brood trout and surplus hatchery steelhead are often available at WILLAMINA POND. *Photograph by Terry Hines.*

whether or not bull trout make a comeback. Know your trout species when fishing here, and release bull trout unharmed.

There are campgrounds at Lookout Point and Hills Creek reservoirs, on Hwy. 58 west of Oakridge, and roughly every 5 miles on Forest Rd. 21 in the Willamette National Forest.

WILLAMETTE RIVER, NORTH FORK. The North Fork is an attractive stream of good size, managed for wild trout. It is restricted to the use of artificial flies throughout its run. About 40 miles long, it joins the Middle Fork 2 miles west of Oakridge, about 35 miles southeast of Eugene.

The North Fork heads in Waldo Lake and skirts the Taylor Burn Lakes area. A good road, Forest Rd. 19, follows the river from the community of West Fir far into the headwaters. Forest Rd. 19 (Aufderheide Forest Drive) is paved all the way to Box Canyon Guard Station, where it joins the South Fork McKenzie Rd. The last 8 miles of the stream to Waldo Lake are off the beaten track, though it is crossed once by trail.

There are good populations of wild rainbow and cutthroat trout in the North Fork, averaging 8 to 12 inches, with some to 17 inches. The lower 12 miles has excellent fly water from July through the fall. Angling pressure is generally light.

This is a lovely forest stream, and official recognition of its merit has won the North Fork state designation as a Wild and Scenic river. Its water is crystal clear and quite cold, too cold for good angling in the spring. But a sunny summer day on this sparkling river is inevitably memorable. Probably due to the river's clarity, the fish here tend to be shy. After arriving riverside, sit and wait awhile before casting. Small flies are best (No. 14 or 16). Caddis imitations are always appropriate.

The only campground on the river is Kiahane, about 20 miles north of Westfir on Forest Rd. 19. There are other camps on Hwy. 58 east and west of Oakridge.

WILLAMINA CREEK. A good little trout stream on the east side of the coast range, flowing into the upper Yamhill River. From McMinnville on Hwy. 18 head north

through Sheridan on the old highway to Willamina. From Willamina, at the mouth of the creek, a paved road heads north, and gravel roads follow the upper stretch.

Willamina has a nice run of winter steelhead, but the creek is closed to steelheading at this time. Abundant wild cutthroat in the 7 to 11 inch range are available for catch and release fishing.

WILLAMINA POND. A 5-acre abandoned log pond in Huddeston Park in Willamina, featuring warmwater fish and stocked trout. Take the Hwy. 18 business loop through Sheridan into the community of Willamina. Turn left at the Rocket Gas Station onto Polk (which runs behind the high school), and follow Polk to the park.

Willamina supports populations of largemouth bass, black crappie, brown bullhead and yellow perch. ODFW stocks catchable rainbows from mid-March through Free Fishing Day, as well as brood trout and surplus winter steelhead when available. No boats or float tubes allowed. Recommended for youngsters.

WILLIAMS LAKE. A 4-acre brook trout lake just north of Taylor Burn Campground north of Waldo Lake. See Whig Lake for road and trail directions. The one-mile trail heads north from the east side of the campground to Williams Lake, which is southeast of Upper Erma Bell Lake. The trail goes on to Otter Lake.

Williams is stocked with brook trout 6 to 12 inches. It is easily fished from shore, and all methods will take fish at times. The area is not accessible until late June.

WILSONVILLE POND. A 3-acre pond west of I-5, south of the Wilsonville Rest Area. From Butteville Rd., take Boones Ferry Rd. north about ½ mile. The pond supports largemouth bass and bluegill.

WIND LAKE. A small hike-in brook trout lake about 2 miles southwest of Government Camp as the crow flies. You'll envy the crow by the time you reach the lake. Wind is on the south side of Tom Dick and Harry Mt. There are two ways in. You can hike one mile to Mirror Lake on Trail 664, then continue on this trail for an additional 1½ miles, crossing the western flank of Tom Dick and Harry above timberline. From there hike three quarters of a mile due east, staying above timberline, and you'll see the lake about 100 ft. below you. A trail leads down to the lake. This hike is about 4 miles and is strenuous.

The second route begins at the parking area of the Multipor ski area. A trail leads southwest, following a ski lift to timberline. (Don't confuse this with the trail that follows another lift southeast up Multipor Mt.) The trail crosses to the south side of the mountain and ends at Wind Lake. This route reaches the lake in a little over 2 miles, but is even steeper than the first.

Wind Lake is stocked with brook trout by air and offers pretty good fishing for fish 6 to 12 inches. Fly fishing is the best method, as the lake is extremely shallow. In some severe winters most of the fish are lost, and it takes a year or two to rebuild the population. It is usually accessible in early June, with some snow left to struggle through.

WITHEE LAKE. A fair warm water lake not far from McMinnville, east of the Yamhill River. From Amity on 99W, head west about 2 miles. The state has an access agreement with the owner of the property, and if anglers act responsibly, the lake will remain open. A sign marks the area. Strictly a bank fishery, Withee supports good size largemouth bass and some crappie. After a big flood you can find all Yamhill species in here. The lake is usually good in spring and summer until the weeds get thick.

WOODBURN POND. A highway borrow pit adjacent to I-5 north of Woodburn. Take the Woodburn Exit and head east on Hwy. 214 to Boones Ferry Rd., north on Boones Ferry about 2 miles, and west on Crosby Rd. Just before the Interstate overpass, turn north onto Edwin Road, which parallels the expressway and leads to the pond. Park at the locked gate, and walk in. There are 14 acres to fish for largemouth bass, bluegill, crappie, and channel cats to 18 inches. The water gets weed choked by late spring.

YAMHILL RIVER. A pretty, rural tributary of the Willamette, flowing 60 miles from the Coast Range to its confluence near Dayton. It offers good spring fishing for wild cutthroat in its upper forks, and bass and panfish primarily in the mainstem. At this time, all trout fishing is catch and release.

The Yamhill flows out of two forks east of McMinnville. The North Fork flows south from the mountains above Yamhill. The South Fork flows north from the Willamina area. Among the first Willamette tributaries to clear, the Yamhill has traditionally been a good choice for the year's first trout outings.

From the lower end, the river can be reached by paved and gravel side roads leading south from Hwy. 99W and north from Hwy. 233. From McMinnville upstream, the South Fork is skirted on the north by Hwy. 18 and is followed through Sheridan and Willamina by the old highway. The North Fork is accessed by Hwy. 47 between Yamhill and Carlton, and is closely followed by a road northwest of Yamhill in the vicinity of Pike.

Wild cutthroat, available for catch and release angling with artificial flies and lures. There's good bank access for trout on the North Fork between Pike and the Flying M Ranch. Bass and panfish are abundant from the McMinnville area to the mouth.

The Yamhill is navigable by small motorboats from the mouth to the old locks above Dayton. There is opportunity for bank fishing at Yamhill Locks Park, where large crappie have been known to hold inside the abandoned lock structure. Check the big eddy below the lock and cascade as well. Bass, bluegill, perch, catfish, trout, and even salmon have been hooked here on occasion. At this time, all fishing (even for catfish) is limited to artificial flies and lures. Check the regulations for a possible relaxation of this restriction. The sloughs in the lower river have excellent crayfish populations.

Steelhead migrate through the river into the forks and other tributaries from mid-January through April. At this time, the entire Yamhill system is closed to steelhead angling. At times when steelheading is permitted, a popular drift on the South Fork is from Ft. Hill to Willamina, and on the North Fork, from Pike to the West Side Rd.

A river gauge reading is available. See Appendix.

ZIGZAG RIVER. A high gradient tributary of the Sandy River, flowing mostly within the Mt. Hood National Forest. The ZigZag offers catch and release fishing for wild cutthroat trout. It is closed to steelhead and salmon fishing. About 12 miles long, the Zigzag joins the Sandy River at the community of Zigzag, on Hwy. 26 about 43 miles east of Portland. Hwy. 26 follows the north bank all the way to its headwaters near Government Camp.

FISHING IN OREGON'S
CENTRAL ZONE

The Central Zone reaches deep into Oregon's heartland, drawing forth all the waters that feed the state's premiere trout fishery, the Deschutes River. These sources include lovely snow-melt pools and their icy outlets, crystalline rivers that pour full-blown out of fern banked springs, desert streams that cut through wild volcanic rock canyons before meandering across the high desert, and a treasure trove of handsome mountain lakes.

Here are many of Oregon's richest cold water angling opportunities in settings of astounding beauty.

The Deschutes itself offers year-round fishing for large rainbow trout in environments as varied as a sage-tufted, rock-rimmed desert canyon, and a flower-bedecked mountain meadow. It is also one of Oregon's top fisheries for summer steelhead, both wild and finclipped hatchery.

The Deschutes' major tributaries are outstanding fisheries themselves. The Metolius—spring-fed, transparent, and cold— throws down the gauntlet to Oregon anglers with the state's most technical fishing for large rainbows, wary browns, and ferocious bull trout. The Crooked River provides one of the state's best winter fisheries for abundant *redband* (the variety of wild rainbow trout found east of the Cascades). Fall River, another spring-fed beauty, offers light-line summer fishing for wary hatchery-bred rainbows.

Reservoirs (Crane Prairie and Wickiup) capture the Deschutes in forested high mountain impundments, offering superior fishing for very large trout—and there's good trout fishing in the big natural lakes of Central Oregon, known as *the Cascade Lakes* (Crescent, Cultus, Davis, East, Elk, Hosmer, Lava, Odell, and Paulina). Paulina, in the crater of a somnolent volcano, produces trophy browns. Hosmer is especially popular with float tube and canoe anglers, who vye with the osprey for the lake's stocked Atlantic salmon and try to outwit its wary old brook trout. Crescent and Odell lakes offer fishing for hefty mackinaw trout and for kokanee—one of the tastiest fishes available in the Northwest. Kokanee are the prime catch at Lake Billy Chinook, a huge reservoir that incorporates the confluence of Deschutes, Crooked, and Metolius rivers in a rugged rimrock setting.

Largemouth bass are thriving in Crane Prairie and Davis lakes, where they were illegally introduced, and anglers are invited to catch and keep unlimited numbers. Largemouth and other warmwater species are also available in Pine Hollow and Prineville reservoirs and in a string of productive

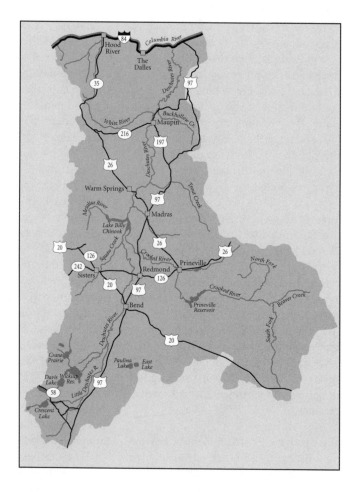

ponds and sloughs along the Columbia River between Hood River and The Dalles.

Highways 26 and 97 provide primary access to the region, with additional paved primary roads leading in from the mid-Willamette valley. Paved or graded two-lane secondary roads lead to most of the big lakes. Most river roads are unpaved but graded. Steep ungraded roads connect basins and lead to smaller lakes, streams, and trailheads.

Access to Central Zone fisheries includes an excellent network of trails, well-signed both at their head and in the backcountry. In addition to stocked trout, many of these high lakes offer ringside views of five gorgeous Cascade peaks: Three Finger Jack, Diamond Peak, and North, Middle, and South Sister—all of which are incorporated into federally designated wilderness areas.

The Central Zone encompasses a generous amount of publicly owned land, including much of the Deschutes and

The Central Zone includes all waters draining into the Columbia River from Bonneville Dam up to and including the Deschutes River.

THE BEST FISHING IN OREGON'S CENTRAL ZONE

BILLY CHINOOK RESERVOIR
Famous for abundant kokanee and trophy-size bull trout, with smallmouth opportunities.

CRANE PRAIRIE RESERVOIR
One of Oregon's premiere fisheries for large rainbow trout (popular with fly anglers), and a burgeoning population of largemouth bass.

CROOKED RIVER
Offers a popular year-round tailrace fishery below Bowman Dam for abundant mid-size redband rainbows.

DAVIS LAKE
Fly fishing only for trophy-size trout in a stunning mountain setting.

DESCHUTES RIVER (Pelton Dam to mouth)
One of America's most productive trout streams and a top producer of summer steelhead.

HIGH LAKES
More than 80 hike-in trout lakes in the Cascade Mountains (most in Deschutes National Forest), offering quality wilderness angling experiences in a variety of spectacular settings.

HOSMER LAKE
Fly fishing only for large brook trout and landlocked Atlantic salmon.

LAVA LAKE
A big scenic lake that grows big rainbow and brook trout, popular with bait anglers.

LOST LAKE (Mt. Hood)
A popular family trout fishing destination with many amenities and a grand view of Mt. Hood.

METOLIUS RIVER
One of the most beautiful and challenging trout streams in Oregon, in a park-like setting of ponderosa pine.

ODELL LAKE
Outstanding fishing for trophy-size mackinaw and some of the best kokanee fishing in the state.

OLALLIE LAKE
The drive-to crown jewel in a lake basin that offers dozens of unique trout fishing opportunities.

PAULINA LAKE
Supports record-breaking brown trout and kokanee in the maw of a volcano.

PINEHOLLOW RESERVOIR
Big largemouth bass are the main attraction, with plentiful bullheads and bluegills as well as stocked rainbows that grow to good size.

PRINEVILLE RESERVOIR
Huge numbers of stocked rainbow trout, as well as abundant smallmouth, bullhead, and crappie, offer year-round fishing.

WICKIUP RESERVOIR
One of Oregon's largest and most productive reservoirs, growing large brown trout, kokanee, and rainbows.

Ochoco national forests, as well as extensive BLM holdings along the Deschutes and Crooked rivers.

Well-maintained campgrounds are plentiful around the big lakes and reservoirs and along most rivers. Primitive campsites are available in the backcountry, and any piece of off-road public land (unless specifically designated to the contrary) may be used for overnight stays.

The community of Bend offers the most complete and sophisticated services and accomodations for visiting ang-lers. Sisters, Camp Sherman, Redmond, Prineville, Madras, Maupin, and Warm Springs also serve fishing visitors. Many of the big lakes of Central Oregon have one or more resorts on their shore. As elsewhere in the state, these are mostly pleasant and comfortable, but modest establishments.

This is high country, with serious winters and cool evenings even in summer. The climate is considerably dryer than on the west side of the Cascades, but a good snowpack accumulates and lingers in the backcountry well into June.

ALLEN CREEK RESERVOIR. A large hike-in lake with good views of the Ochocos, in the northwest corner of Summit Prairie. A mix of BLM and private ranchland surrounds the 200-acre reservoir, which offers good fishing for 6 to 12 inch redband trout. The road into the lake is currently closed to motor vehicles. It is a 1½ mile hike from the parking area.

To negotiate the spur roads that lead to the reservoir you will need an Ochoco National Forest map. From Prineville, follow Hwy. 26 east about 7 miles beyond Ochoco Reservoir, then take County Rd. 23. At the Ranger Station, this road becomes Forest Rd. 22, which leads to Walton Lake. About ⅔ mile beyond Walton, where the road degenerates, take a sharp right heading south, and get out your forest map. Allen is about 9 miles from this point.

This is a remote spot with no facilities. Allen Creek Campground is nearby.

ANTELOPE FLAT RESERVOIR. A desert reservoir that grows big trout in years of average or better rainfall. It is in the Maury Mt. area of Ochoco National Forest, 30 air miles southeast of Prineville.

From Prineville, take the highway toward Paulina, turning south onto Forest Rd. 17 about 8 miles east of the community of Post. The reservoir is about 9 miles south at the head of Bear Creek, about 2 miles beyond Pine Creek Campground. It is wheelchair accessible.

Antelope covers about 170 acres when full, but is sometimes heavily drawn down. During the extreme low-water years of 1987-92, the reservoir was drawn down to 40 acres, its dead storage level, leaving trout vulnerable to the harsh winter of 1992. All fish were lost. But like many desert reservoirs, Antelope is known for growing large trout quickly. The reservoir was restocked in 1993, and fish to 18 inches were available by the end of the season. The average trout at Antelope is about 12 inches, with 18 inchers common, especially following a string of good water years.

The single campground at Antelope Flat is one of the largest in Ochoco National Forest. Set amongst the pines above the reservoir, it offers picnic tables, fire rings, and outhouses, but no water. Camp and boat ramp are at the west end of the reservoir. There are additional campgrounds north at Elk Horn and east at Double Cabin and Wiley Flat.

Antelope Flat is in a big game winter range area. Anglers are urged to be respectful of elk and mule deer and of adjacent private property in order to keep access open to the public. The reservoir is currently open for year-round angling, and winter fishing can be good in dry years. The road in is not plowed, however, so in years with normal snowfall, access is limited to snowmobiles and skis.

BADGER CREEK. A nice trout stream in the White River system, featuring a unique strain of rainbow trout. The creek flows out of Badger Lake on the southeast slope of Mt. Hood, entering Tygh Creek one mile west of the town of Tygh Valley. Tygh Creek empties into White River 3 miles to the east. A falls about 3 miles above the mouth of Badger keeps the creek's rainbows isolated.

About 25 miles long, Badger is accessible by road throughout its lower half. It is crossed by Hwy. 197 at Tygh Valley, and by secondary roads and Forest Rd. 47 east of Tygh Valley. The upper 10 miles is reached by road only at Bonney Crossing Campground and at Badger Lake. A good trail follows the stream through this section.

Bait or spinner and lures will take fish early, and flies do well in summer and fall. A little hiking can result in good fishing. There are campgrounds at Bonney Crossing and at Little Badger Creek. Forest Rd. 2710 connects the two camps.

BADGER LAKE. A good rainbow trout lake on the lower southeast slope of Mt. Hood, accessible by motor vehicles, but not recommended for passenger cars. On no account be fooled by the boat ramp here into thinking you can actually trailer in a boat (or anything else) on this road. It is steep, one-lane, and rutted, with big rocks, and few places wide enough to pass.

From Portland, follow Hwy. 26 east 58 miles, then Hwy. 35 (the Mt. Hood Loop Road) to Bennett Pass. Take Forest Rd. 3550 southeast to Camp Windy. Turn east on Forest Rd. 4860, then north on Forest Rd. 140 to the lake. Watch for signs. Check with the Forest Service for road conditions. The road to Badger is rarely open before July 4. Check with the Forest Service for road conditions.

Two other routes generally clear 2 weeks earlier. From the east, heading into the forest from Wamic, follow the road toward Rock Creek Reservoir, turning south on Forest Rd. 48 before reaching Rock Creek. Take the Forest Rd. 4860 cut-off, heading north to Badger. To reach the lake from the south, take Hwy. 26, Hwy. 216, then a network of forest roads. A navigator with a Mt. Hood Forest map is essential for this one.

Badger is stocked with rainbows and has wild brook trout to 14 inches. Average catch size is 10 inches. There's fair fishing on bait or troll in early summer. In fall, the fish are larger, and fly fishing is the most effective technique. There's a good camp at the lake.

BAKEOVEN CREEK. A small stream entering the Deschutes River below Maupin, where Hwy. 197 crosses the river. It is closed to all angling at this time.

BAKER POND. (Wasco Co.) A stocked trout pond in the White River Wildlife Area southwest of Wamic. From Wamic, head south to Rock Creek Dam Rd., then turn left on Miller Rd., right on Driver Rd., and left on Smock Prairie. The trail to the lake is off Smock Prairie on the right, at about one and a quarter miles.

The pond is spring-fed, with good water quality to support its annual stocking of rainbow fingerlings. Brown bullhead are also present. Though this one-acre pond is ringed with cattails, you won't need a float tube to reach good fishing.

It is open from late April through October. Be aware and respectful of wild game in the area.

BIBBY LAKE. A 16-acre reservoir west of Hwy. 97 at Kent, in Sherman County. It is currently closed to public access but may be re-opened as a pay-to fish destination.

BIG FINGER LAKE. A 5-acre alpine lake in the Deschutes National Forest, off the beaten path and lightly fished. Only 16 feet deep, it is air stocked with brook trout in odd-number years and sometimes winterkills. There are lots of fallen logs around the shoal area.

To reach it from the Mink Lake Basin, head southeast toward Cultus Lake on Trail 33 toward Snowshoe Lake. From the west end of Cultus, follow Trail 16 northwest, cutting north on Trail 33 past Winopee Lake to Snowshoe. See Cultus for complete directions. Big Finger is ¼ mile east of Snowshoe Lake. There is no trail between them. Little Finger Lake, about 2 acres, is another quarter of a mile farther east.

BIG HOUSTON LAKE. An 88-acre lake near Powell Butte, privately owned with no public access. It supports populations of largemouth bass, bluegill, brown bullhead and channel catfish.

BIG MARSH CREEK. A unique wild trout stream and wetland in south central Oregon southeast of Crescent Lake, the highest marshland in the state at elevation 5,000 ft. It joins Crescent Creek south of Hwy. 58, 14 miles northwest of the junction of highways 58 and 97. Forest Rd. 5825, which heads southwest from Hwy. 58 south of Odell Butte, follows the stream's marshy headwaters. Forest Rd. 6020 crosses it east of the railroad crossing at Umli.

The upper creek runs through a large marsh, making the main channel hard to find in places. It supports lots of small brook trout and considerably fewer redband rainbows and browns. Don't expect to catch big fish here, but it's a pleasant stream, and the effects of rehabilitation work here will be interesting to watch over the years.

The main fishery is in the meadow, where restoration efforts have been focused. The meadow has been closed to cattle grazing, the man-made canals have been blocked, and the stream is now flowing in something like its original channel. Willows are returning streamside, and beavers are making a comeback.

There is also good fishing above and below the marsh, including 15 miles of good dry fly water between the marsh and the railroad trestle, with lots of beaver activity (watch for bank holes). The water below the trestle is good but brushy. This stream is in best shape between May and July, after which the water warms and fishing drops off.

BIKINI POND. One of the I-84 ponds adjacent to the Columbia River, at highway mile 75.7 west of Mayer State Park's access road. Between the railroad and the river, it has 4 surface acres. Access is from Exit 76. It may support any of the Columbia River warmwater species. See Columbia River Ponds map.

LAKE BILLY CHINOOK is famous for its abundant kokanee and trophy-size bull trout. Photograph by Dennis Frates.

BILLY CHINOOK RESERVOIR

(a.k.a. Lake Billy Chinook) A large high desert reservoir, famous for abundant kokanee and trophy-size bull trout in the scenic canyon country east of the Cascade Range, about 8 miles southwest of Madras. It is partially administered by Confederated Tribes Warm Springs.

Created by Round Butte Dam (operated by PGE) on the Deschutes River, Billy Chinook covers over 6 square miles and backs up three major Oregon rivers—Deschutes, Metolius and Crooked. Long arms of slack water reach up each stream. The fishery on the Metolius arm is administered by CTWS. This reservoir fluctuates very little, but when it does, the bite is usually off during and immediately after. Call Round Butte Dam for an update. See Appendix.

Kokanee are the primary fishery here, but trout (brown, redband, and bull) make up a portion of the catch. A good population of smallmouth bass and a much smaller number of largemouth are well established, though the bass don't grow to great size. A few chinook may be present, but the fishery for them is closed at this time.

To reach Billy Chinook from Madras, drive south on Hwy. 97. Near Culver, take the road west to Cove Palisades State Park. The route is well signed. The descent to the lake is about 700 ft. From Sisters, follow Forest Rd. 63.

Kokanee are thriving in Billy Chinook. In fact, overpopulation has led to a drop in average size and a bonus bag limit of 25 fish per day. Kokanee are caught throughout the reservoir much of the year, but best fishing is in late spring (May and early June) and again in August and early September when kokanee return to the tributaries to spawn.

The most popular kokanee fisheries are at the confluence of the Crooked and Deschutes rivers, and around Chinook Island in the lower Metolius arm in mid-summer. In late August and early September kokanee begin schooling in the upper reaches of the tributaries, with the Metolius arm turning in the greatest number of catches. (Kokanee in spawning condition are best eaten smoked). Angling methods include trolling flashers (such as the Ford Fender) with a Wedding Ring and corn, and jigging in late summer with white corn and grubs. From mid-season through October, seek kokanee at deeper levels.

Billy Chinook is the only place in Oregon with a trophy fishery for bull trout. Elsewhere in the state, these huge members of the char family must be released unharmed. Current regulations allow anglers here to keep one bull per day, minimum length 24 inches. To preserve this oppor-

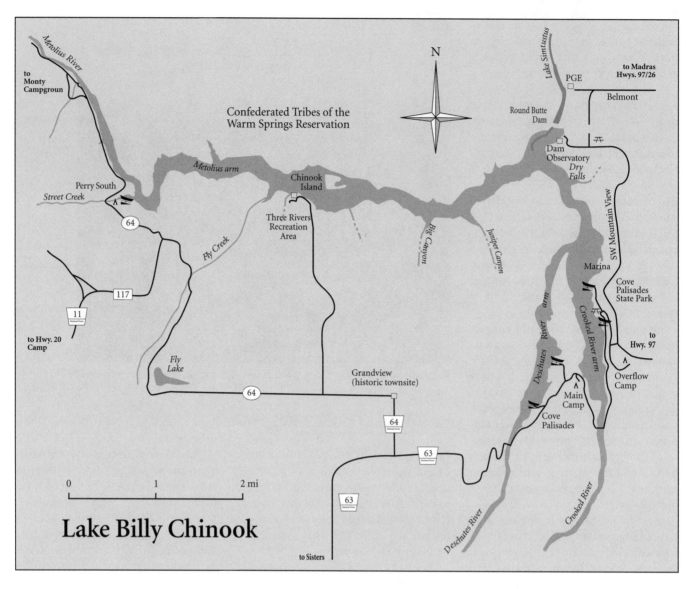

Lake Billy Chinook

tunity, anglers are encouraged to release all but true trophy catches. There are bull trout to 30 pounds in the reservoir. The state record bull trout was caught here in 1988, weighing 20 pounds 8 ounces.

Bull trout are extremely aggressive and prefer large forage. To fish for them, troll large lures (such as Rapalas or wobbling lures) that imitate the movement of minnows and crippled fish. A six-inch long tarpon fly has also been known to get their attention. Best fishing is along the shoreline in spring. If you catch a tagged bull trout, return the tag to the Oregon Dept. of Fish and Wildlife office in Prineville, identifying date caught, location, and length.

Bull trout thrive in very cold water. In fact, unlike true trouts (who eat little when the water temperature gets low), bulls eat voraciously all winter. The Crooked and Deschutes arms of the reservoir are open for trout fishing year-round. When the water begins to warm, more bull trout are found in the cold Metolius arm. The Metolius arm is open for fishing March 1 through October 31. There is a year-round closure on the area from the cable car crossing downstream 350 yards. This is a staging area for bull trout prior to spawning.

The best trout habitat on the lake is upstream from the Island in the cold Metolius arm. Large brown trout are also available in Billy Chinook, and smaller browns and rainbows are commonly caught at the head of each of the three arms. As the surface water warms, bull trout head for the depths, and smaller trout move up into the tributaries. Smallmouth bass take their places near the reservoir shoreline.

Smallmouth bass are found near shore after the water warms above 50º. There are good numbers in the upper reaches of the Deschutes and Crooked River arms, with best fishing in spring. These two arms have better smallmouth habitat (rocks and boulders) than the Metolius arm (which tends to be sandy). The Metolius arm is also colder, so smallmouth activity there picks up later in the season. In the Metolius arm, fish for smallmouth in the coves, where smallmouth are protected from wave action.

Smallmouth feed on young crayfish in spring (May through July), then switch their attention to scuds. Imitations of either can be productive. Some anglers troll for bass, but most cast plugs and lures toward the rocks. There is some bank angling opportunity for bass in the vicinity of the picnic area and between the boat ramps on the Deschutes Arm. The average smallmouth is 10 inches, with the some to 18 inches (3 pounds). There are very few largemouth bass in the lake.

The Metolius arm is managed by Confederated Tribes Warm Springs, and a tribal permit is required to fish it. Daily permits are modestly priced, cover fishing for the entire family, and are also valid on Lake Simtustus. The north shore of the arm is tribal property and is closed to public use. Chinook Island (about midway up the Metolius arm) is also CTWS land, open for day use but closed to camping. Tribal fishing permits are sold at the general store in Camp Sherman, at the sporting goods store and fly shop in Sisters, at Cove Palisades State Park, in stores at the top of the canyon above the park, and from other vendors in Warm Springs and Madras.

Most anglers fish Billy Chinook from boats launched at Cove Palisades State Park on the Crooked River arm or from ramps on the Deschutes arm. There is also a ramp at Perry South Campground, Deschutes National Forest, on the Metolius Arm.

Cove Palisades State Park is the second largest state park in Oregon. It has extensively developed camping and recreational facilities on the Deschutes and Crooked River arms, including r.v. hook-ups, picnic areas, running water, showers, and a swimming beach. Supplies (grocery, tackle, gas), boat and equipment rentals, and a restaurant are available at a private marina on the lower Crooked River Arm. Fishing boats and houseboats are available for rent from two facilities on the lake, Cove Palisades Marina and Three Rivers Marina. See Appendix.

Perry South Campground in Deschutes National Forest offers primitive camping in a shady draw at the Spring Creek inlet on the Metolius Arm. Though it has no drinking water, it does have picnic tables, fire rings, outhouses, and a serenity not available at the State Park. Best access is from Camp Sherman or from Sisters (See map for details). Monty Campground is about 5 miles further upstream from Perry South. The road ends shortly beyond Monty.

Lake Chinook State Airstrip is on the west plateau above the Deschutes Arm. This is a 5000 foot dirt strip running north/south within walking distance of the arm about 700 feet below. Watch out for strong updrafts from the canyon.

BINGHAM LAKES. (Klamath Co.) A series of three hike-in lakes, two miles south

of Crescent Lake. There are no fish in the lakes at this time.

BLACK LAKE. A 4-acre brook trout lake in Hatfield Wilderness (formerly Columbia Wilderness) of Mt. Hood National Forest which provides some good fishing. It's about 18 road miles southwest of Hood River, one mile south of Rainy Lake, off the Rainy Lake Rd. (Forest Rd. 2820). See Rainy Lake for directions. Black Lake is at the end of the road. Contrary to most maps, the road does not continue beyond Black. The lake is off to the right of the road. There is no sign on 2820 indicating the lake is there.

Though small and fairly shallow, this lake can offer good fishing at times for brook trout 7 to 14 inches. Bait will usually produce, especially early in the season, and spinner and bait combinations work well for large fish if retrieved slowly. Flies, either wet or dry, are good late in the season. There are a few campsites at the lake. Bring wet weather gear no matter what the weather map says. Like Wahtum and Rainy lakes, Black is peculiarly situated in relation to weather-generating Mt. Hood so that it is often cloudy and wet here while the sun is shining elsewhere in the area.

BLOW LAKE. A shallow 45-acre trout lake a mile off the road south of Elk Lake. From Bend, follow Century Drive (Hwy. 46) 37 miles south to Six Lakes Trailhead 14, about one mile south of Elk Lake. Blow Lake is an easy one-mile hike over pretty level terrain.

Only 23 feet at its deepest point, it offers good fishing for stocked brook trout 9 to 12 inches. All methods can be effective, with June and the fall months best. There are several natural campsites along the shore. A recommended hike-and-fish for youngsters, with swimming opportunities in July and August when the water temperature warms from refreshing to downright pleasant.

BLOWDOWN LAKE. A small, lightly fished hike-in brook trout lake a mile southeast of Taylor Lake. Take the Taylor Burn Rd. (Forest Rd. 600) from Little Cultus Lake to Irish and Taylor Lakes. This road is very rough and often snowbound until June. From the Pacific Crest Trail crossing at Irish Lake, backtrack exactly one mile. Hike south from the road uphill

¼ mile to the lake.

Blowdown is only about 4 acres, but can produce well. Stocked lightly by air, it generally has a good number of brook trout 8 to 14 inches. All methods work, but it's a good fly-fishing lake. A float tube will be handy, as the shore is brushy. There are no campsites here, but there are good camps at Irish Lake.

BLUE LAKE. (Jefferson Co.) A very deep, pretty lake in the Deschutes National Forest about 16 miles west of Sisters, south of Hwy. 20. It can be seen from the highway as you approach Suttle Lake from the west. Most of the lakeshore is now in private ownership, and it is no longer stocked.

The lake is 65 acres, 300 feet deep, and extremely clear with no natural fish production. For many years it was open to public access, with boat ramps, a resort, and a fishery for stocked rainbow trout. The resort is no longer in operation, and public access is limited to hiking-in from the Corbett sno-park west of the lake.

BLUE LAKE. (Confederated Tribes Warm Springs) An attractive pear-shaped 26-acre lake at the base of the northern slope of Olallie Butte. It is closed to public use.

BOBBY LAKE. A very good brook and rainbow trout lake in the Deschutes National Forest halfway between Odell and Waldo lakes. Although popular, the lake is far enough into the brush to produce consistently.

From Hwy. 58, take the Waldo Lake Rd. (Forest Rd. 5897) north about 6 miles to the Bobby Lake Trailhead (3663). This trail leads east about 2½ miles to the lake. The lake can also be reached from the east by way of Forest Rd. 4652, north of Davis Lake across from North Davis Creek Campground. The trail follows Moore Creek 4½ miles to the lake.

Bobby Lake, with 85 acres, has always been a good producer. There are brook trout to 16 inches here, though the average catch is 10 to 11 inches. It's a good fly lake, but lures and bait will work. It is stocked with both brook trout and rainbows in odd number years.

BOOTH LAKE. A fair brook trout lake in the Mt. Jefferson Wilderness on the southeast slope of Three Fingered Jack. Take the Pacific Crest Trail north from its crossing of Hwy. 20, one mile east of the Hoodoo Ski Bowl turnoff in the Santiam Pass area. A quarter mile north of the highway, Square Lake Trail 65 heads off to the east. Booth Lake is about 2 miles farther, 1½ miles north of Square Lake to the left of the trail.

The lake is about 8 acres and is usually accessible in June. Most of the fish are about 9 inches, with some to 12. It's an easy lake to fish.

BOULDER LAKE. (Confederated Tribes Warm Springs) A good hike-in brook trout lake ½ mile south of Trout Lake on the west edge of Warm Springs Reservation. The lake is accessible only by an unimproved trail which begins at the Trout Lake Rd., about ¼ mile east of Trout Lake Campground.

Boulder is a round, 50-acre lake at elevation 4780 ft. It has a maximum depth of 29 ft., with about ⅓ of its area shoals. There are about 2 miles of shoreline, most of which is quite brushy. The lake is aptly named for the very large boulders that cover most of its bottom. It produces plump brook trout. A CTWS permit is required and may be purchased at the market in Warm Springs. No overnight camping is allowed due to fire danger.

BOULDER LAKE. (White River watershed) A fair rainbow trout lake in the Mt. Hood National Forest on the southeast slope of Mt. Hood. It's about ½ mile hike to the lake from Bonney Camp, which is reached by 6 miles of poor road from Bennett Pass on Hwy. 35. The roads are usually snowbound until July. Approaches from the west clear earlier.

Boulder Lake has about 20 surface acres. A talus pile on the west side of the lake makes a good platform for fly casting. The fish here don't get large, averaging 8 inches. Little Boulder Lake, about half as big, is ½ mile bushwhack southeast and provides good angling for brook trout at times. Both lakes are stocked with fingerlings. There are natural campsites at Boulder Lake.

BRAHMA LAKE. A nice 10-acre brook trout lake off the Pacific Crest Trail in the Deschutes National Forest, north of Irish and Taylor lakes. From the south on Hwy. 58, take the Davis Lake Rd. past Crane Prairie to Forest Rd. 600, which is intersected by the Pacific Crest Trail at Irish

and Taylor Lakes. Brahma is an easy 2-mile hike north.

It offers good angling for brook trout to 15 inches. Average size is around 10 inches. Fly fishing is good, as the lake is quite shallow. Wet bucktails fished with a slow retrieve can be effective. A few natural campsites are available. In early season the mosquitoes in this area are unbelievable. Be prepared. A mosquito helmet can be a godsend here.

BUTTON POND. A one-acre pond associated with the Columbia River at highway mile 65, two miles east of Cascade Locks. It is immediately south of the freeway with limited vehicle parking on an unimproved road paralleling the freeway. Access is from exit 64. See Columbia River Ponds map.

CABOT LAKE. A small lake in the Mt. Jefferson Wilderness on the northern edge of the Deschutes National Forest. Six acres and shallow, it has had a tendency to winterkill, but cutthroat seem able to survive. To reach it from Suttle Lake on Hwy. 20, turn north on Forest Rd. 12, then bear left onto Forest Rd. 1230, which deadends at a trailhead. Trail 3 reaches Cabot in about 1½ miles. Other lakes in the basin (Carl and Shirley) are not stocked.

CACHE LAKE. A lake which is trying to turn back into meadow in the Deschutes National Forest southwest of Suttle Lake on the Jefferson-Deschutes County line. From Hwy. 20, 2 miles east of the Suttle Lake turn-off, follow Forest Rd. 2066 west 2 miles to Forest Rd. 2068, and continue west on 2068 a bit over 2 miles to a short spur which leads to the lake. Look for the spur just before the road makes a sharp hairpin east.

Cache Lake is very shallow, and stocking has been discontinued due to excessive weed growth. Brook trout and cutthroat may still be available for some years, offering good fly fishing in early season. Cache is usually accessible in early summer. There is no campground. Motorboats are prohibited.

CARL LAKE. A good size trout lake in the Metolius River watershed on the eastern edge of Mt. Jefferson Wilderness. From Hwy. 20 about one mile east of the Suttle Lake turn-off, take Forest Rd. 12 north about 4 miles to Forest Rd. 1230, which

branches north at Jack Creek Campground. Follow 1230, the Abbot Butte Rd., 8 miles north to its end, where you will find Trailhead 68. The trail leads 2 miles west to Cabot Lake. Carl is about 2 miles beyond Cabot by way of Trail 68.

Carl is not a rich lake, and its population of stocked cutthroat average 9 to 11 inches. A long deep lake, it can be effectively fished using any technique.

CHARLTON LAKE. A large brook trout lake along the Pacific Crest Trail 2 miles east of Waldo Lake. It is best reached by the Waldo Lake Rd. (Forest Rd. 5897), a paved road leading north from Hwy. 58 about 3 miles west of Odell Lake. Near the north end of Waldo Lake, the road turns sharply to the east and gives way to gravel. This is easy to miss, as a paved road continues north to North Waldo Lake Campground. The quarter-mile trail into the lake is within a mile of the transition to gravel.

Charlton is big, and sometimes the fish are hard to find. Watch for rough water during the day. Brook trout here average 10 to 12 inches with some to 16 inches. Spinners or lures do well, but flies will out-fish both in fall. Peak fishing is just after ice-out and again late in the season. Ice-out is hard to catch, as snow often blocks the roads.

Blueberries are abundant here in late summer, and there are some improved campsites. Motorboats are prohibited.

CHENOWETH CREEK. A small, lightly fished stream about 10 miles long, entering the Columbia at the west end of The Dalles. It is followed by gravel road west to the headwaters. It offers fair catch and release fishing for wild cutthroat (artificial flies and lures only) in late fall and early spring. There's a lot of private property, so ask permission to fish.

CLEAR CREEK. (White River watershed) A fair trout stream flowing from Clear Lake east into the White River in Mt. Hood National Forest. The creek is crossed by Hwy. 26 about 14 miles southeast of Government Camp. Several forest roads follow and cross the stream as well.

Clear Creek has good numbers of rainbow and brook trout in the 7 to 12 inch range, some from Clear Lake. There is no limit on the number of brook trout that may be kept. Fishing is usually good from early season through the summer in the upper section. Irrigation water is diverted from the lower stream. A small portion of the creek is on Warm Springs Reservation land and is signed to that effect.

CLEAR LAKE. (White River watershed) A good trout lake on the east side of Mt. Hood, heavily stocked with legal rainbows. It is about 67 miles from Portland by Hwy. 26. Turn off at a well-signed intersection to the right, about 11 miles past Government Camp. It's a short mile to the lake. A good road follows the lake shore half-way around.

Clear Lake covers just under a square mile most of the season, but is heavily drawn down for irrigation by fall. Stocked rainbow trout (as many as 17 thousand annually) supplement the lake's self-sustaining population of brook trout. Both species average 8 to 12 inches, with some fish to 18 inches. Excess brood trout are also stocked when available.

Trolling and bait fishing are popular, and flies are good early and late in the day. Crayfish are abundant.

There is a nice campground with boat ramp on the east shore of the lake. When the reservoir is low, the ramp is only usable by smaller boats.

CLIFF LAKE. (Wasco Co.) An I-84 pond adjacent to the Columbia River, located at highway mile 74.6. Only one acre, it is immediately east of McClures Lake south of the freeway. There is limited unimproved parking for eastbound traffic only at the east end of the lake. The pond may contain any of the Columbia River warmwater species. See the map of Columbia River Ponds.

CODY PONDS. Three small ponds west of Tygh Valley offering bass and panfish. From Hwy. 197 south of the Dalles, head west 5 miles to the community of Wamic. From there continue west 4 miles on Rock Creek Reservoir Rd. Between 2 small ponds on the right, a road turns north. Follow this a short way to the first 5-acre pond. For the second pond, stay on the main road to Rock Creek Reservoir, and head north on Forest Rd. 466. After one mile, turn right to the pond, which has about 6 surface acres. The third, with 5 acres, is on the north edge of the Reservoir road, about 1½ miles from Rock Creek.

The ponds are all on land managed by ODFW, but the second has only a 10-foot public easement around the shore. All are shallow, with good populations of bluegill and bass. The bass are rather small, with an occasional 16-inch fish tops. A rubber boat or float tube would be handy on the lakes, but they're easily fished from shore. There are no facilities at any of the ponds, but there's a campground at Rock Creek Reservoir. Recommended for youngsters.

CRANE PRAIRIE RESERVOIR

A large, very rich reservoir fed by the waters of the upper Deschutes River. Beautiful and productive for very large rainbows, brook trout, and largemouth bass, it is one of Oregon's premier fisheries. Relatively shallow water, abundant cover, and dense insect populations make this a fly fishing paradise. It covers over 5 square miles, with many interesting arms and bays, historically maintaining a fairly constant water level. Average depth of the reservoir is 11 ft. at full pool, with the old river channels running to 20 ft. deep. Boats or float tubes are necessary to reach good fishing.

When Crane Prairie was flooded in 1920, most of its timber was left standing. Though many of the old stands have deteriorated, silver skeletons of the old forest still rise from the water. Fallen timber forms intricate and extensive log jams. Approximately ten percent of the lake is covered by these stands, which provide excellent fish habitat and, with the bottom ooze and pond weed, produce an enormous supply of fish food, including mayflies, midges, caddis, leeches, scuds and other trout delights. Curiously, damsel flies, whose hatch was a highlight of the fly fishing season here as recently as 1992, have been in short supply, and dragonflies were depleted by commercial harvest of their nymphs a number of years ago.

Crane Prairie is a Wildlife Management Area. Osprey, Canadian geese, assorted ducks, grebes, blue herons, bald eagles, and an occasional sandhill crane are among the many birds that frequent the area .Osprey and eagles nest in the snag forest and do their own share of fishing with consummate skill. Deer, elk, mink, porcupine, and otter can be seen at the water's edge.

Crane Prairie is east of Century Drive (Forest Rd. 46) about 46 miles from Bend. Alternately, one can drive south from Bend about 18 miles on Hwy. 97 to County Rd. 42, Fall River Hwy. Turn off 2½ miles past the Sunriver junction, and continue west approximately 20 miles to Forest Rd. 4270, which is signed for Crane Prairie. Turn right. It is only 4 miles to the east side of

CRANE PRAIRIE's partially submerged old forest and log jams provide habitat for insects and fish. Photograph by Scott Richmond.

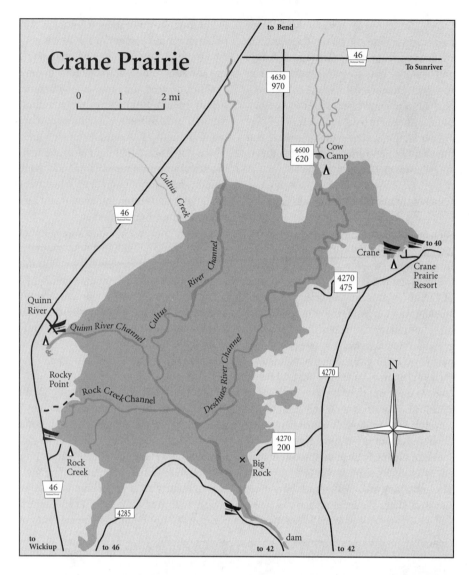

Crane Prairie

0   1   2 mi

to Bend

46
National Forest

To Sunriver

4630
970

4600
620

Cow
Camp

Cultus Creek

46
National Forest

Cultus River Channel

Crane

to 40

4270
475

Crane
Prairie
Resort

Quinn
River

Quinn River Channel

Cultus River Channel

Deschutes River Channel

4270

Rocky
Point

Rock Creek Channel

N

4270

Rock
Creek

4270
200

46
National Forest

× Big
Rock

4285

to
Wickiup   to 46

dam

to 42   to 42

---

the lake. From the Willamette Valley, Eugene offers good access by way of Hwy. 58 to the Davis Lake cutoff (Hwy. 61), which is 3 miles south of the Crescent Lake junction. Take Hwy. 46 north past Davis Lake to the junction with Hwy. 42. Here one may go east to reach Crane Prairie's eastern shore, or proceed north to the campground on the west or the resort on the north shore.

Trout are the biggest draw for Crane Prairie anglers. Trout put on pounds quickly in these rich waters. In good years, the average catch is 12 inches, with many big fish taken daily. Rainbows close to 19 pounds (and 35 inches) and brook trout to 6 pounds have been landed. Five pounders don't even raise eyebrows.

The lake opens for fishing at the end of April, but best trout fishing is often in July and again in September and October. It can still be winter here in May and early June, and August is often slow.

Fly fishing is very popular at Crane Prairie. In early season, before weed growth is excessive, large rainbows (whose natural prey are baby bass and sticklebacks) can be taken on large trolled woolly buggers or big streamers. Callibaetis mayflies hatch from late spring through summer, gradually diminishing in size. Midges and caddis are almost always present in one form or another. Leech imitations can be productive any time, but especially on overcast days and before the sun is on the water. Dragonfly and damselfly nymphs can still be productive. If and when the spectacular damselfly hatches of past years return to Crane, anticipate them from opening day till the end of July. For best results fishing any fly, use a long leader, intermediate line, and in most cases, an excruciatingly slow retrieve. Overcast days are almost always productive.

Trout are also taken on bait. Both Power Bait (all colors) and worms are productive.

Traditionally, bait anglers also fished live dragonfly and damsel nymphs. Keep your bait out of the bottom vegetation. Power Bait and nightcrawlers are both popular.

Spring is the best time to fish with lures here, before natural forage is abundant. Panther Martins, Kwikfish-type lures, Roostertails, and spinner and worm combinations cast and retrieved among the snags can be productive. Rapalas can catch the eye of larger trout. Trolling spoons (and trolling in general) is less effective here than at other big lakes, though some large trout are taken on the troll before weed growth is thick.

As a rule of thumb, in spring and early summer and when the reservoir is high, look for trout close to shore and among the submerged trees. As the water lowers and warms, head for the channels. In early summer you can sometimes locate the channels by sight, but a depth finder is helpful once the weeds thicken. The biggest fish are usually landed in May and June, but there is no off-season here. Occasionally, in a dry cycle, the reservoir gets so low that the lake is closed to angling in late summer to protect the trout from over-fishing.

Largemouth bass, illegally introduced, are thriving and may offer the best bass fishing in eastern Oregon. Though trout seem to be holding their own against these uninvited smolt predators (and competitors for space and food when times are tough), anglers are encouraged to catch and keep their limit whenever possible. Aggressive "keeping" will also help increase the size of the average catch, which is running small due to overpopulation. Most bass run 3 to 4 pounds, with some to 7 pounds.

Try fishing for bass in mornings before trout fishing turns on, or in evenings when most Crane Prairie trout have tucked in for the night. The average catch is 2 to 3 pounds, with 5-pounders not uncommon, and an occasional fish to 7 pounds. Bass can be found throughout the reservoir, though they generally avoid the cool water of the channels and the whole north end. In spring when the reservoir is high and cold, they seem to favor the shallows east of the Deschutes channel and associated backwaters, which tend to be warmer. They are also fished in the protected coves of the southern shore and along the dam. The southwest coves are also good bass haunts, as is Rocky Point (fish either side of the rocky mound on the bottom).

Their main forage prior to the drought in the early '90s was tui chub, which ran 10 to 11 inches. Since the tui population took a dive, bass have been feeding on illegally introduced stickleback. A 3-inch silver lure does a good stickleback imitation. Top water plugs, such as the Rapala or Rebel, especially in silver or gold with a black back, make sense in this weedy environment. Plastic worms are also effective.

Kokanee are well established, though their population grows thin when low water prevents them from reaching their spawning areas in Quinn, Cultus, and upper Deschutes rivers. Troll for them in the Rock Creek vicinity early in the season, and come back in fall to fish schooling kokanee in the channels. Mature Crane Prairie kokanee can reach 20 inches and more.

In addition to the bass, bluegill, black crappie, and three-spine stickleback have been illegally introduced to the reservoir. So far, Crane Prairie's trout seem to be holding their own, but illegal introductions can result in disaster for a trout fishery due to predation on smolts and competition for food. We have only to look at the sad state of Diamond Lake to understand why it is not only illegal—but in the best interest of our sport—not to transport live fish between water bodies.

Crane Prairie is so large and complex, it can be a bit overwhelming at first, but likely looking habitat is more obvious here than at most big lakes. Early in the season when the reservoir is high, fish along submerged shoreline trees, over the flats, and among the old submerged forest. Avoid the colder channels till the water warms. Heading for concentrations of other boats is a reasonable scouting tactic. Position yourself a generous cast away from the casting range of others. Look for brook trout among the old submerged forests near Cultus, Deschutes, Quinn River, and Rock Creek channels early in the season. More sensitive to water temperature than rainbows, brook trout will be the first to move into the cooler channels as things heat up. Information about what's happening at Crane Prairie is available at fly shops throughout Central Oregon and the Willamette Valley. Guides specializing in Crane Prairie are also available through the shops. See Appendix.

There are good boat ramps at Rock Creek. Quinn River Campground, and at and near Crane Prairie Resort. A 10-mph speed limit is in effect. Float tubes can be launched at Rock Creek, Rocky Point, and at the end of Forest Rd. 4270-470. Canoes and float tubes work fine here, but keep a weather eye out. The campground south of the resort has 2 boat ramps. There is a very poor ramp (not recommended) by the dam. The only shore fishing opportunities are around Rock Creek, the dam, and Crane Prairie Resort.

There are 4 campgrounds on the reservoir. Rock Creek and Quinn River campgrounds on the west shore are large and have boat ramps. The campground south of the resort is like a small city, with 140 spaces. The campground at Cow Meadow on the north shore is very small with poor access to the reservoir. The road into Cow Camp is a bit rough, and there is no ramp, though you can slip a shallow draft cartopper or canoe into the Deschutes River and drift down. A campground shows up on the forest map at the dam, but there are no developed sites there. All these camping areas get crowded on weekends and holidays, and individual sites are not very secluded. Cow Meadow sometimes offers the best bet for solitude.

Boats, motors, and canoes can be rented at the resort, and gasoline is available there. The resort also stocks limited general supplies, tackle, and a good selection of flies. It does not offer lodging, but it does have RV hook-ups and showers. The nearest overnight lodging is available at Twin Lakes and in Sunriver, Bend, and LaPine.

For more information about how to fish Crane Prairie, see *Fishing in Oregon's Cascade Lakes* and *Fishing in Oregon's Best Fly Waters*.

CRESCENT CREEK. A trout stream which meanders 40 miles through Deschutes National Forest from Crescent Lake to the Little Deschutes River. Its fish populations are currently depressed, an aftereffect of the drought or possibly due to disease.

Crescent Creek flows east out of Crescent Lake and away from any roads for its first 2 miles. The creek then swings south, paralleling Hwy. 58 for about 3 miles, where it flows through mostly private land. It then turns east again, crossing and leaving Hwy. 58, entering a steep valley in the Deschutes National Forest. Within the for-

est the creek is followed from above by Forest Rd. 61, the shortcut to Lapine and main route to Davis Lake. Crescent Creek is intersected by this road just past the Davis Lake turn-off and trends east through mostly private land until it joins the Little Deschutes River about 5 miles north of the town of Crescent on Hwy. 97.

In past years, the creek has supported healthy populations of brown trout 8 to 14 inches and rainbow trout a little smaller. Big browns and rainbows, once found regularly in this stream, have been conspicuously absent for a number of years.

Best fishing on the creek is in the steep valley. It isn't easy to get down there, and the bank is brushy. Park anywhere along the road and climb down, or bull your way in from a road crossing.

There is a campground at the stream crossing on Forest Rd. 61, and lodging on Hwy. 58.

CRESCENT LAKE. (Klamath Co.) A large deep lake in the Deschutes National Forest, 3 miles south of Odell Lake, offering fair fishing for hefty mackinaw, brown trout, and rainbow, as well as kokanee and whitefish. Just under 6 square miles, with a depth of 280 ft., it's a popular general recreation area, with clear sparkling water and miles of wooded shoreline.

Crescent Lake is about 75 miles southeast of Eugene by Hwy. 58, about 18 miles northwest of the junction of highways 58 and 97. A small community, Crescent Lake Junction, is on Hwy. 58 at the turnoff to the lake, Forest Rd. 60. The forest road reaches the lake in about 2 miles and hugs the western and southern shore for about 5 miles. Forest Rd. 6015 follows the eastern shore.

This big, deep lake grows big, deep-bodied lake trout from 5 to 10 pounds, with some over 20 pounds occasionally landed. A 33-pound mackinaw was landed in 1993. The mackinaw population is currently down following years of low water in the late 1990's, but if good precipitation continues, numbers and size will increase in time (fish that live 30 years take a take a while to grow to size). Minimum keeper size is 30 inches, and mature macks can reach 40 inches.

Ice-out finds the big trout cruising the shallows, and anglers have good success casting spoons from shore, particularly in the Simax Beach area on the northeast side

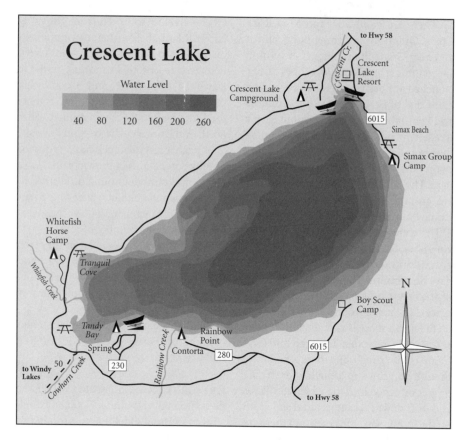

Crescent Lake

Water Level

40 80 120 160 200 260

to Hwy 58

Crescent Cr.

Crescent Lake Resort

Crescent Lake Campground

6015

Simax Beach

Simax Group Camp

Whitefish Horse Camp

Tranquil Cove

Whitefish Creek

Boy Scout Camp

N

Tandy Bay

Spring

Rainbow Point

Contorta

Rainbow Creek

280

6015

to Windy Lakes

50

230

Cowhorn Creek

to Hwy 58

of the lake. Fly anglers participate in the action at this time of year using big leech patterns and dragonfly nymphs. The trick is spotting the fish and casting directly to them. Wearing polaroid glasses helps.

By July, mackinaw begin to school in deep water. Deep trolling with downriggers and lead line along the summer home area

(northwest shore) and along the ledges off Spring and Contorta Point campgrounds (southern shore) is often productive. A depth finder is useful to locate the ledges. If you don't have one, the area offshore from the scout camp, one mile east of Contorta Point, has a straight ledge at 80 feet that is easy to track. Trollers favor lures

that resemble kokanee, the mack's favorite forage. Kwikfish-type lures or fish-imitation plugs like Rebels or Rapala are effective. Fly anglers use big streamers. In spring and fall, trollers often work at depths of 20 to 30 ft. In summer, they go deeper.

A big lead jig, like the Luhr Jensen Nordic, might be effective here, as they have been at nearby Odell. With these jigs, anglers can avoid all the special downrigging gear. The only catch is, of course, being (and knowing you be) directly over the fish in order to get results.

Kokanee are the most popular fishery on the lake. Though less abundant in Crescent than in nearby Odell Lake, they tend to be larger. Fingerling kokanee are planted annually and generally grow to 13 or 14 inches, with some catches to 20 inches. Kokanee move in schools throughout the lake, ending their migration in fall at Crescent Creek near the resort. Check at the resort to learn where the schools have been located and at what depth to fish. Kokanee are generally taken by jigging or by trolling spinner and bait. Light-weight gear with a downrigger offers the best sport. Dodgers and lake trolls are also popular, though they require a heavier rod and line and (consequently) a lighter touch in order to keep the hook from pulling out of the comparatively diminutive kokanee. Like the mackinaw, kokanee numbers are currently down following the low-water cycle, but are on the rebound.

Brown trout continue to be stocked and grow to respectable size in Crescent. Fish to 12 pounds have been taken. Rainbow trout reproduce naturally here, and additional rainbows from the Deschutes hatchery are stocked each year. All angling methods are used, with good success near the creek inlets on the southern shore. Whitefish also show up in the catch. Some anglers regard them as a nuisance, but they make fine eating, especially if smoked. Bank angling opportunities are available on the northwest shore near the road and near the west side campgrounds.

Though a natural lake, Crescent is heavily drawn down for irrigation, and drought can have a significant effect on Crescent fisheries. In dry years, kokanee can't reach their spawning areas, and habitat is significantly diminished for rainbows and browns.

There are three Forest Service campgrounds on the lake shore—Crescent Lake,

The CROOKED RIVER below Bowman Dam offers some of Oregon's best winter trout fishing. Photograph by Dennis Frates.

Spring, and Contorta Point. Each has a boat ramp. Picnic facilities are available at Simax Beach, Tandy Bay, and Tranquil Cove. Housekeeping cabins are available for rent at Crescent Lake Resort, which also has a full-service restaurant, motor boat and canoe rentals, and fishing tackle. Groceries and additional fishing supplies are available at Crescent Lake Junction on Hwy. 58.

For more information, see *Fishing in Oregon's Cascade Lakes*, published by Flying Pencil.

CROOKED RIVER

One of the most productive trout streams in Oregon, carving handsome canyons through the central Oregon desert before joining the Deschutes River in Lake Billy Chinook. The North Fork heads in the Ochoco Mts. about 75 miles east of Prineville. The South Fork heads in the high desert northeast of Brothers on the G.I. Ranch.

The most popular and accessible fishery on the river is concentrated in the seven miles below Bowman Dam. This is a classic tailrace fishery, cooled by releases from Prineville Reservoir. It is estimated that each of the seven miles holds from 2,000 to 8,000 redband rainbows, and while the average size is only 10 to 12 inches, fish over 20 inches and weighing 3 pounds are occasionally taken.

Don't be put off by the water color here. Releases from the reservoir contain a high amount of suspended clay, but that doesn't keep the fish from seeing flies as small as No. 18., even if you can't.

This stretch of the river is open year-round, but best catches are made autumn through spring. Fishing is catch and release with artificial flies and lures only from November 1 to the late April general trout opener. The river gets too warm for good fishing in summer. Midges, scuds, and blue-winged olive mayflies in all life stages offer year-round trout food. Little black stoneflies hatch February through March. Pale morning duns (mayflies) hatch April through September.

To reach this stretch from Prineville, follow Hwy. 27 toward Bowman Dam. Do not head toward Prineville Reservoir. There are a dozen developed access sites below the dam, including ten campgrounds. Paths connect many of the sites.

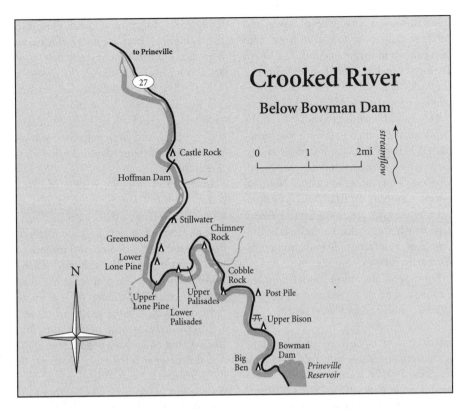

There's generally good casting room from the bank, but the river is easily waded, and crossing over to the west bank is often possible in some places. The rocks are slippery, however, so watch your step.

Another reach of the lower Crooked that offers good angling but considerably more rugged access is the Crooked River Gorge, about 10 river miles south of Lake Billy Chinook. To reach this area, follow the road to Opal Springs off Hwy. 97 south of Culver. Opal Springs is a private water and hydroelectric facility. Anglers may use the private road, which is open during weekdays, but are requested to check in at the facility office. On weekends when the road is closed, park at the rim and walk down to the river (about 1½ miles). Another half mile of public access is available above Opal Springs through the golf course at Crooked River Ranch.

The mainstem above Prineville Reservoir suffers from riparian degradation and heavy irrigation withdrawals. Trout survival in this section is poor during drought years.

Both North and South forks of the Crooked are spring fed, in good shape in their upper reaches, and open to fishing. Check current regulations for special restrictions. Though much of the South Fork flows through BLM land, access is limited by surrounding ranchland. The only drive-

in access is a rough road leading south about 4 miles east of the BLM office on the Post-Paulina Rd. The road shows up on the Ochoco National Forest Map. Driving toward Paulina (east) look for a small sign on the right. The road ends at a BLM site, known as Congleton Hollow, which offers river access and undeveloped campsites. The access is not named on Forest maps. For best fishing, head upstream about 2 miles.

South Fork trout average 12 to 18 inches, and the river is capable of growing fingerlings to 10 inches in a single season. Grindstone lake, a private pay-to-fish reservoir on the South Fork, attests to the stream's capacity to grow big trout. At this time, the South Fork opens in late April and is restricted to artificial flies and lures with a two fish limit.

The North Fork also grows trout to good size. A rough road heading north off the Post-Paulina Rd. about 4½ miles west of the BLM office leads to the only public access on the lower North Fork. The upper Fork is approached by Forest Rd. 42 in the Ochoco National Forest west of Prineville. Follow Forest Rd. 42 to Deep Creek Campground, then get out your topo map. This stretch offers anglers a quality fishing experience, more for the rugged beauty of the canyons than for the abundance of large trout. The North Fork of the Crooked flows through a narrow deep canyon and offers angling for 12 to 15 inch trout, with best catches in spring and fall. The North Fork opens in late April. The confluence of the forks east of Prineville is adjacent to private property, closed to public access.

Developed campgrounds on the Crooked are limited to the stretch immediately below Prineville Reservoir and to Deep Creek Campground near the North Fork on Forest Rd. 42 in Ochoco National Forest. Camping on BLM land is permitted wherever you can find a flat spot free of sage brush and rocks. Be aware that rattlesnakes are a fact of life in canyon country, particularly in summer.

For more information about fishing the Crooked, see *Fishing in Oregon's Best Fly Waters* , published by Flying Pencil.

CULTUS LAKE, BIG. A large deep lake with decent fishing for rainbows and mackinaw (lake trout), about 50 miles southwest of Bend in Deschutes National Forest. Take Century Drive (Forest Rd. 46) south from Bend to the Cultus Lake turnoff, about 10 miles past Elk Lake. Forest Rd. 4635 leads to the lake. The road is paved, and there is a sign for Cultus Lake Resort at the turn-off. From the Willamette Valley, take Hwy. 58 southeast from Eugene to the Davis Lake cutoff (Hwy. 61), which is 3 miles south of the Crescent Lake junction. Then take 46 north past Davis Lake and Crane Prairie to the Cultus turn-off.

Cultus has 785 surface acres and is exceptionally deep and sparkling clear. In places, its blue waters reach a depth of 200 feet. Lurking in these depths are hefty lake

trout from 3 to 7 pounds, with 15 pound fish available. There are fewer mackinaw here than at Odell or Crescent, but there are also generally fewer anglers.

In the first few weeks after ice-out you can find lake trout in the shallows, and even tempt them with a fly (try big dragonfly nymphs and leech patterns). Mackinaw fishing is best in May and from mid-September on.

In July and August, macks head for deeper water. Their primary quarry is whitefish. Trolling flashers with Kwikfish-type lures near drop-offs is a good method. Trollers use lead core line or 6 ounces of lead to get down to the fish, and a fish-finder really helps. The deepest area is from about ½ mile northwest of the lodge (which is located on the southeast shore), right down the middle of the lake. The shallow west end is least productive.

A downrigger is the best way to get to the mackinaw without weighting your line. If you want to try this fishery without investing in a lot of special gear, you might look into a leaded jig like the Luhr Jensen Nordic. There is some indication that these jigs are taken more readily than a trolled lure if you're over the fish. With a fish finder, that's not hard to accomplish.

Cultus also offers pretty good fishing for rainbows, including both stocked trout and a pretty good population of wild fish. Most run 8 to 12 inches, but a few reach 18 inches. Trolling accounts for most catches. The southeast shoreline is a popular area, and sticking close to shore is good advice anywhere on the lake. You might also try working the shelves along the northwest

shore. Fly casting along shore can be productive in late summer and fall. A few brook trout show up around the mouth of Winopee Creek at the northwest end of the lake. Whitefish are abundant and tasty when smoked.

This is a popular general recreation lake in a beautiful setting, though without spectacular mountain views. It has nice swimming areas and is one of the few lakes in the area without a speed limit, so water-skiing and large boat cruising are popular, as is sailing.

Cultus Resort is a pleasant place, with restaurant, boat and motor rentals, cabins, supplies and gas. West Cultus Campground, north of the resort, has a boat ramp. There are also three boat-in or hike-in campgrounds. On the north shore, Little Cove is about 3 miles by water from the resort, and Big Cove is near the lake's midpoint. Trail 16 from Cultus Lake Campground reaches these campgrounds and continues on to Teddy Lakes. West Cultus Campground is at the extreme west end of the lake. Other trails at the west end lead to Teddy Lakes and Corral Lakes. For more information about how to fish Cultus, see *Fishing in Oregon's Cascade Lakes*, published by Flying Pencil.

CULTUS LAKE, LITTLE. A very nice trout lake in the Deschutes National Forest southwest of Bend on the east slope of the Cascade Range. Don't let the "little" fool you. The lake has 170 surface acres. It is about 50 miles from Bend by way Century Drive (County and Forest Rd. 46). From 46, take Forest Rd. 4635 toward Big Cultus. At a little over ½ mile, turn left on Forest Rd. 4630. When the road forks, keep going straight. You are now on Forest Rd. 4636, which reaches Little Cultus in a little over ½ mile. Later in the season, you can approach Little Cultus from Waldo Lake by way of the infamous Forest Rd. 600, which passes Irish and Taylor lakes. See Irish or Taylor for a description of this road.

Little Cultus offers good angling for naturally reproducing brook trout 9 to 10 inches, with an occasional fish to 14 inches. Wild rainbows to 15 inches can be found near the springs in the meadow at the west end of the lake. Best fishing is in early season and again in fall.

Though shoal area predominates, there is a deep hole (50 ft.) toward the west end, and an interesting variety of underwater

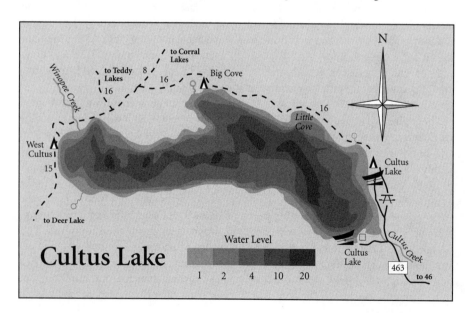

Cultus Lake

environments to fish. Trolling the west end is popular, but there's good fly and spin fishing throughout the lake. Nymphs, or bucktails fished wet can be especially effective late in the season.

There is a boat ramp off Forest Rd. 4636 toward the east end of the lake. A primitive campground a bit farther east beyond the boat ramp has drinking water, tables, fire rings, and outhouses. Other campsites are scattered along the south shore. There is a 10-mph speed limit for motorboats. For more information about fishing Little Cultus, see *Fishing in Oregon's Cascade Lakes*, published by Flying Pencil.

CULTUS RIVER. A very short stream in the Deschutes National Forest, primarily a spawning and rearing area for Crane Prairie rainbows and kokanee. It is about 50 miles southwest of Bend. The river rises from a large spring about 2 miles north of Crane Prairie Reservoir and flows into the north end of the reservoir. The road to Cultus Lake crosses it about mid-way, near Round Mountain. It is rather brushy but carries a lot of water.

There are very few trout of legal size in the stream. It is not recommended for angling except where it enters Crane Prairie.

DARK LAKE. (Confederated Tribes Warm Springs) The middle lake in a chain of five, which also includes Trout, Island, Long, and Olallie. It is accessible only by unimproved trail from either Olallie Lake on the east or Trout Lake on the west. From Trout Lake Campground, it's about a 1½ mile hike. The first quarter mile of trail is a fairly steep uphill grind, but the remaining distance is more easily traveled, passing Island Lake on the way in. The trail from Olallie Lake begins at the southeast end of Olallie and is most easily reached from Olallie Peninsula Campground.

With a maximum depth of 52 feet, Dark Lake is the deepest lake in the chain. It occupies a glacial cirque, its west and south shores abutting a steep talus slope 200 feet high. The shadow of this cliff over the lake and the lake's depth are responsible for its name. Dark Lake is at 4690 ft. and has a surface area of about 22 acres. There isn't a lot of shoal area around the lake. It supports brook trout. A CTWS permit is required to fish. Daily and annual permits are sold at stores on the reservation, at G.I. Joe's throughout the state, and at many fly

DAVIS LAKE is restricted to fly fishing with barbless hooks. Photograph by Scott Richmond.

shops. No overnight camping is allowed due to fire danger.

DARLENE LAKE. A small, deep hike-in brook trout lake in the Windy Lakes area southwest of Crescent Lake. See Crescent Lake for road directions. The trail is ½ mile west of the entrance to Spring Camp, sharing a trailhead with the Windy Lake Trail. It is about 4 miles to Windy. Darlene is about one mile farther on Trail 46. The trail continues east to eventually meet the Pacific Crest Trail.

Darlene covers 11 acres and is 48 feet deep. All angling methods can be used. There are some fair natural campsites at the lake.

DAVIS CREEK. Inundated by Wickiup Reservoir, it is a major cold water inlet to the reservoir, attracting large numbers of whitefish. See Wickiup Reservoir.

DAVIS LAKE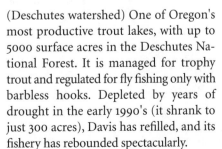

(Deschutes watershed) One of Oregon's most productive trout lakes, with up to 5000 surface acres in the Deschutes National Forest. It is managed for trophy trout and regulated for fly fishing only with barbless hooks. Depleted by years of drought in the early 1990's (it shrank to just 300 acres), Davis has refilled, and its fishery has rebounded spectacularly.

Davis Lake is about 8 miles south of Crane Prairie, 60 miles south of Bend by

way of Century Drive (County and Forest Rd. 46). From the Willamette Valley it is best reached by Hwy. 58, heading east from Eugene. About 3 miles past the turn-off to Crescent Lake, turn left onto County Rd. 61. After about 3 more miles, turn left onto Forest Rd. 46. Turn left at the junction of roads 46 and 62. At the T-intersection, turn right to reach Lava Campground at the north end of Davis. Turn left to reach East and West Davis campgrounds. Neither East or West Davis are on this road, but spur roads to the camps are well signed. Davis Lake is about 220 miles from Portland. In heavy snow years, roads into Davis can still be snow covered in late April and early May. Check with the Crescent Ranger District or Deschutes County Road Department. See Appendix.

Davis was created when volcanic action (less than 3000 years ago) sent a mile-wide, 100 ft. high wall of lava across the bed of Odell Creek. This natural dam formed a roughly round lake that can offer up to 5 square miles of fishable water, all of it under 25 feet deep. Water from Davis seeps through the lava dam (and into Wickiup Reservoir) at a fair rate. The lake is rich with vegetation and thick with insects. Tui chub (a problem in other Oregon lakes) here provide an excellent food source for big trout.

The Davis management plan calls for development of a trout fishery where average angler success is one fish for every three

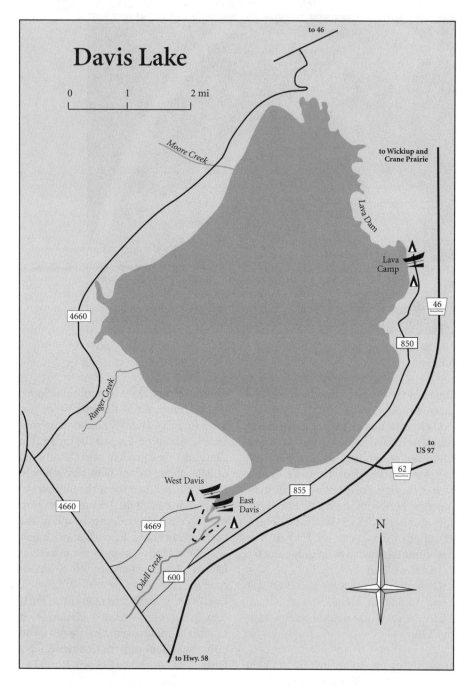

Davis Lake

0   1   2 mi

Moore Creek

to 46

to Wickiup and
Crane Prairie

Lava Dam

Lava
Camp

4660

46
National Forest

850

Ranger Creek

to
US 97

62
National Forest

West Davis

855

4660

East
Davis

4669

N

Odell Creek

600

to Hwy. 58

hours of effort, and where most fish land-ed are more than 15 inches. The lake has consistently met and exceeded this goal, except during the drought years of the early 1990's. The average catch currently is 12 to 16 inches, but fish 24 inches and bet-ter are present. A period of rebuilding Davis' fishery following the drought ended with a final stocking of Klamath rainbows in 1999. Natural reproduction will take over from this point.

Sometime during the late 1990's, large-mouth bass were illegally introduced in Davis. These could pose a threat to the trout fishery, and anglers are urged to catch and kill as many as possible. There is no

limit on the bass harvest. Best bass fishing is along the north shore on either side of the lava flow. The west side of the flow seems to be most productive. The marshy backwater is dynamite in spring. The little cove in the lava flow sometimes attracts schools of chubs, which attract the bass. The emerging vegetation on the east and west sides of the lake look bass-y but haven't been productive so far. Use pop-pers to attract the bass, or present tui imi-tations such as the Conehead Double Bunny or olive Matuka in sizes 4 or 6.

As for the trout, five square miles is a lot of water to cover, but there are some obvi-ously productive areas to target. In early

season, when trout seek warmer water, fish the shallows. The west shore between Moore and Ranger creek inlets is often warmer (submerged springs near Moore raise the water temperature at this time of year). Water temperature is also higher near the lava dam. By mid-summer, when trout seek cooler water, the Odell Creek channel is their refuge of choice. Fish also congregate near the much smaller Ranger and Moore inlets (where springs now keep the water temperature more moderate.) Deep water near the lava flows on the north shore also attracts concentrations of fish, as does the protective cover of weed growth on east and west shores. Try fishing right along the weed edge.

Though its tempting to fish the mouth of Odell Creek in the height of summer when trout are stacked up there like the proverbial cordwood, it's not exactly sport-ing (or in the longterm interest of the fish-ery). Check the water temperature, and if it's high and you've got the means to get out on the lake, consider leaving this area for bank anglers, and as a trout refuge and viewing area.

Davis is ideally suited to fly angling and, except for one five-year period, it has been so regulated since 1939. The lake is too thick with vegetation for effective trolling, and it's not deep enough for dependable still-fishing. Early in the season, leech pat-terns and yellow and white streamers are especially effective. The streamers imitate the tui chub that fatten larger trout here. Retrieve streamers with a quick stripping action. Midges are also abundant early in the year. In May and June, Callibaetis mayfly hatches can provide excellent dry fly opportunities. Dragonfly and damselfly nymph patterns can be productive in June near the reed beds along shore. Use in-creasingly long leaders as the season pro-gresses. By late summer, Davis Lake trout are definitely wiser, since most anglers here practice catch-and-release.

Regulations prohibit fishing while using a motor (i.e. no motor trolling), but you may motor from spot to spot. If you're rowing, paddling, or kicking a float tube, be advised that summer winds can quick-ly turn the lake into a character-building outdoor experience.

There are three campgrounds here, but Lava Campground is closed most of the year (January to September) to protect nesting eagles. Each campground has a boat ramp. In low water years, the Lava ramp is always usable if open, and the East Davis ramp is more reliable than the ramp at West Davis. All the campgrounds have pleasant primitive sites among lodgepole pines. A bridge across Odell Creek not far from the mouth connects East and West campgrounds. Drinking water is available.

For more information about fishing Davis Lake, see *Fishing in Oregon's Cascade Lakes* and *Fishing in Oregon's Best Fly Waters* , published by Flying Pencil.

DEEP CREEK. (Crooked River watershed) A good trout stream with harvest opportunities in the upper Crooked River drainage, Ochoco National Forest. It is about 45 miles east of Prineville. The stream is about 12 miles long and flows from the east into the North Fork of Crooked River about 4 miles east of Big Summit Prairie.

Take Hwy. 26 east from Prineville about 16 miles to Forest Rd. 42, which follows Ochoco Creek to the Ochoco Guard Station. About 12 miles beyond the guard station, swing southeast to Big Summit Prairie. Deep Creek Campground is 3 miles beyond Big Summit, at the confluence of Deep Creek and Crooked River. Forest Rd. 42 continues east, closely following Deep Creek.

The stream supports native rainbows 6 to 10 inches.

DEER LAKE. (Deschutes watershed) A very good early season brook trout and cutthroat lake in the Cultus Lake area southwest of Bend. The lake is about a mile northwest of Little Cultus Lake. Follow directions to Little Cultus Lake, then turn north onto the road that skirts the north shore of Little Cultus. This road leads 2 miles to the Deer Lake trailhead. Deer Lake is about a quarter mile up the trail.

The lake covers 70 acres but is only 20 feet deep at most. It supports stocked cutthroat and brook trout 8 to 12 inches. Bait or cast lures are good in spring, and fly fishing is productive in fall. There are campsites at Big and Little Cultus. Supplies and accommodations are available at Cultus Lake Resort.

DENNIS LAKE. (Deschutes watershed) A real jewel of a brook trout lake, a scenic blue beauty one mile past Irish Mt. on the Pacific Crest Trail. Best route in is to pick up the PCT at Irish Lake. See Irish Lake for road directions. Head north for about 5 miles on the PCT. Dennis is about a quarter mile west of the trail. There is no trail leading to the lake. The PCT reaches Blaze Lake about ½ mile past Irish Mt. A quarter mile farther, it crosses a spring creek. From this point, Dennis Lake is a quarter mile to the northwest and a steep 400 feet above the trail. Carry the Irish Mt. topo map for this one.

Dennis has 11 surface acres and is 42 feet deep. Any method will take trout. If you're fishing from shore, your best bet is to cast flies just beyond the shoal area. Fly anglers won't have trouble with their backcasts here. With a rubber boat or float tube, bait fishing between 15 and 30 feet deep can be very effective. There are fair natural campsites nearby.

DESCHUTES POND. No.1 One of the I-84 ponds adjacent to the Columbia River, located at highway mile 99. It may support any of the Columbia River warmwater species. An old paved road bisects this 3-acre pond, providing excellent vehicle access. It is south of Hwy. 30. See map of Columbia River Ponds.

DESCHUTES POND. No. 2 One of the I-84 ponds adjacent to the Columbia River, at highway mile 98.5. It covers 5 acres and is south of Hwy. 30, with good off-road parking. It may support any of the Columbia warmwater species. See map of Columbia River Ponds.

DESCHUTES POND EAST. One of the I-84 ponds adjacent to the Columbia River. It is between highway miles 99 and 99.8. It has 10 surface acres between I-84 and Hwy. 30. Park along Hwy. 30, not along the freeway. The pond may support any of the Columbia's warmwater species. See the map of Columbia River Warmwater Ponds.

DESCHUTES RIVER

DESCHUTES RIVER:Pelton Dam to the mouth. One of America's most productive trout waters and a top producer of summer steelhead, managed primarily for wild fish. The Deschutes pours into the Columbia River's Lake Celilo about 12 miles west of The Dalles, only a 2 hour drive from Oregon's largest metropolitan area.

This 100-mile stretch of the river drops 1233 feet, carving a canyon 700 to 2200 feet deep out of volcanic rock. Brown palisades rise on either side of the broad stream, and buff-colored hills roll to meet the horizon. The dry air, characteristic of the Cascade rain-shadow, is fragrant with sage, offering a happy alternative to western Oregon's wet-weather angling. Pungent junipers cluster in the draws. This is a land of cliff swallows, meadowlarks, hawks, snakes, and

The average DESCHUTES RIVER steelhead weights 5 to 10 pounds. Photograph by Scott Richmond.

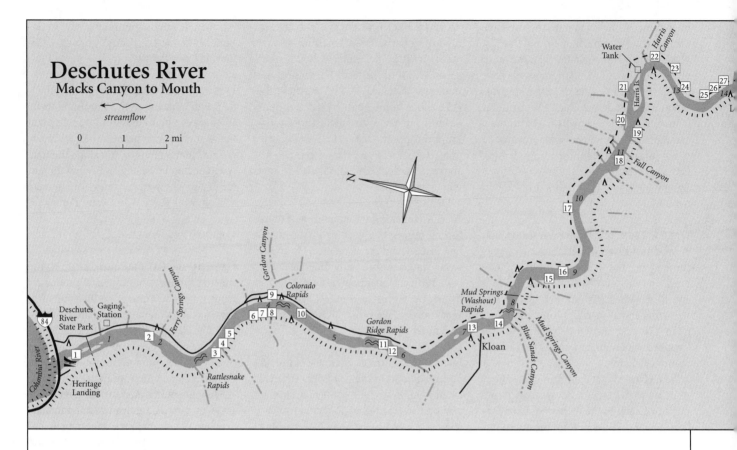

Deschutes River
Macks Canyon to Mouth

streamflow

0   1   2 mi

N

1. Cable Crossing.
2. Sand Hole.
3. Lava Rock Drift.
4. Fence Hole.
5. Twin Island Drift.
6. Merrill Hole.
7. Grasshopper Hole.
8. Ledge Hole.
9. Zeke's Riffle.
10. Wagon Blast Drift.
11. Sharp's Bar.
12. First Green Lt Hole.
13. Bathtub Hole.

14. Traveling Hole.
15. Bedspring Hole.
16. Kortege Corral Drift.
17. Newfound Hole.
18. Second Green Light Hole.
19. Graveyard Hole.
20. Airport Drift.
21. Eddie's Riffle.
22. Tank Hole.
23. Cow Dung Hole.
24. Paranoid Hole.
25. Lockit Drift.
26. Tie Corral Hole.

27. Dead Cow Hole.
28. Steelie Flats.
29. Twin Stumps Hole.
30. Shade Hole.
31. Bull Run Riffle.
32. Dove Hole.
33. Island Riffle.
34. Nookie Rock.
35. Lower Dike.
36. Dike.
37. Brush Hole.

ranging cattle—a dominating landscape guaranteed to restore the perspective of world-weary anglers.

The Deschutes is wide and strong in this stretch, but it offers a variety of fishing environments. There are long slow runs, deep pools, spring creek-like weed beds, gravel bars, boulder pockets, and white water—including 13 major rapids and an impassable falls (Sherars). In the 42 river miles

below Sherars Falls anglers can fish a chain of legendary steelhead holes, welcome runs of spring and fall chinook, and fish a burgeoning population of native rainbows—known as Deschutes redsides. Above Sherars, there is even better shelter, forage, and spawning ground for redsides, as well as additional rich steelhead water.

Steelhead. The Deschutes has been managed for the protection of wild steel-

head since 1979. The average native weighs 5 to 10 pounds. The wild run is supplemented annually with finclipped hatchery stock, and only finclipped steelhead may be kept. After a slump in the early '90s, the wild steelhead population has been steadily growing. As many as 3000 wild steelhead and 5000 hatchery fish have been landed in recent years between Sherars Falls and the mouth—the most popular and pro-

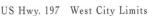
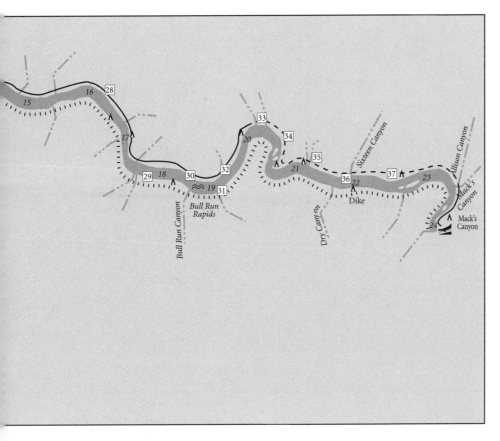

a tight floating line on or just below the surface. The classic technique is to cast at a 45-degree angle to the downstream flow. Follow the fly with your rod tip as it swings across the current, let it hang a moment, then retrieve it with slow, short strips. Brace yourself for a powerful hit. Hold your rod high and perpendicular to the current.

Effective spinners and spoons for steelheading on the Deschutes should be large (sizes 3 to 5) and bright (silver or nickel). Even in summer, the Deschutes is deep and a little off-color. A bit of green tape on the inside of the blade seems to add to its effectiveness. Plugs in a variety of colors (depending on the light) are also effective. For the least damaging catch and release, choose (or replace large hooks with) smaller single or treble hooks.

Remember, only finclipped steelhead may be kept. Be prepared to cut off a lure rather than injure a wild steelhead.

Trout. The Deschutes trout fishery is outstanding. Not only are redsides plentiful (more than 1700 over 7 inches per mile above Sherars Falls) but they're noticeably stronger than trout who don't have to cope with life in such a big, powerful river. The average catch is 8 to 15 inches, and there are many larger.

The Deschutes was once stocked with hatchery rainbows. A decline in the native population encouraged ODFW to abandon the hatchery program after 1978 and

ductive steelhead water in the river.

The earliest steelhead opportunity on the Deschutes is at the mouth in mid-July. When the Columbia water temperature is warm, steelhead bound for home waters elsewhere in Oregon and Idaho slip into the lower Deschutes to cool off. Some wander as far up as Pelton Regulating Dam and may even stay to spawn in Deschutes tributaries. The Clearwater strain is especially hardy and can weigh up to 22 pounds. Most of these migrants eventually drop back out of the Deschutes and continue moving up the Columbia system.

By September, steelhead can be found throughout the river below Pelton. Steelheading at Maupin is generally prime from mid-September through October. Farther upriver, good catches are made through December. The average catch rate is three-quarters of a fish per angler trip. At this time, the river is open to steelheading all year from the mouth to the northern boundary of Warm Springs Reservation, and from April 24 to December 31 from the Reservaton boundary to Pelton Regulating Dam.

All rainbow trout over 20 inches are considered steelhead. To fish for steelhead, you must have a steelhead tag. Except for a short reach from Buckhollow Creek up-

stream to Sherars Falls (a mere 0.9 miles of actually fishable water, intended for use by salmon anglers when salmon fishing is allowed), anglers must use artificial flies and lures for all fishing.

Flies developed especially for the Deschutes steelhead fishery include Doug Stewart's orange and black Macks Canyon (judged to be one of five top producers on the stream). Other classics are Don McClain's Deschutes Demon (yellow, orange and gold), his Deschutes Skunk, and the purple-bodied Dr. Gillis. Randall Kaufmann's Freight Train and Coal Car (variations on the Skunk) are also popular.

Most fly-caught steelhead are hooked on

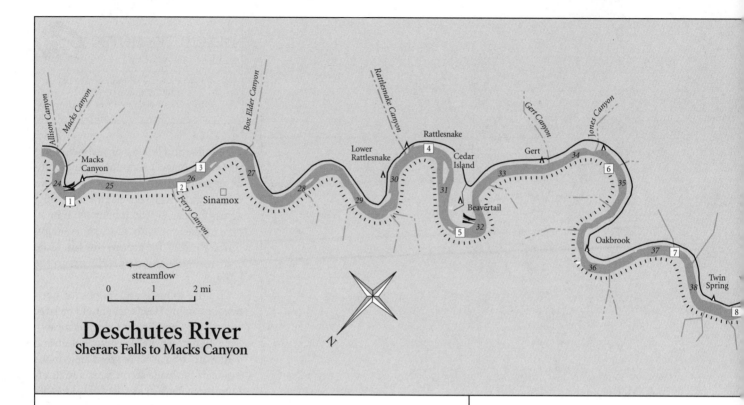

Deschutes River
Sherars Falls to Macks Canyon

streamflow
0   1   2 mi

N

1. *Un-named Hole.*
2. *Ferry Drift.*
3. *Sinamox Hole.*
4. *Rattlesnake Hole.*
5. *Cedar Island Drift.*
6. *Un-named Hole.*
7. *Un-named Hole.*
8. *Ledge Hole.*
9. *Pine Tree Hole.*

to promote the natural generating capabilities of native redsides. For many years now, the river has been a showcase for successful wild trout management. A slot limit allows limited harvest of trout from 10 to 13 inches. Trout larger and smaller must be released unharmed.

Trout fishing is best above Sherars Falls, where there is better spawning gravel and riparian habitat, but the lower river now offers excellent catches as well. During the past decade, special fencing along the lower river has kept cattle focused on a limited number of watering holes. The result has been restoration of the riverbank and renewal of the lower river's native redside population. Some lower river trout move upstream from mid- to late summer, but many stay, and the others return in September. Trout fishing between Beavertail and Macks Canyon remains constant and good throughout the summer. Trout above Sherars are generally slightly larger than those below the falls.

Deschutes redside rainbows predominate, but there are a few bull trout and browns. All bull trout must be released unharmed. Whitefish are abundant and provide good fishing in winter when trout are less active.

At this time, the Deschutes is open for year-round trout fishing from the mouth upstream to the Warm Springs boundary (at about r.m. 69). From the CTWS boundary upstream to Pelton Dam, trout season closes October 31. The most consistent fishing is from February through November.

Salmon. The Deschutes has runs of both spring and fall chinook. The fall chinook population is all wild and currently thriving. ODFW estimated returns of 21,000 fall chinook in 1997, and 11,500 in 1998.

Spring chinook populations, on the other hand, continue to be depressed. The run has been supplemented by a hatchery program since the construction of Pelton

Dam, which blocked natural spawning grounds. In some years, harvest is limited to finclipped spring chinook only; in other years, the fishery is closed entirely. Check with the ODFW district office in The Dalles for salmon fishing opportunities.

Fall chinook begin entering the Deschutes in late July and run through the end of October, though prime catches are made from mid-August to September 30. The quality of the fish as table fare begins to deteriorate about October 1.

Spring chinook enter the river beginning in late March and run through mid-June, peaking between mid-April and mid-May.

The most popular chinook fishery is at and just downstream of Sherars Falls. Angling regulations allow bait to be used from the falls downstream about 3 miles to the upper trestle, though fishable water is actually less than a mile. The precarious-looking structures over the falls are dip-netting platforms, open to use only by members of the Confederated Tribes of Warm Springs.

Boating Access. Much of the Deschutes is accessible only by boat. Anglers drift to a likely spot, anchor near shore or on a gravel bar, then wade to fish. Angling from a floating device is prohibited.

Popular one-day drifts include Warm Springs to Trout Creek (r.m. 97 to r.m. 87), Maupin to Sandy Beach just before Sher-

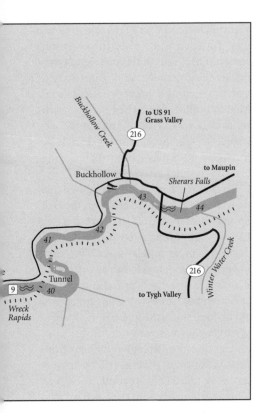

"Washout Rapid," it includes a standing wave and is capable of sinking boats. Don't go through the middle. At this time it is still in transition, and safest routes vary. Scouting is easiest from the west side.

Immediately below Trout Creek, be prepared for a Class 3 rapid and additional heavy water. This stretch is very popular with whitewater rafters in summer.

Except for the broad, flat river mouth, only flat-bottom boats are suitable for the Deschutes (drift boats, rafts, and jet boats). Use of motors on the river above Heritage Landing is subject to a variety of restrictions. Check Oregon Boating Regulations for current information (available from the Oregon State Marine Board). See Appendix.

Boaters are urged to camp only at BLM sites, use the outhouses provided, carry out all refuse, and be mindful of fire restrictions. If you see a young tree, take a moment to water it with the bucket provided nearby for that purpose.

Non-boating Access. Much good water can be reached by a combination of motor vehicle and easy hiking. Deschutes River State Park, off I-84, affords access to angling at the mouth. From the west, take I-84 exit 97 at Celilo and follow Hwy. 206 east to the park. From the east, take I-84 exit 104 at Biggs. Follow Hwy. 97 south and Hwy. 206 west.

There is no motor vehicle access from the mouth to the upper canyon. Anglers can follow the banks for 12 miles upstream through public property on both sides of the river, thanks to purchases of river frontage by the Oregon Wildlife Heritage Foundation, who gave it in trust to the people of Oregon following an enthusiastic grass-roots campaign. The trust specifies continuance of the no motor vehicles policy in the lower canyon.

From Heritage Landing on the west bank, anglers can follow the trail upriver about 2 miles, or walk the railroad grade with caution, keeping to the edge of the

ars Falls (r.m. 51 to r.m. 45), Pine Hollow (below Wreck Rapids) to Beavertail Campground (r.m. 57 to r.m. 31), and Beavertail to Macks Canyon at r.m. 24.

Longer trips include Trout Creek to Maupin and Macks Canyon to the mouth. The trip to the mouth can be done in a day, but you'll regret not having more time for fishing. A large developed boat ramp facility, Heritage Landing is at the mouth on the west bank of the river across from Deschutes River State Park. See the accompanying maps for additional launch and take-out sites.

Except for the drift from Mecca Flat to Trout Creek under most conditions, the Deschutes is not suitable for novice boaters. A boater pass system is in effect throughout the river. All boaters must purchase a daily use pass. Passes are available through the State Parks Department at 525 Trade St. SE, Salem 97310, from their regional office in Portland, and at tackle and supply stores along the river and in metropolitan areas.

From Maupin to the mouth, boaters will encounter four Class 4 rapids and the impassable Sherars Falls. Do not attempt to boat the falls. The only take-out before the falls is at Sandy Beach.

A new major rapid was created by a storm event in 1997 at about r.m. 8 (just after a high wire crossing). Known as

Many anglers use the railroad grade as a trail for moving through the DESCHUTES *Canyon. Photograph by Scott Richmond.*

White Horse Rapids challenges boaters between South Junction and North Junction on the DESCHUTES. Photograph by Richard Grost.

grade. This is a working railroad. On the east bank, a trail suitable for hiking or mountain biking extends upstream 20 miles. Beyond that point the trail deteriorates too much for mountain bikes, but is negotiable for hikers all the way to Mack's Canyon at r.m. 24.

Drive-to access points on the east bank of the river are plentiful from Maupin downstream to Macks Canyon, and upstream to the Deschutes Club Gate. From Sherars Falls to Macks Canyon, there are a number of developed access sites and campgrounds. In addition, in this stretch anglers can simply park along the road and walk over to the river through the sagebrush. The grade between road and river is not very steep. A disabled angler fishing platform at Blue Hole (r.m. 48) washed out in the '96 flood and has been replaced (temporarily perhaps) with a small but serviceable pontoon platform.

At Maupin, near The Oasis Resort on the east bank, a gravel road accesses about 7 miles of river and leads to The Deschutes Club Locked Gate. The public is welcome to fish beyond the gate, but must leave all vehicles (including mountain bikes) at the gate and proceed on foot. The 13-mile trail from the gate to North Junction is an old railroad bed which offers easy hiking. There are more than a half dozen primitive BLM campsites with outhouses along this stretch.

At North Junction, the Burlington Northern railroad track crosses from west bank to east bank. Some anglers continue upstream on foot along the railroad grade as far as South Junction (r.m. 84). Be aware that the railroad grade is private property, that the railroad does have the right to prosecute for trespassing, and that trains do not run on any set schedule. Keep alert for approaching trains and maintenance vehicles.

Additional east bank access is available at South Junction, Trout Creek, Mecca Flat, and Warm Springs. Between North and South Junction, the river's east bank includes a mix of BLM and private land. Respect "No Trespassing" signs. To reach South Junction by car, take Hwy. 197 south from Maupin to the junction with Hwy. 97 (Shaniko). A gravel road heads west to the river. The road down to South Junction is loose gravel and quite steep. There is a primitive BLM campground at South Junction and access to about 1½ miles of good trout water.

Trout Creek is a popular access point with a large developed BLM campground and boat ramp. An old railroad bed trail follows the river from Trout Creek 10 miles upstream to Mecca Flat. The trail proceeds through some private land where BLM has an easement. There are outhouses at intervals along the path. To reach Trout Creek from Warm Springs, continue southeast about 5 miles on US 26 to the canyon rim. Make a hairpin left turn off the highway, then turn right after about 200 yards. Go 3 miles, and make a sharp right turn onto NW Juniper Lane. After another 4½ miles, the road takes a 90-degree right turn, then

a hairpin left, and winds downhill to Gateway. Turn left just before the old train station. There is a subtle road sign pointing to the Deschutes and Trout Creek. Gateway can also be approached from Madras and Maupin. The final approach to Trout Creek is steep and can be extremely rough, though usually do-able by most cars. RV's may have trouble getting back up the grade.

On the west bank, access is limited to a dangerously rough road at Kloan, the Oak Spring Hatchery site off Hwy. 197, and Dry Creek Campground on Confederated Tribes Warm Springs land. A CTWS fishing permit is required to fish at Dry Creek. Permits are reasonably priced and are sold at convenience stores in Warm Springs and at G.I. Joe's stores throughout the state.

At Oak Springs, you can fish for trout and steelhead upstream and down from the Oak Springs Hatchery. To reach the hatchery, take Hwy. 197 south from Tygh Valley, turning left onto the hatchery road about 2 miles south of the White River crossing. Be prepared for a spectacular drop down into the Deschutes canyon. The only other west bank access to the Deschutes in this stretch is at Dry Creek Campground. For access to Dry Creek, see Deschutes River (CTWS) below.

Insect Hatches. The richness of Deschutes insect life is legendary. Big stoneflies (both salmonflies and golden stones) become active in May, emerging in late May and June and producing what some consider to be the best fly-fishing west of the Mississippi. Weighted stonefly nymph patterns are a staple for Deschutes anglers and will produce year-round. Caddis of many varieties are present, hatching in spring and fall but available in other life stages throughout the year. Several varieties of mayflies thrive. Pale morning duns hatch from late-June through mid-July, blue-winged olives October through April. And don't ignore the ever-presence of midges, especially in the evening. See *Fishing in Oregon's Deschutes River* (published by Flying Pencil) for a comprehensive month-by-month hatch chart with fly and presentation recommendations.

Safety. This is a big, swift, dangerous river, and boating and wading must be approached with proper respect. It can kill. Hip boots are not appropriate. If you wear rubber (as opposed to neoprene) waders, be sure to wear a wading belt. A wading staff and properly surfaced wading shoes can be life savers.

Useful Information. The Deschutes fishery is affected by water discharges from Pelton Dam, which are variable in spring. Heavy discharge (or any sudden change) can put the fishery off for several days. Discharge information is available from PGE. River gauge readings are also available. See Appendix. Gauge readings below 6000 are fishable, below 5000 considerably better, but a steady river level over a period of time is more important to good fishing than river velocity.

Experienced Deschutes fishing guides, raft rentals, and float trip services are available in Maupin and at many fly and tackle shops in western Oregon. There's a good fly shop in Maupin.

General supplies and services are available in Warm Springs and Maupin. Overnight accommodations are limited to Maupin.

The only campgrounds with drinking water are at Maupin City Park, Beavertail, and Macks Canyon. All campers along the Deschutes are urged to respect the fragile desert environment, and to camp lightly using wilderness (no trace) camping methods. Open fires are discouraged in this dry country at all times and are prohibited between June 1 and October 1 due to fire danger. For environmental protection, there are outhouses up from the river bank at frequent intervals, even in areas accessible only by boat. Cattle with BLM grazing permits don't seem to bother with such niceties, unfortunately. This here's cow pie country, partner. If watching herds of large animals upsets your casting, you might prefer the stretch above Sherars Bridge.

DESCHUTES RIVER: (Confederated Tribes, Warmsprings Reservation).

Warmsprings Reservation owns the entire Deschutes West bank from 16 miles south of Maupin to Lake Billy Chinook and on up to Jefferson Creek on the Metolius River arm. The only west bank access to the Deschutes in this stretch is at Dry Creek Campground.

To reach Dry Creek from Hwy. 26, drive 3 miles north from Warm Springs toward Kah-nee-ta. A signed road to Dry Creek is on the right. It is 2 miles farther to the campground. When the road forks, keep to the right. At Dry Springs, there is an unim-

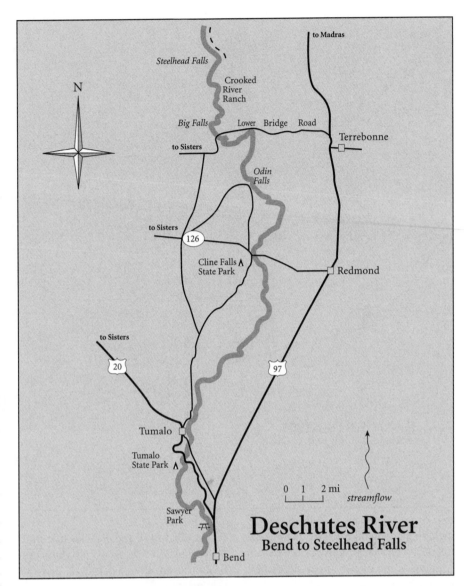

Deschutes River
Bend to Steelhead Falls

proved road (gated and closed to vehicle access) which follows the bank for about 6 miles downstream.

This stretch is open for trout fishing from the last weekend in April through October 31, and for steelhead, till December 31. You will need a tribal permit, available for a reasonable fee at the police station or Rainbow Market in Warm Springs, and at G.I. Joe's stores throughout Oregon.

DESCHUTES RIVER: Bend to Pelton Dam.

Heavily drawn upon for irrigation at times, but offering some opportunities for high quality trout fishing. This stretch of the river is currently open for year-round trout fishing with flies and lures. Wild Deschutes redside rainbows are present, as well as browns, whitefish, and bull trout. Big Falls is the upper limit for bull trout. Regulations currently allow a daily harvest of one bull trout at least 24 inches

in length.

Irrigation withdrawals generally begin in April and continue until October. Temperatures in the reduced flow months can get as high as 80 degrees, forcing trout to migrate to cooler areas near Bend, below Lower Bridge, and wherever else springs offer relief.

From Tumalo to Lake Billy Chinook (about 30 miles), the river flows through a narrow scenic gorge. Well back from the main roads and too shallow for boating due to withdrawals, it offers excellent angling for wild rainbow and brown trout.

The most consistently good fishing throughout in this stretch is below Big Falls, from October until April. Between Big Falls and Lake Billy, the river cuts through BLM and National Forest land. There are access tracks into the gorge and un-named trails, some of which show up on the USGS topographic map of the area,

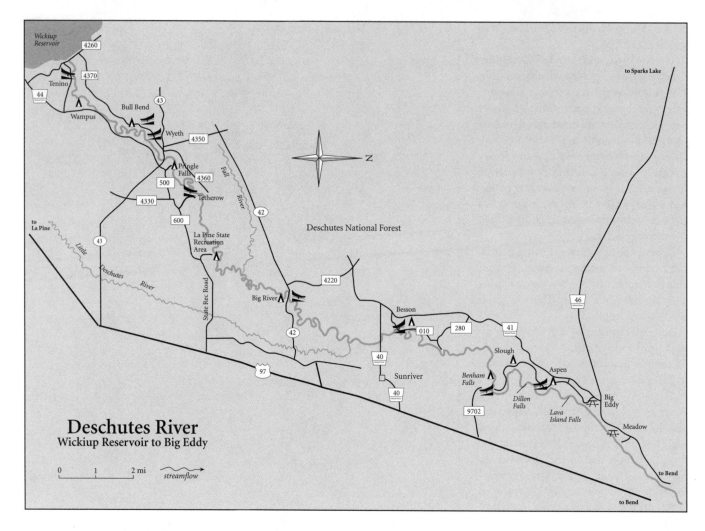

Deschutes River
Wickiup Reservoir to Big Eddy

0   1   2 mi

streamflow

including a long hike down Squaw Creek northeast of Sisters. This remote stretch contains some of the upper river's best trout fishing.

The Steelhead Falls Trail, in the vicinity of Crooked River Ranch, offers hardy anglers access to about 12 miles of high quality gorge fishing. To reach it, turn west off Hwy. 97 (about 10 miles north of Redmond) onto Lower Bridge Rd. Follow signs for Crooked River Ranch. The best bet is to make your way to the development's fire station (don't be shy about asking directions from the occasional passer-by). At the station you can purchase a map of the development and solicit help in locating the trail at the end of River Rd. It's a steep hour's hike to the falls.

Two other opportunities for public access to the river within the development are a BLM recreation site at the end of Sundown Canyon Rd., and another on Foley Waters Rd. There is a BLM camping area adjacent to Crooked Rivers Ranch.

Upstream, the river flows through primarily private land. At this time, landown-

ers are tolerant of anglers who stop in to ask permission to cross over to the gorge. Be courteous, and pack out all refuse to help preserve access.

Public access opportunities pick up again about 15 miles north of Redmond. Lower Bridge, Odin Falls, Tetherow Bridge, and Cline Falls State Park are popular angler access sites. Between Redmond and Bend, the Deschutes can be fished at Tumalo and Sawyer State Parks on Hwy. 97. There is good fly water in this section of the river. Angling from a floating device is prohibited.

DESCHUTES RIVER: Wickiup Reservoir to Bend. A rich, dark, powerful stream, 20-100 feet wide, characterized by deceptively smooth but powerful slicks broken by serious rapids and falls. Wild redside rainbows, browns, and white fish are present, as well as finclipped hatchery rainbows. Trout are significantly smaller here than in the lower river, but they are still plentiful.

The Deschutes is a big river as it emerges

from Wickiup, but its character is distinctly different from that of the lower canyonland. Its power might be missed under a deceptively smooth surface. It flows through fairly open ponderosa pinelands, with sandy banks and tall grass, and through the heart of the high desert community of Bend at the edge of the Deschutes National Forest. Bend is the largest metropolitan area within the river's watershed. For 15 miles upstream from the city, the stream is easily fished from shore, and local anglers drive out the Mt. Bachelor road to try their luck on the evening rise. The river is drawn down substantially in winter to fill Crane Prairie and Wickiup reservoirs.

To reach the river from Bend, take Hwy. 97 south. Secondary and forest roads access both sides of the stream at several locations. In the stretch between Lava Butte and the LaPine State Recreation Area the river flows through much private land, including Sunriver Resort.

This section of the river is regulated from Benham Falls downstream, and from

Benham Falls to Wickiup. Below Benham, trout fishing is open year-round, but restricted to artificial flies and lures. Above Benham, the river is open from late April through October 31. There are no gear restrictions, but non-finclipped rainbows must be released unharmed. Check the regulations for catch limits. All fishing techniques are effective here, though fly fishing is especially popular. A yellow mayfly hatch in June attracts a lot of attention. Wet flies seem to work best during the days, dry flies best in the evenings. Favorite dry fly patterns include stonefly, pale morning dun (mayfly), caddis, and mosquito imitations, with small patterns best in late summer. The big browns are often taken on trout fry imitations. Whitefish are also plentiful and susceptible to all angling methods.

The river is driftable starting about a quarter mile below Wickiup Dam, and angling from a floating device is permitted. There is a good 8-mile drift from below Wickiup to the Pringle Falls area. To reach Pringle Falls from Hwy. 97, turn west on County Rd. 43 north of LaPine. Pringle Falls is not boatable, and the current gets very strong quickly as you near the falls. Keep a sharp watch for warning signs on the river.

One of the finest drifts on this section is the 17 miles from just below the log jam at Pringle Falls to Big River (a.k.a Colonel Patch) Bridge. Another nice drift is from Big River Bridge to the Spring River area. From there to Bend, much of the river is boatable, but check locally for trouble spots. In addition to Pringle Falls, beware of Benham, Dillon, and Lava Island falls. Know where you are putting in and what's between you and the next take-out. These falls have taken the lives of ill-informed boaters. Guides for boating the upper river are available. Check with fly shops in Bend and Sisters.

The river flows through a mix of public and private land in this stretch. Bank fishing opportunities are generally associated with campgrounds and boat ramps. Campgrounds are available along the river beginning at Meadow Camp 4 miles south of Bend. Other campgrounds are Lava Island, Slough Camp, and Benham Falls near the Lava Butte Geological Area, Session Camp near Spring River, Big River Bridge, LaPine State Recreation Area, Pringle Falls, Wyeth, Bull Bend, and Wampus.

Overnight accommodations are plentiful in Bend and between the city and the Deschutes National Forest boundary. Upscale vacation homes and condominiums are available for rent in the resort community of Sunriver, about 12 miles south of Bend.

DESCHUTES RIVER: Crane Prairie Reservoir to Wickiup Reservoir. A beautiful wild trout stream and nursery for Wickiup's brown trout, flowing through flower-bedecked meadowland. To reach it from the east, follow County and Forest Rd. 42 west from Hwy. 97.

This lovely, meandering 3-mile section of the Deschutes offers excellent fishing for brook trout to 5 pounds, a growing number of rainbows, and good numbers of browns. Fishing is restricted to flies and lures, and catch and release only on the rainbows. There is a short season here (June 1 to August 31) to protect spawning trout.

Sheep Bridge Campground is located on the river's east bank. To reach it from the east, turn south off Forest Rd. 42, following signs for Twin Lakes Resort. After ¼ mile, when the main road makes a sharp left turn, continue straight to the camp. There is a wheelchair accessible fishing platform at the Forest Rd. 42 Bridge. Nearest supplies and overnight accommodations are available at Twin Lakes Resort on South Twin.

DESCHUTES RIVER: Headwaters to Crane Prairie. Outlet of Little Lava Lake, which has no inlet streams, but is filled by snow-fed springs. From Little Lava the river flows south, first as a slow, clear slough, then as a sparkling meadow creek, entering Crane Prairie Reservoir after 8 miles.

Whitefish predominate in the slough waters from Lava Lake downstream about 2 miles. The meadow stretch below that, however, is a wonderful stream with firm, small resident rainbow and brook trout. This is a classic small stream, and fishing is rarely disappointing. The river is generally less than 10 feet across and can be waded at almost any point. Fishing is restricted to flies and lures only, but fly fishing is the best method here. Dry flies are almost always effective. Watch your backcast. The small pines along the bank eat flies. Fishing for the rainbows in catch and release

only, but ODFW encourages to catch and keep any number of brook trout.

The Cascade Lakes Hwy. parallels much of the stream. About 2 miles below the Deschutes Bridge Guard Station the road curves west, away from the river. Forest Rd. 40 crosses the river a mile or so below that point, and a mile above the outflow into Crane Prairie. Upstream from this bridge the river flows through a delightful setting of green meadow grass, waist-high lupine, and small pines, with Mt. Bachelor looking on.

Forest Service campgrounds are available at Little Lava Lake, Deschutes Bridge, and Cow Meadow, where the river enters Crane Prairie. Overnight accommodations and supplies are available at Twin Lakes Resort on South Twin.

DEVILS LAKE. (Deschutes Co.) A pretty little lake on Century Drive about 30 miles southwest of Bend. It stretches along the south side of the road about one mile west of Sparks Lake.

Devils Lake is about 40 acres and only 9 feet at its deepest point. Brook trout reproduce naturally here, and catchable rainbows are stocked every couple of weeks during the season.

Fed primarily by a spring creek at its west end, the lake is remarkably clear. During most years, fish are available throughout the lake. If the water gets really low, they will concentrate in the deeper east end. Fly fishing is good when there's a bit of wind to rough up the water, but all methods work. There is not a lot for trout to eat in Devils, so any offering looks good. Light gear is appropriate for these 8 to 11 inches.

No motors are allowed, but a rubber raft or float tube would be helpful. There is a trail from the campground to the east end of the lake. The road to the lake is usually blocked by snow until mid-June. There's a small campground at the lake. Recommended for youngsters. For more informatio, see *Fishing in Oregon's Cascade Lakes*. published by Flying Pencil.

DORIS LAKE. (Deschutes Co.) A large hike-in lake in the Cascades west of Elk Lake, on one of several trails to the Mink Lake Basin. Deep and cold, it provides only fair fishing for brook trout but makes a pleasant day trip. From Forest Rd. 46, about 2 miles past the turn-off to Elk Lake

Some high lakes are so pretty and peaceful, you might forget you hiked up here to fish. Photograph by Lynn Hokanson Welsh.

Resort, watch for Six Lakes Trailhead 14 on the west side of the road. Follow Trail 14 about 3 miles west to Doris Lake, passing Blow Lake at about the half-way point.

Doris has about 90 surface acres and a maximum depth over 70 ft. If you don't bring a raft or float tube, you may wish you had, though fly fishing the shallows near the east and west shores can be productive, especially in fall. It's so pretty here, you could just forget about fishing and enjoy watching the light on the water or do a little (chilly) swimming.

The lake is stocked annually with brook trout fingerlings that grow to 14 inches. There are a several picturesque natural campsites on rocky promontories overlooking the lake and additional camping opportunities at Blow.

EAGLE CREEK. (Columbia Gorge) A trout stream with salmon and steelhead opportunities near the mouth, best known for the scenic trail that follows it from mouth to headwaters. From Wahtum Lake and Table Mountain, it flows through Hatfield Wilderness (formerly Columbia Wilderness), carving a handsome gorge of its own, complete with several stunning cascades. It enters the Columbia River just above Bonneville Dam.

The lower creek can be fished for an eclectic variety of Columbia River salmon and steelhead, who turn in to enjoy its cool water in late summer and early fall. Best fishing at the mouth is in August and September, with some chinook still available in October and later. Historic Old Hwy. 30 crosses the creek near its mouth and offers a good vantage point for viewing spawning salmon. Cascade Hatchery, on the creek a few miles above the mouth, rears coho that are released below Bonneville. The creek itself doesn't have a hatchery run.

To reach the mouth of Eagle Creek from the west on I-84, take Exit 41, signed for Eagle Creek. From the east, take Exit 40, then double back on I-84 heading east to Exit 40. A public road follows the creek to the hatchery intake. Except for hatchery closures, the lower creek can be bank fished from the mouth up to the intake dam. Low flows and the hatchery intake confine salmon and steelhead to the lower stream. By late July they are often further limited to the stretch between the mouth and the railroad bridge, which is watered by backflows from the dam. Fishing in this stretch is governed by Columbia River regulations.

Above the railroad crossing, the stream is open to salmon fishing year-round. Tule chinook, fall chinook, and coho may be present. There are some good salmon holes above the railroad bridge when there's enough water to fill them. Summer steelhead may be present from May through July, and winter steelhead may appear in October and November, but only in small numbers. The current steelhead season here is late May to the end of October.

The upper creek has good fishing for small wild rainbows and cutthroat trout, with brook trout available in the headwaters.

There is a large Forest Service campground and recreation area upstream of the hatchery off Old Hwy. 30. All vehicles both in the park and in parking areas near the mouth must display Forest Service parking permits. Permits are sold by the campground host in summer and at Multnomah Falls . For other permit outlets, see Appendix.

EAST LAKE. A unique fishery in the maw of a dormant volcano in central Oregon, about 25 air miles southeast of Bend. East Lake is one of two lakes within Newberry Crater in the Paulina Mountains of the Deschutes National Forest. The Crater has been designated a National Monument. East Lake is separated from its neighbor, Paulina Lake, by a high ridge. Both lakes produce trophy size brown trout. Especially popular with fly anglers, East also offers good fishing for rainbows, Atlantic salmon, and kokanee.

From Bend, drive south 20 miles on Hwy. 97 to the Newberry Crater turnoff. Turn east on paved Forest Rd. 21, and wind upward about 14 miles to Paulina Lake, then continue east another 3 miles to East Lake.

A mercury health advisory against eating any but the stocked legal rainbows taken from East has decreased this lake's popularity considerably. Though the source of the mercury has been identified as natural (entering the lake through the submerged hot springs), it is no less a concern. For those who fish primarily for sport rather than the freezer, the lake remains an attractive destination.

East is a consistent producer of rainbow trout. In addition to its natives, ODFW stocks about 20,000 rainbows to catch and (safely) eat. The lake has slightly over 1000 surface acres, with broad shoal areas and a maximum depth of 175 feet. This is high country, over 6300 ft. in elevation, and it isn't unusual to find snow on the ground in June. It gets cold up here at night.

Rainbow trout make up 80% of the catch, ranging in size from 10 to 14 inches, though rainbows to 10 pounds have been caught. As for the browns, expert Jim Teeny developed his famous nymph while stalking monster browns in the shallows here. Browns over 20 pounds have been grudgingly dragged from the lake.

Kokanee were first stocked in the lake in 1993 and are now well established. Look for them in the depths to the north, particularly when the lake quiets down in late summer. In fall, when kokanee move into the shallows in search of spawning grounds, they may be still-fished (though the quality of the meat is lower than at other times of year).

Still-fishing takes a lot of trout, but don't go too deep. In early season when the fish are close to the surface, a bobber rig is effective. The hot springs area in the southeast and the north side between the cliffs and Cinder Hill campground are good places to start in early season. Later it pays to go deeper. Bait anglers do best in early season.

Trollers generally work slowly around the shoreline of the lake, going deeper in the warm weather months. Chubs have been the primary natural forage in the past, though kokanee may begin to attract browns in years to come. Kwikfish-type lures and flasher-bait rigs are used, as well as dark colored woolly-worms and Teeny nymphs. S-l-o-w-l-y is the key here. There is a 10-mph speed limit in effect on the lake.

This is a great lake for fly fishing. A rich insect population can turn on a rise at any moment, though evening is the usual time. The shorelines produce well. The southeast shoals get an influx of warm water from volcanic springs that might serve as a magnet to browns in early season. The east shoreline can be very good at evening, but slow during the day. Watch for feeding fish at the surface in the shoal areas along the southern shore.

Stalking big fish which cruise at dusk is an exciting and effective way to tie into a trophy trout. Try the north shore cliffs, east of the red fissure, along the west shore near the white pumice slide, and along the south shore. Try a Teeny nymph in sizes 4 to 6, and hold on tight. A partner on shore spotting from above will improve the odds of success.

Two very attractive Forest Service campgrounds, East Lake and Hot Springs, are on the south shore within stands of ponderosa pine. A third, Cinder Hill, is on the northeast shore. Each campground has a boat ramp. A resort on the east shore offers rustic accommodations, boat rentals, and supplies.

When the lake opens in spring, there is usually a lot of snow around the camps and, sometimes, ice on the lake, but fishing at ice-out fishing can be terrific. Bring

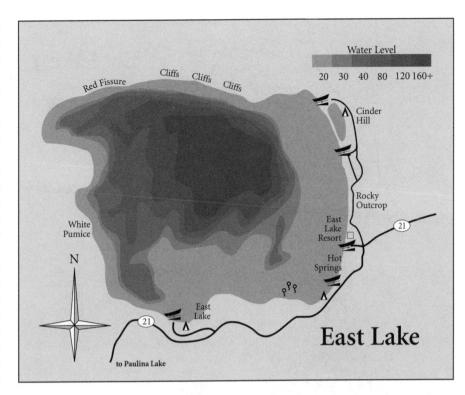

East Lake

plenty of cold weather gear.

For more information, see *Fishing in Oregon's Cascade Lakes*, published by Flying Pencil.

EIGHTMILE CREEK Much longer than its name, this stream flows east about 30 miles from the east edge of Mt. Hood National Forest, crossed by Hwy. 197, before joining Fifteen Mile Creek to enter the Columbia near The Dalles. It is followed for most of its length by gravel and dirt roads.

Used quite a bit for irrigation, it provides some opportunity for catch and release fishing for wild rainbow trout early in the season (artificial lures and flies only). While roads follow the stream closely, there is a lot of private land. Best fishing is in the upper stream in early season. There are no campsites along the lower stream, but there are several in the upper headwaters in the forest, about 17 miles west of Dufur on Forest Rd. 44.

ELK LAKE. (Deschutes Co.) A scenic large lake in the Cascades west of Bend, in the heart of the popular Cascade Lakes recreational area. Brook trout and kokanee are available for anglers, but sailing, wind surfing, and swimming are a big part of the action here. Elk is east of Century Drive (Hwy. 46), about 32 miles southwest of Bend. It can also be reached from the south by forest roads branching off from Hwy. 97

to the east and from Hwy. 58 to the south.

Elk Lake is in a picturesque setting, with the Three Sisters towering over the north end of the lake and Mt. Bachelor dominating the eastern horizon. It is about 1½ miles long from north to south, and ½ mile wide, covering 250 acres. Most of it is over 25 ft. deep, with the southern half considerably shallower than the northern. There is a 65 ft. hole mid-way across the lake opposite Point campground and boat launch.

Fishing here is not the major activity, but it can certainly be good. Brook trout generally range 7 to 14 inches, but trout to 20 inches do show up. Early season offers the best catches, with June the prime month. After a long winter, these fish will take just about anything. Late fall evenings are a good time for taking large fish on a fly, and the weather is generally more dependable. These trout are primarily caught along the shoreline. Stick to water where you can see bottom. In this clear water, that means as deep as 20 feet. Caddis nymphs are the most abundant trout food. Fly anglers will find dark wet patterns a good bet anytime here. Crayfish are also plentiful, so crayfish imitations do well.

Elk has a well established population of kokanee which reproduces naturally. Success rate is high, though the average catch is only 8 to 9 inches since Elk is not a rich lake. Most kokanee are taken at the south

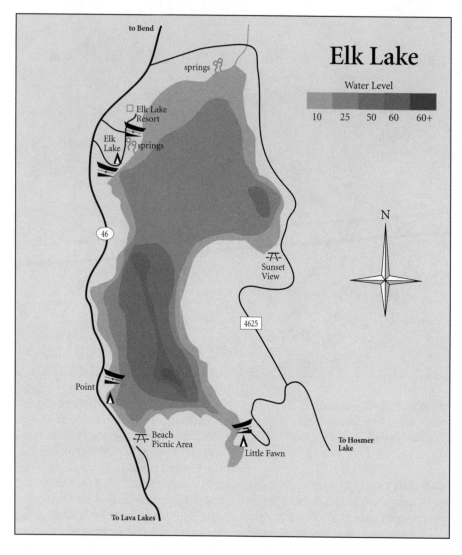

Elk Lake

Water Level

| 10 | 25 | 50 | 60 | 60+ |

N

to Bend

springs

Elk Lake
Resort

Elk
Lake
springs

46

Sunset
View

4625

Point

Beach
Picnic Area

Little Fawn

To Hosmer
Lake

To Lava Lakes

Deschutes about 6 miles below the falls.

The north bank of the upper stream is followed closely by Forest Rd. 42 from the river's source to Fall River Hatchery. Forest Rd. 42 can be reached from Hwy. 97 by taking the Sunriver turn-off, or you may come in from the south from Pringle Falls by way of Forest Rd. 4360. The lower river offers easy hiking south from the hatchery, which is at about the mid-point of the river, or north from the Forest Rd. 4360 bridge which crosses Fall River one mile above its confluence with the Deschutes. In the lower 4 miles, the river flows through a lot of private property.

Fall River is not large, averaging 50 to 75 feet across, but it provides some interesting fly fishing. Spring-fed, it is crystal clear and requires very light tackle. Rainbow, brook trout, and brown trout are present, and the state stocks aggressively with weekly releases of catchable rainbows and brook trout throughout the season. Angling holds steady, as there is no water fluctuation. The average catch runs 7 to 12 inches. Best bet is the water below the hatchery in late June and July. Late afternoon and evening angling is the most productive. Midges, caddis, and a variety of mayflies are trout staples (pale morning and evening duns in summer and fall, mahogany duns mid-summer, and blue-winged olives in winter).

The river is open and fishable year-round except for the stretch from the falls to the Deschutes, which closes September 30 to protect spawning brown trout.

There is a pleasant campground ½ mile below the source springs, though it doesn't have drinking water. Drinking water is available at the hatchery. There are additional campgrounds along the Deschutes. For more information, see *Fishing in Oregon's Cascade Lakes* and *Fishing in Oregon's Best Fly Waters* .

FARRELL LAKE. One of a pair of hike-in brook trout lakes about a mile north of the road between Crescent and Summit Lakes. From Hwy. 58 at Crescent Lake Junction, take Forest Rd. 60 around the northwest shore of Crescent Lake to the Summit Lake turn-off, Forest Rd. 6010 about a quarter mile south of Tandy Bay Campground. Look for the trailhead sign about 4 miles west. The trail to Meek Lake is on the south side of the road. The trail to Farrell is on the north side of the road. The hike in is

end of at the Kokanee Hole. This is an area about 100 feet in diameter which you can find by aligning your boat between a rockslide and the road culvert across from Point Campground. Most anglers take them by deep-trolling a lure tipped with corn at about the 50-ft. level. Jigging a one or two ounce lure is also effective. There is a 25 per day kokanee bag limit to encourage anglers to help keep the population under control.

There is a National Forest guard station at Elk, and several trails to prime high lake fishing areas begin here. See also Horse Lake, Mink Lake. Hosmer Lake is just down the road.

There are quite a few summer homes along the north and northeast shores. A very nice public beach is available at the southern tip of the lake and another on the northwest shore. Both sailing and wind surfing are very popular here. On a fine summer weekend, over a hundred sails will dot the lake. Power boats are allowed, but

there is a 10-mph speed limit.

Elk Lake Resort on the western shore has rustic accommodations, boat rentals, some supplies, and a lunch counter famous for its good milk shakes. This is the center of sailing activity. There is a boat launch at the resort and a public campground to the south. Additional campgrounds are located at the southwest end of the lake off County Rd. 46, and at the southeast end off Forest Rd. 4625. All three campgrounds have boat ramps and drinking water.

In most years, the road to Elk Lake is snow-bound until late May. For more information, see *Fishing in Oregon's Cascade Lakes*, published by Flying Pencil.

FALL RIVER. A beautiful spring-fed stream open to fly fishing only, in the Deschutes National Forest southwest of Bend. Clear and cold, it springs full-blown from the ground about 2 miles northwest of Pringle Falls (on the Deschutes River) and winds its way northeast 8 miles to join the

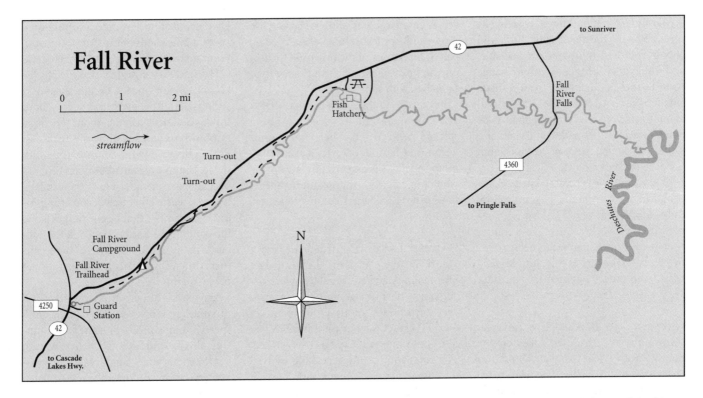

Fall River

0   1   2 mi

streamflow

Turn-out

Turn-out

Fall River
Campground

Fall River
Trailhead

4250

Guard
Station

42

to Cascade
Lakes Hwy.

42

to Sunriver

Fall
River
Falls

Fish
Hatchery

4360

to Pringle Falls

Deschutes River

N

about ½ mile.

Farrell Lake is long and narrow. Four acres and mostly shallow, its brook trout run 8 to 14 inches and average just under a pound. The lake is easy to fish from shore. There are good natural campsites at the west end of the lake. Snell Lake is an eighth of a mile to the east.

FAWN LAKE. A good hike-in brook trout lake east of Diamond Peak Wilderness, about midway between Odell and Crescent lakes. Trails lead to Fawn Lake from the east end of Odell Lake and from Crescent Lake Resort, which is 2 miles south of Hwy. 58. It's about a 3-mile hike from Odell by Trail 44, a little shorter from Crescent Lake.

At elevation 5680 ft., the lake covers 43 acres, with a maximum depth of 27 feet. Brook trout average 12 inches and run to 16 inches. It is stocked in odd-number years. Bait angling is productive early in the year, and flies do best in summer and fall. There are natural campsites. The lake is usually accessible in late June, depending on snow pack.

FROG LAKE. A small trout lake, heavily fished, just off Hwy. 26, 9 miles southeast of Government Camp. The turn-off is well signed. The lake is east of the highway, with a road directly to it, though a short hike is required in spring before the snow clears. Fishing is for rainbow trout. The lake is heavily stocked with legal rainbows annually and often receives a good number of brood trout. All methods are used. Boats can be launched to fish this shallow 11-acre pond, but motors are prohibited. Recommended for youngsters.

GIBSON LAKE. (Confederated Tribes Warm Springs) A 6-acre brook trout lake ¾ mile north of Breitenbush Lake by a trail that starts across from the Breitenbush Lake entry road. Maximum depth here is 14 feet. The lake is stocked semi-annually with brook trout. A permit is not required, and overnight camping is permitted.

GILCHRIST MILL POND. A former mill pond on the Little Deschutes River in the community of Gilchrist. Hwy. 97 skirts the eastern edge of the pond, which is on property currently owned by Crown Pacific. A permit is required to fish there. Stop by the Crown office on Hwy. 97 during weekday business hours to obtain a (free) permit. The pond is not stocked by ODFW, but it supports a variety of warmwater fish as well as migrants from the Little Deschutes.

GOVERNMENT COVE. One of the I-84 ponds adjacent to the Columbia River. Government Cove is 90 acres, located at highway mile 47, two miles east of Cascade Locks. Access is from I-84 at the Herman Creek Exit. As with all the ponds in this series, Government Cove may contain any of the species found in the Columbia, including largemouth and smallmouth bass, crappie, yellow perch, pumpkinseed sunfish, bullhead catfish, and even channel catfish. See Columbia River Ponds map.

GREEN LAKES (Deschutes Co.) A series of three lovely glacial lakes in the Three Sisters Wilderness west of Bend. The lakes are nestled between South Sister and Broken Top Mountains, with South Sister dominating the skyline. They are most commonly reached by a 5-mile hike on a well-marked trail north from North Century Drive (Hwy. 46). The trail begins at a turn-out across from Sparks Lake about 28 miles west of Bend. This trail has an elevation gain of 1000 ft.

An easier but less well known approach is possible from Crater Ditch Creek north of Todd Lake. It's still a 5-mile hike by well-marked, scenic trail, but there is almost no elevation gain. Follow the signs to Todd Lake off Century Drive, but continue past Todd Lake on Forest Rd. 370 (a fair dirt road) about 3 miles to Forest Rd. 380, which branches north toward Broken Top and ends in 1½ miles at the head of Trail 10. There's an impressive view of the blown away south face of Broken Top from the trailhead. Follow Trail 10 an easy 5 miles to Green Lakes.

Middle Green is the largest, covering 85 acres, and it has the best angling. Both wild brook trout and rainbows are available, and run to good size. The rainbows range 10 to 14 inches, the brook trout a shade smaller. North Green is the next largest, about 10 acres and north of the main lake. South Green is the smallest at 8 acres and is the first lake you see from the trail. South is stocked with rainbows.

The setting here is breathtakingly beautiful, a high rocky saddle which is mostly unforested. Fly anglers will have no trouble with their backcast here. At elevation 6500 ft., the snow rarely clears before mid-July. Pack sun screen. At this altitude you'll roast in no time. Good natural campsites are available.

GRINDSTONE LAKES. Two privately owned, pay-to-fish desert lakes on the South Fork of the Crooked about 100 miles east of Prineville. The lakes grow rainbows to 12 pounds and are open for fly fishing only. Contact Kaufmann's Streamborn, Tigard for additional information.

HAND LAKE. A 4-acre trout lake in the Cache Lake Basin, Deschutes National Forest. See Island Lake and Link Lake for directions. From Hwy. 20 north of Sisters, take Forest Rd. 2068 west, then turn right on Forest Rd. 600 to Hand Lake. The lake is 16 ft. deep and is stocked by ground and air with cutthroat and brook trout.

HANKS LAKES. (Deschutes Co.) A series of 3 good trout lakes one mile east of Irish and Taylor Lakes, a short hike from the road. The trailhead is on Forest Rd. 600 about 1½ miles east of the Pacific Crest Trail crossing at Irish Lake. Forest Rd. 600 can be reached from the west by way of Waldo Lake, or from the east by way of Little Cultus Lake. Trail 15 leads north from the road about a ⅓ mile to the west shore of Middle Hanks Lake. West Hanks is to the west, and East Hanks is slightly southeast of Middle. The current Deschutes National Forest map shows the lakes and the trail, but fails to give their names. Middle Hanks is the first lake the trail encounters. The lakes are usually accessible by the end of June.

East Hanks is about 8 acres and stocked with cutthroat. Middle and West are about 6 acres each, stocked with rainbows (Middle) and brook trout (West). Angling success is comparable in all three lakes, with the west lake probably best. All are good on bait or lures most of the time, and fly fishing can be excellent. The trout range 10 to 14 inches, with some larger.

In the area to the north are many lakes and potholes, some of which have been stocked with trout. There are campgrounds at Irish and Taylor Lakes. Mosquito repellent is essential in late spring when the fish may or may not be biting, but hordes of skeeters can be depended upon.

HARVEY LAKE. (Confederated Tribes Warm Springs) A scenic, lightly fished hike-in brook and cutthroat trout lake occupying a narrow flat step between two very steep slopes, about 4 miles south of Olallie Lake. A former road from Warm Springs to the trailhead has been closed. The lake is now only accessible by trail from Breitenbush Campground. The trail begins at the south end of the camp near the inlet. It is a 3-mile hike.

Harvey is at elevation 5400 ft. with 27 surface acres. It is located in a cirque at the base of a 300 ft. talus slope, very similar to Dark Lake to the north, and rivals Blue Lake for beauty. The inlet stream tumbles down from Lake Hilda, 300 feet above. The outlet flow shoots over a 200 foot sheer cliff into Shitke Creek. It has a maximum depth of 40 feet with limited shoal area. The lake has some brook trout along with residual cutthroat trout from earlier stocking programs. A tribal permit is required to fish this lake. Permits are available in Warm Springs and at G.I. Joe's stores throughout Oregon. No overnight camping is allowed due to fire danger.

HAYSTACK RESERVOIR. A fair size reservoir 9 miles south of Madras in Crooked River National Grassland, not especially attractive, but with plentiful bank angling opportunity and an unusually wide choice of fisheries for this area. It is used as a storage reservoir, so there can be considerable daily fluctuation in water level. This kind of fluctuation isn't good for the resident bass, which provide only fair fishing, but Haystack supports an excellent kokanee population and grows good numbers of black crappie and brown bullhead. Stocked rainbows and a few large brown trout are also available.

From Madras drive 8 miles south on Hwy. 97, turning east onto a county road about a mile south of the Culver turn-off. From there it's about 2 miles to Haystack.

Haystack is extremely productive for kokanee 10 to 18 inches. Best catches are in spring and fall. Anglers have success both trolling and bank fishing. About 5000 legal rainbows are stocked annually, with best fishing in spring and fall near the south shore. Crappie are small but plentiful, especially near the inlets. Largemouth bass have established themselves and are reproducing naturally. Best bass fishing is along the dam on the north side. Look for bullheads in the muddy shallows of the southeast corner. Brown trout to 5 pounds are being caught.

Haystack is heavily used by water-skiers in summer. However, there is a 5 mph speed limit near the southeast and southwest shores which should help diminish conflicts between anglers and speedboaters. During drought, the reservoir can be severely depleted.

There is a primitive forest service campground on the east shore. The reservoir is open year-round, but is sometimes frozen over for short periods in winter (though not thick enough for ice fishing).

HERMAN CREEK. A trout stream with small steelhead and chinook runs, entering the Columbia River about 2 miles east of Cascade Locks. It heads about 12 miles upstream in several small lakes in the Wahtum Lake area and is crossed by I-84 just above the mouth. An eclectic variety of Columbia River anadromous fish may be found in the lower creek at any given time. The stretch from the railroad to the Columbia is under Columbia Zone angling regulations.

You must hike in if you want to fish for trout here. A good trail begins at the Columbia Work Center, joining the Herman Creek Trail one mile up the hill. The Herman Creek Trail parallels the mainstem of the creek to the forks, then follows the east fork to the headwaters. Small wild cutthroat can be found all along this stretch, and there are some big holes that may hold larger trout. Trout fishing is catch and release with artificial flies and lures.

There is a hatchery near the mouth of the creek off I-84. A run of fall chinook enters the creek in late August, but angling is prohibited up to the hatchery dam from August 16 through November 30. A small number of summer steelhead enter the stream from June through October. Non-finclipped steelhead must be released unharmed. Check the regulations for bait restrictions during steelheading season.

HICKS LAKE. A small brook trout lake in Mt. Hood National Forest north of Wahtum Lake, about 25 miles southwest of Hood River. Hicks Lake is ½ mile northwest of Wahtum at the head of Herman Creek. Only about 2 acres and shallow, it has frequently winterkilled and is no longer stocked.

HIDDEN LAKE. (Deschutes Co.) A 13-acre lake, sometimes confused with Found Lake, way off the beaten path in the Deschutes National Forest east of Waldo Lake. The lake has a small population of little brook trout. It is on the western slope of Gerdine Butte, about 1½ miles south of Charlton Lake.

HOOD RIVER. A steelhead stream with catch and release trout fishing opportunities. The river is fed by Mt. Hood's east slope glaciers and flows into the Columbia River at the town of Hood River about 50 miles east of Portland.

Steelheading is confined to the lower 4 river miles below Powerdale Dam. Fished mostly by local anglers, this is a genteel fishery. It's customary to ask permission before joining another angler at a steelhead hole. Access to the river within the open area is mostly hike-in except at the upper and lower ends. At the upper end there is bank access near the dam. Park in the PP&L parking lot. A trail follows the river 4 miles to the mouth. At the mouth, park along the dikes or in the PP&L Powerhouse parking lot off Hwy. 35, and walk upstream.

Fishing from boats is discouraged, except between I-84 and the Columbia where there is a boat ramp. Check the regulations for hook and bait restrictions.

Unlike many streams in Oregon, Hood is a free-stone river. Location of gravel bars and holes changes yearly, and dramatically after flood events such as those of '96.

Trout angling is fair in the lower river for both native and stocked fish, catch and release with artificial flies and lures only.

HOOD RIVER, EAST FORK. A wild rainbow trout stream on the southeast slope of

HOSMER LAKE is perfect for float tube fly fishing. Photograph by Scott Richmond.

Mt. Hood, joining the main river about 2 miles north of Dee. It has small wild runs of summer and winter steelhead, but it's closed to steelheading. Trout fishing is catch and release with artificial flies and lures.

The river is closely followed by Hwy. 35, which is clear of snow in late spring. Prior to that, access is from Hwy. 30 at Hood River. Hwy. 281 follows the stream south from Dee, where it joins Hwy. 35 at Parkdale.

There are three campgrounds along the river in Mt. Hood National Forest—Polallie, Sherwood, and Robinhood.

HOOD RIVER, LAKE BRANCH. A summer steelhead and chinook salmon spawning and rearing sanctuary. It is closed to all fishing

HOOD RIVER, WEST FORK. A summer steelhead and chinook salmon spawning and rearing sanctuary. Closed to all fishing.

HOOD RIVER POND. No.1 One of the I-84 ponds adjacent to the Columbia River. Located at highway mile 66.3, this 4-acre pond is accessible to eastbound vehicles only, with parking in a limited unimproved area. It may contain any of the Columbia River species, including largemouth and smallmouth bass, crappie, yellow perch, pumpkinseed sunfish, bullhead and channel cats. See Columbia River Ponds map.

HOOD RIVER POND. No. 2. One of the I-84 ponds adjacent to the Columbia River,

located at highway mile 67. It has 3 surface acres south of I-84, with limited unimproved parking for eastbound traffic only. It may contain any of the Columbia's warmwater species. See Columbia River Ponds map.

HOOD RIVER POND. No. 3 A 3-acre pond south of I-84 adjacent to the Columbia River at highway mile 67. There is limited unimproved parking for eastbound traffic only. It may contain any of the Columbia River species, including largemouth and smallmouth bass, crappie, yellow perch, pumpkinseed sunfish, bullhead catfish, and channel catfish. See Columbia River Ponds map.

HORSESHOE LAKE. (Olallie Lake basin) A pretty, 14-acre brook and rainbow trout lake between Olallie and Breitenbush lakes off Forest Rd. 4220. You can drive right to this scenic beauty. A spit of land juts into the lake from the west shore, giving the lake its characteristic shape. It is stocked with legal trout and is easy to fish from shore. There is a campground at the lake.

Hosmer Lake

One of the richest lakes in the Deschutes National Forest. It grows very large brook trout and deep-bodied landlocked Atlantic salmon. Angling is restricted to fly-fishing only with barbless flies, and fishing for the salmon is catch and release.

To reach Hosmer, drive south from Bend on Century Drive. The turn-off to

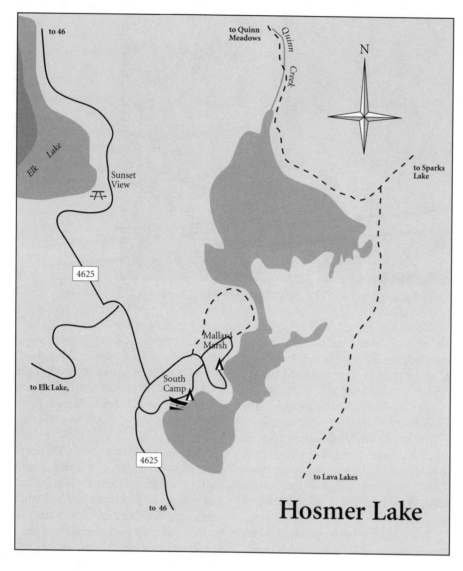

Hosmer Lake

Hosmer is about 3 miles past the entrance to Elk Lake Resort and is well marked. The road reaches the lake in about one mile. Century Drive (County and Forest Rd. 46) can also be reached from the Willamette Valley by driving southeast from Eugene on Hwy. 58 to the Davis Lake turnoff 3 miles past Crescent Lake Junction. Following the signs to Davis Lake will put you on Hwy. 46 heading north. Hosmer is 10 miles north of the Crane Prairie junction. Snow can block access well into May and linger into June.

The lake is consists of two large main pools connected by a long channel through which Hosmer's big fish glide. The pools are thick with submerged weeds, and water lilies hover at the surface. The channel is lined with bullrushes, but is weed free. Even when the bite is off, there is some satisfaction in boating the channel, where big fish are clearly visible at all times. A mid-day tour on the channel is like cruising an aquarium.

Hosmer's dumbbell shape offers many views to the boater. Red Crater (a forested cinder cone) looms over the main pool. Bachelor Butte provides a handsome backdrop to many of the campsites. The Three Sisters guard the back pool. In one cove the water slips into a lava field and disappears. Wildlife abounds, and osprey will put your best fishing efforts to shame. The early riser may slip through the fog and surprise otter, mink, or deer along the shore, while countless marsh birds grumble in the rushes.

Hosmer is a large shallow lake, the channel connecting its two main pools extending north to south. The southern pool is the deeper of the two, yet its maximum depth is only 10 ft. It has two campgrounds on its western shore. The richly organic water limits visibility to about 6 ft. depth. Fish are found throughout this portion of the lake. Most anglers fish near the bullrushes, but good catches are made throughout the pool.

A winding channel almost a mile long leads to the northern pool. Fish in the channel as the main pool warms in late summer. The number and size of fish visible in the channel may tempt you to anchor and fish, but remember, if you can see them, they can see you. Fishing in the channel is best at low light. A side channel branches off towards the northeast, ending at a floodgate which regulates the flow of water into a natural lava sink.

The northern (back) lake covers more area but is generally shallower and cooler, since this is where the inlet stream (Quinn Creek) enters. Few anglers make the trip back here since fish are more abundant closer to the boat ramp. It's pretty, though.

The rich waters of Hosmer have long grown the largest brook trout in Oregon. Brook trout are no longer being stocked, and anglers are encouraged to help tip the population balance toward Atlantics, which provide a better sport fishery (and will grow plumper without competition from the brookies). The Atlantics average 15 inches and may exceed 20 inches. Brook trout (which can live to be 10- 20 years old) have grown to impressive size here and are no fools.

Natural forage in Hosmer includes Callibaetis mayflies, damselflies, midges, leeches, and crayfish. Fish Callibaetis nymphs in the morning, then switch to dries when the hatch begins after the day warms up. Best fishing is from ice-out through mid-July and again in fall, but this is such a great place, you might as well fish it whenever you can get away.

There are two excellent forest campgrounds on the southern pool, with a boat ramp at the southern tip. Only electric motors are permitted on the lake, and the speed limit is 10 mph. This is a great lake for float tubes and canoes. Mallard Marsh Campground at the north end of the lake has a little canoe slip through the bull rushes that leads directly to the channel. For more information, see *Fishing in Oregon's Cascade Lakes*, published by Flying Pencil.

HUSTON LAKES. Two bass and panfish lakes in the Powell Butte half-way between Redmond and Prineville in central Oregon. The lakes are on private land, and neither is currently open for public access.

INDIAN CREEK. (Hood River Co.) A small stream which flows right through the town of Hood River. It is used for agricultural drainage and as an outdoor lab by local high school students.

INDIAN FORD CREEK. (Deschutes watershed) A small creek flowing 11 miles through mostly private land into Squaw Creek north of Sisters. The upper stretch is crossed by Hwy. 20 about 5 miles northwest of town. Its north bank is followed fairly closely by a forest road. The creek supports a few small wild rainbows averaging 6 to 10 inches. There is a nice campground on the upper end at the Hwy. 20 crossing 5 miles west of Sisters. Fishing is restricted to artificial flies and lures.

ISLAND LAKE. (Confederated Tribes of Warm Springs) Fourth in the chain of lakes from Olallie to Trout Lake. This oval lake's name is derived from a one acre island located in the middle. It is accessible only by unimproved trail from either Olallie Lake east or Trout Lake west. See Dark Lake for directions.

Island has about 26 surface acres at elevation 4650 ft. It is the shallowest lake of the chain, with a maximum depth of only 10 feet. Most of the lake is 3 feet deep or less. Brook trout are stocked here. The lake is difficult to fish without a raft or float tube. A CTWS permit is required to fish. Daily and annual permits are sold at the market in Warm Springs, at G.I. Joe's throughout the state, and at many fly shops. No overnight camping is allowed due to fire danger.

IRIS LAKE. One of the I-84 ponds adjacent to the Columbia River, located at highway mile 56. 2. It covers 5 acres at the east end of Viento State Park. Take Exit 56. The lake may contain any of the Columbia's warmwater species. See Columbia River Ponds map.

IRISH LAKE. A scenic trout lake near the summit of the Cascades that you can drive to if you're careful and have a high center vehicle. The access road is not quite a jeep trail, but not a lot better. Irish Lake is midway between Waldo and Cultus Lakes, southwest of Bend in Deschutes National Forest. The Pacific Crest Trail follows the western shore of the lake.

Irish can be approached from either east or west. Access from the east is usually available first. From Bend follow Century Drive (County and Forest Rd. 46) southwest past Lava Lake to the Cultus Lake turn-off. Take Forest Rd. 4630 about 2½ miles to Forest Rd. 600, passing the Cultus Resort turn-off and following signs for Little Cultus Lake. Irish Lake is 6 fairly rough miles west from this point. Drive slowly. From the east, Forest Rd. 20031 leads north from North Waldo Lake Campground towards Taylor Burn. It intersects Forest Rd. 600 one mile west of Irish Lake. This last mile is even worse than the stretch from little Cultus. Irish Lake is at 5500 ft., and the snow lingers until late June most years. This usually blocks the western access.

Irish has 28 acres of clear water and is mostly shallow. The lake is a consistent producer of good size brook trout and is stocked with cutthroat trout from time to time. Brook trout predominate. Trout are typically 8 to 12 inches, but quite a few run to 16 inches or better. Bait angling or lures will work most of the time, but fly angling in the early morning and evening hours produce best results. Brook trout feed in the shoal areas after the sun goes down, and some evenings any fly will entice them. Fishing is best as soon after ice-out as you can get in.

Taylor Lake, a hundred yards south of Irish, is bigger but less productive. Other smaller fishable lakes can be reached by hiking the PCT north, or by taking Trail 15 (Deer Lake Trail) north from Forest Rd. 600 (1½ miles east of the PCT crossing). This area is riddled with lakes and tarns, and hordes of mosquitoes breed in them, especially in early season. Bring repellent and consider head nets.

There is a primitive campground at the lake (no drinking water). Motor boats are prohibited, and there is no boat ramp.

ISLAND LAKE. (Jefferson Co.) An 8 acre lake south of Suttle Lake in Deschutes National Forest west of Link Lake. See Link Lake for directions. Island is 18-ft. deep and supports cutthroat and brook trout.

JEAN LAKE. A 6-acre rainbow trout lake ½ mile northwest of Badger Lake on the southeast slope of Mt. Hood. To reach Jean Lake, drive east from Government Camp on Hwy. 26, and take Hwy. 35 toward Hood River. Six miles from the intersection at Bennett Pass, take Forest Rd. 3550 south-east about 3 miles, then Camp Windy Rd. 3530 northeast a little over a mile past Camp Windy to the Jean Lake Trail. The trail descends about 240 feet in ½ mile. These roads are high and rough. Don't expect to get in before late June.

Jean Lake is about ½ mile northwest and 800 feet above Badger lake. It isn't heavily fished (after you drive the road you'll understand why) and provides very good angling for a small lake. Once stocked with brook trout, it now supports predominantly rainbow trout in the 8 to 9 inch range, with some to 13 inches. There are no campsites at the lake, but there are facilities at Camp Windy.

JEFFERSON CREEK. A pretty stream that heads on the southeast slopes of Mt. Jefferson and flows into the Metolius River at Candle Creek Campground north of Sisters. It serves as a rearing stream for Metolius bull trout and is closed to angling.

JOHNNY LAKE. A brook trout lake in the center of a triangle formed by Waldo Lake, Davis Lake, and Crane Prairie. From the intersection of Century Drive and Hwy. 42, take Forest Rd. 5897 west towards Waldo Lake about 3 miles, then Forest Rd. 200 south for one mile. A trail leading south ½ mile to the lake begins where Forest Rd. 200 cuts sharply back to the east. Johnny has about 20 surface acres and is fairly deep. There is a good campsite at the lake.

KERSHAW LAKE. A 4-acre, lightly fished lake in the Irish Lake area, a good producer for those who find it. It is within a group of small lakes between Little Cultus Lake and Irish. Starting from the trail along the west shore of Middle Hanks Lake, hike north on the trail about ½ mile. See Hanks Lakes for road directions. The lake is east of the trail, and you will cross a depression with a small creek connecting a chain of ponds just before reaching it. Bring the Irish Mt. topo map with you. Total hike from the road is just under a mile.

The lake is 4 acres and 13 feet deep. It has a drop-off ledge along the east side. Try casting over this ledge to bring up the biggest fish. Brook trout average 8 to 10 inches. Mosquitoes are terrible in spring.

KINGSLEY RESERVOIR. (a.k.a. Green Point Reservoir) One of the large lakes in the Hood River area, with 60 surface acres when full, fished for stocked rainbow trout. It is about 11 miles by road southwest of Hood River. Two roads lead west to the reservoir from the community of Oak Grove at the southwest end of Hood River Valley. Look for signs to the reservoir, and stick with the paved road rather than the west-bearing backroad.

More than 13,000 legal rainbows are stocked here annually. The average catch is 10 inches. Bait-fishing and trolling are popular. Non-boating anglers can fish off the gently sloping dam face, and there are other bank fishing spots.

There is a primitive campground at the reservoir with 20 or so sites. Recommended for youngsters.

KOLBERG LAKE. One of the I-84 ponds adjacent to the Columbia River. Kolberg is at highway mile 65.8, with 5 surface acres directly across I-84 from Kolberg Beach State Rest Area. Park at the rest area and walk across the highway. Kolberg may contain any of the Columbia River species, including largemouth and smallmouth bass, crappie, yellow perch, pumpkinseed sunfish, bullhead catfish, and channel catfish. See Columbia River Ponds map.

LAKE CREEK. (Jefferson Co.) A short creek flowing out of Suttle Lake and into the Metolius River south of Camp Sherman. It is one of two Metolius River tributaries open to angling. Rainbows may be fished catch and release, and brown trout are available for harvest. Roads cross the stream near Suttle and near the mouth, but no roads follow it. There is some private land along the lower creek.

The creek divides into three braids that parallel each other about ½ mile apart below Suttle Lake. These are known as the North, Middle, and South Forks, with the middle carrying the most water. They rejoin about a mile up from the mouth. The South Fork flows through a private resort, Lake Creek Resort, near the lower end. Another private resort, The Pines, includes 27 acres on the lower North Fork. Rainbows in the forks can run to 16 inches.

There are forest camps at Suttle Lake and along the Metolius River. Supplies are available at Camp Sherman.

LAURANCE LAKE. A scenic irrigation reservoir on the Clear Creek Branch of the Middle Fork of Hood River, with good

fishing for stocked rainbow trout. Only electric motors are allowed on the lake, which has about 104 surface acres. From Hood River, follow signs to Parkdale. From Parkdale School, it is about 3 miles south to Forest Rd. 2840 (Clear Creek Rd.) This road swings west and reaches the reservoir in another 3 miles.

Flood damage to the entry road (fall 1999) and a tree root disease that poses a safety hazard for users of the campground, day use area, and boat ramp have recently closed the lake to public access. Check with Hood River Ranger District in Parkdale for an update. See Appendix.

Laurance is stocked annually with 20,000 catchable rainbows and supports populations of wild cutthroat and bull trout. Only finclipped trout may be kept. Tributaries to the reservoir, and Clear Branch Creek below the reservoir, are closed to protect the bull trout. Fishing in Laurance is restricted to artificial flies and lures.

This is a pretty and peaceful spot, with a fine view of Mt. Hood. Don't miss the show resident otters put on at sunrise. There is a small campground (no drinking water) with a paved boat ramp. Only electric motors are allowed. There is no charge to park, camp, or launch. Laurance opens for fishing the fourth Saturday in April.

Lava Lake, Big

A scenic spot just off the Cascade Lakes Highway with an excellent trout fishery. It is about 38 miles south of Bend, 20 miles beyond Mt. Bachelor. For early season access it is usually necessary to approach from the east. Drive south from Bend on Hwy. 97 to the Sunriver turn-off, County Rd. 42, which can be followed east to its eventual junction with the Lakes Highway, about 13 miles south of Lava Lake.

Big Lava is a beautiful lake with much of the character of Hosmer Lake to the north. Mt. Bachelor dominates the horizon. A

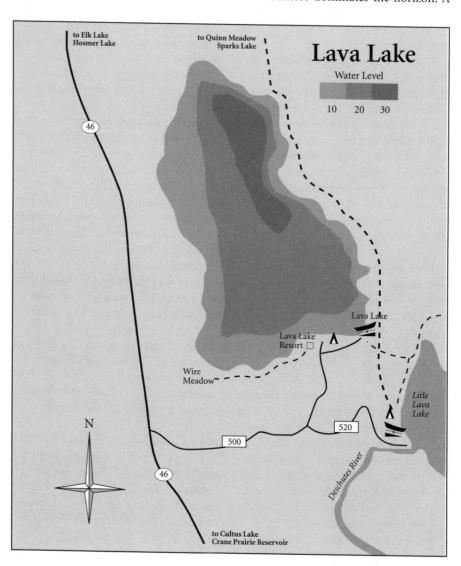

wealth of wildlife adds to the enjoyment of its mountain setting. Although the lake is spring fed, the water is rich with organic material. This forms a food base that grows big fish quickly. Lava is about ½ mile square and 30 feet at its deepest point near the northeast end. Bullrushes line much of the shoreline, and a good deal of shoal water can be effectively fished with a fly.

Rainbows are the predominant catch, ranging 12 to 24 inches, with many 16- to 17-inchers taken. Brook trout currently run smaller, averaging 12 inches, but some 19 inchers are taken. Big Lava has grown trophy brook trout in past years, and there's good reason to suspect the current population will eventually include a good number of challenging old lunkers. Brook trout are no longer stocked here, but there is some natural reproduction. Best fishing for brook trout is just after ice-out and again in fall, though the fall fish are in spawning condition and catch and release is recommended (they don't taste their best at this time, and will serve us all better in the redd than in the pan.).

Bait-fishing is the most popular tactic, and PowerBait is the most popular bait used, replacing Velveeta™, for which Velveeta Point on the northeast shore was named. Trolling picks up in July and August, with spinner-bait combinations effective. Spinners and small Kwikfish-type lures are both popular. In late summer and fall, fly fishing can really pay off, both trolling bright streamers and fishing to the shoreline shelves. Grasshopper imitations are occasionally just what the fish are waiting for.

There is a Forest Service campground and boat ramp on the south shore, and another camp at nearby Little Lava Lake. A rustic resort on the lake has r.v. hook-ups, boat rentals, and supplies. There is a 10-mph speed limit on the lake. For more information, see *Fishing in Oregon's Cascade Lakes*, published by Flying Pencil.

LAVA LAKE, LITTLE. A fair trout lake a quarter mile southeast of Big Lava Lake, headwaters of the Deschutes River. See Big Lava for road directions. Little Lava has 110 surface acres and offers angling for brook trout and stocked rainbows. Whitefish and (too many) chubs are also present.

Rainbow are stocked each year. They run 6 to 5 inches and make up most of the catch. All methods of fishing are used, with

trolling very popular and trolled flies effective. Most fish are caught near the shoreline.

There's a small attractive campground with boat ramp at the lake and more facilities at Big Lava. For more information, see *Fishing in Oregon's Cascade Lakes*, published by Flying Pencil.

LEMISH LAKE. A very good hike-in trout lake in Deschutes National Forest west of Little Cultus lake. From Little Cultus Campground, follow Forest Road 600 west around the south shore of the lake about 2 miles. The trail to Lemish (Trail 19) is on the left. The hike in is less than ½ mile. The trail continues southwest to a junction with the PCT near Charlton Lake.

Some nice brook trout are present in this 16-acre lake, with catches 8 to 16 inches. Lemish is usually good in early season and again in late fall. There's good fly-fishing in evenings. The nearest campground is at Little Cultus.

LILY LAKE. (Deschutes watershed) A nice hike-in trout lake just off the Pacific Crest Trail on the north side of Charlton Butte. It is 2½ miles east of the northern end of Waldo Lake. Pick up the PCT at the northwest end of Charlton Lake (where Forest Rd. 4290 crosses the PCT). Follow the PCT north a bit over a mile to Trail 19, which leads east a short way to Lily. Lily was involved in the Charlton Butte fire of '96. It lost some good trout cover, but half its shoreline is still intact.

This 15 acre lake is fairly rich and has good shoal areas. In places it is over 40 feet deep. Lightly fished, it is a consistent producer using any method. The average catch is 10 inches, with some to 15 inches. It is air stocked with fingerlings, since the lake is not conducive to spawning. Lily is seldom accessible before late June.

LINDSEY POND. One of the I-84 ponds adjacent to the Columbia River at highway mile 54, with 60 surface acres at the mouth of Lindsey Creek. Best parking and access is for westbound traffic at the truck weigh station. See Columbia River Ponds map.

LINE POND. A one-acre pond off I-84 ponds adjacent to the Columbia River at highway mile 68. It is at the Hood River/Wasco County line. It has limited unimproved parking for eastbound traffic

only. See Columbia River Ponds map.

LINK LAKE. A good trout lake 2 miles southwest of Suttle Lake in the Deschutes National Forest. From the Corbett snowpark west of the Suttle Lake turn-off on Hwy. 20, drive west about 2½ miles to Forest Rd. 2076, which leads south. About 2 miles south on this road, a fire road (which may not be marked) leads an eighth of a mile to Link.

The lake has 18 surface acres and reaches a maximum depth of 20 feet. Brook trout predominate, but cutthroat and rainbows may also be present. The fish run 8 to 16 inches. There are several good campsites at the lake.

LITTLE CULTUS LAKE. See **CULTUS LAKE, LITTLE.**

LITTLE DESCHUTES RIVER. A fair brown trout stream with some rainbows flowing 91 miles from its headwaters near Miller Lake in Klamath County to its confluence with the Deschutes River about 15 miles south of Bend. The upper stream, south of Gilchrist, flows through Deschutes National Forest, but much of the lower river flows through private property. County roads cross and parallel much of the stream, however, and road easements provide public access.

The stream is crossed by Hwy. 58 about 15 miles southeast of Odell Lake. From this point, forest roads follow the stream up to its headwaters. Other roads branching off highways 58 and 97 cross and follow the river to Bend.

The Little Deschutes is a meandering, slow-moving stream with deeply undercut banks and a sandy bottom. Big browns to 20 inches lurk in the undercuts, and stealth is advisable as you approach the bank. Casting from as far back as 15 ft. might be necessary, as browns can detect bank vibrations from their cavern hideaways.

Rainbow trout may be present in faster water upstream from LaPine. The river's fish population is considerably down from past years. Fishing for the rainbows is catch and release with artificial flies and lures.

Little Deschutes Campground, the only camp on the stream, is about 15 miles east of Odell Lake.

LITTLE THREE CREEKS LAKE. See **THREE CREEKS LAKE, LITTLE.**

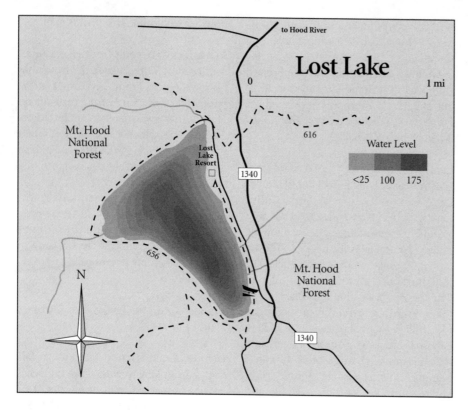

Lost Lake

Water Level

<25 100 175

LIONS POND. A one-acre pond ¼ mile east of Hwy. 97 at the south end of Redmond. It supports largemouth bass, bluegill, brown bullhead, and catchable rainbow trout. It is restricted to fishing by children 14 years or younger and by disabled anglers. A paved jetty at the pond is wheelchair accessible, as is the grassy west bank. The fishery is the project of the Redmond Fire Department.

LONE PINE POND. One of the I-84 ponds adjacent to the Columbia River at highway mile 86.6. It has 5 surface acres north of the freeway and immediately west of Hwy. 197. Parking is difficult, and the east shore of the pond is privately owned. It may contain any of the Columbia's warmwater species. See Columbia River Ponds map.

LONG LAKE. (Confederated Tribes Warm Springs) One of four trout lakes on tribal land in a chain east of Olallie Lake. See also Dark, Island, and Trout. Long is closest to Olallie, accessible by trail from the southeast end of the lake. Fishing here, as for other lakes in the chain, requires a CTWS permit. Daily and annual permits are sold at the market in Warm Springs, at G.I. Joe's throughout the state, and at many fly shops. Camping is not allowed.

LONG LAKE. (Jefferson. Co.) A 16-acre trout lake in Deschutes National Forest east of the Santiam summit. Long Lake is the middle lake in a chain that begins with Square Lake and ends at Round Lake. The best hike in begins at Round Lake. See Round Lake for directions. The trail to Long begins at the end of the Round Lake road. Long is south of the trail, a little over a mile southwest of Round.

Long Lake is ⅓ of a mile long but quite narrow. Its trout are generally small, averaging about 8 inches with some to 15 inches. All methods can be used, but bait and lures are best in early season. There is a small improved tent campground at Round Lake.

LONG POND. One of the I-84 ponds adjacent to the Columbia River, at highway mile 94. It has 27 surface acres, between east and westbound freeway lanes. Best access is from Exit 97 at Celilo, then follow a gravel road west from Celilo Park. It may contain any of the Columbia's warmwater species. See Columbia River Ponds map.

LOST LAKE

(Mt. Hood) A scenic and very popular trout lake on the north slope of Mt. Hood. At 3100 ft., Lost Lake offers a picture postcard view of the mountain. Clear and deep,

with 231 surface acres, it supports three varieties of trout plus kokanee.

Lost Lake is best approached from the east side of Mt. Hood. Take Hwy. 35 south from Hood River to Parkdale. Turn right (west) toward Dee, then turn left onto Lost Lake Rd. The rest of the route is well signed. From Hwy. 26 at Zig Zag, turn left on Lolo Pass Rd. (narrow, steep, and winding) to Lost Lake Rd.

The snow is usually clear in May. Check with Mt. Hood National Forest or Lost Lake Resort for early season road conditions.

Fishing is generally good in the summer and fall. The lake supports natural reproduction of rainbows, brown, and some brook trout, and is heavily stocked with legal rainbows each year (20,000 in 1999). Rainbows are the most frequent catch, averaging 10 inches and running to 16. The browns go to 18 inches.

The lake was last stocked with kokanee 15 years ago, and there is still a small naturally reproducing population. Trolling with flasher and worm is the most popular fishing method, though trolled flies work well on the edge of the shoal areas. Trolling sufficiently slow is rarely a problem, since motors of all kinds are prohibited.

Much of this lake is quite deep (to 200 feet) but there are good shoals in the western lobe of the lake across from the campground. Single eggs and worms are usually effective. Lures will take some of the larger fish, with small Kwikfish-type lures, Hotshots, and flash-type artificial working well. If you're fly fishing, bring along something to imitate the big yellow Hex mayflies that hatch here mid-summer.

An attractive 3-mile trail encircles the lake. Lost Lake Resort at the north end of the lake, has a boat ramp, boat rentals, paddleboats, cabins, and supplies, including a selection of flies. The resort also manages a large Forest Service campground along the eastern shore of the lake. In addition to drive-in camps, there are tent-only site tucked into the side of a forested hill among rhododendrons and bear grass. The resort is open mid-May through mid-October. Recommended for youngsters.

LUCKY LAKE. A pretty good hike-in brook trout lake a mile west of Lava Lake in Deschutes National Forest. From Forest Rd. 46 heading south, Lucky Lake Trail 148 heads off the west side of the highway

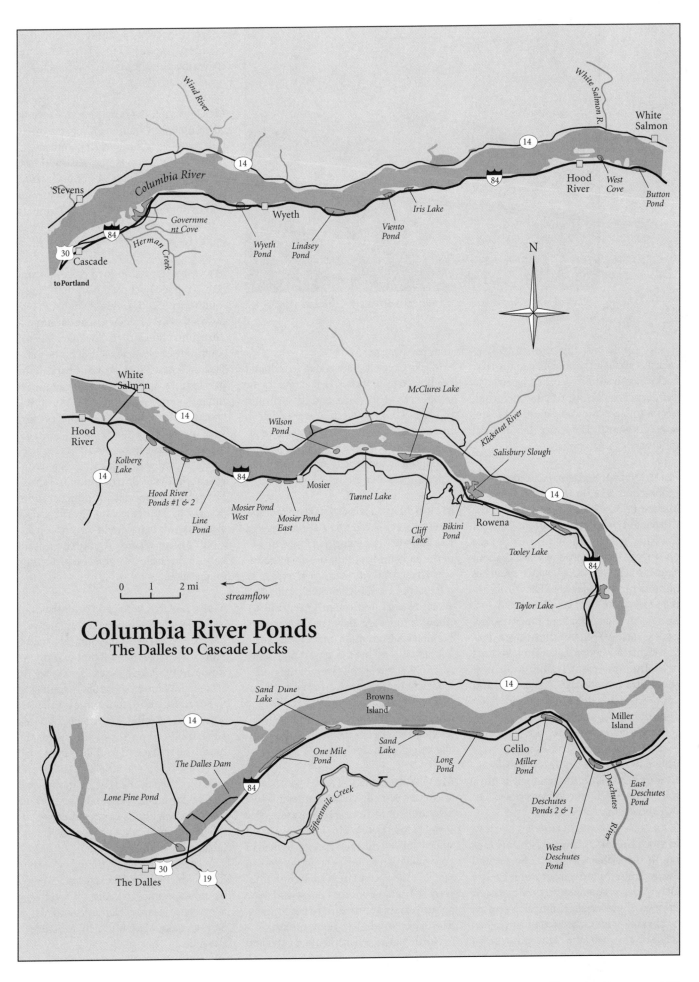

Columbia River Ponds
The Dalles to Cascade Locks

N

0   1   2 mi

streamflow

Wind River

White Salmon R.

Columbia River

14

84

Stevens

Cascade

to Portland

Government Cove

Herman Creek

30

Wyeth

Wyeth Pond

Lindsey Pond

Viento Pond

Iris Lake

Hood River

West Cove

White Salmon

Button Pond

White Salmon

Hood River

14

14

Kolberg Lake

Hood River Ponds #1 & 2

Line Pond

84

Mosier Pond West

Mosier Pond East

Mosier

Wilson Pond

Tunnel Lake

McClures Lake

Klickitat River

Cliff Lake

Bikini Pond

Salisbury Slough

Rowena

14

Tooley Lake

84

Taylor Lake

Sand Dune Lake

Browns Island

14

14

The Dalles Dam

One Mile Pond

Sand Lake

Long Pond

Celilo

Miller Pond

Miller Island

Deschutes Ponds 2 & 1

West Deschutes Pond

East Deschutes Pond

Deschutes River

Lone Pine Pond

84

Fifteenmile Creek

The Dalles

30

19

Bull trout to 20 pounds roam the METOLIUS RIVER year-round. Photograph by Richard Grost.

about ¼ mile past the turn-off to Lava Lake. It's about a 1½ mile hike to the lake. Lucky has 30 surface acres and is over 50 feet deep. Brook trout run 8 to 16 inches. No motors are allowed, so don't pack in your outboard. There are fair natural campsites.

MAIDEN LAKE. A small, deep hike-in brook trout lake on the south slopes of Maiden Peak, a familiar landmark in the Odell and Davis lake area. From Crescent Lake Junction 2 miles south of Odell Lake on Hwy. 58, drive south on Hwy. 58 about 3 miles to County Rd. 61, which branches off to the east and leads to Davis Lake. At the Davis Lake turn off (Forest Rd. 61), turn north and drive about 3 miles to Forest Rd. 4660, which leads northwest. Follow signs to Maiden Lake Trail, about 5 miles from the turn. Trail 41 leads west about 3 miles to the lake. The trail continues west about 2 miles to the Pacific Crest Trail, north of Rosary Lakes.

Only 6 acres but over 20 feet deep, Maiden Lake offers fair fishing for brook trout 6 to 10 inches. The lake is usually accessible in late June, though there is often still some snow. It is no longer stocked, but there is natural reproduction.

MARKS CREEK. A fair trout stream heading in the Ochoco National Forest and flowing into Ochoco Creek 7 miles above Ochoco Reservoir, about 17 miles east of Prineville by Hwy. 26. The creek is crossed by Hwy. 26 at the Ochoco confluence, then followed closely by the highway northeast

to its headwaters.

Marks Creek supports native redband rainbows 6 to 10 inches. Bait angling is the usual method, but lures and flies will also produce. The upper section is good late in the season. In some years this stream almost dries up. There is a Forest Service campground at Cougar and Ochoco Divide on the upper creek.

MARTIN LAKE. A 4-acre hike-in rainbow trout lake, 2 miles south of Three Fingered Jack and a few miles north of Hwy. 20, east of the Santiam Pass summit. Take the Pacific Crest Trail north from Hwy. 20, ½ mile east of Hoodoo Ski Bowl, and hike a short distance to Square Lake Trail 65. About 3 miles on that trail gets you to Booth Lake. Continue a quarter mile north on the trail, and head due west up a draw. Martin is about ⅓ mile west of the trail.

Martin is deep for its size and has rainbows 6 to 12 inches. It's a nice fly fishing lake and a fairly consistent producer. Bait and lures can be effectively used. It is usually accessible in late June.

MATTHIEU LAKES. These hike-in lakes are on the east edge of an impressive lava field south of McKenzie Pass near the Dee Wright Observatory. This lava looks like it spilled out yesterday, an enormous field of gray rubble stretching as far as the eye can see. Take the Pacific Crest Trail south from Hwy. 126 at the Observatory, and hike about 3 miles to the lower (north) lake. The upper (south) lake holds no fish.

North Matthieu Lake, about 6 acres and

not very deep, is a steady producer of medium size rainbows. There is some spawning here, but the lake also gets airdrops of fingerlings.

MCCLURES LAKE. One of the I-84 ponds adjacent to the Columbia River at highway mile 74. It has 50 surface acres, immediately east of Memaloose State Park and Rest Area. Best access is for westbound traffic, with parking available at the rest area. It may contain any of the Columbia's warmwater species. See Columbia River Ponds map.

MEADOW LAKE. A good drive-in trout lake in the Deschutes National Forest southwest of Suttle Lake and south of Hwy. 20, on the west side of Cache Mountain. Turn into the Corbett Sno-park on the south side of Hwy. 20 west of Suttle Lake. Pick up Forest Rd. 2076 at the back of the parking area, and follow it south about 2½ miles. A very rough fire road (Forest Rd. 700, suitable for high-center vehicles only) leads about ¼ mile to the lake.

Meadow Lake has about 16 surface acres and is stocked with brook trout. It is a consistent producer of trout 10 to 16 inches. Fly fishing is especially productive, with best results late in the year. The lake is usually accessible in June, and early season angling is good. There are several pleasant natural campsites. Motors are prohibited on the lake.

MEEK LAKE. A brook and cutthroat trout lake in Deschutes National Forest mid-way between Crescent and Summit Lakes. From Crescent Lake Junction on Hwy. 58 southeast of Oakridge, take Forest Rd. 60 around the western shore of Crescent Lake to Forest Rd. 6010, the Summit Lake Rd. After about 5 miles, and watch for Meek Lake Trailhead on the south side of the road. The lake is just ½ mile off the road by Trail 43.

Rather deep for its 11 acres, it offers fair angling for brook trout and nice size cutthroat. All methods can be effective, although bait probably works best. Fish to 14 inches have been taken here.

In late summer, try fly fishing in Summit Creek, which the trail crosses. Larger brook trout sometimes wander in from the lake. The nearest campground is at Summit Lake. Meek is usually accessible in late June.

One of the most beautiful and challenging fisheries in Oregon, pouring full blown out of a fern carpeted hollow at the base of Black Butte. It is famous for year-round insect hatches and difficult fly fishing. All fish here are wild: rainbow, brown, bull, and brook trout, whitefish, and a spawning run of kokanee. Fishing throughout the river is catch and release for all species. Only barbless flies are allowed from the source to Bridge 99 (attached weights are prohibited, though weighted lines and flies are legal). Below the bridge, both artificial flies and lures may be used. Fishing from boats is prohibited.

To get there take Hwy. 20, northwest from Sisters, or east from the Willamette Valley. Follow signs to Camp Sherman, a small resort community near the Metolius source. From Sisters, turn off Hwy. 20 at Forest Rd. 14. Skirt the west flank of Black Butte, reaching Camp Sherman in about 5 miles. Most campgrounds are on the east bank of the river off Forest Rd. 14. Two campgrounds on the west bank are off the beaten track and may have sites available when others are full.

The Metolius flows about 9 miles through a handsome ponderosa pine forest before entering a canyon. About 20 miles later, it joins the Deschutes River in Lake Billy Chinook. Its source spring can be viewed from a paved stroll-in path about a mile south of Camp Sherman, off Forest Rd. 14. The spring site is well marked.

The river maintains a constant temperature (about 46 degrees) despite the season, fluctuates little in cfs, is unaffected by drought, and always runs clear. Insects hatch prodigiously throughout the year, and the river is open for year-round fishing. The main roads are generally passable even in the depths of winter.

It has been a number of years since trout were last stocked in the Metolius. Redband rainbows are most numerous. The average catch is 13 to 15 inches, with some fish 5 pounds and more. Trout in general (and larger rainbows in particular) are most abundant from the Gorge downstream where there's better instream habitat and more difficult wading. A deep hole at the Canyon Creek confluence often yields large fish.

Bull trout to 20 pounds are in the river

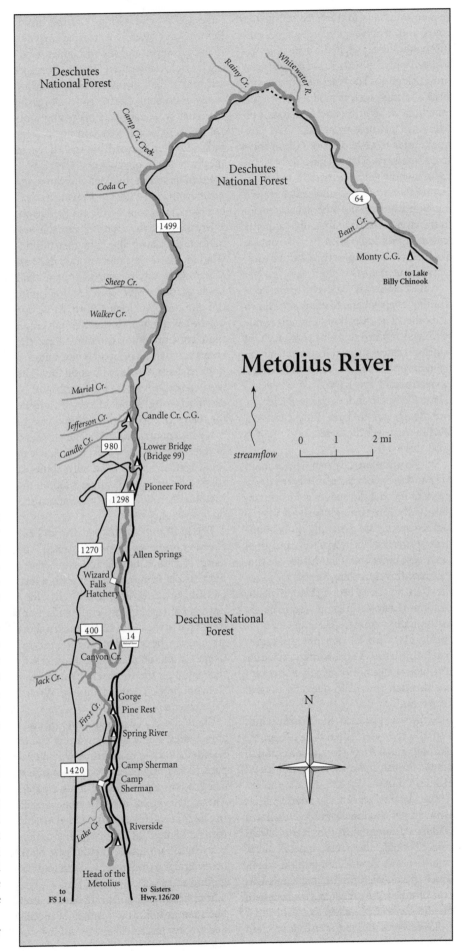

year-round. Look for them beneath bank cover and around submerged structure throughout the river, in the deep holes associated with the bridges, and downstream from Bridge 99. They may be enticed with large offerings, such as mouse and sculpin imitations or big streamers. Additional bull trout and kokanee from Lake Billy Chinook enter the Metolius in fall on their spawning runs. The kokanee in brilliant red spawning colors are a sight to behold (rather than to fish), and die after spawning. Bull trout, on the other hand, remain in the river through winter, their appetite and energy undiminished. Brown trout are also present and numerous, but few anglers pursue them.

Water clarity is one challenge confronting anglers here. Matching the hatch is another. The river flows through a wide variety of mini-environments, each of which produces its own insect hatches on its own time schedule. The three general environments are from Lake Creek to Gorge Campground, Gorge to Bridge 99, and Bridge 99 to Lake Billy Chinook. Within each of these sections there is great variety.

Some of the best fly fishing occurs in May and early July, when big green drake mayflies hatch, followed by golden stoneflies (early July through early October). Golden stones are generally more abundant upstream of Canyon Creek, and green drakes are more abundant below Canyon. Pale morning duns (mayflies) and caddisflies (tan, olive, and brown) are also abundant from early summer on. Caddis hatches on late summer evenings can be spectacular. Smaller mayflies and caddis hatch through fall and winter, including tiny blue-winged olive mayflies (November through April). Midges are present year-round.

Nymphing produces most consistently. Use a long leader tapered to 6X or 7X. Nothing much stirs before 10 a.m., and in winter, the fish and most anglers knock off around 3 p.m.

The Metolius is primarily a bank fishery, with some wading possible. Insulated waders are essential, as the river is always cold. Though the river appears fairly smooth below Gorge Campground, whitewater and downed timber make it treacherous for boats of all kinds. Few people of good sense boat this river.

Easiest wading is in the stretch between Lake Creek and Gorge Campground. Below Gorge, wading is trickier, since the river is powerful and rife with holes. Wading becomes very difficult in the Gorge itself, and in the canyon. However there are many good bank casting spots along the river. Below Bridge 99, good fishing spots are well kept local secrets. You can look for pull-offs along the road, but trails down to the river are not obvious.

From its source, the Metolius flows due north, with Forest Rd. 14 following its eastern bank for about 9 miles to Bridge 99. There is some private property on the west bank in the Camp Sherman area, but beyond that the river flows through national forest, with only two small private land holdings, one below Gorge Campground, the other above Pioneer Ford. At Bridge 99, the pavement ends, and a rough gravel road continues downstream along the river's east bank. This road is best suited to 4-wheel drive vehicles with good tires. The road ends about where the river begins its eastward swing. A trail follows streamside for the next 2 miles, providing access to many nice pools and rapids. The other end of the trail is met by Forest Rd. 64, which leads upstream from Lake Billy Chinook, passing Perry South Campground on the Metolius Arm and Monty Campground on the Metolius itself.

The most popular fishery is from Lake Creek to Bridge 99, a 10-mile stretch. The Gorge is within this stretch, a 2-mile reach inaccessible from above, but with a foot path at river level. Private property along the east bank road limits entry and exit to the Gorge to the north end, though a short stretch can be fished in the vicinity of Gorge Campground. There is also access to the Gorge on the west bank from Lower Canyon Creek Campground to Wizard Falls Hatchery.

There are 8 developed campgrounds along Forest Rd. 14 downstream of Camp Sherman. Each is in an attractive natural park-like setting of big ponderosa pines. The fee-pay camps have drinking water. There are two additional campgrounds (no fee, Canyon Creek and Candle) on side roads off Forest Rd. 1420. Another option is to throw up a tent on the east bank below Bridge 99 wherever you can find flat ground and a place to park.

Supplies and gas are available in Camp Sherman as well as a number of motels and low key resorts. There is a fishing closure near the Camp Sherman store, where large trout are clearly visible, cruising for bread and other trifles tossed by tourists. Wizard Falls Hatchery on the east bank offers an chance to brush up on your species identification skills. The hatchery rears kokanee, Atlantic salmon, brook trout and rainbows. A pond on the grounds opens for youngsters to fish on Free Fishing Weekend.

MIDNIGHT LAKE. A good rainbow trout lake west of Odell Lake and south of Hwy. 58, off the Pacific Crest Trail. Pick up the PCT from a spur road at the northwest end of Odell, and hike about one mile southwest to the lake.

Midnight has about 12 surface acres and is quite deep. It is well stocked with rainbows 6 to 13 inches. It gets fairly heavy use but holds up well, best in early season and again in the fall. Camping and supplies are available at Odell Lake.

MILL CREEK. (Columbia Gorge) A fair-size trout stream that flows through the heart of The Dalles and enters the Columbia River through a culvert at the west edge of town. Fishing is catch and release only with artificial flies and lures. It is crossed by Hwy. 30 near its mouth. The creek heads at the eastern edge of Mt. Hood Forest and flows northeast about 20 miles. It is followed and crossed by many paved and gravel roads. In The Dalles, it may be fished at the road crossings, but adjacent land is all private. Best fishing is in the upper reaches.

MILLER POND. One of the I-84 ponds adjacent to the Columbia River at highway mile 97.5. It has 8 surface acres between I-84 and Hwy. 30, and may contain any of the Columbia's warmwater species. Best access is from Exit 97, then proceed east on Hwy. 30 for one mile. Parking on the freeway is prohibited. See Columbia River Ponds map.

MONON LAKE. A large brook trout lake adjacent to Olallie Lake and bordered on the east by Confederated Tribes of Warm Springs Reservation. From Hwy. 26, about two miles past the Clear Lake turnoff, take Forest Rd. 42 south about 35 miles, following signs to Olallie Lake. Monon is just beyond Olallie on the same road. It can also be reached from the south by about 28 miles of forest road from Detroit. The north road is generally snow-blocked till late June, and the road from the south rarely opens before July.

Monon is over 90 acres and exceptionally clear. It is mostly shallow, but reaches 40 ft. at it deepest point near Olallie Lake, but most of the lake is shallow. Its naturally reproducing population of brook trout (7 to 18 inches) aren't easy to catch.

Motors are prohibited on the lake, and there is no developed campground. There is a full service campground at Olallie on the peninsula that separates the two lakes, and there is one topnotch campsite on a rocky point that juts into the center of Monon, accessible only by boat. Monon offers a good escape from the crowds.

MORAINE LAKE. A pretty but fishless lake in a very scenic area on the south flank of South Sister in Three Sisters Wilderness. Stocking of this lake was discontinued a number of years ago due to frequent winterkill.

MOSIER POND EAST. One of the I-84 ponds adjacent to the Columbia River at highway mile 69. It has 6 surface acres and is immediately east of Exit 69 between I-84 and Hwy. 30. Parking along the freeway is prohibited. The pond may contain any of the Columbia's warmwater species. See Columbia River Ponds map.

MOSIER POND WEST. One of the I-84 ponds adjacent to the Columbia River at highway mile 69. It has 8 surface acres and is bisected by the Union Pacific Railroad south of the freeway. There is limited unimproved parking for eastbound freeway traffic at the west end of the pond. It is also accessible from Hwy. 30 by way of I-84 Exit 69. The pond may contain any of the Columbia's warmwater species. See Columbia River Ponds map.

MUSKRAT LAKE. An 8-acre hike-in trout lake in the Cultus Lake area southwest of Bend. From the east end of Big Cultus Lake, it is a 5-mile hike on the Winopee Lake Trail 16. You can save 3 miles by boating across Big Cultus Lake to the campground at the west end of the lake and picking up the trail to Muskrat. See Cultus Lake for road directions.

Muskrat is a difficult lake to fish. Its brook trout average 8 inches and run to about 15 inches. Fly angling can be good late in summer and fall. An old trapper's cabin survives in good repair. Please help preserve it. Natural campsites are available. It is usually accessible in late June. Mosquitoes can be devilish.

NAP-TE-PAH LAKE. (Confederated Tribes Warm Springs) A 2-acre lake between Olallie and Monon lakes, reached by trail from Peninsula Campground at the south end of Olallie. Maximum depth is 25 feet. Both this lake and a smaller neighbor, Mangriff Lake, are stocked with brook trout. It is a good float tube lake. Although located on CTWS land, no permit is required.

NORTH LAKE. A 6-acre hike-in brook trout lake, 3 miles south of the Columbia Gorge in the northeast corner of Mt. Hood National Forest. It can be reached by a strenuous hike up from the gorge on Trail 411, which heads at the Forest Service campground at Wyeth, 12 miles west of Hood River. The trail ascends 3800 ft. in about 4 miles. For Sunday morning anglers who can't make the grade, as it were, the alternative is to approach the lake from the south. Trail 416 heads at Rainy Lake Campground and gets you there in 1½ miles. (Had you worried there, eh?) See Rainy Lake for road information. North Lake is at 4000 ft.

Fly anglers do well here, as the lake is only 8 ft. at its deepest point. Brook trout average 9 inches, but an occasional 16 incher is taken. The lake is stocked every other year. There are some fair natural campsites around the lake and a good improved camp at Rainy Lake. The road is usually snowbound until mid-June. Check with Mt. Hood Forest Service for early season conditions.

OCHOCO CREEK. A good size stream near Prineville, flowing into Ochoco Reservoir from the east. It is followed closely by Hwy. 26 for 6 miles upstream from the reservoir, then by Forest Rd. 22 to its source at Walton Lake, 14 miles to the northeast. It is accessible for most of its length, but there is some private land in the lower stretch. Ask permission for access.

The creek has wild rainbow trout and is stocked with catchable rainbows in the area around Prineville. Angling is usually good early in the season and again in the fall, with bait the most popular method. The trout range 6 to 12 inches, and the catch rate is good. There are two campgrounds, one at Ochoco Guard Station and the other at the creek's source at Walton Lake.

OCHOCO RESERVOIR. A large reservoir with good fishing for rainbow trout 5 miles east of Prineville. Ochoco covers over 1000 acres and is a popular recreational area. To reach it, drive east from Prineville on Hwy. 26, which follows the north shore.

The reservoir is stocked annually, and rainbows average 10 to 12 inches with some to 15 inches. Large fish are available some years, and anglers often catch their limit. Crappie have been illegally introduced for the second time in recent memory and it is anticipated they will proliferate and eventually lead to smaller average trout size as happened in the '50s. If the experience of the '50s bears out, Ochoco will prove to be too cold for crappie, and they will remain scrawny and not worth the price (spoiling a good trout fishery).

Ochoco is open year-round, and fish are caught in every season, with best catches in spring and fall. Bank angling and trolling are both popular, with most bank anglers working the north shore below the highway. Ice fishing is sometimes possible.

There is a good state park with camping facilities at about mid-point on the reservoir off Hwy. 26. Trailers are prohibited, but there is an RVpark across the highway. Several resorts with rental boats, motors, and supplies are also on the highway.

ODELL CREEK. The outlet stream from Odell Lake, flowing northeast 6 miles from the southeast tip of Odell into Davis Lake. Forest roads parallel it without coming too close for the first 4 miles, and a poor road follows the lower two miles. It is crossed by Forest Rd. 4660 two miles above Davis.

Odell Creek has small populations of wild rainbow and bull trout that may be fished catch and release with artificial flies and lures. Kokanee move through from Odell to Davis, but few are caught in the creek. This is a good creek for whitefish in the fall, but not much of a trout stream. There is a handsome resort with lodge and cabins at the creek source at Odell Lake, and there are forest service campgrounds on each bank of the creek at the Davis Lake inlet.

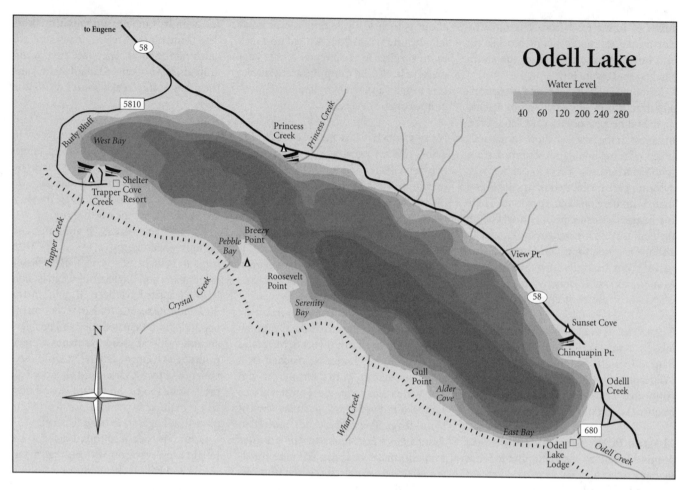

Odell Lake

Water Level

40 60 120 200 240 280

to Eugene

58

5810

Burly Bluff

West Bay

Princess Creek

Princess Creek

Trapper Creek

Shelter Cove Resort

Trapper Creek

Breezy Point

Pebble Bay

Crystal Creek

Roosevelt Point

Serenity Bay

View Pt.

58

Sunset Cove

Chinquapin Pt.

Odelll Creek

N

Wharf Creek

Gull Point

Alder Cove

East Bay

680

Odell Lake Lodge

Odell Creek

ODELL LAKE 🐟

One of the largest natural mountain lakes in Oregon, 5 miles long with over 3300 surface acres, offering outstanding fishing for trophy size mackinaw trout and some of the best kokanee fishing in the state. Odell also supports bull trout and a good population of rainbows. There is no targeted fishery for the bull trout, which must be released unharmed. Angler success rate for all other species is extremely high.

Odell stretches along the east side of

Willamette Pass south of Hwy. 58, distracting drivers with glimpses of sparkling water or churning whitecaps through the dark firs that surround it. Diamond Peak stands guard just 5 miles away on the western horizon. More than thirty creeks and a number of springs feed the lake, keeping its water level constant to within a foot throughout the year. Glacially scoured to over 280 ft. deep near the east end, Odell provides a rich and variable environment for its resident fish populations, all of which are self-sustaining.

Odell Lake is about 70 miles southeast of Eugene by Hwy. 58, and 23 miles northwest of the junction of highways 58 and 97. Hwy. 58 follows its northwest shore for about 5 miles.

The lake was first stocked with mackinaw trout (also known as lake trout), in 1902, and stocking continued through 1965. Mackinaw have been successfully propagating ever since. Lake trout commonly live to be over 20 years old and can exceed 40 pounds. A 30-year-old mack was caught here in 1992. The state record mackinaw came from Odell in 1984, weighing 40 pounds 8 ounces. A 32-pound 6-ounce mackinaw was caught in 1992. Most run 10 to 20 pounds.

In the early years mackinaw preyed primarily on Odell's whitefish and chubs, but today they prey on the growing population of tasty kokanee. One of the tricks anglers use to locate mackinaw (which often hunt in groups) is to first find the kokanee. The bottom of Odell is a varied landscape, with many submerged buttes (observed from the surface as shoals), around which the kokanee cower and dart in schools. One theory is that mackinaw hover just above

the buttes, located east of Princess Creek boat ramp, east of the Hwy. 58 viewpoint, east of Chinquapin Point boat ramp, near the railroad slide on the south shore east of Serenity Bay, and off Burly Bluff near West Bay. Use a depth finder to locate these shoals (at 60 to 90 ft.), or ask the folks at the resorts to point out landmarks that can line you up. They can also usually tell you where mackinaw and kokanee have been schooling lately. Electronic depthfinders and fish finders are very useful at Odell.

The Luhr Jensen Nordic jig has been especially successful here. Most anglers use the No. 060 in silver and fluorescent green with a very sharp treble hook. They locate a likely spot and lower the jig on an 8-pound line, raising it up several feet and letting it flutter down on a slack line. Strikes almost always occur when the lure is falling.

Trolling is effective for picking up single macks cruising through deeper water. Trollers work off the shoals rather than over them, using leaded line with sinkers or downriggers to get to 60- 200 ft., trailing big Kwikfish-type lures, J-plugs, or Silver Hordes. (White and blue lures are supposed to look very kokanee-like down in the depths.) As much as 90% of the catch is taken trolling Kwikfish or Flatfish. Average angler success rate for mackinaw is about one mack per 2 anglers per day. The current catch limit is one mack per day, minimum length 30 inches.

For better numbers and faster action, try for the kokanee. Kokanee are a delicious tasting landlocked sockeye salmon, first stocked in 1931. They are now a very large and self-sustaining population here. Their average size is just 12 inches, with 18-inchers occasionally caught. They are very abundant, and the average size is slipping due to overpopulation. Anglers are encouraged to catch and keep the maximum allowable (25 at this time).

Because of their fine taste, abundance, and ease of catch, most kokanee are sought as meat for the table rather than for sport. Some anglers still-fish for them early in the season using shelled caddis fly larvae, single eggs, or worms. Most folks troll, using a small flasher, 18-inch leader, and a small kokanee lure (such as Wedding Ring or Super Duper) tipped with a piece of worm and a kernel of corn. If you're using heavy gear, you'll need a rubber snubber to absorb some of the shock of the initial hook-

up. A downrigger will enable you to use lighter gear more suited to kokanee size.

Kokanee can provide good sport to anglers who use a downrigger (rather than heavy hardware) to get down to their level, and light gear—a light, sensitive rod, light line (6 pound test monofilament, 4 pound leader), and light terminal tackle (a few fluorescent beads, a tiny spinner with the blade removed, a No. 6 hook, and a single kernel of white corn). The downrigger usually has to be manually released, since the kokanee bite is more subtle than most tension mechanisms can detect. Jigging is also effective and popular, especially using the Nordic in pink pearl or fluorescent green.

In early season, kokanee schools can generally be found within 8 to 20 ft. of the surface. But kokanee prefer water temperatures 50 degrees or colder, and as the lake warms in June they descend to about 50 ft., then to around 75 ft. in July, and down to 100 ft. in August. Towards fall, kokanee move closer to shore, seeking spawning inlets. You can observe kokanee spawning in Trapper Creek, at the Shelter Cove dock, and in Little Creek from mid-September to mid-November. During spawning, best fishing is mid-lake from 40 to 150 ft.

Electronic fish finders can locate where and at what depth the schools are holding, though looking for congregations of boats on the lake and asking other anglers what depth they're fishing is just as effective. Kokanee anglers tend to be generous with information, since there are plenty here for

all. Best fishing is in early morning and late in the day, which suits Odell's temperament perfectly.

Odell Lake is aligned with a major mountain pass and, at elevation 4788 ft., the wind can really whip through, churning up the water. When it does, you want to be safely ashore, perhaps sipping coffee

ODELL LAKE's big macks prey on the lake's abundant kokanee. Photograph courtesy of Shelter Cove Resort.

beside the big stone fireplace at Odell Lodge on the east end of the lake. The weather can change quickly in spring and late fall, so keep a weather eye out. Typically, the lake is calm in the morning, and boating even by canoe can be quite pleasant. (There is, in fact, an annual canoe race on Odell). Afternoons, the wind can be counted on to pick up, a fact which sail boarders have taken note of. Most anglers pack it in afternoons. The lake generally calms again by early evening.

Other species available in Odell include bull trout and rainbows. Both reproduce naturally here and reach good size. Bull trout average 12 to 14 inches and must be released unharmed. The rainbows typically range from 8 to 16 inches with many to 20 inches and better. They can be taken by all methods, though trolling with lure or spinner and bait combinations is most common. Rainbow anglers work the shorelines from mid-June throughout the season, with best catches in fall.

There are excellent campgrounds at the east and west ends of the lake and along the north shoreline. Princess Creek, Trapper Creek, and Sunset Cove campgrounds have boat launches. Pebble Bay Campground is a small tent camp on the south shore, accessible only by boat.

There are two resorts on Odell, one at each end of the lake, each offering accommodations, supplies, tackle, boats and motors. Shelter Cove on the west end has attractive cabins and a deli. The fireplace at Odell Lake Lodge is worth a visit, and you can get an excellent meal there. For more information about fishing Odell, see *Fishing in Oregon's Cascade Lakes*, published by Flying Pencil.

OLALLIE LAKE 🐟

The largest and most popular of over 200 lakes and ponds in the Olallie Lake Scenic Area at the far southern edge of Mt. Hood National Forest. This is a good rainbow trout fishery, with over a dozen other fair to good fishing opportunities within a 3-mile radius.

Olallie is at the western end of a chain of 5 trout lakes connected by Mill Creek, draining east through Confederated Tribes Warm Springs Reservation. The others lakes are on CTWS land but open to public fishing with a tribal permit (See Appendix). See also Long, Dark, Island and Trout.

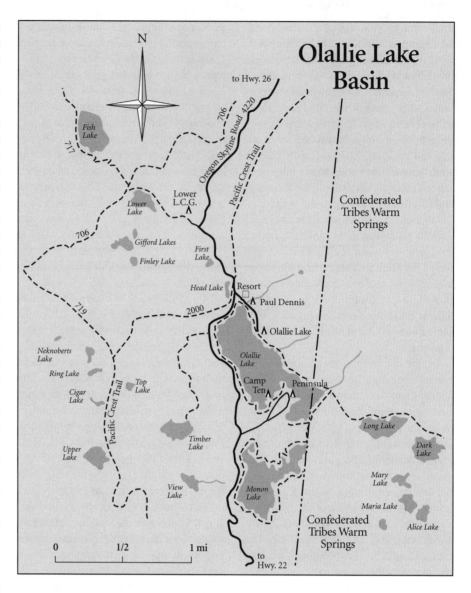

To reach Olallie from Portland, follow Hwy. 26 through Government Camp to Forest Rd. 42, which cuts off from the west side of the highway about 2 miles south of the Clear Lake turn-off. At Warm Springs Meadow, pick up Forest Rd. 4220, which leads to Olallie. The last 12 miles or so are unpaved but good when dry. The way is well signed. This area is snowbound into June most years.

From Salem, follow Hwy. 22 to Detroit Reservoir, then continue east on Forest Rd. 46 past Breitenbush Campground and up the North Breitenbush River. Turn east on Forest Rd. 4220 shortly after passing under the power line. The turn is signed for Breitenbush Lake. Continue north past Breitenbush to Olallie (about 3 miles farther). This road is the shorter but rougher way in to Olallie. The first 4 miles of road are the worst, but no problem if you take it slow

and easy. Alternately, continue north on Forest Rd. 46 about 6 miles to Forest Rd. 4690. Follow 4690 east about 8 miles to Forest Rd. 4220, then backtrack south to Olallie.

Olallie is over a mile long with 188 surface acres, shallow but with some deep spots toward the north and south ends. From June through October you can expect good fishing for rainbow trout and the occasional brook trout that wanders in from the higher lakes. Brood trout from Oaks Springs Hatchery are released here as available (200 to 400 most years), but the average catch is 10 to 14 inches. Slow trolling around the lake about 200 ft. from shore is effective. It'll be easy to bracket your trolling speed, since motors are prohibited. Lures and spinner and bait combinations are popular. Fly fishing can be good in the evenings. Bank anglers do best casting from spots where the bottom drops

most sharply into deeper water

A trail encircles the lake, and trails lead west to other lakes in the basin. The Pacific Crest Trail intersects Forest Rd. 4220 near Olallie's north end. Monon Lake is an easy stroll south from Peninsula Campground. A trail heading east from the southeast end of the lake near Peninsula Campground follows the Mill Creek outlet toward the four other lakes in the chain. The southeast end of Olallie is bordered by CTWS land.

There are three campgrounds on the lake, the largest (Peninsula) on the south shore, the smaller Camp Ten on the west shore, and a boat-in or hike-in camp (Paul Dennis) on the east. There is a boat ramp at Peninsula. A resort at the north end of Olallie has cabins, boat rentals, food and tackle. A map of the Olallie Lake Scenic Area is available.

OLDENBERG LAKE. A 28-acre hike-in brook trout lake in Deschutes National Forest 3 miles south of Crescent Lake. From Crescent Lake Junction on Hwy. 58, take the Crescent Lake Rd. south about 7 miles to Oldenberg Lake Trailhead, ½ mile west of the entrance to Spring Campground. Its about a 3-mile hike to Oldenberg past Bingham Lakes. The trail continues south to Windigo Pass.

The typical trout here is 8 to 10 inches, with some fish to 14 inches. Lures and bait will work during the day, with fly fishing best in the evening, as is usual at most high lakes. Good natural campsites are available, and there are campgrounds at Crescent Lake.

ONE-MILE LAKE. One of the I-84 ponds adjacent to the Columbia River at highway miles 90-91. It has 9 surface acres and is between the east and westbound lanes on I-84. There is no parking for westbound traffic, and parking for eastbound traffic is unimproved and limited. It may contain any of the Columbia's warmwater species. See Columbia River Ponds map.

OTTERTAIL LAKE. (a.k.a. Otter Lake) A 2-acre lake at the head of Green Point Creek, ½ mile east of Wahtum Lake on the opposite side of the ridge. Follow Forest Rd. 2810 from Punchbowl Falls, one mile north of Dee, to the lake. Ottertail supports a population of brook trout.

Several hundred brood trout from Oak Springs Hatchery are released in OLALLIE LAKE. *Photograph by John Ramsour.*

PAULINA CREEK. Outlet stream for Paulina Lake in the Newberry Crater of Paulina Mt. southeast of Bend. The creek can offer fair angling for migrants from Paulina Lake. It is not stocked.

Paulina flows down the western slope of the mountain, and enters the Deschutes River about 6 miles south of Bend. Much of the lower creek flows through private lands. It is followed upstream from Prairie Campground by Trail 56.

Though the lower creek is used for irrigation purposes, it usually retains a flow. Its trout are fair size but scarce, a nice stream to fish on bait or flies. Prairie Campground is on Forest Rd. 2120 three miles east of Hwy. 97. McKay Crossing Campground is 2 miles farther east.

PAULINA LAKE

A big, very productive, very popular lake in the crater of a dormant volcano in the Paulina Mountains, an isolated range east of the Cascades about 20 air miles southeast of Bend. It shares this handsome setting in Newberry Crater with East Lake, separated from East by a high ridge. Paulina is at elevation 6350 ft. and is about 1½ times the size of East Lake. Newberry Crater has been designated a National Monument.

Paulina is managed for trophy browns and kokanee. Its kokanee are the egg source for kokanee fisheries throughout the Northwest. The state record brown was taken from Paulina, and a former state record kokanee was only recently surpassed by a fish taken from Wallowa Lake. Rainbow trout are also present, averaging under 12 inches. All gamefish in Paulina are stocked, as there are no tributaries suitable for spawning. [Note: Unlike East Lake, Paulina does not have a mercury contamination problem.]

To reach Paulina, drive south from Bend on Hwy. 97 about 19 miles to County Rd. 21, which leads to the Crater and its lakes. For a better appreciation of the unique geology here, plan a stop at Lava Lands Visitor Center, a Forest Service interpretive center 8 miles south of Bend on Hwy. 97. You'll pass it on the way to Paulina. The Center is located atop a high, relatively recent cinder cone and presents a good overview of this interesting area.

Newberry is actually a double crater, for both Paulina and East have their own lava dome. Unlike East Lake, Paulina has very little shoal area. It is over 200 ft. deep almost throughout. Even its lava dome comes to within only 60 feet of the surface. The lake's only shoal areas are in the southwest near the resort, and directly across from the resort at the black slide. The cream colored basalt crater walls are clearly visible around the perimeter, and these, combined with the great depth, color

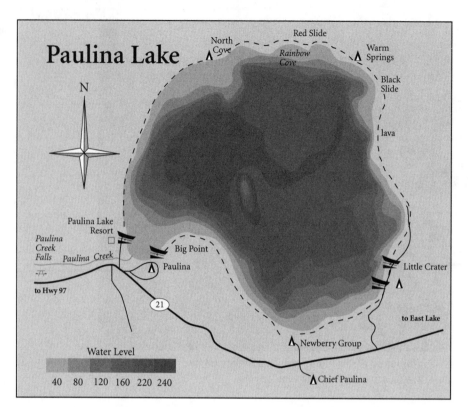

Paulina Lake

N

Red Slide

North Cove

Rainbow Cove

Warm Springs

Black Slide

lava

Paulina Lake Resort

Paulina Creek Falls

Paulina Creek

Big Point

Paulina

Little Crater

to Hwy 97

21

to East Lake

Newberry Group

Water Level

40 80 120 160 220 240

Chief Paulina

An irrigation reservoir, in a pretty setting of pine and oak south of The Dalles, which has turned into a fine fishery for trout, largemouth bass, brown bullhead, and bluegill.

From Hwy. 197 at Tygh Valley, follow Wamic Market Rd. west about 4½ miles, then turn right onto Ross Rd. (about a mile east of Wamic). Keep left at the first intersection, turn left at the "T," and follow Ross to the reservoir's east shore. Pine Hollow is managed cooperatively by ODFW and the irrigation district, with agreement to retain the minimum pool needed to support fish even during drought. At high water the reservoir has 240 surface acres, and though it is heavily drawn down annually, all fish are able to hold over till the reservoir refills.

The reservoir's fish populations appreciate the consideration. Largemouth 4 to 5 pounds are commonly caught, with some approaching 9 pounds. Rainbows grow to 16 inches. Rainbow fingerlings are stocked annually, and legal rainbows are stocked several times each year. Brown bullheads and bluegills are thriving. Look for bass along the shoreline willows. The bullheads favor the southwest corner where there are muddy shallows and submerged woody debris. Bluegills are abundant along the south shore shallows and around the docks when the reservoir is full.

The land surrounding the reservoir is privately owned and has been developed for year-round and vacation homes, but public access to the reservoir has been preserved through the purchase (by ODFW) of a 10 ft. easement encircling the lake. This is a walking and emergency pull-out easement only. Public bank fishing is limited to the area west of the south shore boat ramp and north and south of the east shore ramp.

A 10 mph speed limit on the lake is eased from July 1 through Labor Day to allow waterskiing on the west half of the lake, but the speed limit is retained on the east half to maintain good fishing.

The lake is open for fishing year-round, and the roads are generally clear throughout the winter. The lake frequently freezes thick enough for safe ice fishing. Check with the Forest Service at Maupin for an update on the ice pack.

There are two public boat ramps and a

Paulina's waters an unusual turquoise.

Kokanee are doing quite well in Paulina and make a good contribution to the mid-summer catch. They can be found all over the lake, including the center. These fish run to 22 inches, which is large for the species. The former state record kokanee taken here weighed 3 pounds, 6 ounces.

Two successive record-breaking brown trout came out of Paulina, the most recent in 1993 at 27 pounds 12 ounces. Browns do not reproduce naturally in Paulina, but they do live to be 18 to 20 years old. In addition to providing opportunity for trophy catches, the browns help curb the lake's chub population.

Rainbow trout fingerlings are planted annually and make up the majority of the catch. Most are 9 to 14 inches, though the lake has some lunkers over 5 pounds. Trolling and bait-fishing are a toss-up for popularity, with trolling probably taking the larger fish. Rainbow anglers work the shorelines, usually keeping within depths of 20 ft. or less. Popular trolling and still-fishing areas are off the rocky points on the mid-eastern shore and off the western shore between Red Slide and Paulina Resort. Trollers also work the area southeast of Big Point (the rocky point near the main campground). There is good still-fishing in the little cove between Red Slide and the warm springs. Most of the fly action is over

the weed beds near the warm springs and Black Slide in the northeast, between Red Slide and Rainbow Cove in the northwest, and north of the Clay Banks in the southeast.

There are two drive-to campgrounds on the lake—Paulina Lake Campground at the southwest end and Little Crater Campground on the southeast shore. Both have boat ramps. Little Crater offers the most privacy of the two. In addition, there are two hike-in or boat-in camps on the northeast and northwest shores. Newberry Group Camp on the southeast shore is available by advance reservation. Chief Paulina, across County Rd. 21 from Newberry Group Camp, is a horse camp with corrals and stock water.

There is a rustic log resort with attractive restaurant, cabins, boats, motors, and supplies at the west end of the lake. A few summer homes are located on the south shore. A 7-mile trail (foot traffic only) encircles the lake. Boaters should observe the 10-mph speed limit on the lake and keep a weather eye out, as Paulina gets rough in a blow, and storms can come up in a hurry. Winter holds on long up here, and the campgrounds are often blocked with snow till early June. The weather is usually pleasant by late June in most years, but bring warm clothes. For more information, see *Fishing in Oregon's Cascade Lakes*.

privately operated resort on the east shore. Facilities at the resort include a campground with RV and tent sites, rustic rental cabins, boat and motor rentals, and a general store (groceries, gas, and tackle). Pinehollow is recommended for introducing youngsters to fishing.

PRINEVILLE RESERVOIR

A large reservoir on the Crooked River in Oregon's high desert country, with year-round fishing opportunities for trout, largemouth and smallmouth bass, crappie, and brown bullheads. From Prineville on Hwy. 26, follow signs toward Prineville Reservoir, not toward Bowman Dam. The access road is Juniper Canyon Rd., which reaches the reservoir in about 12 miles.

Prineville Reservoir was created for flood control, irrigation, and municipal water supply and varies considerably in water level annually. At high water, it can cover up to 5 square miles, at low water, under 3 square miles. Lake level varies about 30 feet most years, preventing successful spawning by many of the reservoir's warmwater fish. During drought periods, its fisheries have been lost.

Huge numbers of trout are stocked each year (as many as 170,000 three- to five-inchers). They generally reach 8 inches by August, and 12 to 14 inches by the following spring. Best trout fishing is January through June. When the winter is cold enough, ice fishing can be excellent here. Check with ODFW's Prineville office for an ice pack update.

The reservoir supports abundant populations of brown bullhead and black crappie. Crappie average 8 inches. Best concentrations are up-reservoir from the resort in shallow coves. Good catches are also made off the resort docks. They can be taken on worms and small jigs.

Best bullhead fishing is at the upper end of the reservoir in May and June, and again in September (water temperature 55 to 60 degrees). Bullheads run 6 to 7 inches with some to 10 inches. Worms take most of the catch. There are bullhead bank fishing opportunities by the dam in the south, at Roberts Bay, in Bear Creek arm, and along the road through the Wildlife Area northeast of the resort in spring when the road opens in time. The Wildlife Area road can open as early as mid-March in high water years but can remain closed till the end of

April when the reservoir is low. West end access to this road closes in mid-November.

Smallmouth bass are abundant, but most are less than 12 inches. Regulations require release of smallmouth between 10 and 14 inches. Bigger smallmouth can be found around Owl Creek in the 5 mph zone. The largemouth population has declined as smallmouth have increased. The average largemouth is 3 to 4 pounds, but there are some approaching 7 pounds. Look for largemouth around the woody debris in the upper reservoir and in

Roberts Bay. Habitat additions (submerged juniper bundles) in the Sanford Creek mouth area and about ½ mile above should attract additional bass. Be careful motoring in that area. The Bear Creek arm can also be good for largemouth in spring. In general, most bass (smallmouth and large) move into the upper reservoir in spring to take advantage of nutrients flowing in from the Crooked River. As the water warms. they move downstream.

A boat is really handy here, though there are excellent bank fishing opportunities

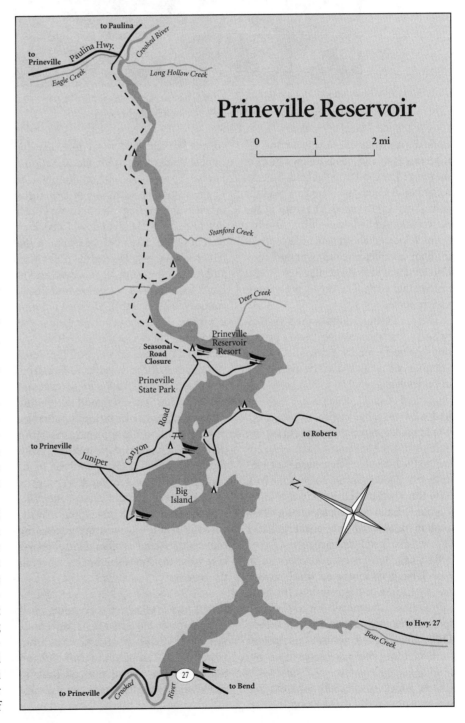

Fishing for brown bullhead catfish is best at the upper end of PRINEVILLE RESERVOIR in May and June. Photograph by Bud Hartman.

along the northeast shore, where Prineville Reservoir State Park roads follow 3 miles of shoreline. The most popular bank fisheries are at Jasper Point, the State Park, and the dam. There are good boat ramps at the State Park and at Jasper Point. Another ramp is located about one mile south of the dam, and there are ramps at the Crook County Park and Prineville Resort east of the state park. The resort rents boats and motors.

There is a campground at the State Park (which accepts reservations) and a private campground run by Prineville Resort. Supplies are available at the resort and in Prineville.

RAFT LAKE. A lightly fished brook trout lake in the Deschutes National Forest, one mile west of Little Cultus Lake. No trails lead to the lake. To reach it, head west a little over 2 miles on Forest Rd. 600, the Irish Lake Rd. Then head north cross-country ½ mile. Refer to the Irish Mountain USGS quad map.. You may hit (smaller) Strider or Lois Lake first. Both have fish.

Raft Lake is 10 acres and about 30 ft. deep. It has good shoal areas which provide fine fly fishing in the evenings. It takes a raft or float tube to get out to the deep spots. There are brook trout 8 to 16 inches. There are some fair natural campsites at the lake. Mosquitoes are fierce in spring.

RAINY LAKE. A 10-acre brook trout lake you can practically drive to, on the east edge of Hatfield Wilderness (formerly Columbia Wilderness) in Mt. Hood National Forest. From Hood River, follow Dee Highway to the community of Dee, turning right and making a hairpin onto Punch Bowl Rd. (toward Punch Bowl Falls). Pick up Forest Rd. 2820 before reaching the falls, heading west. Forest Rd. 2820 twists and turns about 11 miles to a dead end at Black Lake (it does not go beyond Black, contrary to most maps). The road to Rainy is on the right, about a mile before the dead end. There is no sign to Rainy on 2820. The lake is usually accessible in June.

Rainy is shallow, not over 10 feet deep, and provides good fishing for brook trout 6 to 15 inches. This is a good lake for fly fishing. There is a nice little Forest Service campground on the approach road (but invisible from 2820). A ¼-mile trail from the campground leads to the lake. As its name suggests, always bring along your wet weather gear on an outing here. Like Wahtum and Black lakes, Rainy is peculiarly situated in relation to weather-generating Mt. Hood so that it is often cloudy and wet here while the sun is shining elsewhere in the area.

RED LAKE. (Marion Co.) A good small rainbow trout lake in Mt. Hood Forest west of the Olallie Lake Scenic Area. From Lower Lake Campground (off Oregon Skyline Rd. 4220), head south on Trail 719 past Wall and Averill Lakes. See Averill Lake for directions. Red Lake is about 3½ miles from Lower Lake. It is south of the trail, about a quarter mile beyond Averill. For a more direct approach (1½ miles), pick up the Red Lake Trail 719 east of Forest Rd. 380, which cuts off the Clackamas River Rd. (Forest Rd. 46) about 5 miles beyond Breitenbush Hot Springs. There are good natural campsites at Red. It's usually accessible by June.

RED SLIDE LAKE. A small, difficult to find brook trout lake 1½ miles north of Irish Lake, about a quarter mile south of Brahma Lake, which is on the Pacific Crest Trail. See Brahma Lake for directions. No trail leads to Red Slide. You might get lost for a while, as this is tricky terrain with potholes and lakes all about. Happily, many of them hold fish. In addition to Brahma, you stumble across Timmy, Lady, Gleneden, and Pocket. Hiking due west will get you back on the trail anywhere in here. Bringing along the Irish Mt. USGS quad map will help some.

Red Slide has only 2 surface acres but is deep. There aren't a lot of fish here, but the brook trout reach good size. Mosquitoes in this area are fierce in early season.

REYNOLDS POND. A 20-acre pond near Alfalfa, offering fair warmwater fishing. From Alfalfa, about 14 miles east of Bend, follow Alfalfa Market Rd. to Johnson Market Rd., heading south to the landfill. The pond is about ½ mile past the landfill.

Reynolds is very shallow (only 4 ft. in most places), and the fisheries aren't thriving. The pond does support largemouth bass and redear sunfish, and it's a good swimming hole.

It's about 100 yards from the parking area to the pond, so only light boats or float tubes are appropriate. Bank fishing is good, with the south shore accessing the one deep (10 ft.) hole. To avoid snagging your hook, keep an eye out for submerged junipers which have been added to the pond to provide additional fish habitat. Fishing is best in spring. Recommended for youngsters.

ROCK CREEK RESERVOIR. A pretty little reservoir in an evergreen setting with trout, bass, bluegill, and brown bullhead. It is in eastern Mt. Hood National Forest, about 10 miles west of Tygh Valley. From Tygh Valley, follow the paved road to Wamic, continuing west on this road for about 5 miles to the reservoir. It can also be reached by way of a harrowing drive from Hwy. 26, cutting north from Wapinita, crossing the White River at Smock Crossing, then following signs north to the lake.

Rock Creek Reservoir has about 100 surface acres when full but is heavily drawn down each year. Draw-down is well underway by mid-July, and it's tough to get a big boat in beyond that point. Most anglers launch car-top boats year-round.

It is stocked annually with legal rainbow trout, and brood trout are stocked when available. The average catch is 9 to 13 inches, with some to 18 inches. All fishing methods are effective, with bait fishing most common. Trollers do well using Kwikfish-type lures, Triple-Teasers, or spinner and worm rigs. Brown bullhead and largemouth bass populations have steadily gained ground here, with bass to 5 pounds available. Best bass habitat is along the south shore where there are more willows. Bluegills average 8 inches and can be found throughout the reservoir. The reservoir is shallow with lots of accessible shoreline.

Rock Creek Campground on the south shore is well shaded with pine trees. The boat ramp is adjacent to the campground. Recommended for youngsters.

ROSARY LAKES. A series of three hike-in trout lakes on the Pacific Crest Trail one mile north of Odell Lake. Lower Rosary Lake is 2 ½ miles by trail from the PCT crossing of Hwy. 58 at Willamette Pass. The lower lake is 42 acres, the middle 9 acres, and the upper lake 8 acres.

The lower lake has rainbows, brook trout, and cutthroat averaging 8 to 12 inches with some 16 inches or better. The other two have brook trout in the same size range, but less abundant. All are easily fished with a fly. In early season, come prepared for mosquitoes. The trail is snowbound into June most years.

ROUND LAKE. (Jefferson Co.) A sweet spot for trout lake in the Santiam Pass area northwest of Suttle Lake. From Hwy. 20 about a mile beyond the Suttle Lake Resort turn-off, turn left (north) onto Forest Rd. 12, then left onto Forest Rd. 1210, the second left off 12. From there it is about 4 miles to the lake.

Round is only 22 acres but is fairly deep and holds up well. Brook trout, rainbows, and cutthroat (when available) are stocked.

Catching is good for 8 to 12-inchers, as well as a few to 18 inches. There is a small improved campground on the east side of the lake. The Forest Service grants a use permit for a church camp on the west side. Motors are prohibited on the lake.

SALISBURY SLOUGH. A backwater of the Columbia River, off I-84 at highway mile 76. It has about 50 surface acres and can be accessed at Mayer State Park, where there is a concrete boat ramp and ample parking. Take Exit 76. The slough may contain any of the Columbia River species. See Columbia River Ponds map.

SAND LAKE. One of the I-84 ponds associated with the Columbia River, at highway mile 94. Just an acre, it is south of I-84, with limited unimproved parking for eastbound traffic. It may contain any of the Columbia's warmwater species. See Columbia River Ponds map.

SAND DUNE LAKE. One of the I-84 ponds adjacent to the Columbia River at highway mile 9 2.3. This one-acre pond is between the east and westbound freeway lanes. There is no parking for westbound traffic, and only limited parking for eastbound. It may contain any of the Columbia's warmwater species. See Columbia River Ponds map.

SCOUT LAKE. (Hood River watershed) A 3-acre trout lake in a pretty spot, tucked up against a rock wall. It is just south of Wahtum on Forest Rd. 1310. See Wahtum Lake

for directions. Stocked with brook trout, it yields brook trout 7 to 9 inches.

SCOUT LAKE. (Santiam watershed) A small lake ½ mile south of the west end of Suttle Lake. This lake is currently not stocked and is probably fishless. There is a campground is the east shore.

SIMTUSTUS LAKE. (Confederated Tribes Warm Springs) A reservoir created by Pelton Dam, a power dam on the Deschutes River west of Madras. Most fishing here is for kokanee, but browns, smallmouth bass, and the occasional huge rainbow trout are also available. There is also a catch and keep fishery for trophy-size bull trout. A CTWS permit is required to fish here. This is the smaller of two major impoundments on the Deschutes. The second, Lake Billy Chinook, is upriver.

To reach Simtustus from Hwy. 26 at Warm Springs, continue south on 26 about 3 miles to the Pelton Dam turn-off. A paved road leads to Pelton Park on the east shore, where there is a campground and boat ramp. The only other public access to the reservoir is from Indian Park, a campground with boat ramp on the west shore. Ask for directions in Warm Springs when you pick up your fishing permit.

The dam backs up about 7 miles of river, all the way to Round Butte Dam. Angling is almost exclusively by boat, as there is no access to the canyon much above the dam. The lake is stocked with kokanee and brown trout. There's also a good number of smallmouth bass, though few anglers

ROCK CREEK RESERVOIR *rainbows grow to 18 inches. Photograph by Jim Liddle.*

pursue them here.

Fishing is only fair. Most anglers focus on the upper part of the lake, but early and late in the season, fishing is generally good throughout the reservoir.

Trolling is the most popular method, with bait angling the next choice. Rainbow trout average 10 to 12 inches, but there are some larger—much larger. Trout weighing 25 pounds have been taken here. To pursue these big guys, use big lures and stay deep at most times of year. (Here's a chance to see if that fish finder was worth its ticket price).

Bull trout are also present in Simtustus as in Billy Chinook, and current regulations allow you to keep one (at least 24 inches) per day. The average bull trout is 10 to 12 inches, but there are some 3 to 4 pounds.

Lake Simtustus is on CTWS Reservation, and a permit is required to fish it. A daily permit covers the whole family. Permits are available at Rainbow Market in Warm Springs, at other outlets in Warm Springs and Madras, and at G.I. Joe's stores throughout Oregon.

A 10 mph speed limit is in effect on all but the lower three-quarters of the reservoir. Landing boats on the western shore is prohibited, except at Indian Park. Supplies are available in Warm Springs and at Pelton Park. Simtustus was named after a Warm Springs warrior who served as a US Army scout in the Paiute wars of the 1860s and lived on the reservation till his death in 1926.

SISTERS MIRROR LAKE. A very scenic lake in the Wickiup Plains area north of Elk Lake, south of the Three Sisters. The lake is no longer stocked due to frequent winterkills. There are good campsites all around the lake, and fishing in nearby lakes. See Denude, Burnt Top, Nash.

SNELL LAKE. A nice 9-acre hike-in trout lake in the Deschutes National Forest between Crescent and Summit Lakes. Snell can be reached by trail less than ¼ mile northwest of Farrell Lake. See Farrell for directions.

Both cutthroat and brook trout are stocked, but brook trout dominate. Brook trout average 10 to 12 inches, and fish up to 18 inches have been reported. Snell Lake is fairly shallow, and fly fishing is good late in the year. Farrell Lake also supports trout.

SNOW CREEK. A small, clear trout stream joining the upper Deschutes River just above Cow Meadow on the north shore of Crane Prairie Reservoir. Snow Creek flows only about 5 miles from springs northeast of the Deschutes Bridge Guard Station on the Cascade Lakes Hwy. It offers difficult catch and release fishing for rainbows and catch and keep fishing (with no limit) for brook trout.

Spring fed, it is very clear and cold, and light tackle is a must. The fish here will take a fly. No good trail follows the stream, and the banks are very brushy. The upper portion is crossed by Forest Rd. 4270 south of Deschutes Bridge. Forest Rd. 40 to Cow Meadow crosses the creek one mile above its mouth.

SNOWSHOE LAKES. Three remote hike-in trout lakes roughly half-way between Big Cultus Lake and Mink Lake in Three Sisters Wilderness. The area is at least a 7-mile hike from the nearest road. The lakes are north of Winopee Lake on a trail that runs from the west end of Big Cultus Lake to Mink Lake. The trail is usually clear of snow by late June, but bring dry footwear, as the snow melt tends to pool along the Winopee Trail. Unless you are camped in the Mink Lake Basin, you will probably approach from Big Cultus.

First chore is to reach the western end of Big Cultus. Your choices are to hike around the north shore on a good trail, to hike north from road's end near Deer Lake, or to boat across to West Cultus Lake Campground. The latter will save about 3 miles of hiking. From the west end of Big Cultus Lake, take Trail 16 north about 5 miles to Winopee Lake. Here the trail splits. Follow Trail 35, the eastern fork. Lower Snowshoe Lake is about ⅓ mile north of Winopee on the east side of the trail.

This fairly shallow lake is 18 acres, with a rocky ledge that runs along the west shore. Infrequently visited, it has some nice brook trout 8 to 12 inches, with some to 16 inches. All methods of angling can be effective, but this is a great fly fishing situation.

Middle Snowshoe Lake, ¼ mile west of the north end of Lower, is only 3 acres. It's stocked with rainbow trout. Continuing north on the trail ½ mile brings you to Upper Snowshoe Lake, the largest of the group with 30 surface acres. It's also the shallowest, with a maximum depth of only 8 ft., and it occasionally winterkills.

Upper Snowshoe produces medium-size brook trout.

From Upper Snowshoe the trail continues north into the rich Mink Lake Basin, reaching Mink Lake in about 2½ miles. There are many opportunities for anglers willing to explore with rod and map in hand.

SPARKS LAKE. A large fly fishing-only trout lake just off the Cascades Lakes Hwy. 46, directly south of the Three Sisters. The lake is visible from the highway, about 28 miles southwest of Bend and 3 miles beyond Mt. Bachelor Ski Area. A spur road leads to the east shore of the lake.

Sparks Lake covers a lot of area, about 400 acres, and none of it is more than 10 feet deep. A narrow extension of the lake winds south about a mile from the campground into the lava field that created Sparks. The lake is deepest near the lava dam, and fish congregate there when the water warms.

The natural lava dam has always leaked, and Sparks gets low by late summer. It is hard-hit by drought and takes years to recover. Brook trout were still running small in 1999. Cutthroat were added in 1999 and may be stocked annually. Fishing is best right after ice-out if you can make it through the snow.

There is a boat ramp at the end of Forest Rd. 400, but during low water it is sometimes necessary to drag boats to deeper water. Motors are allowed for transportation on the lake, but fishing is prohibited while the motor is operating. This still allows trolling a fly while rowing or wind drifting. A canoe is probably best for exploring Sparks. Hiking the rocky shoreline is almost impossible due to rock walls and crevasses.

There is a day-use area near the boat ramp, but camping is limited to natural sites off Forest Rd. 400 and a couple of sites at the northwest corner of the lake. From the northwest, a canoe can be slipped into Satan Creek and paddled to the lake when the water is high. The road to these campsites turns off the highway ½ mile east of Devils Lake. For more information, see *Fishing in Oregon's Cascade Lakes*, published by Flying Pencil.

SPOON LAKE. (Confederated Tribes Warm Springs) A shallow 2-acre lake on the west side of the Skyline Rd. between

Horseshoe and Breitenbush lakes. A small population of brook trout is present but subject to winterkill. The lake is on CTWS land, but no permit is required to fish. Overnight camping is permitted. See Breitenbush Lake for directions.

SQUARE LAKE. A hike-in trout lake one mile northeast of Santiam Pass on Hwy. 20. Take the Pacific Crest Trail north ¼ mile from its crossing of the highway, ½ mile east of the entrance to Hoodoo Ski Bowl. Trail 65 takes off to the east and reaches the lake in a bit over a mile.

Square lake is 55 acres and fairly deep. It's fished pretty hard, but continues to produce good catches. Brook trout are stocked. Most fish are 8 to 11 inches, with some to 14 inches. A float tube comes in handy. Following the trail along the outlet creek brings you to Long Lake, ½ mile to the east, where there is also good fishing. Good natural campsites are available.

SQUAW CREEK. (Deschutes watershed) Heading on the east slope of the Three Sisters and flowing northeast through the town of Sisters into canyon country. It joins the Deschutes about 3 miles upriver from Lake Billy Chinook. Below Sisters, Squaw Creek flows through its own canyon. Unimproved roads drop down to it at Camp Polk and at several points to the north. These roads are shown on the Deschutes National Forest map.

Much of the creek goes dry during irrigation season. Except in early spring, there is little or no fishing in the upper creek. There is good early angling at the lower end.

STRIDER LAKE. A seldom-fished, deep 3-acre lake above Little Cultus, off the road to Taylor Burn. See directions to Little Cultus Lake. At Little Cultus Lake Campground, follow the primitive Irish and Taylor lakes road (Forest Rd. 600) west about 2 miles. Strider is about ¾ mile past the Lemish Lake Trailhead, on the north side of the road. There is no trail to the lake, but it's a fairly easy half-mile bushwhack north for feisty rainbows. There are a few logs to cast from, and the fishing's generally good along the rock slide, but a raft or float tube comes in handy.

SUMMIT LAKE. (Deschutes watershed) A large alpine lake on the summit between Willamette and Deschutes watersheds. From Crescent Lake Junction on Hwy. 58, drive around the northwest shore of Crescent Lake to Forest Rd. 6010, the Summit Lake Rd. This road leads west about a quarter mile south of Tandy Bay Campground. Summit Lake is a bit over 5 miles by good dirt road. Diamond Peak stakes out the northern horizon, and Sawtooth Mountain the southern. This is a beautiful lake, surrounded by spruce and pine, but like Waldo Lake to the north, the fish come hard here. At an elevation of 5553 ft., the lake is usually snowbound until late June.

Summit is about 500 acres but is not a rich lake, and fishing is only fair. Some anglers do well, but locating the fish here is a problem. Brook and rainbow trout are stocked, and a population of mackinaw is self-sustaining. The altitude and extremely clear water lead to slow growth of the stocked fish. Brook trout average about 10 inches, get up to 18 inches, and are plentiful if you can locate the schools. Trolling in different areas is the best way to do this. Not many large fish are seen. Most rainbows caught are 8 to 10 inches, but fish to 20 inches are present. Both rainbow and brook trout can be taken by fly fishing in early morning and evening. Few anglers try for the mackinaw, but they do show up occasionally on deep trolls. Summit Lake mackinaw rarely exceed 8 pounds.

There's a good campground at the northwest corner, and Summit makes a nice base camp for exploring other smaller lakes. See Windy Lakes, Suzanne, Darlene. The Pacific Crest Trail touches the southwest corner of Summit and crosses the road a quarter mile west of the camp. Bring mosquito repellent.

SUTTLE LAKE. A popular multi-use lake in Deschutes National Forest off Hwy. 20 northwest of Sisters, featuring kokanee, browns and water-skiing. Follow Hwy. 20 (from Albany or Bend). The lake is just 7 miles east of the Santiam Pass summit.

Kokanee (landlocked salmon) are the main feature for anglers on this 240-acre lake. Late May and June are most productive (before other water sports rev up), but fish are taken throughout the season, with bait the favored method. Bait anglers fish perrywinkles or caddis fly larvae as one would a single egg. The kokanee are currently running to 14 inches.

There are a tremendous number of whitefish and a good reproducing population of browns. Browns to 16 inches and an occasional 4 to 5 pounder are taken on lures or bait.

A good family lake, Suttle offers pleasant swimming and opportunities for recreational boating, with an area roped-off for water-skiing. Mosquitoes, for some reason, are a rarity here. Forest Rd. 2070 circles the lake, and there are four boat ramps on the south shore. USFS campgrounds are located at northeast and southwest ends of the lake and on the south shore. Equipment rentals, lodging, supplies, and a restaurant are available at a resort on the northeast shore.

SUZANNE LAKE. One of a pair of good hike-in trout lakes above Crescent and Summit Lakes. The trailhead is ½ mile west of the Spring Campground entrance road at Crescent. It's about a 3-mile hike to the junction with Trail 46. Hike about ½ mile east on 46 to reach Suzanne and her neighbor Darlene. From Summit Lake it's about a 5 mile hike to Suzanne on Trail 46, past Windy Lakes. The trailhead is off the south side of Forest Rd. 6010.

Suzanne has about 14 surface acres and is very deep. Rainbows average 12 inches, with an occasional 18 incher. Brook trout are also stocked, with catches to 16 inches. Fly fishing is good most times other than mid-day.

TAYLOR LAKE. (Deschutes Co.) The larger, but slightly less productive, of a pair of closely nestled Cascade summit lakes known as Irish and Taylor. These are scenic trout lakes you can drive to if you're careful and have a high-center vehicle. The road in is not quite a jeep trail, but not a lot better. Irish and Taylor are mid-way between Waldo and Cultus Lakes southwest of Bend in the Deschutes National Forest. The Pacific Crest Trail follows the west shore. See Irish Lake for directions.

Brook trout predominate, though the lake is occasionally stocked with cutthroat. Fish average 9 to 12 inches, with a few to 16 inches. Taylor's trout usually run slightly smaller than those in Irish, but are generally easier to catch. There's good fly angling here, but be warned—the mosquitoes can be ferocious, especially in spring. Try fishing the ice-out or in early fall to avoid these pests. Motorboats are prohibited on the lake, so plan to row or paddle if you want

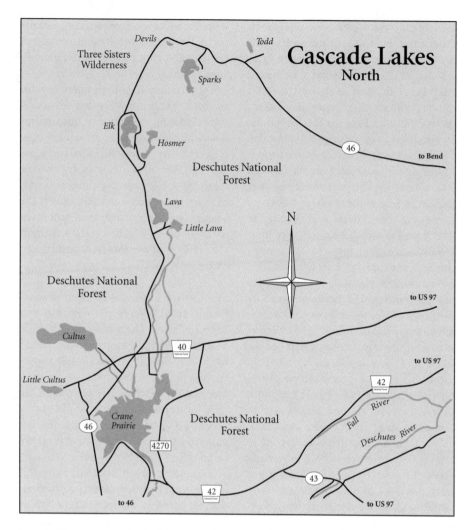

mum depth, is smaller and shallower than North. It provides brook trout 7 to 18 inches. The north lake is a quarter mile northeast of South Teddy and is twice as large and deep. It is stocked with rainbows and brook trout which run to about 13 inches. Both lakes offer excellent fly fishing, but bait and lures are also effective. There are nice campsites at Big Cultus Lake.

THE DALLES POOL. See **COLUMBIA RIVER:** CeliloLake.

THREE CREEKS LAKE. A popular 28-acre trout lake in the Deschutes National Forest on the north slope of the Cascades west of Bend. Cupped in a depression in the mountains at elevation 6500 ft., it receives one of the heaviest snowfalls in the forest. To reach the lake, take Forest Rd. 16 south from Sisters about 15 miles. The road is paved to within ½ mile of lake, and the rest is rough. From Bend it's 24 miles by way of Tumalo Creek Rd. west, then Forest Rd. 4601, following the northwest spur. The last 8 miles of this approach are rough. These roads usually open in mid-June or, in heavy snowpack years, around July 4.

The lake is stocked with catchable rainbows and has a naturally reproducing population of brook trout. The trout run 8 to 15 inches. All fishing methods are used with success. There are two camping areas on the lake, and another a mile north on Forest Rd. 16. A trail leads west from Driftwood Campground, on the north shore of the lake, to Little Three Creeks Lake. This lake is about half the size of Big Three Creeks and has brook trout to 14 inches.

THREE CREEKS LAKE, LITTLE. A wild brook trout lake just beyond Big Three Creeks Lake. About 14 acres and 10 feet deep, it can be reached by Trail 97 from Driftwood Campground at Big Three Creeks. Its brook trout are self-sustaining and reach 14 inches. See Three Creeks Lake for directions.

TIMBER LAKE. A hike-in lake in the Olallie Lake Scenic Area north of Mt. Jefferson, about 100 miles from Portland. From Forest Rd. 4220 (The Oregon Skyline Rd.) about a quarter mile south of the turn-off to Olallie Resort, follow Red Lake Trail 719 west. After about ½ mile, turn left (south) onto trail 733, which reaches Timber in about three quarters of a mile.

to troll. There are good primitive campsites here and at Irish, and the Pacific Crest Trail leads north to other high lakes. See Brahma and Red Slide.

The roads in are generally snowbound till late June or early July. Check with the Forest Service for road conditions.

TAYLOR LAKE. (Columbia River) A popular and productive pond west of The Dalles featuring truly big redear sunfish. It is one of the I-84 ponds adjacent to the Columbia River, offering good angling for largemouth bass, redear sunfish, and crappie. Legal trout and fingerlings are stocked in early season. There is limited unimproved parking for westbound traffic, but best access for parking and boat launching is on Taylor Lake Rd. Take Exit 83 north, then go west on Frontage Rd. to the Taylor Lake Rd. Taylor covers 35 acres. See Columbia River Ponds map.

This is a good place to come in early spring, since it warms sooner than most waters in the area. It's also the place to come to try for the next record redear.

Sunfish to 2 pounds are available. Largemouth bass here reach 5 to 6 pounds. Most people fish along the south shore, but there is a rough trail to the north shore. A boat or float tube comes in handy. There's no boat ramp, but it's easy to launch car-top boats. Recommended for youngsters

TEDDY LAKES. North and South Teddy Lakes are two good hike-in lakes, far enough away to take the pressure off but close enough (if you have a boat) for an easy day hike. The lakes are in the Cultus Lake area about 50 miles southwest of Bend. The Cultus to Mink Lake Trail runs between the lakes about a mile north of the west end of Big Cultus. Start at Big Cultus Lake Campground and follow Trail 16 along the north shore. At the west end of the lake the trail heads north, and South Teddy is one mile up on the west side of the trail. From the campground, it's about 4 miles to the lake. Many anglers use a boat to get to the west end of Big Cultus, then hike the remaining mile.

South Teddy, at 17 acres and 10 ft. maxi-

Timber has 10 surface acres and is fairly shallow. It is stocked by air every few years with brook and rainbow trout. The fish don't get large because of fairly heavy pressure, but fly fishing in late summer and fall can net some nice fish. The setting's real pretty, and the hiking is easy. The road into Olallie Lake usually opens in late June. There are many other small hike-in lakes south and west.

TIMMY LAKE. A tiny rainbow trout lake on the west side of the Pacific Crest Trail in the area north of the Irish-Taylor Lakes group. It's a bit over a mile northeast of the north end of Irish Lake, and ⅓ mile south of Brahma Lake. See Irish and Brahma for directions. The lake is on the top of a knoll and is hard to spot.

Timmy is easy to fish from shore. Only 3 acres but fairly deep, it has produced some big fish in the past. You can expect eager medium size brook trout if you can find the lake. There are other good lakes close by. See Red Slide, Gleneden, Lady, Brahma. A maze of potholes in the area breed confusion and a wretched excess of mosquitoes in spring.

TODD LAKE. A deep brook trout lake 2 miles north of Bachelor Butte in Deschutes National Forest west of Bend. Take Hwy. 46 (Cascades Lakes Hwy.) about 2 miles past the Bachelor Ski Resort parking area to Forest Rd. 370, which joins from the north. At ½ mile, the Todd Lake Rd. heads east. This is blocked to motor vehicles, so you'll have to hike in the last quarter mile.

Todd is 45 acres and up to 60 ft. deep in places. It provides angling for brook trout to 15 inches. For a week or so after the ice melts fishing is hot, but during the rest of the year the fish are hard to catch. A trail encircles the lake. There is a small tent campground and a picnic area on the west shore. Snow may linger here until late June or July.

TOOLEY LAKE. (a.k.a. The Onion Patch) One of the I-84 ponds adjacent to the Columbia River, at highway mile 79. It has 30 surface acres south of the freeway, with limited unimproved parking at the west end of the lake for eastbound traffic only. Most of the north shore is privately owned. It may contain any of the Columbia's warmwater species. See Columbia River Ponds map.

TROUT LAKE. (Confederated Tribes Warm Springs) The lowest of a chain of five good lakes which begins at the southeast end of Olallie Lake. See also Island, Long, and Dark. The lake has a self-sustaining trout population and receives an annual stocking as well. From Warm Springs, follow Hwy. 26 west, then turn left on Rd. P600 (currently signed for "High Lakes"). Follow P600 6½ miles to a fork. Take the left fork (there may be a small Trout Lake sign). Total mileage from Hwy. 26 to Trout lake is 19. 5. If you miss the left fork, you'll end up wandering across a big flat. Turn around.

Trout is at 4600 feet and has 23 surface acres, about in shoals, with a maximum depth of 28 feet. There is a campground here. The lake's outflow is the source of Mill Creek, a tributary of the Deschutes. The CTWS fishing permit required to fish here includes a map showing the route to Trout Lake. Permits are sold at the market in Warm Springs, at G.I. Joe's stores throughout Oregon, and at many fly shops.

TUMALO CREEK. A popular trout stream, about 20 miles long, which flows east from the Three Sisters, joining the Deschutes River north of Bend. It is the municipal water supply for Bend. Several good roads follow the stream and cross it several times. Forest Rd. 4601 picks up the creek about 7 miles from the west end of Bend and parallels the stream for several miles to Tumalo Falls Campground. Here trails follow the major tributaries of the creek west.

The creek has a fair population of small wild trout 7 to 9 inches. Fishing is restricted to artificial flies and lures. The creek is a nice close-in recreation area for Bend residents. Shevlin City Park is on the creek 3 miles northwest of town.

TUNNEL LAKE. One of the I-84 ponds adjacent to the Columbia River, at highway mile 7 2.6. Just one acre, it is immediately west of Memaloose State Park between I-84 and the railroad. Best access is for westbound traffic. It may contain any of the Columbia's warmwater species. See Columbia River Ponds map.

TWIN LAKE, NORTH. (Deschutes Co.) A good size trout lake a mile north of Wickiup Reservoir in the Deschutes Forest southwest of Bend. South Twin, similar in

character and productivity, is a mile south. North Twin is a little over 45 miles from Bend by way of the Cascade Lakes Hwy. 46. For directions, see South Twin.

North Twin is about 130 acres and 60 feet deep. It is stocked heavily with catchable rainbows, and the catch averages 10 inches, with some larger. Bait angling and trolling are both good, and fly fishing is excellent at times. Best fishing is in the shallows except when the water warms. There is a good campground with boat ramp on the north shore of the lake. A short trail at the south end leads to South Twin. Motorboats are prohibited. For more information, see *Fishing in Oregon's Cascade Lakes*.

TWIN LAKE, SOUTH. (Deschutes Co.) A delightful family lake, offering very good fishing, swimming, and other activities and attractions (not the least of which is Wickiup Reservoir just ½ mile north. South Twin is about 40 miles southwest of Bend. Many people fishing Wickiup camp here. From Bend you can drive to the lake by the Cascades Lakes Hwy. 46, taking the Wickiup turn-off (County Rd. 42) east. The Twin Lakes turn-off is one mile past the Deschutes crossing.

Alternately, you may drive south from Bend on Hwy. 97. Take the Sunriver turn-off, which is the east end of County Rd. 42, and follow signs to Crane Prairie or Wickiup Reservoir till you see the Twin Lakes sign. From the Willamette Valley, drive southeast from Eugene on Hwy. 58 to the Davis Lake turn-off, 3 miles past Crescent Lake Junction. Follow Davis Lake signs to the south end of the Cascades Lakes Hwy., and drive past Davis to the Wickiup turn-off, County Rd. 42.

South Twin is about 120 acres and reaches a depth of 55 feet. Stocked with both fingerling and legal rainbows in the spring, it is a consistent producer, especially in spring. The catch average is 9 to 10 inches, and trout to 15 inches are taken.

The lake lends itself to all methods of angling. Bait fishing is popular, but doesn't seem to produce any better than

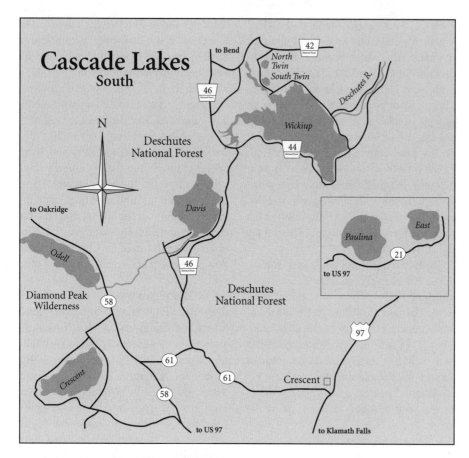

Cascade Lakes
South

(map labels) to Bend · 42 National Forest · North Twin South Twin · 46 National Forest · Deschutes R. · Wickiup · 44 National Forest · N · Deschutes National Forest · to Oakridge · Davis · Odell · 46 National Forest · to US 97 · Paulina · East · 21 · Diamond Peak Wilderness · 58 · Deschutes National Forest · 97 · 61 · Crescent · 61 · Crescent · 58 · to US 97 · to Klamath Falls

---

VIENTO LAKE. One of the I-84 ponds adjacent to the Columbia River, at highway mile 56. It has 4 surface acres at the mouth of Viento Creek, with good access from Viento State Park at Exit 56. It may contain any of the Columbia's warmwater species. See Columbia River Ponds map.

VIEW LAKE. Offering a good view of the many large and small lakes in the eastern half of the Olallie Lake Scenic Area. From Timber lake, head due south, keeping to about the same elevation. You should reach View in about ½ mile. Another option is to bushwhack uphill from the west side of Skyline Rd. (opposite Monon Lake), following View's intermittent outlet creek.

View is stocked every other year by air with brook trout fingerlings. With 7 surface acres, it offers good fishing for trout 8 to 12 inches, but no large fish.

WAHTUM LAKE. The largest hike-in lake (62 acres) in Mt. Hood National Forest, with fair fishing for brook trout. It is within Hatfield Wilderness (formerly Columbia Wilderness), source of the East Fork of Eagle Creek and upland terminus of the scenic Eagle Creek Trail, which begins in the Columbia Gorge. You can drive to within a quarter mile of the lake. The Pacific Crest Trail passes by the rim of the glacial cirque in which the lake is cupped.

Wahtum is 7 miles north of Lost Lake. See Lost Lake for directions to Dee. From the community of Dee southwest of Hood River, drive 3 miles west to Forest Rd. 13, the Lost Lake Rd. At about 10 miles, take Forest Rd. 1310 to the right, and follow it about 6 miles to Wahtum Lake Campground. The lake is to the west, at the bottom of a quarter-mile trail which descends 200 ft. from road level.

Wahtum is exceptionally clear and deep. The lake is most successfully fished from a raft or float tube. Fishing is best in the 10 to 30 ft. shoal areas. Brook trout average 8 inches, with a few to 15.

There are several nice natural campsites beside the lake as well as a primitive campground near the road (fire pits, no water). There's good huckleberry gleaning in late August. Don't neglect to bring rain gear and warm clothes. Like Rainy and Black lakes, Wahtum is peculiarly situated in relation to weather-generating Mt. Hood so that it is often cloudy and wet here while

---

other methods. Many anglers fish too deep, below the oxygen layer, so stay shallow (less than 30 ft. deep). A trail encircles the lake and accesses very good water.

If fishing on South Twin is slack, an arm of Wickiup Reservoir is only 200 yards west. There is a good Forest Service campground, West South Twin, on this arm directly across from Twin Lakes Resort. The resort keeps boats here for use on Wickiup.

Twin Lakes Resort, on the west shore, has extensive facilities, including a variety of accommodations, an RV park with full hook-ups, restaurant, convenience store, laundry, and showers. It also has motor boat, canoe, and paddle boat rentals. South Twin Campground offers pleasant sites north of the resort. There is a short trail to North Twin that starts at the campground. Recommended for youngsters. For more information, see *Fishing in Oregon's Cascade Lakes*, published by Flying Pencil.

TWIN LAKES. (White River watershed) Two good hike-in brook trout lakes 6 miles south of Barlow Pass on the south slope of Mt. Hood, reached by way of the Pacific Crest Trail. The lower lake covers 12 acres,

and the upper or north lake about 10 acres. Follow Hwy. 26 four miles south from its junction with Hwy. 35 to the crossing of the Pacific Crest Trail ½ mile north of Frog Lake. (Watch for a trail sign on the road.) The lower lake is an easy mile hike east and north on the PCT. Turn right off the PCT onto Trail 482. The upper lake is ½ mile farther north on Trail 482.

These lakes are stocked with fingerling brook trout every other year. They are fairly deep (lower, 40 feet; upper, 50 feet) and usually have some holdover fish of good size. The lakes see a lot of angling pressure. There is a campground at lower Twin and one at Frog Lake south of the trailhead.

UPPER LAKE. An easy to reach hike-in brook trout lake in the Olallie Lake area, about 100 miles from Portland. See Olallie Lake for directions. Take the Pacific Crest Trail west about 1½ miles from the trailhead north of Olallie (off the Skyline Rd.)

Upper is stocked by air every few years with brook trout fingerlings. The lake has 8 surface acres and is of moderate depth. It's a good fly fishing lake for brook trout 6 to 12 inches. There are fair natural campsites at the lake.

the sun is shining elsewhere in the area. For other fishing lakes nearby, see Hicks and Scout.

WALTON LAKE. Very popular with Prineville locals, a 25-acre lake in an attractive pine forest. Walton was created by damming a spring creek in the headwaters of Ochoco Creek, a contribution of Isaac Walton League members in the Prineville area. Take Hwy. 26 about 15 miles east of Prineville, then Hwy. 23 toward Ochoco Ranger Station. Just past the station, turn left onto Hwy. 22. Follow signs to the lake.

Walton is at elevation 5150 ft. and has a maximum depth of 25 ft. It is stocked with legal rainbows annually, and catches 8 to 10 inches are taken on bait and lure. A few fish reach 16 inches. Best fishing is in May and June.

Canoes or float tubes are great here. Electric motors are allowed, but this lake is really too small for boats. A trail encircles the lake. Facilities include a wheelchair accessible platform with paved path and a large campground.

WARM SPRINGS RIVER. (Confederated Tribes Warm Springs) The Warm Springs River is open to fishing only in the vicinity of Kah-Nee-Ta Resort. To reach it, drive north from Warm Springs about 10 miles. The way is well signed. The open area is between Kah-Nee-Ta Village Bridge and the marker at the east end of the golf course. A paved road follows the northern bank of the fishing area.

The river is currently stocked with rainbow trout, but there is some question about continuing the stocking program. Check with Warm Springs Fish and Wildlife Department for a stocking update. Anglers are prohibited from using cluster eggs, spinners, wobblers, or any attractor blade or device. A tribal permit specifically for this area is required. Permits are sold at Kah-Nee-Ta and at the market in Warm Springs.

WARREN LAKE. A 5-acre brook trout lake at the head of Warren Creek, which flows north 3 miles into the Columbia River, 9 miles west of the town of Hood River. The lake is a quarter mile from the end of a primitive road southeast of Mt. Defiance. You might want to walk the last mile of road. To reach the trailhead, follow the directions to Bear Lake, but take Forest

Rd. 28 21 when it forks northeast off Forest Rd. 2820. At the next fork, take the left (west) fork. (Here is where you should begin to consider the capabilities of your vehicle). About three quarters of a mile farther, at a T-intersection with the Mt. Defiance Rd., turn right, away from Mt. Defiance. The road ends at a trail crossing. The trail west leads to Warren Lake.

WASCO LAKE. A good brook trout and cutthroat lake below the Pacific Crest Trail 2 miles northeast of Three Fingered Jack in Mt. Jefferson Wilderness. The most direct approach to the lake is 1½ miles by Trail 65, which heads at Jack Lake. The trail passes along the west shore of the lake ½ mile before joining the Pacific Crest Trail north of Minto Pass. See Jack Lake for road directions.

Wasco is at elevation 5150 ft. and has 20 surface acres. The lake is over 20 ft. deep, and all methods will take fish. A hike up to the PCT and back south ½ mile will take you to Catlin and Koko lakes, two small brook trout lakes that are lightly fished.

WEST COVE. One of the I-84 ponds adjacent to the Columbia River, at highway mile 62.3. It covers 10 acres at the west end of Hood River Industrial Park and is accessible from Exit 63. It may contain any of the Columbia's warmwater species. See Columbia River Ponds map.

WHITE RIVER. A good size tributary of the Deschutes, flowing almost 50 miles from its glacial origin on Mt. Hood's south face to its confluence with the Deschutes north of Maupin. To reach it from Portland, follow Hwy. 26 to Mt. Hood, then Hwy. 35, which crosses the upper end of the river. Forest Rd. 48 heads south from Hwy. 35 just beyond the crossing and parallels the river's Iron Creek tributary, reaching the river itself at Barlow Crossing Campground. The primitive Old Barlow Rd. also accesses the river at Barlow Crossing. Forest Rd. 3530 follows the stream's west bank for about 4 miles from Barlow Crossing past White River Station Campground.

East of Mt. Hood National Forest, the river cuts a deep canyon, accessible in the Smock Prairie area. Take Hwy. 216 to a north-bound county road about mid-way between Wapinita and Pine Grove. The canyon is about 2½ miles past the Oak

WALTON LAKE offers easy access to trout in a pretty pine forest. Photograph by Jeffrey Kee.

Grove School.

This road crosses the river and continues north to Wamic. Hwy. 197 crosses the river east of Tygh Valley, and there is pretty good early season trout fishing in the flatland stretch from there to the series of three falls 2½ miles above the Deschutes confluence. Above the falls, rainbows average 7 to 11 inches.

Below the lowest falls, the White River supports Deschutes redbands of size and number equal to the Deschutes itself. In fact, Deschutes regulations apply in this stretch. The falls are 2.5 miles above the Deschutes. Access is by a trail leading downstream from White River Falls State Park, 39 miles south of The Dalles off Sherars Bridge Hwy. 216. The State Park is open for day use only.

Fishing throughout the White River is restricted to artificial flies and lures. Trout above 20 inches are considered to be steelhead, and all non-finclipped steelhead must be released unharmed.

Campgrounds on and near the stream include White River Station, Keeps Mill, Forest Creek, Grindstone, and Devil's Half Acre Meadow.

WICKIUP RESERVOIR

One of Oregon's largest and most productive reservoirs, created by a dam on the upper Deschutes River in Deschutes National Forest. It is about 40 miles southwest

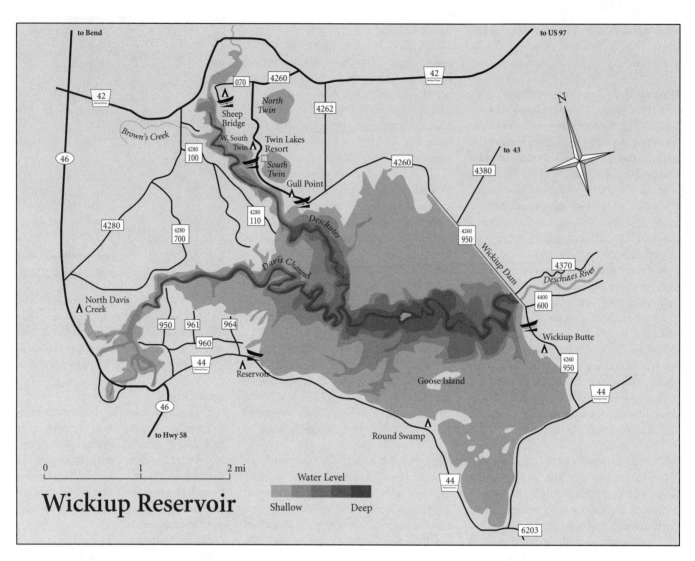

Wickiup Reservoir

of Bend. Wickiup is a fertile lake with large self-sustaining populations of brown trout and kokanee, and a growing population of rainbows. The landlocked coho program here has been abandoned due to unavailability of a hatchery source. A small number of largemouth bass are available. Kokanee are the primary focus of most anglers, but brown trout are the prize catch.

To reach Wickiup from Bend, take Hwy. 97 south to County Rd. 43, north of LaPine. Turn south onto Forest Rd. 4380 about 2. 25 miles beyond Pringle Falls. This road follows all but the west shore of the lake Paved forest roads connect the reservoir to all the major lakes in the area, including Odell, Crescent, and Davis lakes to the south.

Wickiup has nearly 10,000 surface acres when full, but it is primarily an irrigation reservoir and is heavily drawn-down throughout the summer even in years of normal precipitation. During drought, heavier than usual draw-downs work

havoc with the kokanee and rainbows, but brown trout seem able to cope.

Much of the reservoir is under 20 ft. deep, but the old Deschutes channel carves an arc in the lake bed from the Deschutes arm in the north to the southern end of the dam in the east. The river had cut a steep rocky channel, and this now provides a cool deep-water refuge for fish in late summer. The water in this channel is over 60 ft. deep in places, with much irregular structure. A shallower channel leads east from the Davis Creek arm. Deepest water in the reservoir is at the intersection of Deschutes and Davis channels. Unlike Crane Prairie, Wickiup's submerged channels and bottom structure are never obvious. A depth and fish finder is especially helpful here.

Wickiup is very large and, it is generally agreed, difficult to fish. Finding fish is the first challenge. At high water, when kokanee are generally scattered, try fishing along the dam and at the mouth of the De-

schutes channel. In spring the water temperature is uniform, and catches can be made in as little as 10 ft. of water. As drawdown occurs, kokanee move into deeper parts of the channels. Throughout the summer, bait anglers and trollers work the main channels and the dam area. Bait anglers seem to fare best, offering a concoction called the Wickiup sandwich—a pinch of crayfish tail, a chunk of nightcrawler, and a kernel of white corn on a size 8 hook. Trollers use kokanee hardware tipped with nightcrawler or corn. Near the end of August, kokanee assume spawning colors and move into the Deschutes channel. Kokanee spawning grounds are protected by a September 1 to October 31 closure in the Deschutes channel from Gull Pt. boat ramp upstream to Crane Prairie Dam. At this time, kokanee are very abundant, and the average size is a little smaller than other years. Anglers are encouraged to catch and keep the 25 fish per day allowed.

Wickiup's brown trout are imposing—10 to 20 inches, 2 to 3 pounds, with 9 and 10 pounders common enough. The current state record brown, a 26-pounder, was caught here on opening day in 1998. Look for big browns in the old channels where the water is cool and the current serves up the meal, or toward windward shores where forage fish get tossed during or immediately following a blow.

To troll for browns, work at about the 15 ft. depth, trolling shallower as the weather cools. A quick troll imitates the chubs, whitefish, and kokanee these big trout pursue. Casting to the edges of drop-offs, along channel ledges, or wherever there are concentrations of kokanee, etc. is also productive. In spring, fish around Goose Island and along the dam. The waters off Wickiup Butte and at the mouth of the Deschutes channel are also productive. Most browns are caught in the vicinity of the Deschutes channel.

Browns are nocturnal feeders. Consider taking advantage of the "one hour before sunrise" opportunity. Cloudy days and late afternoons till "one hour after sunset" are also productive. As evening approaches, browns venture into the shallows where they are available for fly fishing. Working the points and ledges with a big fly can be worthwhile.

In September browns begin gathering along the Deschutes channel and off Gull Point, feeding enthusiastically prior to spawning (in November and December). In addition to Wickiup's abundant population of chubs, kokanee, and whitefish, they gorge on insects and crayfish. Gold or bronze-finish minnow imitations (Rapala, Rebel, Bomber) seem to pass for chubs. Kwikfish-type lures and large streamers are effective. Crayfish (whole or tails only) are hard to beat.

Rainbows are most plentiful in the reservoir's Davis arm. Whitefish to 4 pounds are also available in quantity

Wickiup is primarily a boat fishery, though non-boating anglers do well in early season at the dam and along the channel. There are good boat ramps at Gull Point and North Wickiup campgrounds at the mouth of the Deschutes arm, at West South Twin Campground on the lower Deschutes Arm, and at Reservoir Campground on the southwest shore. Boats can also be launched at Wickiup Butte Campground on the southeast shore.

Twin Lakes Resort maintains a fleet of rental boats on the Deschutes arm. There is a 10-mph speed limit there and in the Davis Creek arm. Watch out for the pumice flats when the lake is low. It's easy to get stuck.

There are a number of campgrounds around the reservoir. Most of these are left high and dry when the reservoir is drawn down in late season. Gull Point and West South Twin are full-service public campgrounds with access to water throughout the season. Supplies, gas, a restaurant, and accommodations are available at Twin Lakes Resort on the Deschutes arm at the north end of the reservoir. For more information, see *Fishing in Oregon's Cascade Lakes*, published by Flying Pencil.

WILSON POND. One of the I-84 ponds adjacent to the Columbia River, at highway mile 71.4. Privately owned but open to public use with permission, it has 5 surface acres between I-84 and the Union Pacific Railroad. Access is from Hwy. 30. See Columbia River Ponds map.

WINDY LAKES. A group of 4 hike-in lakes not far from the Pacific Crest Trail southeast of Summit Lake. The trail begins on the road about ½ mile south of Tandy Bay Picnic Area on Crescent Lake. It's a fairly steep hike in.

The Windys haven't been very productive, perhaps due to their location at 6000 ft. West Windy is no longer stocked, but the others are stocked with brook trout. The lakes range from 5 to 16 acres and are close together. The best bet is the south lake.

WINOPEE LAKE. A fairly remote 40-acre hike-in lake between Mink Lake Basin and Big Cultus Lake. Winopee supports naturally reproducing populations of rainbow and brook trout and is stocked with additional brook trout. It can provide very good fly fishing for fish 8 to 14 inches.

The lake is about 8 miles by trail from the end of the road at the east end of Big Cultus. Some anglers run a boat to the west end of the big lake, cutting the hike in half.

Winopee has a lot of marshy shoals along the shoreline. A rubber raft or float tube comes in handy. (Old Paint comes in handy for lugging your raft or tube this far.) The lake goes to 30 ft. in places. You can get through the snow in June in most years, but mosquitoes are fierce here in spring. There are other good lakes in the vicinity. See Snowshoe.

WYETH LAKE. An I-84 pond adjacent to the Columbia River at highway mile 50.6. It may contain any of the Columbia River species. It is between I-84 and the railroad, with 6 surface acres, and is one of the few ponds in the series that can be reached by boat from the Columbia. See Columbia River Ponds map.

YAPOAH LAKE. A small high lake that turns out good rainbow trout for the few who hike to it. Yapoah Lake is at 5800 ft., one mile east of Yapoah Crater in the McKenzie Pass area north of North Sister. To reach the lake you can take an unusual hike on the Pacific Crest Trail, heading south through the Dee Wright Observatory's lunar-like lava flow area. Hike a little over 2 miles Matthieu Lakes, then take Trail 95 (Scott Trail) east one mile. From that point the lake is a quarter mile bushwhack due south. The trail in begins high, so there's not a lot of climbing. Bring your USGS Three Sisters Quad map.

Rainbow stocked here grow to 12 inches. The lake has 10 surface acres and is 25 ft. deep. This is fairly open country, and the lake is easy to fish from shore. It's in a scenic area, worth the hike for the splendid view of North Sister.

FISHING IN OREGON'S
SOUTHEAST ZONE

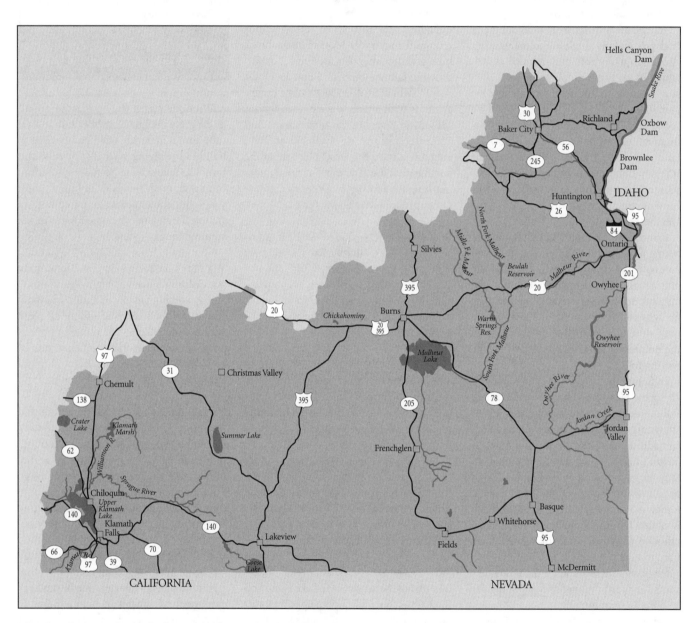

The Southeast Zone includes more than a third of all land in Oregon, but only a tenth of the state's population. The reason for the disparity is the lack of abundant water. But western anglers know that nothing grows fish like a desert climate, and what water there is in Southeast Oregon proves the point.

Trout in the 18-20 inch class are usually available in a dozen desert reservoirs, including Ana, Beulah, Chickahominy, Holbrook, Malheur, Priday, Thompson Valley, Thief Valley, and Warm Springs. Even when drought drains one of these reservoirs dry, a single good growing season can bring the fishery back to trophy size. A string of wet winters can produce fishing bonanzas.

The area's natural lakes also yield big trout. Upper Klamath Lake grows the largest rainbow trout in Oregon. Mann Lake offers the opportunity to catch Lahontan cutthroat in a spectacular desert setting. The zone's major rivers—Ana, Burnt, Chewaucan, Klamath, Malheur, North Fork Malheur, Owyhee, Sycan, Williamson—are also famous producers of large rainbows and brown trout.

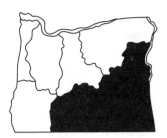

The Southeast Zone includes all tributaries (including their impoundments) of the Snake River system above Hells Canyon Dam; the Silvies River drainage in Grant County; all waters in Malheur and Lake counties; all waters in Harney County except the drainage of the South Fork of the John Day river; and all waters of the Klamath River Basin in Klamath and Lake counties. This zone does not include any portion of the mainstem Snake River. The Klamath River Basin is where all streams and their tributaries drain toward the Upper Klamath Lake or the Klamath River.

THE BEST FISHING IN OREGON'S SOUTHEAST ZONE

AGENCY LAKE
Big redband rainbows and browns.

BEULAH RESERVOIR
A remote reservoir that grows big trout in good water years.

CHICKAHOMINY RESERVOIR
A popular stop-off for big desert trout year-round.

DONNER UND BLITZEN (BLITZEN) RIVER
Quality spring trout fishing in a spectacular wild desert setting.

KLAMATH RIVER
Difficult fishing for large rainbows.

LAKE OF THE WOODS
Abundant kokanee, big browns, and family camping amenities.

MALHEUR RIVER
Take your pick between easy highway access or a remote canyon hike for large rainbow trout.

MALHEUR RIVER, Middle Fork
Remote fishing for wild redband trout and smallmouth bass.

MANN LAKE.
Rare wild Lahontan cutthroat in a spectacular desert setting.

MILLER LAKE
Best brown trout lake fishing in the state.

OWYHEE RIVER
Quality fishing for large rainbows and browns.

SPRAGUE RIVER
Bass, big rainbows, and browns, including some who've never seen an angler.

SYCAN RIVER
Catch and keep rainbows of good size below Sycan Marsh, and unlimited numbers of brook trout above.

UPPER KLAMATH LAKE
Fish for some of Oregon's largest redband rainbow trout in the lake and its tributaries: the Williamson, Wood, and Sprague rivers.

WARM SPRINGS RESERVOIR
Good size trout and a strong population of smallmouth bass in a remote setting.

WILLIAMSON RIVER
Fish for big, wily Klamath Lake migrants below Kirk Bridge, and for wild brook trout and redbands above.

Other Southeast waters are equally productive for bass and panfish. The upper Owyhee River and Owyhee, Gerber, Phillips, Thompson Valley, and Warm Springs reservoirs all have fine warmwater fisheries.

Some lakes and streams in the region are notable not so much for the size of their fish as for their offer of a pleasant refuge from the region's fierce summer heat. Big Creek, the Blitzen River, Dairy Creek, Delintment Lake, Wood River, and upper North and Middle Fork Malheurs are such oases.

A portion of the southern Eagle Cap Wilderness, with its glacial lakes and mountain streams, is also within this zone, as are the waters of Gearhart Mountain, Mountain Lake, and Sky Lakes wilderness areas. Freemont, Winema, and portions of the Ochoco, Malheur, and Wallowa-Whitman national forests are here. The Malheur National Wildlife Refuge, Steens Mountain, Hart Mountain National Antelope Refuge, the Alvord Desert, and Warner Valley Lakes are among Oregon's scenic treasures.

US highways 97 and 395 provide primary north-south access to the region. Highways 20 and 140 are the major east-west routes. Most secondary roads are unpaved. The only towns of any size in this vast area are Klamath Falls, Lakeview, Burns, and Ontario. Most other communities in the Southeast offer little more than a gas station, post office, general store, and maybe a cafe. (Some offer all of the above under a single roof.)

Visitors should come prepared with spare water and gas and would do well to be as self-sufficient as possible. This is a land of wide open spaces, wild windy places, and big fish.

The large northern pool of Upper Klamath Lake, separated from the main body by a narrow natural channel, offering excellent opportunities to catch some of the state's largest redband rainbows and browns. From Klamath Falls take Hwy. 97 north to Modoc Point, then the old Hwy. 162 northwest to Agency Lake, about a 23-mile drive. From Bend, follow Hwy. 97 south to Chiloquin, then take the Klamath Agency cutoff south of town, about a 115-mile drive. A secondary road south of Klamath Agency crosses the narrows and follows the Wood River tributary. Hwy. 162 follows Agency's east shore.

Like Upper Klamath, Agency is primarily a trout fishery. The big fish spawn in Agency's main tributaries, Wood River and Sevenmile Creek. In early spring, troll slowly near the mouths of these streams at the north end of the lake and in the narrows. As the lake warms in June, troll closer to the Wood River mouth. Fishing usually slows by July. Large lures seem to be more productive than bait.

The redbands average 18 to 20 inches, with many 16 to 26 inches and some exceeding 30 inches and 15-pounds, especially in the north. Fishing is traditionally best in the early morning. Large perch and brown bullhead are also available, primarily at the north end of the lake.

Boats can be launched at Henzel Park in the south, at Petric Park on the Wood River, and at the resort on the northeast shore. BLM has acquired property (Agency Ranch) adjacent to the mouth of Wood River. There is a canoe launch near the parking lot and restroom facilities. Fishing in the Wood itself is restricted to artificial flies and lures and is catch and release only. The river is open from late April till the end of October, while Agency is open for year-round fishing. There is currently a one trout per day limit on Agency. There is no limit on bullhead and perch.

Agency can get rough, so stay close to the shore.

ALTNOW LAKE. A privately owned 8-acre bass and panfish pond in Harney County with largemouth bass and bluegill. It is northeast of Drewsey, off Hwy. 20 about 47 miles east of Burns.

The pond is behind the ranch house, and visitors are requested to stop in at the house before fishing. If no one is home, head on down the road to Cottonwood Reservoir instead. There is a user fee, which was instituted due to occurrences of vandalism and excessive littering. Anglers are urged to respect the owner's generosity and help keep this lake available for all.

Small boats can be launched here. Camping at the lake is prohibited.

ANA RESERVOIR. A 60-acre reservoir north of Summer Lake, offering year-round, ice-free fishing for record-breaking hybrid bass and stocked legal trout. The lake is in a popular waterfowl hunting area. It is about 2 miles east of Hwy. 31, 5 miles north of the community of Summer Lake.

Big hybrid bass are the prize catch here, a sterile cross between white and striped bass. Look for them in deep water and wherever there are concentrations of chubs. Bait, lures, and flies are all effective, though bait anglers have some problem with chubs taking their offerings. Regulations restrict hybrid harvest to a 16-inch minimum, and only one bass per 24-hour period. The current official state record hybrid was landed here in 1996, weighing 18½ pounds. Larger hybrids are present, and several were landed in 1998, though none were officially recorded. The only other hybrid bass fishery in Oregon is in Thompson Valley Reservoir.

Ana is stocked annually with legal-size rainbow trout (to compete with the huge chub population) and with trophy-size trout to 2 pounds.

The reservoir offers a very consistent fishery, unaffected by drought, fed by underground streams whose flows remain constant. Their temperature remains constant as well, 58 degrees, which keeps the reservoir ice free for winter fishing. There is no structure to speak of in the lake. The fish just cruise around. Boats can be launched from the beach, but most fish are caught from the bank. Float tube fishing is also popular, especially near the dam. Camping is allowed, though facilities are primitive.

ANA RIVER. A short but excellent trout stream, popular with fly anglers, though not very scenic. It flows south from Ana Reservoir into Summer Lake Marsh. Hwy. 31 leads into the basin, and county roads lead down to the river. It is approached near the marsh by a road east from the community of Summer Lake and, at the reservoir, by the Ana Reservoir Rd. north of town. Good fishing starts immediately downstream of the reservoir. Floating the 5 miles in float-tube or raft can be pleasant and productive. Take out at the county road crossing.

The river maintains a stable, clear, cool flow and a constant 50-60 degree water temperature that produces insect hatches throughout the year. Planted rainbow fingerlings rear in the stream, averaging 8 to 12 inches, with 16- to 18-inch fish common and some to 5 pounds. Small dry fly patterns work best, though streamers imitating chubs may take larger fish. There is a state park picnic area at Summer Lake, with camping available at the reservoir, at natural sites along the river, and at the River Ranch Campground at Summer Lake Wildlife Area.

ANDERSON LAKE. See **WARNER VALLEY LAKES.**

ANNIE CREEK. A spring-fed trout stream that flows out of Crater Lake National Park, tributary to the Wood River. Hwy. 62 follows the creek closely from its headwaters about 5 road miles south of Crater Lake, to its confluence with the Wood north of Fort Klamath. Fort Klamath is near the junction of highways 62 and 232, about 40 miles north of Klamath Falls.

Annie Creek is about 14 miles long and offers good angling for wild rainbow, brown, and brook trout, especially in the lower end. It is not stocked. Fly angling is good in the evenings. The stream has a high pumice content and retains a milky color throughout the year. There is a good campground at its head, off Hwy. 62, with the Pacific Crest Trail passing west of camp.

State licenses are not required to fish in the national park. Fishing permits may be obtained at Park Headquarters on the south rim.

ANTELOPE CREEK. A remote Lahontan cutthroat stream, closed to all fishing to protect the Lahontan, which are listed as a threatened species. The Lahontan population throughout southeast Oregon was devastated by the 1987-92 drought and is still in recovery. There is little good habitat in Antelope, and reopening of the stream to recreational angling is doubtful.

ANTELOPE RESERVOIR. A stark but scenic irrigation reservoir off Hwy. 95 east of Burns Junction near the state line. It is lightly stocked and has some wild redbands from Jordan Creek. There are some very large trout here, but fishing is slow. A mercury health advisory is in effect, the legacy of mining in the area. Blue-green algae has stained the shoreline rocks but is harmless.This is a better destination for solitude than for fishing.

There are a few campsites on the northwest shore, plentiful waterfowl (including impressive sandhill cranes), gorgeous sunsets, and terrific star-gazing opportunities.

ANTHONY LAKE. High in the Elkhorn Mountains of Wallowa-Whitman National Forest. This 19-acre lake is one of many located about 20 miles east of the town of North Powder, which is on Hwy. 30 between LaGrande and Baker.

A good paved road heads west from North Powder, connecting with Hwy. 411, which becomes Forest Rd. 73 and leads to the lake. Hwy. 411 can also be picked up in Haines. Other good forest roads lead in from Ukiah (off Hwy. 395 between Pendleton and John Day). Anthony Lake is the site of a popular ski resort.

Fishing is good for stocked rainbows to 14 inches from early summer through fall. There are also wild brook trout to 10 inches. Fly fishing can be productive, but most anglers troll or cast bait. The lake is 30 feet at its deepest point. There is a boat ramp, but motors are prohibited.

There is a large campground at the lake, and there are camps at tiny Mud Lake and at Grande Ronde Lake to the north. Other lakes in the area include hike-ins Van Patten, Black, and Crawfish. There is a resort at Anthony with accommodations, supplies, and boat rentals. At elevation 7100 ft., ice-out is generally around July 4.

ASPEN LAKE. A 500-acre marsh area west of Klamath Falls, with rumored catches of brown bullhead. To get there, take Lake of the Woods Rt. 140 north from Klamath Falls about 16 miles, turning south onto Aspen Lake Rd. one mile past Rock Creek Ranch. There are no campgrounds in the vicinity.

AUGUR CREEK. A small, wild trout stream, tributary of Thomas Creek and of Goose Lake. It has been closed for a number of years to protect Goose Lake redband trout, which use it for spawning. Goose lake redband are a strain of rainbow trout uniquely suited to withstand the high water temperatures characteristic of desert streams. Goose Lake redband were severely depleted when the lake went dry in 1992 during drought. Studies are currently being conducted to determine how well the redband population is rebounding, and whether or not it can withstand angling pressure. Augur has a good population of small redbands as well as wild brook trout to 10 inches.

BACA LAKE. A 300-acre irrigation reservoir for the Malheur Wildlife Refuge north of French Glen. It is closed to angling.

BALM CREEK RESERVOIR. A good size reservoir near the head of Balm Creek, a tributary of the lower Powder River northeast of Baker. It supports rainbow trout and smallmouth bass. Follow Hwy. 203 about 25 miles north to Medical Springs, then take Forest Rd. 70 east about 10 miles to the reservoir. Forest Rd. 7040 approaches from Hwy. 86 to the south. The turn-off to the reservoir is about 22 miles east of Baker.

The reservoir has about 110 surface acres when full, but it can be severely drawn down in low water years. Trout to 13 inches were available within a season of re-stocking following the most recent drought, and trout exceeding 15 inches are currently available. Balm Creek is at high elevation, and growth rate can be a little slower than at other Eastern Oregon reservoirs. Bait is the most popular method.

Motors may be used to get around, but cannot be operated while fishing. Fishing usually holds up well into mid-summer when the water level drops. There are no improved campsites at the lake, but there is space for trailers. There are two campgrounds on Forest Rd. 67 north and east of the reservoir. Follow Forest Rd. 475 north to the junction with 67.

BEAR CREE. (Chewaucan watershed). A small tributary of the Chewaucan River in Fremont National Forest, joining the main stream near the community of Paisley. You'll find Paisley on Hwy. 31 (Bend to Lakeview) south of Summer Lake. To reach the creek's confluence with the Chewaucan, follow the Chewaucan River Rd. (Forest Rd. 330) south about 6 miles from town. A north-bound gravel road west of town (Forest Rd. 331) crosses the upper stream, as does Forest Rd. 348. The creek flows about 9 miles and offers good fishing for redband and brook trout in late spring and early summer. Its trout run small but are numerous as the creek is lightly fished. Bait is usually best.

BEAR CREEK (Malheur watershed). A tributary of the North Fork Malheur, supporting redband rainbows and brook trout. This Bear Creek flows through a roadless canyon in Malheur National Forest. No trails access the creek, though you can make your way in with the help of cow paths to fish for wild redband 6 to 12 inches, and the occasional fish 14 to 16 inches. The creek flows through rocky terrain dotted with ponderosa pine before breaking out into sagebrush near its mouth. Forest Rd. 1675 (off Forest Rd. 16) crosses the creek near its headwater springs and follows it briefly. North Fork Malheur Trail 381 extends as far as the Bear Creek confluence. See Malheur River, North Fork for information about accessing the trail. Forest Rd. 898 off 1675 approaches Bear Creek near the confluence. Refer to a current edition of the Malheur National Forest map.

BEAR CREEK (Silvies watershed). A tributary of the upper Silvies, entering the river near the community of Seneca on Hwy. 395 between John Day and Burns. About 25 miles long, it is followed east from Hwy. 395 (about 26 miles south of John Day) by Forest Rd. 16. Forest roads 1530 and 1640 access the waters upstream from Parish Cabin.

Lightly fished, the creek produces fair fishing for this part of the country. Bait-fishing is the usual method here, but flies work just fine. May, June, and July are the best months, but fish can be taken later. Parish Cabin Campground is streamside, about 11 miles east of Seneca.

BECKERS POND. A small lake next to the fair grounds in Ontario at Beck-Kiwanis City Park, stocked with bluegill, channel catfish, and largemouth bass. The bluegill are plentiful and eager biters (a great fishery for youngsters). The bass are thriving and reach 15 inches. A path encircling the lake allows easy access.

BENDIRE CREEK. A little-known, lightly fished trout stream, tributary to Beulah

Reservoir, which flows into the reservoir's northeast arm. See Beulah Reservoir for directions from Burns and Vale. Bendire flows about 12 miles from spring-fed headwaters north of Bendire Mountain.

Murphy Reservoir is on Bendire, and hatchery trout move down from Murphy and up from Beulah into the creek. There is about ½ mile of public land along the stream immediately below Murphy, but most of the lower creek flows through the Butler Ranch. Ask permission to fish on ranch property.

Hatchery trout make up most of the catch, averaging 9 to 12 inches, with a few to 16 inches. Bait is most frequently used. Beulah Reservoir has the only improved campground in the area.

BERT LAKE. A small off-trail brook trout lake in the southern Sky Lakes Wilderness of Winema National Forest. Bert is about ¼ mile north of Trail 3712 to Island Lake. To reach the area, follow Rt. 140 northwest from Klamath Falls toward Lake of the Woods. Get out your Winema National Forest map. The trail to Island Lake heads into the wilderness off Forest Rd. 3659 in the Big Meadows area. Bert is about ½ mile from the trailhead, off to the right about ¼ mile.

Only 2 surface acres, it usually has good numbers of brook trout 10 to 11 inches. Though the lake is accessible in late June, fishing is best in fall. In addition to Cold Springs Campground, there are nice campsites at Island Lake, a mile west of Bert.

BEULAH RESERVOIR

(a.k.a. Agency Valley Res.) A large, nutrient-rich irrigation reservoir on the North Fork Malheur capable of growing big trout. It has 2000 surfaces acres when full, though it is severely drawn down during drought. From Juntura, on Hwy. 20 mid-way between Burns and Vale, a gravel road leads north about 15 miles to the reservoir. Roads also lead in from Drewsey on the west, and from Hwy. 26 at Ironside to the north.

Stocked rainbow fingerlings grow to good size here, exceeding 20 inches. It is especially popular with float tube anglers, who fish the shallow upper end around the willows and near the inlets. Large fish are caught on both bait and fly. Whitefish and bull trout are also present.

Open all year, the lake makes a conve-

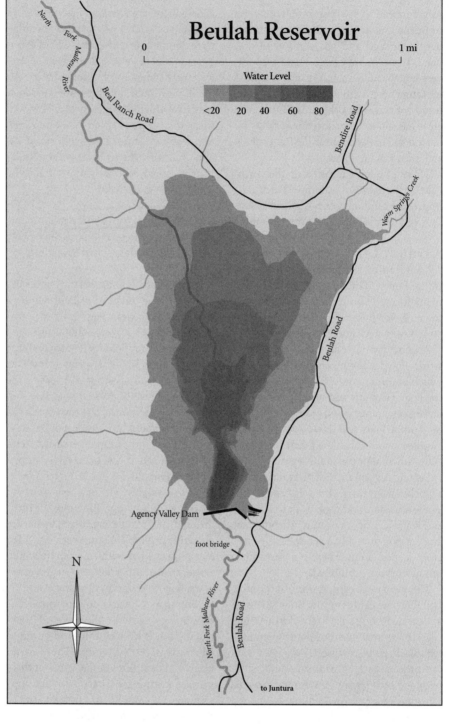

nient base camp for deer hunters. This is a pretty spot for this part of the country, not as stark as Mann or Chickahominy. Castle Rock overlooks the lake from the north, and there is some shade provided by junipers. Ice fishing is not recommended, since the reservoir fluctuates during the winter and ice tends to be thin.

There are generally quite a few campers and trailers here. There's no drinking water, but there are outhouses above the dam. There is no gas station in Juntura at

this time. Closest fuel is at Buchanan to the west, and at Harper Junction east of the reservoir towards Vale.

BIG ALVORD CREEK. A remote stream with a very small population of cutthroat, remnants of an earlier Lahontan stocking program, since discontinued. Closed to all fishing.

BIG CREEK (Malheur watershed). A beautiful wild trout stream in the Logan

Valley of Malheur National Forest, tributary to the Middle Fork Malheur River, with headwaters in the Strawberry Mountains. From John Day, follow Hwy. 395 south 9 miles to Seneca (about 45 miles north of Burns). Turn east on Forest Rd. 16. Big Creek Campground is 18 miles east on Forest Rd. 16, only 2 miles from the creek's mouth. About a mile east beyond the campground turn-off, Forest Rd. 1648 leads further upstream and ends at the head of Trail 377, which follows Big Creek to its headwaters.

Big Creek flows through an open meadow valley with fingers of forest reaching down to the stream. The creek offers good fishing for wild rainbows, brook trout, and whitefish. The trout run small (7 to 10 inches) but are plentiful, due to light pressure. Bull trout are also present and must be released unharmed. Fishing is restricted to artificial flies and lures to limit harm to the bull trout.

Fire damage to the east side of Big Creek from the campground to the wilderness boundary is now completely recovered. There are two established campgrounds on the creek, Big Creek Campground (which has water and charges a user fee) and Murray (no water, no fee). There are many pleasant natural campsites along the creek as well. When camping along the creek, camp well back from fragile streamside vegetation, and use no-trace camping methods.

BLACK LAKE. A small brook trout lake above Anthony Lake in Wallowa-Whitman National Forest. The trail to Black heads east from Anthony Lake Campground, reaching the lake in less than one mile.

BLITZEN RIVER. See **DONNER AND BLITZEN RIVER.**

BLUE JOINT LAKE. See **WARNER VALLEY LAKES.**

BLUE LAKE. (Sprague watershed) A large, deep trout lake in the Gearhart Mt. Wilderness of Fremont National Forest. It's the only lake in the wilderness, though spring-fed creeks are plentiful. The wilderness covers 18,709 acres and is accessed by the 12-mile Gearhart Trail 100, with trailheads at the north-central and southeast boundaries.

Blue Lake is near the northern border at elevation 7031 ft. It's a 2-mile hike to the lake from the northern trailhead, with a 600 ft. elevation gain. The 10-mile hike to the lake from the southeast trailhead involves a 760 ft. climb over 3 miles, followed by a spectacular ridge walk among the volcanic spires of Gearhart Mountain, with views of the area's many meadows, the distant Cascades, and Steens Mountain.

From Lakeview, follow Rt. 140 west to Quartz Mt. Pass, turning north onto Forest Rd. 3660, which leads to the southeast trailhead. To reach the northern trailhead, cut north off Rt. 140 about 4 miles west of Lakeview onto County Rd. 2-16. Turn west onto 2-16A, which follows Thomas Creek into Freemont Forest, becoming Forest Rd. 28. Turn west onto Forest Rd. 3428 at Dairy Pt. Campground and, at the next junction, head north on Forest Rd. 3372 along the Sprague River. A primitive track leads south to the trailhead about 8 miles from the junction.

Blue Lake has 20 surface acres. It is stocked annually with rainbow fingerlings that can reach 16 inches in their short growing season. Bait fishing is most common, and success rate is high. Fly fishing is good later in the season, mornings and evenings.

Trails into the Wilderness are generally clear by mid-June and are usually snow-free till November. There are campsites at the lake. Camp well back from fragile lakeside vegetation, and use no-trace camping methods.

BOSENBERG CREEK. A short tributary of the Middle Malheur River that flows almost totally through private land with no public access. Forest Rd. 16 (Malheur National Forest) crosses the creek at Kimberling Cabin east of the turn-off to Big Creek Campground. Forest roads north of the cabin follow the creek to its headwaters, and there is some access to headwater tributaries. Wild redband are present, but brook trout predominate, with the average catch 9 to 10 inches and some to 12 inches. Best fishing is in May and June.

BOYLE (J.C.) RESERVOIR. (a.k.a. Topsy Reservoir) A 450-acre impoundment on the Klamath River that supports a quality largemouth bass fishery. The reservoir is used to store water for power generation, and fluctuation is heavy, (as much as 3 ft. daily). Nevertheless, it is successfully fished from boat and bank.

Largemouth bass 12 to 16 inches are available. The average catch is 2 pounds, though bass to 6 pounds are present. Best bass habitat is downstream of the Hwy. 66 bridge where the reservoir floods a rocky canyon. Use the lower boat ramp to access this part of the reservoir since boats can't float beneath the bridge. Above the bridge, the reservoir is silty and shallow.

Black and white crappie, yellow perch, and small pumpkinseed sunfish are also available.

The reservoir is lightly fished, and bank anglers seem to stick close to the boat ramps and picnic areas.

Topsy Campground and Boat Ramp are on the south shore of the reservoir, south of Hwy. 66 on Topsy Rd. Topsy campground is a nice facility (maintained by PP&L) with a wheelchair accessible fishing pier that accesses good perch and crappie water.

BRIDGE CREEK (Malheur Lake watershed). A fair trout stream flowing off the west slope of Steens Mt. into the Blitzen River in the southern Malheur Wildlife Refuge northeast of Frenchglen. Frenchglen is at the south end of the Blitzen valley and is reached by Hwy. 205 about 55 miles south of Hwy. 20 from Burns.

To reach the creek, drive toward Page Springs Campground from Frenchglen. Just after crossing the Blitzen River, take a dirt road that leads north. The creek flows out of a low canyon about 3 miles down this road, which leads through mosquito infested marshlands, home to many aquatic birds.

Bridge Creek has native redband trout that average 10 inches. Occasionally much larger fish are present, probably spawners from Baca Lake. Fishing at this time is restricted to artificial flies and lures.

Page Springs Campground has water. Limited supplies and fuel are available in Frenchglen.

BRIDGE CREEK (Silver Lake watershed). A shallow stream flowing about 20 miles from the northern edge of Fremont National Forest into Paulina Marsh, north of the community of Silver Lake. The stream is crossed by Hwy. 31 northwest of town, and by County Rd. 650-N beyond the forest service landing strip southwest of town. Dirt roads south from 650-N access the upper waters.

Redband rainbows predominate in the lower stretch, brook trout in the upper, with the upper waters most productive. Trout reach 10 inches. Best time to fish is spring and early summer. Flies dropped off the vegetation along the pools can be very effective. If the petition to list Goose Lake redband trout succeeds, this fishery will be closed. As it is, Bridge Creek trout get more pressure than the fishery can support. Catch and release is recommended, though not required at this time.

BUCK CREEK. A good eastern Oregon stream, about 20 miles long, heading in the Yamsay Mt. area and flowing into Paulina Marsh near the town of Silver Lake. From LaPine on Hwy. 97, drive about 43 miles southeast on Hwy. 31. The creek is crossed by Hwy. 31 two miles west of Silver Lake. One mile closer to Silver Lake, County Rd. 660 follows the creek west. It leads to Forest Service and logging roads that access the creek's headwaters.

The upper creek has some nice water. It's small, but supports a good population of little brook trout. Redband trout are found in the lower reaches, but most of the land there is private. There are no improved camps, but lots of nice natural campsites.

BULLY CREEK RESERVOIR. An irrigation reservoir that supports bass and panfish, about 8 miles west of Vale (which is 12 miles west of Ontario by way of Hwy. 20). From Vale, drive west on Hwy. 20 about 8 miles, then take a road leading north at Hope School which reaches the reservoir in about 7 miles. The road continues along the northern shore of the reservoir then west up Bully Creek.

White crappie, yellow perch, and largemouth and smallmouth bass offer a self-sustaining fishery. Even following winterkills and severe draw-downs, Bully Creek eventually re-populates. Crappie fishing is best near the upper end where the lake is shallower. There is a nice county park with camping and boat ramps about one mile above the dam.

Little more than a depression in the sagebrush, Bully Creek Reservoir is dedicated to irrigation and has no minimum pool requirement. It was drawn dry in three successive years (1990-92) and winterkilled in the spring of 1993. The reservoir is currently full, but its fisheries are not yet fully recovered.

BUMPHEAD RESERVOIR. A 100-acre irrigation impoundment in Klamath County, east of Klamath Falls near the California line. It is 10 miles northeast of Langell Valley, which is 18 miles south of Bonanza and 3 miles north of Willow Valley Reservoir. Drawn dry in '92 and '94, it has been restocked, and crappie and largemouth bass are re-established, though largemouth are not yet plentiful and are currently small.

BURNT CREEK. A short trout stream about 5 air miles (but many more road miles) southeast of Lakeview. From Lakeview drive north on Hwy. 395 about 5 miles to the intersection of Rt. 140. Take 140 east about 7 miles to Forest Rd. 391, which leads a bit over 3 miles to the creek then parallels it south. It offers marginal fishing for wild redband trout to 12 inches.

BURNT RIVER. Outlet of Unity Reservoir, featuring large trout and smallmouth bass. The river flows east 77 miles, joining the Snake east of Huntington on I-84.

It is followed east by paved county roads from the reservoir downstream 30 miles to Bridgeport. This stretch is cross-ditched for irrigation purposes. From Bridgeport to Durkee on I-84, the river flows through the Burnt River Canyon and is followed by a gravel road. At Durkee the river turns south and is followed by I-84 to Huntington. There are lots of rough fish in this section. Much of the river flows across private lands, so get permission before crossing fences. From Huntington downstream the river is backed up by Brownlee Dam (the Burnt River Arm of Brownlee Reservoir). It is closely followed by the Snake River Road. Anglers park along the road and fish from the bank.

Trout angling right below Unity Reservoir Dam can be excellent at times. Some large trout are scattered through the lower river. Smallmouth bass and crappie are available near the mouth in the Huntington area.

Farewell Bend State Park on Brownlee south of Huntington and Unity Lake State Park north of Unity offer developed camping facilities. Other campgrounds are available in Wallowa-Whitman National Forest along the South Fork 8 miles south of Unity.

BURNT RIVER, SOUTH FORK. One of the most unique trout streams in the area, heading on the east slope of the Blue Mountains and flowing through a mix of pines and firs in Wallowa-Whitman National Forest southwest of Baker City. It is a major tributary of Unity Reservoir.

Only about 12 miles long, the South Fork and is followed by gravel Forest Rd. 6005 to its headwaters. It's crossed by Hwy. 26 about 3 miles above Unity. Several roads follow the river upstream from Unity.

Cold springs provide a stable flow to this pretty stream, keeping water temperatures low and offering good trout habitat throughout the year. The South Fork has a good population of wild rainbows and is stocked with rainbow catchables. Bait-fishing is the most popular method. Two of its tributaries, Elk and Last Chance creeks, offer good fishing as well.

There are four campgrounds on Forest Rd. 6005 within a 3-mile stretch, beginning about 8 miles southwest of Unity.

BURNT RIVER, NORTH FORK. A 25-mile long trout stream, major tributary of Unity Reservoir, located in the southern Wallowa-Whitman Forest. County Rd. 507 leads northwest about 2 miles east of Unity Dam and picks up the North Fork about 2 miles above the reservoir. Dirt roads follow the creek downstream from this crossing to the reservoir. County Rd. 503 follows the river along its best reach, above Whitney.

The North Fork has a good population of wild trout in spring. Above Whitney Valley the river is of high quality and maintains a good flow throughout much of the summer. Below Whitney, water is withdrawn for irrigation, and the stream can get low and warm in summer. Rainbows are typically 6 to 10 inches.

The nearest campground is at Unity Reservoir State Park.

CACHED LAKE. A tiny but productive trout lake off the trail to Eagle Lake, in the Eagle Cap Wilderness of Wallowa-Whitman National Forest. Only 2 acres, it supports a lot of small brook trout. From the end of Forest Rd. 7755, follow the Eagle Creek Trail 1922 north 5.7 miles towards Eagle Lake, gaining 1649 ft. in elevation. One mile south of Eagle Lake, turn east on Trail 1931 for a fairly easy (600 ft. elevation gain) mile to Cached Lake. Snow may block access until July.

To reach this area from Baker or LaGrande, follow Hwy. 203 east. From Baker, follow Forest Rd. 67 northeast to the trailhead. From LaGrande, follow Forest Rd. 77. Both are all-weather roads. Trout season is determined by trail conditions, with best fishing in August and September. Camp well back from fragile lakeside vegetation when in the wilderness, using no-trace camping methods. There are campgrounds on Forest Rd. 77.

CALAMITY CREEK. A small trout stream in the upper Malheur system. It enters the Malheur south of Van, which is on County Rd. 306 east of Silvies. To reach the upper waters, follow County Rd. 309, a primitive track, west from Van. The creek heads in the Malheur National Forest near Calamity Butte. It isn't much of a stream, but it has some has some wild rainbows (to 10 inches) that don't see many of anglers. Rock Springs Campground is off Forest Rd. 17 about 10 miles west of Van.

CAMAS CREEK. A fair trout stream in the Lakeview area. Its headwaters are in Fremont National Forest about 6 miles east of Lakeview, and the creek flows east about 15 miles into Deep Creek. From Lakeview head north 4½ miles on Hwy. 395, turning east onto Warner Canyon Rd. 140. At the junction of Forest Rd. 391 about 7 miles east, the highway hits the creek and follows it east. Several other roads cross it at points where it leaves the main road. It can be reached from Warner Valley by going west from Adel.

In wet years Camas Creek can offer fair fishing after the spring run-off and through early summer, though it has been carrying a lot of sediment in recent years due to overgrazing. Fishing picks up again in fall. The creek supports good numbers of wild rainbows. Most fish caught are around 12 inches, but a few go to 16 inches. Beaver ponds along the creek are worth exploring for larger rainbows. Bait angling is most popular, but flies take fish in late afternoon and evening. Spinners and small lures work well in the larger holes.

CAMP CREEK. (Silvies watershed) A fairly good trout stream, about 14 miles long, entering the Silvies River between Seneca and Silvies near Hwy. 395. Silvies is on Hwy. 395 about 32 miles north of Burns. The creek flows out of Malheur National Forest and joins the Silvies River about 3 miles north of Silvies. Forest Rd. 37, which leaves the highway 4 miles north of Silvies, follows the creek about 6 miles, and Forest Rd. 370 continues to the headwaters.

Camp Creek has a fair number of native

The CHEWAUCAN RIVER *is one of the best trout streams in Fremont National Forest. Photograph by Dennis Frates.*

rainbow trout 9 to 12 inches. Most angling takes place in May and June.

CAMPBELL LAKE. A popular high mountain trout lake in Fremont National Forest. It is stocked with fingerlings, legal rainbows and trophy-size trout as well as excess hatchery brook trout when available.

As the crow flies, Campbell is 34 miles northwest of Lakeview, about half-way between highways 140 and 31. It has a little over 20 acres and is reached by fairly good graded roads. From Paisley on Hwy. 31, follow Forest Rd. 33 south along the Chewaucan River, turning west (right) onto Forest Rd. 28 about 18 miles south of Paisley. Follow Forest Rd. 28 about 8 miles, then turn left on Forest Rd. 033, which leads to Campbell Lake. The road continues on to Dead Horse Lake, a mile farther west.

The time period during which the lake is accessible is fairly short, from July through October. The US Forest Service locks the road gate and doesn't open it until the road is passable. Check with the ranger stations at Bly, Lakeview, or Paisley.

Campbell is tied with Dead Horse lake for best catch rate in the district. On its own, the lake produces few large trout due to poor winter carry-over, but the stocking of trophy-size rainbows should add a little excitement. This is a good fly-fishing lake, but lures or bait also work. Troll slowly with a lot of line. Small boats with trailers can be launched, but motors are prohibited. There is a good camp here. Dead Horse Lake is one mile west.

CAMPBELL LAKE, UPPER. See **WARNER VALLEY LAKES.**

CAMPBELL LAKE, LOWER. See **WARNER VALLEY LAKES.**

CAMPBELL RESERVOIR. A 200-acre reservoir 8 miles northeast of Bly which has been known to support largemouth bass. The reservoir is mostly on private land, though there is some public access across BLM property. It does go dry from time to time, so the status of the fishery is anybody's guess.

CHERRY CREEK. A nice trout stream west of Upper Klamath Lake. When Rt. 140 turns west toward Lake of the Woods, continue north on Forest Rd. 3459 about 4 miles, then west on Forest Rd. 3450. Trail 3708 at road's end follows Cherry Creek for several miles toward its headwaters, then leads to Horseshoe Lake in the Sky Lakes Basin.

Cherry Creek offers very good angling for wild brook trout and doesn't get a lot of pressure. Though not a large stream, it's worth the effort. Sneak tactics may be necessary since these trout tend to be spookier than most.

CHEWAUCAN RIVER. The largest and one of the best trout streams in Fremont National Forest. About 50 miles long, it flows northwest from the mountains southwest of Lakeview, past the town of Paisley, and into the Chewaucan Marsh. The lower end near Paisley is crossed by Hwy. 31. From Lakeview, drive north on Hwy. 395, then turn northwest onto Hwy. 31 at Valley Falls. The stream is followed south from Paisley by Forest Rd. 330, a good graded road. The upper stream and tributaries are followed and crossed by forest roads branching from Forest Rd. 351, which is reached by 330. From Bly, on Rt. 140, follow Forest Rd. 348 to Paisley.

Though no longer stocked, the river has a good population of wild rainbows. Habitat improvement projects seem to have had some impact here. Cut junipers were wired in along the banks in places to stop bank erosion, reduce siltation, and provide cover. Work around the clumps.

The stream is large enough for all fishing techniques. Drifted worms are always a sure bet, but bly anglers do well, too.

There are catfish in the extreme lower stream. Check locally for more information.

There is a good campground at Marster's Spring, about 8 miles south of Paisley. Other campgrounds are available in the headwater area.

CHICKAHOMINY RESERVOIR

A desert reservoir near Burns, managed especially for anglers by the Oregon Department of Fish and Wildlife and BLM, famous for growing big rainbow trout. It can usually be counted on for rainbows 16 to 20 inches, weighing up to 5 pounds.

ODFW holds most, but not all, the water rights to Chickahominy, and the reservoir does go dry some years (such as 1992). Occasional algae blooms have also been known to reduce the trout population from time to time, so it's a good idea to check with ODFW in Hines on the status of the fishery before making the trip. See Appendix.

The 530-acre reservoir within sight of Hwy. 20 near Riley is about 32 miles west of Burns. The gravel access road can be deeply rutted and hazardous to low-center vehicles. This is not a scenic fishery (little more than a depression in the sagebrush), but Chickahominy is stocked with up to 80,000 rainbow fingerlings each spring. In good years, those fingerlings grow about 2 inches per month during the summer. Most serious anglers forgive Chickahominy's shortcomings once they're into a four-pound rainbow.

Anglers use all methods to fish here. There's a boat ramp, and many anglers troll or cast bait. It's an excellent float-tube lake, and fly anglers take advantage of their mobility to fish for the big trout that cruise near the weed beds. But neither boat nor float tube is necessary to do well. There are good wading opportunities at the upper end and in the shallow arms. In spring, the gravel near the boat ramp attracts big rainbows with spawning on their minds.

The reservoir has good populations of dragonflies, scuds, *Callibaetis* mayflies and midges. Dragonfly nymphs are on the move early in the season, and mayflies start hatching in May. The bigger trout also go for leech imitations.

It should be noted that Chickahominy sits among the sagebrush, its banks and the landscape for miles around entirely devoid of trees. The wind can really pick up here in a hurry, and the summers are very hot. Fishing is best in spring (March through May) and again in fall if the water level is high enough. (Even when full, the reservoir is less than 30 ft. deep.) Ice fishing is often a possibility for a couple of months each winter before the road becomes impassable. February fishing can be good though bitterly cold.

Chickahominy's campground has been upgraded in recent years to include more official campsites and more shaded picnic tables. Camping in undesignated sites is discouraged. There is drinking water, and a fee for both overnight and day use during the peak season.

CLOVER LAKE. A small, lightly fished brook trout lake in the southern Mountain Lakes Wilderness in Winema National Forest. It's a 2-mile hike by trail north from the end of the Buck Peak Lookout Rd. Buck Peak is about 12 miles southwest of Lake of the Woods Resort.

The lake is in a basin of potholes at the head of Clover Creek. It's only a couple of acres, but offers good angling for brook trout to 12 inches. Clover is stocked by air with fingerlings in odd-number years. Best fishing is usually in even-number years. Fairly shallow, it's an easy lake to fly fish. Some of the other small lakes in this area just might offer surprises.

COMO LAKE. A very nice lake in the Mountain Lake Wilderness of the southern Winema National Forest. There are three main trails into the basin. From Rt. 140, about 7 miles east of Lake of the Woods, take the Varney Creek Rd. (Forest Rd. 3610) south about 1½ miles, turning left onto Forest Rd. 3637 and right on Forest Rd. 3664. Varney Creek Trailhead 3718 is at the

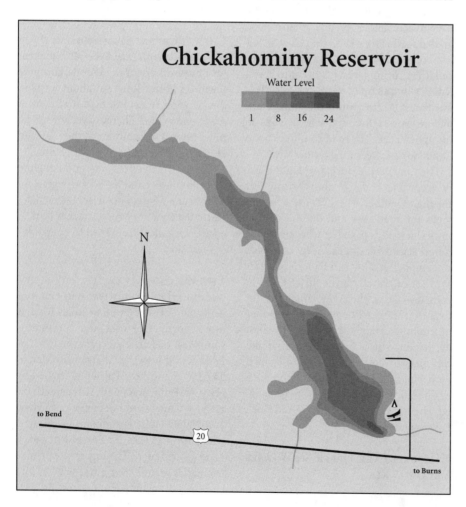

Chickahominy Reservoir

Water Level

1   8   16   24

N

to Bend

20

to Burns

end of the road. It's about a 4 miles to Como Lake.

The lake is 7 acres and quite deep. It's stocked with brook and rainbow trout in odd-number years, with the average catch (best in even-number years) averaging 10 to 14 inches, with a few larger. Bait is best in spring, and all methods can be effective in fall. For other good lakes in the area see Harriette, Echo, South Pass.

COTTONWOOD CREEK (Goose Lake watershed). A redband trout stream northwest of Lakeview, tributary to Goose Lake. Regeneration of Goose Lake's trout population following the 1992 drought led to the re-opening of this fishery in 1998.

COTTONWOOD CREEK (Malheur R. watershed, Malheur Co.) A wild redband trout stream south of Harper Junction on Hwy. 20. Several roads south of Harper Junction approach the creek.

COTTONWOOD CREEK (Goose Lake watershed). A lightly fished trout stream north of Drewsey, dammed to create Cottonwood Creek Reservoir (see below). Below the reservoir, it flows through private ranch land and is not open to public access. Above, a primitive track follows the creek through public land, offering access to good fishing. The trail can be accessed either at Cottonwood Meadows Lake (encircling the lake then following the creek downstream to a trailhead on Forest Rd. 3870), or from a spur road off 3870 two miles west of the north end of Cottonwood Reservoir.

COTTONWOOD CREEK RESERVOIR (Malheur R. watershed). An impoundment north of Drewsey which offers only fair trout angling. Drewsey is reached by paved road north from Hwy. 20, about 47 miles east of Burns. A gravel road leads north from town. Watch for a sign. The reservoir covers about 120 acres.

Cottonwood is stocked with 5,000 rainbow fingerlings annually, which commonly reach 8 to 10 inches, with a few to 12 inches. Crappie were stocked in the early '90s, but so far they have not done well.

COTTONWOOD MEADOWS LAKE. (Goose Lake watershed) In the Fremont National Forest, about 22 miles northwest of Lakeview, a joint project of the National Forest Service and ODFW. From Lakeview, take Rt. 140 about 20 miles west to Forest Rd. 3870. Follow 3870 about 6 miles northwest to the lake. Do not confuse it with Cottonwood Reservoir, a much larger impoundment near Lakeview on lower Cottonwood Creek. The road to Cottonwood Reservoir continues on to the lake, but keep your forest map handy. Forest Rd. 3870 is accessible both from east and west of the lake, but each section of the road dead ends at the lake without allowing through-traffic.

The Meadows Lake is a nice body of water that holds up well during dry years, offering about 42 acres of good fishing. Rainbow fingerlings and legals are stocked each year, and the catch rate is high. The rainbows average 9 to 12 inches with a lot to 15 inches. Brook trout run larger, with most 14 to 16 inches. All methods work, but there's always a slack period in late summer because of algae. Late fall produces good fly fishing.

There are two campgrounds on the lake. Electric motors are allowed on the lake. The road in is usually open by May.

COTTONWOOD RESERVOIR. (Goose Lake watershed). A 900-acre irrigation reservoir on lower Cottonwood Creek, offering good fishing for wild redband trout. From Lakeview, head west on Hwy. 140 about 7 miles. There is a sign indicating the reservoir. The gravel access road heads north from the highway and reaches the lake in about 6 miles. The road continues beyond the upper end of the reservoir, crosses Cottonwood Creek, passes Cottonwood Creek Trailhead (2 miles past the reservoir) and reaches at Cottonwood Meadows Lake (on Freemond Forest Rd. 3870).

The trout fishery here is dependent on the continued good health of the Goose Lake redband population. Depleted (and closed to fishing) during the drought in the early '90s, it is now in good shape and producing fish to 24 inches. The reservoir is drawn down in fall.

Surrounded by trees (and private land), the reservoir is open to public access with the indulgence of the landowners. Clean up after yourself (and others) to preserve access. The boat ramp and dam at the north end offer bank fishing opportunities.

The reservoir is open year-round, though it can get snowed in. Ice fishing is possible when the road's open.

COW LAKES. Two large bass and panfish lakes near the Idaho border south of Ontario, only the upper of which provides angling. Roads approach the lakes from Hwy. 95, just south of Sheaville, or from Jordan Valley. The access road is gravel.

Covering almost 1000 acres, the upper lake supports populations of brown bullhead and white crappie, and some largemouth bass. BLM maintains the facilities here, which include campsites among the cockleburs and mud and a boat ramp. A campground upgrade is being contemplated.

Fishing's best at the west end near the lava bed where the lake is deeper and the weeds are less of a problem.

CRACKER CREEK. A short tributary of the Powder River with wild rainbows and brook trout, entering the river at Sumpter about 30 miles west of Baker. Bull trout are also present and must be released unharmed. From Baker, take Hwy. 7 south and west along the Powder River, following the river to Sumpter. A gravel forest road follows Cracker Creek north about 4 miles, and dirt roads follow its forks.

Fishing in the main creek and its forks is quite good after the spring thaw and holds up well into summer. Heavily stocked in years past, it is now stocked only lightly and has good numbers of wild trout to 10 inches. The nearest campground is at McCully Forks, west of Sumpter.

CRANE CREEK (Malheur watershed). A tributary of the North Fork Malheur with small wild redbands and some large bull trout. It is best known as an access to the upper North Fork Malheur. It joins the North Fork at Crane Crossing in Malheur National Forest, once an old military road fording spot. Forest Rd. 1675 approaches the Crossing from the east. See North Fork Malheur for directions.

The western stretch of the old road is now closed to motor vehicles and used as a hiking trail along Crane Creek. To reach the trailhead from Forest Rd. 16 in Malheur National Forest, follow Forest Rd. 1633 south from Crane Prairie Guard Station. The trailhead is on the east side of the road about a mile from the junction. Crane Prairie is a pretty place in spring.

CRATER LAKE (Powder River watershed). A good brook trout lake high in the southeast corner of Eagle Cap Wilderness in the Wallowa Mountains. Crater Lake is at the head of Kettle Creek, a tributary of the upper East Fork of Eagle Creek, and you'll work hard to get to it. Best route to the lake is from the south from Baker or Halfway. Snow may block access until July. From Baker take Hwy. 203 north to Medical Springs and pick up Forest Rd. 67, which leads to Eagle Creek, meeting it at Tamarack Campground. From here, follow the creek downstream on Forest Rd. 77.

You have your choice of two trails, one a steep but somewhat shorter punishment, and the other a bit longer but not quite as steep. For the eager hiker, Trail 1945 will get you there quickest. Turn up the East Fork of Eagle Creek on Forest Rd. 7740, and follow it about 5 miles north to its end at Kettle Creek Campground. Trail 1945 grinds east following Little Kettle Creek for about 6.6 miles to the lake, switch-backing most of the way and gaining 3000 ft. in elevation—a killer.

The better route in is by Trail 1946. About 6 miles beyond the East Fork junction on Forest Rd. 77, take Forest Rd. 7732 northwest to its end. Trail 1946 leads northeast towards Pine Lake and eventually Crater Lake. This hike is 7.7 miles long, but it's over an interesting ridge route. Total elevation gain is still at least 3000 feet.

Crater Lake covers 12 acres and is only 10 feet at its deepest point. The lake is cupped on a high saddle between Red Mountain and Krag Peak at an elevation of 7500 feet. It produces good catches of brook trout 8 to 13 inches. This is a good place to give your fly rod a workout. The scenery is grand, and the fish are willing.

CRATER LAKE (Rogue watershed). This is a great scenic attraction, but it doesn't grow large fish and attracts few anglers. Filling a somnolent volcano, Crater Lake is the showpiece of Crater Lake National Park. The lake is reached by Hwy. 62 from Medford, and by Hwy. 97 from Klamath Falls or Bend. The park shows up on every map.

The lake is about 5 miles in diameter and 2000 ft. deep. It is no longer stocked, though in the past it was stocked with rainbow trout and kokanee. Anglers are welcome to fish the lake from Cleetwood Cove (at the end of the single trail into the crater) or from Wizard Island. The tour boat that leaves from Cleetwood will drop you off at the island and pick you up later in the day. Camping is prohibited on the island. A state fishing license is not required, and there is no catch limit.

Cleetwood Cove is at the end of the only trail into the crater, on the southwest shore. Check at park headquarters for an update on fishing regulations and access. This is high country, and the snow lingers well into June.

There are two campgrounds in the park, as well as primitive sites in the back-country. The day lodge at the rim has a cafe and some supplies, and the restored lodge offers handsome accommodations and dining.

CRATER LAKE (Malheur watershed). A 2-acre lake in Malheur Wildlife Refuge that has supported largemouth bass and white crappie. The lake periodically winterkills and has not been restocked.

CROOKED CREEK (Wood River watershed). A short tributary of lower Wood River flowing south of Fort Klamath. Only about 5 miles long, it offers fishing for rainbows, browns and brook trout (catch and release with artificial flies and lures). The creek is closely followed north by Hwy. 62 from the junction of the Chiloquin road and Hwy. 97.

There are some big fish in this stream,

The tour boat from Cleetwood Cove ferries anglers out for a day's fishing on CRATER LAKE's Wizard Island. Photograph by Richard T. Grost.

both residents and migrants from Upper Klamath Lake. If you haven't seen big fish for a while or you want to brush up on your fish identification skills, check out the hatchery on the creek 2 miles north of Klamath Indian Agency. There are often some large fish in a hole right by the hatchery, though the creek is closed to fishing on hatchery grounds.

In good water years, fishing can be good in spring and early summer. Mosquitoes are a problem in spring. Much of this creek is on private land, so ask permission to fish.

CROOKED CREEK. (Chewaucan watershed) A small wild redband trout stream between Lakeview and Valley Falls. It flows into the lower Chewaucan River north of Valley Falls. The creek is followed south by Hwy. 395 and is accessible from the west by Hwy. 31. The upper creek is only 10 miles north of Lakeview.

In good water years, fishing is fair for a short time in spring and early summer. The creek is quite small, and bait-fishing produces best. Chandler State Park is on the creek about 5 miles south of Valley Falls.

CRUMP LAKE. A large shallow lake bass and panfish lake at the south end of Warner Valley, due south of Hart Mountain. To reach it, take the gravel road north from Adel toward Plush. When full, Crump has 3200 surface acres.

In drought years, Crump is one of the last lakes in the valley to go dry. It did so in 1992, and its crappie fishery (which boomed in the 1980's) is not yet fully restored. Black and white crappie to 12 inches, the occasional largemouth bass, and brown bullheads are available. Best bullhead fishing is in spring.

Supplies are available at Adel. This is remote country, so check your gas gauge.

CULVER LAKE. An 8-acre brook trout lake in southern Eagle Cap Wilderness, about 6 trail miles from Boulder Park, elevation gain about 2050 ft. From Baker, follow Hwy. 203 then Forest Rd. 67 to Boulder Park, about 45 miles. Take Eagle Creek Trail 1922 into the wilderness, then follow 1921 and 1921A to Culver. Other lakes in the basin include Bear and Lookingglass. Trails are generally accessible by July 4, and fishing is good through September.

DAIRY CREEK (Chewaucan watershed). A nice wild redband trout creek in Fremont National Forest, flowing through a lodgepole pine forest. It offers a cool refuge from the valley heat. Dairy heads on the east slope of Gearhart Mt. in the Gearhart Mt. Wilderness Area, and flows east into the upper Chewaucan River. A major fork of the river, it enters the Chewaucan 18 miles south of Paisley. It is followed and crossed by a network of forest roads. A Fremont Forest map will come in handy. One good route to the upper stream from Lakeview is to take Rt. 140 west 3 miles to a paved road leading north (County Rd. 2-16). About 8 miles north it becomes Forest Rd. 28, which follows Thomas Creek to its headwaters and eventually reaches Dairy Point Campground. Dairy Point is on the creek.

Dairy Creek is no longer stocked, but wild redbands and brook trout 9 to 10 inches are available, with some 12 inches and larger. Bait angling is the preferred method, but there's a lot of nice fly water. Happy Camp is about 2 miles further upstream on Forest Rd. 047.

DEAD HORSE LAKE. A pretty, drive-to, high alpine trout lake in Fremont National Forest east of Dead Horse Rim, overlooking the wild and scenic section of the Sycan River. From Paisley on Hwy. 31, follow Forest Rd. 33 south along the Chewaucan River, turning west (right) onto Forest Rd. 28 about 18 miles south of Paisley. Follow Forest Rd. 28 about 8 miles, then turn left on Forest Rd. 033, which leads to Campbell Lake then, a mile farther, to Dead Horse. There are several trailheads at Dead Horse, including one that leads to (and along) the scenic rim.

Dead Horse Lake is accessible for only a short period, from July through October. The Forest Service locks the gate in spring and doesn't open it until the road is passable. Check with the Ranger Stations at Bly, Lakeview, or Paisley.

About 20 acres, Dead Horse is stocked with legal rainbows, brook trout fingerlings, and trout grown to trophy size. The average catch is 10 inches. Trolling is popular as well as still-fishing with bait, but any method will produce fish. The success rate is pretty high.

Boats can be launched and effectively used, but only electric motors are allowed. There is a small campground at the lake, and hike-in or boat-in camping units are available along the shoreline for a more solitary experience.

DEE LAKE. One of the hike-in lakes in the Island Lake area of Rogue River National Forest, about 10 miles north of Lake of the Woods. From Lake of the Woods on Rt. 140, drive about 5 miles east, then turn north on Forest Rd. 3561 to the Big Meadows spur road (Forest Rd. 3659). This leads west a bit over a mile to a hairpin turn north, on which you will find the Lost Creek Trailhead. Follow Trail 3712 west about 3½ miles to Island Lake. Dee Lake is west of Island Lake.

Dee is not heavily fished and has some nice brook trout. The average size is 10 inches, with some fish to 18 inches taken occasionally. The lake is 14 acres and fairly shallow, stocked by air. It's an excellent fly fishing lake, with best results in August and September. It's usually accessible by late June. There are good campsites at Island Lake to the east. In addition to Island, see Red, Pear, and Camp lakes for additional fishing opportunities.

DEEP CREEK (Warner Valley). A very good redband trout stream southeast of Lakeview, flowing out of Crane Mountain in Freemont National Forest and into Crump Lake near Adel.

To reach the headwaters from Lakeview, follow Hwy. 140 east along Warner Canyon about 6½ miles, then turn right onto Forest Rd. 3915, which reaches Deep Creek in about 20 miles. Turn right onto Forest Rd. 4015 to reach Deep Creek Campground at the confluence of its headwater tributaries.

The creek flows out of the forest into Big Valley, where the Sage Hen Creek Rd. picks it up for about a mile as it leaves the valley. Deep Creek then plunges into a canyon with no road access until it reaches Rt. 140 about 5 miles west of Adel. The highway follows it closely into Adel.

Deep Creek offers very good fishing in late spring and summer for wild trout to 15 inches. There is excellent fly fishing in the stretch west of Adel (along the highway) after the water clears, usually around the beginning of July.

DEEP LAKE (Sky Lakes). A fairly good hike-in brook trout lake in the Sky Lakes Wilderness, Winema National Forest. A popular route into the area begins at Cold Springs Campground on Forest Rd. 3651. To reach the campground from Klamath Falls, follow Rt. 140 north along the lake. Rt. 140 makes a sharp turn west toward

Lake of the Woods (just before Pelican Guard Station). About 3½ miles farther, turn right onto Forest Rd. 3651. Cold Springs is at the end of the road (about 9 miles from the highway).

From the campground, Trail 3709 leads north to Heavenly Twin Lake. At the junction with Trail 3762, take the right fork to Trapper Lake. From there Trail 3734 leads past Donna Lake to Deep. The hike to Deep is about 6 miles. Other approaches are possible. Take along a USGS topographic quad map or the Sky Lakes Wilderness map.

Deep Lake is lightly fished and has a good number of brook trout averaging 9 inches. Not too deep and only 4 acres, it's an easy lake to fish, best in late summer and fall. All methods will take fish. Other lakes in the area include Trapper, Donna, Sonya, Marguerette. The Pacific Crest Trail passes about ½ mile to the west.

DEER CREEK (Powder watershed). A small wild rainbow trout stream, tributary to the upper Powder River west of Baker. It flows about 8 miles from the north into Phillips Reservoir. Hwy. 7 crosses the stream at Mowich Park, a picnic area. Forest Rd. 6550, west of Mowich Park, leads to Deer Creek Campground, and forest roads 6540 and 220 follow the creek to its head. Deer Creek offers good angling for wild rainbow 8 to 9 inches and up to 12 inches. Bull trout are also present and must be released unharmed.

DEER LAKE (Sky Lakes). A trout lake at the southwest end of the Sky Lakes area of the Winema National Forest. A popular route into the basin begins at Cold Springs Campground on Forest Rd. 3651. See Deep Lake for directions to the campground. From Cold Springs, hike a little less than a mile on Trail 3710 to the junction with Trail 3762. The left fork leads to Deer Lake. It's about 6 miles to the lake. Continuing ½ mile on this trail brings you to the Pacific Crest Trail.

Deer is fairly shallow with 5 surface acres. It is stocked by air with fingerling trout that commonly grow to 11 inches with a few larger. Fly fishing is usually good in late summer and fall.

DELINTMENT LAKE. A popular 50-acre trout lake in Ochoco National Forest northwest of Burns, featuring large rain-

DELINTMENT LAKE can offer good angling for rainbows large and small. Photograph by Jeffrey Kee.

bows. Created by a dam on Delintment Creek specifically for recreation, the lake and its surrounding ponderosa pine forest are a welcome oasis in the eastern Oregon landscape.

From Burns, travel south on Hwy. 20 to Hines, then northwest on Forest Rd. 47 to its junction with Forest Rd. 41, about 15 miles from Burns. Forest Rd. 41 reaches the lake in about 35 miles. Additional roads access the lake. Refer to the forest map.

Delintment can offer good angling for large rainbows, but it often winterkills (most recently in 1998-99). Fingerlings are added annually to replace those lost during the winter. The lake is shallow and rich, and fish grow well. Trout average 10 to 14 inches. Larger fish (3 to 4 pounds) are common following warmer, dryer winters. Boats can be launched (5 mph speed limit throughout the lake), and there's a good shoreline for bank casting. It is almost impossible to fish here in late summer due to extensive weed growth.

The campground is large and attractive, with many flat grassy sites tucked discretely among the tall pines. A private concession currently manages the facilities at Delintment, and there is both a day-use and overnight fee. There is a wheelchair accessible fishing dock.

DENIO CREEK. A remote Lahontan cutthroat stream. It is closed to all fishing to protect the Lahontan, which is listed as a threatened species. The trout population is recovering following great losses during

the 1987-94 drought.

DEVIL LAKE (Sprague watershed). An irrigation reservoir with bass and panfish 7 miles southeast of Bly. From Bly, drive east on Rt. 140, then turn south on Forest Rd. 3790 (Fishhole Creek Rd.) Devil is on the west side of the road.

The reservoir normally has about 100 acres. It was once stocked with trout, but they've all but disappeared and there are no plans to re-stock. Fishing is for brown bullhead catfish to 14 inches, a ton of yellow perch, and a few small largemouth bass. Boats are allowed, but there is no ramp. Fishing is generally best in fall. The lake is an unattractive depression in the sage, its banks heavily grazed. You wouldn't want to camp here even if you could.

DOG LAKE. One of the few warmwater fisheries near Lakeview, a large lake in Fremont National Forest. From Lakeview, head west on Rt. 140 about 9 miles. Turn left on County Rd. 1-13. At about 4 miles, turn right on Dog Lake Rd., which passes Drews Reservoir and reaches Dog Lake in about 14 miles.

With about 500 surface acres, Dog Lake provides fair fishing for perch, brown bullhead, small black and white crappie, blue gills, and largemouth bass. There's lots of submerged structure and vegetation, but during high water years, most fish are found in deeper water. Experienced anglers can take trophy-size bass, but few small

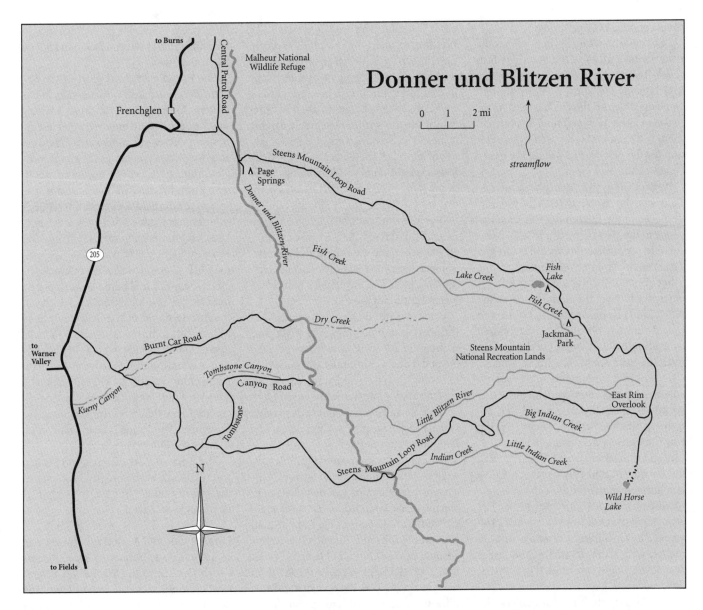

Donner und Blitzen River

0   1   2 mi

streamflow

to Burns

Malheur National
Wildlife Refuge

Central Patrol Road

Frenchglen

Steens Mountain Loop Road

Page
Springs

Donner und Blitzen River

Fish Creek

205

Lake Creek

Fish
Lake

Fish Creek

Dry Creek

Jackman
Park

Burnt Car Road

to
Warner
Valley

Steens Mountain
National Recreation Lands

Tombstone Canyon

Canyon Road

Kueny Canyon

Tombstone

Little Blitzen River

East Rim
Overlook

Big Indian Creek

Little Indian Creek

N

Steens Mountain Loop Road

Indian Creek

Wild Horse
Lake

to Fields

---

bass are present.

The lake is at high elevation in an attractive forest setting. There are two campgrounds, Cinder Hill and Dog Lake. Dog Lake Campground has a boat ramp. There is a 5 mph speed limit on the lake.

DONNA LAKE. A small brook trout lake at the northern end of Sky Lakes Wilderness, Winema National Forest. A popular route into the basin begins at Cold Springs Campground. See Deep Lake for road directions. From Cold Springs follow either Trail 3710 or 3709 north to Heavenly Twin Lake, then continue north on trail 3762 to Trapper Lake. From there Trail 3734 leads to Donna Lake. Donna is east of the trail, slightly north of Trapper and Margurette Lakes. Other approaches are possible. Bring a topographic map (Sky Lakes Wilderness or USGS).

Only 2 acres and 9 ft. deep, Donna provides fishing for brook trout 8 to 14 inches. The lake is stocked every other year. There are good natural campsites and fishing at larger lakes to the south.

DONNER UND BLITZEN RIVER

(a.k.a. Blitzen) A designated Wild and Scenic River System with quality fishing for redband rainbow trout, flowing 40 miles off Steens Mt., through Malheur Wildlife Refuge, and into Malheur Lake. Best access to the river is by trail upstream from Page Springs Campground south of Frenchglen.

To reach Page Springs Campground from Burns, follow Hwy. 205 south to Frenchglen, toward the southern edge of Malheur Wildlife Refuge. Beyond the Frenchglen Hotel at the south end of "town" look for signs to Steens Mt. Loop

Rd. and Page Springs on the left. Access to the trail is through a stile at the far end of the campground. To reach the upper Blitzen by road, continue on Hwy. 205 to the south end of Steens Mt. Loop Rd. Follow the Loop Rd. to Blitzen Crossing (about 13 miles), just downstream from the Indian Creek confluence. Jeep tracks off the South Loop Rd. lead to two other access points where trails lead down to the river. Known as Tombstone and Burnt Car, they are unsigned. The Loop Rd. is generally snowbound until mid-June.

Other than the sheer adventure of finding your way over rough roads and exploring the Blitzen's tributaries, there's little reason to approach the Blitzen from above. The river's larger fish are in the lower reach, though there are plenty of smaller redband upstream. As for solitude, you'll usually have the canyon pretty much to yourself within a couple of miles of Page Springs.

The trail from Page Springs follows the river about 4 miles to the mouth of Fish Creek. This portion of the canyon is easily hiked during low summer flows, though you'll need to ford the creek several times. Between Fish Creek and the Little Blitzen, there is no trail. Be prepared to boulder hop for the privilege of fishing the river's largest trout.

Perhaps this is the place to mention rattlesnakes. Be aware that there are rattlesnakes in the Blitzen canyon and elsewhere in this part of the country. Take reasonable precautions as in other Oregon desert environments. Mosquitoes are the other curse of fishing along the Blitzen, particularly near the marshlands of the refuge, and one of several good reasons to put off your trip till fall. The river is closed to angling below Bridge Creek, about 2 miles downstream of the campground.

The Blitzen's redbands are a desert-adapted fish that can withstand high temperatures, silted bedding gravel, and extremely alkaline waters. During spring run-off the river becomes extremely turbid, and in heavy snowpack years it may not clear until mid-July or later. Mid- to late summer in the Blitzen canyon can be productive for trout but extremely hot. Fall is the most pleasant time to fish here. The average lower Blitzen redband is 10 to 12 inches, with trout 20 inches and larger available. Fishing is restricted to artificial flies and lures.

Though remote for most anglers, the Blitzen can be fished in conjunction with other waters in the area. See Fish Lake, Wildhorse Lake, and Krumbo Reservoir. The Blitzen's tributaries upstream of the wildlife refuge (Fish, Big Indian, and Little Blitzen) offer adventures in rugged hiking for small redbands. Mann Lake is another fishing option within reasonable driving distance once you've come this far. Or you might approach the Blitzen as one activity in an exploration of this fascinating corner of the state. In addition to the lush assemblage of wildlife on Malheur Wildlife Refuge, there are historic sites (Frenchglen Hotel, Round Barn, Pony Express stations, ghost towns), and interesting geologic phenomena (lava tube caves, hot springs, Diamond Craters, and the majestic fault-block Steens Mountain itself).

Donner und Blitzen is German for thunder and lightning. The river was named in 1864 by army troops who crossed it during a thunder storm. Storms in the high Steens (wind, rain, and snow), are legendary and often come up suddenly. Be especially wary of surprise snowstorms in those rare springs when the Loop Rd. opens early.

For fishing the lower river, the most convenient camping is at Page Springs. Upstream, there is a campground called South Steens on the Loop Rd. about three miles east of Blitzen Crossing (the campground isn't on the Blitzen). To reach this campground, drive to the end of the road at Big Indian Creek Gorge. It's a short drive from there to trails along Big Indian and Little Blitzen. Undeveloped (and rather dusty) campsites are available in the vicinity of Blitzen Crossing. There are also campgrounds at Fish Lake and Jackman Park on the upper Steens.

The Frenchglen Hotel (part of the National Park system) offers home-style dining, modest lodging, and the most inviting screened porch for a hundred miles in a refreshing setting of cottonwoods. There are also two pleasant rooms available at Frenchglen Mercantile, whose Buckaroo Room serves sandwiches for lunch and a fine spread for dinner (beef steak after a day's fishing among cattle is strangely satisfying). Higher up the lodging scale, bed & breakfast accommodations are available at the Diamond Hotel and at McCoy Creek Inn. At the other end, you'll find bunks and camp-style facilities at Malheur Field Station, which is at the northern end of the Refuge about 32 miles south of Burns, half-way to Frenchglen. Facilities include RV hook-ups, mobile home rentals, and dorms with kitchens. Dinners are available at the Field Station by advance reservation (a week's notice requested) from the end of April till the end of September. The station is open year-round, with limited lodging in winter.

This is remote, dry country. Carry water, and fill up on fuel before you head out. In the vicinity of the Blitzen, the only fuel stop is in Frenchglen.

DRAKE CREEK. A good small creek east of Lakeview, tributary to Deep Creek, which flows into the Warner lakes near Adel. From Lakeview, follow Hwy. 395 north. Turn east (right) onto Rt. 140 and follow it to Adel. Drake flows into Deep Creek from the north about 6 miles west of Adel. The creek heads on the east slopes of Drake Peak to the northwest, but flows through mostly private property, limiting fishing to the mouth.

Drake Creek supports native redband trout, averaging about 10 inches with an occasional 14-incher.

DREWS CREEK. An early season trout stream with a fair number of wild redband trout. Hwy. 140 crosses it about 23 miles west of Lakeview. It flows out of Fremont National Forest, is dammed to form Drews Reservoir, then flows southeast into Goose Lake. It is open to fishing above the reservoir (with artificial flies and lures only) and is closed to fishing below.

DONNER UND BLITZEN (popularly known as the Blitzen) offers quality fishing for redband rainbows in a desert setting. Photograph by Dennis Frates.

DREWS RESERVOIR. A large irrigation reservoir on Drews Creek, lightly fished for warmwater species by local anglers. It is about 18 miles west of Lakeview on Rt. 140. The reservoir is encircled by gravel and dirt roads.

When full, Drews covers about 4500 acres, but it is heavily drawn down and, in dry years, gets very low. The primary quarry here are big channel cats (to 18 pounds). There are also some white crappie 6 to 10 inches, brown bullhead to 12 inches, and yellow perch to 13 inches. An occasional large rainbow is also taken. There is a boat ramp at the south end of the reservoir.

DUCK LAKE. A low elevation lake that offers early season opportunities for hike-in trout fishing. It has about 20 surface acres, draining into Pine Creek in Hells Canyon National Recreation Area. It sees little angler pressure.

From Joseph, head east 8 miles on the road to Imnaha, then go south about 30 miles on the graded gravel road that becomes Forest Rd. 39. Turn west on (dirt) Forest Rd. 3960 across from Ollokot Campground. Trail 1875 heads south from Indian Crossing Horse Camp, about 8 miles from Ollokot. The trail passes the lake and continues to the southern wilderness trailhead on Forest Rd. 66. To access the lake from the Baker area to the south, follow Hwy. 86 east to Forest Rd. 39. Turn west on Forest Rd. 66 to its junction with Forest Rd. 3960. The trail heads north from the junction. It's a 2-mile hike from either trailhead.

Duck Lake is stocked every other year with rainbow trout which grow to an average 10 inches and may reach 13 inches. Naturally reproducing brook trout are also available. The lake is open all year and, at elevation 5366 ft. (lowest of all natural lakes in Wallowa-Whitman National Forest), provides one of the earliest opportunities in the area for mountain lake fishing, though the road is blocked till the snow melts.

DUNAWAY POND. A one-acre borrow pit on the east side of the highway south of Nyssa, supporting bluegill, largemouth bass, and brown bullhead. From Nyssa (heading toward Owyhee Junction on Hwy. 201), when the road makes a sharp 90 degree turn, veer left onto a gravel road, passing under a viaduct. This road leads to the pond.

DUNCAN RESERVOIR. A 33-acre impoundment on Duncan Creek about 2 miles southwest of Silver Lake with lots of brown bullheads and some trout of good size. From the town of Silver Lake, 40 miles east of LaPine, it's about 6 miles by good gravel road southeast to the reservoir.

Duncan Creek is open year-round to give anglers the opportunity to take trout that leave the reservoir in the spring water release. The creek dries up completely in summer. There are some camping facilities at the reservoir.

DUTCH FLAT LAKE. A small wild brook trout lake in the southern Wallowa-Whitman National Forest west of North Powder. The easiest approach is by way of Trail 1611 above Anthony Lake.

EAGLE CREEK (Powder River watershed). A beautiful stream, once premier chinook water, a tributary of the lower Powder River. It drains a number of the southeastern lakes of Eagle Cap Wilderness and enters the Powder River Arm of the Snake River's Brownlee Reservoir near Richland. Wilderness trails follow its upper waters, and good roads access the lower stream. It supports a population of wild rainbows and is heavily stocked. Angling is good from June to September for trout to 12 inches.

Hwy. 86 crosses Eagle Creek at Richland, and the paved northbound road to Newbridge follows the creek into the Wallowa-Whitman National Forest, becoming Forest Rd. 7735. From Eagle Forks Campground (the confluence of Little Eagle Creek with the mainstem 7 miles north of Newbridge) Trail 1878 follows the mainstem upstream about 5 miles.

To reach the upper creek from Eagle Forks Campground, follow Forest Rd. 7735 up Little Eagle Creek. Pass up the first spur on the left (which reaches Eagle Creek but is rough). Continue to the next fork, and turn left onto Forest Rd. 77, Eagle Creek Rd. This road reaches Eagle Creek at the upper end of Trail 1878.

To reach the upper stream, from Hwy. 86 about 20 miles east of Baker, turn left (north) on County Rd. 852. After about 3½ miles, turn left (north) onto County Rd. 891 (Collins Rd.), then right onto Forest Rd. 7015 (Empire Gulch Rd.), which crosses Eagle Creek shortly after a hairpin turn. Continue north along the creek to road's end. Trail

1922 heads up the creek to Eagle Lake.

One of the prettiest streams in the Wilderness, Eagle Creek has high quality water which flows through scenic canyon and meadow land.

In addition to Eagle Forks Campground on the lower stream, there are two campgrounds on Forest Rd. 77 beside the upper creek, Tamarack and Two Color.

ECHO LAKE. (Powder River watershed) A brook trout lake at the head of Eagle Creek West Fork, in the southern Eagle Cap Wilderness, Wallowa-Whitman National Forest. From Catherine Creek State Park on Hwy. 203 (between LaGrande and Baker) continue south on Hwy. 203, then turn left (east) on Forest Rd. 77 (Eagle Creek Rd.). Trailhead 1934 is on the left about 13 miles from the turn-off. Keep a copy of the forest map open for reference as you negotiate the forest roads. There are many spurs that could mislead you.

Trail 1934 gains 1500 feet elevation before reaching Echo in 5 miles. The trail continues north 1.6 miles to Traverse Lake and connects with other wilderness trails, including an arduous 12.7 mile connection to the lake group at the head of the main Eagle Creek Trail. Echo has 28 surface acres and a maximum depth of 19 feet. At 7100 ft. it is one of the lower lakes in the wilderness. It has an abundant population of small brook trout which take a fly enthusiastically in August and September.

ECHO LAKE (Mountain Lakes Wilderness). A small, fairly good hike-in brook trout lake in the Mountain Lakes Wilderness of Winema National Forest, east of Lake of the Woods.

From Rt. 140, about 7 miles east of Lake of the Woods, take the Varney Creek Rd. (Forest Rd. 3610) south about 1½ miles. Turn left onto Forest Rd. 3637 and right on Forest Rd. 3664. Varney Creek Trailhead 3718 is at the end of the road. Follow Trail 3718 about 4 miles, then take the left fork, Trail 3127, which reaches Harriette Lake in about 1½ miles. Follow the trail around to Harriette's north shore. Echo is left of the trail.

Echo is only about 5 acres and is lightly fished for brook trout 7 to 12 inches, and a few that run larger. Some good size lunkers are reported from time to time. There are fair campsites along the trail near Harriette Lake. Most of the other small lakes in this area are too shallow to support fish.

ELDER CREEK (Chewaucan watershed). A small trout stream south of Paisley, flowing into the upper Chewaucan River. Paisley is about 130 miles southeast of Bend by way of highways 97 and 31. The creek enters the river about 18 miles south of Paisley.

Elder supports native redband rainbows and some brook trout, with few over 8 inches. There are several campgrounds a few miles south of the creek, west of Dairy Creek Guard Station.

ELIZABETH LAKE. A small lake in the southern Sky Lakes area of Sky Lakes Wilderness, Winema National Forest. A popular hike in begins at Cold Springs Campground. See Deep lake for directions. From Cold Springs, take Trail 3710 about 3 miles to Elizabeth Lake, which is ¼ mile north of Natasha lake.

Elizabeth has 5 surface acres and is lightly fished. It is a steady producer of trout to 11 inches. Quite shallow, the lake is best suited to fly angling. Fishing is best in early spring and in fall.

EMIGRANT CREEK. A better than average trout stream, tributary of the Silvies River, flowing 30 miles in the southern portion of Ochoco National Forest near the Malheur Forest boundary. It enters the Silvies 20 miles northwest of Burns.

From Hines on County Rd. 127, look for signs to Delintment & Yellowjacket lakes. The road heads north behind the gas station a the west end of town, crossing Emigrant just before entering Malheur National Forest. Turn left before the crossing, onto Forest Rd. 43, which follows Emigrant upstream past Falls and Emigrant campgrounds. There is a fee to camp at both. At about 15 miles, Forest Rd. 4360 branches to the right and follows the creek to its headwaters. Near its confluence with the Silvies, Emigrant flows through a patchwork of BLM and private ranchland. Primitive roads follow the lower stream, but be careful not to trespass.

Fishing is good in late spring and summer for trout 6 to 8 inches, with the occasional 15-inch catch.

FISH LAKE (Blitzen watershed). A remote but popular lake high on the west slope of Steens Mt. Deer hunters like to camp here in fall. The lake is on the Steens Mt. Loop Rd., which is usually snowbound at its upper elevations until July.

Take Hwy. 205 from Burns south through the Malheur Wildlife Refuge to the tiny community of Frenchglen, a 55-mile trip. To reach the Loop Rd., drive east from Frenchglen towards Page Springs Campground, turning north immediately after crossing Donner Und Blitzen River. Steens Loop Rd. is blocked by a series of gates that are opened successively as the snow melts. It is about 15 miles from Page Springs to Fish Lake.

The lake is tucked within a sparse aspen grove near the rim of Steens Mt., at 7200 ft. Winter hangs on hard here, and there are snow banks and cold nights into early July. The lake is stocked annually with legal rainbow trout, and there is a naturally reproducing population of brook trout. The lake is only about 20 acres, but lots of fish are caught. The rainbows are typically 8 to 10 inches, and an occasional brook trout reaches 3 pounds. Fly fishing can be excellent, especially in the fall. Its outlet stream, Fish Creek (a tributary of the Blitzen) can also be fished a little ways downstream from the lake.

This is a pleasant family lake, with a shallow edge and floating dock beside the boat ramp. There are a number of nice BLM campsites around the lake. There is a fee to camp. Occasionally a strong, steady wind comes up here, and there is little to break it. Storms in the high Steens (wind, rain, and snow), are legendary and often come up suddenly. If the Fish Lake campground is full or too exposed for comfort, there's camping at Jackman Park (a natural meadow) a mile farther up the Loop Rd., and at Page Springs Campground at the base of the mountain near Frenchglen. The gate above Jackman is the last to open. Road conditions permitting, be sure to continue the extra 4 to 5 miles up the Loop Rd. to the Steens Mt. rim for a spectacular view of the Steens escarpment and the desert below.

Fish Lake is ideal for a rubber raft, float tube, or canoe. Motors are prohibited on the lake. Limited supplies, fuel, and accommodations are available in Frenchglen.

FISH LAKE. (Pine Creek watershed). An 86-acre drive-in brook trout and rainbow lake south of Eagle Cap Wilderness in the Wallowa-Whitman National Forest. From Halfway on Hwy. 86, drive east about 12 miles, then turn onto Forest Rd. 29 N, then Forest Rd. 66, heading west about 19 miles to the lake. The road passes Duck and Twin

lakes. Fish Lake is at elevation 6640 ft. and is usually accessible only from July through September.

The lake has a maximum depth of 50 ft. Trout are plentiful here, but on the small side. Brook trout outnumber rainbows 4 to 1, and you'll be lucky to find many over 12 inches. Rainbow fingerlings are stocked every other year, and brook trout reproduce naturally. There's no limit on the brook trout catch.

There's a guard station at the lake and an excellent campground with dispersed campsites, delicious artesian well water, and a good boat ramp. Several interesting trails begin at the campground, including those heading east into the Hell's Canyon Recreation Area.

FLAGSTAFF LAKE. See **WARNER VALLEY LAKES**.

FORT CREEK. A short tributary of Wood River, south of Fort Klamath, crossed by Hwy. 62 about 2 miles south of town near Fort Klamath Park and Museum. It's a very clear, spring-fed creek, accessible by road for most of its 3 mile length. A dirt road takes off north of Klamath Junction and follows the headwaters of the creek to the east. Fishing is catch and release only, for brown trout in its lower reaches, redband rainbows in the upper stream, and the occasional phantom appearance of one of Upper Klamath's big migratory rainbows.

The lower stream flows through land owned by Fort Creek Resort (for use by guests only).

FOURMILE LAKE. A large lake on the east edge of Winema National Forest, 9 miles west of Klamath Lake. It currently supports brook trout, rainbows, and kokanee. The lake is on the divide between the Rogue and Klamath basins, high in the Cascade range. To reach it, take Forest Rd. 3661 north from Rt. 140 at Lake of the Woods Visitor Center. See Lake Of The Woods for directions.

Fourmile has 740 surface acres and a maximum depth of 170 ft. At 5744 ft. elevation, the winters are long and the growing season short. Nevertheless, kokanee are doing almost too well here, with a large self-sustaining population holding the size range to 6 to 10 inches. Kokanee are taken by trolling with large spinners trailing a small baited hook, and by still fishing with eggs on the bottom. They can also be taken on sinking lines using small wet flies and nymphs.

Naturally reproducing brook trout reach 15 inches here and are present in good numbers. Trolling and flies take these speckled trout. Best time to go for the larger ones is in September and October. Stocked rainbow trout reach 18 inches. Best rainbow fishing is in spring and fall. ODFW is considering introducing lake trout. After introduction, it will take 5 to 10 years for these slow-growers to reach catchable size.

The lake is open all year but doesn't get much play in winter. There is no boat ramp, but you can launch from the beach at the campground. Fourmile gets awfully rough at mid-day, so be careful when boating. There is a Forest Service campground at the southern tip of the lake. Trails leading to nearby small lakes begin near the campground. See Badger, Long, Squaw.

FRANCIS LAKE (Klamath L. watershed). A small trout lake north of Pelican Butte Lookout about 4 miles northwest of Point Comfort on the west shore of Upper Klamath Lake. Access is by bushwhack.

From Rt. 140, follow Forest Rd. 33651 toward Cold Springs Campground, and turn west on Lookout Rd. When you reach the lookout, backtrack about 1½ miles by road, and trek north around the butte at constant elevation. The lake is about 1½ miles from the lookout tower. It is within a draw that runs northeast from the butte. Don't confuse it with fishless Gladys Lake, which is ¼ mile northwest.

Francis has 3½ surface acres and is stocked periodically. The typical catch is 8 to 10 inches. Other little lakes in the area aren't stocked.

GERBER RESERVOIR. A large reservoir in south central Oregon between Lakeview and Klamath Falls with excellent populations of yellow perch and white crappie as well as largemouth bass. A state record white crappie came out of Gerber Reservoir at 4-pounds 12-ounces.

To get there from Klamath Falls, take Rt. 140 east 19 miles to Dairy, then County Rd. 70 southeast about 17 miles to Bonanza and Lorella. Head northeast about 8 miles to the reservoir. From Lakeview, take Rt. 140 west to Bly, and follow forest roads. 3752 and 3814 south 10 miles to the lake.

Gerber has over 3800 surface acres when full, but the water level fluctuates even in normal years. In dry years, the fisheries suffer, but a series of good water years results in natural recovery. At this time, the reservoir has been full for several years. There are tremendous numbers of yellow perch to 14 inches and beautiful white crappie in the 14-inch range. Largemouth bass and brown bullheads are also present. Gerber used to be stocked with trout, which grew to good size, but there are no plans to resume that program. Gerber has been popular for ice fishing.

The BLM provides 2 campgrounds with boat ramps, one at the dam and another about 2 miles north. There is a third more primitive boat launch on the Barnes Valley arm at the south end of the reservoir.

GOOSE LAKE. A very large lake that straddles the Oregon-California border about 8 miles south of Lakeview. When full, it covers about 46 square miles. In 1992 it went completely dry, and its population of wild redband trout took refuge where they could in its tributaries. The lake is currently well filled, and fish from the system are repopulating the lake.

HAINES POND. A one-acre pond ¼ mile north of Haines. It supports largemouth bass and is stocked with legal rainbows.

HARRIETTE LAKE. The largest lake in the Mountain Lakes Wilderness of southeast Winema National Forest. It's in a very scenic area, surrounded by tall peaks, with small lakes and potholes close by. From Rt. 140, about 7 miles east of Lake of the Woods, take the Varney Creek Rd. (Forest Rd. 3610) south about 1½ miles. Turn left onto Forest Rd. 3637 and right on Forest Rd. 3664. Varney Creek Trailhead 3718 is at the end of the road. Follow Trail 3718 about 4 miles, then take the left fork, Trail 3127, which reaches Harriette Lake in about 1½ miles.

The lake is at 6750 ft., 63 ft. deep with 70 surface acres. It is heavily visited and heavily fished. Good numbers of brook trout and rainbows are caught, with the average size about 10 inches. A few larger fish to 15 inches show up from time to time. Any method can be effective, with bait-fishing along the west shore most popular. Best angling occurs in spring and fall. Other fishable lakes in the area include Echo, Como, and South Pass.

HART LAKE (Lake Co.). A huge lake in Warner Valley north and downstream from Crump Lake, best known for its crappie fishery. The rugged face of Hart Mt. rises 3000 feet above the lake to the east. Hart Lake is due east of the tiny town of Plush on Rt. 140, 18 miles north of Adel. Adel is 31 miles east of Lakeview. Dirt roads lead north and east from Plush over a dike along the north edge of the lake. A jeep road runs along the east shore and eventually leads back to Rt. 140. The southwest shore is reached by a jeep road that first follows the north shore of Crump Lake. This road leaves the Plush Rd. about 9 miles north of Adel.

Hart Lake covers 10,000 acres in wet years, but can go dry. See Warner Valley Lakes for additional information.

Hart is primarily fished for bullhead catfish and crappie. Fishing for white crappie is popular off the southeast shore, with peak activity in July. In some years, this lake has been known to really turn out crappie, with thousands taken on jigs in a few days. In good years, crappie can run to 14 inches, though the current average is 9 to 10 inches. The lake is due for another crappie bonanza if the wet streak continues.

Bullhead catfish are numerous and of good size. Average weight is one pound, but some tip the scale at 2 to 3 pounds. A favorite bullhead area in the spring is the narrows near the inlet from Crump Lake.

There's not much in the way of trout fishing here, although a few large wild redband rainbows are caught. Largemouth bass have been stocked but aren't thriving. The Warner Sucker, a fish unique to the Warner Valley, is a Federally protected species.

This is remote country, so check your rig, gas, and supplies before you head out.

HEART LAKE (Eagle Creek watershed). A small trout lake in the southern Eagle Cap Wilderness. From Catherine Creek State Park on Hwy. 203 (between LaGrande and Baker), continue south on Hwy. 203, then turn left (east) on Forest Rd. 77 (Eagle Creek Rd.). Keep a copy of the forest map open for reference as you negotiate this road. There are many spurs that could mislead you. Follow signs toward Tamarack Campground, which is on Forest Rd. 7755. Eagle Creek Trail 1922 is at the end of Forest Rd. 7755.

Follow the Eagle Creek Trail about 2½ miles. Trail 1937 to Heart Lake is on the left.

This trail is steep, climbing over 1500 feet in just 1½ miles.

Heart Lake is at the head of Bench Canyon south of the main trail at 7300 ft. It has 3 surface acres and supports rainbow trout to 15 inches, although the average size is about 9 inches. It provides good bait and fly fishing in August and September.

HEART LAKE (Fishhole Lake Basin). A 25-acre rainbow and kokanee lake in a little lake basin in Fremont National Forest about 28 miles west of Lakeview. Follow Rt. 140 to Quartz Mt. Pass, and turn south on Forest Rd. 3715. Heart Lake is about 9 miles from the junction. A primitive road on the right circles through the basin that also includes Spatterdock Lake and Tule Pond. Heart is the southernmost lake on the circle.

Heart is currently full of tui chub, and the quality of fishing here has suffered. Kokanee average 7 to 9 inches and there are some rainbows to 18 inches. Bait is best in early season, with flies effective in summer and fall. The nearest campground is at Lofton Reservoir across the road from the Heart Springs turn-off.

HEAVENLY TWIN LAKES. Two good trout lakes in the Sky Lakes Area near the border between Rogue and Winema national forests. A popular route into the area begins at Cold Springs Campground on Forest Rd. 3651. To reach the campground from Klamath Falls, follow Rt. 140 north along the lake. Rt. 140 makes a sharp turn west toward Lake of the Woods (just before Pelican Guard Station). About 3½ miles farther, turn right onto Forest Rd. 3651. Cold Springs is at the end of the road (about 9 miles from the highway).

Follow Trail 3709 into the lake basin. The trail crosses a small ridge between the two lakes. Trails are usually accessible in late June, with good fishing then and in late summer and fall.

The larger of the two lakes covers about 25 acres and is fairly shallow, a good fly fishing lake. Heavily fished, it is an excellent producer of rainbow and brook trout averaging 10 inches, but fish over 5 pounds have been taken. A rubber boat or float tube would allow you to troll lures for the big ones. The smaller lake covers about 7 acres and is deeper, providing mostly brook trout to 12 inches with occasional larger fish. There are good campsites

around the lakes near the trail and at Isherwood Lake east of Big Twin. Camp well back from fragile lakeside vegetation, and use no-trace camping methods.

HIDDEN LAKE (Powder River watershed). A brook trout lake high in the Eagle Cap Wilderness. The outlet from the lake flows into the East Fork of Eagle Creek. The lake is about 1½ miles northeast of Eagle Lake on the opposite side of a ridge. Best approach is from the south by East Fork Trail 1910.

From Catherine Creek State Park on Hwy. 203 (between LaGrande and Baker) continue south on Hwy. 203, then turn left (east) on Forest Rd. 77 (Eagle Creek Rd.). Keep a copy of the forest map open for reference as you negotiate this road. There are many spurs that could mislead you. About 6 miles beyond Tamarack Campground, turn left (north) onto Forest Rd. 7745 (East Eagle Rd.). Trailhead 1910 is at road's end. About 5½ miles in, follow Trail 1915 to the left. It reaches Moon Lake, then Hidden Lake in about a mile.

Hidden Lake has lots of brook trout and produces well. Best fishing is August through September.

HIGGINS RESERVOIR. A 100-acre impoundment on Camp Creek northeast of Unity. An unimproved road less than one mile east of town heads north off Hwy. 26 toward the reservoir, a 5-mile drive.

Higgins has been stocked with rainbow trout that commonly reach 14 to 15 inches, with 20-inch fish available. Trolling and bait fishing with eggs or worms are most productive. The reservoir is open from late April through October. The access road and most land around the reservoir is privately owned. To preserve public access, be fastidious about packing out your trash and respect private property. Nearest camping facilities are at Unity Reservoir on Hwy. 7.

HIGH LAKE. A 10-acre brook trout lake, highest lake in the Strawberry Mt. Wilderness of Malheur National Forest. It is the source of Lake Creek, nestled in a pretty alpine cirque just above timberline. Spring fed and not too deep, it's a good fly fishing lake, especially in fall. Brook trout reproduce naturally here, with a big catch about 10 inches.

The shortest route to the lake is from the south. At Seneca (on Hwy. 395 north of

Burns) turn east onto Forest Rd. 16, and drive east about 13 miles to the intersection of Forest Rd. 1640. Drive north on 1640 to the end of the road. Trail 385 leads to the lake in about 1½ miles, losing about 600 ft. of elevation in the process. From John Day, follow Hwy. 395 south to the Canyon Creek Rd. (County Rd. 65, Forest Rd. 15). Turn left onto Forest Rd. 16 beyond Parish Cabin Campground, and left again onto Forest Rd. 1640 in about 2 miles.

Alternately, you may hike in from the north by way of Strawberry and Slide Lake. Trail 385 leads from Slide Lake to High Lake, following a scenic route near timberline. Access in early spring may be impossible due to snowbound roads.

HIGHWAY 203 POND. A 10-acre pond north of Baker at the junction of Hwy. 203 and I-84. It is stocked with legal rainbows and supports largemouth bass and bluegills. Crappie may also be present.

HOLBROOK RESERVOIR. A productive 40-acre reservoir on Fishhole Creek 2 miles downstream from Lofton Reservoir. Holbrook is south of Rt. 140 at Quartz Mt. Pass, about 28 miles west of Lakeview. The reservoir is managed for public fishing through a cooperative agreement between a private landowner, ODFW, and the US Forest Service.

Despite efforts to eradicate the tui chubs here, they are thriving, and the trout fishery is suffering. The largest rainbows fatten nicely on the chubs, but there are fewer trout over-all. The reservoir is stocked annually with legal trout and a few of trophy size.

There is a boat ramp, and good catches are made from boat and bank. Most of the land surrounding the reservoir is privately owned. Camping on the private property is prohibited.

HOME CREEK. A short wild redband trout stream, originating on Steens Mountain and flowing 9 miles east into the Catlow Valley. The creek crosses Hwy. 205 about 21 mile south of Frenchglen near Home Creek Ranch (about 7 miles south of the change from pavement to gravel). It flows mostly through BLM land, but the stretch near the highway flows through private property. BLM land touches the highway a tenth of a mile north of the crossing (mid-way through the kinked section). Dirt roads cross the upper creek in at least two places. You'd better have a BLM map in hand to find your way in the headwaters.

Home Creek is best fished in spring and early summer. Redbands to 14 inches are present. Though not required by law at this time, catch and release is recommended to protect this fragile trout population.

HONEY CREEK. A good trout stream which heads on Abert Rim in Fremont National Forest. Its headwaters can be reached from Forest Rd. 3615 or Forest Rd. 3720 before the creek flows into a canyon then through private ranchland (which is closed to public access due to past vandalism). The lowest waters enter a small canyon that begins on the ranch and through which the creek flows toward Plush. Plush is in Warner Valley on Rt. 140 east of Lakeview.

Best fishing on Honey is in the lower stretch, for wild redband and brook trout. However, we have been advised that lower Honey Creek Canyon is particularly rattlesnake infested. (It's so bad that most people never go back twice, even though the fishing is tremendous Our source assures us that this isn't a rumor propagated by the local folks to keep outsiders away from a good thing!)

ISHERWOOD LAKE. A very good 18-acre hike-in lake in the Sky Lakes group of Sky Lakes Wilderness, Winema National Forest. It's a 3½ mile hike north by trail 3710 from Cold Springs Campground. See Heavenly Twin for directions. Near the north end of the largest Heavenly Twin, the Isherwood Trail branches west. Isherwood is on the west side of the trail.

The lake supports brook trout and rainbows 12 to 14 inches. All methods may be used successfully, but fly fishing early and late in the day is especially productive. Campsites are currently limited due to efforts to rehabilitate the lakeshore following years of heavy use. Camp well back from fragile lakeside vegetation, and use no-trace camping methods.

ISLAND LAKE (Island Lake watershed). The largest lake in the Island Lake group of Sky Lakes Wilderness, Winema National Forest. From Lake of the Woods on Rt. 140, drive about 5 miles east, then turn north on Forest Rd. 3561 to the Big Meadows

A generous landowner welcomes the public to fish, but not camp, at HIGGINS RESERVOIR. *Photograph by Dennis Frates.*

spur road (Forest Rd. 3659). This leads west a bit over one mile to a hairpin turn. Trailhead 3712 is at the apex of the turn. Follow Trail 3712 west about 3½ miles to Island Lake. The lake can also be reached by longer trails from Fourmile Lake and the Blue Lake area on the Rogue side.

At elevation 5906 ft., Island has 40 surface acres but is only 17 feet deep at its deepest point near the northern end. Fishing from shore is easy and, more often than not, excellent.

The lake is stocked with brook trout and has natural reproduction. The average catch is 11 inches, with some fish to 18 inches. Fly fishing is the preferred method here, but bait and trolling will also produce. Try tossing a fly into the shoal areas of the island around evening. Campsites are limited due to lakeshore rehabilitation efforts. Camp well back from fragile lakeside vegetation, and use no-trace camping methods.

JENNY CREEK. A good trout stream flowing south of Howard Prairie between the Rogue and Klamath drainages, 16 miles east of Ashland. Rainbows 8 to 10 inches make themselves at home throughout the

creek, and brook trout are present in the lower stream.

The creek flows south, crossed by Hwy. 66 at Pinehurst, and skirts the eastern border of the Siskiyou Mountains, finally reaching Iron Gate Reservoir on the Klamath River about 3 miles south of the California line. A fair stretch of the upper river is followed by the Jenny Creek Rd. south from the southern tip of Howard Prairie Reservoir. Moon Prairie Rd. follows the creek from about one mile to the east from the end of Jenny Creek Rd. to Hwy. 66.

Jenny Creek continues to benefit from large scale habitat enhancement programs. It provides good angling in early spring and again in the fall. There are no improved campgrounds along the creek, but Tub Springs Wayside, about 4 miles west of the crossing on Hwy. 66, has a nice picnic area.

JONES LAKE. See WARNER VALLEY LAKES.

JUNIPER LAKE. A Lahontan cutthroat lake on the east side of Steens Mt. It is about 12 miles north of Mann Lake. See Mann Lake for directions. Juniper is ⅔ the size of Mann, muddier, and considerably less popular as an angling destination. Like Mann, it is stocked bi-annually with hatchery-bred Lahontans. Due to its persistent turbidity and smaller aquatic insect population, it is less popular with fly anglers than Mann. Juniper grows fish of respectable size, and bait anglers do well. There are no facilities at the lake.

KILLAMACUE LAKE. A small high lake in the Elkhorn Range of southern Wallowa-Whitman National Forest west of Haines. The lake is 45 ft. deep with brook trout and small mackinaw. To reach it from Haines, take Hwy. 411 west to Rock Creek, continuing west past Rock Creek Power Station into the forest. The road becomes an unimproved track (Forest Rd. 5520) and follows the North Fork Rock Creek. About 2 miles from the paved road, Trail 1617 leads northwest to Killamacue.

KLAMATH LAKE. See **UPPER KLAMATH LAKE.**

KLAMATH RIVER

In Oregon, a very productive trout stream, flowing only 38 miles within the state before crossing the border into California. Steelhead and salmon runs into Oregon were eliminated by California's Copco Dam in 1917. Within California the Klamath flows an additional 200 miles, entering the Pacific Ocean at the community of Klamath.

The Klamath River is the outlet of enormous Upper Klamath Lake, but flows freely only 18 miles within Oregon borders. The other 20 miles are captured by dams. That the river continues to produce good numbers of large, powerful rainbows is a testament to the vitality of the Klamath—and to its lost potential.

The Klamath River once began at Upper Klamath Lake. A dam at Keno, 17 miles downstream, created Lake Ewauna, a pool that backs up to within a mile of Klamath Lake. The most productive stretch of Oregon's Klamath today is the flow between Keno Dam and J.C. Boyle Reservoir, only

6 miles. Highway 66 parallels this stretch on the south. Park on the highway shoulder and hike down at any point that looks accessible. A number of trails drop into the canyon. This is private timber land, but the public has unrestricted access to the river. The river pours through a relatively steep canyon and features a series of runs and deep holes with intermittent shallow riffles over a bedrock base. You can also enter the canyon at Keno Dam. This stretch is not boatable.

The average fish here is 14 inches, with many to 20 inches, weighing 2 to 4 pounds.

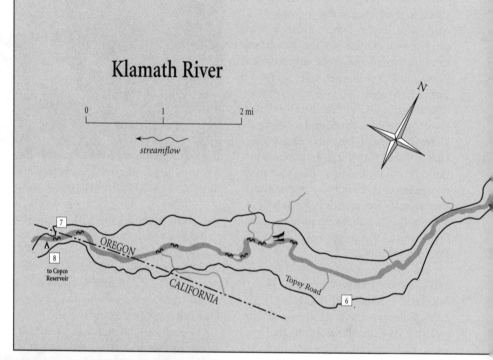

This is heavy water. Fly anglers use big weighted nymphs on sinking or sink tip lines. Spin casters favor Rooster Tails, and bait casters use a heavily weighted worm rig. Check in at the Keno store for additional information and directions.

There is a special closure on this reach from mid-June until the beginning of October, related to the effects of rising water temperature on the trout. As the water climbs toward 70 degrees and the river fills with algae, the fish acquire an unpalatable taste. Trout also lose much of their strength when the water warms and would suffer high mortality if catch and release were practiced.

At J.C. Boyle, Hwy. 66 crosses the reservoir and the river bends southward. The Klamath River Rd. closely follows its west bank to Boyle Powerhouse. In this 5-mile

Steep trails drop down into the KLAMATH canyon, providing access to the river's larger rainbow trout. Photograph by Jeffrey Kee.

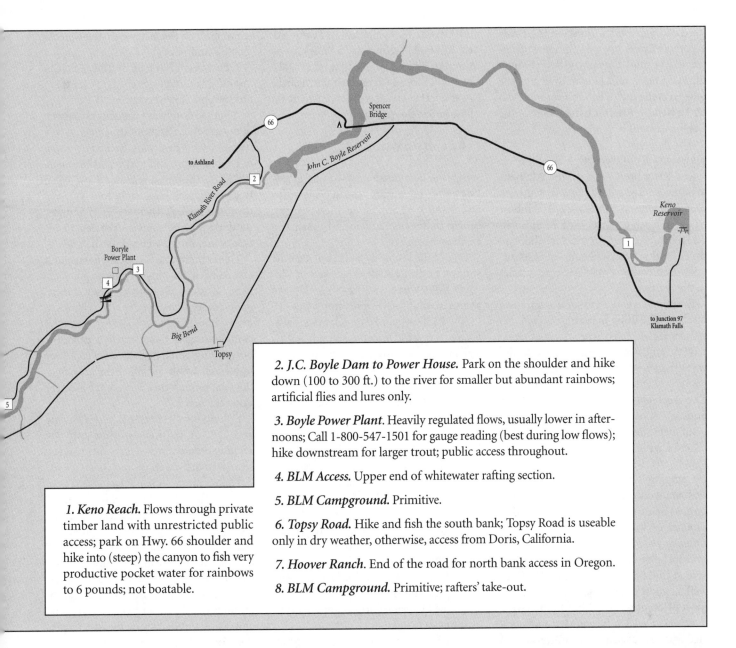

2. *J.C. Boyle Dam to Power House.* Park on the shoulder and hike down (100 to 300 ft.) to the river for smaller but abundant rainbows; artificial flies and lures only.

3. *Boyle Power Plant.* Heavily regulated flows, usually lower in afternoons; Call 1-800-547-1501 for gauge reading (best during low flows); hike downstream for larger trout; public access throughout.

4. *BLM Access.* Upper end of whitewater rafting section.

5. *BLM Campground.* Primitive.

6. *Topsy Road.* Hike and fish the south bank; Topsy Road is useable only in dry weather, otherwise, access from Doris, California.

7. *Hoover Ranch.* End of the road for north bank access in Oregon.

8. *BLM Campground.* Primitive; rafters' take-out.

1. *Keno Reach.* Flows through private timber land with unrestricted public access; park on Hwy. 66 shoulder and hike into (steep) the canyon to fish very productive pocket water for rainbows to 6 pounds; not boatable.

stretch, from J.C. Boyle to Boyle Power House, the river is cool and stable, though its flow is much reduced by diversion into a sluice that carries water to the generating station. The river runs its clearest here, and trout are abundant. Resident trout in this reach are only 8 to 12 inches, but larger fish move through. The flow is augmented by spring outflows from the reservoirs. The riverbed is much the same as in the Keno stretch. Best fishing is from the end of May until mid-June. From J.C. Boyle Reservoir to the Oregon border, angling is restricted to catch and release with barbless flies and lures throughout the year.

Below the powerhouse the river regains its size, and so do the fish, averaging 12 to 15 inches. In 1994, the 11-mile reach from J.C. Boyle Dam to the Oregon border won

federal designation as a wild and scenic river. A portion of this reach is locally known as the Frain Ranch, named for Martin Frain who settled the valley in the late 1800's. The few remaining buildings and the original Frain orchard have been named an Oregon Historical landmark.

Fishing in this section is characterized by very unstable water conditions resulting from Boyle Power Plant. The water usually drops in late evening and rises at 7 or 8 a.m. Once the river rises and stabilizes, good fishing generally resumes. The fish here are larger than those in the Boyle section, but smaller than the Keno trout. Peak fishing in this stretch is from the end of May until mid-June. In early spring and summer stonefly nymphs are generally most effective. Try Polly Rosborough's

Golden Stone and Dark Stone Bucktail or the yellow Bucktail Caddis. In high water years, this section of the river is considerably more difficult to fish. Faster flows, submerged riparian vegetation, and dispersal of the trout population throughout a larger area contribute to the challenge. River gauge readings at Boyle and Keno are available. See Appendix.

The east bank of the Frain reach is accessed by the Topsy road, which heads south from Hwy. 66 east of Spencer Bridge. The road is passable only in dry weather. At other times of the year, the east bank can only be accessed by a road leading in from Copco Reservoir in California.

Public facilities on the Klamath in Oregon are very limited. Rafts can be launched below Boyle Power Plant. The only developed campground is Topsy on J.C. Boyle Reservoir. There are two additional primitive BLM camps. One is mid-way through the Frain reach off Klamath River Rd. The other is at the end of the popular whitewater stretch on the east bank just over the California border.

KRUMBO RESERVOIR. A reservoir on lower Krumbo Creek in the Malheur Wildlife Refuge with a good largemouth bass population and stocked rainbow trout. To reach it, drive south from Burns on Hwy. 205 toward Frenchglen. About 20 miles south of the Malheur Refuge Headquarters turn-off, a road leads east 4 miles to the reservoir.

Krumbo has about 150 surface acres and offers good fishing in spring and fall. No motors are allowed on the lake, but there is a boat ramp (recently improved) and a wheelchair accessible fishing pier. Look for bass around the rushes near the boat ramp. The creek above the reservoir has a fair population of wild rainbows and larger trout that move up from the reservoir. For other fisheries in the vicinity, see Donner Und Blitzen River and Fish Lake.

Camping is prohibited at the reservoir, and you wouldn't want to anyway. Mosquitoes here are fierce (bring a head net). The nearest campground is Page Springs, a pleasant BLM facility on the Blitzen east of Frenchglen. Accommodations are available at the historic Frenchglen Hotel, as well as good family style meals and the most pleasant screened front porch for a hundred miles. The Steens Mt. Inn, associated with Frenchglen Mercantile, also rents a couple of comfortable rooms and serves lunch and dinner. Don't neglect a visit to the handsome Refuge Headquarters.

LAKE CREEK. A fair wild trout stream flowing south out of Strawberry Mt. Wilderness into the Middle Fork Malheur. The creek begins as the outlet of High Lake, 7400 ft. above sea level. It supports redband and brook trout to 11 inches, averaging 9 to 10 inches. Bull trout are also present and must be released unharmed. Bait is prohibited to protect the bulls. There's no limit on the brook trout catch.

At Seneca (on Hwy. 395 north of Burns) turn east onto Forest Rd. 16, which crosses Lake Creek at the intersection of Forest Rd. 924. Watch for a sign to Lake Creek Orga-

nization Camp. At the end of Forest Rd. 924, Trail 378 follows Lake Creek to its source at High Lake, about 4 miles. Lake Creek and McCoy Creek enter the Malheur River together about 2 miles downstream of the Forest Rd. 16 crossing.

LAKE OF THE WOODS

A big lake in an attractive woodland setting, offering a four-season fishery for abundant kokanee, huge brown trout, brown bullheads, largemouth bass, and rainbow trout.

Lake of the Woods is on Rt. 140 near the summit of the Cascade range west of Klamath Lake. Direct routes access the lake from east, south, and west. From Medford, follow Rt. 140 east. From Klamath Falls, follow 140 west. From Ashland, follow signs to the airport, then turn north beyond the runway onto Dead Indian Memorial Rd., which becomes Forest Rd. 363 after entering the Rogue River National Forest. Lake of the Woods is about 35 miles from both Ashland and Klamath Falls, about 45 miles from Medford. It has 1146 surface acres and is 3½ miles long, encircled by roads and a large number of year-round and vacation homes.

Kokanee are abundant and of good size (to 12 inches), offering the best fishery on the lake. Look for concentrations of kokanee in the deep trough along the steep-banked western edge of the lake opposite Sunset Campground. Best fishing is in spring. Most kokanee are caught at a depth of about 30 ft.

Large brown trout to 6 pounds may occasionally snatch your kokanee jig, but these big predators are most likely to be prowling towards evening. (Keep an eye on the regulations for a possible easing of restrictions against fishing after dark here.) Look for browns around structure close to shore.

There's not much natural reproduction of trout, but large numbers of legal-size rainbows are stocked from June through August, with average catches 9 to 14 inches. Hatchery brood stock and rainbows grown to trophy size (2 pounds) further supplement the fishery.

Brown bullheads are abundant and average 8 to 13 inches. They make up over ½ the population in the lake, and anglers are urged to catch and keep as many as possible. There is no limit on bullhead. The best bullhead habitat is at the north and

south ends of the lake where the water is shallow and weedy.

Yellow perch (illegally introduced) are a good focus for youngsters. Look for them around shoreline vegetation.

A limited number of largemouth bass are also available. Catches range from 2 to 5 pounds. The best bass habitat is along northwest shore and in the northeast corner near submerged vegetation and fallen trees. The largest bass can be found among the rushes (sedge). There are also bass under the docks—at the resort and adjacent to private homes on the west side of the lake.

This is pretty cold water for bass, and it takes them a long time to grow to good size here. Consider releasing bass over 12 inches. In addition to giving you the chance to catch that lunker another day, you'll be contributing to the effort to control the burgeoning perch population. Perch prey upon bass smolts, limiting the growth of the bass population, but adult bass prey upon the perch.

Fishing for all species is best in spring and fall, or in the morning and late evening before water-skiers and jet-skiers churn up the water.

There's plenty of bank fishing available. Though there are many year-round and vacation homes around the lake, the entire lakeshore perimeter is open to public access for fishing. Good catches are made all around the lake, including bank areas adjacent to the campgrounds and resort.

There are large Forest Service campgrounds with boat ramps at the north end and near Rainbow Bay on the east. Lake of the Woods Resort at the north end of the lake is open year-round and offers recently renovated cabins, RV hook-ups, a full-service restaurant and bar, boat rentals, and supplies.

Ice fishing is popular here in January and February, and the road is ploughed. Check with ODFW in Klamath Falls or with the resort for an ice pack update.

LITTLE MALHEUR RIVER. A good trout stream, tributary to the North Fork of the Malheur River, with populations of redband and bull trout. Best access is from Hwy. 26 east of Unity. Follow Forest Rd. 16 southwest. Or Forest Rd. 13 from Prairie City. The lower end of the stream flows through private land, but the upper reach (upstream from the Forest Rd. 16 crossing) is within National Forest. Trail 366, which heads at Elk Flat, follows Elk Creek down to the Little Malheur's headwaters.

The Little Malheur joins the North Fork about 5 miles northwest of Beulah Reservoir north of Juntura. It runs generally north-south, draining the south slope of the Blue Mts. Much of the creek is shown on the Malheur National Forest map, flowing near the east edge of the forest, though its headwaters and some tributaries are in Wallowa-Whitman. It offers fair fishing for wild redbands to 11 inches, averaging 6 to 8 inches. Bull trout must be released unharmed, and bait fishing is prohibited to protect the bull trout.

LOFTON RESERVOIR. A 40-acre impoundment in a pine forest on upper Fishhole Creek, with lots of stocked rainbows. It is 30 miles west of Lakeview and about 5 miles northwest of Drews Reservoir. Take Rt. 140 west from Lakeview to Quartz Mt. Turn left (south) onto Forest Rd. 3715, which reaches the Lofton access road in about 5 miles.

Lofton is treated periodically for tui chubs, but is currently offering good fishing for (lots of) stocked fingerling, legal, and trophy-size trout. The average catch is 8 to 12 inches, but the trophies run to 2 pounds.

Lofton Dam maintains a reasonable water level throughout the year, and the reservoir is easily fished from shore. Nevertheless, a rowboat, raft, or float tube can be useful. Only electric motors are allowed on the lake.

Most anglers use bait, but flies and lures can be equally productive. In late summer flies have the edge, as weed growth makes bait-fishing difficult.

There is a US Forest Service campground at the reservoir. Several other small lakes in this area that show up on the Freemont National Forest map might be worth investigating (Spatterdock, Pete's Puddle, Heart). Nearby Holbrook Reservoir is a proven winner. Lofton is recommended for youngsters.

LOOKINGGLASS LAKE. A nice glacial cirque lake within the southern border of Eagle Cap Wilderness, Wallowa-Whitman National Forest. This is one of the easier lakes to hike to in this physically challenging wilderness. It is reached by a spur off the Eagle Lake Trail 1922.

From Catherine Creek State Park on Hwy. 203 (between LaGrande and Baker) continue south on Hwy. 203, then turn left (east) on Forest Rd. 77 (Eagle Creek Rd.). Keep a copy of the forest map open for reference as you negotiate this road. There are many spurs that could mislead you. Follow signs toward Two Color Campground, which is on Forest Rd. 7755. Eagle Creek Trail 1922 is at the end of Forest Rd. 7755. Follow Trail 1922 four easy miles, then cut back south on Trail 1921, climbing 1300 feet in 2.2 miles to the lake.

Lookingglass is 31 acres and 45 ft. deep at elevation 7500 ft. In addition to good numbers of brook trout, it may have carryover mackinaw from a stocking in the early 1970s. Bait or flies will take trout easily, while lures fished deep work best for the mackinaw. Best months are August and September. Remember to pick up a US Forest Service parking pass, required for parking at any Eagle Cap Wilderness trailhead.

LOST LAKE. A small high lake in the Elkhorn Range west of Haines. It supports naturally reproducing brook trout. See Red Mt. Lake for directions to North Fork North Powder River Rd. At road's end, follow Trail 1632 west less than a mile, then turn left (north) onto Trail 1621, which leads first to Meadow Lake then to Lost in about 1½ miles.

LOST RIVER. A sluggish stream with fishing for bass and panfish east of Klamath Falls. The river originates in California. Outlet of one of California's Clear Lakes, it flows northwest in an arc through the Langell Valley, Bonanza, Olene, and Merrill, re-entering California as an inlet to Tule Lake. In the upper stretch from California to Bonanza the stream is split and channeled extensively for irrigation. Rt. 140 parallels the river for a short way at Olene, and county roads follow it for most of the distance from Bonanza downstream. Klamath County has provided a public parking area and bank fishing access. There is public access for boat and bank anglers south of Olene on Crystal Springs Rd.

Lost River offers fishing for a variety of warmwater species, including bass 2 to 7 pounds, brown bullhead, crappie, and pumpkinseed sunfish. Both Sacramento and yellow perch are abundant. A few trout show in the catch but are not common.

Spring is probably the best time to fish, but good catches are made year-round. There are no campsites along the stream.

LUCKY RESERVOIR. A 6-acre desert reservoir, very lightly fished, that can grow big trout in wet years. It is on BLM land southwest of Adel. Take Rt. 140 west from Adel 3 miles, then turn south, fording Deep Creek and following the powerline road 4½ miles to the reservoir. You'll go through four gates. Abide by range rules: leave gates as you find them. Deep Creek isn't fordable until the spring runoff has dropped, usually in June.

Lucky is stocked with rainbows, which can reach 20 inches in good years, though 16 to 18 inches is more common. The water is quite turbid throughout the summer, and fishing is usually very slow. Bait is the most popular method, although fly anglers take fish at times. The reservoir holds up well during droughts.

Large brown trout to 6 pounds may snatch your kokanee jig at LAKE OF THE WOODS. Photograph by Richard T. Grost.

Malheur Reservoir. A large popular irrigation reservoir, privately owned but on public land and open to public use. It is capable of growing good size trout. Malheur is north of Hwy. 26 between Ontario and John Day, approached by 15 miles of dirt road north from Ironside or Brogan, both on Hwy. 26. The reservoir covers up to 2000 acres when full.

Malheur is stocked with hatchery rainbows. During drought, it can go dry, but during wet cycles, fish of all class sizes are available, including some exceeding 20 inches.

The reservoir is open year-round, but fishing is best in spring and fall. Keep in mind that spring in this part of the country can be as early as February, or as late of July. Ideal water temperature is probably the better determinant of good fishing. From 50 to 60 degrees seems to produce the liveliest fishing. The fishery slows when the reservoir warms above 60 degrees (usually from late June through the end of August).

There is one boat ramp on the north shore, with bank fishing possible nearby. You can also launch at other places along the road.

Camping is limited to a few spots near the ramp. Don't expect amenities like trees. This here is sagebrush country. Respect "No Trespassing" signs, clean up after yourself, and be cautious during fire season. Abuse of the reservoir by visiting anglers could lead to its closure.

MALHEUR RIVER

Featuring abundant large trout in a 54-mile flow from the confluence of South and Middle forks to Gold Creek (21 river miles below Juntura). Hatchery rainbows predominate at the upstream end of the mainstem Malheur, with some wild redband rainbows. The average catch is 10 to 14 inches, but lots of fish are 15 to 20 inches by late summer and some reach 25 inches and 6 pounds. Most of these large fish are escapees from Warmsprings and Beulah reservoirs.

From Juntura to Namorf Dam the river supports increasingly more non-game fish than trout—and the 70-mile flow to the Snake River (heavily drawn upon for irrigation) offers little more than catfish opportunities near Vale & Ontario.

The Malheur is artificially controlled by two irrigation dams. Water is captured in Beulah and Warmsprings reservoirs throughout the winter and released into the Malheur channel beginning in late March. There is a reliable flow by mid-April. The flow is maintained throughout the summer then is gradually decreased from September 1 through the end of October. The river is very low thereafter and freezes over in late November.

The Malheur is at its best from mid-April (after snowmelt and high flows) till late June. Good catches continue to be made throughout the summer, but bright sun and very little shade on the water limit active feeding to the deeper holes and to morning and evening. After the river is "turned off" in October, the flow drops from irrigation season highs of up to 5000 cfs to as little as 5 cfs. The river is transformed into a string of pools connected by a small creek. Trout congregate in the larger pools. Anglers who choose to fish at this time of year move from pool to pool using stealth and pond fishing techniques. It's possible to harvest quite a few trout for the freezer during this post-season period, though only one trout over 20 inches may be kept per day.

Don't be discouraged by the river's year-round turbidity. The trout still seem capable of seeing tempting morsels on hook sizes 18-20, though they're a little nearsighted. For best results, take the time to spot fish first, then cast.

Scuds, leeches, damselfly nymphs, crayfish, and minnows provide a staple diet for Malheur trout throughout the year. *Callibaetis* mayflies are available in late spring and early summer. Grasshoppers and

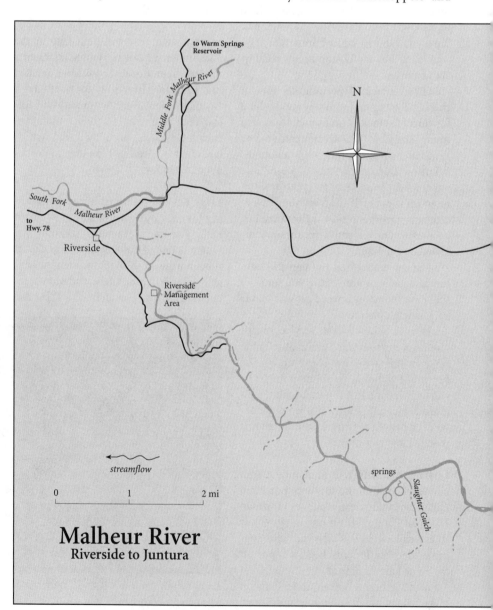

to Warm Springs Reservoir

Middle Fork Malheur River

N

South Fork Malheur River

to Hwy. 78

Riverside

Riverside Management Area

streamflow

0   1   2 mi

springs

Slaughter Gulch

Malheur River
Riverside to Juntura

grasshopper imitations bounced off shore-line vegetation can get excellent results mid- to late summer.

From just above Allen Diversion Dam (4 miles upstream of Juntura) to an abandoned railroad whistle-stop called Riverside (near the South Fork confluence with the Middle Fork), the river flows through a publicly owned roadless area. It can be accessed by foot from Riverside Wildlife Management Area. To reach the Management Area from Juntura (on Hwy. 20), follow the Juntura-Riverside Rd. about 18 miles, continuing beyond the turn-off for Warm Springs Reservoir and crossing the Malheur downstream of the South Fork confluence. About a mile beyond the crossing, turn left onto an unsigned dirt track, and follow it over an abandoned railroad grade and across the sagebrush about a mile to Riverside Management Area. A sign lets you know you've arrived. Park at the lower end of the Management Area, and hike downstream. ODFW owns much of the land along the river through this stretch, and an old railroad grade (tracks and ties removed) offers convenient access almost all the way to Juntura. The Management Area property includes the original

An old railroad grade follows the MALHEUR RIVER through its canyon between Riverside and Juntura. Photograph courtesy of ODFW.

ranch buildings and alfalfa fields, now irrigated to feed deer. Take a moment to water young trees planted along the river. Warning: this trail includes several old timber railroad bridges of questionable stability. They will grow increasingly dangerous with the passing years. Cross carefully. This trail is closed to vehicles, but good sense should lead to the same conclusion. A dispute over

public access to the old railroad grade has been simmering recently, so check with the ODFW office in Hines for an update before setting out to hike the trail.

The river in this section is narrow and flows between rock walls that reflect the sun and can increase air temperature by as much as 20 degrees. Be prepared for 112-degree days here at the height of summer.

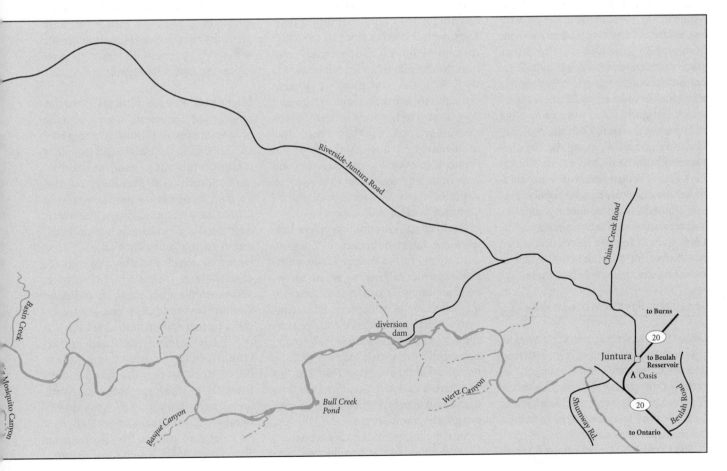

This stretch of the Malheur is boatable from about April 15 to the first of October. Most boaters do the float in a day, taking out at Allen Diversion Dam or at Twin Bridges, downstream about 4 miles from Juntura. Both take-outs are undeveloped spots where the river bank is flat and the road runs close to the stream. This is not a river to float for whitewater thrills—nothing wilder than a few weak Class II rapids. Launch at Riverside Management Area or at the bridge across the South Fork confluence on Riverside-Juntura Rd. Drift boats, personal boats, rubber rafts, and canoes are appropriate for this river. Big rafts can feel a little crowded by rock walls in some places. Be prepared to drag your boat across rocks by mid-summer.

From Juntura to Gold Creek, Hwy. 20 runs along the river. Park in turn-outs along the highway and fish along the road. There are some large fish in this section, though the ratio of trout to carp, dace, and suckers increases below the North Fork confluence. Below Namorf dam, the river is badly polluted by irrigation run-off. Don't eat fish caught in this section.

The only campground on the mainstem Malheur is a small BLM holding at Riverside below the concrete bridge across the Malheur. The site is an old gravel pit without shade or drinking water. Riverside Management Area near the South Fork confluence is open for day use only. There are natural campsites on ODFW property along the old railroad grade trail. Keep an eye out for rattlesnakes when camping or hiking along this trail. There are additional natural campsites along the river between Juntura and Gold Creek. Chukar Park on the Beulah Reservoir Road north of Juntura is another camping option. Fuel and limited accommodations, supplies, and services are available in Juntura. The Oasis Cafe in Juntura serves up the best hamburger for a hundred miles and its owner is a knowledgeable fisherman.

MALHEUR RIVER, MIDDLE FORK

One of Oregon's most productive rivers for wild redband trout and smallmouth bass, and one of the state's best kept angling secrets. It flows primarily through a mix of BLM range and private ranchland, joined by the South Fork near Riverside to form the mainstem Malheur.

The Upper Middle Fork flows 60 miles from headwater tributaries in Logan Valley to its impoundment as Warm Springs Reservoir. Included within this stretch are both a warmwater ranchland reach near the reservoir and a 10-mile scenic segment in Malheur National Forest. Its primary tributaries are Big and Lake creeks, which flow out of Strawberry Mt. Wilderness. They are joined by Summit and Bosenberg creeks in Logan Valley.

To access the upper river and its tributaries, follow Hwy. 395 to Seneca (about 24 miles south of John Day, 45 miles north of Burns). Follow Forest Rd. 16 east. A maze of forest roads provide access to Malheur Ford, but Forest Rd 1641 (2½ miles east of the Bosenburg Creek crossing) leads directly to the Ford. Hike upstream from the Ford along cow trails, or follow the Malheur River National Scenic Trail 303 downstream 7 miles to Hog Flat. The Malheur is a designated Wild and Scenic River from the confluence of its headwater tributaries to the Malheur National Forest boundary about ½ mile below Hog Flat. Malheur Ford has a gravel bottom and is generally "fordable" by most standard-size vehicles. Sports cars and compacts may take on a little water.

The upper Middle Fork Malheur was last stocked with rainbow trout in 1992. These were always outshone by the native redband rainbows. The upper river is now managed for wild fish. Wild rainbows 16 to 18 inches and whitefish are present throughout, and bull trout are present downstream to Bluebucket Creek. Brook trout are available in the upper reach. Bull trout must be released unharmed, and fishing is restricted to artificial flies and lures from Big Creek down to Bluebucket to protect the bulls. Brook trout may be harvested in unlimited numbers.

The Malheur flows through private land from the forest boundary to Hwy. 20 downstream from Drewsey. Public access resumes south of Hwy. 20, where there's excellent fishing for smallmouth. Access to this reach is off Warm Springs Rd. An unmarked dirt road heads east to the river about 7 miles south of Hwy. 20. A second unmarked road reaches the river near the north end of the reservoir. Hike and fish upstream and down. Some anglers float this section in personal boats, but the river can get very low in summer.

Smallmouth bass to 15 inches are present in fair numbers in this 12-mile reach. The smallmouth population does well during wet cycles and is currently thriving. This section can be fished year-round, though best fishing is in spring after the run-off recedes and before the river gets low.

BLM and private property are well mixed in this stretch. Ask permission when in doubt as to land ownership, or walk upstream from the reservoir. Public land borders both sides of the river for about 3 miles upstream from Warm Springs.

Below Warm Springs Reservoir, the Middle Fork Malheur offers an excellent tailrace trout fishery, with trout to 20 inches and up to 3 pounds. To access the river immediately below Warm Springs Reservoir, follow Hwy. 78 east from Burns. At Crane, continue east along Crane Creek-Venator Rd. following the South Fork Malheur. Turn left (northwest) onto Warm Springs Rd. after about 35 miles. Warm Springs dam is about 2 miles upstream. Continue straight at the fork (the left road leads to Warm Springs Reservoir) and park near the old concrete damkeeper's house to fish from the spillway pool to the old wood bridge. The spillway pool offers year-round fishing for all the reservoir species, including trout, channel cats, yellow perch, crappie, and both smallmouth and largemouth bass. The river itself is generally pretty dry after October 15, returning to life with spring spillage or the beginning of irrigation season in mid-April.

MALHEUR RIVER, NORTH FORK. A productive trout stream, flowing from the Blue Mountains of Malheur National Forest and joining the mainstem Malheur at Juntura. It flows 41 miles south before its impoundment as Beulah Reservoir, and another 18 miles below the reservoir to its confluence with the mainstem. The river is designated Wild and Scenic from its headwaters to the southern Malheur Forest boundary, which includes a canyon accessed by trail.

To reach the upper stream from Prairie City on Hwy. 26 (east of John Day), consult a current edition of the Malheur National Forest map. Head south out of Prairie City, then southeast onto County Rd. 62. At about 10 miles, turn left onto Forest Rd. 13, which approaches the North Fork and follows its west bank downstream to Short Creek Ranger Station. A bit more than 2 miles downstream from Short Creek, turn left onto Forest Rd. 1675, which leads to the north end of North Fork Malheur Trail 381. You can also access the trail at Crane Crossing by following 1675 another 3 miles south, turning right onto a spur road that leads over to the river. Crane Crossing can also be approached from the west along an old military road (closed to motor vehicles) that follows Crane Creek.

From Crane Crossing downstream, the North Fork flows through a canyon accessed by Trail 381. The trail follows the river through handsome old growth timber. An additional point of access to the North Fork canyon is off Forest Rd. 898 near the downstream end of the trail at the mouth of Bear Creek.

The North Fork is also accessible at the mouth of the Little Malheur River. Access is by way of Lost Creek Rd., which branches off Bendire Rd. north of Beulah Reservoir. Park at the rim above the confluence and make your way down to the river. Beaten trails follow the North Fork upstream along both banks. The downstream property is posted against trespassing. Refer to BLM's Malheur Recreation Area map to navigate the unsigned roads that lead to the Little Malheur confluence from Beulah Rd. Avoid trespassing on private land.

Wild redbands, rainbow escapees from Beulah, whitefish, and bull trout are present in the river above Beulah. Bull trout must be released unharmed, and fishing is restricted to artificial flies and lures to protect them. The average catch in the upper river is 8 to 10 inches. Redbands in the canyon stretch are commonly 15 to 20 inches.

The upper North Fork flows through a mixed conifer forest from its headwaters to Crane Creek. From Crane to Bear Creek, ponderosa pine and junipers predominate. Below Bear Creek, junipers and sagebrush overtake the landscape.

The lower river below Beulah Dam is followed by a graded gravel road that leads upstream to the reservoir from Juntura on Hwy. 20. This section of the North Fork has trout 9 to 13 inches, with a few to 20 inches. The lower river flows through private ranchland with public access limited to the first quarter-mile below Beulah and to BLM's Chukar Park, 7 miles north of Juntura on Beulah Rd. To reach the river right below the dam, continue north on Beulah Rd., then follow the gravel road behind the gatekeeper's house.

MALHEUR RIVER, SOUTH FORK. A short tributary of the Malheur, flowing north from Malheur Cave and joining the Middle Fork Malheur near Riverside. Most of the land along the river is private property, and the river is heavily drawn upon for irrigation. It is not stocked, and angling is only fair, with best fishing the first month or two in spring.

MANN LAKE

One of the premiere trout fisheries in southeast Oregon and a rare opportunity to catch wild Lahontan cutthroat trout. Mann Lake sprawls at the summit of a gentle saddle in the rain shadow east of Steens Mt. just 10 miles north of the forbidding Alvord Desert. Fishing is restricted to artificial flies and lures. This is a wild and wonderful place if you love open spaces and the vast scale of desert country.

Mann Lake is due east of Frenchglen, but there is no direct route over Steens. From Frenchglen, follow Hwy. 205 south towards Fields. At the Fields-Denio Rd. junction, turn left. Mann is about 39 miles from the junction. The most direct route from Burns on Hwy. 20 is to follow Hwy. 78 southeast, turning right on the Fields-Denio Rd. (two-lane gravel). It's about 100 road miles to Mann Lake from Burns. The lake is west of the road, its presence indicated by a BLM sign.

Mann Lake averages about 275 acres, considerably more or less depending on the weather cycle. Currently, the Lake is larger than average, and trout are responding to the opportunity of more space to feed and grow. The lake is fairly rich and quite shallow, with an average depth of 8 ft. and a maximum depth of 15 ft. Aquatic vegetation flourishes. The water is often somewhat turbid due to gale force winds, which are not uncommon. It takes about 24 hours for the lake to clear after a blow.

Hatchery-grown Lahontan cutthroat are stocked here on a regular basis since there is no natural reproduction at Mann. Lahontans are among the largest and most

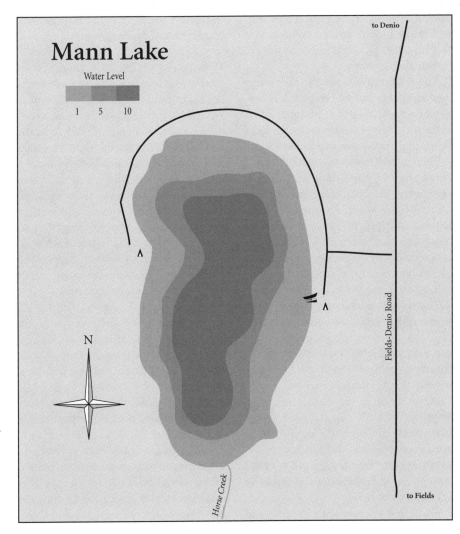

MANN LAKE offers anglers a rare opportunity to fish for big Lahontan cut-throat trout. Photograph by Dennis Frates.

predacious trout in western North America, especially adapted to desert life. A Lahontan in Nevada's Pyramid Lake reached 40 pounds. Mann's Lahontans generally exceed 12 inches, with many to 20 inches. They are not as feisty as rainbows when hooked, but are a handsome-looking fish. Trout under 16 inches must be released unharmed. There is a two-fish harvest limit. Fishing in the tributary streams is prohibited. Algae blooms in mid-summer give the fish an off-taste, but you don't want to be here then anyway.

Anglers begin making the pilgrimage here soon after ice-out (as early as February if the water is open). Fishing drops off as the water temperature climbs, but picks up again in September and October.

There are no forage fish in Mann, but a rich and varied population of aquatic insects thrive here, and trout grow quickly grazing upon them. Dragonflies, damselflies, *Callibaetis* mayflies, and midges are most common. Fly anglers have good success with Woolly Buggers and big nymphs. The midges here grow larger than in most places (hook sizes 10-12 for the nymphs).

There are two boat ramps here, but a boat is really overkill, and even a float tube isn't necessary for good fishing. There are generally plenty of fish close to shore, especially in spring. Try wading out and casting back toward shore.

Mann Lake is on BLM land, with camping on both east and west shores when water level permits. Currently, there are fewer sites due to high water. The south end is bounded by private land with public access prohibited. There is no drinking water here.

The lake is at the top of a low pass, and the wind can really howl through occasionally, which makes fishing either unpleasant or impossible. When it gets like that, drive south to Alvord Hot Springs, on the left side of the road around the mid-point of the Alvord Desert. Fields offers fuel, supplies, and the best burgers and shakes for a hundred miles. This is exceptionally remote country, so top off your gas and water tank prior to heading out, and bring plenty of drinking water.

MARGURETTE LAKE. A good hike-in brook trout lake of about 15 acres in the Sky Lakes group of Sky Lakes Wilderness, Winema National Forest. From Rt. 140 at Pelican Guard Station north of Lake of the Woods, continue north about 10 miles, past Crystal Springs Roadside Rest, turning west on Forest Rd. 3450. At the end of the road, Trail 3708 follows Cherry Creek into the lake basin. At a trail junction about 4 miles in, turn right onto Trail 3762 past Trapper Lake to Margurette, which is an eighth of a mile northwest of Trapper. The trail loops west around the north end of Trapper and leads to Margurette.

Marguerette offers good fishing for medium size brook and rainbow trout. Most fish run 8 to 11 inches, with a few larger. Any method takes fish in spring and summer, but the trout here get finicky in mid-summer. Try casting a large-blade spinner with a worm trailing, retrieving very slowly a yard at a time, letting it settle each time.

Campsites are limited here, as elsewhere in the basin, due to shoreline rehabilitation efforts. Camp well back from fragile lakeside vegetation. For other good fishing opportunities nearby see Donna and Deep.

MCCOY CREEK (Malheur watershed). A tributary of Lake Creek in the headwaters of the Middle Fork Malheur. It flows out of Logan Valley along with Bosenberg and Big creeks. McCoy can be fished for brook trout and some wild redbands. Bull trout may also be present but must be released unharmed.

McCoy flows through mostly private land, but it can be fished from Forest Rd. 16 using the road right of way as access, and from Forest Rd. 1648 which crosses the creek west of Murray Campground. Camp on Lake or Big creeks.

MCCOY CREEK (Blitzen watershed). A tributary of the Blitzen River, flowing northwest off Steens Mt. It joins the Blitzen on Malheur Wildlife Refuge about 14 miles south of the southern border of Malheur Lake. The creek enters the refuge through Diamond Valley, and several miles have been channelized for irrigation. It is open to fishing upstream from the refuge. All Blitzen tributaries open to fishing are restricted to artificial flies and lures.

To reach McCoy, take Hwy. 205 south from Burns toward Frenchglen. The turnoff to Diamond is about 16 miles south of the Refuge Headquarters turn-off. The road reaches the creek about 5 miles to the east. Dirt roads south of the Diamond area follow the creek east for many miles.

McCoy is about 25 miles long and has some good size trout, but it is lightly fished due of its remoteness. Much of the stream flows through private property, and permission to fish is hard to get. Its trout reach 15 inches. McCoy Creek Inn, a handsome old ranch and B&B may allow its guests to fish the creek on ranch property.

MILLER CREEK. A small but good trout stream, outlet of Miller Lake, west of Hwy. 97 at Chemult. The creek is followed west from Hwy. 97 by the Miller Lake Rd. (Forest Rd. 9771), which intersects the highway 6 miles south of Chemult. The entire creek is only 10 miles long. It ends in beaver marsh and percolates into the ground, as do most of the creeks in this area. The upper 4 miles flow within Winema National Forest.

The stream is not stocked, but brown and rainbow trout are well established. The nearest campground is at Miller Lake.

One of the best brown trout fisheries in the state, a deep, clear lake of over 600 acres between Chemult on Hwy. 97, and Diamond Lake. It is reached by 14 miles of good road north of Chemult.

Rainbow and brown trout are stocked annually. The browns are thriving and only lightly fished. Huge numbers of large browns are currently available, with many exceeding 24 inches. Cast lures to shoreline structure, or troll slowly along the shore evenings when the big fish move in to feed. Flies, big streamers, Rapalas, and crayfish imitations can all be effective.

Kokanee are over-abundant, leading to a reduction in average catch size. Most are 6 to 9 inches.

There is a nice campground with boat ramp and picnic facilities is on the northwest shore at Digit Point. Mosquitoes can be a nuisance, but they're not a problem out on the lake itself. Bring repellent and perhaps a head net. Supplies are available at Chemult.

MOON RESERVOIR. A 619-acre irrigation reservoir in a desert setting southeast of Riley, with fishing for largemouth bass, bluegills, crappie, and trout to 18 inches.

From Riley on Hwy. 20, turn south onto Spud Farm Rd. about 2 miles east of town. The approach road is rough and ungraveled dirt, suitable for high-center vehicles only and very muddy in spring.

The reservoir is always drawn down quite low by the end of the irrigation season and can go dry. Once refilled following drought, it can take several years to rebuild its fisheries. Crappie are only now reaching size and quantity suitable for harvest. There are currently some nice size largemouth bass. Look for them around submerged sagebrush and lava rock. The upper end of the reservoir is shallow and silty with little good habitat.

A boat ramp at the north end of the reservoir is suitable for small boats.

MOSQUITO CREEK. A remote Lahontan cutthroat sanctuary stream, closed to all fishing.

MUD LAKE RESERVOI. (Lake Co.). A 170-acre desert reservoir northeast of Adel. Take Rt. 140 about 12 miles east of Adel, and turn onto a dirt road heading north. The reservoir is about 10 miles north. You'd best get a county or BLM map before setting out for it.

The reservoir has been stocked with rainbows, and most are in the 8 to 16 inch range. The fish are of excellent quality but slow biters in this muddy water. Bait is best here. The reservoir is undeveloped, and there are no camping facilities or shade trees.

MURPHY RESERVOIR. A private irrigation reservoir on Bendire Creek, tributary of the North Fork Malheur River and inlet to Beulah Reservoir. It is stocked with rainbow trout. From the north end of Beulah Reservoir, follow the county road north toward Westfall. This is an old military road (public) that winds through a private ranch (leave gates as you find them). At about 4 miles, turn right onto an even more primitive track. It is 2 miles to the reservoir. Don't attempt to navigate these roads till they've dried out for the year, and even then you'll need 4-wheel drive to get to the reservoir.

Murphy is in a long, narrow, steep canyon. There is no boat ramp and no place to camp. Park and fish on the dam, or launch a canoe or float tube at the spillway.

MURRAY RESERVOIR. A rainbow trout lake off Hwy. 26 in western Baker County southeast of Unity. From Baker, follow highways 7 then 26 south about 9 miles beyond the community of Unity. The 45-acre lake is on the north side of Hwy. 26.

Legal rainbows are stocked annually, and bank angling is good for trout 10 to 12 inches. Most anglers use bait. The reservoir is on private property but is open to public use. Be a courteous guest to protect future access. Angling from a floating device is prohibited. Recommended for youngsters, but be careful near the dam.

MYRTLE CREEK (Silvies watershed). A small stream flowing into the Silvies River north of Burns. The creek is within Malheur National Forest and joins the Silvies about 25 miles north of Burns, about 12 miles west of Hwy. 395. To reach it take Hwy. 395 north from Burns about 18 miles to Forest Rd. 31, which cuts west from the highway one mile north of Idlewild Campground. Forest Rd. 31 hits the creek about 12 miles northwest, crossing it 7 miles above the Silvies. Forest roads follow it closely to its headwaters. Downstream, Trail 308 follows the creek almost to the Silvies River, providing the only access.

Myrtle produces a lot of small native redband trout. Best fishing is in spring and summer, with an average catch 6 to 8 inches. There are dispersed campsites north and south of the intersection of Forest Rd. 31 and Hwy. 395.

NATASHA LAKE. An exceptionally pure 6-acre hike-in lake in the southern Dwarf Lakes area of the Sky Lakes group, Sky Lakes Wilderness. See Deep Lake for road directions to the trailhead at Cold Springs Campground. Trails 3709 and 3710 lead from Cold Springs to the basin. Trail 3709 is less steep. Pass between the Heavenly Twins, then turn north onto Trail 3729. Lake Natasha is on the west side of the trail.

The lake is known for its outstanding water quality. It is no longer stocked, though 6 to 9 inch brook trout may still be available. There are good campsites off the trail to the east, at Heavenly Twins and Isherwood, though camping throughout the basin is currently limited due to rehabilitation efforts along the shorelines. Camp well back from fragile lakeside vegetation, and use no-trace camping methods.

NORTH PINE CREEK. A rainbow trout stream, tributary to Pine Creek of the Snake River system, flowing mostly within Hells Canyon National Recreation Area of Wallowa-Whitman National Forest. It can be reached from Baker by taking Hwy. 86 east 51 miles to Halfway. Continue about 9 miles past Halfway to the mouth of North Pine Creek. The mouth is mid-way between the town of Copperfield, where Pine Creek enters the Snake River, and Halfway. From the south, take Idaho Hwy. 11 north from Robinette, crossing the Snake at Brownlee Dam, and continue north to Copperfield. A paved road, Forest Rd. 39, follows the creek north to its headwaters.

North Pine offers 16 miles of water with good road access. Fishing is fair for stocked rainbows and native redbands to 12 inches. Bait is best, but spinner and bait will take fish in murky water. North Pine Campground is 5 miles up from the mouth, and Lakefork Campground is 3 miles farther upstream. A good trail leads west from the latter, following Lake Fork, a tributary of North Pine that offers good fishing as well.

After a flat meander near Rome, the OWYHEE RIVER enters a spectacular whitewater canyon. Photograph by Dennis Frates

OBENCHAIN RESERVOIR. A 40-acre reservoir 10 miles northeast of Bly with fishing for largemouth bass and bluegill. From Bly on Rt. 140, follow Forest Rd. 34 toward Campbell Reservoir, turning left at the road junction before Dutchman Flat. Obenchain is less than 4 miles northwest of the junction.

Privately owned but open to public use, Obenchain supports a dense population of small largemouth bass, though larger bass are beginning to show up. The fishery suffers during the drought but can be counted on to rebound once rains resume and the water level stabilizes. It offers good active fishing for the family. Camping is permitted.

OREGON CANYON CREEK. A tributary of Nevada's Quinn River, flowing out of Oregon Canyon Mountains near Trout Creek Mountains. It offers fishing for hybrid rainbow-cutthroats in a very remote setting at its upper end north of the town of McDermitt. McDermitt is on Interstate 95 near the Nevada border.

The only good fishing is high in the headwaters where the creek flows north before making a horseshoe back toward McDermitt. This part of the upper creek flows through BLM land. Access is hike-in by way of cattle trails.

OWYHEE RESERVOIR. The largest reser-voir in Oregon, created by a dam on the Owyhee River near the Idaho line and fished for abundant largemouth and small-mouth bass, crappie, catfish, and trout. The dam is about 25 miles southwest of Nyssa, 40 miles from Ontario. The reservoir covers about 13,900 acres and winds through 52 miles of spectacular desert canyon that cuts through colorful volcanic rocks—a raw, wild place best explored by boat, and accessed in only three places.

A well-signed road 4 miles west of the town of Owyhee follows the river south to the dam and Lake Owyhee State Park, on the east shore. Unimproved roads approach the canyon from Vale, Adrian and other towns along the Snake River near the border. There are access points at the end of the Dry Creek Rd. on the west side of the lake about 10 miles up from the dam, and at Leslie Gulch on the east side of the lake, by way of the Succor Creek Rd.. This aproach is outstanding for its dramatic rock formations. Refer to the Vale District BLM map.

Owyhee Reservoir State Airport, a dirt strip (1840 ft. x 30. ft) which shows on the sectional, is located at Pelican Point, over 20 miles south of the dam. This strip sees a surprising amount of use. Pilots should give the runway a low pass to check for ruts before landing.

Owyhee's largemouth bass have always attracted a lot of angler attention. During high water cycles, the bass population booms, and larger bass are abundant. The average catch is generally 1 to 2 pounds, but there are many fish in the 5-pound class. There's good fishing around the hot springs at the upper end of the reservoir and in protected coves, which are quick to warm up in spring. Later, bass move out into the main reservoir. Both sinking and surface plugs are effective. Bombers, Sonics, plastic worms, and black eels are popular lures.

Black crappie, which have run 7 to 9 inches and weigh 5 to 8 ounces, are present in abundance. They can be taken on bait, spinner, jigs, or flies. Crappie fishing is best in the Dry Creek arm and downstream.

Smallmouth bass and cat fish are most abundant at the upper end of the reservoir. The area around Leslie Gulch has yielded channel cats to 15 pounds.

Rainbow trout aren't stocked, but some drift in from elsewhere in the basin. Big rainbows occasionally show up in the catch.

During low water years, water fluctua-tion is hard on all the fisheries.

There is a private resort facility about 5 miles east of the dam. Ownership has been in transition, and the resort has been-closed. Call Information (541-555-1212) for Owyhee Lake Resort in Nyssa to check on its availability. In past years, the resort has rented house boats and motorboats and provided supplies, accommodations, restaurant, and trailer parking. A State Park between the resort and the dam has 4 boat ramps and picnic facilities. There are BLM campgrounds below the dam and toward the upper end at Leslie Gulch. Cherry Creek State Recreation Area also has a campground. All the recreation sites above have boat ramps.

The Oregon Departments of Health has issued a mercury contamination health advisory on Owyhee Reservoir fish. Prudent anglers should consider releasing all large fish (who may have built up mercury levels in their body tissue over the years). Check the regulations for complete information.

OWYHEE RIVER

A very productive stream divided into two distinct reaches in Oregon, above and below Owyhee Reservoir. The upper river is fished for smallmouth bass and catfish, the lower river, for large rainbows and browns. The upper reach flows 186½ miles within Oregon from headwaters in the Independence Mountains of northern Nevada, through the remote and rugged canyonland of Idaho and southeast Oregon. The Owyhee joins the Snake River south of Nyssa, across the river from Nampa, Idaho.

The most popular fishery on the Owyhee is the 13 miles downstream from Owyhee Reservoir. This is especially popular with fly anglers, many of whom drive over from the Boise area.

From Ontario On I-84, head south on Hwy. 201 towards Nyssa, then follow signs for Owyhee Reservoir. Owyhee Lake Rd. follows the river from the town of Owyhee to Lake Owyhee State Park at the northern end of the reservoir.

The lower Owyhee, cooled and enriched by releases from the reservoir, offers a year-round tailrace fishery for large rainbow and brown trout. Rainbows grow to six pounds here, with the average catch 12 to 14 inches. Browns average 4 to 6 pounds, with the largest confirmed catch approaching 12 pounds. Larger browns are probably available.

Good fishing is possible year-round in this stretch, except when there's ice on the river (roughly every other winter). Best catching is from mid-October through mid-April, when there are no irrigation withdrawals from the big reservoirs on the middle and north forks. Once irrigation begins, the river jumps from no more than 25 cfs to as much as 250 cfs. River gauge readings are available. See Appendix.

Look for rainbows in the riffles. Look for browns in the slackwater and pools. The biggest browns are usually near the bottom at the head of the pool. Fishing for the browns is catch and release only.

Leech and crayfish imitations can be effective, and anything that resembles a small(er) fish will get the attention of the browns. Midges are present throughout the year, and blue-winged olive mayflies are abundant fall through spring.

The Owyhee runs murky year-round, which means the trout won't notice a heavier line. The river clears somewhat at the end of irrigation season, at which point lighter leaders are appropriate.

This stretch of the Owyhee is only 2 to 4 feet deep, making it easy to fish from the bank. Some anglers float the river in personal boats, but nothing larger is appropriate.

The river flows through public land for its first 10 miles below the reservoir, then comes a patch of private land which includes Snively Hot Springs, followed by a public campground where the hot spring flow enters the river, captured in a few natural rock pools.

From Snively to the dam the river is stocked with 40,000 rainbows annually, and with brown trout every other year. There is a campground at Snively, and natural campsites are available along the river road.

Below Snively the river is heavily drawn down for irrigation, and there is little public access. Bass, crappie, and catfish from the Snake can be present.

The upper river is most famous for whitewater boating, but offers excellent fishing for smallmouth bass. Much of it flows through deep canyons. A popular access to the uppermost waters within Oregon is at Three Forks, confluence of the Middle Fork, North Fork, and Little

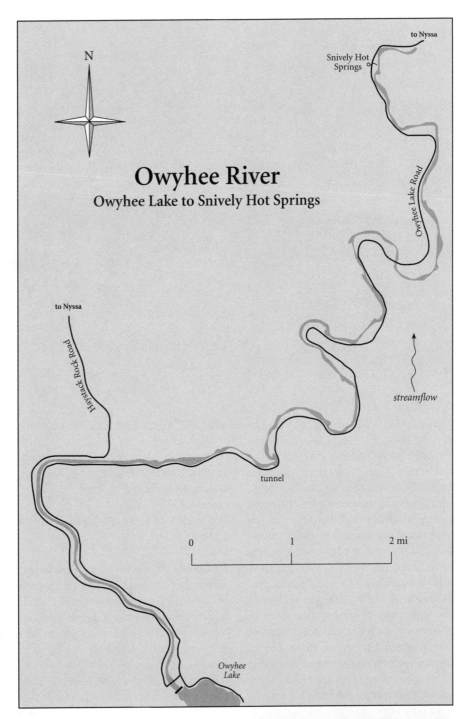

Owyhee rivers. The best approach to Three Forks is from the community of Jordan Valley on Hwy. 95. A gravel road heads east from the highway (called Fenwick Ranch Rd. on some maps), reaching Three Forks in about 28 miles. This stretch of the river is not for the faint of heart. It includes four major rapids (including a Class VI portage). The first 32 mile-flow is through steep-walled canyons. The last 7 miles to the take-out at Rome are frustratingly flat. The wind almost always blows upriver.

The float from Rome to Leslie Gulch is the most popular stretch for boaters. After

Fish for the OWYHEE RIVER's big brown trout near the bottom at the head of pools. Photograph by Dennis Frates.

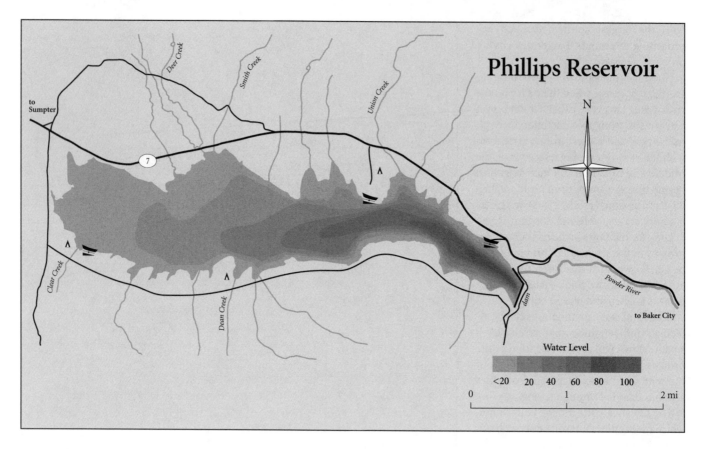

Phillips Reservoir

a 6-mile flat meander, the river enters a spectacular 45-mile long canyon that offers a Class IV rapids, several Class III's, and a variety of geologic and historic wonders, including hot springs and petroglyphs. The final 10 miles involves a work-out across Lake Owyhee to the take-out at stunning Leslie Gulch.

Both smallmouth bass and channel catfish are available in the upper river, with smallmouth to 4 pounds in the more remote reaches. Catfish are most abundant from Rome to the reservoir. Prime floating takes place during spring runoff from April to June. About 2000 people make the trip yearly, encountering some of the nation's most difficult white water and some of its most breathtaking canyonland scenery. The river is designated "Wild and Scenic" from the Oregon boundary to the reservoir. Permits to raft are not required, but users are asked to register with the BLM.

PAIUTE RESERVOIR. A large irrigation reservoir in Guano Valley east of Adel stocked with rainbow trout. From Adel, follow Hwy. 140 east. The reservoir is visible from the highway. Its access road is signed "Antelope Flat." Rainbows were first stocked as fingerlings in spring 1999 and

reached 8 inches by fall. The reservoir is fishable from the bank, but small boats can be launched. There is no boat ramp.

PELICAN LAKE. See WARNER VALLEY LAKES.

PHILLIPS RESERVOIR. A big reservoir on the Powder River capable of growing big trout. Crappie, channel catfish, smallmouth bass, and yellow perch were illegally introduced some years ago, and the yellow perch have dealt a blow to the trout fishery here.

The reservoir is on the upper Powder River about 5 miles east of Sumpter, southeast of Baker. It was created by Mason Dam in 1967. From Baker City, head south on Hwy. 7 to Salisbury, then about 9 miles east toward Sumpter. The reservoir usually covers about 2400 acres and maintains a minimum pool sufficient to maintain its fisheries even during drought.

Troll or still-fish the dam area for trout. The average trout in the reservoir is still 10 to 15 inches, and there are larger trout present. Unfortunately, it is increasingly hard to catch trout due to the overwhelming presence of bait-snatching perch. If you can't fight 'em, you might as well catch

'em. The perch average 7 to 8 inches, with some 11 inches and larger. There is no catch limit on the perch, and the lake is open year-round. Ice fishing is very popular and effective for the perch.

There are two campgrounds on the lake, one at the dam and the second at Union Creek, about 2 miles west. Both are easily reached from the highway, and each has a boat ramp.

PIKE CREEK. A remote Lahontan cutthroat stream. At this time, it is closed to all fishing. Check current regulations.

PILCHER CREEK RESERVOIR. A 140-acre reservoir north of the community of North Powder, offering fishing for rainbow trout and crappie. From Hwy. 84 at North Powder, follow signs toward Anthony Lakes. At about 3 miles, the road to Anthony Lakes makes a sharp left turn. Continue straight (west) another 3 miles to a cutoff on the right (County Rd. 4330, Tucker Flat Rd.) which leads to Pilcher.

Pilcher can go dry during the drought, but is stocked annually with rainbow fingerlings. It also grows nice size crappie. Bullheads have been illegally introduced and will probably thrive here as elsewhere.

There is a boat ramp and a campground set among pine trees.

PINE CREEK. A good trout stream, though isolated and used for irrigation below Halfway. It enters the Snake River below Oxbow Dam. The stream flows 15 miles out of the southeast corner of Eagle Cap Wilderness, to the town of Halfway, then swings east to the Snake. The stretch from Halfway to the Snake River at Copperfield is closely followed by Hwy. 86. Halfway is 51 miles east of Baker on Hwy. 86. A gravel road follows the creek upstream from Halfway to the headwaters, about 11 miles. Cornucopia, a semi-abandoned mining town, is near the end of this road. Most of Pine Creek flows through private lands, so there is little access.

The stream has both stocked rainbows and wild redbands. Rainbows are stocked in the upper stream from Cornucopia to Halfway. In spring, there area good number of larger trout downstream from Halfway, but there is little public access. Later in the season, best fishing is above Halfway. Pine Creek trail follows the upper stream from the end of Country Rd. 413 into Eagle Cap Wilderness.

PINE LAKES. Two small, fairly deep brook trout lakes in the southern Eagle Cap Wilderness, Wallowa-Whitman National Forest. The lakes are about 3 air miles northwest of Cornucopia, which is 10 miles northwest of Halfway on County Rd. 413. Drive as far north on 413 as you can, and you'll reach the Pine Creek Trailhead. Follow Trail 1880 along Pine Creek all the way to the lake, about 7 miles of steady uphill hiking, elevation gain about 2400 ft.

The lakes are side-by-side and quite deep. Upper Pine is the larger, 14 acres with a depth of 70 feet. Lower is only 3 acres, but is 35 feet deep. Each has a good number of brook trout. Bait, flies, and lures all work. These fish aren't fussy. Average size is 10 inches.

POISON CREEK. An 18-mile trout stream originating in Malheur National Forest, followed by Hwy. 395 for about 7 miles north from Burns. The upper waters are accessed by westbound forest roads in the vicinity of Joaquin Miller and Idlewild campgrounds. It offers fair angling for wild trout in spring, with bait most effective. The stream is fairly sluggish and gets low in summer.

POLE CREEK RESERVOIR. An impoundment on a tributary of Willow Creek off Hwy. 26 midway between Unity and Ontario. It is southwest of Brogan (a two-gas station town). Look for a sign to the reservoir on the highway.

An irrigation reservoir of 200 acres when full, it's stocked with 3-inch rainbows that commonly reach 18 inches. Float tubes and car-top boats can be launched, but most anglers bank fish. Fly anglers do well. These fish are finicky for some reason. In this part of the country, only Beulah Reservoir trout are more moody. (If you can figure out what's going on, let me know.) Ice fishing is a possibility, and the reservoir is generally accessible throughout the winter.

POWDER RIVER. A long tributary of the Snake River, heading near Sumpter and winding over 140 miles to the Snake near Richland, which is on Hwy. 86 south of Halfway. The lower 10 miles downstream from Richland make up the Powder River Arm of the Snake's Brownlee Reservoir. Highway 86 follows the next 25 miles upstream, and county roads provide access up to the crossing of Hwy. 203 at river mile 58 northeast of Baker City. The river is designated Scenic from Hwy. 203 up to Theif Valley Reservoir. Access is difficult. Hwy. 30 parallels the river from North Powder to Baker, with many roads leading east to cross or follow the River. From Baker City to Phillips Reservoir, the river is followed by Hwy. 7.

The Powder provides a diversity of angling. In the lower 10 miles from Richland to the Snake, bass, channel cats, crappie and perch predominate. Trolling, casting lures from shore, or bait fishing from boat or bank take fish throughout the season.

Smallmouth bass are among the possible catches when you drop a line in PHILLIPS RESERVOIR. Photograph by Bob Judkins.

The upper river is stocked heavily with rainbows, and a few native redbands are also present. Best angling is in the tail-waters of Mason Dam (Phillips Reservoir) and Thief Valley Dam. Immediately below Thief Valley Dam, trout reach 20 inches, with most 10 to 14 inches. The landowner on the Union County (northeast) side of the river right below Thief Valley allows access to about ¼ mile of river frontage. Watch out for rattlesnakes. There are a couple miles of public access to the Powder below Phillips Reservoir along Hwy. 7, including two developed parking areas with wheelchair accessible trails and several road shoulder turn-outs with trails to the river.

The fish run considerably smaller elsewhere in the system, with the average catch around 10 inches. Above Phillips Reservoir the river has been devastated by gold mining. Hewitt County Park, 2 miles east of Richland, provides boating access to the lower river. Camping is available at Thief Valley and Phillips reservoirs.

POWDER RIVER ARM OF BROWNLEE RESERVOIR. See **SNAKE RIVER.**

POWDER RIVER, NORTH. A redband trout stream, flowing west from the Blue Mountains, entering the Powder River east of the town of North Powder at the junction of highways 84 and 237. North Powder is 20 miles north of Baker. The main stream is followed by paved road for about 7 miles southwest from North Powder. Forest roads access its North Fork and Anthony Fork headwaters north of Anthony Lake. See the Wallowa-Whitman National Forest map, south half, for details.

The stream and its tributaries offer fairly

good angling for native redband rainbows in late spring and summer. Bull trout are also present, but must be released unharmed. The nearest campgrounds are in the Anthony Lake area, with an unimproved camp at Rocky Ford, where the stream flows from the south toward the main road.

PRIDAY RESERVOIR. A very productive fishery for large trout with about 100 surface acres in Warner Valley. It is about 57 miles northeast of Lakeview. From I-395 follow Warner Canyon Rd. 140 east to Adel, then turn north toward Hart Lake and the community of Plush. The reservoir is on the west side of the road about 12 miles beyond Adel.

The reservoir was poisoned in 1992 to remove non-game fish and was re-stocked in the fall of 1992. By spring of 1994 it had trout 18 to 20 inches. It isn't easy to catch them in the reservoir's generally turbid water. The catch rate is slow even with bait.

PUCK LAKES. Two lakes on the east slope of the Cascades, off by themselves between the Sky Lakes Area to the south and the Seven Lakes Basin to the north. Both lakes are stocked. The lakes are accessible by trail from either lake group. For direct access from the east, follow Upper Klamath Lake's westside road, County Rd. 531, to Forest Rd. 3484, 2 miles north of Crystal Springs Campground. Follow 3484 to the end. Trail 3707 (Nannie Creek Trail) reaches the lakes in less than 6 miles.

The northern lake is only 10 acres. The larger southern Puck has about 25 surface acres. Both lakes offer fair fishing for brook trout averaging 10 inches. The lakes are usually accessible in June or earlier and are open as long as trail and weather conditions permit.

RATTLESNAKE CREEK. A small desert stream east of Burns, with wild redbands to 10 inches. It flows about 12 miles from headwaters in Malheur National Forest. From Burns follow Hwy. 20 east about 13 miles, turning north at the cut-off to Harney. A graded gravel road follows the stream from just north of Harney (near the Ft. Harney site) to its headwaters. Late spring and early summer are the best times to fish. Trout average 8 inches.

RED LAKE (Island Lake basin). A shallow lake in the Island Lake group of the Sky Lakes Wilderness, Winema National Forest, about one mile north of Island Lake. Due to frequent winterkill, it will no longer be stocked, though fish may wander in from Island Lake.

RED MT. LAKE. A small lake below Red Mt. in the Elkhorn Range west of Haines. It supports wild brook trout. To reach it, head west from Haines, turning north at Muddy Creek School. About one mile from the school, a road heads west toward Bulger Flat and the North Fork. North Powder River. Follow the North Fork. North Powder River Rd. (Forest Rd. 7301) into the forest about 3½ miles. The trail to Red Mt. is on the south side of the road. The lake is about a mile up the trail.

ROCK CREEK LAKE. A hike-in trout lake on the Elkhorn Ridge northwest of Baker City, in Wallowa-Whitman National Forest. The lake is the source of Rock Creek, which flows northeast to the Powder River through Haines. The trailhead is reached from Haines, on Hwy. 30, by driving west for 10 miles on gravel and dirt roads toward the community of Rock Creek. It's about a 3-mile hike southeast from road's end, following Trail 1626. Another trail, somewhat shorter, approaches from the east from Pine Creek Reservoir west of Wingville.

Rock Creek Lake is at elevation 7600 ft. Although only 35 acres, the lake is over 100 ft. deep. It has a good population of fat little brook trout and skinny mackinaw. The mackinaw run to 20 inches but are not plentiful. You'll have to go deep for them, except right after ice-off. The lake is stocked with rainbows.

ROUND VALLEY RESERVOIR. 150-acre impoundment 15 miles east of Lovella, south of Gerber Reservoir. It has been known to dry up during drought, but it's currently full and well stocked with largemouth bass. Other warmwater species may have been illegally stocked. The reservoir is on BLM land and is open to public access.

SAWMILL CREEK. A short tributary of Silver Creek 29 miles east of Burns, with fair early season fishing for wild redbands. Only about 10 miles long, it flows into Silver Creek about 12 miles north of Riley on Hwy. 20. West of Riley, follow the Silver Creek Rd. north about 20 miles. Sawmill comes in from the northwest and is fol-lowed and crossed by Forest Rd. 45 in Malheur National Forest. The stream has a fair population of small wild redbands averaging 6 to 8 inches.

SCOTTY CREEK. A tributary of the Silvies River supporting wild redband and brook trout. There's beautiful camping in the pine forest and high meadows through which Scotty's tributaries flow within the Malheur National Forest, but fishing for trout of reasonable size is limited to the mainstem reach that is bordered by private land with no public access.

SEVENMILE CREEK. An excellent fly stream, major tributary of Agency Lake, with headwaters in the Cascades southwest of Crater Lake National Park. Despite its name, it is about 18 miles long. From Sevenmile Forest Station on Klamath Lake's Westside Road, paved Forest Rd. 3334 follows about 8 miles of the stream to Sevenmile Marsh. To reach this section from Hwy. 62, turn west onto Nicholson Rd. at Fort Klamath. The lower creek flows into Agency Lake, with an unboatable water level dam at the mouth of the creek.

Most of the lower stream is a canal, and is not fished. Above the canal, fishing is good for rainbow and brown trout. Brook trout are further upstream. Ask permission before fishing in areas where cattle are grazing.

SHERLOCK GULCH RESERVOIR. A good little desert reservoir on BLM land northwest of Plush. It has 10 surface acres and can grow big trout in years when the reservoir is full. To reach it, turn north onto the Sunstone Rd. from Hogback Rd., which runs between Plush and Hwy. 395. The reservoir is about 4 miles northwest of the Sunstone Area. Get local directions before seeking this one out.

Sherlock is stocked annually with rainbow fingerlings and grows trout 8 to 18 inches. The water is always turbid, making bait the most popular method here. Fly fishing is occasionally productive. Winter ice-fishing can be good.

SID LUCE (SID'S) RESERVOIR. A natural lake converted to irrigation reservoir in Warner Valley east of Lakeview. Its excellent rainbow population is lightly fished due to long, difficult access over rough roads. Though only 15 air miles from Lakeview, the drive is over 75 miles one way.

From Lakeview, follow Rt. 140 east to Adel. Turn north following the road toward Hart Lake and the community of Plush. North of Plush, head west toward the Fitzgerald Ranch. The road from Plush to Fitzgerald's is suitable for pick-up trucks. The road through the Fitzgerald property (which is open to public use) is very rough and turns into a power line access road shortly after the ranch buildings.

If there have been recent rains, this road is impassable to all but off-road vehicles. Avoid traveling it before the road dries out in spring to save wear and tear on the road. There are 6 gates on the ranch road. Be sure to leave each as you found it. There are 2 creeks to ford after leaving the ranch, first Snyder (one mile past the ranch) then Colvin (shortly before Sid's).

The 50-acre lake sits in a bowl between Honey and Colvin creeks. It's a rich lake, with lots of insects for trout to forage (similar to Mann Lake in this respect), and stocked rainbow fingerlings show rapid growth, averaging 10 to 14 inches, nice and fat.

Crayfish will eat fish left on stringers in the water, or they can be trapped and eaten themselves. Most anglers use bait and fish from the shore, but a float tube would come in handy. Camping is prohibited. Be advised, too, that Sid's is at the beginning of Southeast Zone rattlesnake country. Walk noisily and carry a big stick.

SILVER CREEK (Harney Lake basin). A long stream northwest of Burns, with trout in its upper waters. It heads in southern Ochoco National Forest a few miles north of Delintment Lake. The creek winds south through forest and high desert to Harney Lake. Hwy. 20 crosses the creek about 28 miles west of Burns near Riley. A paved road leads north from Riley, becoming Forest Rd. 45 upon entering the Ochoco Forest. This road leads to Delintment Lake, and crosses and parallels Silver Creek near the lake. (It first parallels Sawmill Creek, which also has fish.)

Most fishing takes place in the upper creek, north of Delintment and near Allison Ranger Station. Rainbow trout provide good catches in late spring until the water gets low and warm. The fish, mostly caught on bait, are 8 to 10 inches.

A swath in the middle reach of the creek burned in 1990 but is coming back nicely, thanks to restoration work that includes restrictions on grazing. Waist-deep grass, ponderosa pine, and sagebrush characterize the upper basin.

There are two forest campgrounds near the stream in the vicinity of Delintment Lake. Buck Spring Campground is west of Forest Rd. 45 near Sawmill Creek, southwest of Delintment.

SILVER CREEK (Silver Lake watershed). A good trout stream, flowing north from Fremont National Forest west of Hager Mountain, into Paulina Marsh near the community of Silver Lake. The stream is about 16 miles long. It is crossed near its mouth by Hwy. 31, and is followed by graded roads and logging roads to its headwaters. Forest Rd. 288 from Silver Lake reaches the upper stream.

Very low winter flows below Thompson Reservoir practically eliminate any wild population there. The West Fork (above Silver Creek Diversion Reservoir) is lightly stocked and supports a good population of small wild redbands 6 to 10 inches. Best fishing is in June and July.

There is a campground at Silver Creek Marsh on Forest Rd. 288 south of Thompson Reservoir, and two campgrounds at the reservoir.

SILVIES RIVER. A 95-mile flow through private ranchland from headwaters in the southern Blue Mountains south of John Day to Malheur Lake south of Burns. There is almost no public land adjacent to the river. Redband trout are most abundant in the upper river from the headwaters to the confluence with Trout Creek near the community of Trout Creek on Hwy. 395. Public fishing access is limited to easements adjacent to Hwy. 395 or by permission of landowners.

From Seneca downstream, smallmouth bass, yellow perch, brown bullheads, and carp become increasingly abundant. Five-Mile Dam 5 miles north of Burns creates a slackwater pool that offers good fishing for smallmouth bass, brown bullheads, yellow perch, and other panfish. Launch a canoe or fish from the dam. This is also a popular swimming hole. The river flows through private land above and below the dam pool.

SKULL CREEK. The first of three Catlow Valley redband trout streams crossed by the road heading north from Fields towards Burns. The other two are Threemile and Howe creeks. All three are closed to fishing.

SLIDE LAKE (Summer Lake watershed). A 3-acre lake in an interesting geological area of Fremont National Forest, about 12 miles west of Paisley. Follow Hwy. 31 north from Paisley, then turn south on Forest Rd. 29 at the south end of Summer Lake. Forest Rd. 017 to Slide Lake cuts west after about 4 miles. Follow signs to Slide Mt. Geologic Area. It's about 7 miles to the lake. The road is not maintained for low clearance vehicles.

Slide Lake is stocked annually with rainbow fingerlings, and brook trout have been illegally introduced. Both average 9 to 10 inches. There is no limit on the brook trout.

The real interest here is the opportunity to view volcanic geology and resulting earth movement. Slide Mt., once a large dome-shaped volcano, has been scarred by a giant prehistoric slide. The slide can be seen from Hwy. 31 on the way in. Withers Lake, a 5 acre lake about 2 miles to the east, also supports fish. Best access is a mile bushwhack up Withers Creek from Forest Rd. 3360.

SOUTH PASS LAKE. A good hike-in lake, excellent for fly fishing, most productive of all the lakes in Mountain Lakes Wilderness. It is on the eastern edge of the wilderness and may be approached from the west (Lake of the Woods, 9 miles), north (Varney Creek Camp, 7 miles), or south (Clover Creek Rd., 7 miles). From Harriette Lake on the main basin-circling trail, it's a steep 2-mile hike to South Pass Lake on an unmaintained track.

The lake is quite shallow, with 7 surface acres. It is stocked bi-annually with brook and rainbow trout. Fish average 8 to 10 inches with a few larger, and the lake has been known to grow some lunkers. Fly fishing is good here, with best catches in fall and early spring.

The entire basin has suffered from heavy use, and many good campsites are closed due to efforts to rehabilitate lakeside vegetation. Camp well back from the lake, and use no-trace camping methods.

SPALDING RESERVOIR. One of the most productive reservoirs in southeast Oregon, fished for big rainbow trout. Dry spells benefit the fishery here, eradicating troublesome chubs and allowing shoreline

Big migratory rainbow and brown trout can be stalked in SPRING CREEK in late May. Photograph by Richard T. Grost.

vegetation to regenerate—providing good shelter for fish and insects when it submerges during subsequent wet years.

Spalding has 20 surface acres in good years and is surrounded by BLM land. It is 85 miles east of Lakeview. Turn north from Rt. 140 about 20 miles east of Adel, onto a dirt road that skirts the eastern edge of Guano Valley. The reservoir is 19 miles from the highway. Come prepared for remote country.

Spalding grows fish quickly and well, currently offering 20-inch trout. Like other desert reservoirs, Spalding's water tends to be turbid, but it is clearer than many other reservoirs in the county. Both flies and lures can be effective here.

SPENCER CREEK. A very good trout stream, tributary of the Klamath River. It flows 18 miles from spring-fed headwaters south of Lake of the Woods into J.C. Boyle Reservoir on the Klamath west of Klamath Falls. The main creek and its tributaries are followed north by good graded roads from Keno on Hwy. 66.

Spencer Creek is managed as a wild trout stream. Fair numbers of large Klamath River rainbows enter the creek in spring on their spawning run. The creek opens at the end of May to protect spawning trout.

SPRAGUE RIVER

A long, good trout stream with very good brown trout opportunities and largemouth bass, flowing into the Williamson River at Chiloquin about 30 miles north of Klamath Falls. Managed for wild trout, the Sprague flows over 100 miles from east to west.

The Sprague heads on the west slope of Gearhart Mt. and the rimlands to the south, about 30 miles west of Lakeview. Two major forks and Fishhole Creek combine near the town of Bly to form the main stream. Rt. 140 (Lakeview to Klamath Falls) follows the upper half of the river west from Quartz Mt. Pass to the town of Beatty at r.m. 70 on the mainstem.

The north fork provides excellent fly fishing for rainbow, brook, and brown trout in its upper reaches near Sandhill Crossing. The south fork has abundant small brook trout. There are some nice browns in the lower stretches of this fork also. Access to the upper stream involves difficult hiking and difficult fishing conditions, but there are brown trout here who've never seen an angler. Fremont National Forest roads leading north and west from Bly and north from Quartz Mt. Pass provide access to these headwaters. Bring a map.

Largemouth bass are present in the Sprague River Valley reach where the river meanders between the towns of Sprague River and Beatty. Bass fishing is best in mid-summer. A secondary road runs east from Hwy. 858 north of the highway's crossing of the river at the town of Sprague River. This secondary road follows the north bank to a point north of Beatty.

Five miles west of Beatty, Hwy. 858 cuts northwest from Rt. 140 and follows the river all the way to Chiloquin. Chiloquin is on Hwy. 97, about 30 miles north of Klamath Falls. Access to much of the lower

stream is prohibited by landowners, but some grant permission to fish.

The lower Sprague has many rainbows to 3 pounds or better, and good-size browns take a fly appreciatively. Large streamers and bucktails can do the trick. Bait and lures are also effective. Best trout fishing is in late spring and early summer. The final mile of river below Chiloquin Dam is restricted to artificial lures and flies and opens in late May. Above the dam, the river opens in late April.

Sprague River Picnic Area, 5 miles east of Bly, is a nice lunch spot, but camping is prohibited. There are several forest campgrounds on or near the upper forks, including Sandhill Crossing, Lee Thomas, and Campbell Lake. S'Ocholis Campground is on the river 12 miles east of Chiloquin, along Hwy. 858.

SPRING CREEK. A very short tributary of the Williamson River, offering easy spring and summer angling for stocked rainbows and technical fishing for big Williamson River migrants. Only 2 miles long, it flows into the Williamson at Collier State Park, accessible from Hwy. 97 about 4 miles north of Chiloquin. It's primarily a put-and-take fishery with most angling pressure from Crater Lake tourists.

Spring is heavily stocked with legal rainbows annually near the headwaters and in the area above Collier. In addition to these, some sizable redbands and brown trout wander into the stream from the Williamson. The river opens in late May, allowing time for these migrants to spawn undisturbed, but they can be stalked and fished later in spring using fly and spinner techniques.

Collier State Park is a very attractive full service park beside the river, with trailer hook-ups, tent sites, and showers as well as a picnic area. Mosquitoes are ferocious in spring and summer but die down in late summer and fall. Spring is an ideal canoeing stream. You can carry a canoe in from the rest area at the north end and canoe up to the head, or drive to the day-use area at the upper end and drift down to Collier. It's about 1½ miles (2 hrs.) of leisurely drifting in an idyllic forest setting. For other good fishing in the area, see Sprague and Williamson.

SQUAW LAKE (Lake Co.). A 10-acre natural desert lake about 5 miles from Hwy. 31

north of Picture Rock Pass between Summer and Silver Lakes. The road to Squaw heads east from the highway about 4 miles north of the community of Summer Lake. Squaw Lake is very turbid and receives little use by anglers. It is stocked with rainbow fingerlings when there's enough water to support them. The typical fish caught here is in the 8 to 10 inch range. Bait is the most effective method.

STONE CORRAL LAKE. See **WARNER LAKES.**

SUMMIT LAKE. A small mountain lake in the Elkhorn Range west of Haines. It supports wild brook trout. See Red Mt. Lake for directions. The trail to Summit is a little more than a mile beyond the Red. Mt. Lake Trailhead, on the south side of the road. The hike to Summit is about a mile.

SWAMP LAKE. See **WARNER VALLEY LAKES.**

SYCAN RIVER

A tributary of the Sprague River capable of producing very good fishing for rainbows and brook trout during good water years. There are lots of brook trout in its headwaters above Sycan Marsh, with unlimited harvest opportunities at this time.

The Sycan heads on the west slope of Winter Ridge in Fremont National Forest and flows northwest about 20 miles into Sycan Marsh. Leaving the marsh, it flows about 30 miles south to the Sprague at Beatty. In this stretch it forms the border between Fremont and Winema National Forests. It is only lightly fished, probably due to its remoteness and rugged access roads. But the upper river offers very good fly fishing for small wild brook trout in a very pretty setting (if you don't mind cows).

The Sycan is managed as a wild trout stream and has reproducing populations of brown, rainbow, brook, and bull trout. Rainbows are found throughout the stream, but brook and bull trout are mostly in the upper river above the marsh, and the browns are strictly in the waters below the marsh. Know your trout, and release the bulls unharmed. Bull trout are especially numerous near and in Long Creek, a tributary of the upper river.

The Sycan enters the marsh at its southeast corner. Upstream from this point, the river is reached and crossed by many forest roads. Use the Fremont National Forest map to locate road accesses and crossings.

Above the marsh, most fish are 6 to 10 inches, but larger fish exceeding 20 inches are occasionally landed. Some of the finest fly fishing in the area is on the upper Sycan River and its tributaries.

Below the marsh, a maze of rough forest and county roads provide access to the river. Follow County Rd. 1193 north from Beatty. At the first junction, Forest Rd. 347 (to the left) leads to the river and crosses it below Teddy Powers Meadow, a popular take-out for drifters from the marsh. If you continue north instead of left onto Forest Rd. 347, you'll reach Sycan Ford, a rough crossing. A Fremont Forest map will come in handy. Most of the lower 12 miles of river is on private land, and you will need permission to fish.

The waters below the marsh have suffered from overgrazing and excessive irrigation withdrawals. Reduced grazing and habitat restoration work are beginning to help. Designation as a Federal Scenic River has protected the Sycan from further degradation. Most of the fishing in this stretch is concentrated between Torrent Spring (2 miles above Sycan Ford) and the mouth. Early season angling can be quite good for rainbows 10 to 18 inches and for good size browns. The browns are probably spawners from the Sprague River. By summer the stream flow has dropped to the point where water temperature makes fishing unproductive.

There are good campsites along the upper stream. Downstream, camp at Lee Thomas Meadow and the Sandhill Crossing of the North Fork of the Sprague.

TAFT MILLER RESERVOIR. A large irrigation reservoir in the desert country east of Hart Mt. National Antelope Refuge with crappie and a few redband migrants from Rock Creek. The reservoir is about 85 miles south of Burns and 85 miles east of Lakeview. It has 350 surface acres at full pool, but it can get very low during drought. Due to wild fish policy issues concerning Rock Creek, the reservoir is no longer stocked with hatchery trout. Wild redbands from the creek enter the reservoir, but the most consistent fishing is for crappie.

Camping is possible here among the sagebrush and cow pies. Better spots are available at Frenchglen and on the Hart Mt. Refuge, both about 25 miles from the reservoir.

THIEF VALLEY RESERVOIR. An irrigation reservoir on the Powder River capable of growing good-size trout and a mixed bag of warmwater species. It is about 15 miles north of Baker City, about 5 miles east of I-84. It can be reached from the road between Telocaset and Medical Springs. Telocaset is on Hwy. 237 eight miles south of Union and 7 miles northeast of the North Powder Exit on I-84, south of La Grande.

Two miles long and ½ mile wide, Thief Valley has about 200 surface acres at full pool, but it has no minimum pool and goes dry rather frequently. Best fishing is often within a few years after a drought, since non-game fish tend to get the upper hand here even after a complete die-off. In 1999 the reservoir almost went dry, and many fish were lost. Fingerlings stocked in spring generally reach 10 inches by the following October.

Crappie, bullhead, and largemouth bass drift into the reservoir from the Powder River. Bluegill may also be present. Brown bullheads average 9 to 12 inches. Bait-fishing from the bank is popular, with the area near the boat ramp a favorite spot. The county maintains a small park with boat ramp on the reservoir. There are often strong afternoon winds here, so don't kick or paddle too far from shore.

The reservoir is open for angling year-round. Ice fishing is popular, and the success rate can be high some years. There is

Powder River catfish drift into THIEF VALLEY RESERVOIR. *Photograph by Dennis Frates.*

a campground here, but no trees or drinking water.

THOMPSON VALLEY RESERVOIR. A large impoundment capable of providing very good angling for large trout and a growing population of largemouth bass. It is about 12 air miles southwest of Silver Lake in northern Lake County. The reservoir is in the headwaters of the upper east fork of Silver Creek in Fremont National Forest. It is about 14 miles south of the town of Silver Lake, which is on Hwy. 31. Several roads lead south from the highway near the town. Look for signs to the reservoir.

Thompson Valley reaches 2500 surface acres when full. With a maximum depth of only 30 ft. and lots of sunshine, trout food is abundant. Stocked rainbow trout reach 24 inches and about 5 pounds. The average catch exceeds 12 inches.

With fish this big, fly fishing the shallows can provide real thrills. Trolling with spinner and worm is productive, as is still-fishing with worms, cheese or eggs.

Largemouth bass, illegally introduced, are thriving and currently averaging 3 to 4 pounds. Look for them around the submerged wood. Hybrid bass were stocked in '96 and '98 with hopes of establishing a trophy fishery similar to that in Ana Reservoir. So far, no hybrids have been caught.

Thompson is open year-round, and lots of anglers fish through the ice when snow allows access. If the snow's too deep, you may have to hike a short way. Winter anglers stick to bait fished just off the bottom.

There are two US Forest Service campgrounds on the reservoir, each with a boat ramp.

THREE MILE CREEK. (Klamath Lake watershed) A small wild redband and bull trout stream, heading near Puck Lakes in the Cascades west of Fort Klamath. The lower end is crossed by the Westside Upper Klamath Lake Highway about 10 miles out of Fort Klamath. A road heads part way up the stream, and a trail follows the rest of the way. If you choose to fish here, know your trout, and release the bull trout unharmed.

TRAVERSE LAKE. A nice brook trout lake in the southwest Eagle Cap Wilderness. It's at the head of the West Fork of Eagle Creek, one mile above Echo Lake on the same trail. See Echo Lake (Eagle Creek Watershed) for directions.

Brook trout are numerous and of good size. Fly fishing is excellent in August and September, and bait will produce fish at any time. This lake doesn't get much pressure.

TROUT CREEK. About as remote as any you can drive to in Oregon. This creek heads high in the Trout Creek Mts. near the Nevada border and flows north into the desert country southeast of Steens Mt. About 30 miles long, it is so remote it is hardly ever fished. Small, darkly speckled Alvord cutthroat inhabit its bracing upper waters.

Only the upper waters are available for fishing. The lower stream flows through private ranchland. You'll want a good map before heading in here. The BLM Steens Mt. map covers the area well. Four-wheel drive or at least a high center vehicle is strongly recommended, along with a good stock of supplies. Inquire at the State Patrol office in Burns for road conditions prior to attempting this.

A graded road leads east toward Whitehorse Ranch from the Fields to Denio Rd., about mid-way between those two stagecoach stops and one mile north of Tum Tum Lake. This road reaches a gap formed by lower Trout Creek about 6 miles to the east, and follows the lower waters about 8 miles. Unfortunately, the creek flows across private land here.

To reach the upper waters from Whitehorse Ranch Rd. east of Fields, turn right on a graded gravel road before crossing Willow Creek. A road described in previous editions of this book (that reached Trout Creek by way of Oreana Creek) is now officially closed, though there is no gate. The currently open route follows Little Trout Creek up to and beyond its headwaters, a total of about 13 miles, before doubling back north into the big Trout Creek drainage.

Trout Creek offers fair fishing for rainbow trout on bait or flies in the lower waters if you can get permission to fish. There's not a lot of water in the upper creek, and the trout above are generally under 8 inches. There are natural campsites in the aspen groves and plenty of wide open spaces in a setting that feels like you've reached the top of the world.

TWENTYMILE CREEK. A pretty good desert trout stream supporting wild redband trout, flowing east and north from springs near the California line into Warner Valley, about 7 miles south of Adel on Rt. 140.

Twentymile is followed by a gravel road that leads south from Adel to California. The upper stream is accessed by graded roads running northwest from this road toward Big Valley and Big Lake, then on to Rt. 140.

Between the Big Lake Rd. and the Adel-to-California Rd., the stream flows into a canyon. Best fishing for the creek's wild redbands is in this canyon. Fishing is good in spring and summer for trout to 15 inches, but the average is 9 to 10 inches.

TWIN LAKES (Powder River watershed). Two little trout lakes below Elkhorn peak in the Elkhorn Range northwest of Baker. The trail to the lake is at the end of the Lake Cr. Rd. (Forest Rd. 030) which heads north from Deer Creek Campground. Trail 1633 reaches the lakes in about 2 miles. Both rainbows and brook trout are present.

UNITY RESERVOIR. A large and popular irrigation reservoir on the upper Burnt River south of Baker, 3 miles north of the town of Unity. It offers good fishing for rainbow trout and smaller numbers of small smallmouth bass and crappie. From Unity, follow Hwy. 26 northwest about 2 miles, then turn north on County Rd. 245, which reaches the reservoir in about 3 miles

About a 1000 acres when full, Unity provides good catches of rainbows to 16 inches, with the typical fish 9 to 12 inches. Trolling and bait-fishing are both popular, but bait anglers fare better early in the season. It is possible to fish from the bank. The reservoir is too high in elevation to support a productive warmwater fishery. Smallmouth average 11 to 12 inches, and crappie average 6 to 7 inches.

Burnt River flows into the reservoir at the northeast corner. West, Middle, and South forks enter (from north to south) along the west side of the reservoir. Trout fishing is generally best in spring before the water temperature climbs too high, and again in fall. Algae blooms in late summer, but it doesn't seem to affect the fishing. High summer water temperatures, on the other hand, do slow things down.

Unlike some irrigation reservoirs in eastern Oregon, Unity maintains a minimum pool that preserves its fish population even in dry years. Draw-down takes place from July through October, but there is good fishing even when the reservoir is low.

A State Park south of the dam provides welcome shade trees and a campground with boat ramps. It closes at the end of October. When the ice pack is sufficient for safety, ice fishing is popular. Avoid fishing within 200 feet of the dam, since currents there can keep the ice dangerously thin.

UPPER KLAMATH LAKE

Often the largest lake in Oregon (vying with Malheur in wet years), shallow and extremely productive, featuring big wild rainbow trout. With about 64,000 acres, Upper Klamath is connected by a natural strait to 8200 acre Agency Lake. Its primary tributary is the rich Williamson River, and its outlet is the Klamath River. From its southern tip within the town of Klamath Falls, the lake stretches almost 25 miles.

I-97 provides direct access from Bend and from Redding, California and follows a good portion of the east lakeshore. Rt. 140 follows the more popular west lakeshore from Pelican Bay to Klamath Falls. There are no bridges across the lake. Secondary roads east from Rt. 140 access boat ramps and popular fishing areas on the west shore, including Pelican Bay, Odessa Creek, Ball Bay, Shoalwater Bay, and Howard Bay.

Of Klamath Lake's 100 square miles, all but 2 percent is less than 25 ft. deep. This shallow water is high in nutrients and provides a food-rich environment that grows fish quickly. Large rainbows over 20 inches are the main attraction in Upper Klamath, with the average catch a whopping 18 inches. Studies have shown that rainbow trout in this lake reach 20 inches in only 3 years, 26 inches in 5 years. A few 17- to 20-pound rainbows are occasionally caught. The lake's trout population is entirely dependent on natural reproduction, since past fish stocking programs have failed. Hatchery trout proved to be susceptible to a disease organism present in the lake.

By mid-summer the main lake becomes too warm for trout, and the fish move into spring-fed pockets and toward the mouths of tributaries, including the Pelican Bay area and Recreation Creek. Most fishing during the heat of the summer is catch and release, since annual summer algae blooms on the lake tend to give the fish an off-taste.

Bank angling is popular in winter, spring, and fall in Klamath Falls at Moore Park, Pelican Marina, and the Link River outlet. Anglers also fish along Howard

Rainbow trout over 20 inches are the featured attraction in UPPER KLAMATH LAKE. Photograph by Scott Richmond.

(Wocus) Bay in the southwest and near springs on the east shore north of Hagelstein County Park off Hwy. 97. In early spring there is a boat fishery near Eagle Ridge and in Howard (Wocus) and Shoalwater bays. In late April the northern lake opens, and there are active troll fisheries out of Rocky Point and Harriman resorts, at the Recreation Creek inlet of Pelican Bay, and in the narrows between Upper Klamath and Agency lakes. In late summer fish gather in the Fourmile Creek inlet of Pelican Bay, which is cooled by springs, and at the mouths of cooler tributaries.

Klamath Lake has a large native chub population (tui and blue), and bait fishing with chub chunks is popular. Fathead minnows are also present in abundance, as are sculpins and lampreys. All fish bait must be dead. Bait is available at local shops. Trollers use large flasher-type lures or Flatfish and spinner and bait combinations. The Andy Reeker No. 4 has been a standard lure here for years, and Rapalas are popular. Trolling with dead minnows behind a flasher is effective and legal.

Other gamefish available in Upper Klamath include brown bullheads and an increasing abundance of yellow perch. Look for perch near the cold water springs. A few big old sturgeon are occasionally observed, but they are more a phantom presence and curiosity than a targeted sportfish here. Largemouth bass have been introduced but have not thrived. Mullet (Lost River suckers) are a federally protected species and if caught, must be released unharmed.

Klamath Lake is mighty big and can kick

up in even moderate wind. Boat anglers are generally cautious and keep close to shore. There is a public boat launch at Moore Park in Klamath Falls at the south end of the lake. Westside ramps are off Rt. 140 at Howard Bay Observation Pt., Shoalwater Bay Campground, and Odessa Creek Campground. Three additional westside ramps allow boats to launch into tributary streams and drift down to Upper Klamath. They are at Harriman Springs Resort on Harriman Creek, Rocky Pt. Resort on Recreation Creek, and Malone Springs on Crystal Creek.

The only public boat ramp on the east shore is at Hagelstein Park. Boats can also be launched on the Williamson River at Williamson River Resort, and on Agency Lake at Henzel Park, Neptune Resort, and Petric Park. There is a 10 mph speed limit in the channels and resort areas.

Supplies, lodging, and boat rentals are available near the prime fisheries around the lake. Williamson, Wood, Sprague, and Klamath rivers offer outstanding angling alternatives in the immediate area. Lake of the Woods, Fourmile Lake, and Mountain Lakes Wilderness offer additional angling, camping, and hiking opportunities nearby.

UPPER MIDWAY RESERVOIR. A remote 40-acre reservoir on BLM land about 18 miles east of Lorella, stocked with largemouth bass. Heavily drawn down for irrigation and lightly fished, it can grow decent size largemouth bass, weather permitting. It is allowed to go dry during drought and takes about 5 years to rebuild its fish-

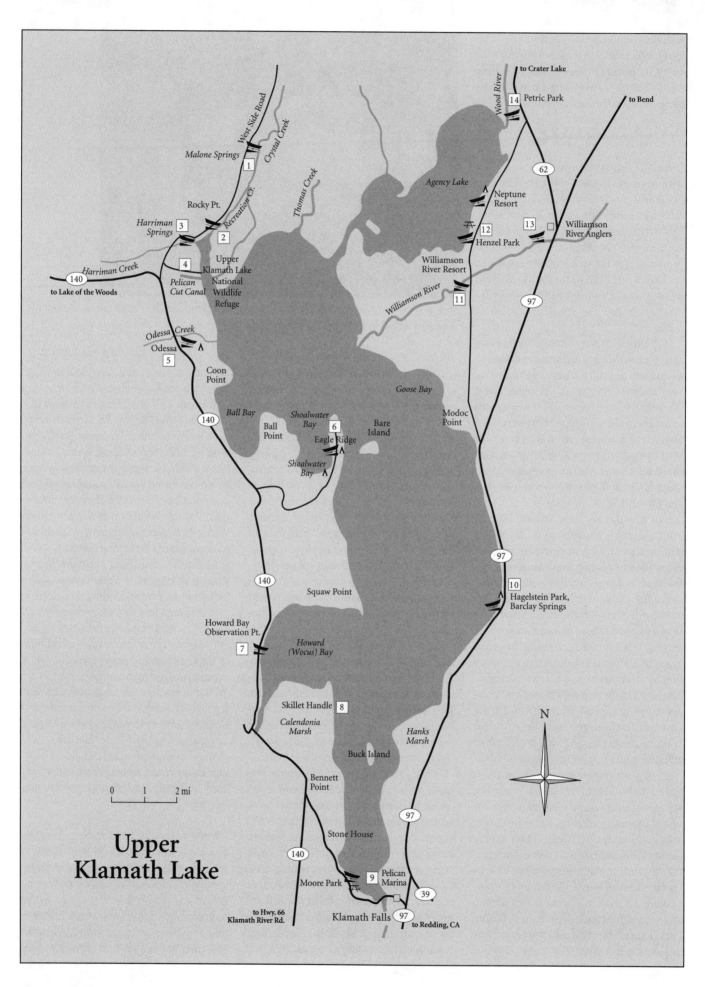

to Crater Lake

Wood River

14 Petric Park

to Bend

62

Agency Lake

Neptune Resort

13 Williamson River Anglers

12 Henzel Park

Williamson River Resort

97

11 Williamson River

West Side Road

Crystal Creek

Malone Springs

1

Recreation Cr.

Thomas Creek

Rocky Pt.

Harriman Springs 3

2

140

to Lake of the Woods

Harriman Creek

4

Pelican Cut Canal

Upper Klamath Lake National Wildlife Refuge

Odessa Creek

Odessa

5

Coon Point

Ball Bay

Ball Point

Shoalwater Bay

6

Eagle Ridge

Shoalwater Bay

Goose Bay

Bare Island

Modoc Point

140

140

Squaw Point

97

97

10 Hagelstein Park, Barclay Springs

Howard Bay Observation Pt.

7

Howard (Wocus) Bay

Skillet Handle 8

Calendonia Marsh

Hanks Marsh

Buck Island

N

Bennett Point

0   1   2 mi

Stone House

97

Upper Klamath Lake

Moore Park 9 Pelican Marina

39

140

to Hwy. 66 Klamath River Rd.

Klamath Falls

97

to Redding, CA

1. *Malone Springs.* Unimproved launch accesses Crystal and Recreation creeks (channels meander through marsh); fish in late summer for big rainbows seeking cool water; good fly fishing; motor up or down.

2. *Rocky Point.* Paved public ramp, dock, facilities for handicapped anglers; adjacent resort offers boat rentals, moorage, gas, and restaurant.

3. *Harriman Springs.* Pay to launch at resort facility; access to Harriman Creek and Pelican Bay.

4. *Pelican Cut Public Access.* Popular with duck hunters; overgrown road along canal accesses Pelican Bay.

5. *Odessa Creek.* Gravel ramp accesses Odessa and Short creeks and Klamath Lake; spring water provides good fishing year 'round

6. *Eagle Ridge/Shoalwater Bay.* Concrete county ramp accesses spring troll fishery in Shoalwater Bay & along Eagle Ridge; bank angling out to point in spring.

7. *Howard Bay (Wocus Bay).* Paved ramp with ample parking accesses spring troll fishery in Howard Bay, Squaw Pt., Eagle Ridge.

8. *Skillet Handle.* Troll the Handle in spring.

9. *Pelican Marina.* Supplies, repairs, moorage.

10. *Hagelstein Park.* Boat ramp for small boats only (under 16 ft).; narrow channel under railroad not passable at low water; accesses spring troll fishery; park along highway and fish the springs.

11. *Williamson River Resort.* Modest fee to launch at private ramp; accesses mouth of Williamson fishery in spring and summer, lower Williamson throughout summer.

12. *Henzel Park.* Concrete public ramp accesses spring and early summer troll fishery.

13. *Williamson River Anglers.* Fly fishing supplies; good information source; pay to launch at private ramp.

14. *Petric Park.* Good boat ramp; motor down to mouth of Wood River; fish Agency Lake.

---

ery. Camping is permitted at the reservoir, which is in a setting of sagebrush and pine.

VAN PATTEN LAKE. A very pretty hike-in trout lake in a scenic area near Anthony Lake. From Haines, head west on Hwy. 411, which becomes Forest Rd. 73. Two miles east of Anthony Lake Guard Station, Trail 1634 leads to Van Patten Lake in about 2 miles.

The lake covers 23 acres and generally offers excellent angling for rainbow and brook trout that occasionally reach 12 inches. Fingerlines are stocked bi-annually. Fishing is good from late spring through fall, and all methods take fish. Campsites are available at Anthony Lakes

VEE LAKE. A nice little 13-acre lake in Fremont National Forest that was created by a small dam to provide fish and goose habitat. The lake is in the North Warner Mts. Northeast of Lakeview. Drive east from Lakeview on Rt. 140 about 15 miles to the North Warner Road (Forest Rd. 3615), and follow it north about 25 miles to the lake.

Vee is shallow and weedy with lots of natural food suitable for growing trout. It is stocked annually, and most catches are 12 to 16 inches. Bait, lures and flies all produce well. Boats with electric motors are allowed on the lake. There are several forest service campgrounds nearby.

WARM SPRINGS RESERVOIR

A large productive reservoir on the Middle Fork Malheur River that grows big trout, smallmouth bass, channel catfish, and yellow perch. From Burns, follow Hwy. 78 east. At Crane, continue east about 35 miles along the Crane Creek-Venator Rd. following the South Fork Malheur. Turn left (northwest) onto Warm Springs Rd. and follow it to the reservoir.

Warm Springs is a little more interesting to fish than some eastern Oregon reservoirs, with lots of bottom relief and rocky structure. It has 4500 surface acres when full. The reservoir begins spilling water in mid-April most years and gets quite low by the end of irrigation season in mid-October. During drought it can go completely dry. After a drought, it takes two seasons before 20-inch trout are again available. Best trout fishing is in spring and fall.

Smallmouth bass run to 4 pounds and take small lures, spinners, and small rubber worms with enthusiasm. Streamers with a lot of color work, too. This is one of the few lakes in the state with channel catfish. Channel cats to 24 inches have been caught here. Brown bullheads are present in larger numbers, but run only to 14 inches, with most just under a pound. There are no improvements at the reservoir. In dry years, it's hard to launch a boat late in the season, but bank fishing at the dam can still be productive. See map page 292.

WARNER VALLEY LAKES. Eleven highly alkaline but life-supporting lakes in an eerie setting of desert vastness. They form a north-south chain across the floor of Warner Valley west of Hart Mountain. From north to south they are Blue Joint, Stone Corral, Lower Campbell, Upper Campbell, Flagstaff, Swamp, Jones, Anderson, Hart, Crump, and Pelican. All are interconnected during high water and can support crappie, brown bullhead, and largemouth bass.

Warner Valley redband trout historically reared in these lakes, but irrigation dams now confine the trout to the tributaries. Reconnection of the tributaries to the lakes for the purpose of restoring redband populations is being considered.

The crappie fishery here during some climate cycles has been the stuff of legends. But it takes a number of years for crappie to grow to size following an event such as the drought of 1988-92. The lakes are now at a record high, with lots of young crappie present. Larger crappie are currently most abundant in Hart and Crump.

The most dramatic approach to the lakes is to drop down into the valley from Hart Mt. From Burns, take Hwy. 205 south, turning east toward Hart about 6 miles south of Frenchglen. Hart Mt. Antelope Refuge Headquarters is 51 miles from the road junction. Take time to visit the Refuge Headquarters, which has a small museum and informative literature relat-

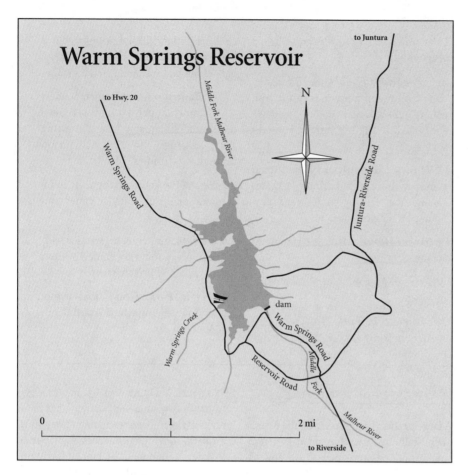

Warm Springs Reservoir

to Hwy. 20

to Juntura

Middle Fork Malheur River

N

Warm Springs Road

Juntura-Riverside Road

Warm Springs Creek

dam

Warm Springs Road

Middle Fork

Reservoir Road

Malheur River

0   1   2 mi

to Riverside

---

ed to this incredible landscape and its wildlife. There is a rustic hot spring south of the headquarters which can be refreshing after the long drive through the desert, though one can't float and take in the view since the pools are walled in with corrugated metal (less for modesty's sake than to thwart the wind). Head down the west slope of Hart Mt. for a stunning vista of Warner Valley.

The first lake to come into view is Upper Campbell, which has been known to cover

4 square miles. Its depth ranges from 10 ft. to less than 4 ft. All the Warner Lakes have been dry at one time or another. During high water their populations intermingle. The lakes were originally stocked in 1971-72 and have been self-sustaining since that time. Five years of good water led to outstanding crappie catches in 1987, especially in Lower and Upper Campbell, with fish 16 to 18 inches and up to 2½ pounds.

During the drought of 1988-92, all the lakes went dry (successively from north to

WILDHORSE LAKE defines remote fishing in Oregon. Photograph by Dennis Frates.

south), but many of the fish survived in a 20 mile slough. In 1993 these washed back into the basin, and the process of repopulation began.

All the lakes are accessible by road. Most angling takes place from the roadside. Frequent high winds across the lakes discourage boating. Aquatic weed growth is heavy by mid-summer. See Hart Lake and Crump Lake for specific information.

WEST SUNSTONE RESERVOIR. A small sometime desert reservoir 2 miles east of Sherlock Gulch Reservoir that produces some nice trout. For directions see Sherlock Gulch Reservoir. West Sunstone has 8 acres when full, but it has had a problem holding water. Stocked rainbow trout here run 8-16 inches. Turbid water makes bait the preferred method.

WILDHORSE LAKE. A cirque lake of about 20 acres on Steens Mt., with wild Lahontan cutthroat trout. Follow Steens Mt. Loop Rd. to the East Rim Viewpoint. Rather than following the Loop west, turn south. At the end of the road, a goat trail leads down to the lake in about a mile, losing 100 ft. in elevation. The scramble down is much easier than the high elevation huff back up. A sign on the road indicates Wildhorse Lake Trailhead.

Wild Horse is in a beautiful setting, a hanging glacial cirque clinging to the rugged Steens. A meadow adjacent to the lake offers pleasant campsites, but winter hangs on hard here. The lake is seldom accessible till August. Lahontans reproduce naturally here, spawning in Wildhorse Creek. A big catch may reach 10 or 12 inches.

WILLIAMSON RIVER

One of Oregon's best opportunities to catch very large wild trout in a river setting, very popular with fly anglers looking for a challenge. The Williamson is a major tributary of Upper Klamath Lake, where those large trout rear and feed. They move into the Williamson and its tributaries to spawn and as a refuge from unfavorable water conditions in the lake. In recognition of its uniqueness, the Williamson was one of the first rivers in Oregon to be managed for the benefit of wild trout.

The Williamson wanders over 70 miles from the Yamsay Mt. area of Winema National Forest, flowing west through Kla-

1. **Williamson River Resort.** Modest fee to launch; fish slack water; run 5 miles to Upper Klamath Lake.

2. **Slack water.** Beginning of slack water.

3. **Water Wheel RV Park.** River access for guests only; fee to launch or take-out; popular float tube drift from here to beginning of slack water.

4. **Williamson River Anglers.** Fly fishing supplies, information, shuttle service; modest fee to launch at private ramp behind motel.

5. **Chiloquin.** Access to .5 miles of NW bank; wadable, but beware of holes; wading staff recommended; boat slide; drift to rapids at Hwy. 97 crossing about 4 miles; novice drift boat water; canoes ok, but skill required.

6. **Pine Ridge.** Private (expensive) fee-pay access to excellent water; old mill site provides good holes & cover.; inquire at Williamson River Anglers at Hwy. 97 rapids.

7. **Collier State Park.** Bank access to west side only; river here is slow flowing and deep with minor rapid below park; mouth of Spring Creek is a popular spot.

8. **Spring Creek.** Launch canoe to fish mouth of Spring Creek.

9. **Primitive Forest Roads.** Off Forest Rd. 9730 reach river used by guides to launch drift boats and canoes; no angling is allowed from a floating device.

10. **East Bank Access.** At dead end, access to 1.5 miles of east bank through State Park and Forest Service land.

11. **Closed Road.** Park and hike road upstream about a mile; long pools offer good rainbow holding water in late summer and fall.

math Marsh, then south into Upper Klamath Lake, entering from the northeast. Its headwaters are in National Forest, but after only ¼ mile it enters private ranchland. Throughout the river, access is limited by extensive private landholdings.

Above Klamath Marsh the Williamson offers spring-fed water, wild rainbows, and brook trout 8 to 15 inches. More than half the property through which it flows is privately owned and closed to public access. The other half is Winema National Forest Land, and accessible, but not obviously so.

The river below Kirk Canyon Falls provides exceptional angling for large native rainbows. Much of the credit for the preservation of this wonderful fishery must go to the efforts of a local fly fishing club which countered a trend of declining fishing that occurred in the late 1950s and early '60s. Their efforts, and those of ODFW, have preserved this trophy trout fishery.

The Williamson's largest rainbows grow to size in the productive waters of Upper Klamath Lake, where 3-year-old fish commonly reach 20 inches or better. The cycle of migration is poorly understood but is probably tied to both spawning and avoidance of warm lake temperatures and high alkalinity in summer. Large fish are generally in the Williamson in good numbers from late June through fall. By late August

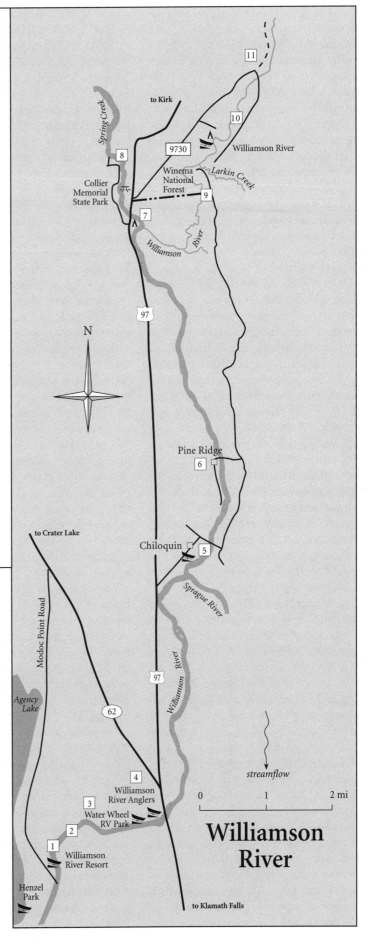

Williamson River

many of these fish have moved into the upper stretches all the way up to the falls. Occasionally, Upper Klamath Lake remains high and cool throughout the summer. On these comparatively rare occasions, fishing in the Williamson is limited to nice (but not trophy) size resident trout.

Eighteen-inch rainbows are ho-hum here, and fish that go well over 10 pounds have shocked many an angler. Good size brown trout are also available in small numbers, particularly below the mouth of Spring Creek. In addition to trout, the Williamson hosts a population of Lost River suckers, locally called mullet, which are a protected species and must be released unharmed.

The Williamson remains high through June, with big-fish fishing best in August and September. Fishing remains good for resident trout through October.

To reach the upper river from Chiloquin, follow the Sprague River Rd. (County Rd. 858) east to Braymill, then turn left on the Williamson River Rd. (County Rd. 600), which crosses the Williamson near the Yamsi Ranch. Head of the River Campground is north of the crossing on Forest Rd. 4648. Within ¼ mile of the head springs the river enters the Yamsi Ranch and is accessible only to the ranch owners and invited or paying guests. Within that quarter mile there are brook trout and some rainbows. The springs themselves are a fine sight, gushing out of a hillside. The pool downstream from the springs is on private property.

The river flows north 27 miles to the marsh, followed up to a mile distant by Forest Rd. 4648 through a mix of private and Winema forest land. Within the forest it is approached from the east by the occasional rough road. You'll need a close reading of the Winema Forest map and an adventurous spirit to make your way, but there's worthwhile fishing in this stretch for the hardy angler.

The reach below the marsh is 38 miles long and is quite different in character from the upper river, though similarly frustrating in terms of public access. Most of the lower river flows through private property, so check locally for permission to fish when property ownership is in doubt.

First good fishing below the marsh is below the falls near the end of Kirk Canyon. County roads follow both sides of the canyon, which is about 200 ft. deep but

accessible. Look for pull-outs and the occasional campsite, indicating rough trails to the river. The best approach is from the vicinity of Williamson River Campground. To reach the campground from Hwy. 97 north of Chiloquin, turn right on Forest Rd. 9730. The road ends about a mile beyond the campground, and a trail follows the river upstream about a mile, past some nice long pools where large rainbows hold in late summer and fall.

A road forking right at the end of Forest Rd. 9730 follows the River's east bank downstream 1½ miles through national forest. Canoes and drift boats can be launched here for a nice float through Collier Memorial State Park. The mouth of Spring Creek at Collier is a popular and productive spot. There are minor rapids below the park. Angling from a floating device is prohibited above Chiloquin.

At Chiloquin, a community off Hwy. 97, there is about ½ mile of public access to the northwest bank. The river is wadable, and boats can be launched for a drift down to the Hwy. 97 crossing. Just below Chiloquin, 11 miles above the mouth, the cooler spring fed waters of the upper river are joined by the warmer waters of the Sprague River at a point known as Blue Hole. This mixing generally results in water temperatures in the lower river that are ideal for trout. A boat can be put in at Blue Hole to float the river below the Sprague confluence. This is flat water, and a canoe is sufficient.

The next access downstream is at the Hwy. 97 crossing. There is a boatable rapids at the crossing. Most anglers take-out at The Rapids Cafe just above, or at Water Wheel RV Park just below the rapids. There is a modest fee to use either pull-out. You can also pay to fish the bank at Water Wheel, or fish for free if you're a paying guest.

The lowest public access to the river is at Williamson River Resort on Modoc Pt. Rd. The river is slack and lake-like at this point, but anglers launch here to fish the slack water or motor down to Upper Klamath. Fishing from a boat is permitted below Chiloquin, but from Modoc Pt. up to Chiloquin, it is prohibited to fish from a motor-propelled craft while the motor is operating (i.e. no trolling).

Leeches, dragonfly nymphs, and baitfish make up the staple diet of Williamson River trout when they're in the lake, and

imitations of these are productive in the river. Woolly Buggers and big streamer flies (especially black and white patterns) catch a lot of big fish. Fly anglers also have good results fishing imitations of the nymph stages of various caddis, mayflies, and midges. Big yellow mayflies present one of the few reliable dry fly opportunities in early July. Williamson River Anglers at the junction of highways 97 and 62 is a good source of local information and supplies.

From the river's mouth up to Kirk Bridge, you can catch and keep one trout per day—except that from Modoc Pt. upstream to Kirk Bridge, trout fishing is catch and release only from August 1 through October 31. At this time of year, the river is often serving as a refuge for a large concentration of Klamath Lake rainbows at a time when the river is low and clear, and angling pressure is at its highest. Fishing from Modoc Pt. upstream is restricted to artificial flies and lures. Barbless hooks are encouraged, though not required. Other special regulations are in effect. Check the current synopsis.

In addition to a couple of RV parks off Hwy. 97, camping is available at Williamson River Campground east of 97, Collier State Park north of Chiloquin, and Kimball State Park at the source of Wood River 3 miles north of Ft. Klamath. There's a nice picnic area on the Wood River at Ft. Klamath.

Accommodations in the area offer pretty slim pickings—a couple of very expensive fishing resorts, and a couple of roadside motels. There is a good cafe in Fort Klamath, a truck stop near Chiloquin, and a cafe with great pies on Hwy. 97 near its crossing of the river. More plentiful supplies and accommodations are available in Klamath Falls, 20 miles or so to the south. For more information, see *Fishing in Oregon's Best Fly Waters*.

Willow Creek (Trout Creek Mts.). A remote Lahontan cutthroat stream which runs out into the desert at White Horse Ranch and dries up. See Whitehorse Creek for directions. Whitehorse Creek Rd., a loop road off Whitehorse Ranch Rd., follows Willow on its southern leg. Best fishing is in the upper reaches. It has been closed to all fishing for a number of years to protect threatened Lahontans. ODFW may re-open it for catch and release fishing. Check the regulations.

WILLOW CREEK (Malheur River watershed). A tributary of the mainstem Malheur, dammed to create Malheur Reservoir. Below the reservoir, non-game fish predominate, but above, the creek offers good fishing for resident redbands and hatchery trout escapees from the reservoir.

See Malheur Reservoir for directions. Willow Creek Rd. follows the creek upstream from the reservoir to the confluence of Middle and South Willow creeks near Ironside on Hwy. 26. Secondary roads follow the forks upstream.

Willow is not stocked but has a good population of resident rainbows. The average catch runs 9 to 10 inches, but some fish to 15 inches are landed. There's little angling pressure.

WILLOW VALLEY RESERVOIR. A remote irrigation reservoir east of Klamath Falls that grows good size Lahontan cutthroat as well as largemouth bass, crappie, and bluegill. It has 500 surface acres when full.

From Klamath Falls follow Rt. 140 to Dairy, then turn right on County Rd. 70 to Bonanza, continuing southeast on Langell Valley Rd. through Lorella and south toward California. As you near the border, watch for the sign to the reservoir, which is east of State Line Rd. on BLM land about 5 miles from the turn-off.

If ideal conditions continue, Willow Valley's crop of Lahontans, currently averaging 11 to 13 inches, should reach 20 inches by summer 2000. Given adequate water, trout gain about an inch a month here. Willow Valley also offers good fishing for largemouth bass. Look for them around the flooded junipers.

It is possible to launch a boat here, though there is no improved ramp.

WITHERS LAKE. A pretty walk-in trout lake in Fremont National Forest below Slide Mt. From Paisley on Hwy. 31, follow County Rd. 3315 west. Pick up Forest Rd. 3360 at the Freemont Forest boundary and continue west about 4½ miles to the trailhead on the left. The lake is about ¼ mile easy walk from the parking area. Withers offers good fishing for a self-sustaining population of brook trout.

WOLF CREEK RESERVOIR. A 230-acre irrigation reservoir south of North Powder, with angling for rainbow trout. From North Powder, follow Wolf Creek Rd. about 4½ miles west to the reservoir. The reservoir has been known to go dry during drought, but it is stocked annually with rainbows, which grow to 12 inches. Crappie may also be present.

Facilities include a county picnic area and boat ramp. The reservoir is drawn down considerably in fall.

WOOD RIVER. A spring-fed, crystal clear trout stream in the Fort Klamath area north of Agency Lake, about 35 miles from Klamath Falls. It offers catch and release fishing for both resident rainbows and browns and for big migrant trout from Upper Klamath. Hwy. 62 crosses the river at Ft. Klamath. Much of the lower stream flows through private land and is best fished by boat.

This is a delightful spring creek, favored by fly anglers. It is generally under 30 feet wide and not too deep, flowing through lush meadowland with undercut banks, log jams, and occasional deep pools. Perfect fly water. Managed for wild trout, it offers fishing for wild rainbows that reach 4 to 5 pounds, as well as some large browns of similar size. Brook trout are also present. The stream flow is consistent throughout the year.

Large trout move into the Wood from June through fall, depending on conditions in Upper Klamath and Agency lakes. Trout migrate out of the lakes when water temperature and alkalinity become oppressive. Best fishing is in August and September when grasshoppers are abundant and the river is running clear. Prior to August, the flow can be cloudy due to snow melt from Crater Lake National Park.

Resident trout are used to a general diet of midges, mayflies, and caddis, but the big migrants are more tempted by larger patterns imitating big baitfish and leeches. Woolly Buggers and Matukas are popular choices.

There is bank access at the Wood River Day use Area off Sun Mountain Rd. and at the Weed Rd. bridge. Only canoes and small boats are appropriate for this river. Boats can be launched at the Day Use Area, Kimball State Park, Loosley Rd. crossing, and Weed Rd. crossing. The most popular float is the 12 miles from Weed Rd. to the mouth, taking out at Petric Park on Agency's northeast shore. Note that the lower 2 miles of the Wood have been restored to a more natural flow from a previously channelized state and now provide much better habitat for redbands as well as other wetland critters.

The float from Kimball to the Forest Service picnic area near Ft. Klamath, or to Hwy. 62 makes a pleasant day's drift. Jackson F. Kimball State Park is at the source spring of the river above the intersection of highways 232 and 62. It has a dirt put-in suitable for raft or canoe. Boats must be hand carried to the water's edge. There is a small tent campground at Kimball. Ft. Klamath Picnic Area has a dock that is wheelchair accessible. Mosquitoes can be thick along the river in summer.

YELLOW JACKET LAKE. A 35-acre impoundment in a ponderosa pine setting on upper Yellowjacket Creek in Malheur National Forest. It is south of the Blue Mountains, about 40 miles northwest of Burns. To get there, turn west off Hwy. 20 south of the Hines Mill (south of Burns), and follow Forest Rd. 47, watching for a road sign.

Yellowjacket offers fishing for rainbow trout 8 to 12 inches. Most anglers fish from shore, but small boats and float tubes can be launched. Ice fishing is possible most winters until the snow gets too deep. Logging operations sometimes keep the road open through the winter. There is an improved campground at the lake.

NORTHEAST ZONE

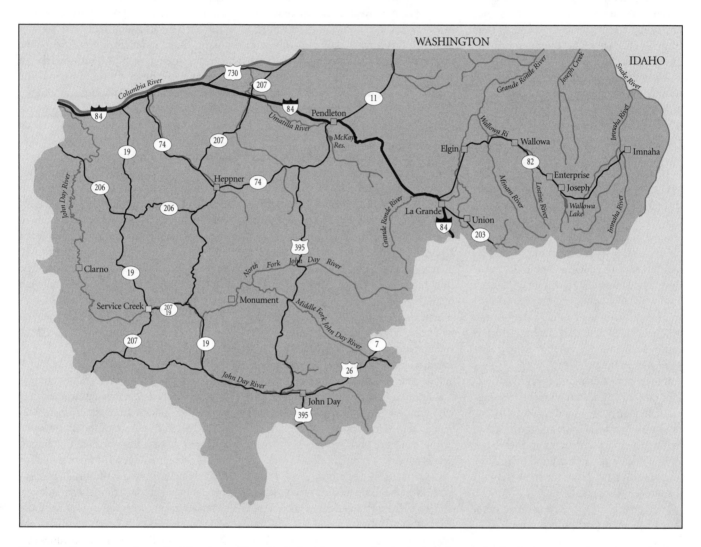

To most Oregon anglers, the Northeast Zone is defined as "far away from here." It is nearly 200 miles from Portland to Pendleton, another 44 miles to LaGrande, and miles more by secondary roads around the scattered uprisings of Wallowa and Blue mountains to reach the premiere fisheries of this region. Yet anglers come, attracted by the very fact of distance from home, work, and other anglers.

They come to hike and fish the nearly 50 trout lakes of the Eagle Cap Wilderness, including several that yield fish of good size (Aneroid, Frances, Frazier, Prospect, Glacier). All yield spectacular scenery, as does Wallowa Lake, with its backdrop of granite peaks, pleasant State Park facilities, trailheads into the wilderness, and Oregon's largest kokanee. Other good but more remote drive-to coldwater fish-

eries include Olive Lake for kokanee and Penland, for big trout.

In autumn, anglers are drawn to the Northeast to fish for steelhead in the Grande Ronde, Wallowa, John Day, and Umatilla rivers. Fall is also the best time to fish the beautiful Wenaha, Catherine Creek, Minam, and Imnaha for big trout—including Oregon's largest populations of bull trout. Fussy about their environment, bull trout (formerly known as *dolly varden*) are threatened with extinction in other Oregon fishing zones, but thrive in the Northeast's exceptionally cold, clean water. The South Fork Walla Walla River offers trout water that is considered unusually pristine even for these parts, reputedly guarded at its mouth by a plethora of rattlesnakes, and in its headwaters by bears.

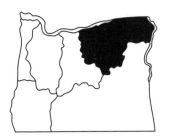

The Northeast Zone includes all waters draining into the Columbia River east of the Deschutes River and all waters draining into the Snake River system up to Hells Canyon Dam. This zone does not include any portion of the mainstem Columbia and Snake rivers.

THE BEST FISHING IN OREGON'S NORTHEAST ZONE

ANEROID LAKE
One of a handful of lakes in Eagle Cap Wilderness that produce larger trout. Others include Frances, Hobo, Prospect and Unit.

CATHERINE CREEK
Good fishing for wild trout and finclipped steelhead.

COLD SPRINGS RESERVOIR
Offers good warmwater fishing during a wet cycle, especially for crappie.

GRANDE RONDE RIVER (lower)
A productive stretch for finclipped steelhead.

IMNAHA RIVER
Excellent rainbow trout fishing in a Wild and Scenic setting.

JOHN DAY RIVER (below Kimberly)
World class angling for smallmouth bass and a premiere summer steelhead fishery.

JOHN DAY RIVER, SOUTH FORK
Features a rebounding redband rainbow population with good access through public land.

McKAY RESERVOIR
Can offer excellent fishing for crappie and other warmwater panfish during high-water years.

STRAWBERRY LAKE
An easy hike for plump trout in an alpine wilderness setting.

UMATILLA RIVER
Good fishing for finclipped summer steelhead, fall chinook jacks, and finclipped coho.

WALLA WALLA RIVER, SOUTH FORK
The most pristine trout water in Northeast Oregon.

WALLOWA LAKE
Currently growing the state's largest kokanee.

WALLOWA RIVER
A popular and accessible stream for trout and finclipped winter steelhead.

WENAHA RIVER
A beautiful wilderness trout stream with plentiful bull trout and big rainbows.

There isn't a lot of warmwater fishing available in this chilly corner of the state, but the John Day River below Kimberly makes up for it with a world-class smallmouth bass fishery. Anglers from around the nation appreciate the combination of remote desert canyons, thrilling whitewater, and abundant smallmouth. Other good warmwater fisheries include Cold Springs Reservoir for crappie and McKay Reservoir, which offers excellent fishing for largemouth bass during wet weather cycles.

The Northeast Zone includes the entire Umatilla National Forest, and portions of the Wallowa-Whitman, Ochoco and Malheur forests. It encompasses four wilderness areas (Bridge Creek, Eagle Cap, Strawberry Mountain, and Wenaha-Tucanon) and two wildlife refuges (McKay Creek, and Philip Schneider on the South Fork John Day).

I-84 cuts diagonally across the zone (between Wallowa and Blue mountain ranges), along which are located the major communities of Pendleton, LaGrande, and Baker City. Paved secondary roads lead to the small communities that serve as gateways to the region's fisheries, most notable of which are Enterprise and Joseph. Most other roads in the zone are unpaved.

Well-maintained trails access most backcountry lakes and streams. Trails into the Wallowas are noted for their steep grade. Pack trains (horse, mule, and llama) are popular and are available through guide services in Joseph, Enterprise, and LaGrande. Minam Lodge, the only commercial facility in the Wallowa-Whitman National Forest, is accessible only by trail or small plane.

Campgrounds are plentiful in the national forests. Wallowa Lake State Park offers a full-service campground with many amenities. There are motels in most communities, with visitor conveniences especially concentrated in the vicinity of Wallowa Lake east of Joseph.

One of the more heavily visited lakes in Eagle Cap Wilderness, offering fishing for larger trout. Aneroid is off the main trail, cradled among high peaks at 7520 ft., six miles from the southern end of Wallowa Lake. Elevation gain is 2320 ft. It is off Trail 1804 which heads south from Wallowa Lake State Park. Snow may block access until July. It has a privately owned camp with cabins on it shores.

The lake has 39 surface acres and supports brook and rainbow trout to 14 inches, averaging 10 inches. Fly fishing is good in August and September. There are good campsites at the lake. Camp well back from the water to preserve fragile vegetation, and use no-trace camping methods.

BARTH QUARRY POND. A lightly fished half-acre pond southeast of Hermiston that dries up during drought but is currently full and stocked. Take Exit 193 off I-84. Head north 50 yards, turn east onto Whitmore Rd. 1.6 miles, then north on Nolan Market Rd. 0.3 mile. Park on the shoulder of the gravel road.

The pond supports crappie and largemouth bass to 3 pounds. L-shaped, the pond abuts a rock cliff on one edge and is brushy on another, but the brush is not impassable. A float tube would be very helpful. Best fishing is up against the brush and just off the rock cliff.

BATES POND. An 8-acre former mill pond about 30 miles northeast of John Day, west of Bates. It is privately owned and its spillway and dam have been declared unsafe. It is closed to public use.

BEAR CREEK (Wallowa watershed). A pretty little wild trout stream flowing out of Bear Lake in Eagle Cap Wilderness. It enters the Wallow River at the town of Wallowa. Fishing throughout the Bear Creek system is restricted to artificial flies and lures.

From Wallowa, the Bear Creek Rd. (Forest Rd. 8250) follows the creek south into Wallowa-Whitman National Forest. Continue south on Spur Rd. 040 to Boundary Campground, and pick up Trail 1653 to follow the creek to its headwaters.

Bear is fairly productive for wild rainbows and brook trout. Bull trout are also present and must be released unharmed.

There's no limit on the brookies. Below the forest boundary, ask permission to access the creek.

BIBBY RESERVOIR. A 16 acre impoundment 5 miles west of Kent on Buckhollow Creek. It supports largemouth bass.

BIG SHEEP CREEK. A tributary of the Imnaha River, lightly fished but supporting excellent populations of wild rainbows and bull trout. All bull trout must be released unharmed. The creek flows 25 miles to its confluence at the town of Imnaha on Hwy. 350.

A primitive road follows the lower 12 miles, but all but the first 1.5 miles flow through private land closed to public access. Ask permission for access. Spur roads off Forest Rd. 39 access portions of the upper creek in Wallowa-Whitman National Forest. Trail 1800 follows the creek 3.5 miles from a trailhead off Forest Rd. 140 downstream to Forest Rd. 3940. This is a very high gradient reach, extremely cold, primarily supporting bull trout.

Trout in the lower creek average 9 to 12 inches, with angling best in late summer and fall. Both bait and flies can be productive. The nearest campground is at Lick Creek on Forest Rd. 39, a couple of miles southeast of the Forest Rd. 140 junction.

BILLY JONES LAKE. A 6-acre hike-in brook trout lake above the tree-line near the top of Hurricane Divide in Wallowa-Whitman National Forest. From Joseph, take the Hurricane Creek Rd. south to Hurricane Creek Campground. Follow Hurricane Creek Trail 1807 south about 7 miles to Trail 1824, a steep 3-mile switchback to Echo Lake. Billy Jones can be reached by hiking south up-ridge one mile from Echo Lake. There is no trail, and snow may block access until July. You'll need good knees if you're hiking back down with a loaded pack.

The lake once supported a population of fine rainbow to 14 inches until someone took it upon themselves to introduce brook trout. The plump, restrained rainbows are now gone, and the prolific brook trout are thriving. Overpopulation and stunting are inevitable.

Bait works well in summer, with flies best in September. The trail is generally open from July through September.

BIRCH CREEK. A tributary of the lower Umatilla River with catch and keep fishing opportunities for rainbow trout. It joins the river at Pendleton. About 30 miles long, it heads in the Pine Grove area south of Pilot Rock. It is followed closely by Hwy. 395 and by secondary roads from Pendleton to Pilot Rock. Most access is through private property. Ask permission to fish. South of Pilot Rock the creek is followed by paved and gravel roads up both the east and west forks. Fishing for wild rainbow is fair to good in early season. There are no campgrounds in the area. The creek has steelhead runs but is closed to steelhead and salmon angling.

BLUE LAKE. (Wallowa watershed) A deep 30-acre hike-in brook trout lake, headwaters of the Minam River in Wallowa-Whitman National Forest. From the community of Lostine east of Enterprise, follow the Lostine River Rd. to the end. The trail to Blue heads south from Two Pan Campground. Follow the Lostine River Trail 1670 about 5.7 miles to Minam Lake. Blue Lake is 0.9 mile south of Minam's southern tip. Take the right fork at the trail junction. Snow may block access until July.

Blue Lake derives its rich color from its 62 ft. depth. It supports a large population of fair size brook trout, which take flies and bait. Trout season is determined by snowpack. August and September are generally the best angling months.

BOARDMAN POND. No. 2 ¼ acre pond on Umatilla National Wildlife Refuge south of I-84. Turn right at the Boardman Exit. When the road dead-ends, work your way over to the pond. It has an excellent bluegill population and reportedly supports crappie and walleye. Pond No. 1 is closed.

BRIDGE CREEK. A scenic stream both near its source and confluence, tributary of the John Day, offering fair trout angling. It flows through a variety of interesting eastern Oregon terrain, including a forest wilderness (Bridge Creek Wilderness, created in 1984), and the Painted Hills of the John Day Formation, a geologic study area.

Bridge Creek originates in springs near Mt. Pisgah in the Ochoco Mountains just south of Mitchell on Hwy. 26 northeast of Prineville. There is an undeveloped campground (Carroll Camp, Ochoco National

Forest) at the head of the creek near Pisgah Springs. The main attraction of the wilderness is North Point, a 600 ft. cliff overlooking central Oregon and the Cascade peaks. The wilderness is a mix of fir, larch, lodgepole, and ponderosa pine, with clearings of sagebrush, grass, and mountain mahogany typical of Oregon's high desert plateau.

To reach Pisgah Springs from Mitchell, follow County Rd. 8 south from Mitchell. It becomes Forest Rd. 22. At the first crossroads, turn right onto Forest Rd. 2630 (Scotts Campground and Allen Cr. Reservoir are to the left). At the next crossroads, the left fork climbs Mt. Pisgah. Follow the right fork, and turn right again onto Forest Rd. 430, which leads to the springs.

To access the Painted Hills reach of Bridge Creek, from Hwy. 26 about 4 miles west of Mitchell, turn north onto Bridge Creek Rd., which follows the creek through the Painted Hills toward its confluence with the John Day near Burnt Ranch. The Painted Hills are handsome red and yellow layered volcanic formations that contain a wealth of fossils and are widely studied for the geologic story they tell—of volcanic eruptions, oceanic inundation, and climatic changes in this area over the past 75 million years.

Bridge Creek provides fair trout angling in May and June after the spring run-off. Other than Carroll Camp in the headwaters, there is no camping streamside. There is a State Picnic Area on Bridge Creek Rd. about 10 miles northwest of Mitchell at the beginning of the Painted Hills, a very pretty spot. This reach of the Creek has been treated to intensive habitat improvement projects. In-stream structure has been added, cattle grazing is being controlled, riparian vegetation is on the rebound, and trout are responding well.

BULL PRAIRIE RESERVOIR. Good trout water within easy reach, offering year-round angling. It's located about 35 miles south of Heppner, about 15 miles north of Spray, in the Umatilla National Forest. From Heppner, drive south on Hwy. 207 to Forest Rd. 2039, which leads 2.5 miles east to the reservoir.

The 27-acre reservoir was built cooperatively by the Forest Service and ODFW in 1961. Fishing has been good for rainbow and brook trout 8 to 13 inches. Trout to 16 inches are occasionally caught.

There is a campground with drinking water and a boat ramp. Motors are prohibited. Ice fishing is popular, but snow depth can make it a trek to get in. Check with Heppner Ranger District, Umatilla National Forest, for an update on the ice and snowpack. Recommended for youngsters.

BUTTE CREEK (John Day watershed). A tributary of the lower John Day River, entering the river near the county line between Gilliam and Wheeler counties. The creek, 27 miles long, heads southeast of Fossil. Its upper waters are crossed and followed by Hwy. 218. The lower creek is approached by a private gravel road leading northwest from Fossil. Get permission to use this road. The road roughens after about 3 miles. After another 2 or 3 miles it can hardly be called a road.

Irrigation withdrawals from the creek lower it considerably in summer. In early spring it's too high for good fishing due to run-off. But in late spring and early summer Butte offers good angling for wild rainbows. Bait-fishing with worms, eggs or grasshoppers is the most common method. There are several state picnic areas on Hwy. 19 north and south of Fossil, but no campgrounds.

CANYON CREEK (Grant Co.). A popular 27-mile long trout stream, tributary to the upper John Day River, which joins the river at the city of John Day. The creek is closely followed by roads throughout most of its length. Hwy. 395 follows it south from the town of John Day about 11 miles. Forest Rd. 15 continues along the creek for another 8 miles, and Forest Rd. 1520 picks up the final 3 miles to Canyon Meadows Reservoir. The few miles of stream above the reservoir are followed by a logging road on the slope to the north.

Wild redband and west slope cutthroat are present both above and below the reservoir. Fishing below the reservoir improves as the gradient flattens out. Cutthroat 12 to 13 inches are present in these lower reaches, as well as brook trout escapees from the reservoir and wild redbands. The cutthroat move further downstream in winter and early spring. Bait fishing is best until water drops in late spring.

Starr Campground is on Hwy. 395, 3 miles south of its intersection with Forest Rd. 15. Wickiup Campground is on Forest

Rd. 15 about 8 miles upstream from the highway intersection, and there is a campground at Canyon Meadows Reservoir.

CANYON CREEK MEADOWS RESERVOIR. A 25-acre impoundment of upper Canyon Creek in Malheur National Forest. For directions, see Canyon Creek. The reservoir was last stocked with rainbows in 1996 and has reproducing populations of brook trout and west slope cutthroat. Angling is good in spring and late fall, but the dam leaks, and the pool drops to low levels during July, August, and September. Efforts to solve the problem haven't been successful, and stocking has been discontinued pending an evaluation of the situation.

All fish run to good size, and winter fishing through the ice can be very good when the snowpack isn't too heavy. The canyon can really pile on the snow. There is a campground with tent sites, drinking water, and a boat ramp.

CARTER SLOUGH. A 2-acre pond northwest of Cove, offering mediocre fishing for largemouth bass, crappie, bluegill, and brown bullhead.

CATCHED TWO LAKE. A 14-acre lake in Eagle Cap Wilderness offering good angling for smaller brook trout. To reach it, follow Trail 1670 about a mile from Two Pan Campground on the Lostine. At about one mile, Trail 1679 forks to the right and leads to Catched Two in about a mile.

The lake is in a very small basin with a little meadow. Tributary streams enter from the northwest. There are no suitable campsites.

A beautiful stream with good fishing for wild trout and finclipped steelhead, flowing into the upper Grande Ronde River north of Union. It heads on the southwest slope of the Wallowa mountains and flows about 32 miles below its forks. It is closely followed by gravel roads southeast from Union for about 10 miles. Forest Rd. 7785 follows the North Fork, and Forest Rd. 600 follows the South Fork.

The creek is open to steelhead angling from the upper Hwy. 203 bridge (above Catherine Creek State Park) downstream. A lot of effort has gone into rebuilding the Catherine Creek run. Good results in the early 1990's were followed by drought, and the run hit an all-time low in 1993-94. Better water years have led to a resumption of the run's recovery.

Access to good steelhead water is limited. Anglers fish at Catherine Creek State Park, at the park in Union, along the highway, and at bridge crossings. There's a popular hole near the Sewage Treatment facility downstream from Union, which allows public access to the creek. All non-finclipped steelhead must be released unharmed.

About 5 miles upstream from the state park, the stream flows through Wallowa-Whitman National Forest. This reach, including the forks, serves as spring chinook spawning grounds, and supports small wild rainbows and bull trout. Anglers are urged not to harass the chinook, and all bull trout must be released unharmed. The upper mainstem and forks are patrolled by State Police in summer, and if illegal salmon fishing becomes a problem, the upper creek will be closed to all angling. The North Fork is especially pretty.

There is a campground at Catherine Creek State Park 8 miles southeast of Union, and another about 5 miles up the North Fork Rd.

CATHERINE CREEK SLOUGH. A privately owned 10-acre fishery east of LaGrande, offering mediocre catches of largemouth bass, brown bullhead, crappie, yellow perch, bluegill, and smallmouth bass.

CAVENDER POND. A private irrigation pond with public access to fish for stocked trout and largemouth bass. The pond sits on the north side of the highway (Kimberly to Long Creek) that runs between highways 395 and 19.

The pond was first stocked in 1998, and between 2 and 3 thousand legal rainbows will be stocked annually. Largemouth bass are established, and other warmwater species may be present.

Cavender has about 15 surface acres. It has a steep drop-off, but float tubes and small row boats can be launched. All motor boats are prohibited. Best fishing is in spring and early summer before water is released for irrigation.

CHESNIMNUS CREEK. A wild steelhead and rainbow trout stream, flowing 25 miles through a remote section of northeast Wallowa-Whitman National Forest west of Joseph. It s closed to steelheading. It joins Joseph Creek from the west near Joseph's confluence with Crow Creek, about 15 miles above Joseph Creek Canyon.

From Enterprise, follow Hwy. 3 north 13 miles, then turn east on Forest Rd. 46, which follows Elk Cr. Turn right onto Forest Rd. 4625. About 3 miles past Vigne Campground, Forest Rd. 4690 (on the right) picks up the stream and follows it to its forks near Thomason Meadow Guard Station. The lower creek flows through mostly private land, but there is public access in the National Forest in the vicinity of Vigne Campground. The trout run small, with some 8 to 12 inches. Best fishing is in spring and fall.

CHEVAL LAKE. A 10-acre brook trout lake in Eagle Cap Wilderness, accessed from the Lostine River Trail. To reach the trailhead, follow the Lostine River Rd. south from the community of Lostine on Hwy. 82. At road's end (about 18 miles), follow Lostine Trail 1670 for 2.8 miles, then take the Elkhorn Creek Trail 1656 five miles to its junction with Trail 1681. Follow this trail south and west to the lake, 2.3 miles. Elevation gain is 3095 ft. over 10.1 miles. Snow may block access until July.

Trout run to 12 inches, though most are smaller. Angling is best in August and September. A fly rod or spin-fishing gear are most effective here.

CHIMNEY LAKE. A very good 30-acre lake with a spectacular chimney formation at one end. The lake is cupped beneath Lookout Mountain in northern Eagle Cap Wilderness. From Hwy. 82, follow the Lostine River Rd. south about 16 miles to Lillyville Horse Camp. Follow Bowman Creek Trail 1651 west 3.6 miles, climbing a steep saddle, then follow Trail 1659 about a mile to Chimney Lake. Snow may block access until mid-July most years, and the first week in August occasionally.

Small brook trout are plentiful and bite eagerly at anything. There's an island in the middle of the lake that seems to attract the fish, but you'll need a float tube to reach it. There are good campsites here, and Chimney Lake makes a nice base camp for exploring other lakes in the area. See Hobo and Wood. Camp well back from fragile lakeside vegetation and follow no-trace camping guidelines.

CHESNIMNUS CREEK flows through a remote section of the Wallowa-Whitman National Forest. Photograph by Nancy Huff.

Capable of providing excellent warmwater fishing when reservoir levels are maintained. About 4 miles east of Hermiston, in Cold Springs Wildlife Refuge, the reservoir fluctuates from about 1500 acres in spring to less than 500 at the end of irrigation season. Best access is from Hermiston. Head east from town, then north to the Refuge.

Cold Springs offers warmwater fish a rich environment with excellent submerged structure when the reservoir is full. White and black crappie 14 to 16 inches are plentiful, and brown bullheads reach 18 inches. Largemouth bass to 8.5 pounds have been caught here, though they aren't plentiful. Lots of big carp and small numbers of yellow perch are also present.

Crappie are the main attraction at Cold Springs and are typically caught by anglers jigging around submerged trees and brush. Bait-fishing is popular near the inlet. Fish the inlet canal for bullhead in summer. Bass are most frequently caught near the riprap dam face in late season after the reservoir has been drawn down. When the reservoir is high, there is a lot of submerged vegetation, including a thick fringe of trees. In late season, fishing is limited to the dam pool, with most catches made near the dam face.

Water levels at Cold Springs can fluctuate considerably, and unexpectedly, due to efforts to keep the Umatilla River flowing at acceptable levels. Check with Hermiston Irrigation District for updates. See Appendix.

A boat or float tube is necessary to get at the best fishing, though anglers do fish from the dam face. The south and east banks are brushy and inaccessible at high pool. There is one boat ramp on the southwest shore. It is safest to use in spring. Though it is usable at low water, large boats can get stuck beyond the end of the ramp. Only electric motors are permitted.

There's no camping allowed at the reservoir. The entire reservoir is open to fishing from March 1 to September 30. From October 1 till the end of February, fishing is permitted only from the dam face and along the inlet canal. At that time of year, the catch is primarily bullheads.

Cold Springs Wildlife Refuge welcomes more than a dozen species of waterfowl and is home to 13 species of hawks and eagles as well as mule deer, coyote, bobcat, and ring-necked pheasant.

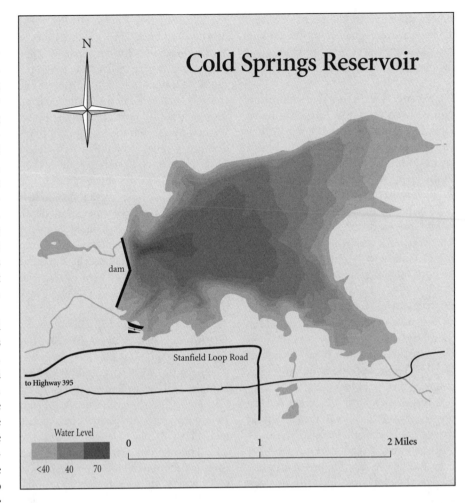

CONFORTH PONDS. (Confederated Tribes of Umatilla) A series of ponds north and south of Hwy. 730 offering fishing for largemouth bass. Other warmwater species may have been illegally introduced by local anglers. Park on the road shoulder. A tribal permit is required. Call the tribal game and fish department for information. See Appendix. Recommended for youngsters.

CRAWFISH LAKE. A 15-acre brook trout lake near the Grant-Baker County Line, a short hike from the road. It is reached from the Baker County side by a 20-mile drive west from the town of North Powder, which is on Hwy. 30 south of La Grande. Follow the signs for Anthony Lake Ski Area. From the ski area, continue west on Forest Rd. 73 about 3 miles to the trailhead, which is on the east side of the road. The lake is a mile hike in.

Brook trout are very plentiful, too plentiful. Take your limit. The fish are stunted from over-population. There is no minimum keeper size. Campgrounds are available near Anthony Lake.

CRESCENT LAKE (Wallowa watershed). A small but very productive brook trout lake in the basin southwest of Wallowa Lake. From Joseph drive around Wallowa Lake to the end of Hwy. 82, one mile south beyond the lake. Hike up the Wallowa River on Trail 1820 for about 6 miles to the intersection of Trail 1821, which leads west and climbs into the lake basin. In 3 miles you'll reach Horseshoe Lake, and the climbing is over. Douglas Lake is 1.5 miles beyond, and Crescent is just north of it across the trail. Total hike is about 10.5 miles, elevation gain 2600 ft.

The basin can also be reached from the upper Lostine River by a hike of about the same distance up the East Fork Lostine River. From the end of the Lostine Rd., hike upstream along the East Fork Trail 1662. It's 6.5 miles to the west end of the Lake Basin at Mirror Lake. Snow may block access until July.

Crescent covers 24 acres and is about 20 feet deep. It supports good numbers of brook trout and holds up well through the season, with fish 7 to 13 inches and some to 15 inches. Larger fish may be taken by float tube at dusk. Flies and lures are effective. There are several good campsites around the lake. Other lakes nearby provide good fishing as well. See Douglas.

CUTSFORTH PONDS. Two small trout ponds in an attractive forest setting in Umatilla National Forest along Willow Creek southeast of Heppner. The ponds are in Cutsforth Park about 20 miles south of the Heppner-Ukiah Road. They cover about ½ acre and are connected by a channel. The ponds are stocked with legal trout in late spring and are fished pretty hard. There is a dock with wheelchair accessible ramp. Camping is permitted. Recommended for youngsters.

DESOLATION CREEK. A nice trout stream, tributary to the North Fork of the John Day, entering the river near Dale on Hwy. 395. This is about 15 miles south of Ukiah. The creek flows about 40 miles, counting the upper forks.

Forest Rd. 10 follows the creek from Dale upstream over 20 miles to the creek fork, then follows the North Fork to its headwaters, continuing several more miles to Olive Lake. From Dale, an unimproved road also follows the east bank of the lower creek closely for about 6 miles before joining Forest Rd. 10. The South Fork has no direct access. Forest Rd. 45 approaches the upper creek area from Susanville.

Desolation Creek has wild redband and bull trout. Bull trout must be released unharmed. Heavy run-off slows the fishing in early spring.

Tollbridge Campground is located near the mouth of Desolation Creek, and there are camping facilities at Olive Lake. A ranger station at Ukiah can provide additional information.

DIAMOND LAKE (Wallowa watershed). A remote brook trout lake north of Tombstone Lake, near the southern border of Eagle Cap Wilderness. The lake is about 20 acres, and its outlet flows into Elk Creek, a small tributary of the upper Minam River. From any direction, it can only be reached by a considerable hike.

Best approach is by Trail 1944, the Middle Fork Trail, which can be reached from Forest Rd. 7787. From Hwy. 203 south of Union take Forest Rd. 77 east about 3 miles to the Catherine Creek turn-off. Follow Forest Rd. 7785 about a mile up the creek

to the Buck Creek Rd. (Forest Rd. 7787) and head up Buck Creek about 4 miles to the trailhead, which is on a hairpin turn. Hike north ½ mile on Trail 1944-A to the main trail, then head east up-slope. The trail follows the middle fork to its head and crosses a saddle north of Burger Butte, about 4 miles from the trail junction. It's another 3 miles downhill to Diamond Lake. Tombstone Lake is .4 mile farther. Total elevation gain is about 1500 ft.

Diamond perches at elevation 6900 ft. It has 11 surface acres and a maximum depth of 24 feet. Angling is usually good for brook trout to 12 inches. August and September are the best months. Flies and lures are equally effective. There's fishing in nearby Tombstone Lake as well. Snow may block access until July.

DOUGLAS LAKE. A 44-acre brook trout lake in the popular lake basin at the headwaters of the West Fork Wallowa River. Douglas is about half-way between Eagle Cap and Matterhorn mountains. From Joseph drive around Wallowa Lake to the end of Hwy. 82, one mile south beyond the lake. Follow Trail 1820 up the Wallowa River for about 6 miles to the intersection of Trail 1821, which leads west and climbs into the lake basin. In 3 miles you'll reach Horseshoe Lake, and the climbing is over. Douglas Lake is 1.5 miles beyond, and Crescent is just north of it. The total trip is about 10 .5 miles with an elevation gain of 2600 ft. Snow may block access until July. These trails get chewed up by pack horses, so be prepared for a bit of mud.

The basin can also be reached by a hike of about the same distance up the East Lostine River. From the end of the Lostine Rd. 18 miles south of the town of Lostine, follow the East Fork Trail 1662 to the west end of the basin at Mirror Lake (6.5 miles). Horses and packers are available at Joseph. You'll want to make reservations for guided trips. Supplies and tackle are available in Enterprise and Joseph.

Fishing for brook trout can be very good in August and September. The lake has about 44 surface acres and a maximum depth of 80 ft. Trout run to 10 inches and are plentiful. Flies and lures are best. This is a good dry fly lake in late July. Other nearby lakes offer good angling. See Crescent, Moccasin, Mirror, Unit, Horseshoe.

EAGLE LAKE. A deep lake at the head of Eagle Creek in the Eagle Cap Wilderness of Wallowa-Whitman National Forest, featuring mackinaw as well as rainbow trout. It's a 7-mile hike up the main Eagle Creek Trail 1922 from the end of the Eagle Creek Rd., with an elevation gain of 2609 ft. See Eagle Creek for directions to the trailhead.

The rainbows reach 12 inches and respond well to flies. The lake trout go to 16 inches and are best taken with deep lures or spinner and bait. Eagle Lake is 90 ft. deep and covers 37 acres. At elevation 7400 ft., the lake is generally only accessible from July through September.

ECHO LAKE (Wallowa watershed). A small brook trout lake high in the Hurricane Creek watershed of Eagle Cap Wilderness, just a ridge to the east of the upper Lostine River. From Joseph, take the Hurricane Creek Rd. south to Hurricane Creek Campground. Follow Hurricane Creek Trail 1807 south about 7 miles to Trail 7775, a steep 3-mile switch-back to Echo Lake. Snow may block access until July.

Echo is at elevation 8320 ft. near the top of Hurricane Divide. It is the source of Granite Creek. Lightly fished, its brook trout have overpopulated the lake and are under 8 inches. There is no catch limit on the brook trout.

The lake is only 7 acres, but almost 50 feet deep. Fishing is fair from late July through September. Bait, lures, or flies can all be effective. Billy Jones Lake, a half-mile bushwhack southeast is also fishable. Keep an eye out and you might spot bighorn sheep and mountain goats.

FRANCES LAKE (Wallowa watershed). One of the more productive lakes in the Eagle Cap Wilderness. Large and scenic, it is cupped on a bench of the Hurricane Divide east of the Lostine River. The old trail to Francis reached the lake in just 4 miles with an elevation gain of about 1000 ft. per mile. An alternative trail is 9 miles with lots of switchbacks. The trailhead is 3 miles south of Lostine Guard Station.

Richer than most lakes at this elevation, Frances has 30 surface acres and is 21 ft. deep. It supports brook trout, which average 10 to 12 inches and occasionally reach 15 inches, and is stocked with rainbows. All methods will take fish. Fly fishing is good in September.

Frances is very scenic, with opportunities to see bighorn sheep and mountain goats.

FRAZIER LAKE (Wallowa watershed). A fairly shallow lake in the headwaters of the West Fork Wallowa River within Eagle Cap Wilderness. From Joseph drive around Wallowa Lake to the end of Hwy. 82, a mile south beyond the lake. Follow the Wallowa River Trail 1820 for about 10 miles to Frazier Lake. This is an easy trail with a total elevation gain of about 1800 ft., much of it spread out along the first 8 miles. The last 2 miles are fairly steep. These trails get chewed up by pack horses, so be prepared for a bit of mud. Little Frazier Lake is above Frazier but holds no fish.

Frazier has about 16 surface acres and offers good fishing for brook trout 7 to 10 inches and larger. Glacier and Prospect lakes to the west also offer good fishing. Horses and guides are available at Joseph.

GLACIER LAKE. A deep, scenic lake high in the Eagle Cap Wilderness at the head of the West Wallowa River. Glacier Lake is cradled in a cirque on the east slope of Eagle Cap, which towers above it.

From Joseph on Hwy. 82, take the road to the south end of Wallowa Lake, where Trail 1820 begins. It's a 12-mile trip up the West Wallowa River to the lake. You can also approach from the north following the East Fork of the Lostine River. Horses and mules are available in Joseph for riding and packing into the high lakes.

Glacier is at elevation 8200 ft. in a beautiful alpine setting. The lake is crystal clear. Fishing for brook trout can be excellent in August and September. The trout run 7 to 15 inches, averaging 10 inches. All methods can be used effectively. Be prepared for sudden snow squalls in late September, though fishing can be best in September and early October. For other fishable lakes in the area, see Prospect, Frazier. Supplies, tackle, and the amenities of civilization are available in Enterprise and Joseph.

GRAND RONDE LAKE. A heavily used trout lake in the Anthony Lake area of the Elkhorn Mountains, within the southern Wallowa-Whitman National Forest. The lake outlet flows north into the Grand Ronde River. The spur road leading to Grand Ronde is on the right about ½ mile beyond the Anthony Lake turn-off.

This 10-acre lake has both rainbow and brook trout and is stocked with rainbows annually. Fishing is good almost anytime after the lake becomes accessible, usually in

FRAZIER LAKE offers some of the best fishing in Eagle Cap Wilderness. Photograph by Ken Witty, ODFW.

late June. Maximum depth is 20 ft. There is a campground on the lake and other good campgrounds at Anthony Lake.

GRANDE RONDE RIVER

GRAND RONDE RIVER: Wallowa River confluence to Snake River. The most popular and productive section of this long river—a 117-mile flow fished primarily for steelhead and including a Wild and Scenic stretch. It is joined by the Wallowa River near Rondowa and by the Wenaha River at Troy.

The Grande Ronde flows over 200 miles from the Blue Mountains southwest of La Grande before crossing into Washington and continuing its flow to the Snake River. Many lower Grande Ronde steelheaders carry licenses for both Oregon and Washington to enable them to take advantage of fishing opportunities on both sides of the state line.

Historically, the Grand Ronde hosted sizable runs of wild salmon and steelhead, all of which were decimated by the usual combination of dams and agricultural and forestry practices. Efforts to restore these runs through hatchery programs, habitat restoration, and angling regulations have begun to show modest success, though the salmon run is still declining.

In recent good years, about 3000 wild

steelhead have returned to the Grande Ronde, along with up to 5000 finclipped hatchery steelhead. Wild fish begin entering in September, while the first hatchery run holds off till October. Another hatchery run enters the river in late winter (February and March), heading for their nursery acclimation pond near Cottonwood Creek in Washington. Only finclipped steelhead may be kept in both Oregon and Washington.

Concentrations of steelhead increase as the river approaches the Snake. The most productive steelhead water is from Cottonwood Creek to the Snake in Washington. In Oregon, best fishing is from the Wallowa confluence to Troy.

A popular access to this section is by boat from the community of Minam on the Wallowa River to Wildcat Creek—a three-day float through the "Wild and Scenic" stretch of the river (Rondowa to Wildcat). Another option is to put in at Palmer Junction on the Grande Ronde about four river miles upstream from the Wallowa confluence.

From Palmer Junction to Wildcat Creek, the river flows through forested canyons that can only be accessed by riverboats. This stretch is suitable for both rafts and drift boats and is popular with whitewater enthusiasts. It is managed by the BLM, which requires floaters to use low-impact camping methods. These include packing out human waste (most folks bring a porta-potty) and discouraging open fires. Campfires are permitted in fire pans only, and campers are asked to pack out campfire ashes.

Below Wildcat the Grande Ronde flows through a mix of State, BLM, private forest, and ranch land and is accessible by road. At Wildcat Creek the river is met by the Wildcat Creek Rd. and by County Rd. 500 (Powwatka Road) from the community of Wallowa. County Rd. 500 follows the river's north bank downstream to the community of Troy and into Washington.

A gravel road out of Troy accesses the south bank downstream for about 3 miles.

It's about 9 river miles from Wildcat to Troy, another 6 to the State Line, and 10 more to the Hwy. 129 crossing in Washington where all roads leave the river. Though floatable, the stretch below Wildcat offers a rocky ride to fish water that's easily accessible from the bank. Most anglers drive to a favorite reach, park at the road side, and walk down to the river. Look for turnouts along the road.

Those who do wish to boat this stretch can put in at Wildcat or Mud Creek, and

pull out 8 or 9 river miles later at Troy. The Troy boat access is a gravel bar on the south bank next to the school. The nearest official take-out below Troy is a long day's drift to the Hwy. 129 crossing in Washington, but there are primitive take-outs at an ODFW area 2 miles below Troy and at a bridge 3 miles below Troy. There is another undeveloped beach take-out about 6 miles beyond the state line. This is a particularly rocky stretch of the river, and wooden boats are not appropriate.

Steelhead season throughout the river is currently September 1 to April 15. Steelheading peaks in October and November before the weather turns really unpleasant, though in warm winters, fishing can be good clear through March. Water conditions for successful fishing usually deteriorate with the spring run-off in March, though fish are generally present throughout the month.

The lower Grande Ronde is fished for trout in spring and summer. Both rainbows and bull trout are present. From Rondowa downstream, a good number of these "trout" are actually finclipped steelhead smolts that fail to migrate, becoming permanent residents of the river. The average catch is 10 to 12 inches, though some exceed 15 inches. Finclipped trout are available for harvest, but wild trout (both rainbow and bull) must be released unharmed. The river above Rondowa has only wild rainbows, and general trout harvest regulations apply.

Smallmouth bass are active in the vicinity of Troy from about mid-June through mid-September. Fish for them in slower water near the shorelines and in deeper, rocky holding water. In winter, anglers at Troy enjoy a fishery for very large whitefish (20 to 25 inches).

Primitive campsites are available at Wildcat Creek and downstream from Troy on north and south banks. Keep an eye out for poison ivy below Wildcat. There's also a Forest Service campground on the Wenaha near Troy.

Troy is a remote community, and though bustling with activity during steelheading and hunting seasons, services can be intermittent. At present, there's gas, a commercial RV and tent campground, and rustic accommodations at a "Shiloh Inn" unlike any other in the otherwise ho-hum motel chain. Positioned at the confluence of the Grande Ronde and Wenaha rivers, it

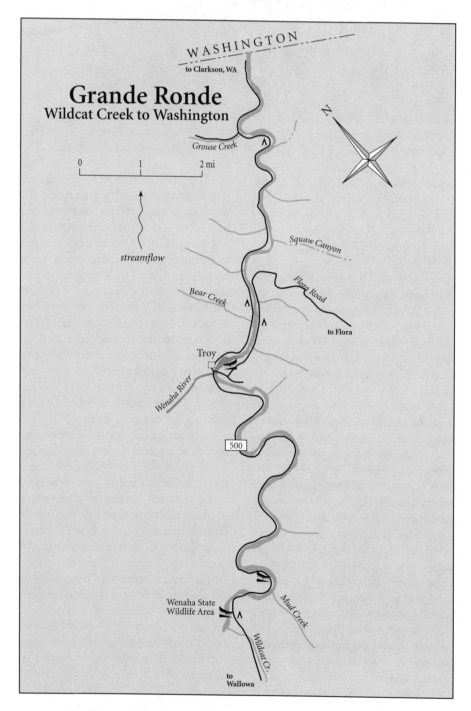

Grande Ronde
Wildcat Creek to Washington

WASHINGTON
to Clarkson, WA

Grouse Creek

0   1   2 mi

N

streamflow

Squaw Canyon

Bear Creek

Flora Road

to Flora

Troy

Wenaha River

500

Wenaha State
Wildlife Area

Mud Creek

Wildcat Cr.

to
Wallowa

consists of very rustic cabins in authentic "fish camp" style, a few rooms above the bar, and an equally authentic camp-style cafe that knows how to feed folks who've been days or weeks in backcountry. Try their feather-light flapjacks or hash browns with gravy. Showers are available for a fee.

GRANDE RONDE: LaGrande to Wallowa River Confluence. A valley flow through agricultural land with some opportunities to fish for wild rainbow trout and a mix of finclipped hatchery and wild steelhead. Only finclipped steelhead may be kept.

Historically, the river was re-channeled in many places throughout the valley, and good trout and steelhead habitat is limited. Habitat and fishing improve below Elgin, where the gradient steepens and the river flows through its natural canyon. Steelhead generally reach LaGrande around January 1.

Both steelhead and trout are fished at Riverside Park off Spruce St. in LaGrande. There is also public access at bridge easements in both LaGrande and Island Park. Many private landowners along the river allow access. Ask permission and be a courteous guest.

Boat fishing is possible from Elgin downstream during high flows. There is an unimproved gravel bar launch opportunity on Clark Creek Rd. in Elgin. Don't underestimate the challenge of taking out at Palmer Junction near the mouth of Lookingglass Creek. The next take-out is at Wildcat Creek. Both driftboats and rafts can be used here, but low water can be a problem.

GRANDE RONDE: Headwaters to LaGrande. Offes fair bank fishing for a mix of hatchery and wild steelhead and for small wild rainbow trout. The river originates at Grande Ronde Lake in the Blue Mountains of Wallowa-Whitman National Forest.

I-84 follows the river west from LaGrande to Hilgard. Hwy. 244 picks up the stream from Hilgard to near Starkey. Forest Rd. 51 and spur roads follow it toward its headwaters.

At this time, steelhead are stocked up to Hilgard Junction State Park on Hwy. 244. The steelheading deadline is at the Meadow Creek confluence near Starkey. Steelhead reach this section of the river in January. Only finclipped steelhead may be kept.

The GRANDE RONDE *is fished for trout and smallmouth bass in spring and summer, steelhead in fall and winter. Photograph by Richard T. Grost*

There's public access to the river from turn-outs on I-84 near the first exit west of LaGrande, at Five Points Creek confluence, and at the weigh station. Hilgard Junction State Park on Hwy. 244 offers access to a good steelhead pool and some nice riffles. The water near Red Bridge State Park is less productive, but it's possible to walk downstream from the park through U.S. Forest Service property to find better fishing. Forest Service landholdings are intermittent and unsigned along the lower portion of this reach. Use a Wallowa-Whitman Forest map to identify public access opportunities.

Trout in this stretch of the river are all wild, and though regulations currently allow some harvest, catch and release is encouraged. Bull trout may be present, particularly near Lookingglass Creek, a bullhead sanctuary. Know your trout, and release bullhead unharmed. Fishing is fair for small rainbow trout from the opening in late spring through summer and fall.

Hilgard Junction and Red Bridge state parks both have camping and day-use facilities in pleasant settings of ponderosa pine and cottonwoods. There are three campgrounds on the upper river—two on Forest Rd. 51 and a third on Forest Rd. 5125.

GREEN LAKE (Minam River watershed). A solitary brook trout lake high in the North Minam River drainage within Eagle Cap Wilderness. Green Lake sits pretty much by itself, 2 miles south of (and about 1800 feet above) the North Minam.

The easiest access is probably up the

Minam River from Red's Horse Ranch, but you have to fly or pack into the ranch. Most backpackers approach from the lakes east of the river. The Bowman Trail 1651 leads west from the Lostine Rd. about 2.5 miles south of Lostine Guard Station. Take Trail 1651 past John Henry Lake and down into North Minam Meadows, then ascend the steep Green Lake Trail (1666) to the lake. The total hike is over 12 miles, with many steep, long pitches. Naturally, you won't suffer from a lot of company once you get there.

The lake is at elevation 7000 ft. in a glacial cirque on the north side of Hazel Mt. It has about 15 surface acres. There are rumors of abundant brook trout to 16 inches. Flies and lures can both be effective. August and September are the best times to be up here. If the hike sounds daunting, horses and guides are available at Lostine.

HAT ROCK POND. A six-acre pond stocked with legal trout and supporting largemouth and smallmouth bass. The pond is at Hat Rock State Park, which provides every facility a state park can offer. Free Fishing Day activities for area youngsters take place here. The park is 98 miles east of Umatilla on Hwy. 730. Recommended for youngsters. Wheelchair accessible.

HOBO LAKE. A small lake stocked with rainbows, high on the east side of Lookout Mt. west of the Lostine River within Eagle Cap Wilderness. Head south 15 miles from Lostine on Hwy. 82 to the Bowman Creek

1. Imnaha to Fence Creek. Private land; access with permission of landowner (most landowners live on premises).

2. Fence Creek to Horse Creek. Private land; road 1000 ft. above river; access with landowner permission.

3. Horse Creek to Cow Creek. Unpaved road along river through public-private mix; USFS land well signed; good trout fishing in holes and pockets from late June; small-mouth plentiful July-Aug.

4. Cow Creek to Eureka Bar. Well maintained trail closely follows river 4 miles to Eureka Bar; moderate gradient; watch for poison ivy.

Trail 1651, about 2.5 miles south of Lostine Guard Station. Climb east on this trail for 3.6 miles to the junction of Trail 1659, which you follow north 1.2 miles to the short spur trail that leads west to Hobo Lake, passing Chimney Lake one mile before Hobo. Total trail mileage is 5.4 miles, and total elevation gain is over 3000 ft., so fuel up before hitting the trail.

Hobo is at 8320 ft and covers 8 acres. It is quite deep for its size. Bait is usually the most productive method, but a wet fly or nymph can do well in the late fall. It can be fished easily from the bank, and there's not much vegetation to catch a back-cast.

HONEYMAN POND. A little pond in a forest setting with opportunities to catch stocked legal rainbows. From Enterprise, follow Hwy. 303 north about 13 miles. Turn right onto Forest Rd. 46. About 6 miles beyond Dougherty Campground, just before the junction with Cold Springs Rd. (4680), turn right onto a spur road (which may not be signed). Honeyman is about ¼ mile farther on the south side of this road. It is stocked with legal rainbows in June. Nat-ural campsites are available at the pond, and there are developed camping facilities at Dougherty and farther east on Forest Rd. 46 at Buckhorn Campground.

HORSESHOE LAKE (Eagle Cap). A gorgeous brook trout lake at the east end of the of Eagle Cap Wilderness lake basin. Horseshoe is the first large lake approached by the trail from the east. From Joseph, drive south around Wallowa Lake to the end of Hwy. 82, a mile beyond the lake. Hike up the Wallowa River on Trail 1820 for about 6 miles to the intersection of Trail 1821, which leads west and climbs into the basin. In 3 miles you'll reach Horseshoe Lake, and the climbing is over. Douglas Lake is 1.5 miles beyond, and Crescent Lake is to the north. The total hike is about 9 miles, with an elevation gain of 2400 ft.

You can also approach from the north along the East Fork Lostine River, Trail 1662. It's 6.5 miles from the end of the Lostine River Rd. to the west end of the basin at Mirror Lake. Snow may block access to either route until July. All these trails can get muddy.

Surrounded by meadows, in the shadow of granite cliffs, the lake has 40 surface acres with maximum depth over 70 ft. There are good reed beds, and brook trout are abundant and fairly easy to catch, though small. Larger fish can be taken in fall, usually on flies and lures. Other lakes in the vicinity include Douglas, Crescent, Moccasin, Lee, Mirror. Horseshoe is usually accessible in early July, and fishing holds up well throughout the season.

ICE LAKE. The deepest lake in Eagle Cap Wilderness. Spectacularly alpine, Ice is perched above the West Wallowa River north of a ridge that separates the river valley from the lake basin. From Joseph, drive around Wallowa Lake to the end of Hwy. 82, one mile south of the lake. Follow the Wallowa River on Trail 1820 for 2.8 miles to the intersection of Trail 1808, which climbs west. Grit your teeth and switch back upslope for 5.1 miles to the lake. Total elevation gain for this stretch is 2300 ft., but the trail is well laid out.

Ice Lake is nestled on the east side of Matterhorn Mt. at elevation 7900 ft. Its

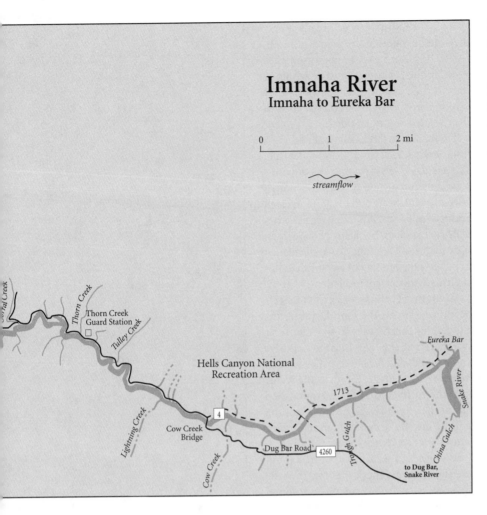

Imnaha River
Imnaha to Eureka Bar

0   1   2 mi

streamflow

Thorn Creek

Thorn Creek Guard Station

Tulley Creek

Hells Canyon National Recreation Area

Eureka Bar

1713

Snake River

Lightning Creek

4

Cow Creek Bridge

Dug Bar Road   4260

Cow Creek

Trough Gulch

China Gulch

to Dug Bar, Snake River

---

bull trout are present from fall through spring. Know your trout, and release the bulls unharmed.

Above Big Sheep Creek the Imnaha is less productive but there are some wild rainbows and plentiful whitefish of good size. Bull trout are in the upper river year-round. The upper river flows through private land up to a 5- mile public easement managed by the U.S. Forest Service. Watch for signs that say "Begin Public Fishing Access." There are turn-outs along the road. The river is deeper in this stretch and is best fished from the bank with spinner and bait, or fly-fished with a nymph. Above Palette, public access continues along the Imnaha River Road to Indian Crossing campground and along Trail 1816 to the headwaters. Best fishing is below the forks (7 miles above Indian Crossing).

Spinner and bait fishing are most popular here, but the river has excellent fly water and is generally wadeable. Golden stoneflies hatch around July, with grasshopper imitations effective in August, and caddis in September and early October.

Like other tributaries of the Snake River System, the Imnaha once hosted sizable runs of chinook salmon and steelhead. These native runs were all but destroyed by hydroelectric dams on the Snake. Efforts to replace the wild runs with hatchery programs have met with some success. Hatchery returns are fair to good. The river is currently open for steelhead up to Big Sheep Creek (at the town of Imnaha). In spring, steelhead are present throughout the open area. Fall fishing is best below Cow Creek Bridge. Best steelheading is after a period of high flows. Steelhead show

basin, possibly created by volcanic action, is over 190 feet deep, and its setting is breathtaking. The lake has about 46 surface acres and lots of fishable shoreline.

Its water is extremely cold but supports brook trout 7 to 11 inches. Bait is best in July, and lures and flies work best by September. Four tributaries enter from the west in a small meadow area, and another from the southeast. There are a couple of natural campsites. Camp well back from fragile lakeside vegetation and use no-trace camping methods. Packers and guides are available in Joseph.

IMNAHA RIVER

A beautiful high gradient stream, tributary to the Snake, with fishing for wild trout and a mix of hatchery and wild steelhead. The Imnaha pours out of the Wallowas, offering an enticing mix of cascades, riffles, glides, and short pools. Designated Wild and Scenic throughout most of its run, it supports good populations of rainbows and bull trout.

The Imnaha flows 75 miles from its headwaters in Eagle Cap Wilderness to its confluence with the Snake River at Eureka Bar, about 22 miles north of the town of Imnaha. From Hwy. 82 at Joseph, it is 32 miles to the river by way of the paved Little Sheep Creek Rd. From there, a good gravel road follows the river upstream for about 45 miles and downstream to within 5 miles of the Snake. A trail (1713) continues from Cow Creek Bridge to Eureka Bar.

Most access to the lower river is in private hands from the town of Imnaha to Fall Creek, though permission to approach the river may be given to courteous anglers who knock at the door. From Fall Creek to Horse Creek, Dug Bar Road follows the river a steep 1000 ft. or more above the stream. This road is dirt and undependable. At Horse Creek, the road returns to the river and follows it to the bridge.

There is excellent fishing throughout this stretch and along the trail. Trail 1713 winds through a narrow canyon in which observant hikers may spot big horn sheep and golden eagles. (Keep an eye out for poison ivy and rattlesnakes..) Rainbow trout are plentiful throughout the year, and

The IMNAHA flows through Hells Canyon Recreation area. Photograph by Dennis Frates.

up at the mouth in mid-September and hold there until the water cools, about mid-October. The best early fall fishing is often in the Snake itself just below the Imnaha confluence. Chinook have also been re-introduced, but in recent years as few as 300 to 400 salmon returned to the Imnaha, and the fishery for them is closed.

There are campgrounds in Wallowa-Whitman National Forest along the Imnaha River Road above Imnaha. Supplies, tackle, and local information are available in Enterprise and Joseph.

JOHN DAY RIVER

JOHN DAY RIVER:Kimberly toColumbia River. One of Oregon's premiere summer steelhead rivers, also offering world class angling for smallmouth bass. The John Day is one of the longest undammed rivers in the lower 48 states. It enters the Columbia River about half-way between Biggs Junction and Blalock on I-84, about 25 miles east of The Dalles. The John Day Dam on the Columbia backs the Columbia 9 miles into the lower John Day Canyon, forming a productive pool (The John Day Arm of Lake Umatilla) that can only be approached from the Columbia due to the presence of Tumwater Falls—a barrier for boats, but not for salmon and steelhead. See Umatilla Lake, John Day Arm for further information about fishing below Tumwater.

Smallmouth bass. Smallmouth bass were first stocked in the John Day in the early 1970s at Service Creek and later at Picture Gorge. From Kimberly to the mouth, the river provides ideal smallmouth habitat, and the fishery has thrived. Smallmouth are fished from March

The highest quality smallmouth fishing on the JOHN DAY is from Service Creek to Tumwater Falls. Photograph by Scott Richmond

through the end of October. In early spring, they can be found in the deeper pools. In later spring, during spawning season, they head for the backwaters and linger along the rimrock ledges. After spawning they can be found throughout this portion of the river, feeding and holding.

The highest quality smallmouth fishing is from Service Creek down to Tumwater Falls. The average catch is 10 to 12 inches with a few fish approaching 6 pounds. Though current regulations don't require it, catch and release on smallmouth over 12 inches will help maintain the quality of this fishery. A catchable slot limit may be implemented to increase the number of larger fish in this stretch. Check current regulations.

Steelhead. There is no hatchery steelhead program on the John Day, but fin-clipped hatchery strays from other river systems enter the river in large numbers and are available for harvest. The ratio of hatchery to wild steelhead in the lower river can reach 50%. Steelhead make good use of the whole river system, migrating well up into the tributaries, though most hatchery strays remain below the forks.

Steelheading seasons vary throughout the river system (check the regs), but the best fishing is from September through December, with peak catches in November. Early season activity is best below Clarno Rapids. Though steelhead remain in the river into early spring, and some portions of the river are open for spring fishing, they are most often spawned out and in poor condition for either sport or harvest.

Access. The John Day flows through a patchwork of private and BLM lands. Watch for signs, and check with nearby landowners when in doubt as to ownership. There are 185 fishable river miles from Kimberly to the mouth. At Kimberly (a community on Rt. 19) the river is augmented by its major tributary, the North Fork. The stretch between Kimberly and Service Creek is both productive and accessible. Rt. 19 follows the river's north bank from the Hwy. 26 junction near picture Gorge to Service Creek, through a checkerboard of public land and private holdings where there is much posted land. Respect no trespassing signs.

Below Service Creek, the river flows through a colorful lava rock canyonland. A designated Scenic Waterway, much of it is accessible only by boat. Rafting is an exciting and practical way to fish the canyon

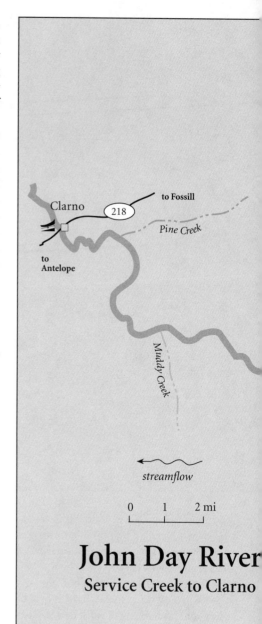

John Day River
Service Creek to Clarno

below Service Creek. For a day's drift, put in at Service Creek (river mile 157, at the junction of routes 19 and 207) and drift 12 river miles to Twickenham (river mile 145). A popular longer drift is from Twickenham to Clarno Rapids (river mile 110 off Hwy. 218 west of Fossil Beds National Monument). Another good day's drift is from Cottonwood Bridge (river mile 40, at the crossing of Hwy. 206) to the mouth of Rock Cr. (river mile 22, east of Wasco).

Whitewater rafting is very popular from Service Creek to Cottonwood Bridge. More than 400 rafts have been known to drift the river in a single day. This stretch includes four Class III rapids (Russo, Homestead, Burnt, and Basalt) and one Class IV (Clarno). At highest spring flow (not rec-

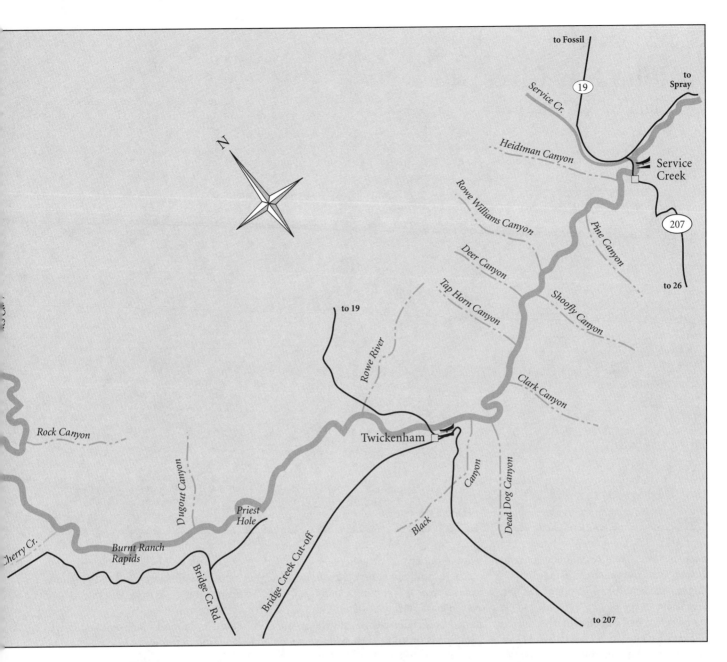

ommended for boating), Clarno can involve a 30 ft. freefall drop. The recommended flow for boating the river is 2000 to 6000 cubic feet per second. Minimum flow for rafts is 1500 cfs. Minimum flow for canoes and other small craft is 500 cfs. River gage information is available. See Appendix.

There is limited public bank access at two BLM-owned sites between Twickenham and Clarno: Burnt Ranch Rapids and Priest Hole. To reach them, follow the Bridge Creek Road north from Hwy. 26. At the fork just before reaching the John Day, turn right to reach Priest Hole (near river mile 136), turn left to Burn Ranch (beween river miles 132 and 133). Be respectful of adjacent private property. Bank access improves again near Clarno Rapids. To reach

Clarno from Hwy. 97, cut south onto Rt. 218 at Shaniko and follow it to the John Day. There is BLM access from just below Clarno to ½ mile above Butte Creek, about 12 river miles. Fished for both smallmouth and steelhead, this is a classic stretch of John Day water, shallow riffles alternating with deep pools.

About 15 river miles from the mouth, gravel roads from Wasco to the west, and Rock Creek to the east, reach the river at Scotts Ford. A gravel road leading west from Mikkalo follows Hays Creek down into the canyon and parallels the river from river mile 30 to river mile 27. Much of this land is private, though there are a few parcels owned by BLM. Ask permission to fish at the nearest ranch if you're in doubt

as to ownership.

There is a BLM campground at Muleshoe Creek, at Sheldon State Park about 10 miles north of Service Creek, and in Ochoco National Forest to the south. Camping is also generally permitted anywhere on BLM land.

JOHN DAY RIVER : Headwaters to Kimberly. A 100-mile flow out of the Strawberry Mountain Wilderness, fished for wild trout and wild summer steelhead in the upper reaches, and for small numbers of smallmouth bass closer to Kimberly. Spring chinook spawn and rear in this section of the river, but the John Day has been closed to salmon fishing since 1977.

The John Day flows only briefly through

John Day River
Kimberly to Service Creek

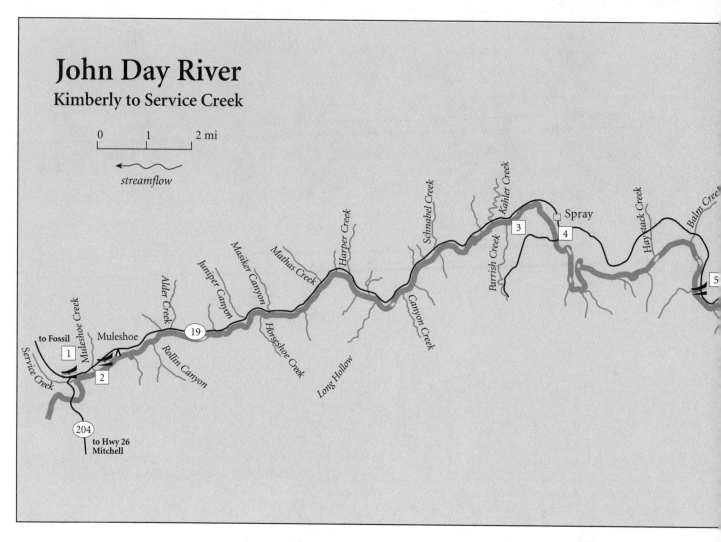

national forest. Good roads follow the river downstream, but much of this reach flows through the private ranchlands of the John Day Valley.

From Kimberly upstream, the river is followed by Hwy. 19 to Dayville, by Hwy. 26 to Prairie City, and by county roads 61 and 14 to its headwaters. In the last 15 miles, the roads turn to dirt and gravel.

For many years, the ranchland portion of this stretch has been inhospitable to trout and steelhead. Barren of sufficient streamside vegetation, the river grows warm in summer, and non-game fish (which prey on trout and steelhead fingerlings) have been a problem. Recently, considerable effort has been devoted to riparian recovery, with good results.

The river is not stocked, but wild rainbows are available, especially in the headwaters. Steelhead reach this stretch in November and December. The river is closed to steelhead angling above Indian Creek. Smallmouth bass are also in this section of the river, but in smaller numbers than

below Kimberly.

Clyde Holliday State Park east of Mt. Vernon provides camping facilities and access to good steelhead water. Though the park is officially closed in winter, and camping is prohibited then, anglers may park and walk in to fish. Trout Farm Campground is near the headwaters, about 16 miles south of Prairie City on County Rd. 62, the road to Drewsey.

JOHN DAY RIVER, MIDDLE FORK. A tributary of the North Fork John Day with fishing for wild redbands, mountain whitefish, and steelhead. It joins the North Fork north of Monument. It has good road access for all but its lower 9 miles, but though it flows through Malheur National Forest, much of the land adjacent to the river is privately owned.

The Middle Fork flows 75 miles from its headwaters east of Prairie City. The head of the Middle Fork is a meandering meadow stream in the vicinity of Bates at about 4800 ft. elevation. It enters a shallow rim-

rock canyon below its headwaters, then moves through a narrow flood plain, remaining more riffle than pool throughout most of its run.

Paved and gravel roads follow the river closely from a few miles below Ritter (on the Ritter-Dale Rd. off Hwy. 395), to its headwaters above Austin Junction (at the Junction of highways 395 and 7) east of Prairie City. It is crossed by Hwy. 395 about 12 miles south of Dale. County Rd. 20 follows the stream from Hwy. 395 southeast past Susanville all the way to Austin Junction. Landowners have been generous along the Middle Fork, but anglers are urged to ask permission to fish and to be courteous guests.

Wild redbands and mountain whitefish 12 to 13 inches provide the primary fishery in this stretch. Bull trout are also present and must be released unharmed. Fishing is good throughout the open trout season. Fly fishing can be effective in summer and fall, with bait best early. Between Hwy. 395 and Hwy. 7, tackle is restricted to a single

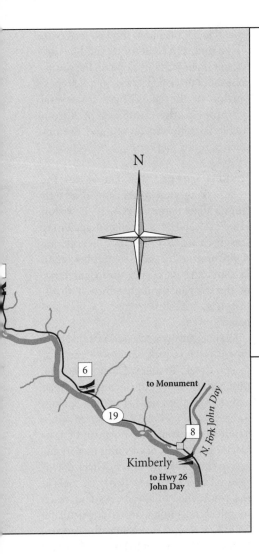

1. *Service Creek.* Gravel bar pull-out and launch for popular drift to Twickenham; bank angling for bass and steelhead.

2. *Muleshoe Creek.* BLM campground and boat ramp; some bank angling for bass and channel catfish; launch for bass and steelhead anglers.

3. *Parrish Creek.* Upper end of Scenic Waterway.

4. *Spray.* Sand launch immediately above county road bridge; private property, modesst fee; be courteous and pack out your litter to insure continued public access.

5. *ODOT Gravel Storage.* Boat launch and pull-out for steelhead & bass anglers.

6. *Mile Post 99.* BLM access; watch for paved turnout; primarily used as launch and pull-out by steelhead anglers; some bank fishing.

7. *Balogna Creek Access.* BLM access; gravel bar boat launch with good bank angling for steelhead and smallmouth.

8. *North Fork Confluence.* Gravel parking area with access to gravel bar boat launch; good bank angling for steelhead (late winter-early spring) and smallmouth (spring-summer).

point hook no larger than 1/4 inch. Lures are prohibited to prevent incidental take of spring chinook. Habitat improvements on the Middle Fork have increased chinook spawning and rearing opportunities, and adult returns have increased, though not to harvestable levels.

Hwy. 395 is the legal deadline for steelheading on the Middle Fork. Most steelhead are hooked in March and early April. No hatchery strays wander this high in the John Day system, so all steelhead fishing on the Middle Fork is catch and release.

The only campground on the river is Middle Fork Campground (Malheur National Forest), on Rt. 20 about 6 miles northwest of Austin.

JOHN DAY RIVER, NORTH FORK. A tributary of the John Day with important salmon and steelhead spawning and rearing habitat. It offers catch and release fishing for wild steelhead but has been closed to salmon fishing since 1977.

The North Fork joins the mainstem at Kimberly on Hwy. 19 after a 113-mile run from the Elkhorn Mountains 20 miles west of Baker City. The upper waters of this fork flow through Umatilla National Forest. This is a big river with a strong flow, yet more riffle than pool throughout most of its run. The best pools are below the confluence of the Middle Fork (at about r.m. 17).

The North Fork has an adequate flow for river boats, and there is some boat angling. Boaters put in at the mouth of Wall Creek and drift to Monument (about 6 miles) or from Monument to Kimberly (about 15 miles).

Much of the river is accessible from nearby roads, though private property may present a problem below Dale. Upstream from Kimberly, a paved road follows the northern bank 15 river miles to Monument. A gravel road continues upstream from Monument as far as r.m. 28 at Birch Creek. The next 11 miles, to Potamus Creek, are roadless. A gravel road follows the river downstream from Dale to Potamus Creek. Dale is on Hwy. 395 south of Ukiah at about the mid-point of the river. Desolation and Camas Creek, both good size tributaries, join the North Fork at Dale.

The North Fork above Dale is followed by paved and gravel forest roads 55 and 5506 for about 11 miles. Above that, Trail 5506 follows the stream through a steep

The JOHN DAY is one of the longest undammed rivers in the United States. Photograph by Scott Richmond

forested canyon to its headwaters in the North Fork John Day Wilderness. The river flows at a moderate gradient over a boulder strewn bed. This is primarily chinook spawning grounds and juvenile steelhead rearing area. Few resident rainbow are present. Anglers are encouraged not to fish for the young steelhead. Bull trout may be found in the deeper pools, but must be released unharmed.

There is fair steelheading in the lower river from the mouth up to the steelhead deadline at the Hwy. 395 bridge at Dale. Steelhead may appear in the North Fork as early as November, but peak activity is in February and March. The season closes after April 15. In most years the river maintains an adequate flow, but it can get very low and clear during winter cold spells, even freezing over. In fact, ice chunks in the river can be a problem to winter anglers.

There is no improved camping on the river below Dale, although you can set up camp anywhere on BLM land. Ukiah Dale State Park offers camping facilities on Hwy. 395, about 8 miles north of Dale. There are four campgrounds on the river in Umatilla National Forest upstream from Dale. Tollbridge Campground is a mile east of Dale. Trough Creek is about 4 miles further east on Forest Rd. 55. Two primitive camps, Gold Dredge and Oriental Creek, are further upstream on Forest Rd. 5506.

JOHN DAY RIVER, SOUTH FORK

An important tributary of the upper John Day River with good fishing for wild redbands and spawning and rearing habitat for steelhead and spring chinook. It is closed to salmon and steelhead fishing.

The South Fork heads in the Snow Mountain area south of Izee (east of Prineville) and flows about 60 miles through high desert country, entering the mainstem from the south at Dayville on Hwy. 26, about 30 miles west of the town of John Day. The South Fork Rd. follows the river from Dayville all the way to Izee.

Land along the first four miles upstream from Dayville is private, but the National Forest Service, BLM, and ODFW own much of the land adjacent to the river above that point, including the Philip W. Schneider Wildlife Management Area (formerly known as Murderer's Creek). There is good public access throughout most of the river.

The river's redband population is responding well to habitat improvement projects within the Management Area both in terms of quantity and size. Redbands to 15 inches and whitefish to 13 inches are present. Take a look at the restored habitat here and ask yourself why more of our streams can't look like this.

The South Fork can be fished all along the South Fork Rd. Park on the road shoulder. It's a fairly short walk to the river in most places. There are unimproved campsites along the stream.

JOHN HENRY LAKE. A shallow, rich lake in the central Eagle Cap Wilderness. It is approached by Trail 1651 which heads about 1.5 miles north of Shady Campground on the Lostine River Rd. Only 13 ft. deep at maximum, John Henry may winterkill some years, but it generally supports a good population of brook trout to 9 inches.

The lakes sits in a basin that contains several small meadows interspersed with alpine timber. A float tube would be useful, but there is a talus slope on the southwest shore that offers access to the deepest portion of the lake. There are several campsites nearby. Camp well back from fragile lakeside vegetation, and use no-trace camping methods.

JOSEPH CREEK. Best known for the breathtaking view of its canyon as seen from a View Point on Hwy. 3 (Lewiston Hwy.). Joseph is a steelhead spawning stream, closed to steelheading, but offering opportunities for nice size rainbows and smallmouth bass. Despite the magnificence of the canyon through which it flows, Joseph is a small brushy stream. Come prepared to wade.

Joseph Canyon is accessed by trail either down Davis Creek, Swamp Creek, or Joseph Creek. To follow Davis or Swamp, turn east off Hwy. 3 onto an unnamed road across from the turn-off to Sled Springs Ranger Station (Forest Rd. 3035). About ¾ a mile east by trail, turn north and follow Davis (Trail 1660), or continue east another 1.5 miles and follow Swamp Creek downstream (Trail 1678). The two trails meet at the confluence of the creeks and reach Joseph about 3 miles farther downstream. To follow Joseph Creek into the canyon, turn east off Hwy. 3 onto Forest Rd. 46 and follow it just a bit beyond the confluence of Chesminus and Crow creeks. Forest Rd. 190 follows Joseph down to the canyon. The road is not well maintained. Trail 1714 follows the creek through the canyon.

Fishing for smallmouth bass is best in late spring and summer below the mouth of Swamp Creek. Best trout fishing is late in the season. There's good fishing for rainbows at the Swamp Creek confluence.

JUBILEE LAKE. A 97-acre impoundment which provides good angling for rainbow trout in an area where lakes are scarce. Jubilee is about 60 miles northeast of Pendleton in Umatilla National Forest. It is at the head of Mottet Creek, about 12 miles north of Tollgate, which is on Hwy. 204. Take Forest Rd. 64 north from Tollgate directly to the lake. Jubilee reaches a depth of 55 ft. Its rainbow are small but numerous. The lake is generally inaccessible until late June.

Jubilee hosts a kids fishing event in late June in cooperation with ODFW and the Forest Service. Lots of catchables are

The SOUTH FORK JOHN DAY flows 60 miles through the high desert, offering excellent public access and good fishing for wild redbands. Photograph by Jeffrey Kee.

stocked prior to the event.

The Forest Service maintains a large campground here with boat ramp. Motors are prohibited on the lake. Recommended for youngsters.

KINNEY LAKE. A 20-acre catfish and rainbow trout lake in the upper Wallowa Valley 5 miles east of Wallowa Lake. From Joseph on Hwy. 82, drive about 5 miles east on paved road 350, the Imnaha Hwy. Turn south onto Tucker Down Rd. and drive 1.5 miles to Kinney Lake Rd., a dirt road that leads east ½ mile to the lake.

Kinney offers good fishing for brown bullheads and stocked rainbow trout. The rainbows are plentiful and average 9 to 13 inches. Bait fishing is most popular here, but there are incredible midge and mayfly hatches, and fly anglers do very well.

This is a private lake to which the public has been granted recreational access. Be a courteous guest. Trashing incidents have been a problem and may eventually lead to closure. Camping, boating, and float tubes are prohibited.

LANGDON LAKE. A fair size lake on Hwy. 204 about half-way between Elgin and Weston at the community of Tollgate. It is privately owned and operated as part of a resort, with angling for patrons only.

LEE LAKE. A small but unusually deep lake in Eagle Cap Wilderness which supports a large naturally reproducing population of small brook trout. To reach Lee, follow Trail 1820 from the power generator south of Wallowa Lake to Trail 1821, which branches west at about 6 miles. The trail reaches Lee in another 4 miles.

Though only 9 acres, Lee reaches a depth of 80 ft. with very little shoal area. The outlet in the northeast corner, used by spawning brook trout, could be productive in fall. The average catch is 8 inches. Rimrock surrounds the lake, and there are no natural campsites.

LEGORE LAKE. One of the highest lakes in Oregon, 30 ft. deep with only 2 surface acres, located in Eagle Cap Wilderness. Access is poor and fishing is marginal. It has been known to winterkill but is stocked with rainbows. Best approach is from the north through Murray Saddle. There are no trails to the lake. The nearest trail ends at the head of Scotch Creek.

LITTLE SHEEP CREEK. A nice little wild rainbow trout stream flowing through much private land. It heads in national forest about 10 miles southeast of Joseph and joins Big Sheep Creek near the town of Imnaha. There is little public access to the lower creek where fishing is best. The upper creek in Wallowa-Whitman National Forest has only marginal trout habitat.

Campgrounds are available at Wallowa Lake State Park and at Lick Creek Campground south of the creek on Forest Rd. 39.

LITTLE STRAWBERRY LAKE. See **STRAWBERRY LAKE, LITTLE.**

LONG CREEK. A tributary of the Middle Fork of the John Day River, about 30 miles long, entering the Middle Fork near Ritter. It heads north of Magone Lake about halfway between the communities of Long Creek and John Day. Hwy. 395 crosses it about 15 miles above its mouth north of the town of Long Creek. The creek is inaccessible downstream from the highway, flowing across private, roadless ranchland. Good gravel roads parallel the upper creek southeast into Malheur National Forest.

Long supports a fair population of wild rainbows and is lightly fished. There's a forest service campground at Magone Lake. Several unimproved campsites are available along the stream.

LONG LAKE (Wallowa watershed). A fair size lake in the headwaters of the North Fork of the Minam River. From the town of Lostine on Hwy. 82 drive south to the end of the road. Take the Trail 1670 along the Lostine River 2.8 miles to the junction with the Elkhorn Trail 1656, which continues southwest. Follow 1656 about 5 miles to a trail junction above Swamp Lake. Follow the trail down to Swamp Lake, and take Trail 1669, which follows the outlet stream about one mile northwest to Long Lake. It's a 10-mile hike on moderately steep trails.

Long Lake is 25 acres, with a reproducing population of brook trout that reach 6 to 12 inches. Fishing is best in August and September. There's also good fishing in Swamp and Steamboat lakes one mile due east of Swamp.

LOST LAKE (Umatilla watershed). A unique hike-in lake near Olive Lake in Umatilla National Forest, stocked with legal rainbows. From Granite on Forest Rd. 73 (west of Phillips Reservoir), follow Forest Rd. 10 west, then Forest Rd. 45 south about ½ mile. Turn left on a unsigned road that ends at a locked gate. Park at the gate and hike about 2 miles to the lake. This is a neat spot—a volcanic bowl against a rocky bluff with a scattering of lodgepole pines. Snow lingers till June.

LOSTINE RIVER. A pretty trout stream heading at Minam Lake, high in the Eagle Cap Wilderness of Wallowa-Whitman National Forest. Crystalline and idyllic within the wilderness, tranquilly majestic in the valley below with its mountainous backdrop, the Lostine flows 31 miles north to join the Wallowa River 2 miles east of the town of Wallowa on Hwy. 82, about 45 miles east of La Grande. The stream is followed 24 miles south by Forest Rd. 8210. The upper river is followed to its source by Trail 1670. Its major tributary, the East Fork, is followed by Trail 1662. Both trails head at Two Pan Campground at the end of the Lostine River Rd. The Lostine Rd. is the jump-off point for several key trails into the Wallowas.

The Lostine is not stocked and provides fair angling for small wild trout in its upper reaches. The average catch is 7-11 inches, with a few larger. Fishing is limited to artificial flies and lures only. Bull trout are present and must be released unharmed. The Lostine is closed to fishing for salmon and steelhead.

There are five forest campgrounds along the Lostine River Rd. from the forest boundary south to road's end. These are heavily used by horse packers—dusty, noisy, crowded with vehicles, and unsuitable for long stays. Don't expect solitude down below. There are many attractive natural campsites along the upper stream, however. Camp well back from fragile streamside vegetation, and follow no-trace camping guidelines

MACK POND. See **R.D. MACK POND.**

MAGONE LAKE. A popular trout lake in Malheur National Forest, about 10 air miles due north of the town of John Day. The lake can be reached by several routes. About 9 miles east of John Day County Rd. 18 leaves Hwy. 26 and runs northeast to the lake. From Hwy. 395 near Mt. Vernon, Forest Rd. 36 winds about 10 miles to the lake.

With 50 acres at elevation 4900 ft., the lake is very rich and 100 ft. deep in places. It is stocked with rainbows and brook trout and is heavily fished for trout to 16 inches. The north end of the lake has good shoal areas where flies will take large fish in the fall.

Magone is open all year. Ice fishing is popular and yields good catches when the ice pack is sufficient. Snow can block access. Check with ODFW in John Day or with the Malheur National Forest Ranger Station for ice pack and road conditions. There is a campground at the lake with drinking water available. Boats can be launched, but there is a 10-mph speed limit on the lake.

MAXWELL LAKE. A pleasant brook trout lake in Eagle Cap Wilderness, approached by trail up the Lostine River. Follow Trail 1674 about 3 miles from the Shady Campground trailhead. The trail is very steep and not suitable for horses.

Covering 16 acres and 50 ft. deep, Maxwell has some good shallows for bank fishing. Deepest water is in the northeast. Tributary inlets enter from the west. Brook trout reproduce naturally in the outlet stream and in subsurface springs in the northern portion of the lake. The fish here are generally small. There are a few natural campsites at the lake. Be sure to camp well back from fragile lakeside vegetation and use no-trace camping methods.

McCORMACH SLOUGH. A 2-mile stretch of Columbia backwater west of Irrigon on the Umatilla National Wildlife Refuge. It offers limited fishing for smallmouth bass and crappie. Dikes have been built to create three separate ponds

From I-84, take Hwy. 730 Exit. Turn left on Patterson Ferry Rd. Trails to the slough are well-signed at every parking lot. Other trails are provided for wildlife viewing. There is a huge mule deer herd on the refuge, as well as a large population of blue herons, several species of ducks, curlews and pelicans. Park at the north end of the slough.

The ponds are rich with good submerged structure to provide habitat, but they are very shallow. Recent stockings seem to have been quickly fished out. The west pond may be full of carp. The others may contain largemouth bass and black and white crappie.

There are two boat ramps, but motors

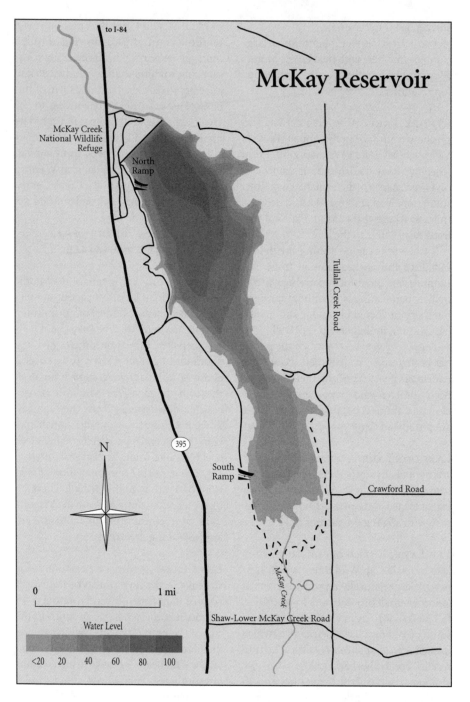

are prohibited. A canoe or float tube would be handy, but there is good bank access.

McGRAW POND. A little pond in the National Forest with drive-in opportunities for stocked trout. From Joseph, follow the main road east toward the Imnaha River. Turn south on Hwy. 395, which becomes Forest Rd. 39. About 3 miles after crossing the Imnaha, turn left onto Forest Rd. 3965 (Hells Canyon Rim Rd.). The pond is about 2 miles farther on the left side of the road. (It doesn't show up on Forest Service maps.) It is stocked with legal rainbows in June.

McKAY CREEK. (Umatilla watershed, pronounced McEye) A tributary of the Umatilla River, captured in McKay Reservoir. The best trout habitat is above the reservoir, where there are some nice riffles and pools that support wild rainbows as well as fish moving into the creek from the reservoir. Only about 5 miles of creek above the reservoir are outside the Umatilla Reservation. For angling on reservation lands, check with the agency at Mission. Best fishing is in early summer.

There is very little angling in the creek below the reservoir because of water fluctuation. Unlike most streams in this district, McKay Creek opens with the early trout opener at the end of April.

McKay Reservoir

Pronounced "McEye," a large reservoir, the heart of McKay Creek National Wildlife Refuge, managed primarily for irrigation and waterfowl. It generally offers excellent fishing for crappie, perch, and brown bullheads, with fair fishing for largemouth bass and some channel cats.

McKay is about 4 miles south of Pendleton. From Hwy. 395, a good gravel road leads east to the reservoir and follows the west shore.

When full, McKay covers about 1300 acres, but it's not unusual for the reservoir to be drawn down to 250 acres in the fall—a little too much water fluctuation for great bass production. During drought years, bass redds in the reservoir's shallows take a beating, the bass population declines, and perch and crappie overpopulate (preying on bass fry). A 3-fish catch limit and 15-inch minimum size requirement for bass help tip the balance in favor of the bass. Largemouth to 9 pounds are currently available.

There's little bottom structure in McKay (a big low spot in the sagebrush), but a brimming reservoir offers good bass habitat around submerged vegetation.

The average crappie is currently 8 inches, and there continue to be lots of yellow perch. Brown bullheads to 15 inches are available, as well as channel catfish.

The entire reservoir is open for public use March 1 to September 30. The southern half remains open throughout the State Waterfowl Season but is closed to fishing.

The reservoir is open for day use only. Camping is prohibited. Of its two boat ramps, only the north ramp is useable when the water is low.

McNary Channel Ponds. Six ponds and connecting channels, covering about 25 acres below McNary Dam on the Columbia River off I-84. They support largemouth bass, catfish, bluegill, and trout.

A combination of backroads and bike paths make the ponds accessible for youngsters riding bikes out from Umatilla or Hermiston. Fishing is good in early spring and summer. To reach the ponds, continue west beyond the fish viewing window at the dam.

The pond area is pleasantly shaded with cottonwoods and willows. Free Fishing Day events take place here every June. Recommended for youngsters. Wheelchair accessible.

Meacham Creek. A 30-mile tributary of the Umatilla River with good fishing for wild rainbow trout, accessible to strong hikers. It heads near Meacham, southeast of Pendleton, and winds through canyons to the east and south. Meacham joins the Umatilla at Gibbon, about 26 miles upstream from Pendleton.

The creek is quite inaccessible. Forest roads leave the Meacham area to the east and stay high on the ridge above the creek. A Union Pacific railroad line follows the creek from Meacham downstream, and anglers can walk the railroad right-of-way to access the creek. It offers good fishing for wild trout. Fishing is restricted to artificial flies and lures only. The lower 5 miles flow within the Umatilla Indian Reservation, and a tribal permit is required.

Meadow Creek. A 24-mile long stream entering the upper Grand Ronde River about 10 miles west of Hilgard, a community on I-84 about 8 miles west of La Grande. It is currently the deadline for steelheading on the Grande Ronde and is a US Forest Service Research Area, closed to all fishing.

Messner Pond. No. 2 A rich pond with nice size largemouth bass and white crappie. It is one mile east of Boardman, with 12 surface acres. To reach the pond from I-84, take the Port of Morrow Exit (No. 165) and drive due north.

Messner is fished primarily for bass and crappie, but since a culvert connects it to the Columbia, it might hold anything, including a lot of carp. Efforts to screen out the carp have been unsuccessful.

Mill Creek (Walla Walla watershed). A beautiful pristine trout stream in its flow through extreme northeast Oregon. Its headwaters are in Washington, but it dips into Oregon for about 7 miles before doubling back to Washington, where it enters the Walla Walla River about 10 miles east of Milton Freewater. Mill Creek is north of the North Fork Walla Walla River. A portion of its flow in Oregon is closed to angling, as it is the source of drinking water for the city of Walla Walla.

Fishing in Mill is for wild redband trout in fast water, with lots of brush to hang you up. But the creek does have a lot of good riffle areas. It abounds with rainbow and bull trout. Bull trout must be released unharmed. Fishing is restricted to artificial flies and lures.

Minam Lake. A fair size brook trout lake in Eagle Cap Wilderness at the head of the Lostine River. While near the head of the Minam River, it does not drain into that watershed. From the community of Lostine east of Enterprise, follow the Lostine River Rd. about 18 miles to its end. Follow the Lostine River Trail 1670 upstream from Two Pan Campground 5.7 miles to Minam Lake. Total elevation gain is about 2000 feet, but it's spread out along the entire hike, making this one of the easier trails in the Eagle Cap. Snow may block access until July.

The lake is at elevation 7400 ft. with 33 surface acres. Maximum depth is 30 ft. Fishing for brook trout is terrific from late July through September, with all methods taking fish. The average catch is 9 to 12 inches, with some to 14 inches. Blue Lake, a mile beyond Minam, also offers good fishing.

Minam River. A major tributary of the Grand Ronde River, heading at Blue Lake, high in Eagle Cap Wilderness, and flowing northwest 50 miles to join the Wallowa River at the town of Minam. Designated a Scenic Waterway, the Minam has limited road access throughout its length. The lower river below the Wilderness is a favorite with rafters. The upper river is a favorite of hikers and horse packers.

The town of Minam is 15 miles east of Elgin, 12 miles west of Wallowa on Hwy. 82. The lower 9 river miles from the mouth to Meads Flat are followed by roads south from Minam. Secondary roads upstream of the Flat are a mile or more from the river and have been closed. Trail access is excellent. Trail 1673 follows the river all the way from Meads Flat to Blue Lake, a distance of over 40 miles. See the Wallowa-Whitman National Forest map for details.

Angling on the Minam is good in late summer and fall. The stream is not stocked but has a good wild population, with rainbows 8 to 15 inches and a few brook and bull trout as well. Bait, flies, and lures will all take fish. As you might expect, the best fishing is away from the roads. Fishing gets

Angling on the Minam River is especially good in late summer and fall. Photograph by Nancy Huff.

underway as soon as the river drops after spring run-off, usually in June. Fishing on the lower river slows by August, but picks up again in September.

The river is closed to salmon and steelhead fishing. There are no drive-in campgrounds along the river. Packers can camp on Bear Creek or on the lower Lostine before heading into the Wilderness. Natural campsites are available in the forest. Supplies, tackle, and local information are available at Enterprise.

Two air strips (at Minam Lodge and Reds Horse Ranch) offer unique access at about the midpoint of the river, just outside the wilderness boundary at the notch above Jim White Ridge. The air strips are deep in the canyon, and private flyers can literally drop right in. Charter flights are available from airports at LaGrande and Enterprise. If you pilot your own craft, check in at Enterprise or call Minam Lodge for a briefing on the approach, and plan your flight for early morning. Red's is no longer open for guests, but its grounds are available for camping. Minam Lodge offers accommodations for humans and horses.

MIRROR LAKE (Wallowa Co.). A scenic trout lake a mile north of Eagle Cap, highest peak in the Wallowas at 9595 ft. The most direct route to it is from the north by way of the East Fork of the Lostine River. From the end of the Lostine Rd., 18 miles south of the town of Lostine, hike upstream along the East Fork on Trail 1662, 6.5 miles to the lake. Total elevation gain is 2000 ft. You can also hike in from Wallowa Lake following trails 1820 and 1810. This route covers about 14 miles.

Mirror Lake is 26 acres with a maximum depth of 77 ft. Brook trout average 10 inches and range from 6 to 13 inches. Other lakes in the basin to the northeast provide good angling as well. You can usually get in by July, but fishing is best in August and September. There are quite a few good campsites. Camp well back from fragile lakeside vegetation, and follow no-trace camping guidelines. See also Moccasin, Glacier, Prospect, Frazier.

MOCCASIN LAKE. A fair size brook trout lake in a lake basin below Eagle Cap in Eagle Cap Wilderness. The hike in can be made from either Wallowa Lake or Two

Pan Campground on the Lostine River. The distance is almost identical. See Mirror Lake for directions. Moccasin is northeast of Mirror. Total trip is about 11 miles, with elevation gain 2400 ft.

Moccasin doesn't have very large fish, but there are lots of them. These brook trout run to 10 inches, and they can be taken easily on bait, lures or flies. Spinner and bait combinations retrieved very slowly will take the largest fish. Other lakes in the basin provide good angling as well. See Mirror, Douglas, Unit, Lilly, Crescent. There's one improved campsite at this centrally located lake, and several other good sites nearby. Camp well back from fragile lake-side vegetation and follow no-trace camping guidelines.

MORGAN LAKE. A former gravel pit, now a pleasant escape from the summer heat high above LaGrande. It offers fishing for stocked trout and crappie. Morgan has 60 surface acres and is perched in hills 5 miles southwest of the city. From Hwy. 30 heading east, turn right onto Gekeler Lane, which becomes C St. in LaGrande. Turn left on Walnut. Just as the road begins to climb, look for a sign to Morgan Lake Game Refuge. The paved road turns to gravel and climbs about 9 steep miles to a plateau. A dirt road on the right leads to the lake.

Morgan is stocked annually with legal rainbows, with the average catch 9 to 12 inches. In 1999 ODFW began an experimental program of adding several hundred trophy size trout as well. Crappie to 10 inches are also available. Fishing is best in early summer. In summer, the bite picks up near sundown. Bait-fishing is the most popular technique. Motors are prohibited on the lake.

This former gravel quarry has been successfully reclaimed, with a fringe of pines and willows on three sides and a grassy dike at the west end. At the east end, trails lead from parking areas down through the trees to picnic tables set among the pines near the lake shore. There are two packed dirt boat ramps at the west end and two paved piers suitable for wheelchair access extending out from the west end dike.

There are both camping and day use facilities. Recommended for youngsters. Wheelchair accessible.

OLIVE LAKE. A good trout and kokanee lake of 160 acres near the headwaters of

Desolation Creek in Umatilla National Forest, about 30 miles west of Baker City. This lake is worth the trip when it's hot in the valley. Gravel and dirt roads approach it from several directions. Forest Rd. 10 leads west about 11 miles from Granite to the lake. Granite can be reached by State Rd. 220 from Hwy. 7 south of Baker. From Dale, on Hwy. 395, head southeast on Forest Rd. 10 up Desolation Creek to the lake. It can also be reached from Susanville to the south.

Olive sits at a cool 6200 ft. elevation. It's over 100 ft. deep and offers good catches of redband rainbows to 15 inches. Brook trout of the same size make up about half the catch. An occasional Lahontan cutthroat is also taken. Trolling and bait fishing are both popular methods here.

Olive also has lots of kokanee, with some to 12 inches but most a little smaller. Try trolling a spinner trailing a small baited hook. Fish deep in spring and summer. Kokanee tend to school, so when you get a strike, stay in the same area. Fall is a good time for catching the larger rainbows on a fly. The lake is also full of crayfish. Throw out a trap near the boat ramp while you're fishing, and bait (or hors d'oeuvres) are practically guaranteed.

This is a very scenic spot, high in the Blue Mountains, surrounded by lodgepole pine and peaks that hold snow throughout the summer.

There's a nice campground with a boat ramp. A fishing pier and the trail around the lake are both wheelchair accessible.

PENLAND LAKE. A remote but accessible (and extremely productive) drive-in trout lake about 25 miles southeast of Heppner. It was built by local private interests but is open to the public. From Heppner, follow County Rd. 678 (the Blue Mountain Scenic Byway) east and south into Umatilla National Forest. About 1.5 miles beyond Cutsforth County Park, turn right onto Forest Rd. 21. At 2.5 miles turn left onto Forest Rd. 2105, which leads to the lake.

There are thousands of trout in this lake, which is open year-round. Fishing is great mornings and evenings. Penland covers 67 acres and is fairly shallow. It can winterkill, but legal trout are stocked after severe winters, and the trout put on weight fast. Trout have been known to grow quite large here.

Good catches are made from the bank and by wading, but trolling in a row boat or canoe is best. Try trolling a dry fly. The lake is too weedy for float tubes. Motors are prohibited on the lake.

An attractive campground set among the big trees offers secluded campsites. Recommended for youngsters.

POCKET LAKE. A small brook trout lake in Eagle Cap Wilderness, perched in a glacial cirque 700 ft. above Moccasin Lake. It is 1.5 miles southeast and 700 ft. above Moccasin. See Moccasin Lake for directions. Follow Lake Creek, the outlet of Moccasin Lake, about ½ mile to a tributary which enters from the south, then bushwhack up this creek to Pocket Lake.

Though only 9 acres, Pocket is very deep for its size. There's not a lot of traffic up here, and the lake produces well for small to medium size brook trout.

POWER CITY PONDS. In Power City Wildlife Area, 4 miles north of Hermiston. The ponds are open to fishing and support largemouth bass and brown bullhead catfish.

PRAIRIE CREEK (Wallowa watershed). A small stream that grows large trout near Enterprise. About 18 miles long, it heads a couple of miles east of Wallowa Lake and flows northwest, joining the Wallowa River at Enterprise. Gravel roads leading east and south from Hwy. 82 between Enterprise and Joseph follow and cross the stream.

The creek has a fair wild trout population. Enriched by nutrients as it passes through agricultural lands, Prairie grows rainbow and brook trout to 18 inches. It is fed by springs and irrigation overflows and maintains a moderate temperature year-round. Bait is the best method early in the year, and flies are good in late summer and fall.

The creek flows almost entirely through private agricultural lands. Ask permission to access the creek and be a courteous guest.

PROSPECT LAKE. A good, small rainbow trout lake at the very head of the West Wallowa River in Eagle Cap Wilderness. It sits below a ridge that separates it from Glacier Lake, ½ mile south. There is no trail to the lake. Hike to Little Frazier Lake (See Frazier Lake) and follow the inlet stream up to Prospect Lake, ½ mile northwest. It's about a 12-mile trip in all.

Prospect is at 8380 ft., so be prepared for cold nights and the possibility of snow showers in September. The lake has been known to have some nice rainbow trout for a small lake, possibly because of its great depth. Though only 14 acres, the lake is over 100 ft. deep. The average catch is 10 to 12 inches, with some fish to 20 inches taken in August and September.

RAZZ LAKE. A small but interesting brook trout lake high in Eagle Cap Wilderness to the north of the popular lake basin south of Wallowa Lake. Razz is about a mile north of Horseshoe Lake at 8100 ft., about 900 ft. above Horseshoe. See Horseshoe Lake for trail directions. Follow Horseshoe's inlet stream upslope one mile

Mirror Lake is nestled beneath Eagle Cap, highest peak in the Wallowas. Photograph courtesy of ODFW.

to the lake. Change your pacemaker batteries before starting out.

The lake is about 14 acres and 26 ft. deep. The brook trout here are 7 to 10 inches. Fishing is good in August and September. Come prepared for snow.

R.D. Mac Pond. An old gravel quarry close to the Grand Ronde River near Island City. The pond is behind the gravel operation off Hwy. 82. It is stocked with fingerlings, legal rainbows, and some larger trout. To reach it, follow Hunter Lane to the first street on the left. Not at all scenic, but youngsters seem to enjoy playing in the gravel pile. (Who can figure kids?) Recommended for youngsters.

Rhea Creek. A good wild trout stream about 35 miles long, flowing into Willow Creek 2 miles east of Ione about 15 miles north of Heppner. Most of its flow is through private property, so ask permission before you fish. Ione is on Hwy. 74, which intersects I-84 east of Arlington. The creek is followed upstream by 20 miles of paved and gravel roads from Ione to the crossing of Hwy. 207 at Ruggs. From there, gravel roads follow the creek to its headwaters.

Rock Creek John Day watershed). A 40-mile tributary of the lower John Day River, with wild rainbow in its upper stretches. It enters the John Day about 15 miles upstream of the John Day mouth. Public access to the lower creek is minimal. Best access is at Anson Wright County Park on State Rd. 207 south of Heppner.

Trout fishing is confined primarily to the upper reaches where there's a fair wild rainbow population. The lower creek is used for irrigation, and there are a lot of non-game fish present.

Roger Lake. A small shallow lake near Aneroid Lake in Eagle Cap Wilderness. Though only 4 ft. deep, warm springs keep the lake from freezing solid and allow a healthy brook trout population to thrive. Though the fish are not large, they are well formed and plentiful. See Aneroid for trail directions. Roger is ¼ mile east of Aneroid and is visible from the trail.

Roulette Pond. A former gravel pit north of Elgin, stocked annually with legal rainbow. Not very scenic, but it's a reliable place to take beginners. Recommended for inroducing youngsters to fishing.

Rowe Creek Reservoir. A 30-acre impoundment stocked with trout. From Hwy. 19 about 10 miles southeast of Fossil, turn south onto the gravel road that leads southwest to Twickenham. The turn is just west of Sheldon Wayside.

Although a private lake, the public has gained access through an agreement made between its owner and ODFW. A 50 ft. strip around the shore is reserved for anglers. Be sure to close the gate behind you.

Rowe is stocked with legal rainbows and is fished very hard by the local folks. The rainbow average 8 to 11 inches with some 15-inch holdovers. The reservoir is open to fishing year-round, but best catches are in spring. There is a 5 mph speed limit on the lake. Camping is prohibited.

Salt Creek Summit Pond. A little pond in Wallowa-Whitman National Forest offering drive-in stocked trout opportunities. (Not shown on National Forest maps.) From Joseph, follow the main road east out of town toward the Imnaha. Turn right (south) on Hwy. 350, which becomes Forest Rd. 39 (Wallow Mt. Loop Rd.). Turn left at the sign for Salt Creek Summit Sno-Park and left at the fork (Forest Rd. 3915). The pond is about ½ mile farther on the east side of the road. The road is usually snow-bound till June.

The pond is stocked annually with legal rainbows and has some fish to 12 inches. There is some carryover following mild winters. This is not a scenic spot (more like a rural parking lot with pond), but it does offer a chance to practice casting with a likelihood of landing trout for the pan.

Searcy Pond (a.k.a. Kinzua Reservoir). A rainbow fishery with a limited open season near the old Kinzua Mill site east of Fossil. It is stocked annually with about 4,000 legal rainbows. The pond is closed to fishing during big game hunting season from August 16 to December 31.

Slide Lake (Strawbery Mt. Wilderness). A small lake high in the Strawberry Mountains south of Prairie City. Strawberry Mountain is an inviting contrast to the arid John Day Valley over which it towers, with its snowy peaks and cool coniferous forest. Follow Main St. (County Rd. 60) south

from Prairie City to Malheur National Forest. Forest Rd. 6001 continues to the trailhead at Strawberry Camp. The upper road is usually poor in early spring. Trail 375 leads south into the wilderness, meeting Trail 372 about ½ mile in. Take this trail about 2 miles to the east, and swing south on Trail 385 to the lake. It's a 4.3 mile hike, steep enough to discourage traffic.

Slide Lake is 13 acres and only 8 feet at its deepest point. It fills a glacial cirque at 7200 ft. but has plenty of aquatic vegetation and grows nice trout. It's not stocked, but has a good self-sustaining population of brook trout. Fly fishing is enjoyable here late in fall, but bring your long johns if you plan to stay for the evening rise. Just south of Slide Lake is Upper or Little Slide Lake, a 3-acre lake that holds a lot of brook trout. It's a bit deeper than the lower lake. The trails to both are generally snow-free by June.

Steamboat Lake. A fair size lake in the headwaters of the North Fork of the Minam River. See Long Lake for directions to Swamp Lake. From Swamp Lake, follow the trail that leads across the saddle to the east, dropping down to Steamboat. It's a 10-mile hike, and the trails aren't too steep.

Steamboat is 30 acres and just over 100 ft. deep. It has a good population of brook trout, but the fish don't get large. Most are 7 to 10 inches with a few larger caught in the late fall. Bait and flies are both productive methods here. Long Lake is a mile west and can be reached by a trail leading down from Swamp Lake.

Strawberry Lake

The largest lake in the Strawberry Mt. Wilderness, reached by a real pretty one-mile hike. The Strawberry Mountains, compact and distinct from other Oregon ranges, rise stately and cool above the arid John Day Valley. Their slopes are covered in dense conifer forest, meadows are carpeted with wildflowers in June, the forest floor with wild strawberries in July. Strawberry Lake is one of several glacial lakes in the wilderness, with a scenic backdrop of snowy crests. It was formed during glacial retreat when steep valley walls collapsed, blocking Strawberry Creek. See also Little Strawberry and Slide.

County Rd. 60 leads south from Prairie City into Malheur National Forest, and Forest Rd. 6001 continues to the trailhead at Strawberry Camp. The upper road is usually poor in early spring. Trail 375 leads south into the wilderness area and skirts the eastern border of Strawberry Lake within a mile. The trail continues south past Strawberry Falls, a 40 ft. cascade, and on to Little Strawberry Lake.

Strawberry is at 6320 ft. and has 31 surface acres, with a maximum depth of 40 ft. The lake offers good angling for naturally reproducing rainbows and brook trout. Both tend to grow nice and plump and run to 16 inches. Fly fishing is best in the southern half of the lake. There are some good deep holes in the center and at the north end. A float tube would be helpful. Fishing is best in early spring and again in late fall. These fish seem to sulk during the middle of the summer.

There is a camping area north of the lake between Strawberry and Little Strawberry. Camp well back from fragile lakeside vegetation, and use no-trace camping techniques.

There are some good deep holes at the center and near the north end of STRAWBERRY LAKE in Strawberry Mt. Wilderness. Photograph by Dennis Frates.

STRAWBERRY LAKE, LITTLE. A small high lake ½ mile south of Strawberry Lake in Strawberry Mt. Wilderness. See Strawberry Lake for directions. Trail 375 leads south into the wilderness, skirts the eastern border of Strawberry Lake, and climbs 1.1 miles to Strawberry Falls. Here a side trail leads east 0.6 mile to Little Strawberry Lake, cupped in a glacial cirque.

Little Strawberry is at elevation 6960 ft. with a handsome craggy backdrop. It covers 4 acres and is 10 ft. deep. It contains large numbers of brook trout, small but easy to catch. There is a camping area to the north between Little Strawberry and Big Strawberry Lakes.

SWAMP LAKE. Fairly shallow and more productive than most lakes in Eagle Cap, offering rainbow trout and a small population of golden trout. It is west of the head of the Lostine River, above and south of Steamboat and Long Lakes. See Long Lake for directions. It's a 9-mile hike on moderately steep trails.

Swamp has about 43 surface acres and is 23 ft. deep. This is one of the few lakes in Oregon that was stocked with golden trout, a beautiful fish native to the high Sierras of California, last stocked in the 1960s. Though not required by regulations, catch and release of goldens is encouraged.

Fishing is generally excellent in August

and September on flies or lures. Still-fishing with worms or eggs will take fish almost anytime. The rainbow average 8 to 12 inches with a few to 15 inches. Both Long Lake and Steamboat Lake are less than a mile away and offer good fishing.

TATONE POND. A one-acre trout pond off Tower Rd. From I-84, take Exit 159 (Tower Rd.). Head north about 50 yards, then turn east on a dirt road and continue about ¼ mile to the parking area. Cross a fence, a railroad track, and another fence. Then walk north about an eighth of a mile.

Tatone is stocked annually with legal rainbows. It can be fished year-round but is best in spring. It is very deep in spots. A float tube could be useful.

TEEPEE POND A little pond in the Wallowa-Whitman National Forest with opportunities to catch stocked legal trout. From Enterprise, follow Hwy. 303 north about 13 miles. Turn right onto Forest Rd. 46. About 3 miles beyond the turn-off to Billy Meadows Guard Station (on Forest Rd. 4670), about a mile past Dougherty Campground, turn left onto Forest Rd. 595. The lake is an eighth of a mile farther on the left side of the road. It is not shown on current National Forest maps. The lake is stocked in June.

THIRTY-MILE CREEK. A wild rainbow creek, tributary of the John Day, flowing through private property. It is actually 39 miles long, entering the John Day at river mile 84, about half-way between highways 206 and 218. There are quite a few trout in the upper creek, but there is no public land adjacent to it. Fish with landowner permission.

UMATILLA FOREST PONDS. A series of former borrow pits, as yet un-named, in the forest in the vicinity of Ukiah. About 15 (of more than 35) are stocked with rainbows legal size and larger. The ponds are off forest roads 52 and 53 south of Ukiah, off Hwy. 244, and off Forest Rd. 54 north of Ukiah. Get a map of the ponds and a stocking schedule from the North Fork John Day Ranger District office in Ukiah.

UMATILLA RIVER

A good steelhead, salmon, and trout stream. The Umatilla enters the Columbia River about 3 miles below McNary Dam at the town of Umatilla. It heads in the northern Blue Mountains and flows west past Pendleton and Hermiston. From Pendleton to the Columbia the stream is easily reached by a paved road that follows it from Rieth to Echo, both of which are on I-84. East of Pendleton, paved and gravel roads follow the stream for another 30 miles, mostly through Umatilla Indian Reservation lands.

Summer steelhead are fished from September through mid-April in the water below the deadline at the Hwy. 11 Bridge in Pendleton. Non-finclipped steelhead must be released unharmed.

Fall chinook and coho were re-introduced into the Umatilla beginning in 1981 following extinction of the native runs 70 years ago. The runs have fluctuated considerably, but coho have done better than chinook. Fall chinook returns have been poor to fair, and only chinook jacks may be harvested. Harvest of adult fall chinook is prohibited. Fall chinook jacks and coho adults and jacks are available for harvest September 1 through November 30 downstream from Stanfield Dam at river mile 32. Spring chinook usually enter the river in late May or early June and may be fished most years during a brief open season that is determined annually based on returns. Call the Pendleton office of ODFW for information about openings. See Appendix. Spring chinook have generally been fished upstream from Stanfield Dam to the forks. Fishing for steelhead and salmon by non-tribal anglers is prohibited within Confederated Tribes of Umatilla boundaries.

The Umatilla has a good population of wild rainbows and a fair population of bull trout. Know your trout, and release the bulls unharmed. Good catches of rainbows are made in the Bingham Springs area upstream from Pendleton. Tribal Permits are required to fish on reservation land and may be purchased at Mission.

There are many irrigation diversion dams on the river which can make boating dangerous during low flows. At all times, only driftboats and rafts are appropriate for the Umatilla due to the river's shallowness. The major dams are Stanfield at r.m. 32, Cold Springs at r.m. 28, Westland at r.m. 27, and Threemile at r.m. 4. All dams should be portaged or otherwise avoided by boaters. Elsewhere, do a good job of scouting before you venture down the river.

Boats may be launched at undeveloped sites at Yoaqum (r.m. 37), Barnhart (r.m. 42), Reith (r.m. 48.5), Prowler Plant gravel bar (rm 51), and at the paved Babe Ruth Ramp across from the ball park (r.m. 52.5).

Bank access at Echo State Park (r.m. 26.5) includes about 100 yards of riprap on the east bank. Bank access at Steelhead

Park (r.m. 9) is a brushy 200 yards on the east bank. From just below Threemile Dam to the mouth, anglers can fish along the Umatilla River Rd. Look for pull-outs along the road. Anglers also fish the river within Pendleton, including the dike on the south bank. There are a number of good steelhead holes within the town.

UMATILLA RIVER, SOUTH FORK. A rather short stream, tributary to the upper Umatilla River, which it joins about 32 miles east of Pendleton upriver from Bingham Springs. Forest Rd. 32 (Umatilla National Forest) follows the lower 3 miles of the fork. Trail 3076 continues up the fork an additional 2 miles. Forest Rd. 3128 follows the upper waters along a ridge about a mile west of the river and could serve as a jump-off for the bushwhacking enthusiast.

The Fork provides good angling for wild trout. Bull trout and rainbows are found in its upper waters. Bull trout must be released unharmed.

Umatilla Forks Campground is about 3 miles above Bingham Springs. There are two additional camps (Elk and South Fork) 3 miles south.

UNIT LAKE. A 15-acre lake in a popular lake basin about 10 trail miles south of Wallowa Lake. It is ½ mile northeast of Horseshoe Lake by trail. See Horseshoe Lake for directions. Unit has brook trout to 11 inches and rainbows to 14 inches. Brook trout predominate.

WALLA WALLA RIVER. A fair steelhead stream south and east of Milton Freewater in the northeast corner of the state. The river heads in Oregon and flows northwest into Washington, meeting the Columbia River a few miles above the Oregon border. About 12 miles of the mainstem river flows through Oregon. The forks are about 5 miles southeast of Milton Freewater.

The river flows right through Milton Freewater and is open for steelhead up to the forks, but, there is little public access to the river. Ask permission to approach the river through the orchards. Marie Dorian County Park, about 4 miles upstream from Walla Walla, accesses good steelhead water.

A few trout are picked up in the mainstem, but most angling for them takes place on the upper forks. The upper South Fork Walla Walla offers some of the most pris-

tine trout water in this part of Oregon, remaining cool all summer. County Rd. 600 out of Milton Freewater (South Fork Rd.) follows the South Fork to the trailhead for Trail 3225 which follows the stream 15 miles into Umatilla National Forest.

WALLA WALLA RIVER, NORTH FORK. A tributary of the Walla Walla joining it about 5 miles east of Milton Freewater. The stream is about 20 miles long, but a road only follows it up about 8 miles through private property. Ask permission to fish. Forest Trail 3222 follows the river to its headwaters, offering the only public angling opportunity. You can reach the trail from Forest Rd. 65 about 4 miles below Deduck Campground off Tiger Canyon Rd., or from the end of a dirt road which follows the lower fork above Milton Freewater. Check the Umatilla National Forest map.

The fork below the forest is heavily used for irrigation, and water gets very low in summer and fall. The North Fork supports bull trout and rainbows. Bull trout must be released unharmed. Best fishing for the rainbow is in early season.

WALLA WALLA RIVER, SO. FORK

An important tributary of the Walla Walla River joining the North Fork about 5 miles east of the city of Milton Freewater. The South Fork is about 30 miles long. Roads follow it upstream about 12 miles. It heads 3 miles south of the upper corner of the state and arcs south through Umatilla National Forest, emerging southeast of Milton Freewater. In the forest it can be fished from Trail 3225, which begins at Harris Park and follows the river to its head near Deduck Campground.

The South Fork offers some of the most pristine trout water in this part of the state. It carries more water than the North Fork and remains cool all summer. Angling holds up well throughout the season. Fishing is good for trout 9 to 12 inches, with some 16 to 18 inch fish present. Bull trout are present in the upper river and must be released unharmed.

The river flows through a deep, rugged canyon. The road is at the canyon bottom. The first three miles up from Harris Park is open to foot traffic and all-terrain vehicles up to Bear Creek Cabin. Above the cabin, only foot traffic is allowed on the trail, which continues to Deduck Springs, about 20 miles. The approach from De-duck Springs involves about 4 miles of steep downhill hiking before reaching fish-able water. Beware: the South Fork Canyon is famous for having rattlesnakes at its lower end and bears at its upper end (es-pecially during ripe berry season). Come if you've got the nerve.

Camping is available at Deduck Camp-ground. A Umatilla National Forest map will be useful.

WALLOWA LAKE

The largest natural lake in northeast Ore-gon, south of Joseph at the foot of the Wal-lowa Mts. It supports record-breaking kokanee, rainbow trout, mackinaw, and bull trout. The lake was formed by the ter-minal moraine of a glacier that carved out the Wallowa River Valley. The moraine forms an immense natural dam on the Wallowa River and towers over 400 ft. above the surface of this 1600-acre lake. To reach the lake drive to Joseph on Hwy. 82, and continue south to the lake. This high-way follows the lake's eastern shore to its southern tip.

Wallowa is a clear, deep lake, with ideal conditions for kokanee and mackinaw. Kokanee (landlocked sockeye salmon) are actually native to the lake but have been supplemented. The kokanee average 9 to 10 inches, but there are some 15 to 20 inch-es and larger. The current state record kokanee came out of Wallowa Lake in 1998, weighing 4 pounds, 14.7 ounces. Large numbers of fish are present, and an-gling is excellent, with best catches in May, June, and the first part of July. Up to 30,000 are caught annually.

Mackinaw are no longer stocked but there are still many in the lake. These are finicky fish, and one catch a day is average for those few who pursue them. A fish finder is helpful here, since the bottom topography is pretty uniform. They can be caught by deep trolling with spinner and lure along a shelf at about 250 ft. The lake is 300 ft. at its deepest point.

Rainbow trout are stocked annually and average 9 inches, with a few reaching 16 inches and larger. Every year a few rainbows over 20 inches are caught. Rainbow are taken both by trolling and still-fishing with bait. Fishing around the edges in the fall often produces nice catches. There are also some nice fish in the river below the dam.

WALLOWA LAKE is currently producing Oregon's largest kokanee. Photograph courtesy of Randy Sampson.

To protect spawning kokanee, all an-gling in the tributaries of the lake (up to the falls on the West Fork and the PP&L intake on the East Fork) is prohibited from September 1 through October 31. Kokanee in their brilliant red spawning colors are quite a sight.

Bull trout were native to Wallowa Lake and have been re-introduced following their extinction here. Bull trout must be re-leased unharmed.

Wallowa Lake is a popular multi-use recreational lake, but users segregate them-selves pretty well. Most kokanee fishing takes place at the northwest end of the lake. Most trout anglers fish the southern shore-line. Water-skiers pretty much stick to the northeast end.

Boats are available for rent at Wallowa Lake State Park on the south end of the lake. Private boats can be launched there and at the county ramp at the north end. There is a full-service campground at the State Park and many private resorts in the vicinity. The south end of Wallowa Lake is a popular jumping-off place for trails into the Eagle Cap Wilderness. Horses and guides are available in Joseph.

WALLOWA RIVER

A popular and accessible trout and steel-head stream, tributary to the Grand Ronde River. The Wallowa flows 80 miles from headwaters in the central lake basin of Eagle Cap Wilderness to its confluence with the Grande Ronde about 16 miles downstream from Elgin. The river feeds Wallowa Lake, skirts the eastern edges of Joseph and Enterprise, and absorbs Lostine and Minam rivers on its journey north and west. Hwy. 82 follows the river from Wal-lowa Lake to the Minam confluence. Trails 1820 and 1804 follow the West and East forks from South Park Picnic Area at Wal-lowa Lake into Eagle Cap.

Steelhead are generally in the river from mid-February into April. The Wallowa's steelhead fishery is composed almost en-tirely of hatchery stock, the original runs of both steelhead and salmon having been decimated by Columbia River dams. The hatchery is west of Enterprise on Spring Creek. The acclimation pond is on Deer Creek above Minam. Steelhead holding in Big Canyon below the Deer Creek facility offer a popular spring fishery. Bank anglers concentrate below the mouth of Spring Creek and in Big Canyon.

Trout fishing throughout the river is ex-cellent from late spring through late fall, with best river conditions generally in Sep-tember and October. The river hosts a population of wild rainbows, with a few brook trout below Enterprise. Bull trout are also present but must be released un-harmed. The average trout runs 8 to 14 inches, with some wild rainbows and bull trout to several pounds. Large whitefish (delicious smoked) are also available and

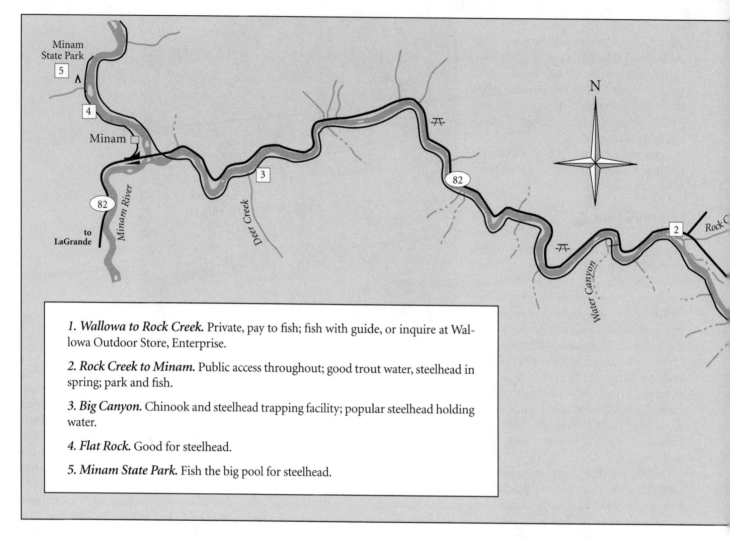

1. *Wallowa to Rock Creek.* Private, pay to fish; fish with guide, or inquire at Wallowa Outdoor Store, Enterprise.

2. *Rock Creek to Minam.* Public access throughout; good trout water, steelhead in spring; park and fish.

3. *Big Canyon.* Chinook and steelhead trapping facility; popular steelhead holding water.

4. *Flat Rock.* Good for steelhead.

5. *Minam State Park.* Fish the big pool for steelhead.

may be fished during trout and steelhead seasons. Below Rock Creek, the "trout" fishery targets hatchery steelhead that fail to migrate. Non-finclipped trout must be released unharmed below Rock Creek. Tackle in the river above Wallowa Lake is restricted to artificial flies and lures to protect the bull trout.

Minam State Park and two waysides offer bank fishing opportunities. Anglers also pull off the highway and fish throughout the canyon from Rock Creek downstream. From the town of Wallowa down to Minam, the river offers especially good fly fishing water. Fairly fast, with a medium size flow, this stretch is characterized by riffles and glides, a liberal distribution of large boulders, a few deep holes, and many excellent wading opportunities.

Boats are rarely launched above Minam. A boat ramp at Minam commits anglers to a 43-mile float to Wildcat Creek on the Grand Ronde, a popular trip generally requiring 2 to 4 days (though it can be done in a long day during high water). There is

no opportunity to take-out before Wildcat at this time. The road into Rondowa (Wallow River confluence) washed out a few years ago and has not yet been repaired.

The best flows for boating and fishing are between 1500 and 3000 cfs. Small craft should be wary of flows above 2500. Refer to the river gauge reading for the Grande Ronde at Troy. See Appendix. Shuttle service is available at the Minam Motel. See Appendix.

Nearest campgrounds are at Minam State Park and in the Wallowa-Whitman National Forest along the Lostine River.

WENAHA RIVER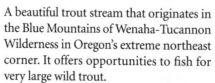

A beautiful trout stream that originates in the Blue Mountains of Wenaha-Tucannon Wilderness in Oregon's extreme northeast corner. It offers opportunities to fish for very large wild trout.

The river flows east about 35 miles and enters the Grande Ronde River at the community of Troy about 30 miles north of the

town of Wallowa. There are no roads near the stream, except for the lower few miles above Troy. Trail 3106, which begins at a trailhead off the road that climbs uphill behind Troy, follows the river for more than 30 miles through the wilderness. Other trails intersect the river higher up, but none is as well maintained. Walking up from the mouth is the best bet. Second best is to follow a trail down to the river from the north to intersect Trail 3106. It's much harder to move up and down the river from trails that enter the river canyon from the south. Refer to the US Forest Service's Wenaha-Tucannon Wilderness map for trail options.

The Wenaha-Tucannon Wilderness is a huge canyonland, popular with horse packers and hunters. A trip into the canyon can yield glimpses of elk, big horn sheep, bears, and golden eagles as well as large steelhead and trout.

The Wenaha River valley is lined with old cottonwoods. The canyon slopes are characterized by rocky outcrops and sage,

Wallowa River
Wallowa to Minam

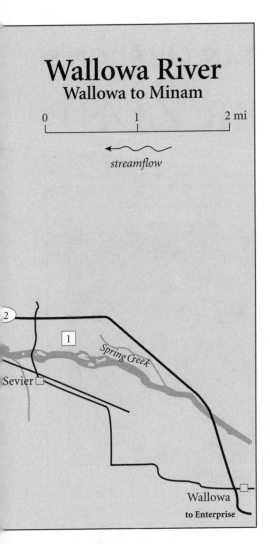

0   1   2 mi

streamflow

Macks Canyon, and Silver Hilton.

There are no developed campgrounds along the stream, but there are natural campsites in the cottonwood stands on occasional riverside flats. Check with Forest Service guard stations for a camping permit during fire season.

WILD SHEEP LAKE. A small lake at the head of Wild Sheep Creek about ¾ of a mile west of Blue Lake. No trails lead to the lake, which supports a naturally reproducing population of brook trout.

WILLOW CREEK. An 80-mile tributary of the Columbia River that flows out of Umatilla National Forest southeast of Heppner and is captured in a reservoir just above town. It is heavily stocked with legal rainbow trout within the city limits.

There's good access to the creek at the park in town. The creek is followed from its mouth to Heppner by Hwy. 74 and southeast from Heppner by county road. There is no stocking above the reservoir, where the creek flows through mostly private property. Recommended for youngsters.

WILLOW CREEK RESERVOIR (Columbia River). An impoundment south of Heppner that grows big trout and plump warmwater fish. It has a maximum pool of 110 acres. Hwy. 206 leads southwest from Heppner to the reservoir access road.

Willow Creek has a nicely balanced population of warmwater fish. There are good numbers of largemouth 15 to 18 inches, lots of 12-inch smallmouth, plump crappies to 9 inches, and pumpkinseed sunfish big enough to fillet. White crappie and brown bullhead are also available. Legal size rainbow trout are stocked annually (since anything smaller are devoured by the warmwater population).

This is a big deep reservoir with good bank access and an angling area where water-skiing is prohibited. The banks are fairly steep, but an old road bed (now closed to vehicles) runs close to the reservoir along the southwest shore and provides access to good bass water. There are

excellent boat ramps, docks, and campground facilities.

WINELAND LAKE (a.k.a. Camp Five). A retired mill pond in the headwaters of Rock Creek in Umatilla National Forest with fishing for stocked trout and a variety of warmwater fish. From Hwy. 207 between Heppner and Spray, head west on Forest Rd. 21 about 13 miles. The pond is on the north side of the road at the old Kinzua Mill site. The lake is stocked with over 5000 legal rainbows annually and has populations of small largemouth bass, nice size bluegill, and small black crappie. There is no boat ramp, but a float tube or cartop boat would be useful.

WOOD LAKE. A very good brook trout lake in the northern Eagle Cap Wilderness, happpily off the beaten track. The trail that leads to Wood is better suited for hikers than for horses.

West of the Lostine River, Wood sits in a nice meadow about a mile north of Hobo Lake. From Lostine on Hwy. 82, head south to the Bowman Creek Trail 1651, about 2.5 miles south of Lostine Guard Station. Climb east on this trail for 3.6 miles to the junction of Trail 1659, which leads north past Chimney Lake and Hobo Lake, reaching Wood Lake 1.5 miles beyond Hobo. The total hike is just over 6 miles, with elevation gain over 3000 ft.

Flies work well in late summer and fall.

dotted with stands of ponderosa pine and fir. Hawthorne and mock orange flower in spring. Sumac burns a brilliant red in autumn. Keep an eye out for poison ivy.

Trout angling is excellent from midsummer through fall. Wild rainbows run to 20 inches, with many 10 to 15 inches. Bull trout are plentiful and big here. Bulls must be released unharmed. The river is easily waded in summer and fall. Good catches can be made from the bank when the river is high in spring.

The Wenaha is open for catch and release steelheading from the Grande Ronde confluence to the mouth of Crooked Fork. Crooked Fork is about 6 miles upstream from Troy. Fly fishing for steelhead is popular. Favorite patterns include the Skunk,

FISHING IN OREGON'S
SNAKE RIVER ZONE

The Snake River forms a significant portion of Oregon's eastern border, flowing north from Napton (south of Ontario) and crossing into Washington northeast of Enterprise. Oregon's Snake offers outstanding fishing for several varieties of catfish, smallmouth bass, largemouth bass, and crappie.

Following the format used in ODFW's angling regulation booklet, this chapter presents Oregon's Snake River fishing opportunities north to south.

We begin our coverage at the Washington state line, moving through wild and scenic Hells Canyon, then follow the river upstream through Hells Canyon Reservoir, Oxbow Reservoir, and Brownlee Reservoir, concluding with the free-flowing flat water stretch above Brownlee.

Oxbow Reservoir. Photograph by Phil Simonski.

SNAKE RIVER

SNAKE RIVER: Hells Canyon Dam to Washington State Line. Perhaps Oregon's wildest Wild and Scenic River, offering some of the best fishing in the state—when you can get to it. Smallmouth bass, channel cats, trout, steelhead, and sturgeon are available in this stretch. The section from the Oregon/ Washington border upstream to the Hell's Canyon Dam is the heart of Hells Canyon Wilderness. Access is the tough part, as this portion of the river runs through spectacular Hells Canyon, an awesome gorge over 6000 ft. deep in places.

In recent years, civilization has encroached on the canyon. Commercial rafting and jet boat operations have flourished. There are many more visitors, and the Forest Service has responded by creating additional facilities to serve them. But access is still limited.

From Oregon, this portion of the river is only approached by road at Hells Canyon Dam and at Dug Bar. From Idaho, roads reach the river at Pittsburg Landing, Wolf Creek and Dry Creek. Dug Bar is about 8 miles above the confluence of the Imnaha. To reach it from Joseph, follow the Imnaha River Rd. east to the community of Imnaha, then follow the river downstream. To get to Hells Canyon Dam, follow Hwy. 86 from Halfway to Copperfield, crossing to Idaho, and following the river downstream on the Idaho side to the bridge. The boat ramp and campground are on the Oregon side. There are no trails upstream or down from the dam area.

The best map for hiking the area is the Hells Canyon National

Recreation map, available at the visitor center in Enterprise and from vendors throughout Oregon and Idaho. There are a number of trails into the canyon. Among those most popular with anglers are the Battle Creek Trail and the Dug Bar Trail. The Battle Creek Trail heads off the Hells Canyon Rim Rd. and reaches the river about 4 miles downstream from the dam. The Dug Bar Trail begins at river level at the end of Dug Bar Rd. several miles upstream from the mouth of the Imnaha. The road is gravel and is passable for passenger cars at low speeds, though higher clearance vehicles may weather the potholes better. The trail follows the river's west bench, sometimes at river level, sometimes high above, all the way to Saddle Creek. The trail is well-maintained. There is also a trail down Saddle Creek which heads on Forest Rd. 4230 off the Imnaha River Rd. A number of other trails begin on spur roads leading east from the Imnaha River Rd. While hiking along the Snake, keep an eye out for poison ivy and rattlesnakes.

Smallmouth bass to 3 pounds and better are plentiful in this stretch. Best smallmouth fishing is late spring to early fall.

Channel catfish are a popular fishery here. The bigger the bait, the bigger the catch. Channel cats to 20 pounds have been taken from this reach.

Rainbow trout are numerous for the first 15 miles below Hells Canyon Dam and range in size from 8 to 20 inches. Tributary mouths are especially productive. Trout over 20 inches are considered steelhead.

Steelhead angling has been improving over the past few years as a result of an intense program of hatchery plants to offset

The Snake River Zone includes all waters of the Snake River from the Oregon-Washington border upstream to the Oregon-Idaho border. The boundary between the Snake River and its tributaries is defined as a straight line across the mouths of all rivers. The Snake River Zone includes the portions of the Burnt and Powder rivers downstream of the Huntington-Richland Road near their mouths and includes the portion of Pine Creek downstream of the Oxbow Bridge.

THE BEST FISHING IN OREGON'S SNAKE RIVER ZONE

HELLS CANYON DAM TO THE STATE LINE
Oregon's wildest Wild and Scenic River with some of the best fishing in the state for smallmouth bass and channel catfish.

HELLS CANYON RESERVOIR
Most popularly fished for smallmouth and crappie, but with a large population of catfish.

OXBOW RESERVOIR
Rivals Brownlee in productivity for smallmouth and crappie.

BROWNLEE RESERVOIR
A nationally known destination fishery for smallmouth bass, crappie, and 7 species of catfish (including huge channel and flathead cats).

SNAKE RIVER (above Brownlee)
Offers world-class fishing for huge catfish.

losses caused by dams. Barbless hooks are required for steelheading. Non-finclipped steelhead must be released unharmed. Most steelhead are caught by trolling hotshots or casting lures. Best fishing is November to February. The most productive water is downstream from the Imnaha in Oregon and in the vicinity of the Grande Ronde confluence a few miles downstream from the state line. A Washington or Idaho license is required to fish north of the state line.

Sturgeon are present in all size classes, including 8 to 9 footers. All sturgeon must be released unharmed.

There is a boat launch and Forest Service campground at Dug Bar. The facility at Pittsburgh Landing in Idaho includes a boat ramp and RV hook-ups. There are also boat-in only facilities at Cache Creek about 9 miles downstream from the dam, and at Kirkwood, near the mid-point of this reach. The Kirkwood facility includes an historic ranch and museum.

Commercial rafting and jet boat operations will take you the whole length of this wild river. Jet boats are available for hire in Lewiston, ID and Clarkston, WA. Guides and outfitters are available in Oxbow, Enterprise, and Joseph. Boaters who want to go it alone should be aware that the river above Kirkwood is suitable for experts only.

SNAKE RIVER: Hells Canyon Reservoir. The lowest reservoir on the Snake River, deep and narrow, fished primarily for smallmouth and crappie but with a large population of catfish. It stretches 21 miles between Oxbow Dam at Copperfield, Oregon, and Hells Canyon Dam at the southern boundary of Hells Canyon Wilderness. Below Hells Canyon Dam, the river runs free through its magnificent gorge, accessed only by trails and intrepid river runners.

To reach the reservoir from Baker, follow Hwy. 86 to Copperfield. From Weiser, Idaho, take I-95 north to Hwy. 71. The highway crosses the reservoir at Brownlee Dam and follows the west shore of Oxbow to Copperfield. There is a boat ramp about one mile downstream from Copperfield Park. A gravel road then a dirt track follow the Oregon shore for about 8 miles. Trail 1890 continues downstream another 7 miles.

At Copperfield, a paved road crosses the reservoir and follows the Idaho shore down to Hells Canyon Dam. There is a boat launch on the Idaho shore at Hells Canyon Park, about 5 miles downstream from Oxbow Dam. At Hells Canyon Dam, the east side road crosses the reservoir to the Oregon shore, leading to Hells Canyon Creek Campground and Boat Ramp. This ramp is used to float Hells Canyon.

Channel cats here average 10 to 14 inch-es and run to 20 inches. Anglers use bait, fishing from both bank and boats. Hells Canyon Reservoir has the smallest populations of crappie and smallmouth of any Snake River reservoir, though good numbers of crappie are caught from the bridge at Copperfield. Bluegills and trout are also present as well as a reproducing population of sturgeon. Sturgeon of all age classes are present in the reservoir, but unlike the Columbia fishery, all sturgeon here must be released unharmed. The sturgeon are found upstream of Copperfield Bridge.

Smallmouth bass are taken on lures and spinners. Bluegill and crappie are caught on jigs or cut bait.

There are campgrounds on the reservoir at Copperfield Park on the Oregon shore, and at Hells Canyon Park in Idaho. There are also several hike-in or boat-in camps on the Oregon shore between road's end and Hells Canyon Dam.

SNAKE RIVER: Oxbow Reservoir A 12-mile impoundment of the Snake River between Oxbow and Brownlee dams, offering outstanding fishing for smallmouth bass, channel cats, and crappie. From Baker City take Hwy. 86 east 70 miles to the community of Copperfield, at the huge bend in the Snake from which the dam gets its name. A paved road follows the reservoir closely from Oxbow upstream to Brownlee.

Since 1994, Oxbow's bass fishery has been regulated specifically to develop a trophy smallmouth bass fishery. The reservoir is open for bass fishing year-round, but from January 1 to July 1, bass fishing is strictly catch and release. This gives the bass time to reproduce without taking males away from their redds. A limit of two bass per day and a keeper slot limit (under 12 inches or over 16 inches) have also contributed to the quality of Oxbow's bass fishery. In recent years, anglers using artificial lures have reported 100-bass days.

The largest bass are caught on plastic lures fished in 20 to 40 feet of water. Lures that imitate wounded minnows (a common product of Brownlee's turbines) have been especially effective. Best colors are pearl, smoke and brown (pumpkin). Look for smallmouth near rocky points that break the current. A medium action bass rod will handle any fish in Oxbow. Fly fishing can also be effective for bass, especially on warm summer evenings. Try poppers or deer hair mice near the riprap banks on

Oxbow offers outstanding fishing for smallmouth bass. Photograph by Phil Simonski.

the Oregon side.

As in Brownlee, the crappie population here has diminished in recent years, though there are still plenty of crappie in the 8- to 10- inch range. Look for them behind the points of land used as campgrounds on the Oregon side. In late April, crappie begin moving into shallow water in search of spawning areas. Small plastic jigs in any color can be effective. By mid-June, most crappie have returned to the deeper water (30 to 40 feet) off the vertical rock walls where they are more difficult to catch. In fall. they move to the deep water in front of the Oxbow turbine intake and remain there throughout the winter.

Channel and flathead catfish have rebounded in Oxbow following closure of the commercial crayfish operations here. Channel cats to 15 pounds are not uncommon and flatheads to 28 pounds have been landed in recent years. Channel cats are more abundant in the upper reservoir, while flatheads are more abundant in the lower reservoir. The best time to fish for these big cats is July and August. The best bait for both species is fresh shrimp. Use the lightest sinker possible to keep your bait on the bottom. In the lower reservoir where the current is slow, no weight is needed.

Bank fishing is available the full length of the reservoir on the Oregon side. On the Idaho side, the only bank fishing area is from the dam deadline to McCormick Park, about a mile. All species can be caught from the bank, but this reservoir is best fished using a boat.

Small boats (up to 20 feet) can be launched at several undeveloped sites off the Oregon shore, but the only developed ramp is at McCormick Park on the Idaho shore at the south end of the reservoir below Brownlee Dam below the bridge. There is a rock island and fast current immediately downstream from the ramp, so launch with caution.

The reservoir fluctuates daily about four feet as well as during the night, so it is best to anchor your boat in five feet of water when you are through fishing for the day. If you don't, you may well be beached come sun-up.

There are developed campgrounds at McCormick Park and at Copperfield on the Oregon shore below Oxbow Dam.

There is a mercury contamination health advisory on all Snake River reservoir fish. Prudent anglers should consider re-

leasing all large fish (which may have built up mercury levels in their body tissue over the years). Check the regulations for complete information.

SNAKE RIVER: Brownlee Reservoir A 57-mile long, 15,000 acre impoundment on the Snake River whose outstanding fisheries for smallmouth bass, crappie, and catfish draw the attention of anglers throughout the western U.S. Brownlee is formed by Brownlee Dam, the uppermost dam in the Hells Canyon dam complex. In addition to the Snake, the dam backs up the Powder River near Richland and the Burnt River near Huntington.

In recent years, smallmouth bass have overtaken crappie as the star attraction here. Catfish are the main event on the upper reservoir. Crappie are still plentiful and popular; and largemouth bass, rainbow trout, yellow perch, and bluegills are also present. Brownlee fisheries are jointly managed by Oregon and Idaho departments of fish and wildlife.

How to Get There. To reach the lower reservoir from Oregon, take Hwy. 86 north from Richland, through Halfway, to Oxbow Reservoir. At Copperfield Campground, turn right and head south along Oxbow to Brownlee Dam. The road crosses the reservoir at the dam and continues south to Woodhead Park in Idaho.

To reach the Powder River arm from Baker City, take Hwy. 86 to Richland. About a half mile east of town, when Hwy. 86 veers left and uphill toward Halfway, continue straight toward Hewitt Park, which is on the Powder River Arm.

To reach mid-reservoir from Richland, turn south on First St., a gravel road signed for Huntington. After crossing the Powder River, continue east on the Snake River Rd., which meets the main reservoir at Swede's Landing. The Snake River Rd. continues south to Spring Recreation Area, then crosses the Burnt River Arm and follows it upstream to Huntington.

To reach Farewell Bend State Park (on the upper reservoir) from Baker, take Hwy. 84 south to the Huntington Exit (Hwy. 30). Continue through Huntington. The road to the park is well signed.

Fisheries. Smallmouth bass are present in good numbers throughout the reservoir, though concentrations are greatest around rocky outcroppings in the lower half. Best fishing for keeper-size bass (12-inch mini-

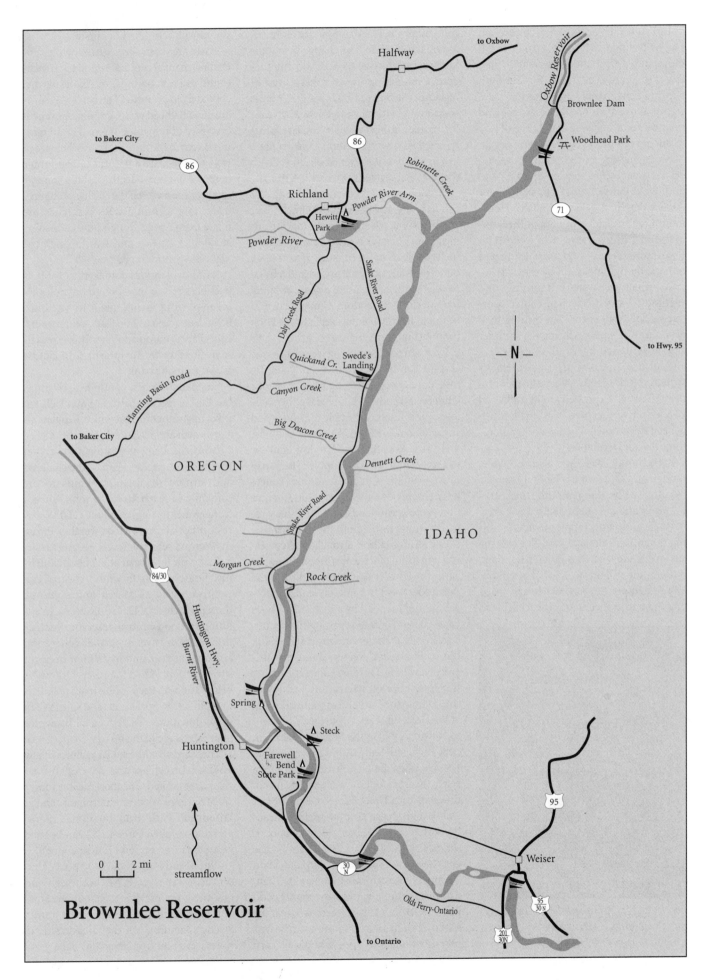

to Oxbow

Halfway

to Baker City

86

Richland

Powder River Arm

Robinette Creek

Oxbow Reservoir

Brownlee Dam

Woodhead Park

71

to Hwy. 95

Hewitt Park

Powder River

Daly Creek Road

Snake River Road

Quicksand Cr.

Swede's Landing

Canyon Creek

Hanning Basin Road

Big Deacon Creek

Dennett Creek

OREGON

IDAHO

Snake River Road

to Baker City

Morgan Creek

Rock Creek

84/30

Huntington Hwy.

Burnt River

Spring

Steck

Huntington

Farewell Bend State Park

95

0 1 2 mi

streamflow

30 N

Weiser

Olds Ferry-Ontario

95 30 N

Brownlee Reservoir

201 30 N

to Ontario

mum) is in early spring (March through May). Starting in March, big smallmouth move into the shallows to spawn then linger to guard their redds. Smallmouth become active when water temperature warms above 55 or 60 degrees. Catch and release is recommended at this time of year to encourage successful regeneration. In summer, the bigger smallmouth move into deeper water where they can be difficult to find. By September and October, look for them at depths of 35 to 75 ft. Smaller smallmouth are available throughout the summer and can give your arm a workout (two-hundred bass days are not unheard of here, though most will be under-size).

Fish shallower water in mornings and evenings. Move to deeper, cooler spots during the heat of the day. Fishing topwater lures after dark during the summer can be very exciting. At all times of year and all times of day, fishing near rocky structure is productive. Crayfish, plentiful near the rocks, can be caught and used very effectively as bait. The smallmouth fishery shuts down when water temperatures dive in December.

Largemouth bass are also available, though nowhere near as plentiful as smallmouth. The best largemouth concentration is in and near the Powder River arm.

White and black crappie provided a fishing bonanza in the late '80s. The average size and annual catch is down these days, but crappie still attract a lot of attention. White crappie 12 to 15 inches and black crappie 9 to 11 inches are still available in

Best fishing for Brownlee's keeper size smallmouth (minimum size 12 inches) is in early spring. Photograph by Jeffrey Kee.

good numbers. Black crappie are more numerous than white. The change in crappie fortune may be due to reservoir fluctuations, over-fishing, or other factors resulting from the current high water. Crappie seem to do better during low water years.

Crappie are most aggressive in late spring during their spawning season. Look for them in 5 to 6 ft. of water over small-gravel beds that are interspersed with rocks. A moderately sloping bank is often a good indicator of adjacent gravel beds. At this time of year crappie will attack almost anything, including a bare hook. Tube baits in sizes 1 and 2 inch, or curly-tail grubs on 1/32 to 1/16 ounce jig heads are popular. Cast and retrieve parallel to the bank, using a short hopping retrieve along the bottom. Crappie can also be found near spawning carp in June. Look for thrashing carp and cast nearby.

Even during spawning season, some crappie can be found in deep water. By mid-June, most spawning activity is concluded, and most crappie leave the shallows. Big schools of crappie may be found suspended off the larger points. Look for them at 12 to 30 ft., though in low light (or when the surface is wind-rippled) they may move to within 5 ft. of the surface. Unlike bass, crappie don't seem to mind fluctuations in reservoir levels, and the fishery remains strong throughout the summer.

Catfish are available throughout the reservoir, but fishing for them is especially popular in the Powder River arm and from the Burnt River arm to Farewell Bend. (A dangerous rapid created by a rock ledge above Farewell Bend prohibits passage further upstream). Boat anglers are most successful, but bank anglers average about one fish every two hours. There are good catfish bank fisheries at Spring Recreation Site downstream from the Burnt River confluence and at the Holcomb Park day use area adjacent to Hewitt Park on the Powder River arm near Richland. Sight-fishing for catfish is possible when the cats are foraging for carp eggs (usually in June). Cast in the vicinity of thrashing carp. Don't fish too deep. The cats will be taking eggs 18 to 30 inches beneath the surface. Flooded bankside vegetation is also a good place to look for big cats. Fly anglers have good success catching catfish on streamers, though most anglers use bait. Crappie (both flesh and guts) makes good bait, and some catfishionados swear by spoiled shrimp. Later in the summer, boaters use fish finders to spot schools of carp

smolts with catfish in hot pursuit.

There are seven species in Brownlee, including channel cats that run 16 to 20 inches and reach 45 pounds, and flatheads that approach 40 pounds. (The current record-breaking flathead was a 42-pounder caught upstream of Brownlee in 1994.) Dead minnows, cut bait, and nightcrawlers work well. Crayfish are a natural catfish forage here and are very effective as bait. In June, cats seem eager to take anything presented, using any technique. Peak catches are made from April through July. Launching at dusk to anchor and fish through the night is a common practice.

Rainbow trout are stocked as soon as possible after ice-off. Though rainbows average 10 to 14 inches, trout to 3 pounds have been taken here in recent years. Bluegill are plump and plentiful, especially in the Powder River arm, and can be fished from the bank

Sturgeon numbers continue to dwindle, but the big fish do spawn at Swan Falls 120 miles upstream from Brownlee. Regulations allow catch and release sturgeon fishing.

Boating. Brownlee is big and can get rough. Most anglers keep to the shallows and around the islands. Winds in the canyon can reach 30 to 70 mph when a front comes through. Call the ODFW district office at Ontario for weather information and reservoir levels. See Appendix.

Reservoir levels can affect boat launching. Draw-downs for flood control can begin as early as March and continue through Memorial Day some years. In addition to flood control, reservoir fluctuations can be driven by power generation any time of year, and by salmon needs in spring or fall. When the reservoir level is below 2060 ft., keep to the main channels to avoid hitting rocks and sand spits. When draw-down exceeds 70 feet, all Brownlee boat ramps are high and dry.

There are no commercial facilities of any kind on Brownlee, and developed boat ramps are limited. The most reliable ramps are at Spring Park near Huntington, and at Woodhead Park in Idaho. Other ramps and undeveloped launch sites can be used when the reservoir level is high enough.

Woodhead Park is the only boat ramp on the lower river. It has both high and low-water ramps. Hewitt Park on the Powder River arm has a high-water ramp. Swede's Landing (on the Oregon side 18 miles upstream from the dam) has a gravel bar launch that requires 4-wheel drive during low water. Spring Recreation Area north of Huntington has a low-water boat ramp with optional launching possible from the gravel bar (using 4-wheel drive) when the reservoir is really low. Farewell Bend State Park south of Huntington has a high-water ramp. Steck Park on the Idaho shore, a BLM facility about 40 miles south of Bowman Dam, has a high-water ramp. Boaters can also put-in at The Oasis, a privately owned ramp on the Olds Ferry-Ontario Rd. Small boats and canoes can slide into the reservoir along Hwy. 201 where the highway follows the reservoir toward Weiser, and the banks are flat. This area is known locally as "The Slides." There are no opportunities to launch a boat on the Burnt River arm.

Bank Access. As with other Snake River fisheries, bank access is limited. There's good crappie fishing from the bank near Brownlee Dam, accessible from Woodhead Park in Idaho. Good catches of crappie as well as catfish can be made from the fishing dock at Hewitt Park on the Powder River arm when boat congestion allows, and from the bank at adjacent Holcomb Park day use area. There's good bank fishing for catfish and bass at Farewell Bend and for all species along the Snake River Road south of Huntington, where you can fish from the rocks or from culverts near the mouth. Ice-fishing is popular at the upper end of Brownlee, where an ice pack 10 inches thick can build up some years.

Camping and Accommodations. There are camping facilities with drinking water at Woodhead Park, Hewitt Park, Spring Recreation Area, Steck Park, and Farewell Bend State Park. Electrical hookups for RV's are available at Woodhead and Farewell Bend. There are commercial campgrounds near the reservoir in Richland (Eagle Valley RV Park) and at The Oasis on the Olds Ferry-Ontario Rd. It's also possible to camp at undeveloped sites (big flat spots between the road and the river) along the river between Farewell Bend and The Oasis. Another option for boaters on the Powder River Arm is to "camp" in a cabin on one of the anchored fishing floats. These floats were anchored in place before the reservoir was flooded and are privately owned, but many are available for public use on a first come first served

basis. Look for floats with a sign reading: "You're welcome to use it, but please leave it as you found it." Respect "No Trespassing" signs. Accommodations, supplies, and services are limited but available in Richland, plentiful in Ontario and Baker City.

Other Useful Information. An Oregon license is required to fish the Powder River Arm. Elsewhere on the reservoir, either Oregon or Idaho licenses are valid. Idaho anglers should remember that Oregon law allows only one rod per angler.

Both Oregon and Idaho Departments of Health have issued a mercury contamination health advisory on Brownlee Reservoir fish. Prudent anglers should consider releasing all large fish (who may have built up mercury levels in their body tissue over the years). Check the regulations for complete information. For reservoir levels, water temperature, and boat ramp availability, contact Idaho Power or Farewell Bend State Park. See Appendix.

SNAKE RIVER: Above Brownlee Reservoir. A shallow, free-flowing stretch of the Snake accessible from both Oregon and Idaho, offering world-class fishing for huge catfish. On the Oregon side, the river is accessible from Hwy. 201 and county roads in the vicinity of Adrian, Nyssa, and Ontario.

The opportunity to catch record-breaking catfish attracts anglers from all over the western U.S. The State Record flathead catfish weighing 42 pounds came out of this stretch of the river in 1994. There are more big flatheads here than in Brownlee Reservoir. Both channel and flathead catfish here average 5 pounds.

This is a springtime fishery, triggered by rising water temperatures and the movement of catfish into the shallows prior to spawning. The spawn takes place in late June, after which it's considerably harder to find and catch the big cats. By July, dispersal of the fish, uncomfortably harsh daytime temperatures (95 to 100 degrees), and an increasingly shallow river discourage fishing. By mid-summer, propeller-driven boats are in danger of grounding on the gravel bars, only 4 to 6 ft. deep even in spring. Shallow-draft boats are appropriate for negotiating this section of the river in every season.

Smallmouth bass and crappie are also present in good numbers. Look for small-

Channel catfish are plentiful throughout Oregon's SNAKE RIVER. *Photograph by Marcia Hartman.*

mouth in the current break at the downstream end of islands and adjacent to riprap. There is currently a 12-inch minimum length for bass. Crappie are generally in the backwaters and slower pools.

Boats can be launched at Payette and Weiser in Idaho, and from ramps and undeveloped slides off County Rd. 201 in the vicinity of Ontario, Nyssa, and Adrian in Oregon. Popular launch spots include The Oasis (a privately owned ramp on the Olds Ferry-Ontario Rd. north of Ontario), the Hwy. 52 Bridge to Payette, Ontario State Park, Nyssa Ramp, and the Adrian Ramp. Small boats and canoes can slide into the river along Hwy. 201 (where the highway follows the reservoir toward Weiser, and the banks are flat). This area is known locally as "The Slides."

In addition to Farewell Bend State Park, there are developed camping facilities at The Oasis, about 2 miles upstream from Farewell Bend. There are also natural campsites available along the river between Farewell Bend State Park and The Oasis (big flat spots between the road and the river).

Both Oregon and Idaho Departments of Health have issued a mercury contamination health advisory on fish taken out of this section of the Snake River. Prudent anglers should consider releasing all large fish (who may have built up mercury levels in their body tissue over the years). Check the regulations for complete information.

FISHING IN OREGON'S
COLUMBIA RIVER ZONE

Columbia River

Primary gathering place of the Northwest's water, draining more than 250,000 acres of land over a 1200 mile journey, the Columbia River is a gathering place of life as well. Its estuary is resident home to greenling, perch, lingcod, and several kinds of rockfish. Largemouth and smallmouth bass, walleye, and many other warmwater species thrive in its backwaters and in the enormous reservoirs created by the huge dams that harness its flow. Plentiful numbers of green and white sturgeon reside in the river and move in and out with the tides and with runs of smelt, herring, shad, and smaller baitfish.

The Columbia is also (and most famously) home to salmon and steelhead, as well as searun cutthroat trout—fish that begin and end their lives in the river or its tributary streams, but who spend most of their adult lives at sea.

Historically, the Columbia's salmon included about 2-million each of spring, summer, and fall chinook, coho, and sockeye. Each of these species, as well as steelhead and searun cutthroat trout, were composed of distinct populations unique to a particular watershed or reach within the Columbia system.

Anglers discovering the Columbia today are still amazed by its extravagant fishing opportunities. But the truth is, dams and habitat degradation have diminished each of these populations—some (like the sockeye and summer chinook, the *June hog*) to near extinction. Unfavorable ocean conditions, misguided hatchery programs, and unbridled harvest in past years further contributed to the decline of these fisheries. Today, a few of the remaining populations have stabilized (though at low levels), while others are still on a downward spiral. Fall chinook (a combination of both hatchery and wild stocks) is the healthiest race of salmon in the Columbia at this time.

To help protect these remaining runs, anglers are asked to accept strict regulation of all Columbia River anadromous fisheries. For years to come, anglers should anticipate variable seasons from year to year, and sudden closures as well as unexpected opportunities. Check for emergency regulations before fishing the Columbia for any of these protected species. See Appendix.

When the fishing season is open in both Oregon and Washington, a license of either state is valid for Columbia River angling except when fishing from the other state's shore. When the Oregon season is closed, a Washington fishing license is not valid on the Oregon side of the state line (mid-channel), and vice-versa. Though most regulations are concurrent at this time, they have been known to vary between the states.

Anglers who are residents of either Oregon or Washington may put-in or take-out from either shore. Non-residents must possess

The COLUMBIA RIVER estuary offers the river's best opportunity to catch keeper-size sturgeon. Photograph by John Ramsour.

a nonresident license for the state in which they are landing.

For regulatory purposes in Oregon, the Columbia is divided into four sections: Buoy 10 line up to Astoria-Megler Bridge, Astoria-Megler Bridge to I-5 Bridge, I-5 Bridge to Bonneville Dam, and Bonneville Dam to the Oregon/Washington border above McNary Dam. Westward from the Buoy 10 line, ocean catch and length limits apply. Oregon and Washington usually adopt the regulations determined annually by the Federal Pacific Fisheries Management Council. The Council has jurisdiction over waters from 3 miles to 200 miles offshore. Regulations are established each year in April, but mid-season closures do occur.

For regulation and management purposes, sloughs and other backwaters of the Columbia are included in either the Northwest, Willamette, or Central zones. In this book, see the Northwest Zone for Beaver, Blind, Bradbury , Brownsmead, Clatskanie, Deer Island, Dibblee, Goat Island, Magruder, Mayger, Prescott, Rinearson, Sandy Island, and Westport sloughs. Refer to the Willamette Zone for Cunningham Lake, Cunningham Slough, Gilbert River, Multnomah Channel, Pete's Slough, Santosh Slough, Scappoose Bay, and Sturgeon Lake. See the Central Zone for a map and description of the string of ponds adjacent to the Columbia from the community of Cascade to the Deschutes River.

The Columbia River Zone includes all waters of the Columbia River upstream from a north-south line through Buoy 10 at the mouth. It includes those portions of tributaries downstream from the main line railroad bridges near their mouths except for the Willamette, Sandy, Hood, Deschutes, and Umatilla river systems.

The Best Fishing in Oregon's Columbia River Zone

Buoy 10
For fall chinook.

Estuary
The best place in the river to catch legal-size sturgeon.

Clatsop Beaches
Best razor clam digging in the state.

St. Helens to the Astoria-Megler Bridge
Spring chinook and a productive summer fishery for keeper sturgeon are the main attractions.

Bonneville Dam to St. Helens
The most popular fisheries anywhere on the river for all Columbia River species.

Lake Celilo
Most popularly fished for walleye, but with outstanding opportunities for smallmouth bass along the riprap.

Lake Umatilla
Has a national reputation for walleye and a fine population of smallmouth bass.

Columbia River: Estuary. (Pacific Ocean to Astoria-Megler Bridge).

Offshore Fisheries. The mouth of the Columbia was once Oregon's number one access to ocean salmon sportfishing. Experienced anglers and charter boats out of the ports of Astoria, Hammond, and Warrenton in Oregon, plus Ilwaco in Washington would start taking big spring chinook just beyond the bar in May. In early summer, offshore anglers pursued the smaller coho, followed by an intense fall chinook fishery from mid-August through Labor Day.

Fishing off the mouth of the Columbia now begins beyond an invisible line between buoys 7 and 4. The offshore salmon season at the mouth is within the regulatory zone designated as "between Leadbetter point (Washington) and Cape Falcon (just north of Nehalem Bay)." Seasons vary drastically from year to year, depending on estimates of run size. In 1994, the salmon season closed in April. In 1998, the season didn't open until August 3. In 1999, it opened July 19.

In general, ocean salmon fishing opportunities are consistently more generous south of Cape Falcon, and boats out of Columbia River ports frequently head

south to take advantage of open seasons elsewhere. Charter boat operations out of Warrenton and Hammond book trips for bottomfish year-round, but generally head south to better fishing grounds south of Tillamook Head.

A powerhouse (literally), the Columbia rushes toward the ocean on an average summer day at a rate of 400,000 cubic feet per second. Its meeting with the ocean is generally anything but pacific. The Columbia River bar is the most dangerous on the Oregon coast. Only 25 feet deep, though dredged to 60 feet in the channel, and relatively narrow, it is subject to swells that can rise higher than the average water depth. More often the exchange of fresh and salt water takes place beneath a smooth surface, but boaters must be alert and mindful of tide, time, and weather. A craft at least 18 ft. long is recommended for bar crossings, and boaters are urged to cross in flood and slack tides only, and to beware of the ebb tide.

Salmon. "Buoy 10" is the name given to the most popular fishery in the Columbia estuary. Charter and private boats traditionally gather to fish fall chinook and coho salmon between buoys 10 and 14, with the majority of boats fishing as close

as possible to the Buoy 10 line.

This is an active salmon feeding area and, on busy weekends in late summer, over 2000 boats might gather along the buoy line, drifting or trolling herring or anchovies on the incoming tide. Fish are also caught on the outgoing tide. In fact, only slack tide is typically unproductive, and even then, some fish are caught. Coho are generally closer to the surface, while chinook are somewhat deeper. At this time, but both wild and hatchery chinook are available for harvest, but only finclipped coho, steelhead, and searun cutthroat may be kept.

Electronic gear is handy for locating salmon, but the presence of rips (the meeting of conflicting currents) and concentrations of bird activity are also good indicators. Bank anglers participate in the Buoy 10 fishery off the south jetty and off Clatsop Spit, where coho catches predominate.

The Buoy 10 fall chinook season traditionally opens in early August after summer chinook (bound for the upper river) have passed through. In years where low returns are expected, the Buoy 10 season closes early or may never open, since it is assumed that too many of the threatened

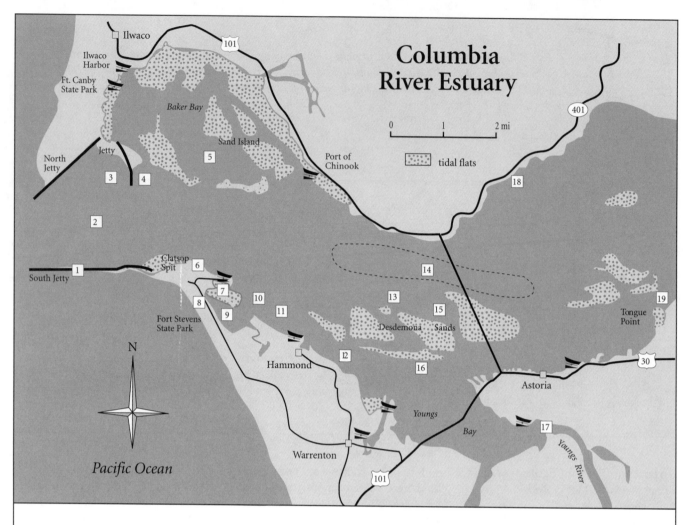

Columbia River Estuary

0 1 2 mi

   tidal flats

1. South Jetty. Fish for salmon at end of jetty; black rockfish and bottomfish mid-jetty, surf perch nearest spit.

2. Buoy 10. Active fall chinook and coho feeding area; give way to commercial traffic.

3. Crab.

4. Crab.

5. Crab, Flounder, Sturgeon.

6. Bank Fish. for crab, salmon, surfperch, flounder.

7. Jetty Sands. Unimproved boat launch off beach.

8. Clatsop Spit. Fish the surf for perch; most productive razor clam digging in Oregon.

9. Crab.

10. Crab.

11. Sturgeon.

12. Sturgeon.

13. Sturgeon.

14. Sturgeon.

15. Desdemona Sands. Submerged sand bar; fish for sturgeon.

16. Sturgeon.

17. Young's Bay. Good ramp accesses spring chinook fishery in bay.

18. Sturgeon. Boat and bank fishery (Washington license required for bank fishery).

19. Sturgeon.

stocks will be caught in this "mixed race" gathering place. The fishery sometimes reopens in mid-September, when it is judged that threatened upriver chinook have left the buoy area.

When the Buoy 10 season closes, fishing is often still permitted upstream from the Astoria-Megler Bridge. Many anglers fish as close to the bridge as possible, but good catches are made throughout the old Columbia River channel (on the Washington side of the river) between the bridge and the point where Washington Hwy. 401 turns away from the river at Knappton.

The average fall chinook weighs about 20 pounds, but upriver brights (wild fall chinook bound for the Hanford Reach) can be 40 pounds and larger.

Spring chinook bound for the lower tributaries (the Willamette and Sandy rivers in Oregon, the Cowlitz, Kalama, and Lewis in Washington) enter the Columbia from January through May. Fish bound for the middle and upper tributaries enter beginning in March.

The estuary fishery for upriver spring chinook has been closed since 1977 to protect endangered stocks and honor Native American treaty obligations. The fishery for lower river spring chinook traditionally began whenever the fish arrived and continued until March 31. In recent years, low returns and Endangered Species Act concerns have resulted in restricted spring chinook fisheries throughout the system. If on-going efforts are successful, all hatchery-bred spring chinook will be finclipped (both in Oregon and Washington), and anglers will be able to fish the spring run with minimal impact on wild stocks.

Charter boats and public boat ramps are available in Hammond, Warrenton, and Astoria. Frozen bait can be purchased at tackle shops near the river, but many anglers call ahead to reserve fresh bait.

Sturgeon. In the late 1800's, Columbia River sturgeon were fished almost to extinction. Today, the Columbia is host to what may be the world's largest concentration of white sturgeon. Less common green sturgeon are also present. The total population below Bonneville Dam is estimated to be about one million.

Conservative regulations and a growing understanding of the sturgeon life cycle are responsible for the come-back. Today we know that the largest sturgeon are generally pregnant females. Minimum and maximum catch lengths protect both juveniles and spawners, and there are daily and annual catch limits.

Sturgeon migration patterns have yet to be understood with certainty. At this point, we only know that sturgeon migrate freely and frequently between ocean and estuary, and roam far from their home waters. Tagged Columbia River sturgeon have been identified as far north as Puget Sound, and as far south as San Francisco Bay.

The Columbia River estuary is the best place in the river to catch legal-size sturgeon. Of the 41,000 legal sturgeon landed in 1998, 30,000 were caught here. The estuary is open to sturgeon fishing year-round, but spring and summer seasons are most popular with anglers. Charter sturgeon trips out of Hammond, Warrenton, and Ilwaco are very popular, and the catch rate is high.

Increased catches generally coincide with the appearance of anchovies in the river intermittently from April to August. Peak sturgeon catches are generally in May, June, and July. Check with local bait shops to determine when the anchovies have arrived, and to place your order for bait. Fresh bait is essential for this fishery and should be ordered at least one day in advance to insure a supply. Sand shrimp are also productive. Normally 12 to 18 baits per person will suffice.

During the peak season, several hundred boats may gather on a single day in the area from Desdemona Sands to Grays Bay Point, with the best bite occurring from low slack to several hours into the flood tide. Tides and thieving sculpin often drive anglers to try several locations per trip.

Anglers fishing sturgeon in the estuary should be especially watchful for barge traffic. It is unlawful (and suicidal) to impede vessels that are restricted to the deep draft channel. To fish for sturgeon, anglers must purchase a sturgeon tag in addition to their regular fishing license, though a sturgeon tag is not required for anglers who purchase a daily fishing license. At this time, the size slot for keeper sturgeon in this section of the river is between 42 and 60 inches. Barbless hooks are required.

Bottomfish. The Columbia Estuary offers varied opportunities for bottom fishing from both boat and bank. The jetties on both north and south sides of the mouth provide access to greenling, rockfish, surfperch, and lingcod. Lingcod may weigh over 20 pounds, and the perch sometimes reach 3 pounds or better. Best catches occur during the incoming tide, using cut herring, shrimp, or clam necks. The surf along the Clatsop beaches south of the estuary is very productive for perch.

Clams. The Clatsop beaches from the south jetty to Seaside offer the best razor clam digging in the state. Clatsop beaches are open to razor clam digging from October 1 to July 14. There are occasional emergency closures when high levels of poisonous demoic acid are detected in area shellfish. Check with the district ODFW office in Astoria.

Minus tides below one foot are usually necessary for good clam digging in general, and spring minus tides are best for razor clams. No license is needed to dig clams in Oregon, and the state's 300 miles of beaches are open to the public.

Tidal information is published daily in the newspapers, and tables for the year are available free at many tackle shops. The Long Beach Peninsula north of Ilwaco, Washington is also famous for razor clams, but a Washington non-resident license is required.

COLUMBIA RIVER: St. Helens to Astoria-Megler Bridge. A 73-mile long, mile-wide swath offering anglers opportunities for sturgeon, spring and fall chinook, coho, steelhead, walleye, and shad, with abundant bass and panfish in adjacent slack water.

Highway 30 follows the river throughout this reach. Secondary roads lead down to the river, which is bordered by agricultural land, narrow beaches, a few private marina and houseboat facilities, and a sprinkling of industry and small town development. There are many access points for both boat and bank anglers. Boat ramps, tackle, and bait are available at Astoria, Rainier, Goble, St. Helens, and other points along Hwy. 30. (Many gas stations and convenience stores sell bait).

Navigational charts of the Columbia River, produced by the National Oceanic and Atmospheric Administration (NOAA) are available through retail map outlets. An up-to-date chart (in hand) is a must for all boaters of the Columbia. In addition to helping you avoid commercial shipping channels, running aground, and losing your way back to the parking lot, the charts also provide a blueprint of the river's submerged structure and its many backwater fishing opportunities.

Sturgeon. The lower Columbia from Astoria to St. Helens includes extremely productive sturgeon water. On the Washington side, excellent catches are made from Megler Pt. to Gray's Bay, within Gray's Bay, off Barlow Pt., and at the mouth of the Cowlitz River. On the Oregon side, anglers fish from Tongue Pt. upstream along the islands adjacent to the shipping channel (keep an eye out for barges). Other popular spots include Three Tree Point, Bugby Hole, Oak Point, the Longview area, Elder Rock, Martins Bluff, Deer Island, and the entire St. Helens area. A deep hole in front of the Trojan Nuclear

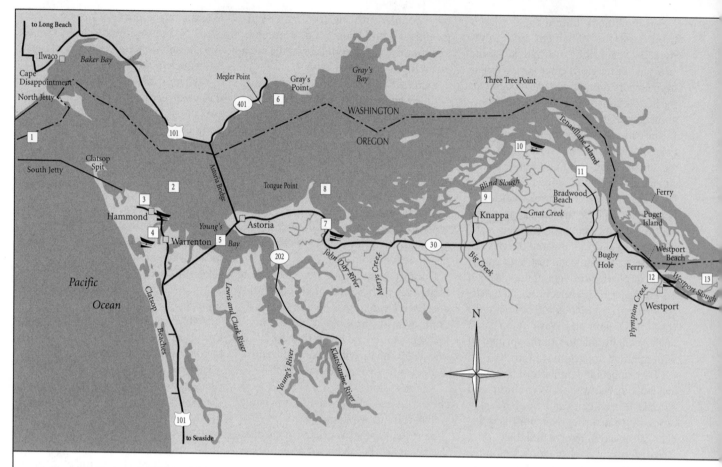

1. Buoy 10. To Astoria Bridge, fish incoming tide for chinook and coho during fall salmon season.

2. Desdemona Sands. Fish troughs north and south of sandbar for sturgeon in June and July.

3. Hammond Boat Ramp. Improved public ramp and moorage; major access to Buoy 10 fishery and to sturgeon through summer.

4. Warrenton Boat Ramp. Improved public ramp and moorage; accesses Buoy 10.

5. Youngs Bay. Selective fishery for netpen-reared spring chinook.

6. Megler Pt. to Gray's Bay. Best sturgeon fishing in estuary at times.

7. John Day Boat Ramp. Improved public ramp is major access to Tongue Point sturgeon fishery.

8. Tongue Point. Fish for sturgeon along islands just off shipping channel.

9. Blind Slough. Hot spot for yellow perch in March and April when anchovies run; selective fishery for net pen chinook in April, finclipped coho in September.

10. Aldrich Point Boat Ramp. Turn off highway at Brownsmead; accesses Clifton Channel and Blind Slough.

11. Clifton Channel. Excellent spot for spring chinook when water is clear and low; good through March or as regs allow.

12. Westport Boat Ramp. Improved single ramp accesses lower Clifton Channel.

13. Seining Grounds. Fish wing jetties for salmon to just above Wallace Is.

14. Wallace Island to Crimms Island. Spring chinook, summer steelhead; bank access at Jones Beach.

15. Barlow Point. Fish for coho jacks, catch and release searun cutthroat, some sturgeon.

16. Lord Island. Fish north side from boat and bank for spring chinook, summer steelhead.

17. Dibblee Beach. Year-round bank plunking for chinook, steelhead; day-use only.

18. Rainier Beach. Plunk for summer steelhead at city park.

19. Cowlitz River. Fish the mouth for sturgeon, summer steelhead, fall chinook, coho, searun cutthroat.

20. Laurel Beach. Plunk for spring chinook and summer steelhead.

21. Prescott Beach & Slough. Plunk from beach for summer steelhead, spring chinook; launch hand carried boat in slough west of beach entrance for bass & panfish; best near mouth & below bluff.

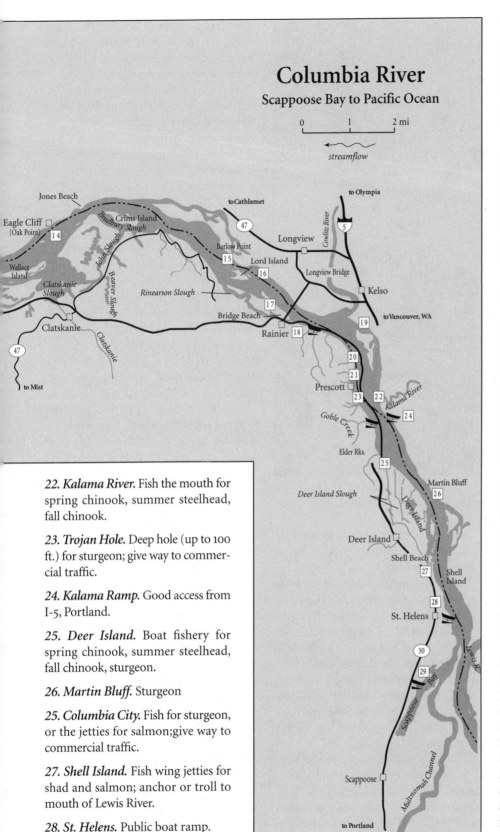

Columbia River

Scappoose Bay to Pacific Ocean

0   1   2 mi

streamflow

Jones Beach

Eagle Cliff
(Oak Point)
14

to Cathlamet

47

to Olympia

Crims Island

Bradbury Slough

Longview

Cowlitz River

5

Wallace
Island

John Slough

Barlow Point

15

Lord Island
16

Longview Bridge

Kelso

Clatskanie
Slough

Beaver Slough

Rinearson Slough

17

Bridge Beach

Clatskanie

Rainier   18

to Vancouver, WA

19

47

Clatskanie

to Mist

20

21

Prescott

23   22

Kalama River

Goble Creek

24

Elder Rks.

25

Deer Island Slough

Martin Bluff
26

Deer Island

Deer Island

Shell Beach

27   Shell
Island

28

St. Helens

30

Lewis R.

29

Scappoose
Bay

Scappoose

Multnomah Channel

to Portland

22. Kalama River. Fish the mouth for spring chinook, summer steelhead, fall chinook.

23. Trojan Hole. Deep hole (up to 100 ft.) for sturgeon; give way to commercial traffic.

24. Kalama Ramp. Good access from I-5, Portland.

25. Deer Island. Boat fishery for spring chinook, summer steelhead, fall chinook, sturgeon.

26. Martin Bluff. Sturgeon

25. Columbia City. Fish for sturgeon, or the jetties for salmon;give way to commercial traffic.

27. Shell Island. Fish wing jetties for shad and salmon; anchor or troll to mouth of Lewis River.

28. St. Helens. Public boat ramp.

29. Scappoose Bay Marine Park. Public ramp accesses lower Multnomah Channel (Coon Island) and Columbia; fish bay for crappie, catfish, bass, perch, crayfish, carp.

Power Plant at Goble can be very productive, as can the water off Columbia City downstream from the St. Helens Boat Ramp. In this stretch of the river, the most productive fishing is May through August, with peak catches in June and July. Most catches at this time of year are from Astoria-Megler Bridge to just above Tongue Point. In summer, few sturgeon are caught between the mouth of the Cowlitz and St. Helens, but winter fishing is best in this stretch, with peak catches in March.

Sturgeon fishing is primarily a boat show. Anglers use depth finders (and the concentration of other boats) to locate likely sturgeon water, then anchor and fish the bottom. The most popular baits are herring, anchovy, and smelt. In 1998, the total estimated sport catch between the estuary and the mouth of the Willamette was 35,000.

Most sturgeon hooked in this reach are legal size (at least 42 inches) or smaller.

Salmon. Spring chinook generally enter the lower Columbia in mid-February, and the fishery is usually open until the end of March, when it closes to allow upriver chinook safe passage. Mid-season closures do occur in low-return years, and complete closures of the spring chinook fishery in the mainstem Columbia have occurred. Plans to finclip all hatchery chinook may result in an extended season by 2002.

Salmon use the shoreline to navigate, so good catches are often made in 10 to 20 feet of water along both Oregon and Washington shores and on either side of the various islands. Favorite spots include the waters just off Shell Island, Shell Beach, Deer Island, Sandy Island, Prescott Beach, Lord Island, Crim's Island, Westport Beach, Puget Island, Tenasillahe Island, and on the Washington side, the mouths of the Lewis, Kalama, and Cowlitz rivers.

Bank angling (locally called bar fishing) is most popular at Shell, Prescott, Laurel, Rainier, Bridge, Dibblee, Jones, and Westport, beaches. An overwhelming number of bar anglers use No. 4 Spin-N-Glo lures. In low-water years, bank and boat angling for spring chinook can be very good from St. Helens down to the Clifton Channel. Most boat anglers troll herring or anchor and use wobbler-type lures. Prawns are also used productively, both trolled and fished at anchor.

Fall chinook and coho fisheries in this stretch of the river are primarily boat shows. Hog lines (regimental formations of anchored boats) form at the mouths of the Lewis, Kalama, and Cowlitz Rivers on the Washington side, with anglers preferring either wobbler-type lures or spinners.

Upriver bright fall chinook heading for the Hanford Reach are the COLUMBIA RIVER'S *showcase fishery. Photograph by Mitch Sanchotena.*

The water just off Shell Island is productive, as is Barlow Point just below the Cowlitz mouth. Bar fisheries for chinook jacks occurs at Prescott, Laurel, and Dibblee beaches in years of good returns. Most coho are caught off the mouth of the Cowlitz. Only finclipped coho may be kept.

In 1998, an estimated 4900 fall chinook were caught in this stretch.

Steelhead. Most summer steelheaders in this stretch of the river fish from the bank until August. In August, steelhead turn into the tributary mouths, where a boat is needed to reach them. In 1998, the estimated catch in the lower Columbia was 4800. Most boat anglers anchor to fish, using wobbler-type lures and rainbow blade spinners. Bank anglers seem to prefer the old standard Spin-N-Glo.

Winter steelhead run up the lower Columbia from November through March. Most anglers prefer to intercept them in the tributaries, rather than tough it out on the blustery Columbia. There is some winter fishing from the beaches, including Shell, Prescott, Laurel, Rainier, Bridge, Dibblee, Jones, and Westport. Only finclipped steelhead may be kept.

Shad. Shad migrate through the lower Columbia heading upriver from mid-May through June. Anglers tap into the run as it passes Shell Island on the Washington side near the Lewis River, and off the wing jetties near Goat Island on the Oregon side of the river. Wing jetty numbers 62, 70, 72, and 77 are especially productive. To identify these jetties, check the Columbia River NOAA chart. Average catch is 5 or 6 fish per person, per trip.

Bass and Panfish. The Columbia River is home to an enormous population of bass and panfish, which inhabit its slackwater, sloughs, and intertidal marshlands. Largemouth and smallmouth bass, white and black crappie, bluegill, yellow perch, channel cats, and brown bullhead are all richly represented. Fishing around rip-rap, pilings, docks, and log rafts is especially productive.

COLUMBIA RIVER: Bonneville Dam to St. Helens A 58-mile stretch, including the greatest variety of opportunity and the most popular fisheries on the river.

About 20 miles upstream from St. Helens, the Columbia is separated from mainland Oregon by Sauvie Island and Multnomah Channel, a long slough that carries a significant flow of the Willamette River to the Columbia. Anglers in the lower portion of this reach access the Columbia at the town of St. Helens, from Scappoose Bay, by launching boats at private ramps along Multnomah Channel and motoring to the Columbia, and from beaches on the east shore of Sauvie Island. When giving directions in this reach, remember that the Columbia makes a hard right at the Willamette River, turning north after a long westward flow.

Upstream of Sauvie Island, the mid-section of this reach is accessed from Kelley Point Park in North Portland at the confluence of the Willamette and Columbia rivers, from boats launched into the Willamette at the north end of the St. Johns Bridge in North Portland, and from public and private marinas off Marine Drive. Marine Drive follows the Columbia's Oregon shore to Blue Lake Park east of Portland. Chinook Landing on the Columbia near Blue Lake has four large paved ramps and lots of parking.

Beyond Blue Lake, the river is followed closely by I-84 to Bonneville and beyond. Interstate exits allow access to the river at Rooster Rock State Park, Dalton Pt., and at The Fishery (5 miles south of Bonneville Dam). There's also bank access at the dam.

Fish counts over the four lower Columbia River dams are available from March through November. See Appendix

Salmon. The primary salmon fishery in this reach of the Columbia is in the fall, and the primary catch is fall chinook. Tule salmon (maturing early) and coho (most of which don't bite once they leave the estuary) are also present. The fall salmon season generally opens August 1, just before the fish arrive. Peak catches are made from the first week in August through the first week in September.

The largest component of the fall run is a wild stock of chinook salmon known as *upriver brights.* These fish historically spawned in the gravel beds of the mainstem Columbia in what is now the Bonneville, John Day, and McNary dam pools.

Displaced but undaunted, they found suitable spawning and rearing habitat in the free flowing Hanford Reach in Washington. The average fish is just over 20 pounds, with 40-pounders caught ever year, as well as an occasional fish to 60 pounds. In 1997, an estimated 162,400 wild adult upriver brights returned to the Columbia. The fishery is supplemented by hatchery-reared chinook.

Best fishing is at tributary mouths where salmon congregate to enjoy the cooler water in August and September. Anglers troll, plunk, and jig with success. On the Oregon side, best fishing is from the mouth of the Sandy River downstream to Government Island and in the vicinity of Hamilton Island near Bonneville Dam. The only bank fisheries for fall chinook are at Warrendale and at Moffett, McCord, and Tanner creeks.

After the majority of upriver brights have passed over the dam, there are still excellent opportunities to catch fall chinook and coho near Bonneville Dam. In years with good water and good returns, the fishery below the dam has remained open or reopened through early October to allow access to these fish. Most are heading for the Bonneville mitigation hatchery on Tanner Creek, but in years of plentiful water, good numbers of wild fall chinook can be found in the vicinity of the gravel bars around Ives and Pierce islands.

Early in the season, plunking is the favorite technique near Bonneville, when the quarry is migrating fish. Later in the season, when salmon are lingering near their spawning grounds, backtrolling a diver with a large Kwikfish-type lure (and a sardine wrap) is more effective. Work this set-up 60 to 90 feet behind the boat (farther in deeper water, shorter in the shallow). Most fish are in 10 to 20 feet of water. Don't be surprised if you connect with an oversize sturgeon incidentally. Be mindful of the fishing closure 150 feet upstream and 450 feet downstream of Tanner Creek, and of the boating deadline associated with the smolt discharge pipe on Hamilton Island. Check for last-minute regulation changes before heading out. The Fishery near Dodson is a good source of information, or call ODFW's office in Clackamas. See Appendix.

The spring salmon fishery is currently limited to the area downstream from the I-5 Bridge (at Portland/Vancouver). A closing date of March 31 further focuses angling effort on the early run, which is composed primarily of fish bound for the Willamette River. Concerns for threatened McKenzie River chinook and low returns in some years have prompted emergency closures. Finclipping all hatchery chinook may extend and stabilize the season for this popular fishery by 2002.

The primary bank fishery for spring chinook takes place off the Sauvie Island beaches, as regulations allow. (This beach fishery has been closed since 1995 but may re-open once anglers can fish selectively for finclipped spring chinook.) Most popular are Reeder Beach (private, fee required), Willow Bar (at mile post 3 or 4), and Walton Beach (at the end of pavement on Reeder Rd.). Boat anglers fish throughout the open area, as well as in Multnomah Channel and the Willamette.

Sturgeon. Sturgeon are fished year 'round in this stretch, and catch numbers are quite high. The greatest concentration of angler effort is focused in the Bonneville area from February through March in conjunction with the arrival of smelt.

Boat angling at Bonneville begins at the boating deadline and continues downstream about 12 miles to Rooster Rock.

Other productive spots include Lady Island at Troutdale, near the I-5 bridge in northeast Portland, at the mouth of the Willamette, and across from Sauvie Island on the Washington side of the river between navigation lights 15 and 23.

The best opportunities to bank fish for sturgeon are at Bradford Island and at the mouth of Tanner Creek at Bonneville, as well as off Sauvie Island beaches. Reeder Beach (privately owned, fee required to fish), North Unit Beach at the very end of Reeder Rd. (public property, about 3 miles beyond the end of pavement), and Willow Bar are especially productive.

Bank angling for sturgeon demands sturdy gear: a 9 to 12 ft. rod, size 4/0+ reel, and 40 to 80 lb. line. Lighter gear is suitable for boat angling, except in the fast water just below Bonneville Dam. Lamprey eels and sand shrimp are favorite baits in winter. They stay on the hook well and are natural baits below the dam throughout most of the year. Smelt and shad strips are effective in season, and some anglers use salmon and pickled herring.

With an estimated life expectancy of 100 years or more, sturgeon have been known to reach lengths of up to 20 feet and weigh as much as 1500 pounds. These days, the

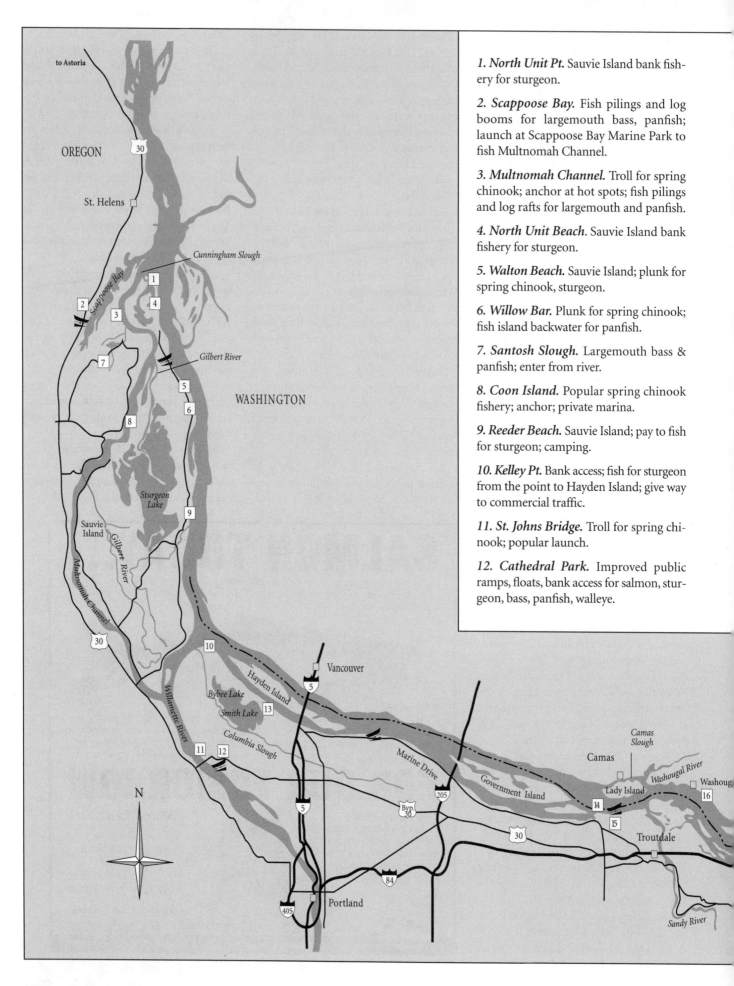

1. **North Unit Pt.** Sauvie Island bank fishery for sturgeon.

2. **Scappoose Bay.** Fish pilings and log booms for largemouth bass, panfish; launch at Scappoose Bay Marine Park to fish Multnomah Channel.

3. **Multnomah Channel.** Troll for spring chinook; anchor at hot spots; fish pilings and log rafts for largemouth and panfish.

4. **North Unit Beach.** Sauvie Island bank fishery for sturgeon.

5. **Walton Beach.** Sauvie Island; plunk for spring chinook, sturgeon.

6. **Willow Bar.** Plunk for spring chinook; fish island backwater for panfish.

7. **Santosh Slough.** Largemouth bass & panfish; enter from river.

8. **Coon Island.** Popular spring chinook fishery; anchor; private marina.

9. **Reeder Beach.** Sauvie Island; pay to fish for sturgeon; camping.

10. **Kelley Pt.** Bank access; fish for sturgeon from the point to Hayden Island; give way to commercial traffic.

11. **St. Johns Bridge.** Troll for spring chinook; popular launch.

12. **Cathedral Park.** Improved public ramps, floats, bank access for salmon, sturgeon, bass, panfish, walleye.

13. Bybee & Smith. Launch canoes to fish for bass and panfish.

14. Government Island. Good fishing up to mouth of Sandy; anchor and spin-fish for coho and chinook jacks in fall; summer steelhead, fall chinook, coho, walleye.

15. Chinook Landing. Improved private ramp; popular access to summer steelhead, sturgeon.

16. Washougal Reef. Fish the rocks for walleye.

17. Cape Horn. Popular sturgeon hole (especially in winter) beneath rocky cliff; give way to barge traffic.

18. Multnomah Falls. Fish for walleye.

19. Outlaw Island. Fish around for sturgeon and walleye.

20. Dodson. Most popular sturgeon fishing on the river.

21. Warrendale. Plunk from beach for summer steelhead, fall chinook.

22. Ives Island. Fish for walleye; anchor for shad on south side of island.

23. Hamilton Island. Fish both sides of channel for fall chinook, summer steelhead.

24. Tanner Creek. Fish cautiously in heavy water from Bradford Is. to mouth of Tanner for sturgeon, walleye, summer steelhead, shad; bank access at mouth.

25. Bradford Island. Fish lower end for sturgeon; bank fishery for shad.

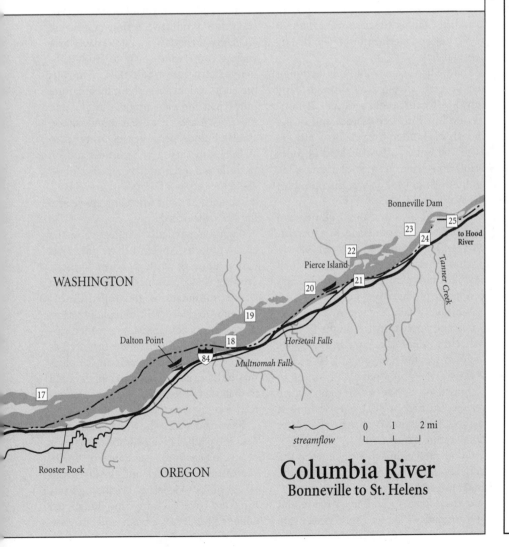

Columbia River
Bonneville to St. Helens

Bank fishing for COLUMBIA RIVER shad is best right below Bonneville Dam. Photograph by Richard Grost.

largest sturgeon are more likely 12 feet and 700 pounds. Catch and release opportunities for these big game fish have attracted anglers from all over the world. Over-size (mostly pregnant female) sturgeon are generally in the gorge below Bonneville in May and June. While the catch and release experience doesn't seem to cause high mortality, it is suspected that the sturgeon do not complete their spawning cycle following the experience. It is not illegal to fish for them, but good sense suggests we should refrain from targeting over-size sturgeon at this time of year.

To avoid hooking over-size sturgeon, use lighter line, smaller hooks, and smaller bait. If the electronic fish-finder indicates you're over large fish, go somewhere else. If you do hook an over-size fish, get your hook out as soon as possible, with minimum handling. Do not remove over-size sturgeon from the water. Turn a hooked fish over on its back, and use your hand to remove the hook from its mouth. Sturgeon have no teeth (though the armor-like plates on its back can do some damage). If a sturgeon has swallowed the bait, cut the line. Single barbless hooks are required for all sturgeon fishing.

Steelhead. The steelhead fishery in this stretch of the Columbia is from May 16 to March 31 from the I-5 Bridge downstream, and from June 16 to March 31 between I-5 and Bonneville Dam. (The brief closure is to promote safe passage of upriver spring chinook.) Summer steelhead make up the bulk of the catch, which is understandable if you've ever been out in the Columbia Gorge in winter.

Steelheading is concentrated near the tributary mouths. On the Oregon side of the river, most fish are caught from Government Island to the mouth of the Sandy River, near Warrendale, and at Hamilton Island and Tanner Creek near the dam. In 1998, only 800 steelhead were landed by sport anglers.

Shad. Shad migrate into this section of the Columbia from May through early July. Most bank angling occurs at Bonneville (off Bradford Island, and at the mouth of Tanner Creek). Boat anglers favor the waters off Ives Island (3 miles below Bonneville on the Washington side), and the Washougal Reef at the mouth of the Washougal River.

Estimated runs of 2 to 4 million shad have passed over Bonneville dam in a single year. The estimated catch in 1998 was 90,000. Anglers use shad darts and small wobblers and spinners. Both plunking and casting are productive.

Walleye. Walleye are now an established and popular fishery in the Columbia below Bonneville. June through early October sees the most angling effort, but walleye are in this stretch and willing to bite as soon as the water temperature reaches the high 30's. The best fishing of the year is often in March, when the water temperature hits 45°.

Good catches are made between the dam and Multnomah Falls, including the water just off Multnomah Falls, inside Ives and Pierce islands, near Outlaw Island, and at the mouth of Tanner Creek. Walleye are also caught around the mouth of the Sandy River near Lady Island, from the lower end of Reed Island to Big Eddy, and on the channel side of Government Island.

The most popular fishery in this stretch is just below Bonneville Dam, where forage fish (and foraging walleye) are most concentrated. But walleye are also caught considerably farther downstream. Catches are made year 'round off Sandy Island (near St. Helens) and in Multnomah Channel (off Rocky Point and Browns Landing, and from Coon Island to Gilbert River). From July to October, walleye are taken off Kelley Point and Jantzen Beach (near Portland) and on the Washington side of the river opposite the mouth of the Willamette.

Though walleye below Bonneville are generally smaller than upriver fish, larger walleye are being caught in this stretch with increasing regularity. Five- and 10-pounders are common, and fish to 15 pounds are sometimes taken. The minimum keeper length is currently 18 inches.

Areas with an irregular bottom are generally most productive. Serious anglers use NOAA river charts to locate the flats where walleye prowl, and sonar to study submerged structure where these ferocious predators wait in ambush for their natural prey (shad and pike minnow smolts, and the occasional trout, steelhead, and salmon smolt). Fish deeper water in spring (18 to 30 feet), and shallower in summer and fall (as little as 8 feet). Walleye are also found along the shores of islands or gravel bars, particularly at night when they move into the shallows to feed.

Jigging is particularly effective in the cooler months. Anglers use weighted jigs either alone or with a worm harness. Trolling is also productive. Spinner and worm combinations are trolled downstream with the current, and plugs resembling natural forage fish are trolled upstream. Most walleye forage fish are between 5 and 8 inches, though smaller plugs may be more effective on brighter days and in shallower water. Trolling is especially effective at night and in the summer.

Bass and Panfish. Most angling for bass and panfish in this section of the river occurs in Scappoose Bay, Santosh Slough, Multnomah Channel, and the lakes and sloughs of Sauvie Island (including Cunningham Lake, Cunningham Slough, the Gilbert River, Pete's Slough, and Sturgeon

Lake). These waters are managed within the Willamette Zone of the state fishing regulations and are included in the Willamette Zone chapter of this book.

Northern Pike Minnow (squawfish). Though this voracious predator of salmon smolts is neither exciting to land nor tasty in the pan, anglers will pursue it in the Columbia as long as Bonneville Power (BPA) continues to offer a cash bounty for each captive (dead or alive) delivered to one of several stations along the river. Below Bonneville Dam, the stations are at the Gleason Boat Ramp (on Marine Drive in Portland) at The Fishery (Exit 34 off I-84), and at Scappoose Bay Marine Park off Hwy. 30.

To participate in the program, register at a station each day before fishing, then return to the station with your catch the same day. The stations issue vouchers, which must be mailed to BPA for payment. At this time, bounties range from $3 to $6 per fish.

The bounty program is an effort by BPA to help control a problem resulting from the presence of hydroelectric dams on the Columbia. Northern pike minnows are thriving thanks to the bonanza of easy forage (dead and wounded smolts) downstream from the dams.

To find out more about the program, and to receive information about how to catch pike minnows, call the Bonneville Power Authority (BPA). Seminars, derbies, and, free fishing kits are available. See Appendix.

In general, a spinning rod and reel loaded with 10-pound line, and plastic worms with twister tails in a variety of colors will get you started. Spoons, spinners, rattling plugs, and baits like chicken liver and nightcrawlers also work well. Plunking, trolling, drift-fishing, and back-bouncing are all effective. Squawfish feed on the bottom in quieter waters or back eddies. Slackwater beside a roiling current is especially productive, since smolts get disoriented in the current and head toward sheltered water. In mid-July, pike minnows spawning in the shallows bite quite aggressively.

Campgrounds. There are few camping opportunities in this increasingly urbanized area. There is a small campground at a Columbia County park on Airport Rd. off Hwy. 30 near the Scappoose Airport. And there are camping facilities at The Fishery, at the opposite end of the reach (5

miles below Bonneville at Dodson). The Fishery also serves as an informal angler's information center for salmon, sturgeon, walleye, shad, and pike minnow fisheries in the upstream portion of this section.

COLUMBIA RIVER: Lake Wallula to Bonneville Four dams obstruct the flow of the Columbia in Oregon east of Portland, transforming the mighty river into a string of reservoirs 147 miles long—Bonneville Pool behind Bonneville Dam, Lake Celilo behind The Dalles Dam, Lake Umatilla behind the John Day Dam, and Lake Wallula behind McNary Dam.

The dams drastically altered the character of the Columbia in this stretch as well as fishing opportunities within it. Salmon, steelhead, sturgeon, and trout, which made up the dominant populations of the pre-dam river, have given way to burgeoning populations of bass, panfish, walleye, and the warmwater forage fish that support them.

BONNEVILLE POOL The last (lowest) reservoir on the Columbia River, fished primarily for sturgeon and walleye, but with a largely untapped opportunity for smallmouth bass. Summer steelhead and fall chinook are also available. The pool stretches about 20 miles between Bonneville Dam and The Dalles Dam.

Crayfish. Photograph by Richard T. Grost.

Steelhead reach this portion of the river in late June, and angling for them continues through late September. Most steelhead in this section of the river are just passing through, heading for the Deschutes, John Day, Snake, and Eastern Washington streams. Best fishing for them in the pool is at the mouths of tributaries (including Hood River on the Oregon side, Wind and White Salmon rivers on the Washington side). Only finclipped steelhead may be kept.

Fall chinook seasons vary dramatically from year to year, depending on predicted run size, and interstate and tribal negotiations. Check with ODFW for current opportunities.

Walleye in the 10-15 pound class are more frequently caught above Bonneville Dam. Photograph by Marcia Hartman.

Smallmouth bass are plentiful around rock structures throughout the COLUMBIA RIVER. *Photograph by Jim Liddle.*

Sturgeon are fished from boat and bank. Favorite boat fisheries are between Cascade Locks and Stevenson WA, at the Dalles below the Interstate Bridge, and in a few scattered areas throughout the pool. Bank anglers fish from rocky points off I-84 where there are safe pull-offs onto the highway shoulder. To avoid hooking oversize sturgeon, use lighter line, and smaller hooks and bait.

Walleye anglers concentrate below the Interstate Bridge at The Dalles, above Hood River Bridge near the Washington shore (you don't need a Washington license), and in the Rowena area west of The Dalles. Launch at Mayer State Park.

Shad are fished primarily in the area below the Interstate Bridge in May and early June.

Most bass and panfish anglers in this area head for the ponds adjacent to the river, but there is an undeveloped fishery for smallmouth around the rock structures along shore. Basket-size rocks hold the bank here, and smallmouth use holes between the rocks to ambush the pool's abundant crayfish. Wind is the main constraint on fishing (a problem for anglers, not for bass). Smallmouth are most active at water temperatures around 45 degrees but will bite at lower temperatures. When shad fry are in the river in September and October, try shad imitations (silver or white). At all times of year, crayfish bait and imitations are the absolute bass favorite. Fish for smallmouth near the warmer surface in spring and in deeper cooler water in summer.

The Columbia is accessible from shore in many places throughout this section, but parking can be a problem due to the divided highway. Parking on the shoulder of I-84 is discouraged except in emergency situations. Alternative parking suggestions are included in the description of each Columbia River pond. Public boat ramps are available at the Port of Cascade Locks, Port of Hood River, Port of The Dalles, and at Mayer State Park. All ramps are concrete.

CELILO, LAKE (a.k.a. The Dalles Pool, between The Dalles and John Day dams) One of four power impoundments on the Columbia River that share a shore with both Oregon and Washington. Fairly shallow and only about 15 miles long, it offers the most productive angling of the four, including good habitat for walleye, plentiful food sources for resident sturgeon, and the powerful attraction of the Deschutes River mouth for both steelhead and salmon.

Fall chinook seasons vary dramatically from year to year, depending on predicted run size, and interstate and tribal negotiations. Check with ODFW for current opportunities. Traditionally, there has been a popular chinook fishery immediately below the mouth of the Deschutes, where Deschutes salmon (as well as those bound elsewhere) enjoy the cool water after their passage over The Dalles Dam. Salmon are most abundant at the Deschutes mouth in August and September. This is a boat fishery, with boats launched at Celilo Park downstream of the mouth, and at Heritage Landing just above the mouth on the Deschutes. You'll need an Oregon Boater's Pass to launch at Heritage Landing. Passes may be purchased at convenience stores in The Dalles and Biggs Junction.

Angling for summer steelhead in Lake Celilo begins July 4th weekend, primarily at the mouth of the Deschutes. There is also a small bank fishery below John Day Dam. All non-finclipped steelhead must be released unharmed.

Sturgeon are fished by boating anglers throughout the pool, and there is a very popular sturgeon bank fishery at Giles French Park below John Day Dam. About 50% of the sturgeon catch for all the reservoirs is made in Lake Celilo.

Walleye are a big fishery here year-round, with peak catches in February and March as the fish prepare to spawn (when the water warms to 45°), and again in summer. Mostly a boat show, best catches are made at the mouth of the Deschutes, and from Rufus up to the deadline below John Day Dam (a 3 to 4 mile stretch). In winter, walleye tend to congregate at the upper end of the pool. Fishing can be especially good from the shallow tailrace at the deadline to the little island, but there are productive eddies and holes throughout the lake, including the Willow Hole, a good ten-mile drift along the north shore downstream of John Day Dam. There is a small bank fishery for walleye from French Giles Park below the dam down to the Rufus gravel pits. There's a good boat ramp off Hwy. 84 at Rufus. In winter, the key to catching walleye is to fish slowly, either jigging (if wind and waves allow) or floating a walleye rig along the bottom. Walleye tend to school up in winter, so locating one fish generally means others are nearby and at the same depth.

Look for smallmouth bass along rock structures in the river and in ponds adjacent to the river. See the map of Columbia River Ponds, p.229. Bass and panfish are also fished in the Rufus gravel pit complex, a network of sloughs and ponds where anglers can walk out on the flats at low tide from access roads off Giles French Park.

Shad are taken at Giles French Park during June and early July.

Umatilla, Lake (John Day Dam Pool) One of four pools in Oregon's chain of Columbia River reservoirs, with a fine population of smallmouth bass and a national reputation for trophy walleye. Of the growing number of walleye fisheries in the state, Lake Umatilla offers the biggest fish and best structure. The state record walleye was pulled out of Lake Umatilla in 1990, weighing 19 pounds 15.3 ounces.

Walleye are year-round residents of the lake. They are found throughout the pool, though most walleye fishing takes place from Arlington upriver to Umatilla. In general, the walleye seem to concentrate upstream in spring, then move downriver throughout the summer to spawn on submerged gravel bars. Anglers use depthfinders to locate popular walleye structures such as submerged islands, rock piles, rocky points, and ledges. Walleye also prowl the isolated flats, which can be identified without sonar by referring to NOAA charts.

In winter when the water is clear, begin looking for them at 20 to 60 ft. In spring as they approach spawning, they can be found at depths of 12 to 25 ft. In summer, most walleye are caught at 20 to 30 ft. depths.

Walleye are sluggish in spring when the water is cold, and slower fishing techniques are appropriate. As the water begins to warm in June, they become aggressive hunters, prowling the flats close to the bottom or hovering in ambush near rocky structures.

In late winter and early spring, jigging is the most popular technique, though floater rigs are also productive. As walleye become more active (especially in the week or so before spawning), power trolling can be effective. Anglers troll at 20 to 30 feet using large plugs that imitate their natural forage (shad, squawfish smolts, sculpin, and the occasional salmon, steelhead, or trout smolt). Best trolling is along the stepped cliffs and ledges that line the river and over the flats. Vibrating blade baits are especially effective in summer.

The walleye fishery accelerates throughout the summer and can be good into November when autumn is mild. Night fishing by the full-moon is especially popular from August on. This is a boat fishery. Bank anglers have had little success. Catches commonly range from 3 to 13 pounds, with occasional 17 pounders.

Lake Umatilla also offers excellent smallmouth bass angling. Tournament catches are on a par with the best in the country. Most smallmouth are caught in the mid-pool area from Fulton Canyon to above Irrigon. There is a popular bank fishery for smallmouth in the town of Umatilla at Umatilla Park. This fishery is open year-round from the footbridge downstream a couple hundred yards. Above the bridge, the fishery is open only during trout and steelhead seasons.

Using plugs and jigs, anglers start taking smallmouth in May and continue throughout the fall. Fish to 6 pounds have been caught, and 3 pounders are not uncommon. Many smallmouth anglers practice catch and release. The warmwater fishery in Lake Umatilla is open year round up to the Hwy. 730 bridge.

Sturgeon are present in Lake Umatilla, but the population is low, and anglers should anticipate fluctuating regulations. At this time there is an annual sturgeon quota, after which fishing is catch and release only.

Salmon and steelhead angling is concentrated at the upper end of the pool around McNary Dam and at the mouths of the tributaries (especially the John Day and Umatilla rivers). Steelhead are present from September through January.

A shad run is fished primarily in the vicinity of Umatilla from April to June. Crappie fishing is popular in fall, particularly in the boat basins, where there's good fishing from the docks.

There are public boat ramps at the mouth of the John Day River, Blalock Canyon, Arlington, Threemile Canyon (located between Arlington and Boardman), Boardman, Patterson Ferry, Irrigon, and Umatilla.

The Blalock Canyon ramp is a good gravel ramp between I-84 and the railroad tracks. Launch into the backwater between the tracks and highway, then motor under the railroad bridge. Blalock is a popular access for a smallmouth bass fishery around the nearby riprap.

Arlington, Boardman, and Umatilla facilities includes concrete ramps, docks, and enclosed boat basins. There is also a beach at the Boardman marina. The Threemile facility is rough and unimproved. Patterson Ferry is unimproved but easy on a vehicle and seldom used. To reach it from Hwy. 730, follow Patterson Ferry Rd. (near McCormach Slough) north onto the grounds of the Umatilla Hatchery. A second smaller marina in Umatilla is located on the Umatilla River upstream from the Hwy. 730 bridge at Umatilla Park.

Bank access throughout the lake is limited due to the proximity of I-84 and the Union Pacific railroad tracks. Best bank access is at the boat basins, except for Blalock and Patterson Ferry. There is also good bank access for crappie, smallmouth bass, and brown bullhead at Umatilla Park near the mouth of the Umatilla River.

Camping and RV facilities are available at Boardman and Umatilla marinas. There is also a developed boat-in campground on the John Day Arm of the lake. Supplies are available in Boardman, Umatilla, Irrigon, and Arlington.

Umatilla Lake, John Day Arm. Cut off from access above by a major falls, accessible only by boat from Lake Umatilla, the last 9 miles of the John Day offer fine fishing in a stunning environment—a narrow canyon with sheer rock walls, and the added attraction (for some) of a full service boat-in campground complete with running water, picnic tables, grassy lawn, and two boat docks. It can get crowded in here, but fishing is excellent for summer steelhead, very good for smallmouth bass, good for channel catfish and brown bullhead, and fair for crappie.

Steelheaders fish the upper 2 miles, where steelhead congregate at the base of Tumwater Falls prior to making a dash for the upper river.

Wallula, Lake (McNary Dam Pool) The easternmost pool in Oregon's string of four Columbia River reservoirs. Most angling effort is devoted to smallmouth bass. Smallmouth are taken near the islands on both Oregon and Washington sides, with catches up to 6 pounds. Walleye, sturgeon, and channel catfish are all present.

Fall chinook and summer steelhead are fished behind McNary Dam at the buoy line from boats launched at the dam. Summer steelhead are fished from late July into January, with peak catches in November. Fall chinook angling is best in September. A second boat ramp is located at Hat Rock State Park, which has camping facilities. Anglers bank fish for salmon at the park behind the dam as well as at a scattering of points along the shore to Hat Rock.

FISHING RESOURCES DIRECTORY

EQUIPMENT & BOATS

Fisherman's Marine & Outdoor
2 LOCATIONS IN PORTLAND AREA
1120 N. Hayden Meadows Dr.   503-283-0044
1900 S.E. McLoughlin Blvd.   503-557-3313

G.I. Joe's
11 LOCATIONS IN OREGON
Beaverton:
3485 SW Cedar Hills Blvd.   503-644-9936
Bend:
63455 Highway 97 North   541-388-3770
Eugene:
1030 Greenacres   541-343-1666
Gresham:
700 NW Eastman Parkway   503-667-3126
Hillsboro:
7280 NW Butler Rd.   503-846-1514
Lake Oswego:
17799 SW Boones Ferry Rd.   503-635-1064
Medford:
2370 Poplar Dr.   541-772-9779
Milwaukie:
15800 SE McLoughlin Blvd.   503-653-5816
Portland:
1140 N. Hayden Meadows Dr.   503-283-0318
3900 SE 82nd Ave.   503-777-4526
Salem:
275 Lancaster Dr. NE   503-334-3366

Stevens Marine
3 LOCATIONS IN OREGON
Medford (River Marine):
2625 Crater Lake Hwy.   541-779-6161
Milwaukie:
18023 SE Addie St.   503-652-1444
Tigard:
9180 SW Burnham St.   503-620-7023

Photograph by Richard T. Grost.

FLY SHOPS

Deschutes River Outfitters   Bend
61115 S. Hwy. 97   888-315-7272
Bend, OR 97702   www.deschutesoutfitters.com
Complete fly angling supplies, outfitters & guides.
Info source for: Deschutes, Crooked, Fall, Cascade Lakes.

Caddis Fly   Eugene
168 W. 6th Avenue   541-342-7005
Eugene, OR 97401   caddiseug@aol.com
Info source for: McKenzie, Willamette, South Santiam,
Deschutes, Umpqua.

NW Flyfishing Outfitters   Gresham
17302 NE Halsey St.   503-252-1529
Gresham, OR 97230   888-292-1137
Info source for: Deschutes, Clackamas, Sandy, Upper
Willamette, McKenzie.

Deschutes Canyon Fly Shop   Maupin
599 S. Hwy. 197, PO Box 334   541-395-2565
Maupin, OR 97037   flyfishingdeschutes.com
Complete fly angling supplies, outfitters & guides.
Info source for: Deschutes.

Countrysport Limited   Portland
126 SW First Ave.   503-221-4545
Portland, OR 97204
International fly fishing outfiters.
Info source for: Clackamas Deschutes, John Day,
McKenzie, Nehalem, Sandy.

Valley Fly Fishers   Salem
153 Alice Ave. So.   503-375-3721
Salem, OR 97302   valfly@open.org
Info source: Willamette, North Santiam, McKenzie.
Flies & materials for bass & panfish.

The Fly Fishers Place   Sisters
151 W. Main   541-549-3474
Sisters, OR 97759   www.flyfishersplace.com
Info source: Crooked, Deschutes, Fall, Metolius, lakes.
Full service fly shop, outfitter, river guides.

Kaufmann's Streamborn, Inc.   Tigard
8861 SW Commercial   503-639-6400
Tigard, OR 97223
www.kman.com • info@kman.com
Info source for all Oregon fisheries. Free 120 page color
catalog. Classes, trips.

The Fly Fishing Shop   Welches
PO Box 368 (Welches Shopping Ctr.)   503-622-4607
Welches, OR 97067   www.flyfishusa.com
Info source: Deschutes, Sandy.
Guided fly fishing trips on Deschutes & Sandy Rivers.

GUIDES

Eagle Cap Fishing Guides   800-940-3688
Mac Huff, Orvis-Endorsed Guide
machuff@oregontrail.net • wallowa.com/eaglecap
Info source for: Imnaha, Minam, Wallowa, Wenaha.
Guided fishing for both gear and fly anglers.

Powder River Tackle   541-523-7143
Phil Simonski, Guide Service
HCR 87 Box 500
Baker City, OR
prphil@bakervalley.net • www.powderriversgs.com
Guided fishing trips on Brownlee, Oxbow, Phillips.

LODGING

Deschutes Motel   Deschutes River
616 Mill St.   541-395-2626
Maupin, OR 97037   dmotel@prinet.net

Lakeside Motel   Detroit Reservoir
110 Santiam Av.   530-854-3376
Detroit, OR 97342

Odell Lake Resort   Odell Lake
East Odell Lake, Hwy. 58, PO Box 72   541-433-2540
Crescent Lake, OR 97425

Shelter Cove Resort   Odell Lake
W. Odell Lake, Hwy. 58, PO Box 52   541-433-2548
Cascade Summit, OR 97425

Powder River B&B   Oxbow Reservoir
HCR 87 Box 500   541-523-7143
Baker City, OR 97814
prphil@bakervalley.net • www.powderriversgs.com

Darlings Resort   Siltcoos Lake
4879 Darlings Loop   541-997-2841
Florence, OR 97439   DarlingsResort.com

Fish Mill Lodges   Siltcoos Lake
4844 Fish Mill Way   541-997-2511
Westlake, OR 97493   fishmill@nwpaclink.com

Westlake Resort   Siltcoos Lake
4785 Laurel Ave., PO Box 25   541-997-3722
Westlake, OR 97707

Twin Lakes Resort   South Twin Lake
PO Box 3550   541-593-6526
Sunriver, OR 97707   twinlakes@bendcable.com

Lonesome Duck   Williamson River
www.lonesomeduck.com   800-367-2540
steveh@lonesomeduck.com

FOR FURTHER INFORMATION

---

fishinginoregon.com

fishinginoregon.com is an online magazine and information source for Oregon anglers. It includes up-to-date river gauge readings, weather forecasts, tide tables, current fishing reports, and many other useful tidbits. It is edited by Scott Richmond.

BUREAU OF LAND MANAGEMENT	503-952-6027
Eugene	541-683-6600
Hines	541-573-4400
Klamath Falls	541-883-6916
Lakeview	541-947-2177
Medford	541-618-2400
North Bend	541-756-0100
Prineville	541-416-6700
Roseburg	541-440-4930
Salem	503-375-5643
Tillamook	541-842-7546
Vale	541-473-3144

OREGON DEPARTMENT OF FISH AND WILDLIFE
Headquarters
2501 SW First St.
Portland, OR 97207

Information Desk	541-872-5268
Recorded Information	503-229-5222

http://www.dfw.state.or.us/ODFWhtml/RecReports

ODFW NW Zone

Astoria	503-338-0106
Florence	503-997-7366
Newport	541-867-4741
Tillamook	503-842-2741

Willamette Zone

Clackamas	503-657-2000
Corvallis	541-757-4186
Salem	503-378-6925
Springfield	541-726-3515

ODFW SW Zone

Roseburg	541-440-3353
Charleston	541-888-5515
Gold Beach	541-247-7605
Central Point	541-826-8774

ODFW Central Region

Bend	541-388-6363
The Dalles	541-296-4628
Klamath Falls	541-883-5732
Prineville	541-447-5111

ODFW SE Region

Hines	541-573-6582
Klamath Falls	541-883-5732
Lakeview	541-947-2950
Ontario	541-889-6975

ODFW NE Region

Enterprise	541-426-3279
John Day	541-575-1167
LaGrande	541-963-2138
Pendleton	541-276-2344

ODFW Columbia River Zone

Clackamas	503-657-2000

US FOREST SERVICE	503-808-2971
Deschutes National Forest	541-383-5300
Bend	541-383-4080
Crescent	541-433-3200
Sisters	541-549-7700
Fremont National Forest	541-947-2151
Bly	541-353-2427
Lakeview	541-947-3334
Paisley	541-943-3114
Silver Lake	541-576-2107
Malheur National Forest	541-575-1731
Bear Valley/Long Cr.	541-575-3000
Burns	541-573-4300
Prairie City	541-820-3800
Mt. Hood National Forest	503-668-1700
Barlow	503-467-2291
Bear Springs	503-328-6211
Estacada	503-630-6861
Hood River	503-352-6002
Ripplebrook	503-834-2275
ZigZag	503-622-3191
Ochoco National Forest	541-416-6500
Big Summit	541-416-6645
Paulina	541-477-6900
Prineville	541-416-6500
Snow Mountain	541-573-4300
Rogue River National Forest	541-858-2200
Applegate	541-899-1812
Ashland	541-482-3333
Butte Falls	541-865-2700
Prospect	541-560-3400
Siskiyou National Forest	541-471-6500
Chetco	541-469-2196
Galice	541-471-6500
Gold Beach	541-247-3600
Illinois Valley	541-592-2166
Powers	541-439-3011
Siuslaw National Forest	541-750-7000
Hebo	503-392-3161
Mapleton	541-902-8526
Oregon Dunes NRA	541-271-3611
Waldport	541-563-3211
Umatilla National Forest	541-278-3716
Heppner	541-676-9187
N. Fk. John Day	541-427-3231
Pomeroy	509-843-1891
Walla Walla	509-522-6290
Umpqua National Forest	541-672-6601
Cottage Grove	541-942-5591
Diamond Lake	541-498-2531
N. Umpqua	541-496-3532
Tiller	541-825-3201
Wallowa-Whitman National Forest	541-523-6391
Baker	541-523-4476
Eagle Cap	541-426-4978
LaGrande	541-963-7186
Pine	541-742-7511
Unity	541-446-3351
Wallowa Valley	541-426-4978

Willamette National Forest	541-465-6521
Blue River	541-822-3317
Detroit	503-854-3366
Lowell	541-937-2129
McKenzie	541-822-3381
West Fir	541-782-2283
Sweet Home	541-367-5168
Winema National Forest	541-883-6714
Chemult	541-365-7001
Chiloquin	541-783-4001
Klamath	541-883-6824
Klamath R.D.	541-885-3400
Crater Lake National Park	541-594-2211

PHONE NUMBERS REFERENCED IN FISHING IN OREGON

Army Corp of Engineers (Applegate and Lost Creek dams)	800-472-2434
Camp Rilea	503-861-4000
Coast Guard, Rogue River Estuary	541-247-7219
Confederated Tribes of...	
Umatilla	541-276-8223
Warm Springs	541-553-1161
Cove Palisades Marina	541-546-3412
Deschutes Co. Road Dept.	541-388-6581
Diamond Lake Information	541-793-3310
Elk River Hatchery	541-332-7025
Ericson, Jim (N. Fk. Nehalem)	503-368-5365
Fans of Fanno Creek	503-648-8621
Farewell Bend State Park	541-869-2365
Giustina Resources	541-485-2050
Hagg Lake shelter reservations	503-681-3692
Hermiston Irrigation District	541-567-3024
(Cold Springs Reservoir & Umatilla River)	
http://mac/.pn.usbr.gov/umatilla/umat.html	
Idaho Power (Snake R. reservoirs)	800-422-3143
(www.idahopower.com)	
Jackson County Parks Dept.	541-776-7001
Johnson's Rock Pit (Necanicum)	503-738-7328
Marine Board, Oregon State	503-378-8587
Minam Motel (Wallowa shuttle)	541-437-4475
Northern Pike Minnow Program	800-622-4519
NMFS Hotline	800-662-9825
(ocean salmon and halibut seasons)	
National Weather Service	503-261-9246
Oregon State Parks and Recreation Dept.	
General Information	503-378-6305
Campgrounds Info	800-551-6949
Reservations (Portland area)	503-731-3411
Reservations (out of area)	800-452-5687
Oregonian Outdoor Report	503-225-5555
	ext. 9010
PGE Fish Line	503-464-7474
Pacific Power & Light (PP&L)	
(Klamath water levels)	800-547-1501
Snake River Information	509-758-0616
Three Rivers Marina	541-546-2939
Tualatin Riverkeepers	503-590-5913
Willamette Falls Fish Report	503-657-2059

APPENDIX 3
ANYBODY HOME?

Chinook ▬▬▬
Coho ▬▬▬
Steelhead ▬▬▬

This chart shows when salmon and steelhead are in Oregon's top salmon and steelhead waters.

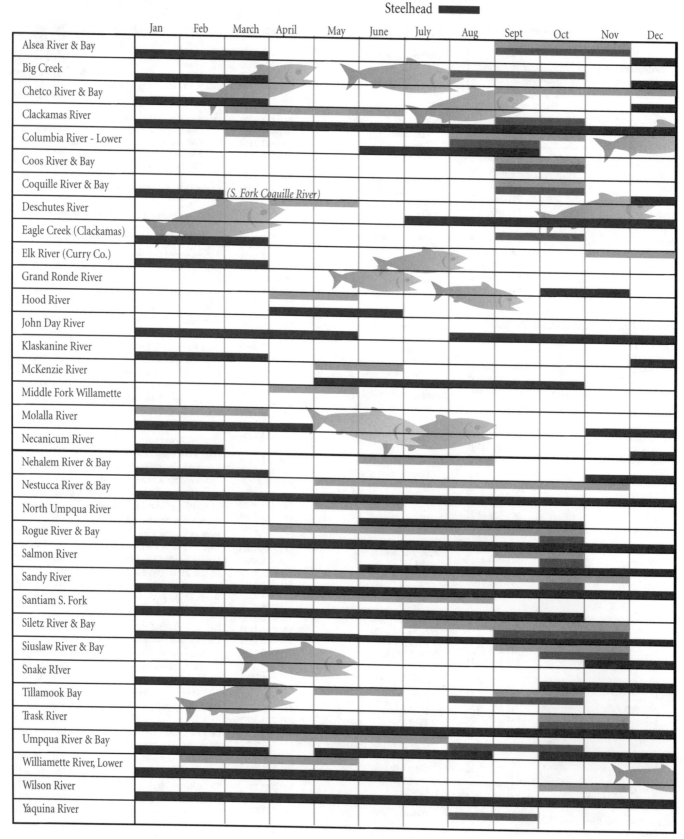

	Jan	Feb	March	April	May	June	July	Aug	Sept	Oct	Nov	Dec
Alsea River & Bay												
Big Creek												
Chetco River & Bay												
Clackamas River												
Columbia River - Lower												
Coos River & Bay												
Coquille River & Bay												
Deschutes River					*(S. Fork Coquille River)*							
Eagle Creek (Clackamas)												
Elk River (Curry Co.)												
Grand Ronde River												
Hood River												
John Day River												
Klaskanine River												
McKenzie River												
Middle Fork Willamette												
Molalla River												
Necanicum River												
Nehalem River & Bay												
Nestucca River & Bay												
North Umpqua River												
Rogue River & Bay												
Salmon River												
Sandy River												
Santiam S. Fork												
Siletz River & Bay												
Siuslaw River & Bay												
Snake River												
Tillamook Bay												
Trask River												
Umpqua River & Bay												
Williamette River, Lower												
Wilson River												
Yaquina River												

RECORD CATCHES IN OREGON

Bass

Largemouth	11 lb. 9.6 oz.	Butte Falls farm pond	4/15/94	Randy Spaur
Smallmouth	7 lb. 9 oz.	Hagg Lake	8/1/97	Raymond Currie
Hybrid striped	18 lb. 8 oz.	Ana Reservoir	2/21/96	John Saunders
Striped	64 lb. 8 oz.	Umpqua River	1973	Beryl Bliss

Catfish

Channel	36 lb. 8 oz.	McKay Reservoir	9/17/80	Boone Haddock
Flathead	42 lb.	Snake R.	6/27/94	Joshua Kralicek
White	15 lb.	Tualatin R.	4/22/89	Wayne Welch
Yellow bullhead	3 lb. 6 oz.	Brownlee Reservoir	6/10/86	Loretta Fitzgerald
Brown bullhead	2 lb. 4 oz.	Eckman Lake	6/10/82	Joshua Spulnik

Crappie

Black	4 lb. 6 oz.	private pond/Corvallis	6/29/95	John E. Doss
White	4 lb. 12 oz.	Gerber Reservoir	5/22/67	Jim Duckett

Panfish

Bluegill	2 lb. 5.5 oz.	Prineville farm pond	5/12/81	Wayne Elmore
Yellow perch	2 lb. 2 oz.	Brownsmead Slough	6/5/71	Ernie Affolter III
Sacramento perch	11.2 oz.	Lost River	5/1/98	Jonathan Cogley
Green sunfish	11 oz.	Umpqua	4/25/91	John L. Baker
Red-ear sunfish	1 lb. 15.5 oz.	Reynolds Pond	8/1/92	Terence Bice
Pumpkinseed sunfish	7.68 oz.	Lake Oswego	7/10/96	Linda Mar
Warmouth	1 lb 14.5 oz.	Columbia R.	12/27/75	Jess Nowel

Salmon

Chinook	83 lb.	Umpqua R.	1910	Ernie St. Claire
(dressed)	62 lb.	Nestucca R.	10/70	Craig Hansen
Chum	23 lb.	Kilchis R.	1990	Roger Nelson
Coho	25 lb. 5 oz.	Siltcoos Lake	11/05/66	Ed Marti
Kokanee	4 lb. 14.7 oz.	Wallowa Lake	6/27/98	Don Exon

Shad

	5 lb. 13 oz.	Columbia R.	5/31/94	Patricia Young

Trout

Brook	9 lb. 6 oz.	Deschutes R. (below Little Lava Lake)	6/21/80	Burt Westbrook
Brown	27 lb. 12 oz.	Paulina Lake	5/21/93	Guy Carl
Bull	23 lb. 2 oz.	Lake Billy Chinook	3/25/89	Don Yow
Searun cutthroat	6 lb. 4 oz.	Siltcoos Lake	8/20/84	Kay Schmidt
Inland cutthroat	9 lb. 8 oz.	N. Fork Malheur R.	4/09/86	Phillip Grove
Golden	7 lb. 10 oz.	Eagle Cap Wilderness	7/16/87	Douglas White
Mackinaw	40 lb. 8 oz.	Odell Lake	9/84	Ken Erickson
Rainbow	28 lb.	Rogue R.	5/19/82	Mike McGonagle
Steelhead	35 lb. 8 oz.	Columbia R.	9/19/70	Berdell Todd

Walleye

	19 lb. 15.3 oz.	John Day Pool	2/20/90	Arnold R. Berg

Whitefish

	4 lb. 14 oz.	Crane Prairie	7/21/94	Roger A. Massey

If you think you have caught a record-breaking fish:

- Photograph a side view of the fish to accompany your record catch application.
- Weigh your catch as quickly as possible on a state certified scale (e.g. supermarket meat department).
- Identify two witnesses you can later ask to sign your application; one witness must be the person weighing the fish.
- Obtain and complete an application, including signatures of witnesses. Coldwater record applications are available at each district ODFW office, or from ODFW, Information and Education Dept., P.O. Box 59, Portland, OR 97207. Warmwater record applications are available from The Oregon Bass and Panfish Club, Contest Manager, P.O. Box 1021, Portland, OR 97207.
- To be eligible, a fish must have been caught legally, in Oregon using hook and line.

FISHERIES FOR YOUNGSTERS

Photograph by Bill Wagner.

Northwest Zone
Alder Lake
Alsea Bay
Big Creek Reservoir
Carter Lake
Clatskanie Slough
Coffenbury Lake
Crescent Lake (Tillamook Co.)
Cullaby Lake
Dune Lake
Elbow Lake
Hebo lake
Klaskanine River
Siltcoos Lake
Tahkenitch Lake
Triangle Lake
Yaquina Bay

Southwest Zone
Canyonville Pond
Cooper Creek Reservoir
Denman Management Area Ponds
Dutch Herman
Eel Lake
Emigrant Lake
Empire Lakes
Expo Ponds
Fish Lake (Rogue watershed)
Galesville Reservoir
Herbert Log Pond
Howard Prairie Lake
Libby Pond

Loon Lake
Millicoma River, West Fork - interpretive Center
Plat I Reservoir
Powers Pond
Selmac Lake
Squaw Lakes
Tenmile Lakes
Umpqua River (shad fishery)

Willamette
Adair Pond
Alton Baker Canal
Benson Lake (Lane Co.)
Blue Lake (Willamette watershed)
Brown-Minto Island Complex
Commonwealth Lake
Delta Ponds
Detroit Lake
Dorena Reservoir
E.E. Wilson Pond
Foster Reservoir
Freeway Ponds
Johnson Creek
Junction City Pond
Little North Santiam River
Mt. Hood Community College Ponds
North Fork Reservoir
Pine Ridge Lake
Roaring River (Santiam watershed)
Roslyn Lake
St. Louis Ponds

Spirit Lake
Tenas Lakes
Trillium Lake
Walter Wirth Lake
Willamina Pond

Central
Blow Lake
Cody Ponds
Devils Lake (Deschutes watershed)
Frog Lake
Kingsley Reservoir
Lions Pond
Lost Lake (Mt. Hood)
Metolius River (Wizard Falls Hatchery)
Ochoco Creek
Pine Hollow Reservoir
Reynolds Pond
Rock Creek Reservoir
Taylor Lake (Columbia River pond.)
Twin Lake, South (Deschutes Co.)
Walton Lake

Southeast Zone
Becker Pond
Lake of the Woods
Lofton Reservoir
Murray Reservoir
Obenchain Reservoir

Northeast Zone
Bull Prairie Reservoir
Conforth Ponds
Cutsforth Ponds
Hat Rock Pond
Jubilee Lake
McNary Channel Ponds
Morgan Lake
Pilcher Creek Reservoir
Penland Lake
R.D. Mack Pond
Roulette Pond
Willow Creek (Morrow Co.)

APPENDIX 6
FISHERIES FOR DISABLED ANGLERS

Northwest Zone
Big Creek Reservoirs
Cleawox Lake
Coffenbury Lake
Devils Lake
Hebo Lake
Lytle Lake
Nehalem River, North Fork:
    Hatchery
Siltcoos Lake
Siuslaw Bay: Rock Dock
Siuslaw River :
    Bender's Landing (r.m. 3)
    Mapleton Dock
Tahkenitch Lake
Tillamook Bay: Garibaldi Coast Guard Pier
Vernonia Lake

Southwest Zone
Applegate Reservoir
Chetco Bay: Jetty
Chetco River: Eastside Ramp on lower Isthmus
Cooper Creek Reservoir
Coos Bay: Eastside Boat Ramp
Coos River, South Fork: Myrtle Tree Ramp
Denman Wildlife Ponds
Eel Lake: Tugman State Park
Empire Lakes
Fish Lake (Rogue River watershed)
Howard Prairie Reservoir
Hyatt Lake
Loon Lake
Rogue River:
    Chinook Park
    Dodge Bridge
    McGregor Park
    Pearce Park
    Schroeder Park
Selmac Lake
Tenmile Lakes

Willamette Zone
Benson Lake (Multnomah Co.)
Blue Lake (Multnomah Co.)
Clackamas River: Indian Henry Campground
Detroit Lake: Detroit Lake State Park
Dexter Reservoir: South bank below dam
E.E. Wilson Pond, Corvallis
Fern Ridge Reservoir
Hagg Lake: Elk Point Picnic Area
Harriett Lake
Junction City Pond
Leaburg Lake
Lost Creek (Clackamas Co.): Lost Cr.
    Campground
    Lost Lake
McKenzie River: Hendrick's Bridge Wayside
Mill Creek: Stewart Grenfell Park
Olallie Lake: Peninsula CG
Prineville Reservoir

While WAHKEENA POND was drained, the Oregon Bass and Panfish Club built a wheelchair accessible fishing platform and installed bottom structure to attract warmwater fish. Photograph by Bud Hartman

Roaring River (Linn Co.): Pier near hatchery
Rock Creek
Roslyn Lake
St. Louis Pond No. 3
Sandy River:
    Dabney State Park
    Oxbow Hatchery
    Oxbow State Park
Santiam River, South :
    Yukwah
    Fern View
Sauvie Island: Inquire at ODFW Headquarters
Timothy Lake
Trail Bridge Reservoir
Trillium Lake
Vernonia Lake
Wahkeena Pond
Walter Wirth Lake
Willamette River:
    Alton Baker Park, Eugene
    Armitage State Park, Eugene
    Brown-Minto Slough Complex
    Cascade Gateway Park, Salem
    Meldrum Bar, Oregon City
Willamina Creek - Blackwell Park
Willamina Pond
Wilsonville Pond
Woodburn Pond

Central Zone
Antelope Flat Reservoir
Billy Chinook, Lake: Cove Palisades State Park
Deschutes River:
    Rd. 42 Bridge (Crane to Wickiup)_
    Blue Hole Campgound (below Pelton)
    Browns Mt. Crossing
Lions Pond
Walton Lake
John Day Arm, Lake Umatilla

Southeast Zone
Alkali Lake Reservoir
Becker's Pond
Boyle Reservoir: Topsy Campground
Brownlee Reservoir: Hewitt Park
Campbell Reservoir
Chickahominy Reservoir
Dead Horse Lake
Delintment Lake
Krumbo Reservoir
Loften Reservoir
Malheur Reservoir
Snake River: Farewell Bend State Park
Summer Lake
Upper Klamath Lake: Moore Park
Williamson River: Collier State Park
Wood River: Fort Klamath Picnic Area
Yellowjacket Reservoir
Wallula, Lake

Northeast Zone
Bull Prairie Reservoir
Camas Creek - Camas Creek State Park
Cold Springs Reservoir
Cutsforth Ponds
Hat Rock Pond
Magone Lake
McCormach Slough
McNary Channel Ponds
Morgan Lake
Olive Lake
Penland Lake
Phillips Reservoir
Pilcher Creek
Thief Valley Reservoir
Umatilla River:
    at forks on east bank south of Hwy. 730
Unity Reservoir

APPENDIX 7
WARMWATER FISHERIES

Yellow perch bite aggressively at HENRY HAGG LAKE. *Photograph by Jim Liddle.*

* = largemouth bass
\+ = smallmouth bass

Northwest Zone
Beaver Creek (Columbia Co.)
Big Creek Reservoirs *
Blind Slough*
Bradbury Slough*
Brownsmead Slough*
Buck Lake
Burkes Lake
Cape Meares Lake*
Cemetery Lake*
Clatskanie Slough
Clear Lake (Clatsop Co.)*
Clear Lake (Lane Co.)
Cleawox Lake*
Collard Lake*
Crabapple Lake*
Crescent Lake (Tillamook Co.)*
Cullaby Lake
Deer Island Slough
Devils Lake (Lincoln Co.)*
Diblees Slough
Eckman Lake*
Goat Island Slough*
Hult Reservoir*
Lost Lake (Westport)*
Lytle Lake*
Magruder Slough
Maple Creek
Marie Lake*
Mayger Slough
Mercer Lake*
Munsel Lake*

Neacoxie Lake
Ocean Lake
Olalla Reservoir*
Prescott Slough*
Rilea Slough*
Rinearson Slough*
Sandy Island Slough
Santosh Slough
Shag Lake
Siltcoos Lake*
Siuslaw Bay
Slusher Lake*
Smith Lake (Clatsop Co.)*
Spring Lake
Sunset Lake*
Sutton Lake*
Tahkenitch Lake*
Town Lake
Triangle Lake*
Trojan Pond
Vernonia Lake*
West Lake
Westport Slough*
Woahink Lake*

Southwest Zone
Agate Reservoir*
Applegate Reservoir*
Babyfoot Lake*
Beale Lake*
Ben Irving Reservoir*
Bradley Lake*
Burma Pond*
Butterfield Lake*
Cooper Creek Reservoir*

Cow Creek+
Davidson Lake
Denman Management*
  Area Ponds
Dutch Herman*
Eel Lake*
Emigrant Lake*
Empire Lakes*
Expo Ponds*
Floras Lake*
Fords Mill Pond*
Garrison Lake*
Galesville Reservoir*+
Hall Lake*
Hoover Ponds*
Horsfall Lake*
Howard Prairie Lake+
Hyatt Reservoir*
Johnson Mill Pond*
Jordan Lake*
Lake Marie
Little Hyatt Lake*
Loon Lake*
Lost Creek Reservoir*+
Medco Pond*
Plat I Reservoir*
Powers Pond
Saunders Lake
Selmac Lake*
Skookum Pond*
Snag Lake*
Squaw Lakes*
Tenmile Lakes*
Triangle Lake
Umpqua River+
Umpqua River, North+
Umpqua River, South+
Willow Creek Reservoir*

Willamette Zone
Adair Pond*
Benson Lake (Columbia Gorge)*
Bethany Lake*
Blue Lake (Willamette watershed)*
Bluegill Lake
Bond Butte Pond*
Brown-Minto Island Complex*+
Bybee Lake*
Canby Pond*
Cleary Pond*
Colorado Lake*
Columbia Slough*
Cottage Grove Ponds*
Cottage Grove Reservoir*
Creswell Ponds*
Cunningham Lake*
Cunningham Slough*

Delta Park Ponds*
Delta Ponds*
Dexter Reservoir*
Dorena Reservoir
Dorman Pond*
Fairview Lake*
Fern Ridge Reservoir*
Foster Reservoir*
Freeway Ponds*
Gilbert River*
Goose Lake*
Government Island Lake*
Green Peter Reservoir*
Grossman Pond*
Hagg Lake*+
Haldeman Pond*
Hills Creek Reservoir
Horseshoe Lake (Willamette)*
Johnson Creek+
Junction City Pond+
Kirk Pond+
Lambert Slough*
Long Tom River*+
Lookout Point Reservoir*
Luckiamute River+
Mary's River+
McKay Creek*+
McNary Lakes*
McNulty Creek*
Mercer Reservoir*
Milton Creek*
Mirror Pond*
Mission Creek Reservoir*
Mission Lake
Muddy Creek (Mary's watershed)*
Multnomah Channel*+
Oswego Creek
Pete's Slough*
Pope Lake
Pudding River*
Rooster Rock Slough*
Santiam River+
Santiam River, South+
Santosh Slough*
Scappoose Bay*+
Skookum Lake (Willamette)
Smith Lake (Lower Columbia)*
St. Louis Ponds*
Sturgeon Lake*
Thomas Creek*
Timber Linn Lake*
Tualatin River*
Walling Pond
Walter Wirth Lake*
Walterville Pond*
Waverly Lake*
Willamette River*+
Willamina Pond*
Wilsonville Pond*

Withee Lake*
Woodburn Pond*
Yamhill River*+

Central Zone
Big Houston Lake*
Bikini Pond*+
Billy Chinook Reservoir*+
Cody Ponds*
Crane Prairie Reservoir*
Davis Lake (Deschutes watershed)*
Deschutes Pond East*+
Deschutes Pond No. 2*+
Deschutes Pond No.1*+
Gilchrist Mill Pond
Government Cove*+
Haystack Reservoir*
Hood River Pond No. 1*+
Hood River Pond No. 2*+
Hood River Pond No. 3*+
Iris Lake+
Kolberg Lake*+
Lions Pond*
Lone Pine Pond*+
Long Pond*+
McClures Lake*+
Miller Pond*+
Mosier Pond East*+
Mosier Pond West*+
One-Mile Lake*+
Pine Hollow Reservoir*
Prineville Reservoir*+
Reynolds Pond*
Rock Creek Reservoir*
Sand Dune Lake*+
Sand Lake*+
Taylor Lake (Columbia River)*
Tooley Lake*+
Tunnel Lake*+
Viento Lake*+
West Cove*+

Southeast Zone
Altnow Lake*
Balm Creek Reservoir+
Becker's Pond*
Boyle (J.C.) Reservoir*
Brownlee Reservoir*+
Bully Creek Reservoir*+
Bumphead Reservoir*
Burnt River+
Campbell Reservoir*
Cow Lakes*
Crater Lake (Malheur watershed)*
Crump Lake*
Devil Lake*
Dog Lake*
Drews Reservoir
Dunaway Pond*

Gerber Reservoir*
Haines Pond*
Hart Lake*
Highway 203 Pond*
Krumbo Reservoir*
Lake Of The Woods*
Lost River*
Malheur River, Middle Fork+
Moon Reservoir*
Obenchain Reservoir*
Phillips Reservoir+
Powder River*+
Round Valley Reservoir*
Silvies River+
Sprague River*
Thompson Valley Reservoir*
Thief Valley Reservoir*
Unity Reservoir+
Upper Midway Reservoir*
Warm Spring Reservoir+
Warner Valley Lakes*
Willow Valley Reservoir*

Northeast Zone
Barth Quarry Pond*
Bibby Reservoir*
Boardman Pond No.2
Carter Slough*
Catherine Creek Slough*+
Cavender Pond*
Cold Springs Reservoir*
Conforth Ponds*
Grande Ronde River+
Hat Rock Pond*+
John Day River+
Joseph Creek+
McCormach Slough+
McKay Reservoir*
McNary Channel Ponds*
Messner Pond No. 2*
Morgan Lake
Power City Ponds*
Willow Creek Reservoir*
Wineland Lake *

Snake River Zone
Brownlee Reservoir*+
Hells Canyon Reservoir*+
Oxbow Reservoir*+
Snake River*+

Columbia Zone
Bonneville Pool*+
Columbia sloughs*+
Lake Celilo*+
Lake Umatilla*+
Lake Wallula*+

INDEX

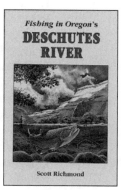